THE *unofficial* GUIDE®
TO South Florida including Miami and the Keys

THIRD EDITION

THE *unofficial* GUIDE®

to South Florida including Miami and the Keys

THIRD EDITION

LEA LANE

WILEY

Please note that prices fluctuate in the course of time, and that travel information changes under the impact of many factors that influence the travel industry. We therefore suggest that you write or call ahead for confirmation when making your travel plans. Every effort has been made to ensure the accuracy of information throughout this book, and the contents of this publication are believed correct at the time of printing. Nevertheless, the publishers cannot accept responsibility for errors or omissions, for changes in details given in this guide, or for the consequences of any reliance on the information provided by the same. Assessments of attractions and so forth are based upon the author's own experience, and therefore, descriptions given in this guide necessarily contain an element of subjective opinion, which may not reflect the publisher's opinion or dictate a reader's own experience on another occasion. Readers are invited to write the publisher with ideas, comments, and suggestions for future editions.

Published by:
John Wiley & Sons, Inc.
111 River Street
Hoboken, NJ 07030

Produced by Menasha Ridge Press

Cover design by Michael J. Freeland

Interior design by Vertigo Design

For information on our other products and services or to obtain technical support, please contact our Customer Care Department within the United States at 800-762-2974, outside the United States at 317-572-3993, or by fax at 317-572-4002.

John Wiley & Sons, Inc. also publishes its books in a variety of electronic formats. Some content that appears in print may not be available in electronic formats.

ISBN 0-7645-9536-9

Manufactured in the United States of America

5 4 3 2 1

CONTENTS

List of maps

ABOUT *the* AUTHOR *and* CONTRIBUTORS

Lea Lane headed up the extensive update for this third edition, working on all chapters. Lea has been a columnist for Gannett Suburban newspapers, a TV travel and lifestyle reporter, managing editor of the newsletter *Travel Smart,* and coauthor of a book on cruises. She writes for magazines and newspapers, including the *New York Times,* and is a major contributor to guidebooks on Belgium, Greece, and Italy, and to *The Unofficial Guide to New York City.* She is the author of *The Unofficial Guide to Bed-and-Breakfasts and Country Inns in New England* and the popular travel guide *Solo Traveler: Tales and Tips for Great Trips.* Lea grew up in Miami Beach and now lives in Miami for most of the year. Her lifestyle Web site is www.sololady.com.

Trish Riley personally inspected and rated every hotel property in the guide. She is an independent journalist who enjoys documenting her travels to help others make the best choices and ensure their traveling pleasure. She also writes about families, health, and environmental issues to bring beneficial information to readers. A member of the American Society of Journalists and Authors and the Society of Environmental Journalists, Trish has had her work published in many newspapers, magazines, and custom publications.

Suzy Buckley, a 13-year resident of South Beach, contributed the shopping and nightlife sections for the Miami-Dade chapter and the nightlife section for the Keys chapter. She is lifestyle editor at *Ocean Drive* magazine in Miami Beach; Miami and Florida editor of *Lucky;* and a contributor to *Departures, Four Seasons,* the *New York Post, Town & Country,* and *Town & Country Travel.* She is also a frequent guest commenting on nightlife and celebrities for E! Entertainment Television and the Travel Channel.

Marli Guzzetta, a native South Floridian, wrote our dining and nightlife sections for Palm Beach and Broward counties. She contributes regularly to *New Times Broward–Palm Beach* and *Miami New Times*. She has also worked at *Family Life, Marie Claire,* and *Out* magazines. Her writing has appeared in *Parenting* magazine, the *South Florida Sun-Sentinel*, the *Houston Press, Cleveland Scene, The Pitch,* and *Gainesville* magazine. Currently, she splits her time between South Florida and Gainesville, where she is a graduate student in the University of Florida's creative-writing program.

Karen Feldman wrote the nightlife and dining sections for our Southwest Florida chapter. Her specialties include food, dining, and travel. Her articles have been published in newspapers and magazines across the country. She's authored two books on fund-raising events for nonprofit groups. Karen lives in Fort Myers, Florida.

INTRODUCTION

◀ ABOUT *this* GUIDE

HEAT IS INTIMATELY ASSOCIATED WITH South Florida, so this thoroughly revised edition of *The Unofficial Guide to South Florida* offers sizzling info on the region's hottest hot spots.

Cool is an apt description of South Florida, too, and right now no area in the States comes close to the trendy, edgy attitude and atmosphere down here. So we scope out both the hottest and coolest aspects for you, from Palm Beach County south along the Atlantic coast through Broward and Miami-Dade counties, across the Everglades to Lee County on the Gulf of Mexico, and south again to the Florida Keys.

South Florida encompasses some of the world's most paradisiacal resort cities, including Greater Miami, Fort Lauderdale, Boca Raton, Delray Beach, Fort Myers, Key West, Naples, and Palm Beach. And nearby, unique wildlife areas include Big Cypress National Preserve, underwater Biscayne Park, and, of course, the amazing Everglades.

Lush, semitropical South Florida is among the fastest-growing regions in the United States. Outstanding beaches and natural areas, trendy hotels and restaurants, exciting shopping opportunities, varied spectator sports and cultural offerings, and unique, world-renowned tourist attractions lure new residents and vacationers alike.

But South Florida isn't all bougainvillea, guava-hued sunsets, and icy mojitos. This guide will help you sort through myriad hotels, restaurants, and sights to find those that best suit your taste and budget. We provide impartial and thorough evaluations of the area's top draws and best-kept secrets, moving beyond boosterism to informed criticism. We tell you if food is mediocre, even in well-known restaurants. We complain about overpriced and inconveniently located hotel rooms. And we keep you away from the crowds and congestion. We point out good values and help you avoid wasting time and money, making your visit more efficient, economical, and fabulous.

HOW UNOFFICIAL GUIDES ARE DIFFERENT

THE UNOFFICIAL GUIDE TO SOUTH FLORIDA is for individuals and families traveling for fun, as well as for business travelers and convention-goers. First-time visitors and Florida-vacation veterans alike will find helpful tips and evaluations that add up to a (wonderfully) unforgettable vacation. Our readers are value-conscious, consumer-oriented adults who seek a cost-effective but comfortable travel style. So unlike most guides, we do more than describe: We spell out alternatives and recommend specific courses of action. We simplify complicated destinations and attractions, giving you control even in the most unfamiliar environments.

We don't provide all the info possible, just the most accessible and useful—unbiased by affiliation with any organization or industry. Our authors and research team are completely independent from the attractions, restaurants, and hotels we describe. We work for you alone because we want you to have the best trip possible.

HOW THIS GUIDE WAS RESEARCHED AND WRITTEN

WHILE MUCH HAS BEEN WRITTEN ABOUT SOUTH FLORIDA, very little has been evaluative. Some guides practically regurgitate the hotels' and restaurants' own promotional material. In preparing this work, we took nothing for granted. Each hotel, restaurant, club, and attraction was visited by a team of trained observers. They conducted detailed evaluations and rated properties and attractions according to formal, tested rating criteria.

While our observers are independent and impartial, they do not claim to have special expertise. Like you, they visited South Florida as tourists or business travelers, noting their satisfaction or dissatisfaction. However, the primary differences between the average tourist and the trained evaluator are the evaluator's skills in organization, preparation, and observation. The trained evaluator is responsible for much more than simply observing and cataloging. Observer teams use detailed checklists to analyze every aspect of attractions, hotel rooms, restaurants, and clubs. Finally, evaluator ratings and observations are integrated with tourist reactions and the opinions of patrons for a comprehensive high-quality profile of each feature and service.

In compiling this guide, we recognize that tourists' ages, backgrounds, and interests will strongly influence their taste in South Florida offerings and will account for a preference for one city or hotel over another. Our sole objective is to provide the reader with sufficient description, critical evaluation, and pertinent data to make knowledgeable decisions according to individual tastes.

COMMENTS AND SUGGESTIONS FROM READERS

WE LEARN FROM OUR MISTAKES AND FROM reader input. Many of you write to us with your own discoveries and lessons learned in South Florida. We appreciate both positive and critical input, and encourage you to continue writing.

How to Contact the Author:

Lea Lane
The Unofficial Guide to South Florida
P.O. Box 43673
Birmingham, AL 35243
unofficialguides@menasharidge.com

Be sure to put your return address on your letter as well as on the envelope—sometimes they get separated. And remember, our work takes us out of the office for long periods, so forgive us if our response is delayed.

Reader Survey

At the back of our guide you'll find a short questionnaire concerning your South Florida visit. We encourage you to clip the questionnaire along the dotted line and mail it to the above address.

The *Unofficial Guide* Web Site

The Web site of the *Unofficial Guide* Travel and Lifestyle Series, providing in-depth information on all *Unofficial Guides* in print, is at **www.theunofficialguides.com.**

HOW INFORMATION *is* ORGANIZED

YOUR CHOICE OF HOTEL (OR CONDO) WILL SHAPE your South Florida vacation more than any other decision. Therefore, we devote an initial section to hotels and other lodging options. To facilitate touring, we present information on attractions, restaurants, and nightlife geographically, dividing the region into six smaller areas.

Sparkling *Miami,* with its Latin and European influences, is becoming a 24-7 city and no longer merely a winter retreat. Today, Miami-Dade County lures people year-round from around the globe and provides an active cultural scene and the famed clubs and beaches of Miami Beach. New artsy neighborhoods are developing rapidly.

The *Florida Keys* conjure up black-and-white images of Humphrey Bogart in *Key Largo,* or Ernest Hemingway imbibing at Sloppy Joe's and penning another masterpiece in his Key West study. Today the Keys offer sun, fun, and historic sites to enjoy, and the islands' major cruise port draws more than a million visitors each year, including divers and sportfishers.

Palm Beach County is the winter home for the Kennedys, Trumps, and thousands of multimillionaires whose names haven't yet made the tabloids. But Palm Beach County is also a thriving community of arts and history, where young families and active retirees coexist. Development after development sidles westward from the ocean toward the Everglades. Yet some coastal areas remain pristine.

Broward County, with its myriad new communities, offers waterways and beaches, the world's second-largest cruise port, a state-of-the-art airport, and one of the largest outlet shopping malls (more than 200 stores) in the world.

The Broward beaches of Hollywood, Dania Beach, Fort Lauderdale, Pompano Beach, and Deerfield Beach have been designated the first of Florida's favorable "Blue Wave" beaches.

Southwest Florida is booming as a tourism and retirement destination, but one that emphasizes nature and ecology. With its million-plus acres of nature sanctuaries, tourists can still explore virginal Florida and observe wildlife thriving in natural settings.

Adjacent *Everglades National Park* is the vast backyard of outdoor Florida. The as-yet-unspoiled wetlands of the largest national park east of the Rockies are home to a dazzling array of flora and fauna, and no South Florida vacation is complete without a visit.

MAPS AND PROFILES

TO HELP YOU ASSESS YOUR TRAVEL OPTIONS throughout South Florida, we've organized material using several formats. Maps of each region allow you to plan efficient touring. Easy-to-read profiles help you determine what to see and do. Here's the sort of information to expect:

HOTELS With so many lodging choices, our maps, ratings, and rankings help you focus and decide. We don't go on, page after page, describing lobbies and rooms. Instead, we concentrate on the major variables: location, size, room quality, services, amenities, and cost.

ATTRACTIONS We've provided detailed profiles of the best attractions in each South Florida destination. We rate each attraction by age group to help you decide which attractions are right for you. And we provide recommendations on other things to do nearby so you can plan a full day of sightseeing.

RESTAURANTS We provide detailed profiles of a variety of the best restaurants in South Florida—from informal to posh—and even offer suggestions for when to go and what to order.

ENTERTAINMENT AND NIGHTLIFE We spotlight the best bars, clubs, and lounges throughout South Florida, indicating what sort of crowds, music, and prices to anticipate.

SPECIAL FEATURES

OUR GOAL IS TO GIVE YOU WHAT YOU NEED for a maximum South Florida travel experience, so this *Unofficial Guide* offers:

- An overview of South Florida's history, to put things in perspective
- "Best ofs"—savvy opinions on everything from beaches to golf, from museums to the best views
- Well-organized, easy-to-read listings of attractions and shops, keyed to your interests
- Practical tips and inside information that locals know but tourists usually don't
- Maps to help you find what you want and avoid what you don't
- Expert advice on avoiding South Florida negatives, such as crime, traffic, crowds, sunburn, and expense
- Easy-to-read hotel information
- Our favorite restaurants and clubs
- A detailed index

florida area map

ALABAMA

GEORGIA

29

85

10

319

19

10

10

231

Fort Walton
Beach

CENTRAL
TIME

10

98

98

EASTERN
TIME

★ Tallahassee

19
27

Pensacola

Destin

Panama City

319

98

Perdido
Key

Panama City Beach

98

27

Apalachicola

St. George
Island

*Apalachee
Bay*

Gulf of Mexico

THE UNITED STATES

FLORIDA

0   50 mi
0   50 km

N

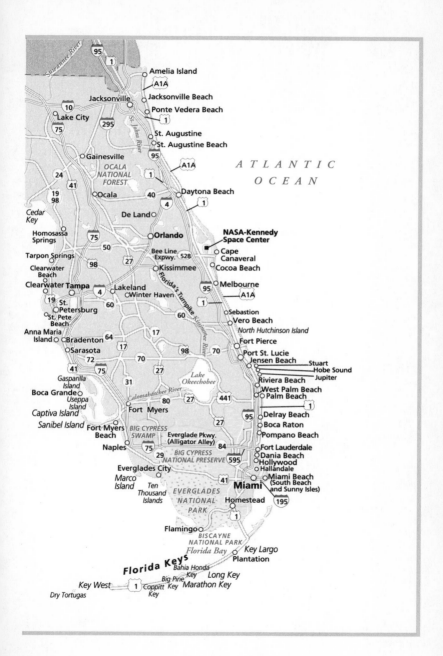

PART ONE

PLANNING *your* VISIT

HOW *it all* STARTED

IN TRUE AMERICAN FASHION, WAVES OF immigrants and entre-preneurs created South Florida's vibrant mix of Native Americans, Cuban fishermen, European artists, corporate honchos, Haitian refugees, northern snowbirds, Latin American businesspeople, and just about anyone else from anywhere, longing for sun and fun.

For generations, South Florida was stereotyped as a haven for retirees rocking on the front porches of its many beach hotels. Today, seniors—and people of all ages—are likely to be rocking in clubs or rock climbing on gym walls—and swinging tennis rackets and nine-irons, boating and diving, and enjoying South Florida's extensive cultural offerings.

In the 20th century, residents from the Northeast left snow and slush behind and opted for the sunshine of Florida's Atlantic Coast. Mid-westerners settled in communities along the Gulf of Mexico. In the 21st century, it's all about sexy energy, no matter where you were born or when, creating a spirited South Florida demographic mix.

THE QUEST FOR YOUTH

THE EARLIEST SETTLERS WERE MIGRATORY Native Americans drawn to the region 10,000 years ago, like many since, by warm weather and good fishing. From hunter-gatherer tribes developed towns and, ul-timately, societies, the remnants of which—pottery, burial mounds in downtown Miami—await curious contemporary visitors.

However, South Florida was changed forever with the arrival of one 16th-century Spanish immigrant, and Hispanic influence in the region expanded exponentially.

Ponce de León never found the Fountain of Youth, but he did claim what is now Southwest Florida for Spain, in 1521 (on his second voyage to Florida). Wounded by Native Americans shortly after arriving, he and his expedition withdrew and sailed for Cuba, where he died shortly after landing.

Spanish settlement and political rule continued in Florida for 300 years. Spanish missions undertook the conversion to Catholicism of the indigenous Calusa Indians. The tribe of fierce warriors, whose roots can be found along the coastal and barrier islands as far back as 5000 BC, was ultimately wiped out by war and disease.

The 1783 Treaty of Paris granted the Spanish authority to protect Florida's coast and shipping routes. Yet although the Spanish language and Catholic faith had long distinguished Florida from English settlements to the north, the young United States bought the territory of Florida from Spain in 1821.

The First Seminole War (1816–18) prompted the acquisition. The Seminoles (literally, "separatists") retreated from Georgia to the wilds of Florida in the 18th century. They drew the ire of General Andrew Jackson for harboring escaped slaves. The war merely drove the Seminoles southward, and two wars followed, fought largely in South Florida's Everglades, before most remaining Seminoles were resettled in the West.

TRACKING FLORIDA

PALM BEACH AT THE END OF THE 19TH century was an isolated area of private estates and broad beaches, a prime site for a mogul's winter vacation home. When Henry Flagler, a founding partner in Standard Oil, first brought his rail line to Palm Beach in 1893, he chose not to continue south into Miami, 65 miles away.

Julia Tuttle, a businesswoman and citrus farmer, was born in Cleveland, but she settled on the north bank of the Miami River in 1891. She soon resolved to find a railroad magnate who would build a line south to Miami. When the 1894–95 frost depleted crops in Palm Beach, Tuttle sent a simple but eloquent message to Flagler: a single orange blossom. Flagler decided to take his train farther south and completed the line to Miami on April 15, 1896. Legend has it that all 300 Miami residents turned out to greet the locomotive.

Before the turn of the century, Miami was printing a newspaper. Soon churches and schools were established, and the city was calling itself "America's Sun Porch." Flagler extended his railroad to Key West, at the southern tip of Florida, in 1912.

In the 1920s, a land boom developed from Palm Beach to the Keys, and the real estate market was as sizzling as the Florida sun. Low-priced South Florida land sites were offered for sale across the nation. But alas, much land consisted of swamps—many lots were under water, and some didn't even exist. So began South Florida's reputation as an area of fast-talking salesmen (a reputation, some would say, that is still deserved).

But nature intervened in 1926, when a hurricane devastated the area. Those garrulous salesmen took their pitches elsewhere, and South Florida suffered hard financial times. Art Deco hotels did rise in South Beach in the late 1930s and early 1940s, however, establishing Miami as a winter-vacation destination, along with fancier Palm Beach.

WORLD WAR II TO THE PRESENT

MILITARY PERSONNEL TRAINING IN MIAMI enjoyed Florida's sun and sand on rest-and-relaxation leave, and at the end of World War II, many returned to establish homes and families, taking advantage of Veteran's Administration low-interest-rate mortgages and low down payments. The construction industry—and the entire area—entered another boom; hotels, homes, and apartments sprang up like tropical foliage after a rainstorm.

Air-conditioning was not yet ubiquitous, so many hotels and restaurants were shuttered during the hot and humid summers. Traffic slowed considerably, and the area was but a series of sleepy Southern towns waiting to wake again in the cooler months.

In the 1950s, the region was largely a winter home for wealthy families from the Northeast and Midwest. Major hotels were built in Miami Beach, and tourism thrived in this pre-jet era, before Caribbean islands drew away vacationers.

Stable economic times fueled a condo boom in the 1960s, and high-rises towered along the Atlantic Ocean in Miami-Dade and Broward counties, where beachfronts were sacrificed to developers. With highways expanding, some Broward County neighborhoods became bedroom communities for Miami's workers. The Southwest Coast and Keys developed slowly but steadily, their natural beauty left mainly unspoiled.

Cuban Immigration

In 1960, Fidel Castro came to power in Cuba (only 90 miles south of Key West), triggering the first wave of Cuban immigration. The Cuban Missile Crisis of October 1962 again put South Florida in the news, when Castro's guns and Russia's missiles were aimed at the region.

Four decades later, Miami has become what many consider the most Latin city in the United States, where strong, hot *café cubano* is the wakeup drink of choice for more than half the population. Calle Ocho (Eighth Street), the main street of this community, has become a destination for tourists and a center of life for three generations of Cuban Americans.

The 1970s

Fort Lauderdale developed as a city but gained fame (and notoriety), as the nation's spring-break capital, annually hosting some 350,000 college kids from all over the country. The film *Where the Boys Are,* starring George Hamilton and Connie Francis, began a tradition of beer guzzling and wet-T-shirt contests that continues today. But many students discovered beaches elsewhere, much to the joy of locals and other tourists, and Fort Lauderdale focused on the quiet delights of living between the Intracoastal Waterway and Atlantic Ocean.

Miami, meanwhile, became a major player in international banking and business as the gateway to Latin America. Huge office buildings were erected along Brickell Avenue, a combination of Wall Street and Park Avenue, with a lush tropical edge. But despite the new soaring skyline, Miami's historic downtown languished.

Cities and towns continued to grow elsewhere in the region. Key West, long a sleepy, fishing and port town, was enlivened by an influx of artistic types and an active gay community. In Southwest Florida, retirement enclaves and well-off neighborhoods were developed neatly along the gulf, avoiding the overzealous building of East Coast Florida.

Notoriety and Another Boom

South Florida saw its share of problems in the 1980s. Massive Cuban immigration, the resultant tent cities where newly arrived Cubans lived for months, and horrendous crime statistics straight out of TV's *Miami Vice* marked the decade.

All the while, growth continued, Miami's South Beach blossomed, and the once-seedy Art Deco District started attracting photographers, models, and wannabes. The fashion press posed gorgeous men and women against a backdrop of pastel hotels, white sand, and turquoise sea. The publicity worked, and huge numbers of tourists began arriving daily from Germany, Scandinavia, Great Britain, and elsewhere in Europe, enlivening the international mix.

Disaster Strikes Again

Hurricane Andrew hit South Florida in 1992, causing nearly $20 billion in damage. Many Miami-area families whose homes were devastated by the monster hurricane relocated to Broward and Palm Beach counties or Florida's southwest coast.

The area made tremendous efforts to rebuild itself, and as the century ended, South Florida was again a world-class tourist destination—extending now across the state to Southwest Florida and down through the Florida Keys.

SOUTH FLORIDA TODAY

THE YEAR 2000 SAW THE SAGA OF ELIAN GONZALEZ played out on nightly newscasts as the boy's immigrant family and Cuban father vied for custody of him. Stories of Florida consumer scams and political graft also made headlines, and the year ended with the drama of hanging chads in the disputed presidential election of 2000.

Following September 11, 2001 came the revelation that some terrorists had lived in Florida, as well as the discovery of anthrax in Palm Beach. Worries hung in the air like humidity in August.

But the region cleaned up its act. South Florida—from coast to coast—saw lower crime figures and an improved quality of life. Today, leisure and business travel have increased, convention centers are doing big business, and hotels and motels are full. People are not only traveling to South Florida, they are buying second homes, as the real estate market has boomed.

Nothing, it seems, can beat incredible winter climate, fresh ocean breezes, and hotels and restaurants charged with a tropical energy. Shopping areas in South Florida can compete with any elsewhere, cultural venues are increasingly sophisticated, and tourist attractions grow ever more spectacular. South Florida is a 21st-century destination for the world, and it's getting better every year.

MIAMI-DADE COUNTY   In the new millennium, Miami is an ever-more-vital business center for Latin America. It has also become the "cruise capital of the world," with dozens of ships calling the beautiful port home; the city's huge airport is the number-one gateway for both cargo and passengers traveling to the Caribbean and Latin America.

Miami Beach's diverse community has gone from mainly Jewish to half Hispanic, a change that began in the late 1970s when the Jewish community began its trek northward into Broward and Palm Beach counties. And the average age of residents has since dropped from 69 to 41!

South Beach today draws an international crowd of clubbers and fashionistas, and the energy and sexiness of SoBe, as it's known, is spilling over into all parts of the city. Besides the resurgence of the city's Art Deco corridor, outlying communities continue to grow, each with its own character.

THE FLORIDA KEYS   Though still isolated by geography, the Florida Keys are today more accessible than ever, thanks to transportation and communication connectivity. Visitors to the Keys, many of whom come for world-class diving and fishing, tend to stay longer and to opt for historic hotels and bed-and-breakfasts over high-rise condos. The relaxed character of the Keys remains a major draw, and locals take pride in the lazy tropical character of their towns.

PALM BEACH COUNTY   Legend has it that Palm Beach was so named after the remnants of a Spanish ship carrying a load of coconuts from Trinidad washed ashore. (Some locals joke that rich white nuts are still coming there, but we don't agree, of course.)

Since Henry Flagler's time, Palm Beach has been synonymous with grand lifestyles. Gated waterfront mansions hide behind walls covered in purple and scarlet bougainvillea. Shops, clubs, and galleries seem exclusive (and often are).

Palm Beach County remains a bastion for the wealthy—and for vacationers seeking a bit of luxury for themselves. One city on the south end of the county has grown incredibly: Boca Raton. In Spanish, the name means "rat's mouth," supposedly a term sailors used to describe a hidden rock that destroys ship's cables. But "mink's mouth" might be more appropriate in this ever-expanding upscale community, as elegant homes and condos with $1 million–plus price tags sprawl westward from the ocean.

BROWARD COUNTY What was once a solitary strip of beach development 1.5 miles long is today only part of Greater Fort Lauderdale, which encompasses 30 municipalities and 1,200 square miles. The area extends from the Atlantic Ocean to the depths of the Everglades and from Palm Beach County to Miami-Dade County.

Investors and taxpayers have spent big bucks in Greater Fort Lauderdale, including a major expansion and renovation of Fort Lauderdale Hollywood International Airport.

The area is now a self-contained tourist destination, with museums, a performing-arts center, and the Intracoastal Waterway, a system of canals that draws boaters from around the world.

SOUTHWEST FLORIDA On Florida's Gulf of Mexico, Lee and Collier counties and the cities of Fort Myers, Fort Myers Beach, Marco Island, and Naples are popular tourist destinations. More than two million tourists visit Southwest Florida each year. When inventor Thomas Edison, auto tycoon Henry Ford, and tire mogul Harvey Firestone made Fort Myers their winter home a hundred years ago, the population of the city was less than a thousand. Today, the county has almost half a million residents, approximately twice what it had ten years ago, and the population practically doubles during winter months.

unofficial **TIP**
Winter months are the best time to visit the Everglades (it's the dry season, so mosquitoes are usually scarce, and alligators and herons congregate around the remaining water).

THE EVERGLADES Thanks to growing interest in ecotourism, more South Florida vacationers are including the "Rivers of Grass" on their itineraries. Though development still threatens the Everglades, Floridians have cultivated great pride in this fragile environmental wonder. A multibillion-dollar restoration plan, approved by Congress in 2000, aims to ensure that Everglades National Park continues to lure travelers for years to come.

WHEN *to* GO

THE CORRECT SEASONING

FROM LATE NOVEMBER THROUGH EARLY APRIL, South Florida's subtropical climate offers almost-perfect blue skies, warm sunshine, and low humidity.

The winter season generally starts just before Christmas and ends just after Easter. Christmas week, the busiest week of the year, pushes tourist facilities, restaurants, and hotels to their limit throughout South Florida. The period between Thanksgiving and Christmas, however, offers manageable crowds at attractions, beaches, and restaurants—and finding a reasonably priced hotel room is easier.

While crowds recede after New Year's Day, things pick up in mid-January, as northerners and midwesterners settle into their winter digs. The winter peak season continues through Easter, and that week is almost as crowded as the winter holidays.

South Florida's Average Monthly Temperatures Degrees Fahrenheit

MONTH	HIGH	LOW
January	74°	63°
February	76°	63°
March	77°	65°
April	79°	68°
May	83°	72°
June	85°	76°
July	88°	76°
August	88°	77°
September	86°	76°
October	83°	72°
November	79°	67°
December	76°	67°

The Summer Season

Yes, summers smolder, but breezes off the water usually cool things a bit. The Miami area has traditionally been a major summer destination for South Americans who head north to shop and escape their winter weather. Action picks up in June, and the summer season continues through mid-August, when kids head back to school. The July 4th and Labor Day weekends see great crowds.

This is the rainy season, characterized by ferocious (though usually brief) afternoon thunderstorms, high temperatures, and often equally high humidity. Though less of a long-range consideration, hurricane season runs from June through November—one more reason to make refundable or transferable reservations.

The intense sun and high temperatures can be oppressive, but most natives pay more attention to a weather forecast's humidity levels than the day's high temperature (80% humidity or below is comfortable; the high 90s is not).

For comfort, as well as crowd and thunderstorm avoidance, touring, tennis, golf, and sightseeing should be done early in the day or late in the afternoon.

But don't let tales of heat and humidity keep you away. We definitely recommend South Florida's off-season. Remember that just about everything indoors is air-conditioned. (In fact, locals keep cotton sweaters handy, as many public places are over–air-conditioned.) Unless you plan to run a marathon or trek through the Everglades, those few minutes outdoors won't hurt anyone.

In return, you'll find hotel prices are lower than in the winter. With moderately priced airfares, a summer getaway weekend in South Florida is definitely doable.

Soft Shoulders

The two "shoulder" periods between the major tourist seasons—mid-April through early June and September through mid-December—offer the best chances of avoiding large crowds, packed attractions, and expensive lodging. The weather is usually pleasant and dry (though rainier than the winter months).

unofficial **TIP**
If you're driving into South Florida on a weekday, avoid hitting town between 7:30 a.m. and 9 a.m., and 4 p.m. to 6 p.m. Time your arrival or departure to midday hours (although in season, highways and expressways seem gridlocked all day long). The Florida Turnpike makes a terrific alternate route to the Florida Keys, bypassing Miami and mucho traffic. Keep a map handy and look for similar side-road alternatives when plotting your route. Last but not least, try Miami's Metrorail. It could save you a lot of time, not to mention the hassle of finding a parking space.

Note, however, that the shoulder season isn't entirely outside South Florida's June-to-November hurricane season. Statistically, chances are fairly low that one of the huge tropical storms will hit during your visit—and if it does, there will be plenty of warning. Evacuation routes are well marked, and media weather coverage is seemingly omnipresent.

CROWD CONTROL

MOST POPULAR TOURIST SIGHTS are busiest on Saturdays. The winter season is by far the busiest time of year at most attractions, but kid-friendly places such as the Seaquarium in Miami, Butterfly World in Broward, and Lion Country Safari in Palm Beach may not be as crowded, compared with summer.

Avoid driving in South Florida's rush-hour traffic, especially on the Florida Turnpike (also called Ronald Reagan Turnpike), Interstate 95, US 1, Interstate 75, and US 41 (also called Tamiami Trail) from the East Coast to the Gulf Coast.

In the Miami area, expect equally heavy traffic on the two east–west expressways that connect with I-95 near downtown: the Dolphin

Expressway (FL 836) and the Airport Expressway (FL 112). US 1 below downtown is the only direct route to Coconut Grove, Coral Gables, and points south; rush-hour gridlock is the norm.

█ GATHERING INFORMATION

BEFORE YOU LEAVE HOME

WHEN PLANNING YOUR TRIP, CHECK OUT organizations dedicated to helping you make the most of your time.

VISIT FLORIDA HEADQUARTERS ☎ 888-7-FLA-USA; **www.visitflorida. com;** Visit Florida Headquarters, 661 East Jefferson Street, Suite 300, Tallahassee, FL 32301. Vacation guides are available in versions for France, Germany, Spain, the United States. and the United Kingdom.

MIAMI-DADE COUNTY Visitor Service Center at the Greater Miami Convention and Visitors Bureau, 701 Brickell Avenue, Suite 2700, Miami, FL 33131; ☎ 800-933-8448 or 305-539-3000; **www.tropicoolmiami.com.**

THE FLORIDA KEYS Monroe County Tourist Development Council, ☎ 800-FLA-KEYS; **www.fla-keys.com.**

PALM BEACH COUNTY Palm Beach County Convention & Visitors Bureau, 1555 Palm Beach Lakes Boulevard, Suite 800, West Palm Beach, FL 33401; ☎ 561-233-3000; fax 561-471-3990; **www.palmbeachfl.com.**

BROWARD COUNTY Greater Fort Lauderdale Convention & Visitors Bureau, 100 East Broward Boulevard, Suite 200, Fort Lauderdale, FL 33316; ☎ 800-22-SUNNY (in the U.S. and Canada) or 954-765-4466; fax 954-765-4467; **www.sunny.org.**

SOUTHWEST FLORIDA Lee Island Coast Visitor & Convention Bureau, 12800 University Drive, Suite 550, Fort Myers, FL 33907; ☎ 800-237-6444; **www.leeislandcoast.com.**

TOURISM ALLIANCE OF COLLIER COUNTY 3050 Horseshoe Drive, #218, Naples, FL 34104; ☎ 800-688-3600 or 239-403-2384; **www.paradise coast.com.**

HIGHWAY HELP: OFFICIAL FLORIDA WELCOME CENTERS FOR MOTORISTS

I-95	7 miles north of Yulee on I-95 South ☎ 904-225-9182; fax 904-225-0064
I-75	4 miles north of Jennings on I-75 South ☎ 386-938-2981; fax 904-938-1292
I-10	16 miles west of Pensacola on I-10 East ☎ 850-944-0442; fax 850-944-3675
US 231	3 miles north of Campbellton; ☎ 850-263-3510 (phone/fax)
The Capitol	Plaza Level, Tallahassee, 32301 ☎ 850-488-6167; fax 850-414-2560

INFORMATION ON VACATION

Publications for Visitors

The *Miami Herald* is Miami's only daily newspaper, while the *South Florida Sun-Sentinel* does the job for Broward County. Both papers provide Friday editions with comprehensive information on entertainment, restaurants, nightclubs, happenings for kids, art reviews, and goings-on about town. Try to grab a Friday edition before heading south, or go online to **www.herald.com** or **www.sun-sentinel.com.**

Another source for listings is the weekly *New Times*, an alternative newspaper available free from street boxes as well as from a wide variety of clubs, bars, and shops around town. It carries listings for both Miami-Dade and Broward counties.

Other publications available at newsstands and hotel lobbies include *Metro Metro*, the area's main monthly magazine; *City and Shore*, a bimonthly; *Ocean Drive*, a glossy South Miami Beach magazine that chronicles the comings and goings of celebrities and beautiful people; *South Beach*, a bimonthly with a more artistic slant on SoBe life; and *Travel Host*, a visitors' guide with information on shopping, dining, clubs, pay-per-view television, and maps.

In Palm Beach, the local newspaper is the *Palm Beach Post;* however, both the *Herald* and the *Sun-Sentinel* include the Palm Beach area in their weekly listings on Friday. Other South Florida daily newspapers include Fort Myers's *News-Press* and Naples's *Naples Daily News*. The area's magazines include *Florida Journal*, *Fort Myers Life*, *Gulfshore Life*, *Southwest Florida Business Magazine*, and *Times of the Islands/Shore* and *Island Living*.

Radio

Aside from the usual babble of format rock, talk, easy listening, and country music stations, South Florida is home to a few radio stations that really stand out for high-quality broadcasting. Scanning the dial may produce a pleasant surprise—and make the gridlock bearable when you're stuck in traffic.

SOUTH FLORIDA RADIO STATIONS	
SOUTH FLORIDA	
Format	Frequency
Christian contemporary	89.7 FM
Country	99.9 FM
Easy listening, jazz	93.9 FM
Electronica, dance	93.1 FM
Hip-hop, rap, R&B	96.5 FM, 99.1 FM
Jazz, Latin	88.9 FM

SOUTH FLORIDA RADIO STATIONS (CONTINUED)

SOUTH FLORIDA (CONTINUED)

Format	Frequency
Latin	98.3 FM
Public radio	91.3 FM
Rock	94.9 FM
Sports radio	560 AM
Top 40	100.7 FM

SOUTHWEST FLORIDA

Format	Frequency
Rock	96.1 FM
Alternative country 1	107.1 FM
Alternative country 2	105.5 FM
Public radio	90.1 FM

INFORMATION AND ACCESS FOR DISABLED VISITORS

MOST PUBLIC PLACES IN SOUTH FLORIDA now offer facilities for visitors with physical disabilities, including wheelchair access. Following the passage of the federal Americans with Disabilities Act (ADA) in 1990, the issue of access gained a higher profile in Miami. Even small Art Deco hotels in South Beach are now outfitted with elevators, ramps, and bathroom railings to make their rooms wheelchair accessible. Plus, many buses are now equipped with lowering platforms that allow wheelchair-bound passengers to board. Even in Everglades National Park, all the walking trails are wheelchair accessible.

Florida state law requires that guide dogs be permitted in all establishments. Also, motorists must yield to people with white canes and guide dogs.

Out-of-state vehicles displaying disability parking permits/plates issued by another state are allowed to park in spaces designated for persons with disabilities.

TRANSPORTATION SERVICES FOR THE DISABLED

MIAMI-DADE COUNTY

Special Transportation Services (☎ 305-263-5406)

PALM BEACH

Dial-A-Ride Yellow Cab (☎ 561-689-2222)

TRANSPORTATION SERVICES FOR THE DISABLED (CONTINUED)

BROWARD

Paratransit (☎ 954-357-6794 or 954-347-8400 for schedules and routes)
Tri-Rail TDD (☎ 800-874-7245)

SOUTHWEST FLORIDA

Comfort Service (☎ 239-995-8313)
Elite Transportation (☎ 239-275-8726)
Good Wheels (10075 Bavaria Road, Fort Myers; ☎ 239-768-2900)
United Way Helpline (7275 Concourse Drive SW, Fort Myers;
    ☎ 239-433-5000 or 941-433-5154 TDD)

South Florida Organizations Serving People with Disabilities

The Deaf Services Bureau (Gables One Tower, 1320 South Dixie Highway, Suite 760, Coral Gables; ☎ 305-668-4407 voice/TDD or TTY 305-668-3328; fax 305-670-4811) provides interpreter services, advocacy, information, personal counseling, special-needs assistance, and a 24-hour crisis hotline: ☎ 305-668-4694 (TDD). The bureau is open Monday, Tuesday, Thursday, and Friday, 9 a.m.–5 p.m.; Wednesday, 9 a.m.–noon. **The Deaf Service Center of Southwest Florida** (1860 Boy Scout Drive, #B-208, Fort Myers; ☎ 239-461-0334, fax 239-462-0434) performs a similar function to the west.

The Florida Relay Service (200 South Biscayne Boulevard, Suite 600, Miami; ☎ 800-955-8770 or 800-955-8771 TDD) serves as a liaison for deaf and hard-of-hearing visitors with TDDs who need to contact persons without TDD-equipped phones. The service operates 24 hours a day, seven days a week.

The State of Florida Division of Blind Services (401 Northwest Second Avenue, Suite S714, Miami, ☎ 305-377-5339; and 2830 Winkler Avenue, Suite 207, Fort Myers, ☎ 239-278-7130) provides services to visually impaired people.

Paraplegics and other physically disabled people needing referrals to services in the Miami area can contact **D-SAIL, the Metro-Dade Disability Services and Independent Living,** (1310 Northwest 14th Street, Miami; ☎ 305-547-5444).

WEB SITES RECOMMENDED BY THE SOCIETY FOR THE ADVANCEMENT OF TRAVEL FOR THE HANDICAPPED

www.access-able.com	Access-Able Travel Source
www.disabilitytravel.com	Accessible Journeys
www.accessiblevans.com	Accessible Vans of America
www.wheelchair-getaways.com	Wheelchair Getaways

The **Disability Affairs** section of the Broward County Equal Opportunity Office (115 South Andrews Avenue, Fort Lauderdale; ☎ 954-357-6500) operates in accord with the ADA. Also of note are the county's **Advocacy Center for Persons with Disabilities** (☎ 954-967-1493), **Disabilities Helpline** (☎ 954-527-5751), and **Emergency Management office** (☎ 954-831-3916 and 954-357-6402).

SOUTH FLORIDA DESTINATIONS: WHICH *is* RIGHT *for* YOU?

GLITZ OR NATURE? ROUGH SEAS OR CALM? Wild nightlife (models and playboys) or night wildlife (alligators and herons)? South Florida offers it all. We've already outlined each of the geographic zones in South Florida and shared the recent history of each. Below, we examine further the character of each region and the atmosphere and activities you will find there, so that you can focus your travel time on the things that most appeal to you. (We omit the Everglades here because, despite its vastness, lodging and amenities are understandably limited.)

MIAMI-DADE COUNTY

BRIGHTLY LIT SKYSCRAPERS UNDER A HUGE Miami moon, palms and shops and bikinis along Ocean Drive—hey, this great city is in its heyday, right now!

In Miami-Dade, "Miami Beach" is the glamour name. And in Miami Beach, South Beach—SoBe—is the most glamorous of all. Don't miss touring the Art Deco hotels or strolling down Ocean Drive to people-watch. Fashion designer Gianni Versace was murdered on the front steps of his palatial estate, which has become a macabre must-see for celebrity-watchers on this otherwise-upbeat street. Nearby, Rollerbladers and sunbathers people Lummus Park.

Though famous (or infamous), SoBe is really only a two-mile strip on the south end of Miami Beach. Miami-Dade is much more, with burgeoning neighborhoods and municipalities, including Central Miami Beach, North Miami Beach, Brickell, Little Havana, Little Haiti, Coral Gables, Coconut Grove, and the new city of Aventura, all integral parts of greater Miami. Downtown is developing artsy enclaves and becoming a destination.

Each area has its own flavor and much to offer tourists, and new neighborhoods are developing all around. The communities of Surfside, Bal Harbour, and Sunny Isles are still dominated by Jewish and Canadian tourists and retirees, but visitors come from around the world.

In mid–Miami Beach, two 1950s temples to excess, the Fontaine-bleau and the Eden Roc, are still megahotels. Not quite the hot spots they once were—Frank Sinatra, Harry Belafonte, Milton Berle, and Nat King Cole once starred in their showrooms—both are nevertheless oceanfront and have been extensively updated.

THE FLORIDA KEYS

A STRING OF TINY ISLANDS CURVING AT THE tip of Florida, between the Atlantic and the Gulf of Mexico, the Keys are connected to the mainland by a series of long causeways. The Florida Keys are paradise for those who enjoy fishing, snorkeling, and diving around the only coral reef in the continental United States.

Day-trippers generally only make it to Upper Keys, around Key Largo, but the Middle Keys, such as Marathon, are perfect for lazing and fishing. At the end of the line is Key West; the gingerbread-Victorian houses, museums, and renowned sunsets are worth the journey.

unofficial **TIP**
Many families vacation off-season in the Keys, where during high season (from late November until Easter) it can be just as crowded as mainland Florida. Before you go, check when cruise ships are in. Avoid Key West during those times, if possible, as the crowds are overwhelming.

PALM BEACH COUNTY

PALM BEACH COUNTY HAS CLOSE TO 150 golf courses—more than any other in the nation—as well as the Palm Beach Polo and Country Club, where Prince Charles has played the game. Trendy Worth Avenue is a delightful corridor of tiles, staircases, sculptures, archways, and hidden lanes lined with some 200 boutiques and charming, intimate restaurants. Cultural attractions include the Kravis Center, the Norton Museum, and the original mansion of Henry Flagler.

Think Trump, Kennedy, and Pulitzer—Palm Beach denizens who live in style, and in the public eye. Most Palm Beach residents are less famous, but just as rich—megabucks property owners who enjoy the Atlantic Ocean at their back door and private clubs as their playgrounds.

If you want to live in the same high style for a while, the Breakers in Palm Beach and the Boca Raton Hotel and Resort are two elegant old hotels, each redone at tremendous expense. If you just want to look the part, Palm Beach thrift shops are the way to go, offering last year's designer outfits at garage sale prices. We found a black cashmere sweater with rhinestone appliqués for $40—perfect for New Year's celebration.

As you head west from the ocean, dozens of more affordable condominium and townhome complexes provide a (somewhat) toned-down lifestyle. West Palm Beach is undergoing a development renaissance that attempts to preserve the charm while upping the excitement.

BROWARD COUNTY

BROWARD COUNTY IS PALM BEACH'S LESS haughty neighbor to the south. More than 500 daily arrivals and departures are scheduled at Fort Lauderdale Hollywood International Airport. Recently redone at a cost of about $700 million, it's user friendly and fast growing.

Port Everglades, just minutes from the airport, is second only to Miami as a cruise-ship hub. While winter holiday vacations find the area busier than ever, summer family vacations in Greater Fort Lauderdale are increasingly popular. Families from Europe and South America frequent the area. Las Olas Boulevard and Riverwalk, with its Broward Performing Arts Center, are charming pedestrian thoroughfares.

Many tourists come via package tie-ins to Disney vacations. Sophisticated, upscale visitors will target the Saint Regis, a five-star hotel on Fort Lauderdale Beach; the business-oriented Renaissance offers a convenient location; and the Seminole Hard Rock Hotel and Casino is a 750-room property on the Seminole Indian Reservation in Hollywood.

Sawgrass Mills is the world's largest discount and entertainment mall, with more than 2,780 brand-name and designer outlets, discount stores, specialty shops, and restaurants.

The Fort Lauderdale area is also a haven for golfers, with more than 50 affordable courses, including municipal, public, semiprivate, private, and various nighttime driving ranges. Boaters enjoy the crisscrossed canals of the Intracoastal Waterway.

SOUTHWEST FLORIDA

CONFEDERATE GENERAL ROBERT E. LEE NEVER visited the area, but the Lee Island Coast, settled in 1887, was named for him. Today, tourists flock to Lee County's hot spots: Captiva and Sanibel Islands, Boca Grande, Bonita Springs, Cape Coral, Fort Myers, Fort Myers Beach, Lehigh Acres, North Fort Myers, and Pine Island. Farther south along the Gulf of Mexico are Naples, a long-standing popular tourist draw, and Marco Island, near the Everglades.

Gulf Coast beaches are powdery white, and many are part of sprawling parks offering recreational settings. These Gulf beaches offer some of the greatest shelling in the world (so famous with collectors that the shelling posture has been dubbed the "Captiva Crouch" and the "Sanibel Stoop").

In Naples alone, accommodations range from small bed-and-breakfasts to the Ritz-Carlton, with its three-story spa. Area tennis and golf facilities consistently rank among the best in the country. Babcock Wilderness Experience in Boca Grande and Everglades National Park (home to 1.5 million acres of the largest wetland ecosystem in the country) are havens for those inclined to explore natural environments and view endangered species.

The entire west coast is a prime vacation area for midwesterners, as well as Canadians who eschew the glitzier Atlantic vacation destinations for the charm and calmer beauty of the southwest Gulf Coast.

BEFORE *you* GO OUTSIDE: CONSIDERATIONS *for* RECREATION

HANDLING FLORIDA WEATHER

FLORIDA'S TRADEMARK HEAT AND HUMIDITY are usually mitigated by a breeze off the ocean, so they don't feel as oppressive as a major northern city in a summer heat wave. While the breezes are augmented by the ubiquitous air-conditioning, we agree that living or vacationing in the South Florida climate takes some getting used to.

Summer storms—complete with world-class lightning shows—can be a daily occurrence and usually strike in late afternoon. Plan your exercise and recreation for the morning to avoid storms as well the heat of midafternoon.

Even if you do little more than walk to your car in a parking lot, you are exposed to the strong rays of a tropical sun, so always use sunscreen. Check with a dermatologist if you have sensitive skin or don't know which SPF to buy. Remember to cover those "danger zones": the back of the neck, the shoulders, the face, and behind the ears. If thinning hair is a problem, cover your scalp or wear a hat—head sunburn hurts.

Reapply sunscreen when sweat or water washes the original application away. Increase your exposure gradually over the course of your trip; don't plan a full day at the beach right away. Remember: South Florida shares the same latitude as the Sahara Desert.

Dehydration, like sunburn, is a constant threat in Florida's hot summer, but it's as easily avoided. Carry a bottle of water around with you, and keep hydrated. Avoid sweet, caffeinated, and alcoholic drinks—colas and fruit drinks don't hydrate as well as water, and alcohol or even tea can dry you out.

Lastly, dress appropriately. When that tropical sun bakes down during summer months, you'll be much more comfortable in loose-fitting pastels and whites than in darker hues.

Pest Control

Because South Florida rarely experiences freezing temperatures, residents contend with a plethora of insects year-round. But don't be shocked by the huge cockroaches called palmetto bugs. The good news: They're only active at night, they don't crawl on you, and they don't bite or make noise.

Another local insect with a notorious reputation—this one more well deserved—is the mosquito. But if your stay in South Florida revolves around the beach, mosquitoes aren't much of a problem. Ocean breezes keep the pesky critters at a minimal level all year long.

The worst place of all for mosquitoes is the Everglades, except in the winter—and even then it's a good idea to use insect repellent, which is readily available at retail outlets and visitor centers.

During the summer, many South Florida residents listen closely to local news broadcasts for reports of mosquito activity. Long, wet periods of rain often result in a predictable explosion in the mosquito population. If one is on the way, consider rescheduling any extended outdoor activities that you're planning away from the beach.

One particularly awful result of a heavy infestation of mosquitoes is encephalitis. It is not a common disease in Florida, and most summers see no cases reported. However, another mosquito-borne illness, West Nile virus, has made headlines in recent years.

During periods of mosquito infestation, health officials advise taking these precautions:

- Avoid outdoor activities between dusk and dawn, when mosquitoes are most active.

- If you must be outside at night, wear long pants and long-sleeved shirts, as well as insect repellent on exposed skin.

- Avoid water—especially standing water—at night.

GOLF AND TENNIS

HEAT AND HUMIDITY MAKE FOR A REAL workout on the golf course or tennis court, so most local golfers and tennis players try to opt for early-morning, late-afternoon, or evening games.

Weekends, when local residents hit the links, are always busy regardless of season, and getting a morning tee time is difficult. Plan on teeing off either before 9 a.m. or after 4 p.m.

Besides heat, be wary of sudden tropical rainstorms. Florida is the lightning capital of the world, and a golf course is a terrible place to be in a thunderstorm. Even before the storm rolls in, consider heading for the clubhouse. And don't seek shelter under a tree: If you're caught outside, seek a lower elevation.

BEACH PRECAUTIONS

ON FLORIDA BEACHES, RED FLAGS WARN you not to swim, although beaches are rarely closed and swimmers may choose to ignore the warning. Yellow flags mean caution; ask the lifeguard

unofficial **TIP**
Choose a hotel with lighted tennis courts, so you'll be able to play as much as you want. Consider playing golf late in the afternoon, when courses offer reduced fees for afternoon play. And ask your hotel to book tee times or court reservations in advance of your arrival whenever possible.

to tell you the specific hazard (jellyfish or riptide, for example). However, the most common hazard on the beach isn't rough water or bad weather—it's the sun. Cloudy days pose a particular hazard because beachgoers often underestimate the exposure their skin receives and end up burned.

Riptides, also called undertows, usually occur when winds are blowing ashore from 15 to 20 miles an hour, creating a break offshore that drains water from the beach. Even if you're a strong swimmer, don't fight a riptide. Rather, swim with the undertow parallel to the beach. Eventually, you'll break free.

Panic is far more dangerous than riptides themselves. The same is true for cramps and other swimming hazards. Sometimes as tides come in, swimmers find themselves in deeper water, realize they can't touch bottom, and panic. It is wise to cast frequent glances ashore (or to children playing in the waves) and to position yourself near a lifeguard. If an incident does occur, shouting will draw a quick response from shore. Tread water and wave your arms, but don't panic.

Pale-pink jellyfish can appear on Florida's shores at any time but are more common in the winter. Portuguese men-of-war, bluish-purple translucent creatures as beautiful as Tiffany glass, are more common in the summer. Both have tentacles that sting. Yellow warning flags indicate their presence in the water. If they wash ashore, avoid stepping on them—the tentacles still sting. If you get stung, go to a lifeguard for help or, if you are feeling really unwell, a hospital emergency room. In the absence of help, don't touch the tentacle; instead, scrape it away from your skin using a credit card or something similar, and treat the sting with vinegar.

Sea lice—actually the spores of Portuguese men-of-war—are invisible creatures that cause an itchy rash called swimmers' eruption. The rash lasts about a week and can be treated with cortisone lotion. Avoid seaweed or anything else floating in the water, since the spores usually come ashore on a host.

Stingrays, another potential hazard, bury themselves in the sand. Occasionally, swimmers step on them, and the barb on the end of a stingray's tail, while it isn't poisonous, is usually dirty and poses an infection risk.

Finally, what about everybody's beach fear: sharks? Shark attack is the least of your worries at the beach—in Florida or elsewhere. Attacks are very rare. Nevertheless, shark sightings are taken very seriously. Often the Coast Guard will investigate and clear nearby beaches.

Other hazards? Take care not to get lost. Lots of children—and adults—manage to lose their bearings and thus are separated from their companions, cars, or possessions. Make note of some permanent landmark (a building, lifeguard stand, or the like) to use as a reference point. Likewise, take precautions not to roam when snorkeling and diving, and always mark your location with a diving flag so you're not run over by a boat. Finally, don't exceeding your physical limits by swimming too far from shore.

SCUBA DIVING: LEARNING HOW

EVERY YEAR, MORE THAN A MILLION PEOPLE travel to the Florida Keys to scuba dive at the only coral reef in the continental United States.

To dive you must be at least 12 years old, pass a swimming test, and be fit enough to take on the rigors of handling and donning scuba gear in a rocking boat. Even if you are not a strong swimmer, you're nearly weightless once you're in the water, so in some ways scuba diving is easier than snorkeling.

How to Get Certified

To become a scuba diver, you need to be certified by an organization such as the Professional Association of Diving Instructors (PADI), the YMCA, or the National Association of Underwater Instructors (NAUI). Certification requires classroom work, passing a written final exam, pool work, and two checkout dives with your instructor. Then you get a diving card that lets you rent equipment and dive anywhere in the world. If your trip to South Florida is leisurely, you can become certified in three to four days.

In two long morning sessions, you go through the text, watch some videotapes, take quizzes, and take the final exam. Next comes the pool work, in which new divers learn how to assemble their gear, accomplish underwater rescue, clear their masks, and perform other skills necessary to master the sport. If fewer than four students take the class, it usually takes a long afternoon to complete the session.

unofficial **TIP**
Buy the PADI dive manual and a dive table at a local dive shop, and read up before you come down.

The final step is two two-tank practice dives with the instructor. You do the drills in the ocean that you learned in the pool. After you've sucked four tanks of air, you're certified. Total cost? Around $300, which includes all equipment except a mask, fins, and snorkel—an additional $100.

What if you're on a tighter schedule and don't want to spend valuable time in South Florida sitting in a classroom and swimming in a pool? You can do everything but the checkout dive at home and get a transferral document from your instructor that states you've completed all your course work and pool work. Then come to Florida to do your checkout dives. The total cost to become certified, however, is usually higher that way.

Another option is a resort diving course: You practice in a swimming pool, then go out on a dive boat and jump in with a certified instructor who stays with you the whole time. If you want to find out whether or not scuba diving is for you, this is the way to go.

After You're Certified

After certification, how much does it cost to go diving? The typical price is $35–$50 for a two-tank, half-day outing with two 60-minute dives, usually at two locations. A novice will also have to rent diving gear: a weight belt, two tanks, a regulator (the critical device that fits in your mouth and controls airflow from the oxygen tank), and a buoyancy-control device (an inflatable vest usually called a BCD). Figure on another $32 a day.

If you plan to dive often, it pays to buy your own gear. The key component is the regulator; list prices for quality units start around $600, but you might find a good unit on sale at around $450. A good vest will cost $300, and with the exception of mask, fins, and snorkel, that's all most divers need to purchase.

unofficial **TIP**
Don't buy weight belts and tanks (flying with them isn't a good idea), unless you live next to the water or you have your own boat.

Diving is a safe sport, but take it seriously. Always dive with a buddy, and always watch that person. Find a dive instructor who's certified by one of the major diving organizations, and make sure he or she has the same attitude toward safety.

DEEP-SEA FISHING

GOING TO SEA TO BATTLE BIG FISH SUCH AS marlin, tuna, sailfish, and shark is a major attraction for Sunshine State visitors. In fact, Florida is called the sportfishing capital of the United States. One big consideration for aspiring deep-sea fishers is what sort of outing to select. Below, we detail your options. (Remember, each dictates prolonged sun exposure, so be prepared.)

Trolling

To see a sailfish do an aerial rumba—eight feet above the water while hooked to the end of your line—go fishing by charter boat, sometimes called trolling. Fifty-foot powerboats leave daily with groups of six to eight anglers on full- or half-day trips from marinas up and down the South Florida coast and the Keys.

A half-day charter averages around $450, and no experience is necessary. On the way out to the fishing grounds, the boat's mate baits the hooks, arranges the lines on outriggers on the side of the boat (to prevent individual lines from tangling), and talks to the customers about the vagaries of hooking the big one. He also gives explicit instructions on what to do when a fish strikes.

Once all the lines are out and the boat is over the fishing grounds, the craft "trolls" at a slow speed until a fish is hooked. Depending on the bait, tackle, and depth of the hook, rods react differently when a fish strikes; it's up to the mate to spot the action, set the hook, and get the rod into the hands of a customer.

The captain will slow the boat until the fish is landed—or cuts the line and escapes. In fact, with the declining population of billfish such as marlin and sailfish, catch and release is the norm on most charter boats.

Trolling is passive. If a fish strikes, the mate sets the hook and passes the rod to an angler seated in a fighting chair, who just has to work the reel. The goal of a fishing charter is to catch fish, and the captain will use his local knowledge of reefs, wrecks, currents, and weather to position the boat in a favorable spot. (He's also on the radio talking to other skippers doing the same thing.)

Trolling trips typically land barracuda, bluefin tuna, bonito, king mackerel, mako shark, and wahoo. While the captain will move the boat from location to location, there are no guarantees you'll come back from your trip with a trophy.

Finding a Charter Boat

A referral is the best way to select a charter. But first-time visitors without local contacts still have a chance of finding a charter boat with a crew that works hard and shows a good attitude.

At least a day before you plan to go on a deep-sea charter, head for a marina around 5 p.m., when the boats are returning from their afternoon and all-day runs. Killing time on the docks—watching the pelicans and the post-trip action—is a South Florida tradition, and your key to locating a good charter boat.

As the boats pull in, happy or disgruntled customers (sometimes both) disembark. Depending on the success of the trip, the mate will unload a variety of fish for admiration by folks like you.

Note which boats are bringing in big sportfish, ask about rates, and try to find a crew you're comfortable with. But before you select a charter boat and leave a deposit for the trip, arrange with your captain to set the hooks and

unofficial **TIP**
If you're staying at a place with a kitchen, this is the time to buy fresh fish fillets.

release the fish. Negotiate terms to enhance the experience. Otherwise, the mate hooks the fish and all you do is crank them in.

Drift Boats

Charter boats aren't your only deep-sea fishing alternative: Drift boats (also called party boats) are larger than charter boats and transport 30–40 anglers at a time to an offshore reef. Once there, the captain turns off the engine, the boat begins to drift in the current, and the fishing lines go over the side—often with amusing results when the lines begin to cross.

Drifting is the least-expensive way to deep-sea fish. You use a conventional rod and reel baited with squid or mullet for bottom fishing, throw the line over the side, and wait for a bite. Most people who go out on drift boats are fishing for dinner; species typically caught include redtail and yellowtail snapper, flounder, barracuda, grouper, and pompano.

You'll also get to know your neighbor as you stand elbow to elbow on the side of the large boat and pass your rods back and forth in an effort to untangle your lines. When things get really complicated, a crew member shows up to straighten it all out.

Just like charter boats, drift boats have crews that bait customers' hooks and gaff (spear) the catch after it's reeled in close to the boat. Beginners get plenty of help and advice—from both the crew and fellow party-boaters—and tackle is available for rent on the boat. Bring your own rod, and a typical three-and-a-half-hour excursion is $35; if you rent tackle, it's around $50.

It's a bad sign, but not unheard of, for a poker game to start up in the cabin of the drift boat. Locals will tell you the fish don't bite like they used to, but that may just be a fish tale.

Light-tackle Fishing

In light-tackle fishing, a style popular in the Keys, a guide takes up to four anglers out in an open 25-foot boat. Using LORAN (a long-range navigation system that allows a boat to reach a precise location), the guide will go anywhere from 10 to 70 miles offshore looking for reefs and wrecks. Many guides take customers to their own secret spots.

After reaching a promising location, the guide throws out chum (cut or ground bait) to attract fish: blackfin tuna, permit, cobia, and other hard-fighting species. The fish come up right behind the boat, and it doesn't take a high level of skill to land them. The captain baits the hook, then the angler tosses the bait into the melee and hooks up. The total cost for an all-day trip is typically $500–$700 for up to four anglers.

Sight Fishing

Also called flats fishing, this type of angling calls for skill and patience. One or two customers and a guide in a 17-foot open boat are "poled"—or pushed by the guide, who sits in an elevated chair with a long pole—through water that's only 18 inches deep or shallower.

Flats fishing takes place in calm settings, with wading birds and clear water, so you can see an incredible amount of sea life. The absence of a motor lets you approach all kinds of creatures.

When a large predator such as a barracuda, bonefish, or permit is spotted—remember, this is called sight fishing—it's up to the angler to present the bait or fly to the prey. You see the fish in advance, so you stalk them. Flats fishing is primarily done with a fly rod, and the guides are teachers, though customers participate fully.

Sight fishing, however, isn't for anglers who judge a trip by the number of fish they catch; most people catch and release. But there can be plenty of action: When you cast a fly in front of a barracuda, it charges, jumps, and does figure-eights out of the water. Typical costs for sight-fishing trips are $350–$500 for a full day and $250–$300 for a half-day; no more than two anglers can split the cost because the boats are so small.

Fishing Seasons

In South Florida, charter and drift boats go out daily, and customers can catch something at any time of year. But spring and fall offer better chances of landing a big fish—or at least seeing more action. May and June are excellent for tarpon, fish that are all muscle. Guides are booked a year in advance during tarpon season.

In general, better fishing occurs when the water temperature is above 72° Fahrenheit. In the winter, when the sea temperature drops below 70°, the only thing that will bite reliably is barracuda.

THE BEST *of* SOUTH FLORIDA

FLORIDA TOURING HAS LONG BEEN ASSOCIATED with sun, surf, and sport. Throughout the region, the standards for relaxation and recreation are high, but some are higher than others. Below is our best-of list for South Florida. For more information on each venue, see complete listings in each chapter.

Best Beaches

- **Bahia Honda State Park (Bahia Honda Key, the Florida Keys)**

- **Hollywood Beach (Hollywood, Broward County)**

- **Captiva Beach (Captiva, Lee Island Coast, Southwest Florida)**

- **Cayo Costa State Park (off Captiva Island, Lee Island Coast, Southwest Florida)**

- **Crandon Park (Key Biscayne, Miami-Dade County)**

- **Haulover Beach (Miami Beach, Miami-Dade County) for nude beach**

- **Lover's Key State Park (Fort Myers Beach, Lee Island Coast, Southwest Florida)**

- **Lummus Park Beach (South Beach, Miami-Dade County)**

- **Naples Beach (Naples, Collier County, Southwest Florida)**

Best Shelling

- **Captiva Island (Lee Island Coast, Southwest Florida)**

- **Sanibel Island (Lee Island Coast, Southwest Florida)**

Best Golf

- **Biltmore Hotel (Coral Gables, Miami-Dade County)**
- **The Breakers (Palm Beach, Palm Beach County)**
- **Fiddler's Creek (Naples, Collier County, Southwest Florida)**
- **Doral Country Club (Miami, Miami-Dade County)**
- **Emerald Dunes Golf Course (West Palm Beach, Palm Beach County)**
- **PGA National Resort and Spa (Palm Beach Gardens, Palm Beach County)**
- **Tiburon Golf Club (Naples, Collier County, Southwest Florida)**

Best Tennis

- **Delray Beach Tennis Center (Delray Beach, Palm Beach County)**
- **Holiday Park (Fort Lauderdale, Broward County)**
- **David Park (Hollywood, Broward County)**

Best Diving

- **Artificial Reef program (Fort Lauderdale, Broward County)**
- **Biscayne National Park (off south Miami-Dade County)**

Best Sportfishing

- **The Florida Keys**
- **Miami Beach**
- **Palm Beach County**

Best Drift Fishing

- **Flamingo Fishing (Fort Lauderdale, Broward County)**

Best Museums for Adults

- **Billie Swamp Safari and Ah-Tah-Thi-Ki Museum, Big Cypress Reservation (west of Fort Lauderdale, Broward County)**
- **Fort Myers Historical Museum (Fort Myers, Southwest Florida)**
- **Norton Museum of Art (Palm Beach, Palm Beach County)**
- **Flagler Museum (Palm Beach, Palm Beach County)**
- **The Wolfsonian-FIU (Miami Beach, Miami-Dade County)**

Best Museum for Children

- **Museum of Discovery and Science—Blockbuster IMAX Theater (Fort Lauderdale, Broward County)**

Best Museum for Fishermen

- IGFA Fishing Hall of Fame and Museum (Dania Beach, Broward County)

Best Performing Arts Venues

- Broward Theater of the Performing Arts (Fort Lauderdale, Broward County)

- Philharmonic Center for the Arts (Naples, Southwest Florida)

- Kravis Center (Palm Beach, Palm Beach County)

- Miami Performing Arts Center (from fall 2006, Miami-Dade County)

Best Modes of Transportation

- Water Taxi (Fort Lauderdale, Broward County)

- Rickshaws (Coconut Grove, Miami-Dade County)

Best Views of Nature

- Babcock Wilderness Adventures (Punta Gorda, Lee Island Coast, Southwest Florida)

- J.N. "Ding" Darling National Wildlife Refuge (Sanibel Island, Lee Island Coast, Southwest Florida)

- Everglades Holiday Park (Fort Lauderdale, Broward County)

- Anne Kolb Nature Center (Hollywood, Broward County)

Best View of Beautiful People

- South Beach (Miami Beach, Miami-Dade County)

Best Iconic Dining Choices

- Grill Room on Las Olas (Fort Lauderdale, Broward County)

- Norman's (Coral Gables, Miami-Dade County)

- Joe's Stone Crab (Miami Beach, Miami-Dade County)

Best Shopping

- Sawgrass Mills (Sunrise, Broward County)

- Fifth Avenue South (Naples, Collier County, Southwest Florida)

- Bal Harbour Shops (Miami Beach, Miami-Dade County)

- Merrick Park (Coral Gables, Miami-Dade County)

Best Tree

- Banyan tree at Thomas A. Edison Winter Home (Fort Myers, Lee County, Southwest Florida)

A (Subjective) List of 15 South Florida Favorites

- Sunday on Lincoln Road, Miami Beach—flea market with an assortment of "art," street cafes with fresh juices, dog walking, and orchids

- The mansions along the Intracoastal Waterway, the Atlantic, and the Gulf. Rent a convertible, smear on some sunscreen, put on your favorite music, and cruise along either coast, gawking at some of the most varied, fantastic gardens and mansions in the world. A dream drive in more ways than one. And as long or short as you like.

- The "Old Downtowns," now thriving with low-rise, high-style restaurants, shops, and galleries: Clematis in West Palm; Fort Myers; Hollywood; Las Olas in Fort Lauderdale; and Worth Avenue in Palm Beach

- The mangrove forests at Oleta River State Park in North Miami and the J. N. "Ding" Darling National Wildlife Refuge on Sanibel Island

- Cabaret at the Colony Hotel, Palm Beach—dinner entertainment that is a jewel in a jewel-box hotel

- Bill Baggs Park, by the lighthouse on the tip of Key Biscayne, for a memorable picnic; and Sonesta Resort on Key Biscayne, for an afternoon of pampering and yellow-flower treatments in the spa

- Walking along Biscayne Bay, Miami, from Brickell Bay Drive to Brickell Key, at sunrise or sunset

- Diva Duck, an amphibious craft that takes you on a short tour-cruise from Palm Beach mansions right into Lake Worth, complete with an opera singer and duck whistles to "quack up" incredulous gawkers

- Sanibel beaches—shelling in the early morning, watching the loggerhead turtles nest in the evening

- Española Way in Miami Beach, just off Washington Avenue at 16th Street, a short 1920s street of fanciful Mediterranean architecture, shops, and restaurants

- The gingerbread houses of Key West, built over 100 years ago

- Dining alfresco in winter, then attending a cultural event at the Lincoln or Jackie Gleason theaters in Miami Beach, the Kravis Center in Palm Beach, or the Broward Performing Arts Center

- The International Book Fair, held in downtown Miami in November, where you can chat with your favorite authors and immerse yourself in things bookish

- Fairchild Tropical Gardens, Miami, for a concert on a moonlit night

- The Tamiami Trail, the picturesque old road between the Florida coasts from Miami to Naples; in winter it's lined with napping gators, egrets, ibises, and ospreys.

- Bonnet House Museum and Gardens, Fort Lauderdale—quirky old mansion by a lagoon with surprisingly good art, and monkeys in the banyan trees

SOUTH FLORIDA
for CHILDREN

SUNSHINE STATE VACATION ACTIVITIES WITH big appeal for children range from butterfly watching to hands-on science museums, from first-class zoos to a wooden roller coaster, from nature walks among hundreds of alligators to beaches, beaches, beaches.

Most families with children visit South Florida during the summer months, when the region is hot and humid. So before starting off on a day of touring or a visit to the beach, head off potential problems.

SUNBURN, OVERHEATING, AND DEHYDRATION Sunburn in young children can cause lifelong problems. Doctors advise putting on sunscreen every morning before breakfast. Sweat, friction, and rain dilute it, so it must be reapplied throughout the day.

An SPF of 15 and above is appropriate for tanned skin, 30 and above for fair skin. Don't forget to put sunscreen on the neck, tops of shoulders, tops of feet, and scalp if hair is thin or absent. Look for ingredients such as the UVA blocker Parsol 1789 (avobenzone). Remember sunglasses and hats, and be especially careful outdoors between 11 a.m. and 3 p.m.

Don't count on keeping small children properly hydrated with soft drinks and water from fountains. Long lines at popular attractions often make buying refreshments problematic, and water fountains are not always handy. What's more, excited children may not tell you or even realize that they're thirsty or overheated. We recommend using a stroller for young children and carrying plastic water bottles.

THE BEACH Don't let kids swim alone; don't even leave them alone on the beach. Practice the buddy system (good advice even for adults), as it's easy to become disoriented in the water. Pay attention to lifeguards, who warn of hazards like riptides. For more information on the hazards of the beach and ocean swimming, see our section on swimming in "Before You Go Outside: Considerations for Recreation" (pages 25–27).

BLISTERS Wear comfortable, well-broken-in shoes or sandals. If you or your children are unusually susceptible to blisters, carry some pre-cut moleskin bandages (available at drugstores); they offer the best possible protection, stick great, and won't sweat off. When you feel a hot spot, stop, air out your foot, and place a moleskin over the area before a blister forms.

Sometimes small children won't tell their parents about a developing blister until it's too late. We recommend inspecting the feet of preschoolers at least twice a day. Athletic socks, which absorb perspiration, might be your best bet.

GLASSES If you want your smaller children to wear sunglasses, or if they wear prescription glasses, it's a good idea to affix a strap or string to the frames so the glasses won't get lost and can hang from the neck when kids are indoors. Look for sunglasses with an ultra-violet coating.

WHERE TO GO WITH KIDS

THE *UNOFFICIAL GUIDE* RATING SYSTEM for attractions includes an "appeal by age group" category indicating a range of appeal from one star (don't bother) up to five (not to be missed).

To get you started, we've provided a list, county by county, of 30 attractions in South Florida most likely to appeal to kids—but keep your children's personal interests in mind when touring. These offer exposure to nature, glimpses of native or exotic wildlife, a sense of what Florida was like in its early days, and educational opportunities from a kid's point of view.

Top Attractions for Kids

MIAMI-DADE COUNTY

Biscayne National Park
Everglades National Park–Shark Valley Tram Tour
Gold Coast Railroad Museum
Historical Museum of South Florida
Metrozoo
Miami Museum of Science–Space Transit Planetarium
Monkey Jungle
Parrot Jungle and Gardens
Seaquarium

FLORIDA KEYS

East Martello Museum
Fort Zachary Taylor State Historic Site
John Pennekamp Coral Reef State Park
Key West Aquarium
Natural History Museum of the Florida Keys
Tram Ride (Key West)
Treasures (Key West)

PALM BEACH COUNTY

Lion Country Safari

BROWARD COUNTY

Ah-Tah-Thi-Ki Museum

Butterfly World

Flamingo Gardens

Hurricane wooden roller coaster

IGFA Fishing Hall of Fame and Museum

Museum of Discovery and Science–Blockbuster IMAX Theater

Young at Art Museum

COLLIER COUNTY

Everglades City and Everglades National Park

LEE COUNTY

Babcock Wilderness Experience

Centennial Park

Imaginarium

Manatee Park

Thomas Edison and Henry Ford Winter Estates

HOW *to* AVOID CRIME *and* KEEP SAFE *in* PUBLIC PLACES

CRIME TIME

YOU DON'T HAVE TO BE A FAN OF TV'S *CSI: Miami* to know that Miami has a reputation for crime. Blame it on a lot of things: the city's geographical (and some say moral) position on the edge of the continent; a drug-smuggling industry that turns over as much as $12 billion a year; a proliferation of guns in the hands of its citizenry (the bloodiest shootout in FBI history took place in Miami, and Florida has some of the most liberal gun-ownership laws in the country); a crush of immigrants fleeing dictators throughout Latin America (a situation that also spawned several racial disturbances in the last two decades); and an increase in crimes against tourists.

The good news is that crime statistics for all of South Florida, Miami-Dade included, are down. Way down. Some experts even say that Miami is safer now than in the 1920s, when gangsters like Al Capone were muscling in on illegal nightclubs and casinos. A local historian notes that Miami's crime rate was three times as high per capita in 1925 as it was in the early 1980s, when the town earned the nickname "Murder Capital USA."

Tourist communities want visitors to come, enjoy, and go away happy—every time a visitor files a police report, a town's image is sullied. Consequently, South Florida cities allot significant resources for law enforcement as a public-relations investment.

Still, savvy travelers know that you don't take chances on vacation that you don't take at home. Do you wander about marginal areas of your hometown late at night? Do you flash wads of bills or impressive jewelry without a second thought? Well, don't do it here.

Below, we outline some important precautions that will ensure you have a safe vacation.

AIRPORT TO YOUR HOTEL

WHILE THE MIAMI INTERNATIONAL AIRPORT (MIA) Expressway whisks you the eight miles to Miami in about as many minutes (except during rush hour), getting to the expressway isn't so easy if your rental-car agency is located on a side street outside the airport—and a lot of them are. You can choose a rental-car company based on its easy access to the expressway instead of its rates, or take a taxi or shuttle van to your hotel and have your rental car delivered to you there. However, while the neighborhoods around the airport can be confusing, signs to the expressway have been improved, and rental agencies are careful to provide detailed directions when they send you on your way.

Today, all rental cars are virtually indistinguishable from private vehicles; they carry regular license plates and no stickers. Most car-rental offices are equipped with TVs that continuously show videos instructing customers on how to avoid becoming a crime victim; the offices also provide customers with detailed written information on avoiding crime. Many Miami car-rental agencies also provide a car phone at no additional charge, and some rent them; you pay for calls by the minute.

Finally, the Tourist Oriented Police Squad (TOPS) patrols the Miami airport area; look for the marked squad cars patrolling the roadways and neighborhoods surrounding MIA. In addition, the Tourist Robbery Abatement Program (TRAP) assigns police officers to patrol areas frequented by tourists, such as the airport, car-rental parking lots, and nearby neighborhoods.

Tips for the Road

Area police departments, eager to help tourists and improve a poor image, offer the following advice for drivers, wherever they are traveling:

- Don't read a road map at an intersection—it attracts attention. Go to a restaurant or well-lit parking lot, and read the map there. In parking lots, park near entryways to malls or shopping centers, or under bright lights.

- If you're bumped from behind by another car, it could be a criminal trying to trick you into pulling over by staging an accident. Keep going.

- Another scam: Criminals will wave and point at your tires, acting like good Samaritans who only want to warn you that one of your tires is bad. Their goal is to get you to stop and get out of your car—so that they can rob you, or worse. Rely on road noise and drag to alert you to flat tires. If something happens, drive to a safe, lighted area before stopping and leaving your car.

- At stoplights, leave room between you and the vehicle ahead. If someone approaches your car, you have room to make a U-turn. Also, it's best to keep your windows rolled up when in stop-and-go traffic. And keep luggage in the trunk: Criminals look inside cars at traffic lights, and if they see luggage, they'll know you're a tourist.

- Don't let your guard down in areas that appear safe. Crime can happen anywhere.

- Drive carefully and with uncommon courtesy. Overloaded highways and long commutes can produce road rage, which can range from vulgar gestures to physical confrontation and can makes criminal of ordinary drivers. Signal lane changes or turns; don't let parking spaces turn you into an ogre. Drive with patience and be defensively courteous to preclude potentially volatile incidents.

HAVE A PLAN

THIS SECTION IS PRESCRIPTIVE. IT IS UNLIKELY any of the scenarios described below will play out on your vacation—anywhere. Nevertheless, a few simple precautions can help ensure your safety and, moreover, afford you an added measure of confidence.

ON THE STREET You present a less-appealing target when you're with other people. If you must be out alone, act alert, stay in well-lit areas, and have at least one of your arms and hands free. Pickpockets and purse snatchers gravitate toward preoccupied folks—the kind found plodding along staring at the sidewalk, with both arms encumbered by bags or packages.

If you have to ask directions, shopkeepers are a good bet. When venturing away from beaches and other tourist areas, cameras, guidebooks, and fanny packs are dead giveaways that you're a tourist. Visible jewelry, even if you know it's fake, attracts the wrong kind of attention. Men, keep your billfolds in a front pants or coat pocket. Women, keep your purses tucked tightly under your arm—if you must carry one; if you're wearing a jacket, put it on over the strap of your shoulder bag. And invest in neck or belt pouches to hide valuables.

Want to take extreme precaution? Carry two wallets: one inexpensive one in your hip pocket or purse containing about $20 in cash and some expired credit cards, and another with your valid credit cards (hide the bulk of your cash elsewhere on your person). If you get mugged, remember to hand over the decoy wallet, not the other.

IF YOU'RE APPROACHED Police will tell you that criminals have the least amount of control over their intended victims during the first few moments of an initial approach. A good strategy, therefore, is to short-circuit the crime as quickly as possible.

If a mugger starts by demanding your money, for instance, quickly take out your billfold (preferably your fake one), and hurl it as far as you can in one direction while you run shouting for help in the opposite direction. The odds are greatly in your favor that the criminal will prefer to collect your billfold rather than pursue you. If you hand over your wallet and just stand there, you'll likely be asked for your watch and jewelry next.

SECONDARY CRIME SCENES Under no circumstances, police warn, should you ever allow yourself to be taken to another location, or a "secondary crime scene" in police jargon. This move, they explain, provides the criminal more privacy and, consequently, more control. A mugger can rob you on the street very quickly and efficiently. If an attacker tries to take you to another location, whether by car or on foot, it is a certain indication that there's more in store than robbery. In most cases, even if the thief has a gun or knife, your chances are better if you run away.

unofficial **TIP**
Don't believe what a criminal tells you, even if it's something you desperately want to believe, such as "I won't hurt you if you come with me." No matter how logical or benign it sounds, assume the worst.

ON PUBLIC TRANSPORT When riding a bus, take a seat as close to the driver as you can. Likewise, on the subway or elevated train, sit near the driver's or attendant's compartment. These employees can summon outside help in the event of trouble.

IN CABS While it's unlikely you'll need to hail a cab on the street in Miami or elsewhere in South Florida, you are somewhat vulnerable if you do. Particularly after dusk, call a reliable taxi company and stay inside while they dispatch a cab to your door. When your cab arrives, check the driver's certificate, which must by law be posted on the dashboard.

It's a smart move to address the cabbie by his or her last name or mention the number of the cab. This alerts the cab driver to the fact that you are paying attention to your surroundings. Not only will this contribute to your safety, it will keep your cabbie from trying to run up the fare.

Familiarize yourself with the most direct route to your destination ahead of time. If you can say, "South Beach via the Julia Tuttle Causeway, please," the driver is less likely to charge you more by taking a circuitous route.

If you need to catch a cab at the train station or at one of the airports, use the taxi queue. Taxis in the official queue are properly licensed and regulated. Don't accept an offer for a cab or limo from a stranger in the terminal or baggage-claim area. At best, you will be significantly overcharged for the ride.

Personal Attitude

You can be the victim of a crime, and it can happen to you anywhere. If you go to a restaurant or nightspot alone, use valet parking or park in a well-lit lot. If you have no choice but to use a dark parking lot, never be reluctant to ask for an escort.

Pride and righteous indignation imperil your survival. This is especially difficult for many men, particularly when in the presence of women. No matter whether you are approached by an aggressive drunk, an unbalanced street person, or an actual criminal, the rule is the same: Forget your pride and break off contact as quickly as possible.

Self-defense

In a situation in which it is impossible to run, be prepared to defend yourself. Most policemen insist that a gun or knife is not much use to the average person; the weapon can easily be turned against the victim. Additionally, concealed firearms and knives are illegal in most jurisdictions. The best self-defense device for the average person is pepper spray. Not only is it legal in most states, it's nonlethal and easy to use. The spray should be able to fire about eight feet, and it should come with a protector cap so it won't go off by mistake in your purse or pocket. Carefully read the directions that come with the product, paying particular attention to how it should be carried and stored, and how long the active ingredients will remain potent. If you wish to test-fire the canister, make sure you do so downwind while wearing a rubber glove.

Avoid dropping pepper spray into the bowels of your purse when you leave your hotel room or your car.

THE HOMELESS

NEAR LARGE PUBLIC BUILDINGS IN DOWNTOWN Miami, you'll sometimes see people draped in blankets or in sleeping bags, their possessions piled up next to them. Sometimes they'll come up to your car and ask for change at long lights.

These are mainly single men and women, a disproportionate number of whom are people with mental illnesses, substance addictions, or physical disabilities.

Studies show that homeless people have lower rates of conviction for violent crimes than the population at large, so they should not instill fear in tourists. Should you give the homeless money? That's a personal decision. However, to insure that your generosity is not squandered, consider simply donating a lump sum to local charities that benefit the homeless. Those moved to get more involved in the nationwide problem of homelessness can send inquiries—or a check—to the National Coalition for the Homeless, 1612 K Street NW, Suite 1004, Washington, DC 20006.

THINGS NATIVES *already* KNOW

CUSTOMS AND PROTOCOL

SOUTH FLORIDA TAKES CASUALNESS TO EXTREMES that can startle folks from colder, stuffier climes—and we're not referring to the profusion of topless bathers on South Beach.

Attire

Casual, cool, lightweight, and colorful clothing is the norm throughout South Florida. The usual outfit for men and women during the day is T-shirt and shorts. Natural fibers—silks, cottons, and linens—are coolest, allowing skin to breathe in hot, humid weather.

Professionals, however, still opt for suits, and shirts and ties are necessary for important business meetings whether the temperature is 90° or 9°, and whether the site is New York City or Naples, Florida. Barely-there tops or T-shirts with inappropriate messages won't work any better in South Florida boardrooms or banks than they do elsewhere.

Nighttime it's glitz up and go, casual or elegant. But even in South Florida, a jacket or sweater can be a necessity for formal places (and in cold air-conditioning).

Even southern portions of Florida occasionally suffer cold spells. A lightweight jacket, cotton sweaters, and long pants become the clothes of choice during December, January, and February. We also suggest a rainproof jacket year-round.

Eating in Restaurants

Again, *casual* is the byword when it comes to dining in most Florida restaurants. (If you're not sure, call to ask if there's a dress code.) Don't feel intimidated by unfamiliar menus or a waitstaff that doesn't speak English; many Latin restaurants offer menus in both Spanish and English, and you only need to point to place your order. Similarly, many French restaurants offer bilingual menus. And during the season in Broward County, you will find many French-speakers.

EARLY BIRDS Forget worms—get the early-bird specials. Though much maligned by late-night comics, these offer cheaper meals, served earlier than normal dining times and sometimes (but not always) made up of smaller portions. Often these meals are three courses, and diners can take home leftovers.

Most restaurants run their early birds until 6 or 7 p.m., while some offer *early* early birds, which are served somewhere around 3 or 4 p.m. Not everyone who takes advantage of these specials fits the retiree stereotype—some are just bargain hunting or enjoying a South Florida tradition.

Tipping

Is the tip you normally leave for good service at home appropriate in South Florida? Yes. Here are some guidelines:

PORTERS AND SKYCAPS A dollar a bag.

CAB DRIVERS If the fare is less than $8, give the driver the change and a dollar. Example: If the fare is $4.50, give the cabbie fifty cents and a buck. If the fare is more than $8, give the driver the change and $2. If you are asking the cabbie to take you only a block or two, the fare will be small, but your tip should be large ($3–$5) to make up for his wait in line and to partially compensate him for missing out on a better-paying fare. Add an extra dollar if the driver does a lot of luggage handling.

PARKING VALETS Two dollars is plenty if the valet is courteous and demonstrates some hustle. A dollar will do if the service is just OK. Only pay when you check your car out, not when you leave it.

BELLMEN When a bellman greets you at your car with one of those rolling luggage carts and handles all of your bags, $5 is about right. The more luggage you carry yourself, of course, the less you can tip.

WAITERS Whether you're dining in a coffee shop, an upscale eatery, or your hotel room, the standard gratuity ranges from 15% to 20% of the tab, not counting sales tax. At a buffet or brunch where you serve yourself, leave a dollar or two for the folks who bring your drinks. Some restaurants, however, are adopting the practice of automatically adding a 15%–18% gratuity to the bill, so check before leaving a cash tip.

COCKTAIL WAITERS/BARTENDERS In this case, you tip by the round. For two people, a dollar a round; for more than two people, two bucks a round. For a large group, use your judgment: Is everyone drinking beer, or is the order long and complicated? Tip accordingly.

HOTEL MAIDS On checking out, leave a dollar or two per day for each day of your stay, provided the service was good. Maids depend on tips the same way other service help does, but because you don't usually see each other, they often get overlooked.

unofficial **TIP**
Places in South Florida that drop surcharges on quarter rolls include banks and Publix food stores. Our advice: Buy a few rolls before hitting town, tuck them in a corner of your luggage, and generously resupply your pocket or purse with quarters each day. It may be worth your while to visit one of the city's parking garages to pick up a prepaid card good for Miami's electronic parking meters. Call the Miami Parking Authority at ☎ 305-373-6789 or visit its Web site, **www.miamiparking.com**, for details.

Bring Lots of Quarters

Because parking meters are everywhere, you can't survive without quarters—lots of them. The demand for two-bit pieces is so intense, in fact, that some businesses in the Miami-Dade area charge each other a $1 surcharge on a $10 roll of quarters.

Some areas now have metered-parking systems in which you pay at a ticketing machine and leave a timed ticket in your car.

Going Native

First, a definition: A South Florida native is anyone who has lived in town at least five years or so. In other words, this is an area of transients. As a result, visitors to Palm Beach or Naples, to Fort Myers or Miami, to Fort Lauderdale or Key West needn't feel concerned about not fitting in. Keep in mind that this region hosts millions of visitors a year from all over the world, and most leave wanting to return.

Yet, if it's important to you not to look like a vacationer, we offer the following tongue-in-cheek advice for fitting in in Miami:

1. Pronounce Miami's name "My-AM-uh," the way folks did when Miami was more Anglo than Latin. Problem is, a lot of natives may not understand what you're saying.

2. Never ever admit to visiting the Everglades.

3. Be obsessive, if not maniacal, about the Dolphins, Heat, Marlins, or Panthers.

4. Be drop-dead beautiful and strut your stuff on Ocean Drive in South Beach. An eye-catching option for ladies: Strap on a thong bikini and cruise through Lummus Park on Rollerblades.

5. Sit alone at a sidewalk cafe and engage in an intense conversation—on your cell phone.

6. Men: For a night of clubbing, sport an earring, ponytail, and gold Rolex while attired in a tux jacket, gaudy Bermuda shorts, and no socks.

7. For women on the town, try an orchid behind the ear, a low-cut blouse, a skirt slit up the thigh, or a silk nightgown; other options include anything in a bright floral pattern or leopard skin, or a tight leather miniskirt.

8. Leave the dog at home, unless you go strolling on Lincoln Road in Miami Beach. But a parrot perched on your shoulder or a boa constrictor draped over an arm is a sure indication you're not from Duluth.

9. Hire a hot-pink Rolls Royce and a driver when clubbing. The hot wheels idling outside (and blocking traffic) make a statement.

10. Never eat green Key lime pie. It should be chartreuse—more yellow than green.

¿HABLA ESPAÑOL?

A Crash Course in Spanish for Anglos

Though many would say otherwise, the official language of South Florida is English. Most people speak rudimentary English even if their native tongue is Spanish.

But it's possible on rare occasions (say, your car breaks down, or you're in a small shop or restaurant) to find yourself in a situation where there's no one around who speaks English.

If you find yourself trying out your high school Spanish with a non–English speaker, remember: Speak slowly and clearly. Charades and hand gestures have been known to bridge language gaps. The critical ingredient to cross-cultural communication is a sense of humor. And it's a great idea to carry a phrasebook.

Here is a sampling of phrases to learn before you come:

Hola. ¿Como estas? **(OH-lah. Como es-TAHS?)** Hello. How are you?

¿Donde esta la playa? El aeropuerto? **(DON-day es-tah lah PLY-yah? El arrow-PWER-to?)** Where is the beach? The airport?

¿Es muy lejos? **(Es moo-ey LAY-hohs?)** Is it very far?

Esta bien. **(Es-tah bee-en.)** Okay.

Quiero el café sin azucar, por favor. Quiero arroz con pollo y una cerveza. **(Kee-err-o el cah-FEY seen a-ZOO-car, pour fah-vor. Kee-err-oh rose cone POY-yo ee oon-a ser-VAY-sah.)** I would like a coffee without sugar, please. I'd like chicken with rice and a beer.

*No puedo hablar español.***(No PWAY-doh ab-lar es-pan-NYOL.)** I can't speak Spanish.

No se. **(No say.)** I don't know.

Dime. **(DEE-may.)** Tell me.

Dame. **(DAH-may.)** Give me.

Gracias. **(GRAH-see-ahs.)** Thank you.

¿Cuanto cuesta? **(Kwan-toe KWES-tah?)** How much is it?

A Cuban-Coffee Primer

You'll see crowds huddling around open windows in front of the restaurants that line Calle Ocho in Little Havana and dot the rest of Miami. From these cafe windows wafts the same aroma of Cuban coffee that hits you when you enter the MIA terminal

In the mornings, workers stop by the windows for a cup of espresso with steamed milk. In late afternoon, the men in their *guayaberas* (loose-fitting shirts) gather to talk politics and drink thimblefuls of black, sweetened espresso. Some of the locals call it "jet fuel."

Here's a java glossary of *café cubano* in ascending order of potency.

Café con leche—usually a morning drink. About one part coffee to four parts steamed whole milk. Usually served *con azucar* (with sugar) and very sweet. Ask for it *sin azucar* (without sugar) to add your own to taste. For more of a kick, drink it *oscuro* (dark).

Cortadito—smaller than a *café con leche*. About one part espresso to two parts milk.

Colada—a cup of straight, hypersugared espresso served with about five plastic thimble-sized cups for sharing. Only the truly intestinally fortified would venture to drink one solo.

For gifts or to replicate Cuban coffee in your espresso machine at home, Café Bustelo and Café Pilon are two of the most popular brands of espresso and are available in almost all local supermarkets and stores.

PART TWO

ACCOMMODATIONS

▌ DECIDING WHERE *to* STAY

LOCATION, LOCATION: AN OVERVIEW
OF YOUR OPTIONS

YOUR MOTIVE FOR VISITING SOUTH FLORIDA will naturally influence your choice of hotel. However, whether you're traveling for business or pleasure, to watch people or alligators, your primary consideration should be location. A lengthy commute to your meeting, to a museum, or to the beach in South Florida's notoriously bad traffic is an unnecessary and unreasonable headache. Though there are hotels all over South Florida—some stuck in quite-improbable places—we deal primarily with those hotels that are located in areas of concentrated tourist activity, business activity, or both. Besides your itinerary and, of course, budget, a cursory knowledge of the various South Florida communities with significant hotel concentrations will help you select the right location for you.

Miami-Dade County

Miami is a colorful, diverse city with pockets of dense, poor communities as well as world-class destinations. Downtown is primarily a business district, although many new condominiums currently under construction are expected to create an urban residential environment in downtown. While there is a nice variety of hotels near the airport, the most interesting areas for visitors are Coconut Grove, Coral Gables, and Miami Beach.

Hotels in **downtown Miami** are close to the Port of Miami, the Orange Bowl, city government, the airport, and Miami's business and financial center. The Miami Beach Convention Center is a 15-minute commute under optimal traffic conditions. Downtown Miami is not particularly active after business hours, however, and the choice of restaurants and nightspots is decidedly limited compared with that of

south beach accommodations

1. Aqua Hotel and Lounge
2. Avalon Hotel
3. Beach Plaza Hotel
4. Bentley Hotel
5. Blue Moon
6. Brigham Gardens
7. Cardozo Hotel
8. Casa Grande Suite Hotel
9. The Catalina Hotel and Beach Club
10. The Chesterfield Hotel
11. Clevelander Hotel
12. Clinton Hotel South Beach
13. Comfort Inn and Suites South Beach
14. Days Inn South Beach
15. Doubletree Surfcomber
16. Essex House Hotel
17. Holiday Inn South Beach Resort
18. The Hotel
19. Hotel Astor
20. The Hotel Chelsea
21. Hotel Delano
22. Hotel Impala
23. Hotel Ocean
24. Hotel Riande Continental
25. The Hotel Shelley
26. Hotel Victor
27. Lily Guesthouse
28. Loews Miami Beach Hotel
29. The Marlin
30. The Mercury Resort and Spa
31. Nassau Suite Hotel
32. National Hotel
33. Park Central Imperial Hotels
34. Ritz-Carlton South Beach
35. Sanctuary South Beach
36. Sonesta Beach Resort
37. The Tides
38. Tudor Hotel
39. Waldorf Towers Hotel
40. The Whitelaw Hotel

miami beach, surfside, bal harbour, and sunny isles accommodations

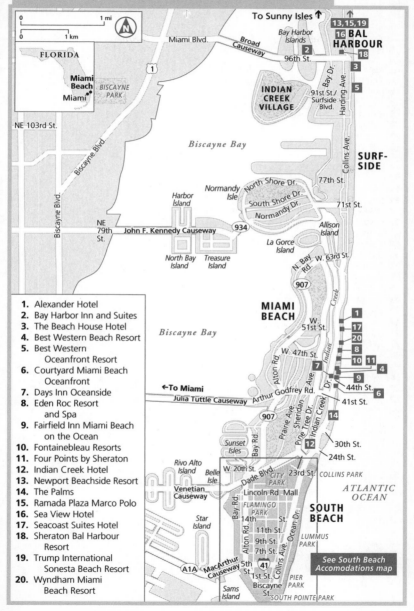

1. Alexander Hotel
2. Bay Harbor Inn and Suites
3. The Beach House Hotel
4. Best Western Beach Resort
5. Best Western Oceanfront Resort
6. Courtyard Miami Beach Oceanfront
7. Days Inn Oceanside
8. Eden Roc Resort and Spa
9. Fairfield Inn Miami Beach on the Ocean
10. Fontainebleau Resorts
11. Four Points by Sheraton
12. Indian Creek Hotel
13. Newport Beachside Resort
14. The Palms
15. Ramada Plaza Marco Polo
16. Sea View Hotel
17. Seacoast Suites Hotel
18. Sheraton Bal Harbour Resort
19. Trump International Sonesta Beach Resort
20. Wyndham Miami Beach Resort

downtown miami accommodations
coral gables, coconut grove, west miami

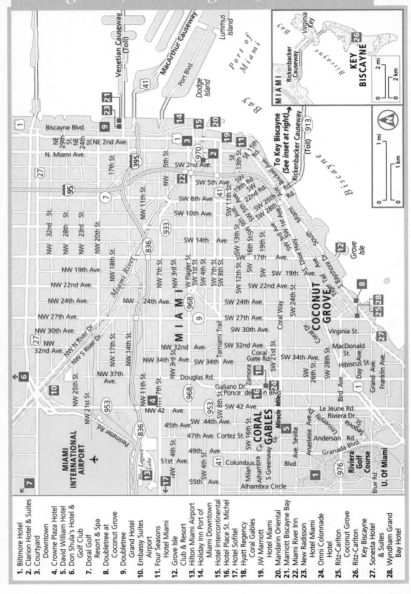

1. Biltmore Hotel
2. Clarion Hotel & Suites
3. Courtyard Downtown
4. Crowne Plaza Hotel
5. David William Hotel
6. Don Shula's Hotel & Golf Club
7. Doral Golf Resort & Spa
8. Doubletree at Coconut Grove
9. Doubletree Grand Hotel
10. Embassy Suites Airport
11. Four Seasons Hotel Miami
12. Grove Isle Club & Resort
13. Hilton Miami Airport
14. Holiday Inn Port of Miami Downtown
15. Hotel Intercontinental
16. Hotel Place St. Michel
17. Hotel Sofitel
18. Hyatt Regency Coral Gables
19. JW Marriott Hotel Miami
20. Mandarin Oriental
21. Marriott Biscayne Bay
22. Miami River Inn
23. New Radisson Hotel Miami
24. Omni Colonnade Hotel
25. Ritz-Carlton Coconut Grove
26. Ritz-Carlton Key Biscayne
27. Sonesta Hotel & Suites
28. Wyndham Grand Bay Hotel

florida keys accommodations

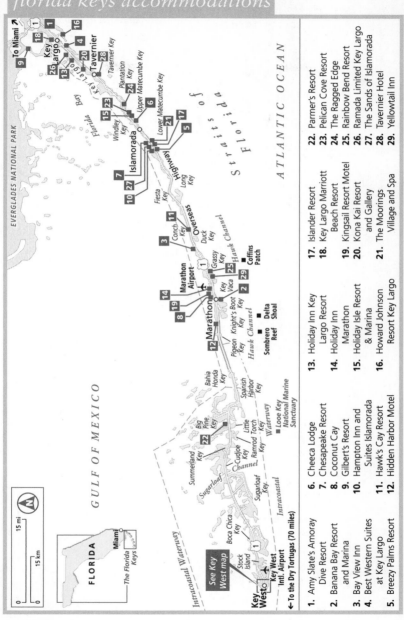

1. Amy Slate's Amoray Dive Resort
2. Banana Bay Resort and Marina
3. Bay View Inn
4. Best Western Suites at Key Largo
5. Breezy Palms Resort
6. Cheeca Lodge
7. Chesapeake Resort
8. Coconut Cay
9. Gilbert's Resort
10. Hampton Inn and Suites Islamorada
11. Hawk's Cay Resort
12. Hidden Harbor Motel
13. Holiday Inn Key Largo Resort
14. Holiday Inn Marathon
15. Holiday Isle Resort & Marina
16. Howard Johnson Resort Key Largo
17. Islander Resort
18. Key Largo Marriott Beach Resort
19. Kingsail Resort Motel
20. Kona Kai Resort and Gallery
21. The Moorings Village and Spa
22. Parmer's Resort
23. Pelican Cove Resort
24. The Ragged Edge
25. Rainbow Bend Resort
26. Ramada Limited Key Largo
27. The Sands of Islamorada
28. Tavernier Hotel
29. Yellowtail Inn

key west accommodations

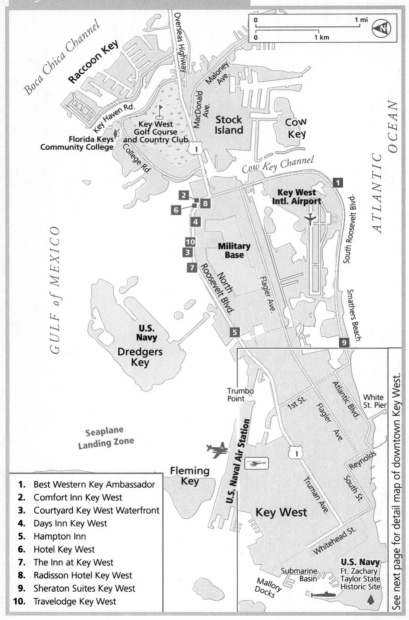

1. Best Western Key Ambassador
2. Comfort Inn Key West
3. Courtyard Key West Waterfront
4. Days Inn Key West
5. Hampton Inn
6. Hotel Key West
7. The Inn at Key West
8. Radisson Hotel Key West
9. Sheraton Suites Key West
10. Travelodge Key West

See next page for detail map of downtown Key West.

key west downtown accommodations

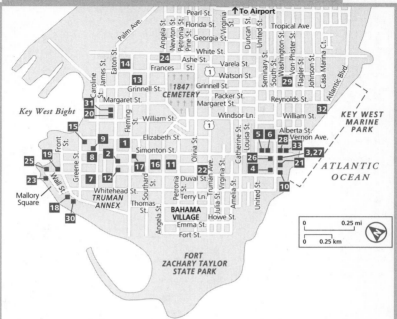

1. Ambrosia House
2. Artist House
3. Atlantic Shores Resort
4. Avalon Bed and Breakfast
5. Best Western Hibiscus Motel
6. Blue Marlin
7. Crowne Plaza La Concha
8. Curry Mansion Inn
9. Cypress House
10. Dewey House
11. Duval House
12. Eaton Lodge
13. Eden House
14. Frances Street Bottle Inn
15. Garden House
16. Gardens Hotel
17. Heron House
18. Hilton Key West Resort and Marina
19. Hyatt Key West Resort and Marina
20. Island City House Hotel
21. La Mer Hotel
22. La Te Da Hotel
23. Ocean Key Resort & Marina
24. Palms Hotel
25. Pier House
26. Southernmost Hotel
27. Southernmost on the Beach
28. Spanish Gardens
29. Suite Dreams
30. Sunset Key Guest Cottages at Hilton Key West Resort
31. Westwinds Inn
32. Wyndham Casa Marina Resort
33. Wyndham Reach Resort

palm beach and west palm beach accommodations

1. The Bradley House Hotel
2. The Breakers Palm Beach
3. Chesterfield Palm Beach
4. Colony Palm Beach
5. Crowne Plaza Singer Island
6. Doubletree Hotel
   Palm Beach Gardens
7. Embassy Suites
   Palm Beach Gardens
8. Four Seasons Resort
   Palm Beach
9. Hampton Inn
   West Palm Beach
10. Heart of Palm Beach Hotel
11. Hibiscus House B&B
12. Hilton Palm Beach Airport
13. Hilton Singer Island
    Oceanfront Resort
14. Holiday Inn Express
15. Hotel Biba
16. Inns of America Palm
    Beach Gardens
17. La Quinta Inn
    West Palm Beach
18. Marriott West Palm Beach
19. PGA National Resort
20. Portside on the Inlet
21. Radisson Suite Inn
    Palm Beach Airport
22. Ritz-Carlton Palm Beach

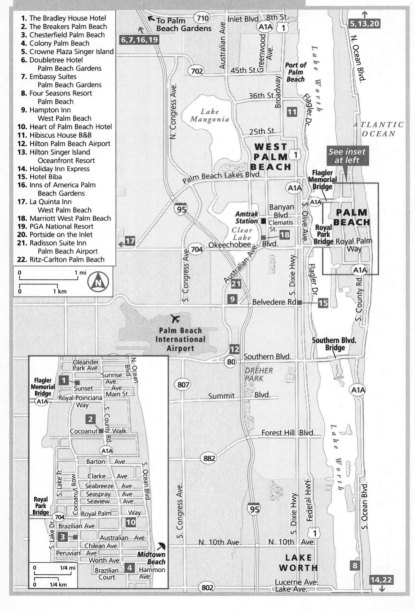

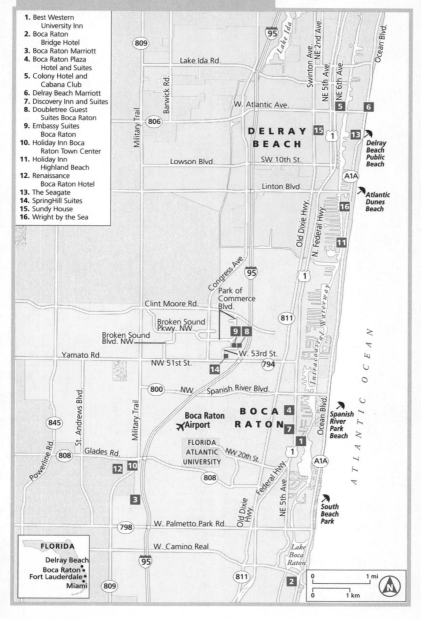

boca raton and delray beach accommodations

1. Best Western
   University Inn
2. Boca Raton
   Bridge Hotel
3. Boca Raton Marriott
4. Boca Raton Plaza
   Hotel and Suites
5. Colony Hotel and
   Cabana Club
6. Delray Beach Marriott
7. Discovery Inn and Suites
8. Doubletree Guest
   Suites Boca Raton
9. Embassy Suites
   Boca Raton
10. Holiday Inn Boca
    Raton Town Center
11. Holiday Inn
    Highland Beach
12. Renaissance
    Boca Raton Hotel
13. The Seagate
14. SpringHill Suites
15. Sundy House
16. Wright by the Sea

broward county accommodations

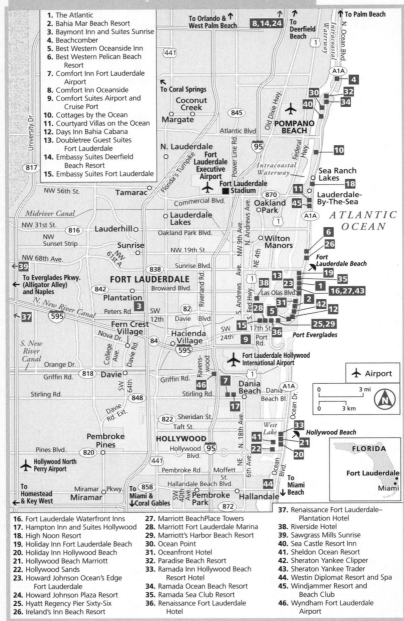

1. The Atlantic
2. Bahia Mar Beach Resort
3. Baymont Inn and Suites Sunrise
4. Beachcomber
5. Best Western Oceanside Inn
6. Best Western Pelican Beach Resort
7. Comfort Inn Fort Lauderdale Airport
8. Comfort Inn Oceanside
9. Comfort Suites Airport and Cruise Port
10. Cottages by the Ocean
11. Courtyard Villas on the Ocean
12. Days Inn Bahia Cabana
13. Doubletree Guest Suites Fort Lauderdale
14. Embassy Suites Deerfield Beach Resort
15. Embassy Suites Fort Lauderdale

16. Fort Lauderdale Waterfront Inns
17. Hampton Inn and Suites Hollywood
18. High Noon Resort
19. Holiday Inn Fort Lauderdale Beach
20. Holiday Inn Hollywood Beach
21. Hollywood Beach Marriott
22. Hollywood Sands
23. Howard Johnson Ocean's Edge Fort Lauderdale
24. Howard Johnson Plaza Resort
25. Hyatt Regency Pier Sixty-Six
26. Ireland's Inn Beach Resort

27. Marriott BeachPlace Towers
28. Marriott Fort Lauderdale Marina
29. Marriott's Harbor Beach Resort
30. Ocean Point
31. Oceanfront Hotel
32. Paradise Beach Resort
33. Ramada Inn Hollywood Beach Resort Hotel
34. Ramada Ocean Beach Resort
35. Ramada Sea Club Resort
36. Renaissance Fort Lauderdale Hotel

37. Renaissance Fort Lauderdale– Plantation Hotel
38. Riverside Hotel
39. Sawgrass Mills Sunrise
40. Sea Castle Resort Inn
41. Sheldon Ocean Resort
42. Sheraton Yankee Clipper
43. Sheraton Yankee Trader
44. Westin Diplomat Resort and Spa
45. Windjammer Resort and Beach Club
46. Wyndham Fort Lauderdale Airport

naples accommodations

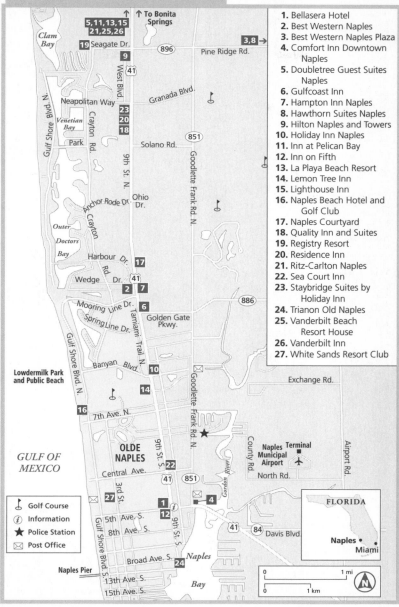

1. Bellasera Hotel
2. Best Western Naples
3. Best Western Naples Plaza
4. Comfort Inn Downtown Naples
5. Doubletree Guest Suites Naples
6. Gulfcoast Inn
7. Hampton Inn Naples
8. Hawthorn Suites Naples
9. Hilton Naples and Towers
10. Holiday Inn Naples
11. Inn at Pelican Bay
12. Inn on Fifth
13. La Playa Beach Resort
14. Lemon Tree Inn
15. Lighthouse Inn
16. Naples Beach Hotel and Golf Club
17. Naples Courtyard
18. Quality Inn and Suites
19. Registry Resort
20. Residence Inn
21. Ritz-Carlton Naples
22. Sea Court Inn
23. Staybridge Suites by Holiday Inn
24. Trianon Old Naples
25. Vanderbilt Beach Resort House
26. Vanderbilt Inn
27. White Sands Resort Club

fort myers accommodations

1. Best Western Airport Inn Fort Myers
2. Clarion Inn Fort Myers
3. Comfort Inn (Boatways Rd.)
4. Comfort Inn (S. Cleveland Ave.)
5. Country Inn & Suites Fort Myers
6. Courtyard Fort Myers
7. Days Inn South
8. Fairfield Inn Fort Myers
9. Fort Myers Inn
10. Hampton Inn Fort Myers
11. Hilton Garden Inn
12. Holiday Inn Select Airport
13. Homewood Suites Hotel
14. Howard Johnson Inn
15. La Quinta Inn
16. Quality Hotel
17. Ramada Limited Fort Myers
18. Ramada Riverfront
19. Residence Inn Fort Myers
20. Suburban Lodge of Fort Myers
21. Super 8 Motel
22. Wellesley Inn and Suites
23. Winyah Hotel and Suites

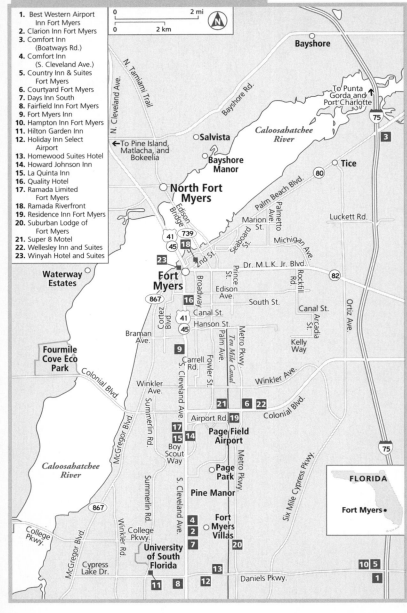

fort myers beach accommodations

1. Beacon Motel and Gift Shop
2. Best Western Beach Resort
3. Carousel Inn on the Beach
4. Casa Playa Beach Resort
5. DiamondHead Beach Resort
6. Dolphin Inn
7. Edison Beach House
8. Gullwing Beach Resort
9. Holiday Court Motel
10. Holiday Inn Fort Myers Beach
11. Lani Kai Island Resort Hotel
12. Lighthouse Island Resort
13. Lovers Key Beach Club and Resort
14. Mariner's Lodge and Marina
15. Matanzas Inn
16. Neptune Inn
17. Outrigger Beach Resort
18. Pink Shell Beach Resort
19. Pointe Estero Resort
20. Ramada Inn Beachfront
21. Sandpiper Gulf Resort
22. Sandy Beach Hideaway
23. Shipwreck Motel

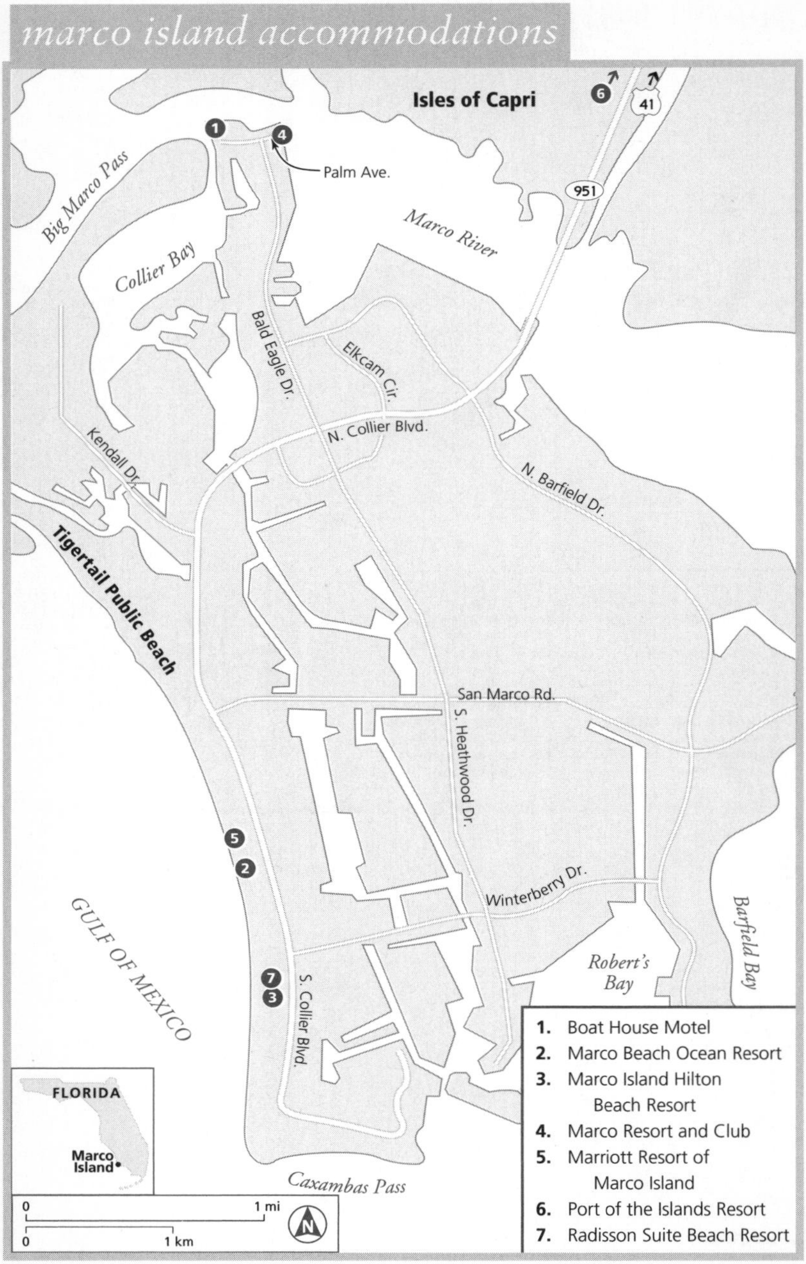

marco island accommodations

Isles of Capri

6 ↗   41 ↗

Palm Ave.

951

Big Marco Pass

Marco River

Collier Bay

Bald Eagle Dr.

Elkcam Cir.

N. Collier Blvd.

N. Barfield Dr.

Kendall Dr.

Tigertail Public Beach

San Marco Rd.

S. Heathwood Dr.

Winterberry Dr.

Barfield Bay

Robert's Bay

GULF OF MEXICO

5
2

7
3

S. Collier Blvd.

FLORIDA

Marco Island •

Caxambas Pass

| 0 | 1 mi |
| 0 | 1 km |

Ⓝ

1. Boat House Motel
2. Marco Beach Ocean Resort
3. Marco Island Hilton
   Beach Resort
4. Marco Resort and Club
5. Marriott Resort of
   Marco Island
6. Port of the Islands Resort
7. Radisson Suite Beach Resort

sanibel and captiva accommodations

1. Anchor Inn and Cottages of Sanibel
2. Beachview Cottages
3. Best Western Sanibel Gateway
4. Blue Dolphin Cottages
5. Captiva Island Bed and Breakfast
6. Caribe Beach Resort
7. Casa Ybel Resort
8. The Colony Resort
9. Country Inn and Suites Sanibel Gateway
10. Forty/Fifteen Resort
11. Holiday Inn Sanibel Island
12. Hurricane House
13. Island Inn
14. Jensen's Twin Palm Cottages and Marina
15. Kona Kai Motel
16. Mitchell's Sand Castles
17. The Palm View
18. Palms of Sanibel
19. Periwinkle Cottages of Sanibel
20. Sandpiper Inn Sanibel Island
21. Sanibel Beach Club II
22. Sanibel Inn
23. Sanibel's Seaside Inn
24. Seahorse Cottages on Sanibel
25. Shalimar Cottages and Motel
26. Sundial Beach Resort
27. Tarpon Tale Inn
28. Tropical Winds Motel and Cottages
29. Tween Waters Inn
30. Waterside Inn on the Beach
31. West Wind Inn

Miami Beach, Coral Gables, or Coconut Grove. Hotels situated near the airport are convenient to Coral Gables, downtown Miami, Fort Lauderdale, major expressways, and Pro Player Stadium (home of the Miami Dolphins). National-chain accommodations near the airport are scattered around a 16-square-mile area crisscrossed by expressways.

Coconut Grove has a long history as a hipster hangout, and although it has been commercialized, it still provides a nice evening of culture and interesting dining and shopping. It's an upscale bay-side community framed on the west and south by Coral Gables. Coconut Grove is convenient to a number of attractions, including Fairchild Tropical Garden, Miami Seaquarium, Parrot Jungle, and Vizcaya Museum and Gardens. Key Biscayne and various Biscayne Bay marinas are also easily accessible from Coconut Grove.

Coral Gables is an international destination for the well-heeled with fat pockets, and it also makes for an enjoyable afternoon or evening of shopping, dining, and cultural activities for those who are properly prepared (that is, those who can afford it!). It's located about two miles south of the airport and four miles southwest of downtown. A banking and trade center as well as one of Miami's loveliest residential suburbs, Coral Gables is also home to the University of Miami, the Miracle Mile shopping district, and many of the area's finest restaurants. Miami Beach and the Miami Beach Convention Center are a complicated 30- to 50-minute commute from Coral Gables.

Miami Beach is situated on a barrier island east of downtown Miami. The Art Deco District, extending from 5th Street northward along the beach to 15th Street, represents Miami Beach at its finest. Hotels here are small, independently owned, and architecturally distinctive in the Deco-Caribbean style of Miami Beach's original tourist boom. While parking is virtually nonexistent, dozens of restaurants and clubs are within easy walking distance—and so is the beach. The Miami Beach Convention Center is a 20- to 30-minute walk or a 5- to 10-minute cab ride away. Hotel rooms, and particularly baths, in the Art Deco District may be smaller than you would find in a chain hotel, but they are often beautifully appointed. On Miami Beach to the north of the official historic district (from 5th to 15th streets), many hotels in the Art Deco style eventually melt into larger hotels, and may or may not have been recently renovated. To muddy the waters for travelers and travel agents, many hotels north of the designated historic district claim in their promotional literature to be in the Art Deco District. If you want to stay in the heart of the Art Deco District, confirm that your hotel is located across from Lummus Park (beachfront) or on Collins Avenue (one block west of the beach) between 5th and 15th streets. Miami Beach is home to buff boys and bare babes—the beach is a mecca for the body gods and goddesses, and the clubs are manna from heaven for the night people.

While all sorts of celebrities can be found here, the community is becoming particularly popular with the hip-hop and rap crowds.

In Miami Beach, Collins Avenue north of Arthur Godfrey Road to the Kennedy Causeway (71st Street) is the home of this town's fabled hotel giants. Though many of the great hotels are gone and others have been renamed or replaced by skyward-stretching condominiums, the Fontainebleau Resorts and the Eden Roc, among others, still invite visitors to relive the zenith of Miami Beach's golden age. Huge, commanding, and magnificent after 40 years, these hotels almost single-handedly saved this part of Miami Beach from decline. Each of the great hotels offers elaborate swimming pools, landscaped gardens, meeting facilities, shopping arcades, and a variety of restaurants. The nightlife and restaurants of South Beach are a 10- to 30-minute drive away, depending on traffic. The Miami Beach Convention Center is 10 to 20 minutes by cab or convention-sponsored bus.

Bal Harbour is an isolated oceanside bastion of affluence and beauty. Large, modern, well-maintained hotels alternate with equally imposing condominiums. The Bal Harbour Shops, which make up one of the most diverse and tasteful shopping venues in the Southeast, are situated at the 96th Street end of the area. Nearby to the north is Haulover Park and Marina, featuring deep-sea fishing and kite flying as well as a nice beach. The airport and Miami Beach Convention Center are about 40–55 minutes away by car.

Across the Haulover Cut (back on the mainland) are **Sunny Isles** and **Golden Shores.** These areas were developed during the late 1950s and early 1960s and are characterized by small, motel-sized properties with exotic themes ranging from space travel to the Suez Canal. Although there are some nice rooms here, many of the properties have seen better days. The area is pretty remote unless you are bound for the Calder Race Track or Pro Player Stadium.

The Florida Keys

The Keys are most popular for fishers and those who like to dive the Coral Reef . . . at least until you reach **Key West,** 100 miles from the mainland. Once a paradise for artists and writers, the city has evolved into a destination that is especially popular among gay tourists. Large hotels crowd the waterfront, and their shops encroach on historic Duval Street, replacing some of the charm with new uglies and too many people. But many of the historic homes nearby have been renovated into guesthouses, each with its own charm and style. As a tourist magnet, Key West offers many excellent restaurants to choose from, crafts created by local artisans, and millions of T-shirts.

Palm Beach County

Palm Beach is home or getaway to some of the nation's wealthiest citizens, and many have lived or vacationed here for generations. The city remains protected from the outside world by bridges as well as an ambience that keeps outsiders from venturing too far into this privileged territory. But for those who dare (and have sufficiently deep pockets), the hotels have a well-worn elegance and charm. A small shopping area offers fine dining and boutique shopping in a village atmosphere.

Singer Island is a world apart from tony Palm Beach, though it's just a short swim north of the illustrious island. Perhaps established as a working people's getaway, the older cottages and rentals are much more modest, though nice. In recent years, many of the older properties have been bought and torn down, giving way to a beachfront of high-rises with famous names. Sad to see the old fade away, but locals seem to appreciate the developments in the name of progress for financial benefits to the community.

Most travelers may feel more comfortable staying in **West Palm Beach,** where downtown hotels offer the most nearby excitement, or in **Boca Raton** and **Delray Beach,** with their few, not-too-crowded beach hotels and some exceptional historic bed-and-breakfasts and hotels. Boca is more ritzy, while Delray offers a pleasant, quaint downtown area that often comes alive with street fairs and festivals.

The southeast coast of Florida is currently undergoing many changes, with older properties being replaced by newer, taller, more expensive ones. Some people are concerned that it may become cost-prohibitive to visit these coastal cities soon, and the beach is expected to be completely obscured by fancy hotels and condominiums.

Broward County

In northern Broward, **Pompano Beach** offers good value and a wide, golden beach, while **Lauderdale-By-The-Sea** offers a quaint, convenient village atmosphere—great for vacationers without cars.

Day or night, **Fort Lauderdale Beach** is a hot spot for the young crowd—the shops and restaurants around Las Olas Boulevard tend to attract well-heeled sophisticates. The town's historic district features not only the Broward Center for the Performing Arts and the Museum of Discovery and Science, but a few good restaurants and night clubs as well.

Hollywood offers an interesting study of a town trying to reinvent itself. Its renovated downtown area provides a pleasant stroll among shops and eateries, although some seem high priced for the area, grabbing for that tourist dollar. Unfortunately, the downtown area is more than a walk from the beach, where there are only a few restaurants and T-shirt shops besides the water itself.

Southwest Florida and the Everglades

Everglades City is a fishermen's village famous for its stone crabs and alligators. Digs here are simple, many without phones, but some of them offer an aged charm. Folks are friendly, and time passes gently if you enjoy exploring quiet natural waterways filled with dolphins, manatees, and mullet. This out-of-the way place is one of the few places where you can still taste the rustic beauty of old Florida. We love it.

Marco is a tidy, remote island village that serves as a popular winter residence for the wealthier set. **Naples** was once a similar vacation haven but is quickly evolving into a commercial city. Visitors can enjoy the finest in four- and five-star beach-area hotels, as well as prime dining and shopping. The long-standing residential foundation of well-heeled citizens has taken care to preserve the natural ambience of the fast-growing city—great tracts of natural habitat are protected to provide for the multiple species of birds and other fauna and flora that reside there. Vacationers can join eagles at the beach or commune with hundreds of passing flocks at the Audubon Society's Corkscrew Swamp Sanctuary bordering the Everglades.

Bonita Springs is a small city sandwiched between Naples and Fort Myers, with just a few hotels overlooking vast preserves of ocean-front wetlands and parklands, providing a peaceful and relaxing getaway.

In contrast, **Fort Myers Beach** is terribly congested except toward the southern tip, a resort and residential area. It's a big getaway for mid-westerners, but it is also notable as a place with many European immigrants, particularly among those who own the vacation properties.

Sanibel and **Captiva** are well-known vacation spots. Sanibel is also well guarded by savvy residents who understand the great value of preserving the native growth of trees, grasses, and ground cover. The result is a peaceful oasis, with small hotels and cottages dotting the shorelines instead of wall-to-wall concrete blocking the views and the breezes. Beaches here are less crowded than elsewhere in South Florida, and dolphins are frequently seen offshore. Captiva is much smaller than Sanibel and more crowded, although there are still a number of private residences lining the waterfront. In the village area near the western tip of the island, new development creates a glut of civilization—tall McMansions, both private homes and rentals, have replaced smaller, older homes, increasing the density of population.

Fort Myers itself is an aged little town that is faintly scenic along its waterfront, with an authentic village atmosphere all the more charming for its lack of polish and renovation. Downtown hotels provide a respite for business travelers, although the airport is located about half an hour away, southeast of the city. The airport is well served by the many hotels that line Interstate 75.

Pine Island and **Matlacha** are a pair of islands strung together off the coast of Fort Myers near Cape Coral. Matlacha provides an interesting land bridge to Pine Island and is lined with funky hotels, galleries, shops, restaurants, and rustic cottages favored by fishermen and artists. Pine Island is still a rural farming community, producing a rich collection of mangoes, avocados, and star fruit on a small, sparsely populated strip of land. **Bokeelia,** at the tip of the island that reaches into Charlotte Harbor, offers a few small rentals that provide a peaceful and remote island getaway.

GETTING *a* GOOD DEAL
on a ROOM

HIGH SEASON VERSUS LOW SEASON

HIGH SEASON IN SOUTH FLORIDA RUNS FROM Christmas through Easter. Additionally, some hotels observe a second high season from mid-June through mid-August, known as the family season. Room rates for many hotels are 25%–50% higher during these times of year. September, October, November (excluding the Thanksgiving holiday), and the first two weeks of December are the best times for obtaining low rates. Be aware, though, that large conventions can drive rates up regardless of the season. Check with the convention and visitors bureau to make sure your visit does not fall during a big meeting or trade show.

SPECIAL WEEKEND RATES

ALTHOUGH WELL-LOCATED HOTELS TYPICALLY charge higher rates, it's not impossible to get a good deal and a convenient location, at least relatively speaking. For starters, most downtown hotels that cater to business, government, and convention travelers offer special weekend discount rates that range from 15% to 40% below normal weekday rates. You can find out about weekend specials by calling the hotel or consulting your travel agent.

GETTING CORPORATE RATES

MANY HOTELS OFFER CORPORATE rates (5%–20% off "rack rates," hotel-industry lingo for standard nondiscounted rates). Usually you do not need to work for a large company or have a special relationship with the hotel to obtain such deals. Simply call the hotel of your choice and ask for their corporate rates. Many hotels will guarantee you the discounted rate on the phone when you make your reservation. Others may make the rate conditional on your providing some sort of bona fides—for instance, a fax on your company's letterhead requesting the rate, or a company credit card or business card on check-in. Generally, the screening is not rigorous.

HALF-PRICE PROGRAMS

THE LARGER ROOM DISCOUNTS (35%–60%) in South Florida are available through half-price hotel programs, often called travel clubs. Program operators contract with an individual hotel to provide rooms at deep discounts, usually 50% off the rack rate, on a space-available basis. "Space available," in practice, generally means that you can reserve a room at the discounted rate whenever the hotel expects to be at less than 80% occupancy. A little calendar sleuthing to help you avoid citywide conventions and special events will increase your chances of choosing a time for your visit when discounts are available.

Most half-price programs charge an annual membership fee or directory subscription charge of $25–$125. Once enrolled, you are mailed a membership card and a directory that lists all the hotels participating in the program. Examining the directory, you will notice immediately that there are a lot of restrictions and exceptions. Some hotels, for instance, black out certain dates or times of year. Others may only offer the discount on certain days of the week or require you to stay a certain number of nights. Still others may offer a much smaller discount than 50%.

Some programs specialize in domestic travel, some specialize in international travel, and some do both. The more established operators offer members between 1,000 and 4,000 hotels to choose from in the United States. All of the programs have a heavy concentration of hotels in California and Florida, and most have a very limited selection of participating properties in the Northeast. Offerings in other regions of the United States vary considerably. The programs with the largest selection of hotels in South Florida are Encore, Travel America at Half Price (Entertainment Publications), International Travel Card, and Quest.

Encore	☎ 800-638-0930
Entertainment Publications	☎ 800-285-5525
International Travel Card	☎ 800-342-0558
Quest	☎ 800-638-9819

One problem with half-price programs is that not all hotels offer a full 50% discount. Another slippery problem is the base rate against which the discount is applied. Some hotels figure the discount on an exaggerated rack rate that no one ever pays. A few participating hotels may deduct the discount from a supposed superior or upgraded room rate, even though the room you get is the hotel's standard accommodation. Though hard to pin down, the majority of participating properties base discounts on the rate published in the *Hotel and Travel Index* (a quarterly reference work used by travel agents) and work within the spirit of their agreement with the program operator. As a rule, if you travel several times a year, you will more than pay for your program membership in room-rate savings.

A noteworthy addendum to this discussion is that deeply discounted rooms through half-price programs are not commissionable to travel agents. In practical terms, this means that you must ordinarily make your own inquiry calls and reservations. If you travel frequently, however, and run a lot of business through your travel agent, he or she will probably do your legwork, lack of commission notwithstanding.

PREFERRED RATES

IF YOU CANNOT BOOK THE HOTEL OF YOUR choice through a half-price program, you may search for a lesser discount, often called a preferred rate. Such a rate could be a deal made available to travel agents to stimulate their booking activity or a discount initiated to attract a certain class of traveler. Most preferred rates are promoted through travel-industry publications and are often accessible only through an agent.

We recommend sounding out your travel agent about possible deals. Be aware, however, that the rates shown on agents' computerized reservation systems are not always the lowest available. Zero in on a couple of hotels that fill your needs in terms of location and quality of accommodations, then have your travel agent call for the latest rates and specials. Hotels are almost always more responsive to agents, who represent a source of additional business. There are certain specials that hotels will disclose only to travel professionals, and agents can sometime secure rooms even when a property is supposedly booked solid.

WHOLESALERS, CONSOLIDATORS, AND RESERVATION SERVICES

IF YOU DO NOT WANT TO JOIN A PROGRAM or buy a discount directory, you can still take advantage of the services of a wholesaler or consolidator. Wholesalers and consolidators buy rooms, or options on rooms (room blocks), from hotels at a low negotiated rate. They then resell the rooms at a profit through travel agents and tour packagers, or directly to the public. Most wholesalers and consolidators have a provision for returning unsold rooms to participating hotels but are disinclined to do so. The wholesaler's or consolidator's relationship with any hotel is predicated on volume: If he or she returns rooms unsold, the hotel might not make as many available the next time around. Thus, wholesalers and consolidators often offer rooms at bargain rates, anywhere from 15% to 50% off rack, occasionally sacrificing profit margin in the process, to avoid returning the rooms to the hotel unsold.

When wholesalers and consolidators deal directly with the public, they frequently represent themselves as "reservation services." When you call, you can ask for a rate quote for a particular hotel or, alternatively, ask for their best available deal in the area where you prefer to stay. If there is a maximum amount you are willing to pay, say so. Chances are the service will find something to suit you, even if it has to shave a dollar or two off its own profit. Sometimes you will have to pay for your room by credit card when you make your reservation; other times you will pay as usual, when you check out. Listed below are several services that frequently offer substantial discounts:

Accommodations Express ☎ 800-444-7666;
www.accommodationsexpress.com

Central Reservation Service ☎ 800-555-7555;
www.crshotels.com

Hotel Reservations Network ☎ 800-964-6835;
www.180096hotel.com

TurboTrip ☎ 800-473-7829;
www.turbotrip.com

TRAVELER INFORMATION GUIDE

A COMPANY CALLED TRAVELER DISCOUNT GUIDE (TDG) publishes a book of discount coupons for bargain rates at hotels throughout the state of Florida. These books are available free of charge in many restaurants and motels along the main interstate highways leading to the Sunshine State. Since most folks make reservations prior to leaving home, picking up the coupon book en route does not help much. For $3 ($5 Canadian), however, the company will mail you a copy (third class) before you make your reservations. If you call and use a credit card, TDG will send the guide first class for $3. Write or call:

Traveler Discount Guide
4205 NW Sixth Street
Gainesville, FL 32609
☎ 352-371-3948 or 800-332-3948
www.travelerdiscountguide.com

CONDOMINIUM DEALS

A LARGE NUMBER OF CONDO resorts and time-shares in South Florida rent to vacationers for a week or even less. Bargains can be found, especially during off-peak periods. Reservations and information can be obtained from Condolink, ☎ 800-733-4445.

The majority of area condos that rent to visitors also work with travel agents. In many cases, condo owners pay an enhanced commission to agents ,who rent the units for reduced consumer rates. It's worth a call to your travel agent.

FINDING DEALS ON THE INTERNET

WHOLESALERS, PACKAGERS, AND MANY OTHER travel and lodging players operate on the Internet, as do specialized Web travel vendors. By far the easiest way to scout room deals on the Internet is through **www.travelaxe.com.** At Travelaxe, you can download free software (which only runs on PCs, not Macs) that scans the better Web sites selling discounted rooms. You enter your proposed check-in and checkout dates (required) as well as preferences concerning location and price (optional), then click "Search." The program scans a dozen or more vendor sites and presents the discounted rates for all hotels in a chart for comparison. Note that the prices listed in the chart represent the total you'll pay for your entire stay, not the rate per night. If you decide to book, you deal directly with the site offering the best price. The software doesn't scan the individual hotel Web sites, so if you have a specific hotel in mind, you might want to check its site also. We've run a number of tests on the Travelaxe program and found that it usually delivers the best prices available on the Internet.

Finally, for Internet shopping, consider **www.priceline.com.** There you can tender a bid for a room. You can't bid on a specific hotel, but you can specify location ("downtown Miami," "Miami Beach," etc.) and the quality level you want, with ratings expressed in stars. If your bid is accepted, you will be assigned to a hotel consistent with your location and quality requirements, and your credit card will be charged in a nonrefundable transaction for your entire stay. Notification of acceptance usually takes less than an hour. We recommend bidding $60–$75 per night for a three-star hotel and $85–$110 per night for a four-star.

HOW TO EVALUATE A TRAVEL PACKAGE

HUNDREDS OF SOUTH FLORIDA PACKAGE VACATIONS are offered to the public each year. Packages should be a win-win proposition for both the buyer and the seller. The buyer only has to make one phone call and deal with a single salesperson to set up the whole vacation: transportation, rental car, lodging, meals, attraction admissions, and even golf and tennis. The seller, likewise, only has to deal with the buyer once, eliminating the need for separate sales, confirmations, and billing. Because selling vacation packages is an efficient way of doing business, and because the packager can often buy individual package components (such as airfare, rental car, and lodging) in bulk at a discount, savings in operating expenses realized by the seller are sometimes passed on to the buyer so that, in addition to convenience, the package is also an exceptional value. In any event, that is the way it is supposed to work.

All too often, in practice, the seller realizes all of the economies and passes nothing on to the buyer in the way of savings. In some instances, packages are loaded with extras that cost the packager next to nothing but that run the retail price of the package sky high. When considering a package, first choose one that includes features you are sure to use. Whether you use all the features or not, you will most certainly pay for them. Second, if cost is a greater concern than convenience, make a few phone calls and see what the package would cost if you booked its individual components on your own. If the package price is less than the à la carte cost, the package is a good deal; if the costs are about the same, the package is probably worth it for the convenience.

HELPING YOUR TRAVEL AGENT HELP YOU

WHEN YOU CALL YOUR TRAVEL AGENT, ASK if he or she has been to your South Florida destination. If the answer is no, either find another agent or be prepared to give your travel agent a lot of direction. Do not accept recommendations at face value. Check out the location and rates of any suggested hotel, and make certain that the hotel is suited to your itinerary. Travel agents unfamiliar with South Florida may try to plug you into a tour operator's or wholesaler's pre-set package. This essentially allows the travel agent to set up your whole trip with a single phone call and still collect an 8%–10% commission. The problem with this scenario is that most agents will place 90% of their South Florida business with only one or two wholesalers or tour operators, greatly reducing your choices. Often travel agents will use wholesalers who run packages in conjunction with airlines, like Delta's Dream Vacations or American's Fly-Away Vacations. Because of the wholesaler's exclusive relationship with the carrier, these trips are often more expensive than packages offered by high-volume wholesalers who work with a number of airlines in the South Florida market.

To help your travel agent get you the best possible deal, do the following:

1. Determine where you want to stay in South Florida and, if possible, choose a specific hotel. This can be accomplished by reviewing the hotel information provided in this guide and by writing or calling hotels that interest you.

2. Check out the South Florida travel ads in the Sunday travel section of your local newspaper, and compare them to ads running in the newspapers of one of South Florida's key markets, such as New York, Philadelphia, or Boston. Often you will find deals advertised in these newspapers that beat the socks off those in your local paper.

3. Call the wholesalers or tour operators whose ads you have collected. Ask any questions you might have concerning their packages, but do not book your trip with them directly.

4. Tell your travel agent about the packages you find, and ask if he or she can get you something better. The packages in the paper will serve as a benchmark against which to compare alternatives proposed by your travel agent.

5. Choose from among the options that you and your travel agent have uncovered. No matter which choice you select, have your travel agent book it. Even if you go with one of the packages in the newspaper, it will probably be commissionable (at no additional cost to you) and will

provide the agent some return on the time invested on your behalf. Also, as a travel professional, your agent should be able to verify the quality and integrity of the package.

IF YOU MAKE YOUR OWN RESERVATION

AS YOU POKE AROUND TRYING TO FIND a good deal, there are several things you should know. First, always call the hotel in question as opposed to the hotel chain's national toll-free number—quite often the national call center is uninformed of local specials. Always ask about specials before you inquire about corporate rates, and do not be reluctant to bargain. If you are buying a hotel's weekend package, for example, and want to extend your stay into the following week, you can often obtain at least the corporate rate for the extra days. Do your bargaining, however, before you check in, preferably when you make your reservations.

HOTELS *and* MOTELS: RATED *and* RANKED

ROOM RATINGS

TO SEPARATE PROPERTIES ACCORDING TO THE relative quality, tastefulness, state of repair, cleanliness, and size of their standard rooms, we have grouped hotels and motels into classifications denoted by stars. Star ratings in this guide apply to South Florida properties only and do not necessarily correspond to ratings awarded by AAA, Mobil, or other travel critics. Because stars have little relevance when awarded in the absence of commonly recognized standards of comparison, we have tied our ratings to expected levels of quality established by specific American hotel corporations.

Star ratings apply to room quality only and describe the property's standard accommodations. For most hotels and motels, this

WHAT THE RATINGS MEAN		
★★★★★	Superior Rooms	Tasteful and luxurious by any standard
★★★★	Extremely Nice Rooms	What you would expect at, say, a Hyatt Regency or Marriott
★★★	Nice Rooms	Holiday Inn or comparable quality
★★	Adequate Rooms	Clean, comfortable, and functional without frills—like a Motel 6
★	Super Budget	These exist but are not included in our coverage

means a room with either one king bed or two queen beds. In an all-suite property, the standard accommodation is either a one- or two-room suite. In addition to standard accommodations, many hotels offer luxury rooms and special suites, which are not rated in this guide. Star ratings for rooms are assigned without regard to whether a property has restaurants, recreational facilities, entertainment, or other extras.

In addition to stars (which delineate broad categories), we also employ a numerical rating system. Our rating scale is 0–100, with 100 as the best possible rating, and 0 as the worst. Numerical ratings are presented to show the difference we perceive between one property and another. On Miami Beach, for instance, rooms at the Beach House Hotel, the Courtyard Miami Beach Oceanfront, and the Whitelaw Hotel all received three stars. In the numerical ratings, the Beach House Hotel is rated a 73, the Courtyard a 72, and the Whitelaw Hotel a 67. This means that within the three-star category, the Beach House and the Courtyard are comparable, and both have slightly nicer rooms than the Whitelaw.

Cost estimates are based on the hotel's rack rates for standard rooms. Each dollar sign ($) represents $50. Thus a cost symbol of "$$$" for a given hotel means that a room (or suite) will be about $150 a night.

WHAT'S IN A ROOM?

THERE IS, OF COURSE, A DISCERNIBLE STANDARD of quality and luxury that differentiates Motel 6 from Holiday Inn, Holiday Inn from Marriott, and so on. In general, however, most hotel guests notice cleanliness, state of repair, and decor but fail to appreciate that some rooms are better engineered than others.

Contrary to what you might suppose, designing a hotel room is (or should be) a lot more complex than picking a bedspread to match the carpet and drapes. Making the room usable to its occupants is an art, a planning discipline that combines both form and function. No one wants to spend several days in a room whose decor is dated, garish, or even ugly. But beyond the decor are variables that determine how livable a hotel room is. We have seen some beautifully appointed rooms that are simply not well designed for human habitation. Here are a few of the things our researchers check that you may want to start paying attention to:

ROOM SIZE While some smaller rooms are cozy and well designed, a large and uncluttered room is generally preferable, especially for a stay of more than three days.

TEMPERATURE CONTROL, VENTILATION, AND ODOR The guest should be able to control the temperature of the room. The best system, because it's so quiet, is central heating and air-conditioning controlled by an in-room thermostat. The next best system is a room-module heater and air conditioner, preferably controlled by an automatic thermostat but usually by manually operated button controls. The worst system is central heating and air without any kind of guest control.

The vast majority of hotel rooms have windows or balcony doors that have been permanently secured shut. Though there are some legitimate safety and liability issues involved, we prefer windows and balcony doors that can be opened to admit fresh air. Also, rooms should be free of odors and smoke and not feel stuffy or damp.

ROOM SECURITY Better rooms have locks that require an encoded plastic card instead of the traditional lock and key. Card-and-slot systems essentially allow the hotel to change the combination or entry code of the lock with each new guest who uses the room. A burglar who has somehow acquired a key to a conventional lock can afford to wait until the situation is right before using the key to gain access. Not so with a card-and-slot system. Though larger hotels and hotel chains with lock-and-key systems usually rotate their locks once each year, they remain vulnerable to hotel thieves much of the time. Many smaller or independent properties rarely rotate their locks.

In addition to an entry-lock system, the door should have a deadbolt, and preferably a peephole and a chain that can be locked from the inside (a chain by itself is not sufficient). Windows and balcony doors, if any, should have secure locks.

SAFETY Every room should have a fire or smoke alarm, clear fire instructions, and preferably a sprinkler system. Bathtubs should have a nonskid surface, and shower stalls should have doors that either open outward or slide side-to-side. Bathroom electrical outlets should be high on the wall and not too close to the sink. Balconies should have high, sturdy rails.

NOISE Most travelers have occasionally been kept awake by the television, partying, or amorous activities of people in the next room, or by traffic on the street outside. Better hotels are designed with noise control in mind. Wall and ceiling construction is substantial, effectively screening routine noise. Carpets and drapes, in addition to being decorative, also absorb and mute sounds. Mattresses, mounted on stable platforms or sturdy bed frames, do not squeak even when challenged by the most passionate and acrobatic of lovers. Televisions are enclosed in cabinets, with volume governors, thereby rarely disturbing guests in adjacent rooms.

In better hotels, the air-conditioning and heating system is well maintained and operates without noise or vibration. Likewise, plumbing is quiet and positioned away from the sleeping area. Doors to the hall and adjoining rooms are thick and well fitted to better keep out noise.

DARKNESS CONTROL Ever been in a hotel room where the curtains would not quite come together in the middle? Thick, lined curtains that close completely in the center and extend beyond the dimensions of the window or door frame are required. In a well-planned room, the curtains, shades, or blinds should almost totally block light at any time of day.

LIGHTING Poor lighting is an extremely common problem in American hotel rooms. The lighting is usually adequate for dressing, relaxing, or watching television but not for reading or working. Lighting needs to be bright over tables and desks, and alongside couches or easy chairs. Because so many people read in bed, there should be a separate light for each person. A room with two queen beds should have an individual light for four people. Better bedside reading lights illuminate a small area so that if you want to sleep and someone else prefers to stay up and read, you will not be bothered by the light. The worst situation by far is a single lamp on a table between beds. In each bed, only the person next to the lamp will have sufficient light to read. This deficiency is often compounded by light bulbs of insufficient wattage.

In addition, closet areas should be well lit, and there should be a switch near the door that turns on lights in the room when you enter. A seldom seen but desirable feature is a bedside console that allows a guest to control all or most lights in the room from bed.

FURNISHINGS At bare minimum, the bed(s) must be firm. Pillows should be made with nonallergenic fillers, and in addition to the sheets and spread, a blanket should be provided. Bedclothes should be laundered with a fabric softener and changed daily. Better hotels usually stock rooms with extra blankets and pillows as a matter of course or provide them on request, and sometimes place a second top sheet between the blanket and the spread.

There should be a dresser large enough to hold clothes for two people during a five-day stay. A small table with two chairs, or a desk with a chair, should be provided. The room should be also equipped with a luggage rack and a three-quarter- to full-length mirror.

The television should be color and cable-connected and, ideally, should have a volume governor and remote control. It should be mounted on a swivel base and preferably enclosed in a cabinet. Local channels should be posted on the set, and a local TV program guide should be supplied.

The telephone should be TouchTone, conveniently situated for bedside use, and on it or nearby there should be easy-to-understand dialing instructions and a rate card. Local White Pages and Yellow Pages should be provided. Better hotels also have phones in the bath and equip all phones with long cords.

Well-designed hotel rooms usually have a plush armchair or sleeper sofa for lounging and reading. Better headboards are padded for comfortable reading in bed, and there should be a nightstand or table on each side of the bed(s). Nice extras in any hotel room include a small refrigerator, a digital alarm clock, and a coffeemaker.

BATHROOM Two sinks are better than one, and you can't have too much counter space. A sink outside the bath is great when two people bath and dress simultaneously. Sinks should have drains with stoppers.

Better bathrooms have both tubs and showers with nonslip bottoms. Tub and shower controls should be easy to operate. Adjustable showerheads are preferred. The bath needs to be well lit and should have an exhaust fan and a guest-controlled bathroom heater. Towels should be large, soft, fluffy, and provided in generous quantities, as should hand towels and washcloths. There should be an electrical outlet for each sink, conveniently and safely placed.

Complimentary shampoo, conditioner, and lotion are pluses, as are robes and bath mats. Better hotels supply their bathrooms with tissues and extra toilet paper. Luxurious baths feature a phone, a hair dryer, and sometimes a small television or even a hot tub.

VENDING There should be free ice and a drink machine on each floor. Welcome additions include snack machines and sundries machines (which dispense combs, toothpaste, and the like), though they're often absent from large hotels with 24-hour restaurants and shops.

HOW THE HOTELS COMPARE

HERE'S A HIT PARADE OF THE NICEST ROOMS in South Florida. We've focused strictly on room quality and excluded any consideration of location, services, recreation, or amenities. (As previously noted, though, we strongly recommend that your business or touring itinerary influence your lodging choice.)

With each edition of the *Unofficial Guide,* we include new properties and adjust ratings to reflect such positive developments as guest-room renovation and improved maintenance and housekeeping in hotels already listed. (Poor maintenance and lapses in housekeeping standards can affect ratings negatively.)

However, even with the best of intentions and the most conscientious research, we cannot inspect every room in every hotel. What we do, in statistical terms, is take a sample: We check out several rooms selected at random in each hotel and base our ratings on those. The inspections are conducted anonymously and without the knowledge of the property's management. Our researchers strive for impartiality, but you will naturally apply your own prejudices when evaluating a hotel's decor and amenities. The key to avoiding a disappointing stay is to do some advance snooping around. We recommend that you ask to be sent a photo of a hotel's standard guest room before you book, or at least get a copy of the hotel's promotional brochure. Be fore-warned, however, that some hotel chains use the same room photo in their promotional literature for all hotels in the chain, and that the rooms in a specific property may bear no resemblance to the brochure photo. When you or your travel agent calls, ask how old the property is and when the room you are being assigned was last renovated. If you arrive and are assigned a room inferior to that which you had been led to expect, demand to be moved to another one.

How the Hotels Compare in Miami-Dade County

HOTEL	STAR RATING	QUALITY RATING	COST ($ = $50)
BAL HARBOUR			
Sheraton Bal Harbour Resort	★★★★½	93	$$$$$$−
Sea View Hotel	★★★★	89	$$$$+
COCONUT GROVE			
Grove Isle Club and Resort	★★★★★	97	$$$$+
Wyndham Grand Bay Hotel	★★★★½	93	$$$$+
Doubletree at Coconut Grove	★★★★	83	$$$
Sonesta Hotel and Suites	★★★½	80	$$$−
CORAL GABLES			
Biltmore Hotel	★★★★★	98	$$$$+
Omni Colonnade Hotel	★★★★½	95	$$$$$$
Hyatt Regency Coral Gables	★★★★½	94	$$$$$$+
Hotel Place St. Michel	★★★★	89	$$$−
David William Hotel	★★★★	86	$$$$−
KEY BISCAYNE			
Ritz-Carlton Key Biscayne	★★★★★	99	$$$$$$$$$$$$+
Sonesta Beach Resort	★★★★	84	$$$$
MIAMI			
Four Seasons Hotel Miami	★★★★★	98	$$$$$$$+
Mandarin Oriental	★★★★★	98	$$$$$$$$+
Ritz-Carlton Coconut Grove	★★★★★	98	$$$$+
Hotel InterContinental	★★★★½	90	$$$$
JW Marriott Hotel Miami	★★★★½	90	$$$$$

How the Hotels Compare in Miami-Dade County (continued)

HOTEL	STAR RATING	QUALITY RATING	COST ($ = $50)
MIAMI (CONTINUED)			
Doral Golf Resort and Spa	★★★★	89	$$$
Doubletree Grand Hotel	★★★★	84	$$$$
Hotel Sofitel	★★★½	82	$$$$$–
Embassy Suites Airport	★★★½	81	$$+
Marriott Biscayne Bay	★★★½	80	$$$
Crowne Plaza Hotel	★★★½	77	$$$$–
Hilton Miami Airport	★★★	74	$$
Miami River Inn	★★★	74	$$
Radisson Hotel Miami	★★★	74	$$$–
Courtyard Downtown	★★★	70	$$+
Clarion Hotel and Suites	★★★	69	$$
Holiday Inn Port of Miami Downtown	★★★	65	$$
MIAMI BEACH			
Ritz-Carlton South Beach	★★★★★	99	$$$$$$$$$
Loews Miami Beach Hotel	★★★★½	95	$$$$$$$$–
Sanctuary South Beach	★★★★½	95	$$$$$$$+
The Tides	★★★★½	95	$$$$$$$
Hotel Delano	★★★★½	94	$$$$$$$
Bentley Hotel	★★★★½	93	$$$$
Hotel Astor	★★★★½	93	$$$
Wyndham Miami Beach Resort	★★★★½	92	$$$$–
The Palms	★★★★½	90	$$$$$$
Alexander Hotel	★★★★	89	$$$$
Eden Roc Resort and Spa	★★★★	89	$$$$
Hotel Ocean	★★★★	89	$$$$
The Marlin	★★★★	89	$$$$$
The Hotel	★★★★	87	$$$$+
Casa Grande Suite Hotel	★★★★	86	$$$$$$+
Hotel Impala	★★★★	85	$$$$
Hotel Victor	★★★★	85	$$$$$$$$$+
Blue Moon	★★★★	84	$$$–

How the Hotels Compare in Miami-Dade County (continued)

HOTEL	STAR RATING	QUALITY RATING	COST ($ = $50)
MIAMI BEACH (CONTINUED)			
Fontainebleau Resorts	★★★★	84	$$$$$$–
The Mercury Resort and Spa	★★★★	83	$$$$
Clinton Hotel South Beach	★★★½	82	$$$$
Park Central Imperial Hotels	★★★½	82	$$$$–
Waldorf Towers Hotel	★★★½	82	$$$$–
Aqua Hotel and Lounge	★★★½	80	$$
Bay Harbor Inn and Suites	★★★½	80	$$$–
Doubletree Surfcomber	★★★½	80	$$$$$–
Nassau Suite Hotel	★★★½	80	$$$
National Hotel	★★★½	80	$$$$
Cardozo Hotel	★★★½	75	$$$
The Catalina Hotel and Beach Club	★★★½	75	$$$$$–
Four Points by Sheraton	★★★½	75	$$$$–
Lily Guesthouse	★★★½	75	$$$$–
Avalon Hotel	★★★	73	$$$+
The Beach House Hotel	★★★	73	$$$–
Clevelander Hotel	★★★	73	$$$–
Comfort Inn and Suites South Beach	★★★	73	$$$
Courtyard Miami Beach Oceanfront	★★★	72	$$$+
The Chesterfield Hotel	★★★	70	$$$$
Fairfield Inn Miami Beach on the Ocean	★★★	70	$$
Hotel Riande Continental	★★★	70	$$$–
Indian Creek Hotel	★★★	70	$$
Newport Beachside Resort	★★★	70	$$
Seacoast Suites Hotel	★★★	70	$$
Essex House Hotel	★★★	69	$$$–
The Hotel Chelsea	★★★	68	$$$$
The Whitelaw Hotel	★★★	67	$$$$
Holiday Inn South Beach Resort	★★★	66	$$$+
The Hotel Shelley	★★★	66	$$$
Brigham Gardens	★★★	65	$$
Beach Plaza Hotel	★★½	64	$$$$

How the Hotels Compare in Miami-Dade County (continued)

HOTEL	STAR RATING	QUALITY RATING	COST ($ = $50)
MIAMI BEACH (CONTINUED)			
Best Western Beach Resort	★★½	64	$$
Best Western Oceanfront Resort	★★½	64	$$$+
Days Inn South Beach	★★½	64	$$+
Ramada Plaza Marco Polo	★★½	64	$$+
Days Inn Oceanside	★★½	63	$$
Tudor Hotel	★★½	63	$$−
MIAMI LAKES			
Don Shula's Hotel and Golf Club	★★★★	85	$$$
SUNNY ISLES BEACH			
Trump International Sonesta Beach Resort	★★★★½	90	$$$$$$

How the Hotels Compare in the Florida Keys

HOTEL	STAR RATING	QUALITY RATING	COST ($ = $50)
DUCK KEY			
Hawk's Cay Resort	★★★★	83	$$$$$
ISLAMORADA			
The Moorings Village and Spa	★★★★★	98	$$$$$−
Cheeca Lodge	★★★★½	92	$$$$$$$$
Islander Resort	★★★★	89	$$$$−
Pelican Cove Resort	★★★	71	$$$
Chesapeake Resort	★★★	70	$$$$
The Ragged Edge	★★★	70	$$+
Breezy Palms Resort	★★★	67	$$
The Sands of Islamorada	★★★	66	$$$−
Hampton Inn and Suites Islamorada	★★½	64	$$$$+
Holiday Isle Resort and Marina	★★½	62	$$$−

How the Hotels Compare in the Florida Keys (cont'd)

HOTEL	STAR RATING	QUALITY RATING	COST ($ = $50)
KEY LARGO			
Kona Kai Resort and Gallery	★★★★★	97	$$$$+
Key Largo Marriott Beach Resort	★★★★	83	$$$$
Amy Slate's Amoray Dive Resort	★★★	74	$$$
Ramada Limited Key Largo	★★★	72	$$$–
Best Western Suites at Key Largo	★★★	70	$$$–
Holiday Inn Key Largo Resort	★★½	64	$$+
Gilbert's Resort	★★½	62	$$
Howard Johnson Resort Key Largo	★★½	60	$$$$$–
KEY WEST			
Sunset Key Guest Cottages at Hilton Key West Resort	★★★★★	98	$$$$$$$ $$$$$$$$$–
Dewey House	★★★★	85	$$$$
Heron House	★★★★	85	$$$$
Hyatt Key West Resort and Marina	★★★★	85	$$$$$$
La Mer Hotel	★★★★	85	$$$$
Gardens Hotel	★★★★	83	$$$$$
Hilton Key West Resort and Marina	★★★★	83	$$$$$$$$–
Pier House	★★★½	82	$$$$
Suite Dreams	★★★½	82	$$$$–
Wyndham Casa Marina Resort	★★★½	82	$$$$$$
Island City House Hotel	★★★½	81	$$$$–
Ambrosia House	★★★½	80	$$$
Avalon Bed and Breakfast	★★★½	80	$$
Crowne Plaza La Concha	★★★½	80	$$$$$–
Ocean Key Resort and Marina	★★★½	80	$$$$$$$+
Sheraton Suites Key West	★★★½	80	$$$$$$$–
Wyndham Reach Resort	★★★½	75	$$$$+
Frances Street Bottle Inn	★★★	74	$$
La Te Da Hotel	★★★	74	$$+
Southernmost Hotel	★★★	74	$$+
Southernmost on the Beach	★★★	74	$$$+

How the Hotels Compare in the Florida Keys (cont'd)

HOTEL	STAR RATING	QUALITY RATING	COST ($ = $50)
KEY WEST (CONTINUED)			
Artist House	★★★	72	$$$$
Curry Mansion Inn	★★★	72	$$$$
Garden House	★★★	70	$$$–
Eaton Lodge	★★★	69	$$$–
Duval House	★★★	66	$$$$–
Best Western Key Ambassador	★★★	65	$$$
Courtyard Key West Waterfront	★★★	65	$$$+
Cypress House	★★★	65	$$$$–
The Inn at Key West	★★★	65	$$$–
Westwinds Inn	★★★	65	$$$–
Comfort Inn Key West	★★½	64	$$
Eden House	★★½	64	$$$–
Hampton Inn	★★½	64	$$+
Palms Hotel	★★½	64	$$
Radisson Hotel Key West	★★½	64	$$+
Spanish Gardens	★★½	64	$$$–
Travelodge Key West	★★½	64	$$$
Atlantic Shores Resort	★★½	63	$$$–
Best Western Hibiscus Motel	★★½	63	$$$$–
Blue Marlin	★★	50	$$$–
Days Inn Key West	★★	50	$$
Hotel Key West	★★	47	$$
LITTLE TORCH KEY			
Parmer's Resort	★★★	70	$$
MARATHON			
Banana Bay Resort and Marina	★★★½	82	$$$
Holiday Inn Marathon	★★★	74	$$
Rainbow Bend Resort	★★★	73	$$$$–
Yellowtail Inn	★★★	72	$$+
Bay View Inn	★★½	64	$$

How the Hotels Compare in the Florida Keys (cont'd)

HOTEL	STAR RATING	QUALITY RATING	COST ($ = $50)
MARATHON (CONTINUED)			
Coconut Cay	★★½	64	$$
Hidden Harbor Motel	★★½	64	$$
Kingsail Resort Motel	★★½	64	$$
TAVERNIER			
Tavernier Hotel	★★½	64	$$–

How the Hotels Compare in Palm Beach County

HOTEL	STAR RATING	QUALITY RATING	COST ($ = $50)
BOCA RATON			
Renaissance Boca Raton Hotel	★★★★½	90	$$$$
Embassy Suites Boca Raton	★★★★	84	$$
Boca Raton Marriott	★★★★	83	$$$$–
SpringHill Suites	★★★½	82	$$–
Doubletree Guest Suites Boca Raton	★★★½	80	$$–
Holiday Inn Boca Raton Town Center	★★★½	79	$$$–
Boca Raton Bridge Hotel	★★★½	75	$$$
Boca Raton Plaza Hotel and Suites	★★★	68	$+
Discovery Inn and Suites	★★½	64	$+
Best Western University Inn	★★	50	$$–
BOYNTON BEACH			
Holiday Inn Express	★★½	62	$$
DELRAY BEACH			
Sundy House	★★★★	89	$$$$
Delray Beach Marriott	★★★★	85	$$$$$
Colony Hotel and Cabana Club	★★★½	78	$$+
The Seagate	★★★½	78	$$+
Wright by the Sea	★★★½	75	$$$$+

How the Hotels Compare in Palm Beach County (continued)

HOTEL	STAR RATING	QUALITY RATING	COST ($ = $50)
HIGHLAND BEACH			
Holiday Inn Highland Beach	★★★½	79	$$$
PALM BEACH			
The Breakers Palm Beach	★★★★★	99	$$$$$$$–
Four Seasons Resort Palm Beach	★★★★★	99	$$$$$$$$
Ritz-Carlton Palm Beach	★★★★★	99	$$$$$$$$ $$$+
Chesterfield Palm Beach	★★★★½	95	$$$$
Colony Palm Beach	★★★★	85	$$$+
Heart of Palm Beach Hotel	★★★½	82	$$$
The Bradley House Hotel	★★★	68	$$$–
PALM BEACH GARDENS			
PGA National Resort	★★★★	89	$$$
Doubletree Hotel Palm Beach Gardens	★★★½	82	$$$–
Embassy Suites Palm Beach Gardens	★★★½	75	$$$–
Inns of America Palm Beach Gardens	★★½	64	$$–
PALM BEACH SHORES			
Portside on the Inlet	★★★	70	$$
SINGER ISLAND			
Crowne Plaza Singer Island	★★★★	84	$$$
Hilton Singer Island Oceanfront Resort	★★★½	82	$$$
WEST PALM BEACH			
Marriott West Palm Beach	★★★½	80	$$$–
Hilton Palm Beach Airport	★★★½	75	$$$–
Hibiscus House B&B	★★★	74	$$
Hotel Biba	★★★	73	$$$–
Radisson Suite Inn Palm Beach Airport	★★★	65	$$+
Hampton Inn West Palm Beach	★★½	57	$$$$

How the Hotels Compare in Broward County

HOTEL	STAR RATING	QUALITY RATING	COST ($ = $50)
DEERFIELD BEACH			
Embassy Suites Deerfield Beach Resort	★★★½	80	$$$$–
Howard Johnson Plaza Resort	★★½	64	$$$–
Comfort Inn Oceanside	★★½	60	$$+
FORT LAUDERDALE			
The Atlantic	★★★★½	94	$$$$$$$$–
Hyatt Regency Pier Sixty-Six	★★★★½	90	$$$$
Marriott Harbor Beach Resort	★★★★½	90	$$$$+
Renaissance Fort Lauderdale Hotel	★★★★	84	$$$$$
Marriott Fort Lauderdale Marina	★★★★	83	$$$$+
Sheraton Yankee Trader	★★★½	82	$$$$–
Marriott BeachPlace Towers	★★★½	81	$$$$$–
Riverside Hotel	★★★½	80	$$$
Embassy Suites Fort Lauderdale	★★★½	78	$$$$
Sheraton Yankee Clipper	★★★½	75	$$$
Wyndham Fort Lauderdale Airport	★★★½	75	$$$
Bahia Mar Beach Resort	★★★	74	$$$$
Best Western Pelican Beach Resort	★★★	74	$$$$$$–
Doubletree Guest Suites Fort Lauderdale	★★★	74	$$$
Fort Lauderdale Waterfront Inns	★★★	74	$$
Ireland's Inn Beach Resort	★★★	74	$$$–
Comfort Suites Airport and Cruise Port	★★★	73	$$$+
Oceanfront Hotel	★★★	72	$$$$+
Holiday Inn Fort Lauderdale Beach	★★★	65	$$$
Days Inn Bahia Cabana	★★½	62	$$$$
Best Western Oceanside Inn	★★½	57	$$–
Ramada Sea Club Resort	★★	52	$$
Howard Johnson Ocean's Edge Fort Lauderdale	★★	47	$$$–
HOLLYWOOD			
Westin Diplomat Resort and Spa	★★★★½	93	$$$$$

How the Hotels Compare in Broward County (continued)

HOTEL	STAR RATING	QUALITY RATING	COST ($ = $50)
HOLLYWOOD (CONTINUED)			
Hampton Inn and Suites Hollywood	★★★	70	$$$–
Comfort Inn Fort Lauderdale Airport	★★★	69	$$–
Hollywood Sands	★★★	67	$$$
Sheldon Ocean Resort	★★	55	$$–
HOLLYWOOD BEACH			
Hollywood Beach Marriott	★★★★	89	$$$$$–
Holiday Inn Hollywood Beach	★★★	67	$$+
Ramada Inn Hollywood Beach	★½	40	$$
LAUDERDALE-BY-THE-SEA			
Courtyard Villas on the Ocean	★★★½	80	$$$$–
High Noon Resort	★★★½	79	$$$$–
Windjammer Resort and Beach Club	★★★	66	$$$$–
PLANTATION			
Renaissance Fort Lauderdale–Plantation Hotel	★★★★	84	$$$$
POMPANO BEACH			
Cottages by the Ocean	★★★	70	$$+
Beachcomber	★★★	66	$$$–
Ocean Point	★★½	63	$$$$
Paradise Beach Resort	★★½	60	$$
Ramada Ocean Beach Resort	★★½	60	$$$–
Sea Castle Resort Inn	★★½	58	$+
SUNRISE			
Sawgrass Mills Sunrise	★★★½	78	$$+
Baymont Inn and Suites Sunrise	★★★	70	$$+

How the Hotels Compare in Southwest Florida

HOTEL	STAR RATING	QUALITY RATING	COST ($ = $50)
BOCA GRANDE			
Boca Grande Club	★★★½	80	$$$–
BONITA SPRINGS			
Trianon Bonita Bay	★★★★½	95	$$$–
Baymont Inn Bonita Springs	★★★	73	$+
Hampton Inn Bonita Springs	★★★	68	$$–
Holiday Inn Express Hotel and Suites	★★★	68	$$–
Bonita Beach Resort Motel	★★★½	64	$+
Tradewinds	★★½	64	$$+
Comfort Inn Bonita Springs	★★½	60	$+
Flamingo Motel	★★½	60	$$
CAPE HAZE			
Palm Island Resort	★★★★	84	$$$$$$–
CAPTIVA			
Tween Waters Inn	★★★	72	$$$+
Captiva Island Bed and Breakfast	★★★	70	$$$–
Jensen's Twin Palm Cottages and Marina	★★★	68	$$$
EVERGLADES CITY			
Everglades City Motel	★★★	68	$$–
Everglades Spa-Fari and Lodge	★★★	71	$$
Ivey House Inn	★★★	72	$$$
Rod and Gun Club Lodge	★★★	70	$$
Captain's Table Lodge and Villas	★★½	64	$$–
FORT MYERS			
Hilton Garden Inn	★★★½	80	$$$
Country Inn and Suites Fort Myers	★★★	75	$$
Suburban Lodge of Fort Myers	★★★	66	$+
La Quinta Inn Fort Myers	★★½	64	$$–

How the Hotels Compare in Southwest Florida (continued)

HOTEL	STAR RATING	QUALITY RATING	COST ($ = $50)
FORT MYERS (CONTINUED)			
Holiday Inn Select Airport	★★★½	80	$$$
Homewood Suites Hotel	★★★½	78	$$$$
Courtyard Fort Myers	★★★	74	$$$–
Hampton Inn Fort Myers	★★★	74	$$$–
Fairfield Inn Fort Myers	★★★	73	$$
Country Inn and Suites Sanibel Gateway	★★★	72	$$$–
Residence Inn Fort Myers	★★★	70	$$$
Best Western Airport Inn Fort Myers	★★★	69	$$
Comfort Inn (Boatways Road)	★★★	68	$$–
Ramada Riverfront	★★★	68	$$–
Wellesley Inn and Suites	★★★	67	$$–
Winyah Hotel and Suites	★★★	67	$$–
Best Western Sanibel Gateway	★★★	65	$$
Clarion Inn Fort Myers	★★½	64	$+
Fort Myers Inn	★★½	64	$+
Super 8 Motel	★★½	63	$$
Quality Hotel	★★½	60	$+
Ramada Limited Fort Myers	★★½	58	$$
Comfort Inn (South Cleveland Avenue)	★★½	56	$$–
Howard Johnson Inn	★★½	56	$$
Days Inn South	★★	54	$$–
FORT MYERS BEACH			
Gullwing Beach Resort	★★★★½	90	$$$$+
Lovers Key Beach Club and Resort	★★★★½	90	$$$$–
Pointe Estero Resort	★★★★	87	$$$$–
DiamondHead Beach Resort	★★★★	84	$$$$
Edison Beach House	★★★★	83	$$$–
Pink Shell Beach Resort	★★★½	80	$$$$
Casa Playa Beach Resort	★★★½	80	$$+
Beacon Motel and Gift Shop	★★★	72	$$+
Outrigger Beach Resort	★★★	71	$$$–

How the Hotels Compare in Southwest Florida (continued)

HOTEL	STAR RATING	QUALITY RATING	COST ($ = $50)
FORT MYERS BEACH (CONTINUED)			
Sandpiper Gulf Resort	★★★	71	$$
Holiday Inn Fort Myers Beach	★★★	70	$$+
Best Western Beach Resort	★★★	68	$$+
Carousel Inn on the Beach	★★★	68	$$
Lani Kai Island Resort Hotel	★★★	65	$$$$−
Matanzas Inn	★★★	65	$$
Neptune Inn	★★★	65	$$
Lighthouse Island Resort	★★½	64	$$
Sandy Beach Hideaway	★★½	64	$+
Ramada Inn Beachfront	★★½	63	$$−
Mariner's Lodge and Marina	★★½	62	$+
Dolphin Inn	★★½	60	$$−
Holiday Court Motel	★★½	60	$$
Shipwreck Motel	★★½	60	$$
NAPLES			
Ritz-Carlton Naples	★★★★★	100	$$$$$$$
Registry Resort	★★★★½	95	$$$$$$+
Trianon Old Naples	★★★★½	95	$$$−
La Playa Beach Resort	★★★★	87	$$$$$$$
Bellasera Hotel	★★★★	84	$$$$
Inn at Pelican Bay	★★★★	84	$$$−
Naples Beach Hotel and Golf Club	★★★★	84	$$$$−
Hilton Naples and Towers	★★★★	83	$$$+
Inn on Fifth	★★★★	83	$$$$
Vanderbilt Beach Resort House	★★★½	82	$$+
Naples Courtyard	★★★½	78	$$
Doubletree Guest Suites Naples	★★★½	77	$$$−
Vanderbilt Inn	★★★½	75	$$$
Residence Inn Naples	★★★	72	$$$−
Hawthorn Suites Naples	★★★	70	$$+
Staybridge Suites by Holiday Inn	★★★	70	$$+

How the Hotels Compare in Southwest Florida (continued)

HOTEL	STAR RATING	QUALITY RATING	COST ($ = $50)
NAPLES (CONTINUED)			
Sea Court Inn	★★★	69	$+
Best Western Naples Plaza	★★★	67	$$$
Quality Inn and Suites	★★★	67	$$
Hampton Inn Naples	★★★	66	$$$$
Best Western Naples	★★★	65	$$
Lighthouse Inn	★★★	65	$$–
White Sands Resort Club	★★★	65	$$
Gulfcoast Inn	★★½	64	$+
Comfort Inn Downtown Naples	★★½	64	$$
Lemon Tree Inn	★★½	64	$$
Holiday Inn Naples	★★	50	$$
PINE ISLAND			
Bokeelia Tarpon Inn (Bokeelia)	★★★★	89	$$$$$$
The Beachouse Lodge (Bokeelia)	★★★	74	$$
Bayview Bed and Breakfast (Matlacha)	★★★	72	$$
Bridge Water Inn (Matlacha)	★★★	70	$$
The Sun and the Moon Inn (Matlacha)	★★★	70	$$
Tarpon Lodge (Pineland)	★★★	70	$$
Jug Creek Cottages (Bokeelia)	★★	55	$$–
SANIBEL			
Casa Ybel Resort	★★★★	89	$$$$$$–
Hurricane House	★★★★	84	$$$$+
Island Inn	★★★½	82	$$$+
Sanibel's Seaside Inn	★★★½	82	$$$$+
West Wind Inn	★★★½	82	$$$$–
Sanibel Inn	★★★½	80	$$$$
Shalimar Cottages and Motel	★★★½	78	$$$$–
Sundial Beach Resort	★★★½	78	$$$$$
Tarpon Tale Inn	★★★½	78	$$$$–
Waterside Inn on the Beach	★★★½	76	$$$$

How the Hotels Compare in Southwest Florida (continued)

HOTEL	STAR RATING	QUALITY RATING	COST ($ = $50)
SANIBEL (CONTINUED)			
Caribe Beach Resort	★★★½	75	$$+
The Palm View	★★★	74	$$
Sandpiper Inn Sanibel Island	★★★	74	$$−
The Colony Resort	★★★	72	$$$
Sanibel Beach Club II	★★★	71	$$
Anchor Inn and Cottages of Sanibel	★★★	70	$$
Beachview Cottages	★★★	70	$$$
Holiday Inn Sanibel Island	★★★	70	$$$
Kona Kai Motel	★★★	69	$$
Seahorse Cottages on Sanibel	★★★	69	$$
Blue Dolphin Cottages	★★★	68	$$
Tropical Winds Motel and Cottages	★★★	68	$$$
Forty/Fifteen Resort	★★★	65	$$$
Palms of Sanibel	★★★	65	$$$−
Periwinkle Cottages of Sanibel	★★★	65	$$
Mitchell's Sand Castles	★★½	64	$$$

THE BEST DEALS

HAVING LISTED THE NICEST ROOMS IN TOWN, let's reorder the list to rank the best combinations of quality and value in a room. As before, the rankings are compiled without consideration of location or the availability of restaurants, recreational facilities, entertainment, or amenities. Once again, each lodging property is awarded a value rating on a 0–100 scale. The higher the number, the better the value.

We recently had a reader complain to us that he had booked one of our top-ranked rooms in terms of value and had been very disappointed in the room. We noticed that the room the reader occupied had a quality rating of ★★½. We would remind you that the value ratings are intended to give you some sense of value received for dollars spent. A ★★½ room at $50 may have the same value rating as a ★★★★ room at $100, but that does not mean the rooms will be of comparable quality. Regardless of whether it's a good deal or not, a ★★½ room is still a ★★½ room.

Listed below are the best room buys for the money, regardless of location or star classification, based on averaged rack rates. Note that sometimes a suite can cost less than a standard room.

The Top 30 Best Deals in Miami-Dade County

HOTEL	STAR RATING	QUALITY RATING	COST ($ = $50)
1. Hotel Place St. Michel	★★★★	89	$$$–
2. Aqua Hotel and Lounge	★★★½	80	$$
3. Hotel Astor	★★★★½	93	$$$
4. Blue Moon	★★★★	84	$$$–
5. Doral Golf Resort and Spa	★★★★	89	$$$
6. Embassy Suites Airport	★★★½	81	$$+
7. Wyndham Miami Beach Resort	★★★★½	92	$$$$–
8. Don Shula's Hotel and Golf Club	★★★★	85	$$$
9. Miami River Inn	★★★	74	$$
10. Biltmore Hotel	★★★★★	98	$$$$+
11. Ritz-Carlton Coconut Grove	★★★★★	98	$$$$+
12. Fairfield Inn Miami Beach on the Ocean	★★★	70	$$
13. Doubletree at Coconut Grove	★★★★	83	$$$
14. Grove Isle Club and Resort	★★★★★	97	$$$$+
15. Sonesta Hotel and Suites	★★★½	80	$$$–
16. Bentley Hotel	★★★★½	93	$$$$
17. Indian Creek Hotel	★★★	70	$$
18. Clarion Hotel and Suites	★★★	69	$$
19. Hilton Miami Airport	★★★	74	$$
20. Hotel InterContinental	★★★★½	90	$$$$
21. Bay Harbor Inn and Suites	★★★½	80	$$$–
22. Tudor Hotel	★★½	63	$$–
23. Brigham Gardens	★★★	65	$$
24. Newport Beachside Resort	★★★	70	$$
25. Seacoast Suites Hotel	★★★	70	$$
26. David William Hotel	★★★★	86	$$$$–
27. Marriott Biscayne Bay	★★★½	80	$$$
28. Nassau Suite Hotel	★★★½	80	$$$
29. Wyndham Grand Bay Hotel	★★★★½	93	$$$$+
30. Alexander Hotel	★★★★	89	$$$$

The Top 20 Best Deals in the Florida Keys

HOTEL	STAR RATING	QUALITY RATING	COST ($ = $50)
1. Avalon Bed and Breakfast	★★★½	80	$$
2. Kona Kai Resort and Gallery	★★★★★	97	$$$$+
3. Frances Street Bottle Inn	★★★	74	$$
4. The Moorings Village and Spa	★★★★★	98	$$$$$–
5. Breezy Palms Resort	★★★	67	$$
6. Holiday Inn Marathon	★★★	74	$$
7. Tavernier Hotel	★★½	64	$$–
8. Banana Bay Resort and Marina	★★★½	82	$$$
9. Ambrosia House	★★★½	80	$$$
10. Parmer's Resort	★★★	70	$$
11. Islander Resort	★★★★	89	$$$$–
12. La Te Da Hotel	★★★	74	$$+
13. Yellowtail Inn	★★★	72	$$+
14. Southernmost Hotel	★★★	74	$$+
15. Heron House	★★★★	85	$$$$
16. The Ragged Edge	★★★	70	$$+
17. Hidden Harbor Motel	★★½	64	$$
18. Kingsail Resort Motel	★★½	64	$$
19. Palms Hotel	★★½	64	$$
20. Key Largo Marriott Beach Resort	★★★★	83	$$$$

The Top 10 Best Deals in Palm Beach County

HOTEL	STAR RATING	QUALITY RATING	COST ($ = $50)
1. Embassy Suites Boca Raton	★★★★	84	$$
2. SpringHill Suites	★★★½	82	$$–
3. Doubletree Guest Suites Boca Raton	★★★½	80	$$–
4. Boca Raton Plaza Hotel and Suites	★★★	68	$+
5. PGA National Resort	★★★★	89	$$$
6. Colony Hotel and Cabana Club	★★★½	78	$$+
7. Discovery Inn and Suites	★★½	64	$+

The Top 10 Best Deals in Palm Beach County (cont'd)

HOTEL	STAR RATING	QUALITY RATING	COST ($ = $50)
8. Doubletree Hotel Palm Beach Gardens	★★★½	82	$$$–
9. Hibiscus House B&B	★★★	74	$$
10. The Seagate	★★★½	78	$$+

The Top 10 Best Deals in Broward County

HOTEL	STAR RATING	QUALITY RATING	COST ($ = $50)
1. Comfort Inn Fort Lauderdale Airport	★★★	69	$$–
2. Sawgrass Mills Sunrise	★★★½	78	$$+
3. Fort Lauderdale Waterfront Inns	★★★	74	$$
4. Sea Castle Inn	★★½	58	$+
5. Hyatt Regency Pier Sixty-Six	★★★★½	90	$$$$
6. Riverside Hotel	★★★½	80	$$$
7. Marriott Harbor Beach Resort	★★★★½	90	$$$$+
8. Cottages by the Ocean	★★★	70	$$+
9. Holiday Inn Hollywood Beach	★★★	67	$$+
10. Wyndham Fort Lauderdale Airport	★★★½	75	$$$

The Top 30 Best Deals in Southwest Florida

HOTEL	STAR RATING	QUALITY RATING	COST ($ = $50)
1. Bonita Beach Resort Motel	★★★½	64	$+
2. Sea Court Inn	★★★	69	$+
3. Trianon Bonita Bay	★★★★½	95	$$$–
4. Trianon Old Naples	★★★★½	95	$$$–
5. Baymont Inn Bonita Springs	★★★	73	$+
6. Marco Resort and Club	★★★½	79	$$
7. Port of the Islands Resort	★★★½	80	$$
8. Suburban Lodge of Fort Myers	★★★	66	$+
9. Naples Courtyard	★★★½	78	$$

The Top 30 Best Deals in Southwest Florida (cont'd)

HOTEL	STAR RATING	QUALITY RATING	COST ($ = $50)
10. Lighthouse Inn	★★★	65	$$–
11. Comfort Inn (Boatways Road)	★★★	68	$$–
12. Edison Beach House	★★★★	83	$$$–
13. Holiday Inn Express Hotel and Suites	★★★	68	$$–
14. Quality Hotel	★★½	60	$+
15. Sandpiper Inn Sanibel Island	★★★	74	$$–
16. Clarion Inn Fort Myers	★★½	64	$+
17. Sandy Beach Hideaway	★★½	64	$+
18. Wellesley Inn and Suites	★★★	67	$$–
19. Casa Playa Beach Resort	★★★½	80	$$+
20. Inn at Pelican Bay	★★★★	84	$$$–
21. Everglades City Motel	★★★	68	$$–
22. Vanderbilt Beach Resort House	★★★½	82	$$+
23. Sanibel Beach Club II	★★★	71	$$
24. The Palm View	★★★	74	$$
25. Tarpon Lodge	★★★	70	$$
26. Fort Myers Inn	★★½	64	$+
27. Lovers Key Beach Club and Resort	★★★★½	90	$$$$–
28. Bayview Bed and Breakfast	★★★	72	$$
29. Hampton Inn Bonita Springs	★★★	68	$$–
30. Ramada Riverfront	★★★	68	$$–

Hotel Information Chart: Miami-Dade County

Alexander Hotel ★★★★
5225 Collins Avenue
Miami Beach, FL 33140
☎ 305-865-6500
FAX 305-341-6553
www.alexanderhotel.com

QUALITY RATING   89
COST ($ = $50) $$$$

Aqua Hotel and Lounge ★★★½
1530 Collins Avenue
Miami Beach, FL 33139
☎ 305-538-4361
FAX 305-673-8109
www.aquamiami.com

QUALITY RATING   80
COST ($ = $50) $$

Avalon Hotel ★★★
700 Ocean Drive
Miami Beach, FL 33139
☎ 305-538-0133
FAX 305-534-0258
www.avalonhotel.com

QUALITY RATING   73
COST ($ = $50) $$$+

Bentley Hotel ★★★★½
510 Ocean Drive
Miami Beach, FL 33139
☎ 305-938-4600
TOLL-FREE 877-236-8510
www.thebentleyhotel.com

QUALITY RATING   93
COST ($ = $50) $$$$

Best Western Beach Resort ★★½
4333 Collins Avenue
Miami Beach, FL 33140
☎ 305-532-3311
FAX 305-531-5296
TOLL-FREE 800-832-8332
www.bestwestern.com

QUALITY RATING   64
COST ($ = $50) $$

**Best Western
Oceanfront Resort** ★★½
9365 Collins Avenue
Miami Beach, FL 33154
☎ 305-864-2232
FAX 305-864-3045
TOLL-FREE 800-327-1412
www.bwoceanfront.com

QUALITY RATING   64
COST ($ = $50) $$$+

Cardozo Hotel ★★★½
1300 Ocean Drive
Miami Beach, FL 33139
☎ 305-535-6500
FAX 305-532-3563
TOLL-FREE 800-782-6500
www.cardozohotel.com

QUALITY RATING   75
COST ($ = $50) $$$

Casa Grande Suite Hotel ★★★★
834 Ocean Drive
Miami Beach, FL 33139
☎ 305-672-7003
FAX 305-673-3669
TOLL-FREE 800-402-2272
www.casagrandesuitehotel.com

QUALITY RATING   86
COST ($ = $50) $$$$$$+

**The Catalina Hotel and
Beach Club** ★★★½
1732 Collins Avenue
Miami Beach, FL 33139
☎ 305-674-1160
FAX 305-672-8216
TOLL-FREE 877-762-3477
www.catalinahotel.com

QUALITY RATING   75
COST ($ = $50) $$$$$–

Clinton Hotel South Beach
★★★½
825 Washington Avenue
Miami Beach, FL 33139
☎ 305-938-4040
www.clintonsouthbeach.com

QUALITY RATING   82
COST ($ = $50) $$$$

**Comfort Inn and Suites
South Beach** ★★★
1238 Collins Avenue
Miami Beach, FL 33139
☎ 305-531-3406
FAX 305-538-0850
TOLL-FREE 877-523-5672
www.choicehotels.com

QUALITY RATING   73
COST ($ = $50) $$$

Courtyard Downtown ★★★
200 SE Second Avenue
Miami, FL 33131
☎ 305-374-3000
FAX 305-374-4263
www.miamicourtyard.com

QUALITY RATING   70
COST ($ = $50) $$+

Days Inn Oceanside ★★½
4299 Collins Avenue
Miami Beach, FL 33140
☎ 305-673-1513
FAX 305-538-0727
www.daysinnmiamibeach.com

QUALITY RATING   63
COST ($ = $50) $$

Days Inn South Beach ★★½
100 21st Street
Miami Beach, FL 33139
☎ 305-538-6631
FAX 305-674-0954
TOLL-FREE 800-451-3345
www.daysinnsouthbeach.com

QUALITY RATING   64
COST ($ = $50) $$+

**Don Shula's Hotel and
Golf Club** ★★★★
6842 Main Street
Miami Lakes, FL 33014
☎ 305-821-1150
FAX 305-820-8190
www.donshulahotel.com

QUALITY RATING   85
COST ($ = $50) $$$

Bay Harbor Inn and Suites ★ ★ ★ ½
9660 East Bay Harbor Drive
Miami Beach, FL 33154
☎ 305-868-4141
FAX 305-867-9094
www.bayharborinn.com

QUALITY RATING   80
COST ($ = $50) $$$−

The Beach House Hotel ★ ★ ★
9449 Collins Avenue
Surfside, FL 33154
☎ 305-535-8600
FAX 305-535-8601
TOLL-FREE 800-327-6644
www.thebeachhousehotel.com

QUALITY RATING   73
COST ($ = $50) $$$−

Beach Plaza Hotel ★ ★ ½
1401 Collins Avenue
Miami Beach, FL 33139
☎ 305-531-6421
FAX 305-534-0341
www.beachplazahotel.com

QUALITY RATING   64
COST ($ = $50) $$$$

Biltmore Hotel ★ ★ ★ ★ ★
1200 Anastasia Avenue
Coral Gables, FL 33134
☎ 305-445-1926
FAX 305-913-3159
www.biltmorehotel.com

QUALITY RATING   98
COST ($ = $50) $$$$+

Blue Moon ★ ★ ★ ★
944 Collins Avenue
Miami Beach, FL 33139
☎ 305-673-2262
FAX 305-534-5399
www.bluemoonhotel.com

QUALITY RATING   84
COST ($ = $50) $$$−

Brigham Gardens ★ ★ ★
1411 Collins Avenue
Miami Beach, FL 33139
☎ 305-531-1331
FAX 305-538-9898
www.brighamgardens.com

QUALITY RATING   65
COST ($ = $50) $$

The Chesterfield Hotel ★ ★ ★
855 Collins Avenue
Miami Beach, FL 33139
☎ 305-531-5831
FAX 305-535-9665
TOLL-FREE 877-762-3477
www.thechesterfieldhotel.com

QUALITY RATING   70
COST ($ = $50) $$$$

Clarion Hotel and Suites ★ ★ ★
100 SE Fourth Street
Miami, FL 33131
☎ 305-374-5100
FAX 305-381-9826
www.choicehotels.com

QUALITY RATING   69
COST ($ = $50) $$

Clevelander Hotel ★ ★ ★
1020 Ocean Drive
Miami Beach, FL 33139
☎ 305-531-3485
FAX 305-531-3953
TOLL-FREE 800-815-6829
www.clevelander.com

QUALITY RATING   73
COST ($ = $50) $$$−

**Courtyard Miami Beach
Oceanfront** ★ ★ ★
3925 Collins Avenue
Miami Beach, FL 33140
☎ 305-538-3373
FAX 305-538-7077
TOLL-FREE 800-321-2211
www.marriott.com

QUALITY RATING   72
COST ($ = $50) $$$+

Crowne Plaza Hotel ★ ★ ★ ½
950 NW LeJeune Road
Miami, FL 33126
☎ 305-446-9000
FAX 305-441-0725
TOLL-FREE 800-HOLIDAY
www.ichotelsgroup.com

QUALITY RATING   77
COST ($ = $50) $$$$−

David William Hotel ★ ★ ★ ★
700 Biltmore Way
Coral Gables, FL 33134
☎ 305-445-7821
FAX 305-913-1933
www.davidwilliamhotel.com

QUALITY RATING   86
COST ($ = $50) $$$$−

Doral Golf Resort and Spa ★ ★ ★ ★
4400 NW 87th Avenue
Miami, FL 33178
☎ 305-592-2000
FAX 305-594-4682
www.doralresort.com

QUALITY RATING   89
COST ($ = $50) $$$

**Doubletree at
Coconut Grove** ★ ★ ★ ★
2649 South Bayshore Drive
Coconut Grove, FL 33133
☎ 305-858-2500
FAX 305-858-5776
TOLL-FREE 800-222-TREE
www.doubletree.com

QUALITY RATING   83
COST ($ = $50) $$$

Doubletree Grand Hotel ★ ★ ★ ★
1717 North Bayshore Drive
Miami, FL 33132
☎ 305-372-0313
FAX 305-372-9455
TOLL-FREE 800-222-TREE
www.doubletree.com

QUALITY RATING   84
COST ($ = $50) $$$$

Hotel Information Chart: Miami-Dade County (cont'd)

Doubletree Surfcomber ★★★½
1717 Collins Avenue
Miami Beach, FL 33139
☎ 305-532-7715
FAX 305-532-7280
TOLL-FREE 800-222-TREE
www.doubletree.com

   QUALITY RATING   80
   COST ($ = $50) $$$$$–

Eden Roc Resort and Spa ★★★★
4525 Collins Avenue
Miami Beach, FL 33140
☎ 305-531-0000
FAX 305-674-5555
www.edenrocresort.com

   QUALITY RATING   89
   COST ($ = $50) $$$$

Embassy Suites Airport ★★★½
3974 NW South River Drive
Miami, FL 33142
☎ 305-634-5000
FAX 305-635-9499
www.embassysuites.com

   QUALITY RATING   81
   COST ($ = $50) $$+

Four Points by Sheraton ★★★½
4343 Collins Avenue
Miami Beach, FL 33140
☎ 305-531-7494
FAX 305-532-2490
www.starwoodhotels.com/
fourpoints

   QUALITY RATING   75
   COST ($ = $50) $$$$–

**Four Seasons Hotel
Miami** ★★★★★
1435 Brickell Avenue
Miami, FL 33131
☎ 305-358-3535
FAX 305-358-7758
TOLL-FREE 800-819-5053
www.fourseasons.com/miami/
index.html

   QUALITY RATING   98
   COST ($ = $50) $$$$$$$+

**Grove Isle Club and
Resort** ★★★★★
4 Grove Isle Drive
Coconut Grove, FL 33133
☎ 305-858-8300
FAX 305-858-5908
www.groveisle.com

   QUALITY RATING   97
   COST ($ = $50) $$$$+

The Hotel ★★★★
801 Collins Avenue
Miami Beach, FL 33139
☎ 305-531-2222
FAX 305-531-3222
TOLL-FREE 877-THE HOTEL
www.thehotelofsouthbeach.com

   QUALITY RATING   87
   COST ($ = $50) $$$$+

Hotel Astor ★★★★½
956 Washington Avenue
Miami Beach, FL 33139
☎ 305-531-8081
FAX 305-531-3193
www.hotelastor.com

   QUALITY RATING   93
   COST ($ = $50) $$$

The Hotel Chelsea ★★★
944 Washington Avenue
Miami Beach, FL 33139
☎ 305-534-4069
FAX 305-672-6712
TOLL-FREE 877-762-3477
www.thehotelchelsea.com

   QUALITY RATING   68
   COST ($ = $50) $$$$

Hotel Ocean ★★★★
1230 Ocean Drive
Miami Beach, FL 33139
☎ 305-672-2579
FAX 305-672-7665
www.hotelocean.com

   QUALITY RATING   89
   COST ($ = $50) $$$$

Hotel Place St. Michel ★★★★
162 Alcazar Avenue
Coral Gables, FL 33134
☎ 305-444-1666
FAX 305-529-0074
www.hotelplacestmichel.com

   QUALITY RATING   89
   COST ($ = $50) $$$–

Hotel Riande Continental ★★★
1825 Collins Avenue
Miami Beach, FL 33139
☎ 305-531-3503
FAX 305-531-5602
www.hotelesriande.com

   QUALITY RATING   70
   COST ($ = $50) $$$–

**Hyatt Regency
Coral Gables** ★★★★½
50 Alhambra Plaza
Coral Gables, FL 33134
☎ 305-441-1234
FAX 305-441-0520
www.hyatt.com

   QUALITY RATING   94
   COST ($ = $50) $$$$$$+

Indian Creek Hotel ★★★
2727 Indian Creek Drive
Miami Beach, FL 33140
☎ 305-531-2727
FAX 305-531-5651
www.indiancreekhotel.com

   QUALITY RATING   70
   COST ($ = $50) $$

**JW Marriott Hotel
Miami** ★★★★½
1109 Brickell Avenue
Miami, FL 33131
☎ 305-329-3500
TOLL-FREE 800-228-9290
www.marriott.com

   QUALITY RATING   90
   COST ($ = $50) $$$$$

Essex House Hotel ★ ★ ★
1001 Collins Avenue
Miami Beach, FL 33139
☎ 305-534-2700
FAX 305-532-3827
www.essexhotel.com

QUALITY RATING   69
COST ($ = $50) $$$–

**Fairfield Inn Miami Beach
on the Ocean** ★ ★ ★
4101 Collins Avenue
Miami Beach, FL 33140
☎ 305-673-3337
FAX 305-673-3660
TOLL-FREE 800-777-9533
www.marriott.com

QUALITY RATING   70
COST ($ = $50) $$

Fontainebleau Resorts ★ ★ ★ ★
4441 Collins Avenue
Miami Beach, FL 33140
☎ 305-538-2000
FAX 305-674-4608
www.fontainebleauresorts.com

QUALITY RATING   84
COST ($ = $50) $$$$$$–

Hilton Miami Airport ★ ★ ★
5101 Blue Lagoon Drive
Miami, FL 33126
☎ 305-262-1000
FAX 305-267-0038
TOLL-FREE 800-HILTONS
www.hilton.com

QUALITY RATING   74
COST ($ = $50) $$

**Holiday Inn Port of Miami
Downtown** ★ ★ ★
340 Biscayne Boulevard
Miami, FL 33132
☎ 305-371-4400
FAX 305-372-2862
TOLL-FREE 800-HOLIDAY
www.ichotelsgroup.com

QUALITY RATING   65
COST ($ = $50) $$

**Holiday Inn
South Beach Resort** ★ ★ ★
2201 Collins Avenue
Miami Beach, FL 33139
☎ 305-779-3200
FAX 305-532-1403
TOLL-FREE 800-356-6902
www.miamisouthbeachresort.com

QUALITY RATING   66
COST ($ = $50) $$$+

Hotel Delano ★ ★ ★ ★ ½
1685 Collins Avenue
Miami Beach, FL 33139
☎ 305-672-2000
FAX 305-532-0099
www.delano-hotel.com

QUALITY RATING   94
COST ($ = $50) $$$$$$$$

Hotel Impala ★ ★ ★ ★
1228 Collins Avenue
Miami Beach, FL 33139
☎ 305-673-2021
FAX 305-673-5984
TOLL-FREE 800-646-7252
www.hotelimpalamiamibeach.com

QUALITY RATING   85
COST ($ = $50) $$$$

Hotel InterContinental ★ ★ ★ ★ ½
100 Chopin Plaza
Miami, FL 33131
☎ 305-577-1000
FAX 305-577-0384
www.intercontinental.com

QUALITY RATING   90
COST ($ = $50) $$$$

The Hotel Shelley ★ ★ ★
844 Collins Avenue
Miami Beach, FL 33139
☎ 305-531-3341
FAX 305-535-9665
TOLL-FREE 877-762-3477
www.hotelshelley.com

QUALITY RATING   66
COST ($ = $50) $$$

Hotel Sofitel ★ ★ ★ ½
5800 Blue Lagoon Drive
Miami, FL 33126
☎ 305-264-4888
FAX 305-262-9049
www.sofitel.com

QUALITY RATING   82
COST ($ = $50) $$$$–

Hotel Victor ★ ★ ★ ★
1144 Ocean Drive
Miami Beach, FL 33139
☎ 305-428-1234
FAX 305-421-6281
www.hotelvictorsouthbeach.com

QUALITY RATING   85
COST ($ = $50) $$$$$$$$$+

Lily Guesthouse ★ ★ ★ ½
835 Collins Avenue
Miami Beach, FL 33139
☎ 305-535-9900
FAX 305-535-0077
www.lilyguesthouse.com

QUALITY RATING   75
COST ($ = $50) $$$$–

**Loews Miami Beach
Hotel** ★ ★ ★ ★ ½
1601 Collins Avenue
Miami Beach, FL 33139
☎ 305-604-1601
FAX 305-531-8677
www.loewshotels.com

QUALITY RATING   95
COST ($ = $50) $$$$$$$$–

Mandarin Oriental ★ ★ ★ ★ ★
500 Brickell Key Drive
Miami, FL 33131
☎ 305-913-8288
TOLL-FREE 866-888-6780
www.mandarin-oriental.com

QUALITY RATING   98
COST ($ = $50) $$$$$$$$+

Hotel Information Chart: Miami-Dade County (cont'd)

The Marlin ★ ★ ★ ★
1200 Collins Avenue
Miami Beach, FL 33139
☎ 305-604-3595
FAX 305-673-9609
www.marlinhotel.com

QUALITY RATING   89
COST ($ = $50) $$$$$

Marriott Biscayne Bay ★ ★ ★ ½
1633 North Bayshore Drive
Miami, FL 33132
☎ 305-374-3900
FAX 305-375-0597
www.marriott.com

QUALITY RATING   80
COST ($ = $50) $$$

The Mercury Resort and Spa
★ ★ ★ ★
100 Collins Avenue
Miami Beach, FL 33139
☎ 305-398-3000
FAX 305-398-3001
TOLL-FREE 877-786-2732
www.mercuryresort.com

QUALITY RATING   83
COST ($ = $50) $$$$

Radisson Hotel Miami ★ ★ ★
1601 Biscayne Boulevard
Miami, FL 33132
☎ 305-374-0000
FAX 305-374-0020
www.radisson-miami.com

QUALITY RATING   74
COST ($ = $50) $$$–

Newport Beachside Resort ★ ★ ★
16701 Collins Avenue
Miami Beach, FL 33160
☎ 305-949-1300
FAX 305-947-5873
www.newportbeachsideresort.com

QUALITY RATING   70
COST ($ = $50) $$

Omni Colonnade Hotel ★ ★ ★ ★ ½
180 Aragon Avenue
Coral Gables, FL 33134
☎ 305-441-2600
FAX 305-445-3929
www.omnihotels.com

QUALITY RATING   95
COST ($ = $50) $$$$$$

**Ritz-Carlton
Coconut Grove** ★ ★ ★ ★ ★
3300 SW 27th Avenue
Miami, FL 33133
☎ 305-644-4680
FAX 305-644-4681
TOLL-FREE 800-241-3333
www.ritzcarlton.com

QUALITY RATING   98
COST ($ = $50) $$$$+

**Ritz-Carlton
Key Biscayne** ★ ★ ★ ★ ★
455 Grand Bay Drive
Key Biscayne, FL 33149
☎ 305-365-4500
FAX 305-365-4505
TOLL-FREE 800-241-3333
www.ritzcarlton.com

QUALITY RATING   99
COST ($ = $50) $$$$$$$$$$$$+

**Ritz-Carlton
South Beach** ★ ★ ★ ★ ★
1 Lincoln Road
Miami Beach, FL 33139
☎ 786-276-4000
FAX 786-276-4100
TOLL-FREE 800-241-3333
www.ritzcarlton.com

QUALITY RATING   99
COST ($ = $50) $$$$$$$$$

**Sheraton Bal Harbour
Resort** ★ ★ ★ ★ ½
9701 Collins Avenue
Bal Harbour, FL 33154
☎ 305-865-7511
FAX 305-864-2601
www.sheratonbalharbour
resort.com

QUALITY RATING   93
COST ($ = $50) $$$$$$–

Sonesta Beach Resort ★ ★ ★ ★
350 Ocean Drive
Key Biscayne, FL 33149
☎ 305-361-2021
FAX 305-361-3096
www.sonesta.com/keybiscayne

QUALITY RATING   84
COST ($ = $50) $$$$

Sonesta Hotel and Suites ★ ★ ★ ½
2889 McFarlane Road
Coconut Grove, FL 33133
☎ 305-529-2828
FAX 305-529-2008
www.sonesta.com/coconut_grove

QUALITY RATING   80
COST ($ = $50) $$$–

Waldorf Towers Hotel ★ ★ ★ ½
860 Ocean Drive
Miami Beach, FL 33139
☎ 305-531-7684
FAX 305-672-6836
www.waldorftowers.com

QUALITY RATING   82
COST ($ = $50) $$$$–

The Whitelaw Hotel ★ ★ ★
808 Collins Avenue
Miami Beach, FL 33139
☎ 305-398-7000
FAX 305-398-7010
TOLL-FREE 877-762-3477
www.whitelawhotel.com

QUALITY RATING   67
COST ($ = $50) $$$$

**Wyndham Grand Bay
Hotel** ★ ★ ★ ★ ½
2669 South Bayshore Drive
Coconut Grove, FL 33133
☎ 305-858-9600
FAX 305-859-2026
www.wyndham.com

QUALITY RATING   93
COST ($ = $50) $$$$+

Miami River Inn ★ ★ ★
118 SW South River Drive
Miami, FL 33130
☎ 305-325-0045
FAX 305-325-9227
TOLL-FREE 800-468-3589
www.miamiriverinn.com

QUALITY RATING 74

COST ($ = $50) $$

Nassau Suite Hotel ★ ★ ★ ½
1414 Collins Avenue
Miami Beach, FL 33139
☎ 305-532-0043
FAX 305-534-3133
www.nassausuite.com

QUALITY RATING 80

COST ($ = $50) $$$

National Hotel ★ ★ ★ ½
1677 Collins Avenue
Miami Beach, FL 33139
☎ 305-532-2311
FAX 305-534-1426
www.nationalhotel.com

QUALITY RATING 80

COST ($ = $50) $$$$

The Palms ★ ★ ★ ★ ½
3025 Collins Avenue
Miami Beach, FL 33140
☎ 305-534-0505
FAX 305-534-0515
www.thepalmshotel.com

QUALITY RATING 90

COST ($ = $50) $$$$$$

**Park Central
Imperial Hotels** ★ ★ ★ ½
640 Ocean Drive
Miami Beach, FL 33139
☎ 305-538-1611
FAX 305-534-7520
www.theparkcentral.com

QUALITY RATING 82

COST ($ = $50) $$$$–

Ramada Plaza Marco Polo ★ ★ ½
19201 Collins Avenue
Miami Beach, FL 33160
☎ 305-932-2233
FAX 305-935-5009
TOLL-FREE 800-272-6232
www.ramada.com

QUALITY RATING 64

COST ($ = $50) $$+

Sanctuary South Beach ★ ★ ★ ★ ½
1745 James Avenue
Miami Beach, FL 33139
☎ 305-673-5455
FAX 305-673-3113
www.sanctuarysobe.com

QUALITY RATING 95

COST ($ = $50) $$$$$$$+

Sea View Hotel ★ ★ ★ ★
9909 Collins Avenue
Bal Harbour, FL 33154
☎ 305-866-4441
FAX 305-866-1898
www.seaview-hotel.com

QUALITY RATING 89

COST ($ = $50) $$$$+

Seacoast Suites Hotel ★ ★ ★
5101 Collins Avenue
Miami Beach, FL 33140
☎ 305-865-5152
FAX 305-868-4090
TOLL-FREE 800-969-6329
www.seacoastsuites.com

QUALITY RATING 70

COST ($ = $50) $$

The Tides ★ ★ ★ ★ ½
1220 Ocean Drive
Miami Beach, FL 33139
☎ 305-604-5070
FAX 305-604-5180
TOLL-FREE 800-OUTPOST
www.thetideshotel.com

QUALITY RATING 95

COST ($ = $50) $$$$$$$$

**Trump International
Sonesta Beach Resort** ★ ★ ★ ★ ½
18001 Collins Avenue
Sunny Isles Beach, FL 33160
☎ 305-692-5600
FAX 305-692-5601
www.sonesta.com/sunnyisles

QUALITY RATING 90

COST ($ = $50) $$$$$$

Tudor Hotel ★ ★ ½
1111 Collins Avenue
Miami Beach, FL 33139
☎ 305-534-2934
FAX 305-531-1874
TOLL-FREE 800-843-2934
www.south-beach-hotels-tudor.com

QUALITY RATING 63

COST ($ = $50) $$–

**Wyndham Miami Beach
Resort** ★ ★ ★ ★ ½
4833 Collins Avenue
Miami Beach, FL 33140
☎ 305-532-3600
FAX 305-534-7409
www.wyndham.com

QUALITY RATING 92

COST ($ = $50) $$$$–

Hotel Information Chart: The Florida Keys

Ambrosia House ★ ★ ★ ½
615–622 Fleming Street
Key West, FL 33040
☎ 305-296-9838
FAX 305-296-2425
www.ambrosiakeywest.com

| QUALITY RATING | 80 |
| COST ($ = $50) | $$$ |

**Amy Slate's Amoray
Dive Resort** ★ ★ ★
104250 Overseas Highway
Key Largo, FL 33037
☎ 305-451-3595
FAX 305-453-9516
TOLL-FREE 800-4-AMORAY
www.amoray.com

| QUALITY RATING | 74 |
| COST ($ = $50) | $$$ |

Artist House ★ ★ ★
534 Eaton Street
Key West, FL 33040
☎ 305-296-3977
FAX 305-296-3210
TOLL-FREE 800-582-7882
www.artisthousekeywest.com

| QUALITY RATING | 72 |
| COST ($ = $50) | $$$$ |

Bay View Inn ★ ★ ½
3 North Conch Avenue
Marathon, FL 33050
☎ 305-289-1525

| QUALITY RATING | 64 |
| COST ($ = $50) | $$ |

**Best Western
Hibiscus Motel** ★ ★ ½
1313 Simonton Street
Key West, FL 33040
☎ 305-294-3763
FAX 305-293-9243
TOLL-FREE 800-972-5100
www.bestwestern.com

| QUALITY RATING | 63 |
| COST ($ = $50) | $$$$– |

**Best Western
Key Ambassador** ★ ★ ★
3755 South Roosevelt Boulevard
Key West, FL 33040
☎ 305-296-3500
FAX 305-296-9961
TOLL-FREE 800-432-4315
www.keyambassador.com

| QUALITY RATING | 65 |
| COST ($ = $50) | $$$ |

Cheeca Lodge ★ ★ ★ ★ ½
81801 Overseas Highway
Islamorada, FL 33036
☎ 305-664-4651
FAX 305-664-5427
TOLL-FREE 866-591-ROCK
www.cheeca.rockresorts.com

| QUALITY RATING | 92 |
| COST ($ = $50) | $$$$$$$$ |

Chesapeake Resort ★ ★ ★
83409 Overseas Highway
Islamorada, FL 33036
☎ 305-664-4662
FAX 305-664-8595
TOLL-FREE 800-338-3395
www.chesapeake-resort.com

| QUALITY RATING | 70 |
| COST ($ = $50) | $$$$ |

Coconut Cay ★ ★ ½
7196 Overseas Highway
Marathon, FL 33050
☎ 305-289-7672
FAX 305-289-0186
TOLL-FREE 877-354-7356
www.coconutcay.com

| QUALITY RATING | 64 |
| COST ($ = $50) | $$ |

Curry Mansion Inn ★ ★ ★
511 Caroline Street
Key West, FL 33040
☎ 305-294-5349
FAX 305-294-4093
TOLL-FREE 800-253-3466
www.currymansion.com

| QUALITY RATING | 72 |
| COST ($ = $50) | $$$$ |

Cypress House ★ ★ ★
601 Caroline Street
Key West, FL 33040
☎ 305-294-6969
FAX 305-296-1174
TOLL-FREE 800-525-2488
www.cypresshousekw.com

| QUALITY RATING | 65 |
| COST ($ = $50) | $$$$– |

Days Inn Key West ★ ★
3852 North Roosevelt Boulevard
Key West, FL 33040
☎ 305-294-3742
FAX 305-296-7260
www.daysinn.com

| QUALITY RATING | 50 |
| COST ($ = $50) | $$ |

Eden House ★ ★ ½
1015 Fleming Street
Key West, FL 33040
☎ 305-296-6868
FAX 305-294-1221
TOLL-FREE 800-533-KEYS
www.edenhouse.com

| QUALITY RATING | 64 |
| COST ($ = $50) | $$$– |

Frances Street Bottle Inn ★ ★ ★
535 Frances Street
Key West, FL 33040
☎ 305-294-8530
FAX 305-294-1628
TOLL-FREE 800-294-8530
www.bottleinn.com

| QUALITY RATING | 74 |
| COST ($ = $50) | $$ |

Garden House ★ ★ ★
329 Elizabeth Street
Key West, FL 33040
☎ 305-296-5368
FAX 305-292-1160
TOLL-FREE 800-695-6453
www.the-garden-house.com

| QUALITY RATING | 70 |
| COST ($ = $50) | $$$– |

Atlantic Shores Resort ★ ★ ½
510 South Street
Key West, FL 33040
☎ 305-296-2491
FAX 305-294-2753
TOLL-FREE 888-324-2996
www.atlanticshoresresort.com

QUALITY RATING   63

COST ($ = $50) $$$–

Avalon Bed and Breakfast ★ ★ ★ ½
1317 Duval Street
Key West, FL 33040
☎ 305-294-8233
FAX 305-294-9044
TOLL-FREE 800-848-1317
www.avalonbnb.com

QUALITY RATING   80

COST ($ = $50) $$

**Banana Bay Resort and
Marina** ★ ★ ★ ½
4590 Overseas Highway
Marathon, FL 33050
☎ 305-743-3500
FAX 305-743-2670
TOLL-FREE 800-226-2621
www.bananabay.com

QUALITY RATING   82

COST ($ = $50) $$$

**Best Western Suites at
Key Largo** ★ ★ ★
201 Ocean Drive
Key Largo, FL 33037
☎ 305-451-5081
FAX 305-451-4173
TOLL-FREE 800-462-6079
www.bestwestern.com

QUALITY RATING   70

COST ($ = $50) $$$–

Blue Marlin ★ ★
1320 Simonton Street
Key West, FL 33040
☎ 305-294-2585
FAX 305-296-1209

QUALITY RATING   50

COST ($ = $50) $$$–

Breezy Palms Resort ★ ★ ★
80015 Overseas Highway
Islamorada, FL 33036
☎ 305-664-2361
FAX 305-664-2572
www.breezypalms.com

QUALITY RATING   67

COST ($ = $50) $$

Comfort Inn Key West ★ ★ ½
3824 North Roosevelt Boulevard
Key West, FL 33040
☎ 305-294-3773
FAX 305-294-5739
TOLL-FREE 877-424-6423
www.choicehotels.com

QUALITY RATING   64

COST ($ = $50) $$

**Courtyard Key West
Waterfront** ★ ★ ★
3031 North Roosevelt Boulevard
Key West, FL 33040
☎ 305-296-6595
FAX 305-296-8351
TOLL-FREE 888-869-7066
www.marriott.com

QUALITY RATING   65

COST ($ = $50) $$$+

Crowne Plaza La Concha ★ ★ ★ ½
430 Duval Street
Key West, FL 33040
☎ 305-296-2991
FAX 305-294-3283
TOLL-FREE 800-745-2191
www.laconchakeywest.com

QUALITY RATING   80

COST ($ = $50) $$$$$–

Dewey House ★ ★ ★ ★
504 South Street
Key West, FL 33040
☎ 305-296-6577
FAX 305-294-2108
TOLL-FREE 800-354-4455
www.lamerhotel.com

QUALITY RATING   85

COST ($ = $50) $$$$

Duval House ★ ★ ★
815 Duval Street
Key West, FL 33040
☎ 305-294-1666
FAX 305-292-1701
TOLL-FREE 800-223-8825
www.duvalhousekeywest.com

QUALITY RATING   66

COST ($ = $50) $$$$–

Eaton Lodge ★ ★ ★
511 Eaton Street
Key West, FL 33040
☎ 305-292-2170
FAX 305-292-4018
TOLL-FREE 800-294-2170
www.eatonlodge.com

QUALITY RATING   69

COST ($ = $50) $$$–

Gardens Hotel ★ ★ ★ ★
526 Angela Street
Key West, FL 33040
☎ 305-294-2661
FAX 305-292-1007
TOLL-FREE 800-526-2664
www.gardenshotel.com

QUALITY RATING   83

COST ($ = $50) $$$$$

Gilbert's Resort ★ ★ ½
107900 Overseas Highway
Key Largo, FL 33037
☎ 305-451-1133
FAX 305-451-4362
TOLL-FREE 800-274-6701
www.gilbertsresort.com

QUALITY RATING   62

COST ($ = $50) $$

Hampton Inn ★ ★ ½
2801 North Roosevelt Boulevard
Key West, FL 33040
☎ 305-294-2917
FAX 305-296-0221
TOLL-FREE 800-960-3054
www.hamptoninnkeywest.com

QUALITY RATING   64

COST ($ = $50) $$+

Hotel Information Chart: The Florida Keys (cont'd)

Hampton Inn and Suites Islamorada ★★½
80001 Overseas Highway
Islamorada, FL 33036
☎ 305-664-0073
FAX 305-664-0807
TOLL-FREE 800-HAMPTON
www.hamptoninn.com

QUALITY RATING   64
COST ($ = $50) $$$$+

Hawk's Cay Resort ★★★★
61 Hawk's Cay Boulevard
Duck Key, FL 33050
☎ 305-743-7000
FAX 305-743-5215
TOLL-FREE 888-443-6393
www.hawkscay.com

QUALITY RATING   83
COST ($ = $50) $$$$$

Heron House ★★★★
512 Simonton Street
Key West, FL 33040
☎ 305-294-9227
FAX 305-294-5692
TOLL-FREE 888-861-9066
www.heronhouse.com

QUALITY RATING   85
COST ($ = $50) $$$$

Holiday Inn Marathon ★★★
13201 Overseas Highway
Marathon, FL 33050
☎ 305-289-0222
FAX 305-743-5460
TOLL-FREE 800-HOLIDAY
www.ichotelsgroup.com

QUALITY RATING   74
COST ($ = $50) $$

Holiday Isle Resort and Marina ★★½
84001 Overseas Highway
Islamorada, FL 33036
☎ 305-664-2321
FAX 305-664-2703
TOLL-FREE 800-327-7070
www.holidayisle.com/hi.html

QUALITY RATING   62
COST ($ = $50) $$$−

Hotel Key West ★★
3850 North Roosevelt Boulevard
Key West, Fl 33040
☎ 305-294-6681
FAX 305-294-5618

QUALITY RATING   47
COST ($ = $50) $$

Island City House Hotel ★★★½
411 William Street
Key West, FL 33040
☎ 305-294-5702
FAX 305-294-1289
TOLL-FREE 800-634-8230
www.islandcityhouse.com

QUALITY RATING   81
COST ($ = $50) $$$$−

Islander Resort ★★★★
82100 Overseas Highway
Islamorada, FL 33036
☎ 305-664-2031
FAX 305-664-5503
TOLL-FREE 800-753-6002
www.islanderfloridakeys.com

QUALITY RATING   89
COST ($ = $50) $$$$−

Key Largo Marriott Beach Resort ★★★★
103800 Overseas Highway
Key Largo, FL 33037
☎ 305-453-0000
FAX 305-453-0093
www.marriottkeylargo.com

QUALITY RATING   83
COST ($ = $50) $$$$

La Te Da Hotel ★★★
1125 Duval Street
Key West, FL 33040
☎ 305-296-6706
FAX 305-296-3981
TOLL-FREE 877-528-3320
www.lateda.com

QUALITY RATING   74
COST ($ = $50) $$+

The Moorings Village and Spa ★★★★★
123 Beach Road
Islamorada, FL 33036
☎ 305-664-4708
FAX 305-664-4242
www.mooringsvillageandspa.com

QUALITY RATING   98
COST ($ = $50) $$$$$−

Ocean Key Resort and Marina ★★★½
0 Duval Street
Key West, FL 33040
☎ 305-296-7701
FAX 305-295-7016
TOLL-FREE 800-328-9815
www.oceankey.com

QUALITY RATING   80
COST ($ = $50) $$$$$$$+

Pier House ★★★½
1 Duval Street
Key West, FL 33040
☎ 305-296-4600
FAX 305-296-7569
TOLL-FREE 800-327-8340
www.pierhouse.com

QUALITY RATING   82
COST ($ = $50) $$$$

Radisson Hotel Key West ★★½
3820 North Roosevelt Boulevard
Key West, FL 33040
☎ 305-294-5511
FAX 305-296-1939
TOLL-FREE 800-333-3333
www.radisson.com/keywestfl

QUALITY RATING   64
COST ($ = $50) $$+

The Ragged Edge ★★★
243 Treasure Harbor Road
Islamorada, FL 33036
☎ 305-852-5389
TOLL-FREE 800-436-2023
www.ragged-edge.com

QUALITY RATING   70
COST ($ = $50) $$+

Hidden Harbor Motel ★★½
2396 Overseas Highway
Marathon, FL 33050
☎ 305-743-5376
TOLL-FREE 800-362-3495
www.hiddenharbormotel.com

QUALITY RATING   64
COST ($ = $50) $$

Hilton Key West Resort and Marina ★★★★
245 Front Street
Key West, FL 33040
☎ 305-294-4000
FAX 305-294-4086
TOLL-FREE 800-445-8667
www.keywestresort.hilton.com

QUALITY RATING   83
COST ($ = $50) $$$$$$$$–

Holiday Inn Key Largo Resort ★★½
99701 Overseas Highway
Key Largo, FL 33037
☎ 305-451-2121
FAX 305-451-5592
www.holidayinnkeylargo.com

QUALITY RATING   64
COST ($ = $50) $$+

Howard Johnson Resort Key Largo ★★½
102400 Overseas Highway
Key Largo, FL 33037
☎ 305-451-1400
FAX 305-451-3953
TOLL-FREE 800-654-2000
www.hojokeylargo.com

QUALITY RATING   60
COST ($ = $50) $$$$$–

Hyatt Key West Resort and Marina ★★★★
601 Front Street
Key West, FL 33040
☎ 305-809-1234
FAX 305-292-1038
www.hyatt.com

QUALITY RATING   85
COST ($ = $50) $$$$$$

The Inn at Key West ★★★
3420 North Roosevelt Boulevard
Key West, FL 33040
☎ 305-294-5541
FAX 305-294-7932

QUALITY RATING   65
COST ($ = $50) $$$–

Kingsail Resort Motel ★★½
7050 Overseas Highway
Marathon, FL 33050
☎ 305-743-5246
FAX 305-743-8896
www.marathonfla.com

QUALITY RATING   64
COST ($ = $50) $$

Kona Kai Resort and Gallery ★★★★★
97802 Overseas Highway
Key Largo, FL 33037
☎ 305-852-7200
FAX 305-852-4629
TOLL-FREE 800-365-7829
www.konakairesort.com

QUALITY RATING   97
COST ($ = $50) $$$$+

La Mer Hotel ★★★★
506 South Street
Key West, FL 33040
☎ 305-296-6577
FAX 305-294-2108
TOLL-FREE 800-354-4455
www.lamerhotel.com

QUALITY RATING   85
COST ($ = $50) $$$$

Palms Hotel ★★½
820 White Street
Key West, FL 33040
☎ 305-294-3146
FAX 305-294-8463
TOLL-FREE 800-558-9374

QUALITY RATING   64
COST ($ = $50) $$

Parmer's Resort ★★★
565 Barry Avenue
Little Torch Key, FL 33042
☎ 305-872-2157
FAX 305-872-2014
www.parmersplace.com

QUALITY RATING   70
COST ($ = $50) $$

Pelican Cove Resort ★★★
84457 Overseas Highway
Islamorada, FL 33036
☎ 305-664-4435
FAX 305-664-5134
TOLL-FREE 800-445-4690
www.pcove.com

QUALITY RATING   71
COST ($ = $50) $$$

Rainbow Bend Resort ★★★
57784 Overseas Highway
Marathon, FL 33050
☎ 305-289-1505
FAX 305-743-0257
TOLL-FREE 800-929-1505
www.rainbowbend.com

QUALITY RATING   73
COST ($ = $50) $$$$–

Ramada Limited Key Largo ★★★
99751 Overseas Highway
Key Largo, FL 33037
☎ 305-451-3939
FAX 305-453-0222
TOLL-FREE 800-272-6232
www.ramada.com

QUALITY RATING   72
COST ($ = $50) $$$–

The Sands of Islamorada ★★★
80051 Overseas Highway
Islamorada, FL 33036
☎ 305-664-2791
FAX 305-664-2886
www.sandsofislamorada.com

QUALITY RATING   66
COST ($ = $50) $$$–

Hotel Information Chart: The Florida Keys (cont'd)

Sheraton Suites Key West ★★★½
2001 South Roosevelt Boulevard
Key West, FL 33040
☎ 305-292-9800
FAX 305-294-6009
TOLL-FREE 800-45-BEACH
www.sheratonkeywest.com

QUALITY RATING 80
COST ($ = $50) $$$$$$–

Southernmost Hotel ★★★
1319 Duval Street
Key West, FL 33040
☎ 305-296-5611
FAX 305-294-8272
TOLL-FREE 800-354-4455
www.southernmosthotel.com

QUALITY RATING 74
COST ($ = $50) $$+

**Southernmost
on the Beach** ★★★
508 South Street
Key West, FL 33040
☎ 305-296-6577
FAX 305-294-8272
TOLL-FREE 800-354-4455
www.southernmostonthe
beach.com

QUALITY RATING 74
COST ($ = $50) $$$+

Spanish Gardens ★★½
1325 Simonton Street
Key West, FL 33040
☎ 305-294-1051
FAX 305-294-2505
TOLL-FREE 888-898-1051
www.floridakeys.net/
spanishgardens

QUALITY RATING 64
COST ($ = $50) $$$–

Suite Dreams ★★★½
1001 Von Phister Street
Key West, FL 33040
☎ 305-292-4713
FAX 305-296-5590
TOLL-FREE 800-730-2483
www.oldtownsuites.com/
suitedreams

QUALITY RATING 82
COST ($ = $50) $$$$–

**Sunset Key Guest Cottages at
Hilton Key West Resort** ★★★★★
245 Front Street (registration + launch)
Key West, FL 33040
☎ 305-292-5300
FAX 305-292-5395
TOLL-FREE 888-477-7786
www.sunsetkeycottages.hilton.com

QUALITY RATING 98
COST ($ = $50) $$$$$$$$$$$$$$–

Tavernier Hotel ★★½
91865 Overseas Highway
Tavernier, FL 33070
☎ 305-852-4131
FAX 305-852-4037
TOLL-FREE 800-515-4131
www.tavernierhotel.com

QUALITY RATING 64
COST ($ = $50) $$–

Travelodge Key West ★★½
3444 North Roosevelt Boulevard
Key West, FL 33040
☎ 305-296-7593
FAX 305-294-5246
TOLL-FREE 800-578-7878
www.travelodgekeywest.com

QUALITY RATING 64
COST ($ = $50) $$$

Westwinds Inn ★★★
914 Eaton Street
Key West, FL 33040
☎ 305-296-4440
FAX 305-293-0931
TOLL-FREE 800-788-4150
www.westwindskeywest.com

QUALITY RATING 65
COST ($ = $50) $$$–

**Wyndham Casa Marina
Resort** ★★★½
1500 Reynolds Street
Key West, FL 33040
☎ 305-296-3535
FAX 305-296-4633
TOLL-FREE 800-626-0777
www.casamarinakeywest.com

QUALITY RATING 82
COST ($ = $50) $$$$$$

Wyndham Reach Resort ★★★½
1435 Simonton Street
Key West, FL 33040
☎ 305-296-5000
FAX 305-296-2830
www.wyndham.com

QUALITY RATING 75
COST ($ = $50) $$$$+

Yellowtail Inn ★★★
58162 Overseas Highway
Marathon, FL 33050
☎ 305-743-8400
FAX 305-743-9014
TOLL-FREE 800-605-7475
www.yellowtailinn.com

QUALITY RATING 72
COST ($ = $50) $$+

Hotel Information Chart: Palm Beach County

Best Western University Inn ★★
2700 North Federal Highway
Boca Raton, FL 33431
☎ 561-395-5225
FAX 561-338-9180
www.bestwestern.com

QUALITY RATING   50
COST ($ = $50) $$–

Boca Raton Bridge Hotel ★★★½
999 East Camino Real
Boca Raton, FL 33432
☎ 561-368-9500
FAX 561-362-0492

QUALITY RATING   75
COST ($ = $50) $$$

Boca Raton Marriott ★★★★
5150 Town Center Circle
Boca Raton, FL 33486
☎ 561-392-4600
FAX 561-395-8258
TOLL-FREE 888-888-3780
www.marriott.com

QUALITY RATING   83
COST ($ = $50) $$$$–

**Boca Raton Plaza Hotel and
Suites** ★★★
2901 North Federal Highway
Boca Raton, FL 33431
☎ 561-395-6850
FAX 561-368-7964
TOLL-FREE 800-228-2828
www.bocaratonplaza.com

QUALITY RATING   68
COST ($ = $50) $+

The Bradley House Hotel ★★★
280 Sunset Avenue
Palm Beach, FL 33480
☎ 561-832-7050
TOLL-FREE 800-822-4116
www.bradleyhousehotel.com

QUALITY RATING   68
COST ($ = $50) $$$–

The Breakers Palm Beach
★★★★★
1 South County Road
Palm Beach, FL 33480
☎ 561-655-6611
FAX 561-659-8403
TOLL-FREE 888-BREAKERS
www.thebreakers.com

QUALITY RATING   99
COST ($ = $50) $$$$$$$–

Chesterfield Palm Beach ★★★★½
363 Cocoanut Row
Palm Beach, FL 33480
☎ 561-659-5800
FAX 561-659-6707
TOLL-FREE 800-243-7871
www.chesterfieldpb.com

QUALITY RATING   95
COST ($ = $50) $$$$

**Colony Hotel and
Cabana Club** ★★★½
525 East Atlantic Avenue
Delray Beach, FL 33483
☎ 561-276-4123
FAX 561-276-0123
TOLL-FREE 800-552-2363
www.thecolonyhotel.com

QUALITY RATING   78
COST ($ = $50) $$+

Colony Palm Beach ★★★★
155 Hammon Avenue
Palm Beach, FL 33480
☎ 561-655-5430
FAX 561-832-7318
TOLL-FREE 800-521-5525
www.thecolonypalmbeach.com

QUALITY RATING   85
COST ($ = $50) $$$+

**Crowne Plaza
Singer Island** ★★★★
3200 North Ocean Drive
Singer Island, FL 33404
☎ 561-842-6171
FAX 561-848-6842
TOLL-FREE 800-327-0522
www.oceanfrontcp.com

QUALITY RATING   84
COST ($ = $50) $$$

Delray Beach Marriott ★★★★
10 North Ocean Boulevard
Delray Beach, FL 33483
☎ 561-274-3200
FAX 561-274-3202
TOLL-FREE 877-389-0169
www.marriottdelraybeach.com

QUALITY RATING   85
COST ($ = $50) $$$$$

Discovery Inn and Suites ★★½
2899 North Federal Highway
Boca Raton, FL 33431
☎ 561-395-7172
FAX 561-750-7351

QUALITY RATING   64
COST ($ = $50) $+

**Doubletree Guest Suites
Boca Raton** ★★★½
701 NW 53rd Street
Boca Raton, FL 33487
☎ 561-997-9500
FAX 561-994-3565
TOLL-FREE 800-222-TREE
www.doubletree.com

QUALITY RATING   80
COST ($ = $50) $$–

**Doubletree Hotel
Palm Beach Gardens** ★★★½
4431 PGA Boulevard
Palm Beach Gardens, FL 33410
☎ 561-622-2260
FAX 561-624-1043
www.doubletreewest
palmbeach.com

QUALITY RATING   82
COST ($ = $50) $$$–

**Embassy Suites
Boca Raton** ★★★★
661 NW 53rd Street
Boca Raton, FL 33487
☎ 561-994-8200
FAX 561-994-9518
TOLL-FREE 800-EMBASSY
www.bocaratonembassy.com

QUALITY RATING   84
COST ($ = $50) $$

Hotel Information Chart: Palm Beach County (cont'd)

Embassy Suites Palm Beach Gardens ★★★½
4350 PGA Boulevard
Palm Beach Gardens, FL 33410
☎ 561-622-1000
FAX 561-626-6254
TOLL-FREE 800-EMBASSY
www.embassysuites.com

QUALITY RATING 75
COST ($ = $50) $$$−

Four Seasons Resort Palm Beach ★★★★★
2800 South Ocean Boulevard
Palm Beach, FL 33480
☎ 561-582-2800
FAX 561-547-1374
www.fourseasons.com

QUALITY RATING 99
COST ($ = $50) $$$$$$$

Hampton Inn West Palm Beach ★★½
1505 Belvedere Road
West Palm Beach, FL 33406
☎ 561-471-8700
FAX 561-689-7385
TOLL-FREE 800-HAMPTON
www.hamptoninnwestpalm beach.com

QUALITY RATING 57
COST ($ = $50) $$$$

Hilton Singer Island Oceanfront Resort ★★★½
3700 North Ocean Drive
Singer Island, FL 33404
☎ 561-848-3888
FAX 561-848-4299
TOLL-FREE 800-443-4077
www.hiltonsingerisland.com

QUALITY RATING 82
COST ($ = $50) $$$

Holiday Inn Boca Raton Town Center ★★★½
1950 Glades Road
Boca Raton, FL 33431
☎ 561-368-5200
FAX 561-395-4783
www.holidayinn.com

QUALITY RATING 79
COST ($ = $50) $$$−

Holiday Inn Express ★★½
480 West Boynton Beach Boulevard
Boynton Beach, FL 33435
☎ 561-734-9100
FAX 561-738-7193
TOLL-FREE 888-271-6540
www.hieboynton.com

QUALITY RATING 62
COST ($ = $50) $$

La Quinta Inn West Palm Beach ★★
5981 Okeechobee Boulevard
West Palm Beach, FL 33417
☎ 561-697-3388
FAX 561-697-2834
TOLL-FREE 800-333-1492
www.lq.com

QUALITY RATING 50
COST ($ = $50) $$

Marriott West Palm Beach ★★★½
630 Clearwater Park Road
West Palm Beach, FL 33401
☎ 561-833-1234
FAX 561-833-4689
www.marriott.com

QUALITY RATING 80
COST ($ = $50) $$$−

PGA National Resort ★★★★
400 Avenue of the Champions
Palm Beach Gardens, FL 33418
☎ 561-627-2000
FAX 561-227-2595
www.pga-resorts.com

QUALITY RATING 89
COST ($ = $50) $$$

Ritz-Carlton Palm Beach ★★★★★
100 South Ocean Boulevard
Manalapan, FL 33462
☎ 561-533-6000
FAX 561-588-4202
www.ritzcarlton.com

QUALITY RATING 99
COST ($ = $50) $$$$$$$$$$$+

The Seagate ★★★½
400 South Ocean Boulevard
Delray Beach, FL 33483
☎ 561-276-2421
FAX 561-243-4714
TOLL-FREE 800-233-3581
www.seagatehotelbeachclub.com

QUALITY RATING 78
COST ($ = $50) $$+

SpringHill Suites ★★★½
5130 NW Eighth Avenue
Boca Raton, FL 33487
☎ 561-994-2107
FAX 561-994-0226
www.springhillsuitesbocaraton.com

QUALITY RATING 82
COST ($ = $50) $$−

Heart of Palm Beach Hotel ★★★½
160 Royal Palm Way
Palm Beach, FL 33480
☎ 561-655-5600
FAX 561-832-1201
TOLL-FREE 800-523-5377
www.heartofpalmbeach.com

QUALITY RATING   82
COST ($ = $50) $$$

Hibiscus House B&B ★★★
501 30th Street
West Palm Beach, FL 33407
☎ 561-863-5633
FAX 561-863-5633
TOLL-FREE 800-203-4927
www.hibiscushouse.com

QUALITY RATING   74
COST ($ = $50) $$

Hilton Palm Beach Airport ★★★½
150 Australian Avenue
West Palm Beach, FL 33406
☎ 561-684-9400
FAX 561-689-9421
TOLL-FREE 800-HILTONS
www.hilton.com

QUALITY RATING   75
COST ($ = $50) $$$–

Holiday Inn Highland Beach ★★★½
2809 South Ocean Boulevard
Highland Beach, FL 33487
☎ 561-278-6241
FAX 561-278-7133
TOLL-FREE 800-HOLIDAY
www.ichotelsgroup.com

QUALITY RATING   79
COST ($ = $50) $$$

Hotel Biba ★★★
320 Belvedere Road
West Palm Beach, FL 33405
☎ 561-832-0094
FAX 561-833-7848
TOLL-FREE 800-789-9843
www.hotelbiba.com

QUALITY RATING   73
COST ($ = $50) $$$–

Inns of America Palm Beach Gardens ★★½
4123 Northlake Boulevard
Palm Beach Gardens, FL 33410
☎ 561-626-4918

QUALITY RATING   64
COST ($ = $50) $$–

Portside on the Inlet ★★★
206 Inlet Way
Palm Beach Shores, FL 33404
☎ 561-842-1215
TOLL-FREE 800-730-2156
www.portside1.com

QUALITY RATING   70
COST ($ = $50) $$

Radisson Suite Inn Palm Beach Airport ★★★
1808 South Australian Avenue
West Palm Beach, FL 33409
☎ 561-689-6888
FAX 561-683-5783
www.radisson.com/westpalmfl

QUALITY RATING   65
COST ($ = $50) $$+

Renaissance Boca Raton Hotel ★★★★½
2000 NW 19th Street
Boca Raton, FL 33431
☎ 561-368-5252
FAX 561-750-5437
TOLL-FREE 800-468-3571
www.marriott.com

QUALITY RATING   90
COST ($ = $50) $$$$

Sundy House ★★★★
106 South Swinton Avenue
Delray Beach, FL 33444
☎ 561-272-5678
FAX 561-272-1115
www.sundyhouse.com

QUALITY RATING   89
COST ($ = $50) $$$$

Wright by the Sea ★★★½
1901 South Ocean Boulevard
Delray Beach, FL 33483
☎ 561-278-3355
FAX 561-278-2871
www.wbtsea.com

QUALITY RATING   75
COST ($ = $50) $$$$

Hotel Information Chart: Broward County

The Atlantic ★ ★ ★ ★ ½
601 Fort Lauderdale
Beach Boulevard (FL A1A)
Fort Lauderdale, FL 33304
☎ 954-567-8020
FAX 954-567-8040
TOLL-FREE 800-325-3535
www.starwood.com/luxury

QUALITY RATING 94
COST ($ = $50) $$$$$$$–

Bahia Mar Beach Resort ★ ★ ★
801 Seabreeze Boulevard
Fort Lauderdale, FL 33316
☎ 954-764-2233
FAX 954-523-5424
TOLL-FREE 800-333-3333
www.bahiamarhotel.com

QUALITY RATING 74
COST ($ = $50) $$$$

**Baymont Inn and
Suites Sunrise** ★ ★ ★
13651 NW Second Street
Sunrise, FL 33325
☎ 954-846-1200
TOLL-FREE 877-BAYMONT
www.baymontinns.com

QUALITY RATING 70
COST ($ = $50) $$+

**Comfort Inn Fort Lauderdale
Airport** ★ ★ ★
2520 Stirling Road
Hollywood, FL 33020
☎ 954-922-1600
FAX 954-923-5363
www.choicehotels.com

QUALITY RATING 69
COST ($ = $50) $$–

Comfort Inn Oceanside ★ ★ ½
50 South Ocean Drive
Deerfield Beach, FL 33441
☎ 954-428-0650
FAX 954-427-2666
www.choicehotels.com

QUALITY RATING 60
COST ($ = $50) $$+

**Comfort Suites Airport and
Cruise Port** ★ ★ ★
1800 South Federal Highway
Fort Lauderdale, FL 33316
☎ 954-767-8700
FAX 954-767-8629
TOLL-FREE 877-424-6423
www.choicehotels.com

QUALITY RATING 73
COST ($ = $50) $$$+

**Doubletree Guest Suites
Fort Lauderdale** ★ ★ ★
2670 East Sunrise Boulevard
Fort Lauderdale, FL 33304
☎ 954-565-3800
FAX 954-561-0387
TOLL-FREE 800-222-TREE
www.doubletree.com

QUALITY RATING 74
COST ($ = $50) $$$

**Embassy Suites
Deerfield Beach Resort** ★ ★ ★ ½
950 Ocean Drive
Deerfield Beach, FL 33441
☎ 954-426-0478
FAX 954-360-0539
TOLL-FREE 800-EMBASSY
www.embassyflorida.com

QUALITY RATING 80
COST ($ = $50) $$$$–

**Embassy Suites
Fort Lauderdale** ★ ★ ★ ½
1100 SE 17th Street Causeway
Fort Lauderdale, FL 33316
☎ 954-527-2700
FAX 954-760-7202
TOLL-FREE 800-EMBASSY
www.embassysuites.com

QUALITY RATING 78
COST ($ = $50) $$$$

**Holiday Inn Fort Lauderdale
Beach** ★ ★ ★
999 Fort Lauderdale Beach Blvd.
(FL A1A)
Fort Lauderdale, FL 33304
☎ 954-563-5961
FAX 954-564-5261
TOLL-FREE 800-HOLIDAY
www.holidayinnftlauderdale.com

QUALITY RATING 65
COST ($ = $50) $$$

Holiday Inn Hollywood Beach
★ ★ ★
2711 South Ocean Drive
Hollywood Beach, FL 33019
☎ 954-923-8700
FAX 954-923-7059
TOLL-FREE 888-258-6466
www.ichotelsgroup.com

QUALITY RATING 67
COST ($ = $50) $$+

**Hollywood Beach
Marriott** ★ ★ ★ ★
2501 North Ocean Drive
Hollywood Beach, FL 33019
☎ 954-924-2202
FAX 954-925-1411
TOLL-FREE 866-306-5453
www.marriott.com

QUALITY RATING 89
COST ($ = $50) $$$$$–

**Hyatt Regency
Pier Sixty-Six** ★ ★ ★ ★ ½
2301 SE 17th Street Causeway
Fort Lauderdale, FL 33316
☎ 954-525-6666
FAX 954-728-3541
www.hyatt.com

QUALITY RATING 90
COST ($ = $50) $$$$

Ireland's Inn Beach Resort ★ ★ ★
2220 North Atlantic Boulevard
Fort Lauderdale, FL 33305
☎ 954-565-6661
FAX 954-565-8893
TOLL-FREE 800-347-7776
www.irelands.com

QUALITY RATING 74
COST ($ = $50) $$$–

**Marriott
BeachPlace Towers** ★ ★ ★ ½
21 South Fort Lauderdale Beach Blvd.
Fort Lauderdale, FL 33316
☎ 954-525-4440
FAX 954-767-1100
TOLL-FREE 800-845-5279
www.marriott.com

QUALITY RATING 81
COST ($ = $50) $$$$$–

Beachcomber ★ ★ ★
1200 South Ocean Boulevard
Pompano Beach, FL 33062
☎ 954-941-7830
FAX 954-942-7680
TOLL-FREE 800-231-2423

QUALITY RATING 66
COST ($ = $50) $$$−

Best Western Oceanside Inn
★ ★ ½
1180 Seabreeze Boulevard
Fort Lauderdale, FL 33316
☎ 954-525-8115
FAX 954-527-0957
TOLL-FREE 800-528-1234
www.bestwestern.com

QUALITY RATING 57
COST ($ = $50) $$−

**Best Western
Pelican Beach Resort** ★ ★ ★
2000 North Atlantic Boulevard
Fort Lauderdale, FL 33305
☎ 954-568-9431
FAX 954-565-2622
TOLL-FREE 800-525-6232
www.pelicanbeach.com

QUALITY RATING 74
COST ($ = $50) $$$$$$−

Cottages by the Ocean ★ ★ ★
3309 SE Third Street
Pompano Beach, FL 33069
☎ 954-956-8999
FAX 954-956-8995
www.4rentbythebeach.com

QUALITY RATING 70
COST ($ = $50) $$+

**Courtyard Villas
on the Ocean** ★ ★ ★ ½
4312 El Mar Drive
Lauderdale-By-The-Sea, FL 33308
☎ 954-776-1164
FAX 954-491-0768
www.courtyardvilla.com

QUALITY RATING 80
COST ($ = $50) $$$$−

Days Inn Bahia Cabana ★ ★ ½
3001 Harbor Drive
Fort Lauderdale, FL 33316
☎ 954-524-1555
www.bahiacabanaresort.com

QUALITY RATING 62
COST ($ = $50) $$$$

**Fort Lauderdale
Waterfront Inns** ★ ★ ★
521 Fort Lauderdale Beach Blvd.
(FL A1A)
Fort Lauderdale, FL 33304
☎ 954-564-4341
FAX 954-565-9564
TOLL-FREE 800-543-2006
www.waterfrontinns.com

QUALITY RATING 74
COST ($ = $50) $$

**Hampton Inn and Suites
Hollywood** ★ ★ ★
2500 Stirling Road
Hollywood, FL 33020
☎ 954-922-0011
FAX 954-929-7118
TOLL-FREE 800-333-1492
www.hamptoninn.com

QUALITY RATING 70
COST ($ = $50) $$$−

High Noon Resort ★ ★ ★ ½
4424 El Mar Drive
Lauderdale-By-The-Sea, FL 33308
☎ 954-776-1121
FAX 954-776-1124
www.highnoonresort.com

QUALITY RATING 79
COST ($ = $50) $$$$−

Hollywood Sands ★ ★ ★
2404 North Surf Road
Hollywood, FL 33019
☎ 954-925-2285
TOLL-FREE 800-269-6192

QUALITY RATING 67
COST ($ = $50) $$$

**Howard Johnson Ocean's Edge
Fort Lauderdale** ★ ★
700 Fort Lauderdale Beach Blvd.
(FL A1A)
Fort Lauderdale, FL 33304
☎ 954-563-2451
FAX 954-564-8153
TOLL-FREE 800-327-8578
www.hojoftlaud.com

QUALITY RATING 47
COST ($ = $50) $$$−

Howard Johnson Plaza Resort
★ ★ ½
2096 NE Second Street
Deerfield Beach, FL 33441
☎ 954-428-2850
FAX 954-480-9639
TOLL-FREE 800-426-0084
www.hojo.com

QUALITY RATING 64
COST ($ = $50) $$$−

**Marriott Fort Lauderdale
Marina** ★ ★ ★ ★
1881 SE 17th Street
Fort Lauderdale, FL 33316
☎ 954-463-4000
FAX 954-527-6705
TOLL-FREE 800-433-2254
www.marriott.com

QUALITY RATING 83
COST ($ = $50) $$$$+

**Marriott Harbor
Beach Resort** ★ ★ ★ ★ ½
3030 North Holiday Drive
Fort Lauderdale, FL 33316
☎ 954-525-4000
FAX 954-766-6152
TOLL-FREE 800-222-6543
www.marriottharborbeach.com

QUALITY RATING 90
COST ($ = $50) $$$$+

Ocean Point ★ ★ ½
1208 North Ocean Boulevard
Pompano Beach, FL 33062
☎ 954-782-5300
FAX 954-946-1853

QUALITY RATING 63
COST ($ = $50) $$$$

Hotel Information Chart: Broward County (cont'd)

Oceanfront Hotel ★ ★ ★
440 Seabreeze Boulevard
Fort Lauderdale, FL 33316
☎ 954-524-8733
FAX 954-467-7489
www.ftlauderdaleoceanfront.com

QUALITY RATING   **72**
COST ($ = $50)   **$$$$+**

Paradise Beach Resort ★ ★ ½
1380 South Ocean Boulevard
Pompano Beach, FL 33062
☎ 954-785-3300
FAX 954-785-8031

QUALITY RATING   **60**
COST ($ = $50)   **$$**

**Ramada
Ocean Beach Resort** ★ ★ ½
1350 South Ocean Boulevard
Pompano Beach, FL 33062
☎ 954-941-7300
FAX 954-941-7300
TOLL-FREE 800-272-6232
www.ramada.com

QUALITY RATING   **60**
COST ($ = $50)   **$$$–**

Ramada Sea Club Resort ★ ★
619 Fort Lauderdale Beach Blvd.
(FL A1A)
Fort Lauderdale, FL 33304
☎ 954-564-3211
FAX 954-561-1252
TOLL-FREE 800-327-9478
www.seaclubresort.com

QUALITY RATING   **52**
COST ($ = $50)   **$$**

**Renaissance Fort Lauderdale
Hotel** ★ ★ ★ ★
1617 SE 17th Street
Fort Lauderdale, FL 33316
☎ 954-626-1700
FAX 954-626-1717
TOLL-FREE 800-468-3571
www.marriott.com

QUALITY RATING   **84**
COST ($ = $50)   **$$$$$**

**Renaissance Fort Lauderdale–
Plantation Hotel** ★ ★ ★ ★
1230 South Pine Island Road
Plantation, FL 33324
☎ 954-472-2252
FAX 954-308-4600
TOLL-FREE 800-468-3571
www.renaissanceplantation.com

QUALITY RATING   **84**
COST ($ = $50)   **$$$$**

Riverside Hotel ★ ★ ★ ½
620 East Las Olas Boulevard
Fort Lauderdale, FL 33301
☎ 954-467-0671
FAX 954-462-2148
TOLL-FREE 800-325-3280
www.riversidehotel.com

QUALITY RATING   **80**
COST ($ = $50)   **$$$**

Sawgrass Mills Sunrise ★ ★ ★ ½
13400 West Sunrise Boulevard
Sunrise, FL 33323
☎ 954-851-1020
www.sawgrasshotel.com

QUALITY RATING   **78**
COST ($ = $50)   **$$+**

Sea Castle Resort Inn ★ ★ ½
730 North Ocean Boulevard
Pompano Beach, FL 33062
☎ 954-941-2570
FAX 954-941-3150

QUALITY RATING   **58**
COST ($ = $50)   **$+**

Sheldon Ocean Resort ★ ★
1000 North Surf Road
Hollywood, FL 33019
☎ 954-922-6020
FAX 954-922-6218
www.sheldonoceanresort.com

QUALITY RATING   **55**
COST ($ = $50)   **$$–**

Sheraton Yankee Clipper ★ ★ ★ ½
1140 Seabreeze Boulevard
Fort Lauderdale, FL 33316
☎ 954-524-5551
FAX 954-524-0777
TOLL-FREE 800-958-5551
www.sheratonclipper.com

QUALITY RATING   **75**
COST ($ = $50)   **$$$**

Sheraton Yankee Trader ★ ★ ★ ½
321 Fort Lauderdale Beach Blvd.
(FL A1A)
Fort Lauderdale, FL 33304
☎ 954-467-1111
FAX 954-462-2342
TOLL-FREE 800-958-5551
www.sheratontrader.com

QUALITY RATING   **82**
COST ($ = $50)   **$$$$–**

**Westin Diplomat Resort and
Spa** ★ ★ ★ ★ ½
3555 South Ocean Drive
Hollywood, FL 33019
☎ 954-602-6000
FAX 954-602-7000
www.starwoodhotels.com

QUALITY RATING   **93**
COST ($ = $50)   **$$$$$**

**Windjammer Resort and
Beach Club** ★ ★ ★
4244 El Mar Drive
Lauderdale-By-The-Sea, FL 33308
☎ 954-776-4244
FAX 954-351-9153
www.windjammerresort.com

QUALITY RATING   **66**
COST ($ = $50)   **$$$$–**

**Wyndham Fort Lauderdale
Airport** ★ ★ ★ ½
1870 Griffin Road
Fort Lauderdale, FL 33304
☎ 954-920-3300
TOLL-FREE 866-235-9330
www.wyndham.com

QUALITY RATING   **75**
COST ($ = $50)   **$$$**

Hotel Information Chart: Southwest Florida

Anchor Inn and Cottages of Sanibel ★★★
1245 Periwinkle Way
Sanibel, FL 33957
☎ 239-395-9688
TOLL-FREE 866-469-9543
www.sanibelanchorinn.com

QUALITY RATING   70
COST ($ = $50) $$

Baymont Inn Bonita Springs ★★★
27991 Oakland Drive
Bonita Springs, FL 34135
☎ 239-949-9400
FAX 239-948-0480
TOLL-FREE 866-999-1111
www.baymontinns.com

QUALITY RATING   73
COST ($ = $50) $+

Bayview Bed and Breakfast ★★★
12251 Shoreview Drive
Matlacha, FL 33993
☎ 239-283-7510

QUALITY RATING   72
COST ($ = $50) $$

The Beachouse Lodge ★★★
7702 Bocilla Lane
Bokeelia, FL 33922
☎ 239-283-4303
www.beachousefl.com

QUALITY RATING   74
COST ($ = $50) $$

Beachview Cottages ★★★
3325 West Gulf Drive
Sanibel, FL 33957
☎ 239-472-1202
FAX 239-472-4720
TOLL-FREE 800-860-0532
www.beachviewsanibel.com

QUALITY RATING   70
COST ($ = $50) $$$

Beacon Motel and Gift Shop ★★★
1240 Estero Boulevard
Fort Myers Beach, FL 33931
☎ 239-463-5264
FAX 239-463-5972

QUALITY RATING   72
COST ($ = $50) $$+

Bellasera Hotel ★★★★
221 Ninth Street
Naples, FL 34102
☎ 239-649-7333
FAX 239-649-6233
TOLL-FREE 888-627-1595
www.bellaseranaples.com

QUALITY RATING   84
COST ($ = $50) $$$$

Best Western Airport Inn Fort Myers ★★★
8955 Daniels Parkway
Fort Myers, FL 33912
☎ 239-561-7000
FAX 239-561-5963
TOLL-FREE 800-780-7234
www.bestwestern.com

QUALITY RATING   69
COST ($ = $50) $$

Best Western Beach Resort ★★★
684 Estero Boulevard
Fort Myers Beach, FL 33931
☎ 239-463-6000
FAX 239-463-3013
TOLL-FREE 800-336-4045
www.bestwestern.com

QUALITY RATING   68
COST ($ = $50) $$+

Best Western Naples ★★★
2329 Ninth Street North
Naples, FL 34103
☎ 239-261-1148
FAX 239-262-4684
TOLL-FREE 800-243-1148
www.bestwestern.com

QUALITY RATING   65
COST ($ = $50) $$

Best Western Naples Plaza ★★★
6400 Dudley Drive
Naples, FL 34105
☎ 239-643-6655
FAX 239-643-4063
TOLL-FREE 888-679-6655
www.naplesbestwestern.com

QUALITY RATING   67
COST ($ = $50) $$$

Best Western Sanibel Gateway ★★★
20091 Summerlin Road
Fort Myers, FL 33908
☎ 239-466-1200
FAX 239-466-3797
TOLL-FREE 800-WESTERN
www.bestwestern.com

QUALITY RATING   65
COST ($ = $50) $$

Blue Dolphin Cottages ★★★
4227 West Gulf Drive
Sanibel, FL 33957
☎ 239-472-1600
FAX 239-472-5906
TOLL-FREE 800-648-4660
www.ivacation.com

QUALITY RATING   68
COST ($ = $50) $$

Boat House Motel ★★★
1180 Edington Place
Marco Island, FL 34145
☎ 239-642-2400
FAX 239-642-2435
www.theboathousemotel.com

QUALITY RATING   74
COST ($ = $50) $$

Boca Grande Club ★★★½
5000 Gasparilla Road
Boca Grande, FL 33921
☎ 941-964-2211
FAX 941-964-0193
www.bocagrandeclub.com

QUALITY RATING   80
COST ($ = $50) $$$–

Hotel Information Chart: Southwest Florida (cont'd)

Bokeelia Tarpon Inn ★★★★
8241 Main Street
Bokeelia, FL 33922
☎ 239-283-8961
FAX 239-283-8215
TOLL-FREE 866-TARPON2
www.tarponinn.com

QUALITY RATING   89
COST ($ = $50) $$$$$

Bonita Beach Resort Motel
★★★½
26395 Hickory Boulevard
Bonita Springs, FL 34134
☎ 239-992-2137
FAX 239-947-2305

QUALITY RATING   64
COST ($ = $50) $+

Bridge Water Inn ★★★
4331 Pine Island Road
Matlacha, FL 33993
☎ 239-283-2423
FAX 239-282-8440
TOLL-FREE 800-378-7666
www.bridgewaterinn.com

QUALITY RATING   70
COST ($ = $50) $$

Carousel Inn on the Beach ★★★
6230 Estero Boulevard
Fort Myers Beach, FL 33931
☎ 239-463-6131
FAX 239-463-1811
TOLL-FREE 800-613-9540
www.carouselbeachinn.com

QUALITY RATING   68
COST ($ = $50) $$

Casa Playa Beach Resort ★★★½
510 Estero Boulevard
Fort Myers Beach, FL 33931
☎ 239-765-0510
FAX 239-765-0514
TOLL-FREE 800-569-4876
www.casaplayaresort.com

QUALITY RATING   80
COST ($ = $50) $$+

Casa Ybel Resort ★★★★
2255 West Gulf Drive
Sanibel, FL 33957
☎ 239-472-3145
FAX 239-472-2109
TOLL-FREE 800-276-4753
www.casaybelresort.com

QUALITY RATING   89
COST ($ = $50) $$$$$–

**Comfort Inn
(South Cleveland Avenue)** ★★½
11501 South Cleveland Avenue
Fort Myers, FL 33907
☎ 239-936-3993
FAX 239-936-7234
TOLL-FREE 877-424-6423
www.choicehotels.com

QUALITY RATING   56
COST ($ = $50) $$–

Comfort Inn Bonita Springs ★★½
9800 Bonita Beach Road
Bonita Springs, FL 34135
☎ 239-992-5001
FAX 239-992-9283
TOLL-FREE 877-424-6423
www.choicehotels.com

QUALITY RATING   60
COST ($ = $50) $+

**Comfort Inn
Downtown Naples** ★★½
1221 Fifth Avenue South
Naples, FL 34102
☎ 239-649-5800
FAX 239-649-0523
TOLL-FREE 800-382-7941
www.choicehotels.com

QUALITY RATING   64
COST ($ = $50) $$

Days Inn South ★★
11435 South Cleveland Avenue
Fort Myers, FL 33907
☎ 239-936-1311
FAX 239-936-7076
TOLL-FREE 800-329-7466
www.daysinn.com

QUALITY RATING   54
COST ($ = $50) $$–

DiamondHead Beach Resort
★★★★
2000 Estero Boulevard
Fort Myers Beach, FL 33931
☎ 239-765-7654
FAX 239-765-1694
TOLL-FREE 888-627-1595
www.diamondheadfl.com

QUALITY RATING   84
COST ($ = $50) $$$$

Dolphin Inn ★★½
6555 Estero Boulevard
Fort Myers Beach, FL 33931
☎ 239-463-6049
FAX 239-463-2148
www.dolphininn.net

QUALITY RATING   60
COST ($ = $50) $$–

**Everglades Spa-Fari and
Lodge** ★★★
201 W. Broadway
Everglades City, FL 34139
☎ 239-695-3151
FAX 239-695-3335
www.banksoftheeverglades.com

QUALITY RATING   71
COST ($ = $50) $$

Fairfield Inn Fort Myers ★★★
7090 Cypress Terrace
Fort Myers, FL 33907
☎ 239-437-5600
FAX 239-437-5616
TOLL-FREE 800-228-2800
www.marriott.com

QUALITY RATING   73
COST ($ = $50) $$

Flamingo Motel ★★½
4330 Bonita Beach Road
Bonita Springs, FL 34134
☎ 239-992-7566
FAX 239-992-0409
TOLL-FREE 888-377-9317
www.flamingobonita.com

QUALITY RATING   60
COST ($ = $50) $$

Captain's Table Lodge and Villas ★★½
102 E. Broadway Street
Everglades City, FL 34139
☎ 239-695-4211
FAX 239-695-2633
www.captainstablehotel.com

QUALITY RATING   64

COST ($ = $50) $$–

Captiva Island Bed and Breakfast ★★★
11509 Andy Rosse Lane
Captiva, FL 33924
☎ 239-395-0882
FAX 239-395-0862
TOLL-FREE 800-454-9898
www.captivaisland.com

QUALITY RATING   70

COST ($ = $50) $$$–

Caribe Beach Resort ★★★½
2669 West Gulf Drive
Sanibel, FL 33957
☎ 239-472-1166
FAX 239-472-0079

QUALITY RATING   75

COST ($ = $50) $$+

Clarion Inn Fort Myers ★★½
12635 South Cleveland Avenue
Fort Myers, FL 33907
☎ 239-936-4300
FAX 239-936-2058
TOLL-FREE 877-424-6423
www.choicehotels.com

QUALITY RATING   64

COST ($ = $50) $+

The Colony Resort ★★★
419 East Gulf Drive
Sanibel, FL 33957
☎ 239-472-5151
FAX 239-472-3541
TOLL-FREE 800-342-1704
www.colonyonsanibel.com

QUALITY RATING   72

COST ($ = $50) $$$

**Comfort Inn
(Boatways Road)** ★★★
4171 Boatways Road
Fort Myers, FL 33905
☎ 239-694-9200
FAX 239-690-0180
TOLL-FREE 877-424-6423
www.choicehotels.com

QUALITY RATING   68

COST ($ = $50) $$–

**Country Inn and Suites
Fort Myers** ★★★
9401 Marketplace Road
Fort Myers, FL 33912
☎ 239-454-0040
FAX 239-454-6006
TOLL-FREE 888-201-1746
www.countryinns.com

QUALITY RATING   75

COST ($ = $50) $$

**Country Inn and Suites
Sanibel Gateway** ★★★
13901 Shell Point Plaza
Fort Myers, FL 33908
☎ 239-454-9292
FAX 239-454-9159
TOLL-FREE 800-456-4000
www.countryinns.com/
sanibelfl_gateway

QUALITY RATING   72

COST ($ = $50) $$$–

Courtyard Fort Myers ★★★
4455 Metro Parkway
Fort Myers, FL 33916
☎ 239-275-8600
FAX 239-275-7087
TOLL-FREE 888-236-2427
www.marriott.com

QUALITY RATING   74

COST ($ = $50) $$$–

**Doubletree Guest Suites
Naples** ★★★½
12200 Tamiami Trail North
Naples, FL 34110
☎ 239-593-8733
FAX 239-593-8734
TOLL-FREE 800-222-TREE
www.doubletree.com

QUALITY RATING   77

COST ($ = $50) $$$–

Edison Beach House ★★★★
830 Estero Boulevard
Fort Myers Beach, FL 33931
☎ 239-463-1530
FAX 239-765-9430
TOLL-FREE 800-399-2511
www.colliercounty.com

QUALITY RATING   83

COST ($ = $50) $$$–

Everglades City Motel ★★★
310 Collier Avenue (FL 29)
Everglades City, FL 34139
☎ 239-695-4224
FAX 239-695-2557
TOLL-FREE 800-695-8353
www.evergladescitymotel.com

QUALITY RATING   68

COST ($ = $50) $$–

Fort Myers Inn ★★½
3511 Cleveland Avenue
Fort Myers, FL 33901
☎ 239-936-1959
FAX 239-936-6973

QUALITY RATING   64

COST ($ = $50) $+

Forty/Fifteen Resort ★★★
4015 West Gulf Drive
Sanibel, FL 33957
☎ 239-472-1232
FAX 239-472-1232
www.fortyfifteen.com

QUALITY RATING   65

COST ($ = $50) $$$

Gulfcoast Inn ★★½
2555 Tamiami Trail North
Naples, FL 34103
☎ 239-261-6046
FAX 239-261-5742
TOLL-FREE 800-330-0046
www.gulfcoastinnnaples.com

QUALITY RATING   64

COST ($ = $50) $+

Hotel Information Chart: Southwest Florida (cont'd)

Gullwing Beach Resort ★★★★½
6620 Estero Boulevard
Fort Myers Beach, FL 33931
☎ 239-765-4300
FAX 239-765-5755
TOLL-FREE 888-627-1595
www.gullwingfl.com

QUALITY RATING   90
COST ($ = $50) $$$$+

**Hampton Inn
Bonita Springs** ★★★
27900 Crown Lake Boulevard
Bonita Springs, FL 34135
☎ 239-947-9393
FAX 239-947-3966
TOLL-FREE 800-HAMPTON
www.hamptoninn.com

QUALITY RATING   68
COST ($ = $50) $$–

Hampton Inn Fort Myers ★★★
9241 Marketplace Road
Fort Myers, FL 33912
☎ 239-768-2525
FAX 239-786-6049
TOLL-FREE 800-426-7866

QUALITY RATING   74
COST ($ = $50) $$$–

Hilton Naples and Towers ★★★★
5111 Tamiami Trail North
Naples, FL 34103
☎ 239-430-4900
FAX 239-430-4901
TOLL-FREE 800-HILTONS
www.hiltonnaples.com

QUALITY RATING   83
COST ($ = $50) $$$+

Holiday Court Motel ★★½
925 Estero Boulevard
Fort Myers Beach, FL 33931
☎ 239-463-2830

QUALITY RATING   60
COST ($ = $50) $$

**Holiday Inn Express Hotel and
Suites** ★★★
27891 Crown Lake Boulevard
Bonita Springs, FL 34135
☎ 239-948-0699
FAX 239-948-0676
TOLL-FREE 800-HOLIDAY
www.ichotelsgroup.com

QUALITY RATING   68
COST ($ = $50) $$–

**Holiday Inn Select
Airport** ★★★½
13051 Bell Tower Drive
Fort Myers, FL 33907
☎ 239-482-2900
FAX 239-210-2450
TOLL-FREE 800-HOLIDAY
www.ichotelsgroup.com

QUALITY RATING   80
COST ($ = $50) $$$

Homewood Suites Hotel ★★★½
5255 Big Pine Way
Fort Myers, FL 33907
☎ 239-275-6000
FAX 239-275-6601
TOLL-FREE 800-CALL-HOME
www.homewood-suites.com

QUALITY RATING   78
COST ($ = $50) $$$$

Howard Johnson Inn ★★½
4811 Cleveland Avenue
Fort Myers, FL 33907
☎ 239-936-3229
FAX 239-939-0424
TOLL-FREE 800-446-4656
www.hojo.com

QUALITY RATING   56
COST ($ = $50) $$

Island Inn ★★★½
3111 West Gulf Drive
Sanibel, FL 33957
☎ 239-472-1561
FAX 239-472-0051
TOLL-FREE 800-851-5088
www.islandinnsanibel.com

QUALITY RATING   82
COST ($ = $50) $$$+

Ivey House Inn ★★★
107 Camellia Street
Everglades City, FL 34139
☎ 239-695-3299
FAX 239-695-4155
www.iveyhouse.com

QUALITY RATING   72
COST ($ = $50) $$$

**Jensen's Twin Palm Cottages
and Marina** ★★★
15107 Captiva Drive
Captiva, FL 33924
☎ 239-472-5800
FAX 239-472-9263
www.jensen-captiva.com

QUALITY RATING   68
COST ($ = $50) $$$

La Quinta Inn Fort Myers ★★½
4850 South Cleveland Avenue
Fort Myers, FL 33907
☎ 239-275-3300
FAX 239-275-6661
TOLL-FREE 866-725-1661
www.lq.com

QUALITY RATING   64
COST ($ = $50) $$–

Lani Kai Island Resort Hotel ★★★
1400 Estero Boulevard
Fort Myers Beach, FL 33931
☎ 239-463-3111
FAX 239-463-2986
TOLL-FREE 800-237-6133
www.drfun.com/lani-kai

QUALITY RATING   65
COST ($ = $50) $$$$–

Lemon Tree Inn ★★½
250 Ninth Street South
Naples, FL 34102
☎ 239-262-1414
FAX 239-262-2638
TOLL-FREE 888-800-LEMON
www.lemontreeinn.com

QUALITY RATING   64
COST ($ = $50) $$

Hampton Inn Naples ★ ★ ★
3210 Tamiami Trail North
Naples, FL 34103
☎ 239-261-8000
FAX 239-261-7802
TOLL-FREE 800-HAMPTON
www.napleshamptoninn.com

QUALITY RATING   66
COST ($ = $50) $$$$

Hawthorn Suites Naples ★ ★ ★
3557 Pine Ridge Road
Naples, FL 34109
☎ 239-593-1300
FAX 239-593-1301
www.hawthornnaples.com

QUALITY RATING   70
COST ($ = $50) $$+

Hilton Garden Inn ★ ★ ★ ½
12600 University Drive
Fort Myers, FL 33907
☎ 239-790-3500
FAX 239-790-3501
TOLL-FREE 800-STAY-HGI
www.hiltongardeninn.com

QUALITY RATING   80
COST ($ = $50) $$$

**Holiday Inn
Fort Myers Beach** ★ ★ ★
6890 Estero Boulevard
Fort Myers Beach, FL 33931
☎ 239-463-5711
FAX 239-463-7038
TOLL-FREE 800-HOLIDAY
www.ichotelsgroup.com

QUALITY RATING   70
COST ($ = $50) $$+

Holiday Inn Naples ★ ★
1100 Tamiami Trail North
Naples, FL 34102
☎ 239-263-3434
FAX 239-261-3809
TOLL-FREE 800-325-1135
www.hinaples.com

QUALITY RATING   50
COST ($ = $50) $$

Holiday Inn Sanibel Island ★ ★ ★
1231 Middle Gulf Drive
Sanibel, FL 33957
☎ 239-472-4123
FAX 239-472-0930
TOLL-FREE 800-HOLIDAY
www.ichotelsgroup.com

QUALITY RATING   70
COST ($ = $50) $$$

Hurricane House ★ ★ ★ ★
2939 West Gulf Drive
Sanibel, FL 33957
☎ 239-472-1696
FAX 239-472-1718

QUALITY RATING   84
COST ($ = $50) $$$$+

Inn at Pelican Bay ★ ★ ★ ★
800 Vanderbilt Beach Road
Naples, FL 34108
☎ 239-597-8777
FAX 239-597-8012
TOLL-FREE 800-597-8770
www.naplesinn.com/pelicanbay

QUALITY RATING   84
COST ($ = $50) $$$–

Inn on Fifth ★ ★ ★ ★
699 5th Avenue South
Naples, FL 34102
☎ 239-403-8777
FAX 239-403-8778
TOLL-FREE 888-403-8778
www.naplesinn.com/fifth

QUALITY RATING   83
COST ($ = $50) $$$$

Jug Creek Cottages ★ ★
8135 Main Street
Bokeelia, FL 33922
☎ 239-283-0015

QUALITY RATING   55
COST ($ = $50) $$–

Kona Kai Motel ★ ★ ★
1539 Periwinkle Way
Sanibel, FL 33957
☎ 239-472-1001
FAX 239-472-2554
TOLL-FREE 800-820-2385
www.konakaimotel.com

QUALITY RATING   69
COST ($ = $50) $$

La Playa Beach Resort ★ ★ ★ ★
9891 Gulf Shore Drive
Naples, FL 34108
☎ 239-597-3123
FAX 239-597-6278
TOLL-FREE 800-237-6883
www.laplayaresort.com

QUALITY RATING   87
COST ($ = $50) $$$$$$$

Lighthouse Inn ★ ★ ★
9140 Gulf Shore Drive North
Naples, FL 34108
☎ 239-597-3345
FAX 239-597-5541

QUALITY RATING   65
COST ($ = $50) $$–

Lighthouse Island Resort ★ ★ ½
1051 Fifth Street
Fort Myers Beach, FL 33931
☎ 239-463-9392
FAX 239-765-5297
TOLL-FREE 800-778-7748
www.lighthouseislandresort.com

QUALITY RATING   64
COST ($ = $50) $$

**Lovers Key Beach Club and
Resort** ★ ★ ★ ★ ½
8771 Estero Boulevard
Fort Myers Beach, FL 33931
☎ 239-765-1040
FAX 239-765-1055
TOLL-FREE 877-798-4879
www.loverskey.com

QUALITY RATING   90
COST ($ = $50) $$$$–

Hotel Information Chart: Southwest Florida (cont'd)

Marco Beach
Ocean Resort ★ ★ ★ ★ ★
480 South Collier Boulevard
Marco Island, FL 34145
☎ 239-393-1400
FAX 239-393-1401
TOLL-FREE 800-715-8517
www.marcoresort.com

QUALITY RATING 98
COST ($ = $50) $$$$$$

Marco Island Hilton
Beach Resort ★ ★ ★ ★
560 South Collier Boulevard
Marco Island, FL 34145
☎ 239-394-5000
FAX 239-394-8410
TOLL-FREE 800-HILTONS
www.marcoislandhilton.com

QUALITY RATING 88
COST ($ = $50) $$$$–

Marco Resort and Club ★ ★ ★ ½
1202 Bald Eagle Drive
Marco Island, FL 34145
☎ 239-394-2777
FAX 239-394-2777

QUALITY RATING 79
COST ($ = $50) $$

Mitchell's Sand Castles ★ ★ ½
3951 West Gulf Drive
Sanibel, FL 33957
☎ 239-472-1282
www.mitchellssandcastles.com

QUALITY RATING 64
COST ($ = $50) $$$

Naples Beach Hotel and
Golf Club ★ ★ ★ ★
851 Gulf Shore Boulevard North
Naples, FL 34102
☎ 239-261-2222
FAX 239-261-7380
TOLL-FREE 800-455-1546
www.naplesbeachhotel.com

QUALITY RATING 84
COST ($ = $50) $$$$–

Naples Courtyard ★ ★ ★ ½
3250 Tamiami Trail North
Naples, FL 34103
☎ 239-434-8700
FAX 239-434-7787
TOLL-FREE 800-321-2211
www.marriott.com

QUALITY RATING 78
COST ($ = $50) $$

The Palm View ★ ★ ★
706 Donax Street
Sanibel, FL 33957
☎ 239-472-1606
FAX 239-472-6733
TOLL-FREE 877-472-1606
www.palmviewsanibel.com

QUALITY RATING 74
COST ($ = $50) $$

Palms of Sanibel ★ ★ ★
1220 Morningside Drive
Sanibel, FL 33957
☎ 239-395-1775
FAX 239-395-3379
TOLL-FREE 877-749-5093
www.palmsofsanibel.com

QUALITY RATING 65
COST ($ = $50) $$$–

Periwinkle Cottages
of Sanibel ★ ★ ★
1431 Jamaica Drive
Sanibel, FL 33957
☎ 239-472-1880
FAX 239-472-5567
www.periwinklecottages.com

QUALITY RATING 65
COST ($ = $50) $$

Quality Hotel ★ ★ ½
2431 Cleveland Avenue
Fort Myers, FL 33901
☎ 239-332-3232
FAX 239-332-0590
TOLL-FREE 877-424-6423
www.choicehotels.com

QUALITY RATING 60
COST ($ = $50) $+

Quality Inn and Suites ★ ★ ★
4055 Tamiami Trail North
Naples, FL 34103
☎ 239-649-5500
FAX 239-430-0422
TOLL-FREE 877-424-6423
www.choicehotels.com

QUALITY RATING 67
COST ($ = $50) $$

Radisson Suite Beach Resort
★ ★ ★
600 South Collier Boulevard
Marco Island, FL 34145
☎ 239-394-4100
FAX 239-394-0419
TOLL-FREE 800-333-3333
www.marcobeachresort.com

QUALITY RATING 74
COST ($ = $50) $$$$–

Registry Resort ★ ★ ★ ★ ½
475 Seagate Drive
Naples, FL 34103
☎ 239-597-3232
FAX 239-597-3147
TOLL-FREE 800-247-9810
www.registryresort.com

QUALITY RATING 95
COST ($ = $50) $$$$$$+

Residence Inn Fort Myers ★ ★ ★
2960 Colonial Boulevard
Fort Myers, FL 33912
☎ 239-936-0110
FAX 239-936-4144
www.marriott.com

QUALITY RATING 70
COST ($ = $50) $$$

Residence Inn Naples ★ ★ ★
4075 Tamiami Trail North
Naples, FL 34103
☎ 239-659-1300
FAX 239-659-2300
TOLL-FREE 888-236-2427
www.marriott.com

QUALITY RATING 72
COST ($ = $50) $$$–

Mariner's Lodge and Marina ★★½
17990 San Carlos Boulevard
Fort Myers Beach, FL 33931
☎ 239-466-9700
FAX 239-466-6116
TOLL-FREE 800-211-9099
www.marinerslodge.com

QUALITY RATING   62
COST ($ = $50) $+

**Marriott Resort of
Marco Island** ★★★★
400 South Collier Boulevard
Marco Island, FL 34145
☎ 239-394-2511
FAX 239-642-2672
TOLL-FREE 800-438-4373
www.marcoislandmarriott.com

QUALITY RATING   85
COST ($ = $50) $$$$–

Matanzas Inn ★★★
414 Crescent Street
Fort Myers Beach, FL 33931
☎ 239-463-9258
FAX 239-765-9258
TOLL-FREE 800-462-9258
www.matanzasinn.com

QUALITY RATING   65
COST ($ = $50) $$

Neptune Inn ★★★
2310 Estero Boulevard
Fort Myers Beach, FL 33931
☎ 239-463-6141
FAX 239-463-7503
TOLL-FREE 888-333-2310
www.neptuneinn.com

QUALITY RATING   65
COST ($ = $50) $$

Outrigger Beach Resort ★★★
6200 Estero Boulevard
Fort Myers Beach, FL 33931
☎ 239-463-3131
FAX 239-463-6577
TOLL-FREE 800-655-8997
www.outriggerfmb.com

QUALITY RATING   71
COST ($ = $50) $$$–

Palm Island Resort ★★★★
7092 Placida Road
Cape Haze, FL 33946
☎ 941-697-4800
FAX 941-697-0696
TOLL-FREE 800-824-5412
www.palmisland.com

QUALITY RATING   84
COST ($ = $50) $$$$$$–

Pink Shell Beach Resort ★★★½
275 Estero Boulevard
Fort Myers Beach, FL 33931
☎ 239-463-6181
FAX 239-463-1229
TOLL-FREE 888-222-7465
www.pinkshell.com

QUALITY RATING   80
COST ($ = $50) $$$$

Pointe Estero Resort ★★★★
6640 Estero Boulevard
Fort Myers Beach, FL 33931
☎ 239-765-1155
FAX 239-765-0657
TOLL-FREE 888-627-1595
www.pointeestero.com

QUALITY RATING   87
COST ($ = $50) $$$$–

Port of the Islands Resort ★★★½
25000 Tamiami Trail East
Naples, FL 34114
☎ 239-394-3101
FAX 239-394-4335
www.portoftheislandsresort
andmarina.com

QUALITY RATING   80
COST ($ = $50) $$

Ramada Inn Beachfront ★★½
1160 Estero Boulevard
Fort Myers Beach, FL 33931
☎ 239-463-6158
FAX 239-765-4240
TOLL-FREE 800-206-2723
www.ramada.com

QUALITY RATING   63
COST ($ = $50) $$–

Ramada Limited Fort Myers
★★½
4760 South Cleveland Avenue
Fort Myers, FL 33907
☎ 239-275-1111
FAX 239-275-3104
TOLL-FREE 800-272-6232
www.fortmyers-ramada.com

QUALITY RATING   58
COST ($ = $50) $$

Ramada Riverfront ★★★
2500 Edwards Drive
Fort Myers, FL 33901
☎ 239-337-0300
FAX 239-337-1530
TOLL-FREE 800-833-1620
www.ramadariverfront.com

QUALITY RATING   68
COST ($ = $50) $$–

Ritz-Carlton Naples ★★★★★
280 Vanderbilt Beach Road
Naples, FL 34108
☎ 239-598-3300
FAX 239-598-6690
TOLL-FREE 800-241-3333
www.ritzcarlton.com

QUALITY RATING   100
COST ($ = $50) $$$$$$$

Rod and Gun Club Lodge ★★★
200 Broadway
Everglades City, FL 34139
☎ 239-695-2101

QUALITY RATING   70
COST ($ = $50) $$

Sandpiper Gulf Resort ★★★
5550 Estero Boulevard
Fort Myers Beach, FL 33931
☎ 239-463-5721
FAX 239-765-0039
TOLL-FREE 800-584-1449
www.sandpipergulfresort.com

QUALITY RATING   71
COST ($ = $50) $$

Hotel Information Chart: Southwest Florida (cont'd)

Sandpiper Inn
Sanibel Island ★★★
720 Donax Street
Sanibel, FL 33957
☎ 239-472-1529
FAX 239-472-0967
TOLL-FREE 877-22-PIPER
www.sandpiperinnsanibel.com

QUALITY RATING   74
COST ($ = $50) $$–

Sandy Beach Hideaway ★★½
2870 Estero Boulevard
Fort Myers Beach, FL 33931
☎ 239-463-1080

QUALITY RATING   64
COST ($ = $50) $+

Sanibel Beach Club II ★★★
205 Periwinkle Way
Sanibel, FL 33957
☎ 239-472-4526
FAX 239-472-0079
TOLL-FREE 800-330-1593
www.tkenoyer.com/sanibel.html

QUALITY RATING   71
COST ($ = $50) $$

Seahorse Cottages
on Sanibel ★★★
1223 Buttonwood Lane
Sanibel, FL 33957
☎ 239-472-4262
FAX 239-466-6149
www.seahorsecottages.com

QUALITY RATING   69
COST ($ = $50) $$

Shalimar Cottages and
Motel ★★★½
2823 West Gulf Drive
Sanibel, FL 33957
☎ 239-472-1353
FAX 239-472-6430
TOLL-FREE 800-995-1242
www.shalimar.com

QUALITY RATING   78
COST ($ = $50) $$$$–

Shipwreck Motel ★★½
237 Old San Carlos Boulevard
Fort Myers Beach, FL 33931
☎ 239-463-2381 or 463-4691
FAX 239-463-2040
www.motelfortmyersbeach.com

QUALITY RATING   60
COST ($ = $50) $$

Sundial Beach Resort ★★★½
1451 Middle Gulf Drive
Sanibel, FL 33957
☎ 239-472-4151
FAX 239-472-8892
TOLL-FREE 800-965-7772
www.sundialresort.com

QUALITY RATING   78
COST ($ = $50) $$$$$

Super 8 Motel ★★½
2717 Colonial Boulevard
Fort Myers, FL 33907
☎ 239-275-3500
FAX 239-275-5426
TOLL-FREE 800-800-8000
www.super8.com

QUALITY RATING   63
COST ($ = $50) $$

Tarpon Lodge ★★★
13771 Waterfront Drive
Pineland, FL 33945
☎ 239-283-3999
FAX 239-283-7658
www.tarponlodge.com

QUALITY RATING   70
COST ($ = $50) $$

Trianon Old Naples ★★★★½
955 Seventh Avenue South
Naples, FL 34102
☎ 239-435-9600
FAX 239-261-0025
TOLL-FREE 877-482-5228
www.trianon.com

QUALITY RATING   95
COST ($ = $50) $$$–

Tropical Winds Motel and
Cottages ★★★
4819 Tradewinds and Jamaica Drive
Sanibel, FL 33957
☎ 239-472-1765
FAX 239-472-1765
TOLL-FREE 866-646-1731
www.sanibeltropicalwinds.com

QUALITY RATING   68
COST ($ = $50) $$$

Tween Waters Inn ★★★
15951 Captiva Road
Captiva, FL 33924
☎ 239-472-5161
FAX 239-472-0249
TOLL-FREE 866-893-3646
www.tween-waters.com

QUALITY RATING   72
COST ($ = $50) $$$+

Wellesley Inn and Suites ★★★
4400 Ford Street Extension
Fort Myers, FL 33916
☎ 239-278-3949
FAX 239-278-3670
www.wellesleyinnandsuites.com

QUALITY RATING   67
COST ($ = $50) $$–

West Wind Inn ★★★½
3345 West Gulf Drive
Sanibel, FL 33957
☎ 239-472-1541
FAX 239-472-8134
TOLL-FREE 800-824-0476
www.westwindinn.com

QUALITY RATING   82
COST ($ = $50) $$$$–

White Sands Resort Club ★★★
260 Third Street South
Naples, FL 34102
☎ 239-261-4144
FAX 239-649-5891

QUALITY RATING   65
COST ($ = $50) $$

Sanibel Inn ★★★½
937 East Gulf Drive
Sanibel, FL 33957
☎ 239-472-3181
FAX 239-472-5234
TOLL-FREE 800-965-7772
www.sanibelinn.com

QUALITY RATING   80
COST ($ = $50) $$$$

Sanibel's Seaside Inn ★★★½
541 East Gulf Drive
Sanibel, FL 33957
☎ 239-472-1400
FAX 239-472-6518
TOLL-FREE 800-965-7772
www.seasideinn.com

QUALITY RATING   82
COST ($ = $50) $$$$+

Sea Court Inn ★★★
40 Tamiami Trail North
Naples, FL 34102
☎ 239-435-9700
FAX 239-435-0369
TOLL-FREE 800-325-7595
www.bestlodgingswflorida.com

QUALITY RATING   69
COST ($ = $50) $+

**Staybridge Suites by
Holiday Inn** ★★★
4805 Tamiami Trail North
Naples, FL 34103
☎ 239-643-8002
FAX 239-643-8069
TOLL-FREE 800-238-8000
www.staybridge.com

QUALITY RATING   70
COST ($ = $50) $$+

**Suburban Lodge of
Fort Myers** ★★★
10150 Metro Parkway
Fort Myers, FL 33912
☎ 239-938-0100
FAX 239-938-0370
www.suburbanhotels.com

QUALITY RATING   66
COST ($ = $50) $+

The Sun and the Moon Inn ★★★
3962 Pine Island Road
Matlacha, FL 33993
☎ 239-283-3192
TOLL-FREE 888-321-3192
www.sunandmoon.net

QUALITY RATING   70
COST ($ = $50) $$

Tarpon Tale Inn ★★★½
367 Periwinkle Way
Sanibel, FL 33957
☎ 239-472-0939
FAX 239-472-6202
TOLL-FREE 888-345-0939
www.tarpontale.com

QUALITY RATING   78
COST ($ = $50) $$$$−

Tradewinds ★★½
26385 Hickory Boulevard
Bonita Springs, FL 34134
☎ 239-992-2111

QUALITY RATING   64
COST ($ = $50) $$+

Trianon Bonita Bay ★★★★½
3401 Bay Commons Drive
Bonita Springs, FL 34134
☎ 239-948-4400
FAX 239-948-4401
TOLL-FREE 800-859-3939
www.trianon.com

QUALITY RATING   95
COST ($ = $50) $$$−

**Vanderbilt Beach
Resort House** ★★★½
9225 Gulf Shore Drive North
Naples, FL 34108
☎ 239-597-3144
FAX 239-597-2199

QUALITY RATING   82
COST ($ = $50) $$+

Vanderbilt Inn ★★★½
11000 Gulf Shore Drive
Naples, FL 34108
☎ 239-597-3151
FAX 239-597-3099
TOLL-FREE 800-643-8654
www.vanderbiltinn.com

QUALITY RATING   75
COST ($ = $50) $$$

**Waterside Inn
on the Beach** ★★★½
3033 West Gulf Drive
Sanibel, FL 33957
☎ 239-472-1345
FAX 239-472-2148
TOLL-FREE 800-741-6166
www.watersideinn.net

QUALITY RATING   76
COST ($ = $50) $$$$

Winyah Hotel and Suites ★★★
2038 West First Street
Fort Myers, FL 33901
☎ 239-332-2048
FAX 239-332-2058
www.winyah.com

QUALITY RATING   67
COST ($ = $50) $$−

PART THREE

MIAMI-DADE COUNTY

THE MAGICAL CAPITAL
of the AMERICAS

WE ALL KNOW MIAMI OFFERS THE WILD LIFE of South Beach, on the edge of the Atlantic. But what most don't appreciate is the wildlife just to the west, in the Everglades: Miami is the only metro area near two national parks and a preserve.

This combo of natural and human wonders helps to make this city special, and in demand. Rising skyscraper condos and hundreds of towering cranes attest to the lure.

Close your eyes and imagine Miami, and you'll come up with endless alluring visions: broad sands and fire-lit sandcastles along the moonlit Atlantic; palm-fringed, neon-lit bridges and the eye-popping skyline across Biscayne Bay; Art Deco hotels shimmering in the sun; sidewalks jammed with slender Europeans, buff models holding tiny pugs, and Lycra-clad Rollerbladers; symphonies and theatre performed on Lincoln Road; DJs and long-haired, long-legged Latinas and continentals clubbing until daybreak; towering cruise ships gliding past Spanish-style mansions; and artists and entrepreneurs dining under the stars and palms in January, near buzzy art galleries open till midnight.

That's Miami, right now. But Miami also evokes cocaine, Al Capone, *Miami Vice,* and *CSI: Miami.* This legendary city wears its reputation for beauty and illegal pleasure like jasmine perfume. A subtropical haven of the Americas, Greater Miami is nevertheless a city of 2 million, with about 10 million visitors a year, a city of incredible wealth and embarrassing poverty, and all the modern-day menaces that entails. Miami, where it seems more people speak Spanish than English and dozens of other languages blend in the balmy air, epitomizes the American spirit for retirees and immigrants from around the world, who have chosen it for new homes—maybe second or third homes.

Miami appears to be an international destination that doesn't require a passport. This melting pot can seem a discordant clash of cultures, best ignored in the rush to familiarity at the beach, a convention hall, or suburban communities up the coast. But Miami's mix of new buildings, new ideas, and ethnicities works, gloriously. It offers—now—the chance to luxuriate in a warm, vibrant, and gregarious milieu, where news from Havana, Caracas—or Paris—can overshadow the latest scandal in Washington.

In this section, we offer suggestions that reveal the essence of this sensual, seductive city that's reaching its ripe, heady prime. We give you explicit directions on how to visit Little Havana; where to sample the best in Haitian or Middle Eastern or fusion-Caribbean cuisine; and where you can walk down streets and hear not only Spanish but Creole, French, German, Russian, and Yiddish spoken within a single block. We'll introduce you to a vivid street life like that of no other city.

A BRIEF HISTORY

AT THE CONFLUENCE OF BISCAYNE BAY AND THE MIAMI RIVER, on Brickell Key, lies a mysterious pile of stones known as the Miami Circle. Recently unearthed during a building excavation for a luxury condo, and now protected, the site was created thousands of years ago by the area's earliest inhabitants, the legendary Tequesta Indians. The nearby Brickell Avenue drawbridge—often up as fishing and pleasure boats head between bay and river—flaunts a towering statue topped by one of these native settlers. They fished, hunted, and traded here in the mosquito-infested swamps, but little else is known. In more recent history, not much more than a hundred years ago, pioneers came from the north.

Miami vibrates with an enterprising spirit and at a frenetic pace, embodied in everything from family-owned grocery stores to huge corporations and banks. This hard-charging business community reflects the first Cuban refugees fleeing the Castro regime in the late 1950s—entrepreneurial and professional classes who often arrived penniless but brought with them the skills and drive to become successfully self-employed in their adopted country.

Historically Miami's pattern has been boom and bust. After all, the city was founded only a century ago on a long-shot business gamble that paid off. Through the decades that followed, Miami has ridden a roller coaster of dizzying successes and precipitous declines.

While South Florida's mild winters attracted visitors from the North during the mid- and late 1800s, it took an idea from a Cleveland businesswoman named Julia Tuttle to create the city of Miami. After resettling on the north bank of the Miami River in 1891, Tuttle began to plan her city—and worked to find a railroad magnate who would extend a line south to the tip of the Florida peninsula.

Henry M. Flagler constructed a line that reached Palm Beach in 1893, but he said he wasn't interested in extending it another 66 miles to tiny Miami. That is, until the winter of 1894–95, when a killer freeze destroyed most of Florida's valuable citrus crops—but cold didn't extend as far south as Miami. Legend holds that Tuttle sent Flagler a single orange blossom—a simple, eloquent, and final plea to extend his railroad line.

Whether the legend is true or not, Flagler changed his mind, and the line to Miami was completed on April 15, 1896. All 300 residents of Miami turned out to greet the locomotive—and a new era.

The Early 20th Century

Within a few months, a newspaper rolled off the press, local citizens voted to incorporate the town, streets were laid out, and churches and schools were established. The city was already promoting itself as "America's sun porch."

A modest boom ensued during the early years of the 20th century. Swamps were drained, marking the beginning of the demise of the Everglades; Government Cut—the future Port of Miami—was dug across the lower end of Miami Beach to improve access to Miami's harbor; and Flagler extended his railroad farther south to Key West in 1912.

Thousands of people threw out their wool coats, packed up, and moved south to take advantage of the year-round warmth and sunshine of Miami. In 1915, the citizens of Miami Beach voted to incorporate. The south end of the island already boasted several casinos, and holiday hotels began sprouting up on South Beach.

The Roaring '20s

Then the 1920s arrived, along with developers who carved up nearby farmland into subdivisions. The city's population doubled between 1920 and 1923 as dozens of new communities sprang up.

This was also the era of Prohibition; rumrunners thrived along South Florida's impossible-to-patrol coast. Mobsters moved in and operated with virtual immunity from the law. The city's reputation teetered on both the moral and geographical edge of America.

Miami in the early 1920s was real estate–crazy. Prices spiraled as property changed hands once, twice, three times. But most of the profits were on paper. Toward the end of 1925, sales at Coral Gables began to decline, and railroads announced an embargo of all but essential freight so they could repair their tracks, cutting off the supply of building materials.

The Pendulum Swings

But it took an act of nature to deliver a near-knockout blow. A hurricane struck on September 17, 1926, killing more than 100 people and leaving Miami in chaos. Houses were smashed, businesses destroyed, and boats tossed onto dry land. National headlines screamed, "Miami Is Wiped Out!" And the pessimistic press became self-fulfilling prophecy.

Over the next few years, Miami's population fled northward. Local leaders went bankrupt. But it wasn't all bad news: Some money came to Miami from outsiders who purchased Hialeah Park race-track, the city's aviation industry was born, and airports were built. During the Great Depression, the Civilian Conservation Corps constructed Greynolds and Matheson Hammock parks.

Slowly, tourism began to pick up in the 1930s, especially in Miami Beach, where new, modern hotels and apartments proliferated on Collins Avenue. Northerners swarmed south again to escape cold winter—and the Depression. More than 500 Art Deco structures were built, and tourists flocked to futuristic Miami Beach.

War . . . and Another Boom

The recovery didn't last long. The Japanese bombing of Pearl Harbor in 1941 and the U.S. declaration of war killed tourism. Nor did it help when a German U-boat torpedoed a tanker in full view of the Florida coast in February 1942. The city's hotels were empty.

That is, until the soldiers came to be trained in the warm climate of South Florida. By the end of 1942, the military had turned 147 hotels into barracks and many hotels into temporary hospitals for wounded soldiers. GIs trained on Miami Beach and German prisoners of war were interned at camps in suburban Kendall and Homestead.

After the war, thousands of former soldiers returned to South Florida with their families, became students on the GI Bill, and crowded the University of Miami. There was a new housing boom in the city. Farms were transformed into suburbs, and by the end of the 1950s the population of Greater Miami was nearing 1 million. The future of Miami looked good.

A Revolution Revolutionizes Miami

But Miami was to change radically after Fidel Castro deposed Cuban dictator Fulgencio Batista in 1959. After Castro declared himself a socialist, confiscated property, and nationalized many island businesses, thousands of Cubans left Havana daily—many with nothing more than the clothes they wore. Most of them came to Miami. Almost overnight, entire neighborhoods filled with people speaking only Spanish.

After the failed CIA-led Bay of Pigs invasion of Cuba in 1961 (still a sore subject for many exiled leaders) and the Cuban missile crisis of 1962 (in which Russia agreed to remove its missiles in return for a U.S. promise not to invade Cuba), Cuban exiles found themselves in Miami to stay. Over the years, thousands more political refugees fled Cuba on "freedom flights" to Miami, expanding the city's Hispanic population base. By 1973, the Cuban population of Miami had swelled to 300,000.

In the 1960s and 1970s, another wave of people moved to Miami: Jewish retirees from the north. By 1975, 300,000 Jews lived in Greater Miami, making the city's Jewish community second only to New York's in size. Most concentrated in Miami Beach, and today that city still hosts American Jews, many retired, during the winter months. But it is also host to the world.

Ethnic Tensions

Miami, alas, developed new problems in the second half of the 20th century. Urban renewal and hard-charging Cubans were squeezing out Miami's African American community, and many jobs were taken by recent immigrants. In 1968, Miami had its first race riot when Liberty City exploded just as Richard Nixon was delivering his acceptance speech at the Republican National Convention in Miami Beach. Long after the riot ended, racial tensions simmered.

Although a recession in the early 1970s was a setback, Miami was booming again at the end of the decade. Money poured into the city to satisfy America's demand for illegal narcotics. Yet at the same time, the legitimate business community prospered; the Cuban community, no longer made up of penniless refugees, thrived and ran successful enterprises throughout Miami. The city had turned into an international banking center as money flowed in from Latin America, rapid-transit construction was under way, and the downtown area was being revitalized.

Then, in 1980, blacks and disadvantaged Miamians rioted after a Tampa jury acquitted a white policeman of murdering a black man, Arthur McDuffie. New immigration trends compiled existing racial tension. Haitian "boat people" landed almost daily on South Florida beaches. Fidel Castro announced that anyone who wanted to leave Cuba could do so—and Miami Cubans sailed to Mariel Harbor, Cuba, to help would-be immigrants. They were forced to bring back inmates of Cuba's prisons and mental institutions. The city struggled under 125,000 new "Marielito" refugees, who drew scorn from the first wave of Cuban exiles. Many new refugees settled in South Beach, compounding the neighborhood's economic doldrums; most Miamians avoided the district of 1930s hotels and apartments at night.

Some Anglo residents of Miami grew angry, and many cars sported bumper stickers that read, "Will the last American leaving Miami please bring the flag?" A variation of white flight had set in, and Anglo residents began to leave Miami, often heading north to Broward County and beyond.

The early 1980s were turbulent years in Miami. Drug dealers pumped more than $10 billion into the economy, and the sale of handguns soared—as did the city's murder rate. In 1981, 621 people died violently in Dade County, and Miami earned a national reputation as "Murder Capital USA."

Miami Vice and a Jet-set Destination

But as it has with every other crisis, Miami bounced back. A new building boom started downtown. The city's image improved dramatically in 1984, when *Miami Vice* premiered on national television and revealed a city steeped in glamorous danger and lush, tropical beauty. In 1985, the city elected its first Cuban-born mayor, Xavier Suarez. The new Bayside Marketplace attracted tourists and shoppers downtown, and Pope John Paul II paid a visit in September 1987.

In the late 1980s, South Beach started a spectacular comeback. Hundreds of millions of dollars were spent renovating the Art Deco hotels and apartment buildings from the 1930s and 1940s. These whimsical buildings—which now compose a designated historical area—are today home to hotels, artists' lofts, trendy restaurants, oceanfront cafes, art galleries, clubs, and theaters. Jet-set celebrities are South Beach, aka SoBe, regulars.

MIAMI TODAY

MIAMI HAS CLEANED UP ITS ACT AND REDUCED crime against tourists. But some problems are not so easy to alleviate. Despite Miami's multicultural identity, ethnic divisions among African Americans, Anglos, Central Americans, Cubans, and Haitians are often appallingly clear, particularly outside the city's more integrated, affluent, and touristy neighborhoods. And the political scene reflects this division.

Travel industry experts say that in spite of the problems and the new era of global terrorism, Miami's future as a tourist destination remains superb: South Americans continue to be a rapidly expanding market for Florida tourism, and safety and security in the state far surpasses that of most Latin American countries. About half of the city's tourists are internationals, increasingly Europeans, looking to spend their strong euros. And North Americans, seeking warmth and fun, are a nonstop, low-cost flight away.

Miami's emphasis now is on culture—art, music, theater, dance—and the city's once-deficient performing-arts offerings are catching up big-time. These include the new Miami Performing Arts Center, designed by Cesar Pelli, rising on the Miami side of the MacArthur Causeway; the Miami Art Museum and the Miami Museum of Science and Planetarium, both moving to Bicentennial Park on Biscayne Bay; Art Basel Miami Beach, the American outpost of the world's greatest art sale and show; the expanding downtown districts of galleries and studios; a lively theater scene; concert, dance, and lecture series; the country's biggest book fair; and dozens of major festivals: There's more here culturally than anyone can possibly fit in.

MIAMI NEIGHBORHOODS

MANY OF MIAMI'S NEIGHBORHOODS ARE officially cities in their own right, and each has a distinctive character. Most can be explored on foot, but a car is still indispensable for getting from one neighborhood to another.

The following list of Miami's most popular neighborhoods starts in South Miami Beach; continues north along the ocean to Sunny Isles; crosses Biscayne Bay to North Miami and Aventura; and turns south to Little Haiti, downtown (with its new urban neighborhoods), Little Havana, Coral Gables, and cities in south Dade County.

SOUTH BEACH

CREATED YEARS AGO AS A PLACE FOR NORTHERNERS to escape cold winters and the Great Depression, South Miami Beach (now usually called South Beach or SoBe or even SoFi, for "south of Fifth") is a 23-block area on the tip of Miami Beach. The architecture is intentionally whimsical—a collage of Art Deco, streamlined moderne, and Spanish Mediterranean–revival styles adapted to the South Florida climate. And clusters of towering glass condos along Biscayne Bay now add a 21st-century dimension.

South Beach remains sizzling. The preservation movement that began in the early 1980s has produced a kaleidoscope of more than 800 fancifully decorated buildings in lollipop colors, many edged in neon at night. This is the first entire district in the 20th century to be placed on the National Register of Historic Places.

And it's fun. The streets are filled with fashion models and photographers, pouty young Europeans, spandexed fitness fanatics, and second-home owners and retirees hanging on as home prices keep going up. Also a requisite stop for celebs, South Beach is justifiably called the American Riviera. (Nowadays, in fact, you might even hear the actual Riviera called the European SoBe!)

Drawbacks? On weekends traffic slows to a crawl, and parking induces heartburn. While South Beach has a reputation for being safe, auto break-ins are a problem, so don't leave anything of value in your car. And keep a couple of dollars handy for valet parking. Many Miamians taxi to South Beach to avoid the hassle, particularly for festivals, which cram onlookers shoulder–to–(bare) shoulder.

South Beach hotels range from funky to lavish, usually with small rooms. Don't assume that a recently renovated exterior is an indication that the rooms got a face-lift, too. As with many of the folks on the street, facades are what counts.

The nightclub and street scenes go on all night, seven nights a week. If you're a light sleeper, rent a room on the upper floors, away

unofficial **TIP**
Don't miss an evening stroll down **Ocean Drive,** where the best Art Deco architecture faces the Atlantic and the beautiful people strut their stuff. End at South Point Park and watch the cruise ships going out to sea from Government Cut, under a Miami moon.

from the elevator and street—you may miss the ocean view, but you're more likely to get some Zs. For more on SoBe hotels, see Part Two, Accommodations.

If the constant procession of hardbodies, neohippies, perma-tanned geriatrics, punk rockers, and portfolio-carrying fashionistas isn't enough to keep you entertained, try SoBe's eclectic spread of boutiques, outdoor cafes, nightclubs, art galleries, restaurants, and bookstores. Stop into the architecturally interesting **Wolfsonian-FIU** museum to see grand examples of 19th- and 20th-century design.

Check out **Española Way,** a narrow Mediterranean fantasy of a street created in the 1920s, off Washington Avenue between 14th and 15th streets. The Sunday sidewalk market is especially delightful, spilling from the **Lincoln Road Mall.** It's a fun fair of art, artifacts, food, and plantings, all sold alfresco. But any day is a hoot on this street, which is filled with shops and galleries and action. And at night, the pedestrian street turns into an umbrella-covered open-air dining scene, lined with crowded cafe after cafe, perfect for people watching.

Seeking artsy pleasures beyond hedonism? The **Lincoln Theatre** hosts (in season) the New World Symphony, an academy composed of gifted young musicians led by Michael Tilson Thomas, and the newly refurbished **Colony Theater** is once again a precious Art Deco venue for cultural pleasures. The nearby **Jackie Gleason Theater of the Performing Arts** (locals call it TOPA) brings major shows to town.

CENTRAL MIAMI BEACH

THE MILE-LONG STRETCH OF MIAMI BEACH above Lincoln Road still reflects the 1940s and 1950s. Outrageous, ostentatious hotels and condos loom over the beach and Collins Avenue, from the ultrachic Delano to the **Fontainebleau,** a curving mass of 1950s "Miami Modern" designed by Morris Lapidus. But hotels along this strip are rapidly being converted to condo-hotels, or just condos, as the world seems to want in on all the fun.

More than ever, Miami Beach is a mix of commercial properties (hotels, restaurants, bars, grocery stores, travel agencies, and so on) and residential properties (mostly large condominium and apartment buildings). And the art scene is growing quickly.

Many of Miami Beach's wealthiest residents live west of Collins Avenue. Stroll or rent a bike to view exclusive homes along pine-tree-lined Alton Road, Pine Tree Drive, North Bay Road, and La Gorce Drive. Many former apartment buildings along Indian Creek have been turned into Art Deco condos and hotels popular with gay locals and visitors. Boat cruises of Biscayne Bay, with waterfront views of the homes, are available at the marina across from the **Eden Roc Hotel.**

In the 21st Street area, now called Collins Park, you'll find the excellent **Bass Museum,** an enhanced new library, and the **Miami City Ballet Rehearsal Hall** (where you can watch the dancers practice through big windows), all across from the ocean. A boardwalk along the beach stretches about 20 blocks north from here.

NORTH BEACH

ALONG THIS STRETCH OF FL A1A, A COMFORTABLE, low-key ambience contrasts with the high-octane pulse of South Beach. The communities of **Surfside, Bal Harbour,** and **Sunny Isles,** once dominated by Jewish and Canadian tourists and retirees, now house the rest of the world as well. Exclusive enclaves tower alongside small motels with easy access to the beach. The seemingly endless succession of high-rise waterfront buildings comprises the original "condo canyons" of Miami.

The **North Shore State Recreation Area,** between 91st and 95th Streets, is one of the few places in Miami that allows topless bathing—although European women tend to doff their tops all along Miami Beach's wide shoreline.

Tony Bal Harbour reflects big, big money. **Bal Harbour Shops,** amid lush foliage in a famed indoor-outdoor mall, offers expensive designer goods and has earned a reputation as one of the country's great shopping experiences.

Haulover Beach Park is where boats were once hauled over to the Intracoastal Waterway from the Atlantic. Today it offers uncrowded beaches—including a nude beach—a marina, kayak rentals, and a great place to fly kites.

At the northern end of Miami Beach, condo-lined Sunny Isles used to be a busy, tacky commercial strip with a "main street" along Collins Avenue and motels decked out with fake camels and dunes. Enjoy the whimsy of the few remaining theme structures before the chain hotels and luxury condos buy them out.

Wolfie Cohen's Rascal House, a restaurant and sandwich shop in Sunny Isles, is a remnant of the past, and one of Miami Beach's quintessential monuments to eating (along with Joe's Stone Crab in South Beach).

NORTH MIAMI–NORTH MIAMI BEACH

COMMUNITIES SURROUNDING BISCAYNE BAY (across the water from Miami Beach) and north toward Broward County include the bland, the luxurious, and the gritty.

Incorporated in 1995, **Aventura** is an upscale residential and shopping mecca featuring high-rises, luxurious single-family homes, and lush tropical landscaping that hugs the Broward County line. This booming enclave of 23,000 residents on the Intracoastal Waterway is a magnet for young families, retirees, and single professionals. A new town center, modern and dramatic, is going up, designed by the famed Miami architectural group Arquitectonica International.

While the 4.3-mile **Don Soffer Aventura Fitness Trail** is a major attraction for exercise buffs, the town's major attraction is the gargantuan **Aventura Mall,** the biggest shopping center in the Miami area, with more than 250 stores.

Around the area are a variety of interesting destinations, some of them world-famous. **Hialeah Park,** where thoroughbreds once raced, has lush landscaping and 400 pink flamingos. **Opa-Locka** was founded by real estate genius and aviation pioneer Glenn Curtiss in the 1920s, and although an economically struggling neighborhood today, it contains restored Moorish-influenced architecture. At **Miami Jai-Alai,** also founded by Curtiss in the 1920s, place wagers on teams of men who play a sort of high-speed racquetball with basket gloves—worth a peek, and a bet.

The **Ancient Spanish Monastery** is a European complex erected stone by stone here in the subtropics, and a surprise treat. And the 23,000-square-foot **Museum of Contemporary Art (MOCA)** mounts world-class exhibitions and offers jazz on some weekends.

Major sporting venues such as **Calder Race Track** (horse racing), the **Golf Club of Miami,** and the **Pro Player Stadium** (formerly Joe Robbie Stadium and home of the Miami Dolphins) are in the vicinity.

LITTLE HAITI

IMMIGRANTS FROM HAITI ARE A MAJOR ETHNIC group in Miami, and a visit to Little Haiti is a chance to encounter this rich Caribbean culture. Yet the neighborhood's name promises more than it can deliver: This is no well-defined Chinatown or Little Italy, but an amorphous community with few architectural features to make it stand out from the rest of sprawling Miami. Look for bright paintings and wall art in a typically Haitian style.

The best bet for first-time visitors is the **Caribbean Marketplace** (5927 NE Second Avenue). The open-air marketplace—planned, alas, for demolition when a modernized marketplace takes its place—was designed to resemble the Iron Market in Port-au-Prince. During the day, visits to neighborhood churches and restaurants are safe, but unfortunately we can't recommend visiting the area at night.

NORTH OF DOWNTOWN: THE EAST SIDE ARTS DISTRICTS, THE DESIGN DISTRICT, MID-MIAMI, AND WYNWOOD

COMFORTABLE RESIDENTIAL COMMUNITIES near Biscayne Bay, such as Miami Shores, Morningside, and Belle Meade, are now joined by emerging neighborhoods, some so new that their names are still up for grabs. East Side, Upper East Side, Wynwood, Biscayne Landing, the Performing Arts District, and MidTown are just a few appellations for this growing area. Warehouses, worn motels, parking lots, and unused railroad tracks are morphing into clusters of galleries, new restaurants, shopping, and high- and low-rise condos, with adjoining retail and pedestrian-friendly walkways and electrified trams.

You could spend days exploring the excitement of these newly vibrant, artsy, urban neighborhoods. New galleries and restaurants are opening constantly in the Wynwood area, which some call "the SoHo of the South." For instance, try not to miss the Rubell collection, an outstanding grouping of contemporary art in Wynwood.

DOWNTOWN MIAMI

DOWNTOWN MIAMI, FOR DECADES SO DEPRESSED that it could have been renamed "downtrodden Miami," is slowly evolving into a 24-7 city center. Streets are still lined with cut-rate shops hawking electronics, luggage, jewelry, and clothes, but glamorous new condo skyscrapers and condo conversions of downtown buildings will soon add thousands of full-time residents. The free **MetroMover** gets you around to the new Macy's and the pyramid-topped City Hall, and past the Spanish-style Freedom Tower and the Gusman Center for the Performing Arts.

Bayside, the open-air shopping center in Bayfront Park on Biscayne Boulevard (next to the American Airlines Sports Center, home of the Miami Heat), offers boat rides into the sunset and a festive atmosphere throughout the day.

What else? A few exotic eateries, small Latin American cafes, and the Miami Art Museum at **Metro-Dade Cultural Center** are already in place.

At night, most of downtown Miami is still as dead as last night's salsa and chips—except for the glorious, jaw-droppingly exotic **Gusman Center for the Performing Arts,** with stars on the ceiling and a peacock perched on a backlit Moorish facade surrounding the stage. Formerly the Olympia Theater, a landmark movie palace from the 1920s, the building has been refurbished to its former glory and is the scene for many of the city's cultural pleasures, including dance, lectures, and film festivals.

unofficial **TIP**
The **Seybold Building,** in the city center, houses dozens of jewelry stores and artisans, where you can find some excellent discounts.

Happily, the Gusman Center is slowly acquiring new neighbors and a better atmosphere. Museums will be moving to a newly designed Museum Park along the bay. The new **Miami Performing Arts Center,** between the MacArthur and Venetian causeways, becomes a reality in 2006. Improved landscaping and lighting and a revitalized baywalk along the Miami River are turning this downtown into a pulsing presence, both night and day.

And street fairs, a farmers' market, and continuous festivals like the great **Miami Book Fair,** at the booming downtown campus of Miami Dade Junior College, increasingly draw many downtown.

SOUTH OF DOWNTOWN MIAMI– BRICKELL AVENUE

BRICKELL AVENUE IS MIAMI'S FIFTH AVENUE and Wall Street in one. The wide thoroughfare is lined by the largest group of international banks in the United States and a parade of high-rises, fine hotels, and condos perched among sculpture-filled piazzas, fountains, and lush South Florida foliage from the Miami River (the southern border of downtown) to Coconut Grove. The collection of banks is partially the result of political instability throughout Latin America in the late 1970s, when Miami became a safe haven for corporate money and a new corporate-banking center.

The area is home to seasonal international visitors and longtime locals with bucks. One famous condo is the **Atlantis,** designed by the famed Arquitectonica International group and an icon of the 1980s TV show *Miami Vice;* its gaping square in the center of the building includes a palm tree, Jacuzzi, and red spiral staircase. Nearby **Brickell Key** offers luxury condos and the Mandarin Oriental Hotel, and charming pastel-hued **Brickell Village** is a growing pedestrian-friendly neighborhood, with condos, restaurants, galleries, and boutiques, just west of Brickell Avenue.

LITTLE HAVANA (CALLE OCHO)

CUBANS HAVE MADE A TREMENDOUS IMPACT on Miami over the last decades and remain the largest and most visible ethnic group in the city. However, the streets of Little Havana (located a few miles west of downtown and centered on SW Eighth Street) offer mostly neighborhood shops, not tourist destinations. In fact, the name "Little Havana" is misleading: While the words suggest a self-contained ethnic enclave, the reality is an amorphous neighborhood without strict boundaries that doesn't look very different from other parts of Miami.

unofficial **TIP**
Visit Little Havana for lunch or dinner at **Versailles Restaurant** (3555 SW Eighth Street; ☎ 305-444-0240), open Sunday–Thursday, 8 a.m.–2 a.m.; Friday, 8 a.m.–3:30 a.m.; and Saturday, 8 a.m.–4:30 a.m. It's huge, cheap, and easy to find, and parking is ample.

Yet old men in guayabera shirts still play dominoes in Domino Park, and you'll also see plenty of examples of "Spanglish": signs and billboards that charmingly mix English and Spanish, like one motel's boast, "Open 24 Horas."

The best place for a stroll in Little Havana is **Calle Ocho** (KAH-yeh OH-cho, Spanish for "Eighth Street"), where streetside counters sell *café cubano* (thimble-sized cups of sweet, highly charged Cuban coffee that Anglos call "jet fuel") and the odor of cigars being rolled and bread baking fills the air. Memorial Boulevard, a newly created pedestrian greenway along SW 13th Avenue, is where the locals stroll.

Two sites reflect on recent Cuban history. To honor the disastrous Bay of Pigs invasion in the 1960s, an eternal flame burns at the **Brigade 2506 Memorial** at SW Eighth Street and SW 13th Avenue. And you can now see perhaps the most famous and controversial shrine in Little Havana—the little two-bedroom house where 6-year-old Elian Gonzalez stayed with his relatives for six months after the harrowing raft journey from Cuba that killed his mother. He's back in Cuba with his father, but the house remains a museum.

CORAL GABLES

EARNING ITS NICKNAME, "THE CITY BEAUTIFUL," the Gables is one of America's first planned communities. Dating from the 1920s, this gracious enclave is filled with upscale commerce, expensive Mediterranean-style homes, manicured lawns, and lush foliage. The layout of the place, however, resembles a maze, with street names in Spanish written on small white stones at ground level—impossible to read at night. As a result, it's easy to get lost. **Coral Way** connects Miami to the Gables, starting on the northern end as a banyan-shaded commercial street and becoming a grand residential way. The charming **Merrick House and Gardens,** at Coral Way and Toledo Street, was built in the 1890s and is the boyhood home of the man who planned the Gables, George Merrick.

Other intriguing sites include the **Venetian Pool,** a freshwater-coral-rock lagoon carved out of a quarry (bring a swimsuit, a towel, and five bucks); the glamorous Spanish-style **Biltmore Hotel,** built in the 1920s and fabulously restored after decades of neglect (it has one of the largest pools anywhere and a famous Sunday brunch around the fountain in the courtyard); and the **Miracle Mile,** a half mile of expensive shops, restaurants, and boutiques, all newly enhanced. Peek inside the restored **Omni Colonnade Hotel;** the rotunda and lobby feature lots of marble. The building was the former office of George Merrick.

Merrick Park, a vast new indoor-outdoor village shopping area, rivals Bal Harbour for fashionable stores, fine restaurants, and high-end atmosphere.

And the **University of Miami,** offers such attractions as lush grounds to stroll; the Lowe Art Museum; the Ring Theatre; Gusman Concert Hall; and the Bill Cosford Cinema, showing independent foreign films.

COCONUT GROVE

"THE GROVE," MIAMI'S FORMER BOHEMIAN quarter, today mixes trendy bars and restaurants, galleries and boutiques, and decidedly young crowds. Although not as fashionable as South Beach, Coconut

Grove offers people-watchers another outstanding opportunity to sit at an outdoor cafe and watch guys drag tourists around in rickshaws, fashion victims strut their stuff, in-line skaters weave through bumper-to-bumper traffic, and hip-looking cops ride by on mountain bikes. The west section of the Grove includes an area originally settled by Bahamians, one of the oldest African-American communities in Florida.

The Barnacle, on the bay across from the Coconut Grove Playhouse, is considered the oldest house in Miami, and you can stroll through its shaded tropical gardens at no charge.

Shoppers can browse New Age bookstores, lingerie stores, a surfboard boutique, a Harley-Davidson dealership, and flower shops. **CocoWalk,** a multilevel mall done in pink and beige, features movies, chain restaurants, and a courtyard with live music on evenings and weekends.

The outrageous, satirical **Mango Strut,** in which locals dress up and parade in a mockery of the year's events; the huge, famed **Coconut Grove Art Fair;** and the now-venerable **Coconut Grove Playhouse** all add luster and creative energy to this tropical haven of sailboats on the bay and lushly landscaped bungalows.

KEY BISCAYNE

UNLESS YOU'VE GOT A YACHT, THE ONLY WAY to reach this tropical island ten minutes from downtown is via the Rickenbacker Causeway ($1 toll). The island, more like New York's Hamptons than SoBe, features some of the best public beaches in the Miami area—broad and duned, with calm waters, they're perfect for swimming. The **Miami Seaquarium,** the city's sea-mammal sanctuary, is located on Virginia Key, the island that the causeway crosses before reaching Key Biscayne (and until the 1950s the only area where black residents could swim and sunbathe legally). On the 5-mile-long causeway, visitors can pull over, park their cars, and rent sailboards, kayaks, and Jet Skis for zooming around the placid waters of Biscayne Bay.

unofficial **TIP**
For those traveling with pets, the beaches of Biscayne Bay allow dogs.

In the spring, the **NASDAQ-100 Open** features top-seeded tennis players in a well-regarded tournament.

Two state parks are located on Key Biscayne. At the tip, **Bill Baggs Cape Florida State Park** offers 406 acres of tropical plants and serene beaches and a 19th-century lighthouse, one of the oldest structures in South Florida. There is a nominal fee to enter. For swimming, we recommend **Crandon Park,** with its wide expanses of sand and calm waters. Pack a lunch and swimming gear. Public restrooms are available for changing.

KENDALL AND PINECREST

AS YOU CONTINUE SOUTH IN DADE COUNTY, A FEW attractions are worth the drive. The premier tourist destination is **Metrozoo,** still a world-class zoo even after the devastation wrought by Hurricane Andrew in 1992. Other nearby attractions will appeal to train and airplane buffs, respectively: the **Gold Coast Railroad Museum** and the **Weeks Air Museum.**

The Falls, on South Dixie Highway, is the most glamorous of the many area shopping arcades—water and foliage are lushly used to counterpoint restaurants, boutiques, and major stores, such as Bloomingdale's.

HOMESTEAD AND FLORIDA CITY

ABOUT AN HOUR SOUTH OF DOWNTOWN MIAMI, Homestead is growing rapidly as an affordable residential location. It has fully recovered from the devastation of Hurricane Andrew, when thousands left the area. Homestead used to be populated by a feisty mix of Florida crackers, farm workers, and military retirees who had served in the former Homestead Air Force base. Today, northerners and commuters are moving in to escape spiraling housing prices in Miami.

Known mainly for its produce farms and easy entrance to the **Everglades,** the **Keys,** and coral-reef-rich **Biscayne National Park,** the area has also retained a taste of an earlier era that becomes more special through the years.

Simple pleasures include antiquing on **Krome Avenue; Cawley Square,** with turn-of-the-20th-century architecture and a tearoom that serves lunch; **The Aviary,** a bird shop worth a peek; cinnamon buns, fruit pies, and milkshakes at **Knaus Farm,** run by Mennonites; **Redland Fruit and Spice Park,** 35 acres where you can walk amid 500 varieties of subtropical plantings, including fruits, spices, herbs and nuts; and you-pick-'em strawberries and tomatoes, the gathering of which is a luscious, cost-effective activity for families at many of the farms in the area.

To cool off, local families enjoy **Homestead Bayfront Park,** with its saltwater tidal pool, playground, and picnic area. And a fledgling arts community includes **ArtSouth,** on Krome Avenue, with studios and galleries. You can take classes, see artists at work, and attend stage performances.

Other nearby attractions may seem a bit offbeat but give a true sense of South Florida life. They include the **Monkey Jungle** and the **Coral Castle,** a three-acre complex carved out of local coral rock from 1920 to 1940 by a lovelorn Latvian immigrant. (Folk art to some, kitsch to others!) And at night, South Dade offers laid-back lounges with local music to relax from all the stimulation.

Florida City, two miles southwest of Homestead, is the southernmost city on the Florida peninsula, and aside from agriculture, its claim to fame is being the entrance to the Everglades. Local eateries and lodging cater to the nature-loving crowd.

GATHERING INFORMATION

FOR ADDITIONAL INFORMATION ON ENTERTAINMENT, sightseeing, maps, shopping, dining, and lodging in Greater Miami, call or write the **Visitor Service Center at the Greater Miami Convention and Visitors Bureau** (701 Brickell Avenue, Suite 2700, Miami 33131; ☎ 800-933-8448 or 305-539-3034).

Ask for a free copy of *Greater Miami and The Beaches Vacation Planner,* a biannual publication with nearly 200 pages of information, including basic stuff such as post office locations, annual rainfall, language services, colleges and universities, hospitals, and real estate agents.

If you need specific information, ask for it when you call or write. For example, if you're planning on staying at a hotel or motel away from traditional tourist haunts and need to know if it's in a safe neighborhood, the folks at the Visitor Service Center can help. And of course, check out the Internet for information on your particular interests.

WHERE TO FIND TOURIST INFORMATION IN MIAMI

IF YOU'RE SHORT ON MAPS OR NEED MORE information on sightseeing, restaurants, hotels, shopping, or things to do in the Greater Miami area, pick up maps and brochures at:

- Miami International Airport A Tourist/Information Center on Level 2, Concourse E, across from the hotel, is open 24 hours a day.
- Greater Miami Convention and Visitors Bureau (701 Brickell Avenue, Suite 2700; ☎ 305-539-3800) It's not particularly convenient for visitors who just want to pick up a map, but the view from these 27th-floor offices is spectacular. Park in the garage, and don't forget to have your parking validated.
- Miami Beach Chamber of Commerce (333 41st Street, Miami Beach; ☎ 305-672-1270) is open Monday–Friday, 9 a.m.–5 p.m.
- Coconut Grove Chamber of Commerce (2820 McFarlane Road, Coconut Grove; ☎ 305-444-7270) is open Monday–Friday, 9 a.m.–5 p.m.
- Sunny Isles Resort Association (17070 Collins Avenue, Suite 266B, at the Milam's Supermarket shopping center; ☎ 305-947-5826) is open Monday–Friday, 9 a.m.–2 p.m.
- Greater Homestead/Florida City Chamber of Commerce (43 North Krome Avenue, Homestead; ☎ 305-247-2332 [Miami], 800-388-9669 [Florida and U.S.]) is open Monday–Friday, 8:30 a.m.–5 p.m.
- Area Sears stores There are tourist information centers at Aventura Mall, 19505 Biscayne Boulevard, Aventura; ☎ 305-935-1110; Coral Gables, 3655 SW 22nd Street (Coral Way at Douglas Road), Coral Gables; ☎ 305-460-3400; Miami International Mall, 1625 NW 107th Street,

Miami; ☎ 786-845-9502; and Westland Mall, 1625 West 49th Street, Hialeah; ☎ 305-364-3800. Most are open Monday–Saturday, 10 a.m.–9 p.m., and Sunday, noon–6 p.m.

▌ ARRIVING

BY PLANE

VIRTUALLY ALL FOREIGN VISITORS FLY INTO Miami International Airport (MIA), but domestic flyers have a choice: Fort Lauderdale Hollywood International Airport, a smaller facility, is well worth considering. It's only 30 minutes north of downtown Miami, close to Interstate 95, and convenient for folks headed to Miami Beach because they can skip the major highways by taking FL A1A south. While not as close to most Miami destinations as its big brother to the south, this airport offers peace of mind to visitors who are anxious about safety when they drive to and from Miami International. For more information, see Part Four, Broward County.

MIA is the ninth-largest airport in the United States, and number three in the number of international passengers it handles. More airline companies (100) fly into this airport than any other in the country, averaging more than 1,400 takeoffs and landings a day. MIA has service to every major city in Latin America and the Caribbean, as well as connections to Europe and the Middle East. All told, MIA makes connections to about 200 cities on five continents; more than 33 million passengers fly in and out of the facility each year.

The Dade County–owned airport has embarked on a $5.4 billion expansion program scheduled to be completed in 2007. Improvements will include increasing the number of gates to nearly 140, adding three new passenger concourses, upgrading baggage-handling systems, and doubling the amount of retail space. But the second-floor departure level of the horseshoe-shaped terminal is already jammed with boutiques, bookstores, a hotel (with 260 rooms), bars, gift shops, restaurants, and a culturally diverse flow of people from around the world.

unofficial **TIP**
If you're faced with a long walk between terminals, take the elevator to Level 3 for a "horizontal escalator" that will save wear and tear on your feet.

In spite of its size, however, MIA is an easy airport to navigate. From your gate, follow signs to the baggage area on the lower level; bus, taxi, SuperShuttle service, passenger car pickup, and rental car limos are outside the door. Directly across the street is a multilevel garage for short-term parking.

Renting a Car at Miami International Airport

Some visitors are more concerned about personal safety after they leave the airport than they are in the air. While we think Miami's bad reputation for visitor safety is largely undeserved, the airport is located about 8 miles west of downtown Miami in a confusing, economically depressed, and crime-ridden area.

Most Miami vacationers rent cars if they don't bring their own, and most MIA rental-car agencies are located outside the airport. Shuttles will take you to them safely, but getting to your hotel is more confusing. Poor highway signs and a landscape with few landmarks (at least to out-of-town visitors) compound the problem of finding your way out of a rental agency.

When you rent your car, get a map and explicit directions from the agency clerk to the closest highway that leads to your final destination. And read "How to Avoid Crime and Keep Safe in Public Places" on pages 37–42 for advice on how to keep from being an easy mark for crooks as you drive around Miami. Hang on to the rental-agency map: When returning your car, it will come in handy on the confusing and poorly marked roadways around MIA.

SuperShuttle

Another alternative for getting out of MIA without your own car or ride from a friend is SuperShuttle, a van service that can accommodate up to 11 passengers at a clip. It operates 7 days a week, 24 hours a day, and fares are lower than taxis. Rates begin around $10 per person (free for children ages 3 and under) for downtown hotels and Coral Gables, $12 for South Beach, and $14–$16 for mid–Miami Beach destinations. Call ☎ 305-871-2000 the day before your return flight to arrange a ride back to the airport; keep in mind the shuttle typically makes two additional stops before heading to MIA, so schedule your pickup time accordingly.

BY CAR

MOST DRIVERS TO MIAMI ARRIVE FROM THE north via **I-95,** which begins south of downtown and continues north along the Atlantic seaboard all the way to Maine; it's the major north–south expressway on the East Coast.

Florida's Turnpike, a toll highway that starts near Orlando and Walt Disney World, runs down the center of the Florida peninsula, then heads east to Fort Pierce on the Atlantic coast. From there, the road parallels I-95 south to Miami. The Homestead Extension of Florida's Turnpike skirts Greater Miami to the west. This is the route to take if you're headed to the Keys.

Another major highway, **I-75,** better known as the Everglades Parkway, funnels motorists to Miami from Naples, Fort Myers, Saint Petersburg, Tampa, and other points along Florida's west coast. **US 41,** also called the Tamiami Trail and Alligator Alley, connects Miami and the Everglades to the west.

US 1 is the stoplight-laden road that I-95 and Florida's Turnpike replaced, but the old highway is still intact, a diversion from highway driving. Though it's not a practical route for visitors on a tight schedule (traffic lights, shopping centers, and congestion often slow traffic to a crawl, and the road is regarded as one of the most unpleasant driving experiences in South Florida), US 1 still affords glimpses of beaches, palm trees, occasional Florida kitsch, and plenty of strip shopping centers.

FL A1A is even better for folks weary of interstates—but, alas, even slower. Much of this venerable state highway runs directly along the beach. For visitors who fly into Fort Lauderdale Hollywood International Airport and are headed to Miami Beach, A1A is the way to go . . . if you're not in a rush.

The following north–south route may sound complicated, but it's much faster than either US 1 or A1A: Driving north to Miami from the Keys on US 1, get on Florida's Turnpike, Homestead Extension, in Florida City; US 1 between here and Miami is often unpredictably congested. Then take FL 874 North (the Don Shula Expressway) to FL 826 North (the Palmetto Expressway); next, go east on the Dolphin Expressway (FL 836), which goes past Miami International Airport and links up with I-95 near downtown Miami.

The Penalty for Getting Lost: More on Driving around Miami

Greater Miami is a sprawling metropolis crisscrossed by busy expressways passing through neighborhoods that can change character from gentrified to seedy within a block. Sooner or later most visitors fall victim to Miami's infuriating lack of street signs and inadequate highway signs. Many visitors aren't prepared for the sharp contrasts that exist between trendy places near the beach and economically disadvantaged neighborhoods west of Biscayne Boulevard in Miami. Don't be fooled; the difference in safety may not be as wide as you think (both areas are relatively safe, but always be wary of pickpockets and opportunists).

BY TRAIN

AMTRAK OPERATES A SMALL, MODERN TERMINAL near Hialeah Park, northwest of downtown Miami. It's not very convenient if your destination is the beach or downtown Miami—and the neighborhood is a bit rough. A Metrorail station (☎ 305-770-3131 for transit information) is about eight blocks away. Outside the terminal, board Metrobus L, which takes you to the elevated-train station; the fare is $1.50 plus 50¢ for a transfer to the above-ground train.

unofficial **TIP**
Check the bulletin board inside the train station for current bus, Metrorail, Metrobus, and driving information.

The terminal is located at 8303 NW 37th Avenue; for recorded arrival and departure information, call Amtrak at ☎ 800-872-7245. For ticket prices and reservations, call ☎ 305-835-1222. To reach the station by car from I-95, take NW 79th Street west to NW 37th Avenue, and turn right;

the station is a few blocks north, where the street dead-ends. Signs will help direct you.

GETTING TO THE PORT OF MIAMI

ONE OF MIAMI'S GREAT SIGHTS IS CRUISE SHIPS floating from the port down Government Cut toward the Atlantic. Miami is the "Cruise Capital of the World," with more than 3 million passengers a year sailing from the Port of Miami, the home of about two dozen cruise ships—the world's largest year-round fleet. Cruise passengers can choose from the world's most popular ports of call on sea vacations ranging from 3- and 4-day excursions to voyages up to 11 days. Destinations include exotic ports in the Caribbean, South America, the coastal resorts of Mexico, the Bahamas, and Key West. Passengers enjoy tropical weather year-round virtually from the start of their voyages—a big attraction for vacationers from northern climates and a key to Miami's leadership in the cruise industry.

For cruise passengers flying into Miami International Airport who booked a cruise with airfare included, getting to the ship is easy: Representatives from cruise-ship operators, holding signs, greet passengers as they enter the passenger terminal. Luggage is transferred automatically to the ship, and passengers board motorcoaches for the quick trip (less than 30 minutes) to the dock. Your luggage is later delivered to your stateroom.

If you booked your own flight to Miami, don't expect to be greeted by an official from the cruise line. Instead, proceed to the lower level, pick up your luggage, step outside, and take a cab to the Port of Miami. Taxi rates are $21 for up to five passengers.

If you're driving, the Port of Miami is easy to find: It's located on Dodge Island in Biscayne Bay between Miami and Miami Beach, and can be reached from Miami via Port Boulevard. From I-95, take Exit 2A to downtown and follow the signs to Biscayne Boulevard; Port Boulevard is next to Bayside Marketplace. From I-395 (Exit 2D east on I-95, toward Miami Beach), take the Biscayne Boulevard exit south to downtown and follow signs to the Port of Miami. Parking is located in front of the terminals for $10 a day, payable prior to embarking. Have your cruise tickets

unofficial **TIP**
Folks who drive to the Port of Miami or who book their own airfare and aren't whisked to their ship on a bus can take advantage of a wider range of duty-free goods at **Miami Duty Free (MDF),** a clean, uncluttered shop located at 125 NE Eighth Street in downtown Miami. Just present your cruise or flight ticket to the security guard, select and pay for your goods, and MDF will deliver them to your plane or ship on the day of departure. Items include liquor, perfumes, Wedgwood china, Waterford crystal, and Rolex watches, all at prices 20%–40% below retail. Salespeople at MDF speak seven languages; the shop is open 10 a.m.–6 p.m. daily. For more information, call ☎ 305-377-0104.

handy, and drop off your luggage at the terminal before parking; the luggage will be sent to your cabin.

The Port of Miami has 12 recently renovated air-conditioned cruise-passenger terminals that are wheelchair accessible and feature duty-free shopping, ground-level customs clearance, and easy access to cars, buses, and taxis. Two new cruise docks have just been developed, increasing the port's size and convenience. In addition, the terminals are color coded and marked with the name of the ship, which makes it easy for folks driving to the port to find the right one. Long-term parking is across from the terminals. Due to increased concerns about terrorism, security measures have been adopted that prevent noncruising visitors from boarding the ships before they sail.

GETTING AROUND

THE MAJOR HIGHWAYS

IMMEDIATELY SOUTH OF DOWNTOWN, I-95 ends and merges with **US 1,** also called South Dixie Highway. US 1 swings southwest along Biscayne Bay through congested suburbs that include the cities of Coral Gables, Cutler Ridge, Homestead, Kendall, Perrine, and South Miami. South Dixie Highway is infamous for its seemingly endless number of traffic lights and horrendous traffic jams.

Forming Greater Miami's western border is **Florida's Turnpike, Homestead Extension.** Folks heading south from Miami and Miami Beach to visit southern Dade County's attractions—or to tour the Florida Keys, Key Biscayne, or the Everglades—should skip US 1 and take **FL 836** (the Dolphin Expressway) to Florida's Turnpike and head south toward Homestead on this toll road.

Other major highways that visitors to Miami need to know about include **FL 112,** aka the Airport Expressway, a toll road that links Miami International Airport with I-95 and Miami Beach; FL 836, the major east–west link connecting Florida's Turnpike, MIA, I-95, downtown Miami, and South Miami Beach; **FL 826,** or the Palmetto Expressway, a major commuter route that runs north–south between MIA and Florida's Turnpike before heading east to I-95 in North Miami; and **FL 874,** the Don Shula Expressway, which links the Palmetto Expressway and Florida's Turnpike in South Miami.

I-95

Interstate 95 is the north–south route connecting all major highways in South Florida . . . and when traffic isn't backed up ten miles by construction delays or an accident, travelers can breeze from Coconut Grove in the south to North Miami, the airport, and Miami Beach in minutes.

miami at a glance

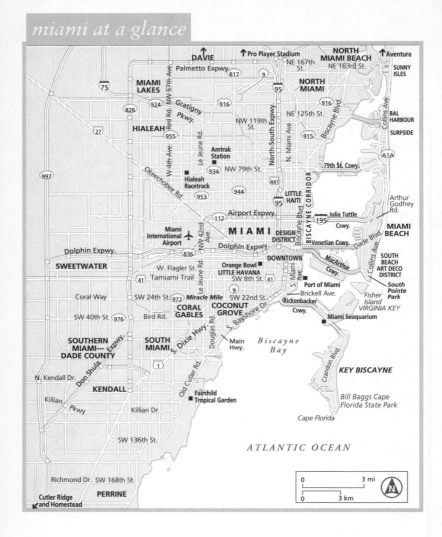

Poor signage, confusing detours, and a peculiar mix of drivers indigenous to South Florida can induce soaring blood pressure and moments of terror—even in experienced drivers who routinely handle the frustrations of driving in other big American cites.

Study a road map carefully before venturing out, check the *Miami Herald* for a listing of construction delays and lane closures (often scheduled at night, causing backups that rival rush-hour traffic snarls), avoid driving in rush-hour traffic, and drive defensively.

CAUSEWAYS TO MIAMI BEACH

THE CITY OF MIAMI BEACH IS ON A BARRIER island across Biscayne Bay from Miami. Getting on and off the island means crossing long bridges, called causeways. You've got a number of choices to make.

GETTING TO SOUTH BEACH The best-known link between Miami and its sister city across the bay is the **MacArthur Causeway.** This toll-free (but not drawbridge-free) road provides a high-speed link between downtown Miami and South Beach (the southern end of Miami Beach). From downtown, the MacArthur Causeway is easy to find. Take **Biscayne Boulevard** (US 1) north a few blocks past Bayside Marketplace, and bear right onto the multilane highway that crosses the bridge. (A landmark: the ugly orange *Miami Herald* building anchors the causeway to the mainland on the left.) From I-95, take **I-395** (Exit 2D), which puts you directly on the MacArthur Causeway to Miami Beach.

Along the way you cross Watson Island (the home of the newly expanded Parrot Jungle Island and Children's Museum). You'll pass the Port of Miami on the right, and glamorous Palm and Star islands on the left, with multimillion waterfront mansions. Ritzy Fisher Island has its own little ferry that crosses Government Cut from the causeway, so that only those invited can come over.

When you reach Miami Beach, Fifth Street and the Art Deco District are straight ahead; bear left onto **Alton Road** if your destination is farther north and you want to miss the congestion of Collins Avenue (Miami Beach's main drag); bear right to reach the Miami Beach Marina, South Pointe Park, and Joe's Stone Crab.

One final note: The return trip from Miami Beach to Miami at sunset into night offers one of the most impressive and beautiful cityscapes in the world—especially on weekends, when cruise ships are framed by the lights of multicolored high-rises in the background.

GETTING TO MID–MIAMI BEACH The **Julia Tuttle Causeway** (I-195) is the main link between I-95, Biscayne Boulevard, and mid–Miami Beach; it's definitely the route to take if you want to avoid the congestion of downtown Miami and the almost 'round-the-clock insanity of South Beach. It's also a straight shot from MIA; **FL 112,** the Airport Expressway, changes route numbers when it crosses I-95 and becomes I-195 as it heads east over the Tuttle Causeway toward Miami Beach.

The causeway drops you off at **41st Street** (Arthur Godfrey Road) on Miami Beach; continue straight to **Indian Creek Road** and turn right if you're going south. If you're headed north, turn left on **Collins Avenue** (FL A1A). The Julia Tuttle Causeway is a very convenient and usually uncongested way to get on and off Miami Beach, and the one the *Unofficial Guide* research team used the most when rooming on Miami Beach. Although the view of Miami's skyline is good from the Julia

Tuttle Causeway, it isn't as impressive as the MacArthur Causeway's up-close, heart-stopping panorama of cruise ships and high-rises.

Farther north, the **John F. Kennedy Causeway** (FL 934) connects **NE 79th Street** in Miami with **71st Street** in Miami Beach (surprise: the street-numbering systems in the two cities are close but don't quite match). While this is a good route to take if you're traveling to or from Biscayne Boulevard and Miami Beach, it's not a good choice for hooking up with (or leaving) I-95. Getting on and off the interstate from 79th Street in Miami is confusing at best—and it's a grim-looking neighborhood that most out-of-town visitors would rather avoid. Take the Julia Tuttle Causeway instead.

GETTING TO MIAMI BEACH NORTH The **Broad Causeway** (NE 123rd Street) links North Miami to Surfside and Bal Harbour at **96th Street** on Miami Beach. It passes through a congested downtown shopping district on the mainland, then crosses northern Biscayne Bay before reaching Bay Harbor Islands and Miami Beach. Due to the traffic lights and congestion along **NE 125th Avenue** on the mainland side, the Broad Causeway isn't a fast way to reach I-95 from Miami Beach.

Farther north, the **Sunny Isle Causeway** (FL 826) connects **NE 163rd Street** in North Miami Beach (which, confusingly enough, is on the mainland) to Sunny Isles on Miami Beach around **170th Street.** It's a major route to and from Haulover Beach Park, the Oleta River State Recreation Area, and Florida International University's Bay Vista campus. The **William Lehman Causeway** (FL 856), just below the Broward County line, connects **Biscayne Boulevard** in North Miami Beach to **192nd Street** on Miami Beach. Neither of these two causeways is a major route for out-of-town visitors.

AN ALTERNATIVE ROUTE TO SOUTH BEACH There's one other route to Miami Beach we need to mention: the **Venetian Causeway,** the original bridge that linked the town with Miami. Located just north of the MacArthur Causeway, it's a narrow two-lane bridge that crosses several artificial islands in Biscayne Bay. While not a particularly convenient route (the MacArthur Causeway is usually faster), the Venetian is a pretty drive, a great bicycling or jogging route, and worth exploring if you have the time. This causeway is also the route to take during rush hour when traffic is backed up for miles on the MacArthur Causeway.

The Miami side of the Venetian Causeway is tucked in behind condos and shopping malls just north of the *Miami Herald* building, and can be tough to find the first time. The Miami Beach side connects drivers with **Dade Boulevard,** just above Lincoln Road Mall. Turn right on Washington Avenue to reach South Beach, and go straight along Dade Boulevard to Collins Avenue.

Parking

Miami forces people to use their cars: Public transportation is limited, and the city is too spread out to make walking convenient. With all those cars in circulation, one question arises quickly, especially on a trip to South Beach or Coconut Grove on a Saturday night: Where do you park? You could take a cab, the alternative used by many Miami residents out for a night on the town.

But if you must park, be sure to carry quarters, or invest in an electric-meter parking card, available at city parking garages. Call the Miami Parking Authority at ☎ 305-373-6789 or visit **www.miami parking.com** for details.

Also, valet parking is a way of life in South Florida. A dollar or two will cover a tip, usually added to a basic fee of about $5 depending on the venue.

TAXIS AND PUBLIC TRANSPORTATION

Taxis

Miami isn't an easy place to hail a cab. If you need one, a phone call is your best bet.

Taxis are usually plentiful outside the terminals at Miami International Airport; the rate is $1.70/mile. Expect to pay about $21 for a trip from the airport to downtown and $23 to Coconut Grove. Flat-rate fares are available to Miami Beach south of 63rd Street ($22–$24), Miami Beach between 67th Street and 87th Terrace ($29), Miami Beach between 87th Terrace and Haulover Park ($34), Miami Beach between Haulover Park and the Broward County line ($41), and Key Biscayne ($36). Trips to other destinations in and around Miami can range from $25 on up.

POPULAR CAB COMPANIES	
Metro	☎ 305-888-8888
Super Yellow	☎ 305-885-1111
Tropical	☎ 305-945-1025
Yellow	☎ 305-444-4444

Buses, Trains, and Trams

Miami, like a lot of large cities, jumped on the mass-transit bandwagon, building an elevated-train system (in lieu of a subway, an engineering no-no in South Florida due to the region's high water table, which also rules out basements) and a downtown "People Mover." Yet the fledgling systems have a long way to go before native Miamians—and visitors to the area—can abandon their cars and rely on public transportation to get around. Our advice to visitors is to come in your own car or rent one after you reach Miami.

Metrorail, Miami's futuristic above-ground train system, is a 21-mile-long, one-line system that runs from Hialeah in northwest Miami south through downtown to Kendall, a suburb southwest of the city. It's clean and modern, but it really doesn't go where most visitors want to be—Miami Beach and the airport being two prime examples.

Moreover, the limited system hasn't really caught on with the local clientele (many of whom refer to the system as "Metrosnail"—the trains run about every 20 minutes). While Metrorail was once burdened with an unsafe reputation, security guards have since cleaned up most of the crime. Still, the line passes through some neighborhoods that visitors will likely avoid.

On the other hand, a ride on downtown's free **Metromover**—nicknamed the People Mover—is a minitour of Miami. A Disneyesque automated monorail scoots around downtown, treating you to spectacular views of the city, Biscayne Bay, and, off in the distance, the Atlantic Ocean. The system includes two out-and-back connections (in spite of their names, they're not loops) to the Brickell Avenue business district to the south (Brickell Loop) and to the Omni Hotel to the north (Omni Loop). It's a practical, clean, and safe system for getting around.

The People Mover is the best tourist bargain in South Florida, and it hooks up with the Metrorail system. But unless you're staying downtown and don't plan to venture to other parts of Miami, this small transportation system won't replace your need for a car.

Miami's **Metrobus** system operates throughout Dade County, serving about 200,000 riders a day on 70 routes. Most of the lines radiate out of downtown Miami and run at least twice per hour between 6 a.m. and 7 p.m. weekdays, less often on weekends. The bus system is also the only public transportation in Miami Beach. Our advice: Short-term visitors should stick to their cars, taxis, or feet and leave the complicated, relatively slow bus system to commuters.

Visitors can cruise South Beach on the **ElectroWave,** Florida's first electric-shuttle system. Shuttles stop every 6–11 minutes at 38 designated stops on Washington Avenue between 16th Street and South Pointe Drive and along Collins Avenue between 16th Street and Dade Boulevard. The minibuses seat up to 22 passengers with wraparound seating and air-conditioning, and allow visitors more-convenient access between municipal parking lots and local hot spots. The shuttle operates 20 hours a day, every day of the year. The fare is cheap, too: a quarter each way.

BUSINESS *versus* BEACH

WHILE MOST OF THE 10 MILLION VISITORS TO Miami come to bask in the tropical sun, about a third arrive for conventions and business. People visiting on business especially need to find a hotel that's convenient, avoid traffic hassles, and know Miami's best restaurants. We can help.

Convention Venues

The massive million-square-foot **Miami Beach Convention Center** is South Florida's major exhibition site. The smaller **Coconut Grove Expo Center,** located in the hip neighborhood south of downtown Miami, specializes in consumer-oriented exhibitions such as home shows, health-and-fitness expos, and gun-and-knife shows. Numerous hotels and other venues host smaller groups.

Sites that draw national conventions include:

- Miami Convention Center in downtown Miami: 37 meeting rooms and the 28,000-square-foot Riverfront Hall

- Hyatt Regency Miami adjacent to the Convention Center: 80,000 square feet of meeting and banquet rooms and the 12,000-square-foot Regency Ballroom

- Radisson Centre near Miami International Airport: 120,000 square feet of meeting, exhibition, and banquet space

- Doral Ocean Beach Resort in Miami Beach: 45,000 square feet of meeting space

- Doral Resort and Country Club in Miami: 75,000 square feet of meeting and banquet facilities

- Fontainebleau Resorts in Miami Beach: 190,000 square feet of meeting and exhibit space

The Miami Beach Convention Center

Expanded and renovated in 1990 at a cost of more than $92 million, the Miami Beach Convention Center is South Florida's premier convention locale. The 1.1-million-square-foot center is one of the best-designed convention facilities in the United States,and can handle up to four conventions at a time.

Spanning four city blocks near Miami Beach's Art Deco District, the center is only minutes from the beach, Lincoln Road, and great restaurants, and it's less than a half hour from Miami International Airport (allow more time during rush hour). The center is located on Washington Avenue between 17th Street and Dade Boulevard; although massive, it is not visible from Miami Beach's main drag, Collins Avenue.

With all its meeting rooms on one level, the center's main floor, with 500,000 square feet, either can be configured as a vast, centralized facility with four points of access or can be subdivided into four separate halls of approximately 125,000 square feet each. A skywalk with lounges, bars, and meeting rooms spans the halls, giving convention-goers a bird's-eye view of the space.

Surrounding the exhibit area are 70 separate meeting rooms for a total of 145,000 square feet of flexible space. All are fully carpeted and divided by soundproof walls. The meeting rooms can accommodate as few as 100 or as many as 2,000 convention attendees.

unofficial **TIP**
Take advantage of hotel shuttle buses or take a cab during large conventions. Or head for the 2,000-space parking garage on 17th Street (a block south toward Lincoln Road Mall); trying to find street parking within walking distance can be frustrating.

The exhibit areas and meeting rooms are well marked and easy to find. Parking around the center, however, is difficult; the adjacent 800-space lot fills up quickly.

For dining, head down Washington Avenue into the heart of South Beach, where a wide range of high-quality eateries, bistros, and fast-food venues are close by. In addition, Lincoln Road Mall, a block south of the convention center between 16th and 17th streets, offers a wide range of trendy restaurants, bars, and shops.

ElectroWave, Miami's minibus service, makes a stop near the convention center on Washington Avenue and provides easy transportation south into the Art Deco District; the electric buses run every 6–11 minutes, 20 hours a day.

For more information on the Miami Beach Convention Center, call ☎ 305-673-7311.

The Coconut Grove Expo Center

Located south of downtown Miami, at 2700 Bayshore Drive in Coconut Grove, this 150,000-square-foot hall accommodates shows of up to 18,000 attendees. Set on the shores of Biscayne Bay, with a backdrop of sailboats in the nearby marina, the center is 15 minutes from downtown Miami and less than half an hour from Miami International Airport.

The main hall is divisible into five halls measuring from 7,000 to 50,000 square feet and features an eight-window ticket booth. Two 30-foot-wide doors roll up to ceiling height at the north and south ends of the hall to enable easy access for service vehicles and exhibitors. All exhibition space is ground level, making it easy to roll or carry equipment through the doors from the parking lot. In addition, two concession stands are located in the main hall, and there is a full-service restaurant on the premises. A 1,000-plus-car parking lot surrounds the hall.

For more information on the Coconut Grove Expo Center, call ☎ 305-579-3310.

AT *the* SEASHORE

LIFE'S A BEACH

GRAB YOUR LOTION AND HEAD FOR THE OCEAN, because with more than 10 miles of wide, palm-tree-studded beaches, Miami Beach is justly known for sand and surf, and it keeps getting better.

All the beach is open to the public and staffed by lifeguards in colorful deco-style stations during daylight hours from 1st to 14th streets; at 21st, 35th, 46th, 52nd, and 64th streets; and at North Shore State Recreation Area and Haulover Beach Park.

Who Goes Where?

South Beach, especially 10th through 12th streets, is topless friendly, while gay sun-worshipers tend to favor the beach around 21st Street. South Beach also attracts Germans, Italians, Hispanics (of course), the young and the restless, Eurotrash, and glitterati the world over.

The War Zone is the old name for the tip of land below Fifth Street down to Government Cut (the shipping channel leading to the Port of Miami). Now it's called **SoFi** ("south of Fifth"). This used to be mostly surfer turf, but the neighborhood is undergoing rapid change as the Art Deco District trendiness, chains and boutiques, and ultra-luxury high-rise and loft condos push south. There's a park on the ocean side between Second and Third streets where folks gather at sunup for tai chi; upgraded **South Ponte Park** is great for sunsets.

Beachgoing families tend to flock to blocks numbered in the 20s, 30s, 40s, and north. A wooden boardwalk now extends from 15th to the 50s behind many of the huge hotels that line the beach; you'll see assorted, mostly tanned bodies strolling and jogging by.

Mid–Miami Beach, centered around 41st Street, is an upscale commercial strip and has one of the largest concentrations of Lubavitcher Jews in the state. Farther north, **Surfside** attracts a mixed population and is also a popular destination for Canadian and Scandinavian tourists. The epicenter of Canadian tourism is **Hollywood,** just over the line in Broward County.

For folks looking to sunbathe in the raw, **Haulover Beach Park** (just past Bal Harbour) has a clothing-optional section at the north end of its mile of sand. The adjoining park features picnic areas, a marina, and plenty of parking.

Sunny Isles, located above Haulover Beach, has a lovely park beach with sea-grape trees and sand dunes (which are about as high above sea level as you'll get in Miami). It's a popular spot for families.

Beyond Miami Beach

Key Biscayne's **Crandon Park,** ten minutes from the Miami mainland, offers miles of wide, white, calm Atlantic beach and is free of parking problems; it's a popular destination for families and picnickers.

For swimming, windsurfing, or Jet Skiing in the shallow, placid waters of Biscayne Bay, pull over on the **Rickenbacker Causeway** that connects Key Biscayne to the mainland. It's a popular beach destination for local residents, featuring shade trees and picnic tables close to the water. And it's okay to bring the dog.

In **North Miami Beach** (which, confusingly enough, is a suburb of Miami located on the mainland), the **Oleta River State Recreation Area** has a small, sandy man-made beach on the shores of Biscayne Bay and the Intracoastal Waterway. It's an oasis of quiet surrounded by condos. South of Coral Gables and east of the Miami suburb of Kendall, **Matheson Hammock Park** offers a small beach on Biscayne Bay with a terrific view of the Miami skyline and an outdoor restaurant.

Where to Put the Car

The farther south along Miami Beach you go, the harder it is to find a place to leave the car; on weekends, it can be nearly impossible unless you arrive early. Along Miami Beach, metered public parking lots, beach access, and restrooms are provided along Collins Avenue

1st Street (at Washington Avenue, South Pointe Park)

6th to 14th Streets, Lummus Park

21st Street

35th Street

46th Street (next to the Eden Roc Hotel)

53rd Street

64th Street

73rd Street (across from the North Shore Community Center)

79th to 87th Streets (North Shore State Recreation Area)

93rd Street (Surfside)

96th Street (Bal Harbour)

108th Street (Haulover Park)

167th Street (next to the Holiday Inn)

SWIMMING

MIAMI BEACH OFFERS 10 MILES OF WHITE-SAND beaches along the ocean from **South Pointe Park** in South Beach north to **Sunny Isles Beach** at 192nd Street. On crowded weekends, the water is often less congested than the shoreline, but those hoping to swim for fun or fitness might find it easier to choose another beach.

Other options for ocean swimming include **Haulover Beach** (just north of Bal Harbour between 163rd and 192nd Streets; $5 per car), **Crandon Park** on Key Biscayne ($4 per car; $1 toll on the Rickenbacker Causeway), and **Bill Baggs Cape Florida State Park** (also on Key Biscayne; $4 per car).

The clear waters of Biscayne Bay are shallow and usually calm; the most popular beaches are along the Rickenbacker Causeway. Picnic tables, shade trees, and no restrictions on pets make these beaches extremely popular with local residents; the waters are also popular with kayakers and windsurfers (the beach after the first bridge on the causeway is informally called Windsurfer Beach).

If you're looking for a non-saltwater experience, but your hotel doesn't have a pool, the **Venetian Pool** at 2701 DeSoto Boulevard in Coral Gables (☎ 305-460-5306) should be on your itinerary. Originally excavated to supply limestone for early Coral Gables homes, this large, coral-rock pool offers a tropical lagoon–like setting, with caves, waterfalls, and stone bridges. (Another beautiful Coral Gables pool is the gigantic one at the Biltmore Hotel.) In winter, the pool is open Tuesday–Sunday, 10 a.m.–4:30 p.m.; closed Mondays; call for summer hours. Admission for residents is $4.25 for adults, $3.25 for children ages 12 and under; nonresidents pay $9.50 for adults and $5.25 for children ages 3-12; no children under age 3 are permitted. A cafe offers a full luncheon menu.

SCUBA DIVING

FOR MORE EXPERIENCED CERTIFIED DIVERS, Miami is a destination that offers an extensive line of natural reefs that parallels the entire length of Dade County. Miami is also home to one of the largest artificial reef programs in the world.

It started in 1972 with the sinking of the *Biscayne,* a 120-foot-long freighter that formerly hauled bananas from South America. The ship was the first of many wrecks (including barges, tugboats, naval vessels, and private yachts) sunk for the enjoyment of sport divers. While the shallowest reefs near Miami are 30 feet down, wreck diving starts at 35 feet and goes down to about 130 feet. Private dive boats can lead visiting divers on tours of the wrecks and reefs, including night dives.

In Sunny Isles is **H2O Scuba,** which offers four-hour, two-tank dive trips at 8:30 a.m. and 1:30 p.m. on weekends and at 9 a.m. and 1 p.m. on weekdays; the cost is $55 per person without equipment, $65 with two tanks, and $100 with all equipment. A certification course is $275. For more information, call H2O at ☎ 305-956-3483.

SNORKELING

THE CLOSEST PLACE TO MIAMI WITH SHALLOW reefs is **Biscayne National Park,** an underwater park located a few miles east of Florida City in southern Dade County; it's about an hour's drive from downtown Miami. The requirements for snorkeling are minimal: the ability to swim and a desire to see aquatic life up close.

At Biscayne National Park, three-hour snorkeling trips (two hours of travel, one hour exploring the reef) leave daily at 1:30 p.m., weather permitting; the cost is $35 for adults and $30 for children ages 12 and under and includes all the equipment you need. Call ☎ 305-230-1100 to make a reservation. See our profile of Biscayne National Park (page 187) for more information.

A small reef is located off **Miami Beach** between Third and Sixth Streets in South Beach, 70 yards offshore and 16 feet down. Check with a lifeguard for the exact location and be sure to take out a diving flag to warn boaters that you're swimming in the area.

SAILBOATS AND SAILING SCHOOLS

TO SET SAIL ON THE CALM, SHALLOW WATERS of Biscayne Bay, head for **Sailboats of Key Biscayne,** located at the Aquatic Rental Center (1275 NE 79th Street, Miami) in the Pelican Harbor Marina (north side of 79th Street Causeway). Keelboat sloops, ranging in size from 20–25 feet, each with a small outboard engine (gas included), rent for $35 an hour with a two-hour minimum, $130 for a half day, and $190 for a full day. Dingy sailboats, Sunfish, and Hobie Holder 12's (holds two people) cost $30 per hour. Also available with advanced notice: motorboats, kayaks, and large sailboats with licensed captain. Never sailed before? **Key Biscayne Sailboat School** offers a ten-hour sailing course for $350 per person (each additional person pays $100). The course includes four two-hour lessons with an instructor; the last two hours you embark by yourself. For more information, visit **www.arcmiami.com.**

Another option: **Dinner Key** in Coconut Grove is another nearby destination well known for sailboat rentals and sailing lessons, and it is a good jumping-off point for sailing Biscayne Bay. For more information, call ☎ 305-579-6980.

CANOEING AND KAYAKING

VISITORS TO MIAMI CAN RENT CANOES AND kayaks to explore the backwaters of Biscayne Bay. The visual rewards range from close-up views of gorgeous waterfront estates to glimpses of Everglades-worthy wilderness located in Miami's backyard.

While 854-acre **Oleta River State Park** is virtually surrounded by high-rises, visitors can rent canoes and explore the quiet waters that surround the park—and possibly sight a manatee, a gentle giant of a water mammal. Admission to the park is $4 per car (up to eight people); canoe and paddleboat rentals are $12 per hour. One-person kayaks rent for $12 per hour. A $20 deposit and a driver's license are also required. Boat rentals are available weekdays, noon–5 p.m.; and weekends, 9 a.m.–5 p.m. The park is located off Sunny Isles Boulevard between Miami Beach and the mainland (North Miami Beach). For more information, call ☎ 305-919-1846.

Some of the world's most extensive mangrove forests can be explored by canoe at **Biscayne National Park,** near Florida City in southern Dade County. Canoe rentals are available 9 a.m.–4:30 p.m. for $12 an hour, $31 for a half day, and $62 for a full day; the price includes paddles and life jackets. Folks with their own canoes can launch for free. Call ☎ 305-230-1100 for more information.

■ SPORTS *and* RECREATION

FITNESS CENTERS AND AEROBICS

MIAMI'S LARGER HOTELS GENERALLY OFFER fitness facilities. The **Sports Club/LA,** in the Four Seasons Hotel on 14th Street and Brickell Avenue, is an ultradeluxe fitness center and spa that offers any and all spa treatments, overlooking a four-story waterfall. However, few of Miami's charming Art Deco–era hotels have added workout rooms.

Fortunately, many Miami fitness centers are coed and accept daily or short-term memberships. The **Olympia Gym and Fitness Center,** located at 20335 Biscayne Boulevard in North Miami Beach, features two free-weight areas, fixed weights, StairMaster machines, and aerobics classes. Daily membership is $15. Call ☎ 305-932-3500 for more information.

The **Downtown Athletic Club,** at 200 South Biscayne Boulevard (on the 15th floor of the Southeast Financial Building), boasts a 32,000-square-foot facility that includes free weights, exercise bikes, treadmills, an indoor track, a basketball court, a whirlpool, and racquetball courts. The daily rate is $16. Members qualify for two and a half hours of free parking per day while working out; for more information, call ☎ 305-358-9988.

Gold's Gym of Coral Gables, at 3737 SW Eighth Street, offers free and fixed weights, StairMasters, Lifecycles, and a treadmill. Membership is $12 a day and $40 for two weeks; call ☎ 305-445-5161 for more information.

South Beach Ironworks, at 1676 Alton Road, offers memberships for $15 a day, $30 for three days, and $60 a week. Facilities include a complete gym (with both free and fixed weights) and aerobic studios, but no sauna or whirlpool. For more information, call ☎ 305-531-4743.

TENNIS

THE PREMIER PUBLIC TENNIS FACILITY IN THE Miami area may be the **Tennis Center at Crandon Park,** on Key Biscayne (☎ 305-365-2300), which offers 17 hard courts, 8 clay courts, and 2 grass courts. Hourly rates during the day for hard courts are $3 per person ($6 per person for clay). Only the hard courts are lighted; the night rate is $5 per person, per hour. Advance reservations are accepted.

The **Key Biscayne Tennis Association,** at 6702 Crandon Boulevard, has seven clay and two hard courts that can be rented up to two days in advance. The courts are open Monday–Thursday, 8 a.m.–9 p.m.; Friday–Sunday, until 6 p.m.; hourly rates are $6 per person; only two clay courts and the two hard courts have lights. Call ☎ 305-361-5263 for more information.

On Miami Beach, **Flamingo Park Center,** at 1000 12th Street, has 19 clay courts, all lighted for night play. The daytime rate is $8 per hour; at night it's $9.50 per hour. Same-day reservations may be made in person, not by phone. Call ☎ 305-673-7761 for more information.

Farther up the beach in Surfside, **A&M Tennis/Surfside Tennis Center and Pro Shop,** at 88th Street and Collins Avenue, features three hard courts and a fully staffed pro shop. Hours are Monday–Friday, 10:30 a.m.–9 p.m.; Saturday and Sunday, 9 a.m.–5 p.m. The hourly fee is $4 per person in daylight and $4.75 at night; reservations are accepted, and the staff will find you a playing partner if you need one. Lessons and programs are available. Call ☎ 305-866-5176 for more information.

In addition, the City of Miami and the Metro-Dade County Parks and Recreation Department operate more than 250 tennis courts between them. Court locations include popular visitor destinations such as **Haulover Park** and **North Shore Park** (Miami Beach), **Peacock Park** (Coconut Grove), **Tamiami Park** (next to Florida International University), and **Tropical Park** (at the Palmetto Expressway).

GOLF

THE PEAK SEASON FOR GOLF IN SOUTH FLORIDA runs Thanksgiving through mid-April. Midmorning tee times are the most popular and usually require reservations. During the week, singles can frequently catch up with a game because of no-shows. Weekends, when local residents hit the links, are always busy (regardless of season), and getting a morning reservation is difficult. Plan on teeing off before 1 p.m. so you're not racing the sun, which sets around 5 p.m. in midwinter.

The summer months are hot and humid, so reserve a tee time either before 9 a.m. or after 4 p.m. to play nine holes; avoid the links between 1 p.m. and 3 p.m. In addition to sweltering heat, afternoon thunderstorms frequently roll across Dade County. Note that many courses offer reduced greens fees for afternoon and evening play.

If possible, vacationers should reserve tee times when booking their hotels; some hotels block off tee times at nearby courses for their guests. Reservations at two municipal courses (Biltmore and Grenada) can be secured up to 24 hours in advance at no charge by calling ☎ 305-669-9500. Golfers on extended stays in Dade County might consider subscribing to the municipal reservation service to secure preferred times farther in advance; the fee is $42.50 (tax included) a year. Call ☎ 305-460-5364 for more information.

Biltmore Golf Course

ESTABLISHED: 1926   STATUS: MUNICIPAL COURSE

1210 Anastasia Avenue, Coral Gables 33134; ☎ 305-460-5364
www.biltmorehotel.com

Tees

- **Championship: 6,642 yards, par 71, USGA 71.5, slope 119**
- **White: 6,240 yards, par 71, USGA 69.7, slope 116**
- **Red: 5,820 yards, par 71, USGA 73.3, slope 122**

Fees   Daily, $79; twilight (after 2 p.m.), $50; includes cart; $9 (9 holes)

Facilities   Clubhouse, full-service pro shop with custom club-building and club-repair capabilities, restaurant, locker rooms, driving range, putting greens, sand trap area, lessons, tennis courts, Biltmore Hotel

Comments   Redesigned in 1992, the Biltmore Golf Course is in excellent shape. Today, the course hosts the Coral Gables Open and the Orange Bowl International Junior Golf Championship.

Miami Springs Golf and Country Club

ESTABLISHED: 1923   STATUS: PUBLIC COURSE

650 Curtiss Parkway, Miami Springs 33166; ☎ 305-805-5180; www.miamisprings.com/golf

Tees

- **Championship: 6,741 yards, par 71, USGA 72.5, slope 120**
- **White: 6,476 yards, par 71, USGA 72.0, slope 116**
- **Red: 5,836 yards, par 72, USGA 72.5, slope 122**

Fees   Daily, $26.75; after 4 p.m., $21.50; includes cart.

Facilities   Pro shop, restaurant, banquet facility for up to 700, lounge, lighted driving range, lessons

Comments   The Country Club in Miami Springs was opened by the City of Miami in 1923. The 18-hole championship par-71 course features challenging sand traps and a tropical ambience throughout its 6,741 yards. Home of the original Miami Open from 1925 until 1955, Miami Springs is now the annual host of the prestigious North-South Tournament. Less than five minutes from Miami International Airport and area hotels, Miami Springs has become a favorite among business travelers in Miami. With its low seasonal rates and extensive facilities, the manicured championship course welcomes visitors to Miami's tropical world of golf.

Country Club of Miami

ESTABLISHED: 1961   STATUS: PUBLIC COURSE

6801 Miami Gardens Drive, Miami 33015; ☎ 305-829-8456

Tees

WEST COURSE

- **Blue: 7,017 yards, par 72, USGA 74, slope 130**
- **Red: 6,139 yards, par 72, USGA 72, slope 124**
- **White: 6,527 yards, par 72, USGA 70.1, slope 127**

EAST COURSE

- **Blue: 6,351 yards, par 70, USGA 70.8, slope 127**

- **Gold: 5,991 yards, par 70, USGA 69.1, slope 123**
- **Red: 5,052 yards, par 70, USGA 69.2, slope 118**
- **White: 5,557 yards, par 70, USGA 66.7, slope 118**

Fees Weekdays, $29; weekends, $40. Twilight fees are available.

Facilities Two grass driving ranges (one lighted), two pro shops, on-course beverage service, lessons, turn-key tournament operation, full-service restaurant, banquet room, men's and women's locker rooms

Comments South Florida's premier public golf facility. Site of former National Airlines Open, the 1991 Senior PGA Tour National Qualifying School, and Regional USGA events such as the Mid-Am qualifier.

Doral Resort and Country Club

ESTABLISHED: 1961   STATUS: RESORT COURSE

4400 NW 87th Avenue, Miami 33178;
Silver Course Clubhouse: 5001 NW 104th Avenue;
☎ 305-592-2000; www.doralgolf.com

Tees

THE BLUE MONSTER

- **Gold: 7,288 yards, par 72, USGA 74.5, slope 130.**
- **Blue: 6,701 yards, par 72, USGA 72.2, slope 125.**
- **Red: 5,392 yards, par 72, USGA 73, slope 124.**
- **White: 6,281 yards, par 72, USGA 69.7, slope 118.**

GOLD COURSE

- **Gold: 6,602 yards, par 70, USGA 73.3, slope 129.**
- **Blue: 6,209 yards, par 70, USGA 70.7, slope 124.**
- **Red: 5,179 yards, par 70, USGA 71.4, slope 123.**
- **White: 5,747 yards, par 72, USGA 68.7, slope 120.**

RED COURSE

- **Gold: 6,146 yards, par 70, USGA 70.2, slope 121**
- **Blue: 6,058 yards, par 70, USGA 69.9, slope 118**
- **Red: 5,096 yards, par 70, USGA 70.6, slope 118**
- **White: 5,596 yards, par 72, USGA 67.6, slope 114**

WHITE COURSE

- **Gold: 7,171 yards, par 72, USGA 75.1, slope 133**
- **Blue: 6,679 yards, par 72, USGA 72.5, slope 128**
- **Red: 5,026 yards, par 72, USGA 70.7, slope 130**
- **White (men's): 6,085 yards, par 72, USGA 69.4, slope 116**
- **White (ladies'): 6,085 yards, par 72, USGA 72.7, slope 135**

SILVER COURSE

- **Gold: 6,557 yards, par 71, USGA 72.5, slope 131**
- **Blue: 6,197 yards, par 71, USGA 70.9, slope 128**
- **Red: 4,738 yards, par 71, USGA 67.1, slope 117**

- **White: 5,589 yards, par 72, USGA 68.7, slope 123**

Fees Blue Course: $200 weekdays, $210 weekends; White Course: $200 weekdays and weekends; Red Course: $165 weekdays, $175 weekends; Gold Course: $165 weekdays, $175 weekends; Silver Course: $165 weekdays, $175 weekends. Greens fees are significantly lower off-season; call for rates.

Facilities One of the world's largest pro shops, driving range, four putting greens, the world-class Doral Spa, on-course snack bar, three full-service restaurants, 15-court tennis facility, Doral golf learning center with Jim McLean, caddies available, fishing in the course lakes. The clubhouse for the Silver Course was recently renovated; the new facilities are extensive.

Comments The home of the famous Doral "Blue Monster" and the Doral-Ryder Open, this is one of the premier golf courses in the country. The Gold Course was redesigned by Raymond Floyd (original designer of the Blue Monster). With the tropical Miami climate and four championship courses, this Florida destination is a winner. Serene lakes and cypress trees line the fairways.

Fontainebleau Golf Club

ESTABLISHED: 1970   STATUS: PUBLIC COURSE

9603 Fontainebleau Boulevard, Miami 33172; ☎ 305-221-5181

Tees

EAST COURSE

- **Championship: 7,035 yards, par 72, USGA 73.3, slope 122**
- **Men's: 6,647 yards, par 72, USGA 71.6, slope 117**
- **Ladies': 5,586 yards, par 72, USGA 71.5, slope 119**

WEST COURSE

- **Championship: 6,944 yards, par 72, USGA 72.5, slope 120**
- **Men's: 6,650 yards, par 72, USGA 71.2, slope 118**
- **Ladies': 5,565 yards, par 72, USGA 71, slope 118**

Fees Weekdays, $15 ($12 after 3 p.m.); weekends, $19.50 ($15 after 3 p.m.); $5 cart fee

Facilities 36-hole championship course, driving range, snack bar, pro shop, lessons

Comments Mark Mahanna designed this public course popular with locals.

Hollywood Beach Golf & Country Club

ESTABLISHED: 1930   STATUS: PUBLIC COURSE

1600 Johnson Street, Hollywood 33020; ☎ 954-927-1751; www.hollywoodbeachgolf.com

Tees

- **Championship: 6,336 yards, par 70, USGA 69.7, slope 117**

- **Men's: 6,024 yards, par 70, USGA 68.5, slope 114**
- **Ladies': 5,494 yards, par 70, USGA 71.5, slope 112**

Fees Weekdays, $25; weekends, $30; cart included.

Facilities Pro shop, clubhouse restaurant, 35-room full-service hotel, locker rooms, pool

Comments This famous Florida club was designed by Donald Ross in 1930. It was completely renovated in 1995.

International Links of Miami

ESTABLISHED: 1960   STATUS: PUBLIC COURSE

1802 NW 37th Avenue, Miami 33125; ☎ 305-633-4583

Tees

- **Championship: 7,173 yards, par 72, USGA 73.5, slope 132**
- **Men's: 6,821 yards, par 71, USGA 72.1, slope 127**
- **Ladies': 5,534 yards, par 71, USGA 71.2, slope 118**

Fees $100–$145; includes cart.

Facilities Pro shop, restaurant-lounge, banquet facility for up to 200, lighted driving range, lessons from pros, rental equipment

Comments Formerly Melreese Golf Course, International Links of Miami is an outstanding 18-hole championship par-71 course with 14 holes bordering the water. Rated as one of the finest municipal golf courses in the country, International Links has hosted a U.S. Women's Amateur Public Links sectional qualifier, the National Clergymen's Tournament, the National Baseball Players' Tournament, and the Regional Handicapped Tournament.

Miccosukee Golf & Country Club

ESTABLISHED: 1970   STATUS: SEMIPRIVATE COURSE

6401 Kendale Lakes Drive, Miami 33183; ☎ 305-382-3930; www.miccosukeeresort.com/golf

Tees

MARLIN COURSE

- **Blue: 3,359/3,334 yards, par 36**
- **White: 3,120 yards, par 36**
- **Red: 2,743 yards, par 37**

DOLPHIN COURSE

- **Blue: 3,319 yards, par 36**
- **White: 3,060 yards, par 36**
- **Red: 2,579 yards, par 36**

BARRACUDA COURSE

- **Blue: 3,360 yards, par 36**
- **White: 3,092 yards, par 36**
- **Red: 2,702 yards, par 37**

Fees In season: $39–$45; $35–$45 after 10 a.m.; $35 after 1 p.m.; $25 after

3 p.m. Cart fee: $40 weekdays; $60 weekends. Call for summer rates.

Facilities Three championship 9-hole courses, 40-stall lighted driving range, 12-court (6 lighted) tennis facility, two Olympic-sized pools, kiddie wading pool, swimming lessons, men's and women's locker rooms, banquet facility, and bar and grill

Comments This club was built in 1970 and is considered one of the best courses in Greater Miami. Remodeled after Hurricane Andrew, with $2 million going to repair the clubhouse and golf course, it has been host to several LPGA tour events and PGA qualifiers for the Doral-Ryder Open and the Honda Classic.

Miami Shores Country Club

ESTABLISHED: 1937   STATUS: PUBLIC COURSE

10000 Biscayne Boulevard, Miami Shores 33138; ☎ 305-795-2366

Tees

- **Gold: 5,793 yards, par 71, USGA 69.7, slope 119**
- **Blue: 6,373 yards, par 71, USGA 70.6, slope 120**
- **White: 6,096 yards, par 71, USGA 69.1, slope 116**
- **Red: 5,442 yards, par 72, USGA 71.3, slope 121**

Fees $60–$100; cart included.

Facilities Clubhouse with three banquet rooms seating up to 450, pool, tennis courts, pro shop, lighted driving range, golf school, men's and women's locker rooms, spacious lounge area available for lunch and dinner

Comments Miami Shores is one of the oldest clubs in Miami, with elevated tees and greens that are small and well bunkered.

WALKING AND RUNNING

WHEN AN ERRAND REQUIRES A TRIP OF TWO or three blocks or longer, most Miami residents reach for their car keys. As a result, except for paths along the waterfronts and under the Metrorail tracks, Miami isn't a friendly city for strolling or walking for exercise. Folks looking for a place to stretch their legs may have to drive to get there.

Perhaps the greatest walking destination in Dade County is **Miami Beach.** Lincoln Road is exciting at night, with fountains, foliage, and a mix of people and their pets. The low-rise Art Deco apartments just south of Lincoln Road, with their decorative doorways and trim, are fabulous backdrops for a leisurely sidewalk stroll. From sunup to sundown, the sparkling white beach is popular for a long walk. From 21st to 51st streets, the wooden boardwalk behind the hotels is a favorite destination. For a more structured walking tour that's also informative and fun, take the **Art Deco Walking Tour** of South Beach, which starts Wednesday, Friday, Saturday, and Sunday mornings at 10:30 a.m. and every Thursday at 6:30 p.m. The cost is $20 (tax deductible), and the tour lasts 90 minutes. It begins at the Art Deco Welcome Center at the Ocean Front Auditorium located at 1001 Ocean Drive; reservations aren't required.

On Miami Beach, the boardwalk between 15th and 51st streets, as well as anywhere along the beach itself, offers the best—and safest— running surfaces. Above 30th Street the beach gets narrow, and it's often hard to find a packed track through the sand (unless you don't mind getting your feet wet near the surf, where the sand is packed down by the waves). North of **North Shore State Recreation Area** (between 79th and 87th streets), a path runs parallel to the beach behind the narrow boardwalk toward Bal Harbour; its wide, packed surface is excellent for running.

On the mainland, **Coconut Grove** and **Coral Gables** offer fine places to stretch your legs along Miracle Mile, with lots of shops and Florida architecture. For a longer walk, take the paved bicycle path that follows **Biscayne Bay** south along Bayshore Drive, Main Highway, Ingraham Highway, and Old Cutler Road.

A good destination for runners and joggers is the bike path that starts in **Coconut Grove** and continues south along Biscayne Bay; watch out for cyclists and cars as you cross the many intersections along the route. In Coral Gables, start walking from the **Miracle Mile** west toward City Hall. The neighborhood gets really lush; energetic strollers can view famous landmarks such as the Merrick House (the former home of Coral Gables' founder), the ritzy Colonnade Hotel, the Venetian Pool, and the Biltmore Hotel.

The **Rickenbacker Causeway** to Key Biscayne has a path—and great views—excellent for a run that can reach marathon lengths if you continue around the island. And right under the Metromover, from **Dadeland** to downtown, is a landscaped ribbon of path for running, walking, in-line skating, or biking.

Although it costs $15 to get in, **Fairchild Tropical Garden** is filled with paths that meander past specimen plantings and a lake.

Farther from Miami, **Everglades National Park** offers unlimited opportunities for walks—at least during the winter months. when the mosquitoes are dormant. **Shark Valley,** about 35 miles west of Miami on US 41, has a long, wide paved path that makes a 15-mile loop into the glades, as well as a short nature path near the visitor center.

Near the park's southern entrance outside Florida City, strollers can choose from a wide number of paved and wooden pathways that show off the best of the Everglades' unique topography, flora, and wildlife.

BICYCLING

THE GOOD NEWS FOR BIKERS: MIAMI-DADE COUNTY is flat. The bad? It can be hot and humid, and with congestion and a decentral-ized layout, devising a long ride is problematic. Road riders out for long-distance spins must often negotiate bumper-to-bumper traffic, share the road with rude drivers, and deal with the city's infuriating lack of street signs.

And unless you're into beach riding (which is hard on equipment), mountain bikers will find little off-road cycling—and certainly no mountains.

In the summer, cyclists should watch for approaching afternoon thunderstorms, which can be fearsome, with lots of lightning. During the summer, try to confine long rides to the early morning hours or you'll risk heat exhaustion; carry plenty of water, and take sunblock and insect repellent along for the ride. On the other hand, the winter months offer ideal cycling conditions.

Where to Rent a Bike

Mountain bikes and beach cruisers are available for rental at **Miami Beach Bicycle Center,** 601 Fifth Street (at Washington Street, ☎ 305-674-0150). Rental rates start at $20 per day or $70 per week.

Mangrove Cycles, at 260 Crandon Boulevard on Key Biscayne (☎ 305-361-5555), rents one-speed bikes for $8 for two hours, $12 a day, and $35 a week; mountain bikes rent for $15 for two hours, $20 a day, and $45 a week. The shop is open Tuesday–Saturday, 9 a.m. to 6 p.m., and Sunday, 10 a.m.–5 p.m., but is closed on Mondays.

Road Riding

For eye-pleasing scenery and enough tree cover to ward off the subtropical sun, consider **Coconut Grove.** You'll feel as if you're in a village, and dense foliage such as bougainvillea and hibiscus shades the worst of the sun's effects. For a longer spin on skinny tires, follow the bike path south along Bayshore Drive, Main Highway, Ingraham Highway, and Old Cutler Road—note, though, that most serious riders will want to stay off the path and ride in the street; the paved path is often broken up by tree roots and is better suited for fat tires and one-speed rental bikes.

If you're rolling along for pleasure, figure on turning back around 152nd Street (Coral Reef Drive). From this point south, the foliage is sparse as the greenery still hasn't fully recovered from Hurricane Andrew, almost 15 years ago.

For a more energetic ride—and the biggest climb in Dade County—take the **Rickenbacker Causeway** to Key Biscayne. Pedaling to the top of the bridge offers stunning views, and a ride around the island is long enough to provide a real workout. A ride to and around Key Biscayne, with a stop at the beach, remains a Sunday-morning favorite with area roadies.

Mountain Biking

All is not lost in mountainless Dade County—although good riding emphasizes handling over aerobics.

The premier off-road destination is just over the line in Broward County: **Markham County Park** (☎ 954-389-2000), located near the intersection of I-75 and I-59, west of Fort Lauderdale. The park features whoop-de-whoops along single-track trails; Jeep roads; low hills in the woods; and black, sticky mud guaranteed to keep intermediate and advanced riders entertained. The park charges a $1 entrance fee on weekends and holidays.

Dade County offers three smaller destinations for off-road rambles. **Amelia Earhart Park** in Hialeah offers trails easier than those in Markham County Park and has single-tracks through woods, open fields, soft sand, and mud. **Greynolds Park,** off West Dixie Highway in North Miami Beach, has a 1.6-mile course that local riders like to jam around. **Haulover Park** offers three short rides in the woods—but avoid riding through the field or you'll be picking thorns out of your inner tubes.

*un*official **TIP**
For more details on off-road rides in southeast Florida, pick up a copy of *Mountain Bike! Florida,* by Steve Jones (Menasha Ridge Press).

Oleta River State Park (across from Sunny Isles in North Miami; ☎ 305-919-1846) offers off-road paths for mountain bikers and an extensive system of dirt roads worth exploring. Admission to the area is $5 per vehicle. While there's no additional charge to ride the trails, helmets are required.

HIKING

FOR UNSPOILED WILDERNESS RAMBLES BY FOOT, savvy hikers drive west to legendary **Everglades National Park,** but only during the cooler months. Clouds of mosquitoes make hot-weather visits to the Everglades uncomfortable.

Shark Valley, about a 90-minute drive from downtown Miami, offers a 15-mile paved walkway to an observation tower; admittedly, this is a long trek for all but the most ardent walkers. But a shorter out-and-back hike still offers glimpses of wildlife and views of the Everglades' unique fauna and topography. An unpaved nature trail is near the visitor center.

For a more varied look at the Everglades, head toward Homestead and the park's southern entrance leading to Flamingo. While it's a longer drive, it's still a manageable day trip, and you will leave with a much better sense of what the subtle Everglades are all about. A number of paved and elevated wooden pathways that radiate from the road to Flamingo lead visitors to hammocks (small islands of elevated land and mangrove), views of the seemingly endless sawgrass prairie, and tropical jungles.

Prepared with heavy boots and experience in using a compass and topographic map, hikers can explore this amazing and precious "River of Grass"; again, winter months—the dry season—are best. Rewards include wildlife sightings: dozens of bird species including herons and osprey and, of course, gators. Pull over anywhere along the road and head off toward a hammock. Park rangers at the main visitor center near the entrance can offer advice on exploring.

SPECTATOR SPORTS

SOUTH FLORIDA GOT ITS BIG START IN SPORTS when the opening of the railroad made it possible for major-league baseball teams to come south for spring training. Next, the construction of the Orange Bowl brought in top-level college and professional football teams. To take full advantage of the many team sports, check the *Miami Herald*'s sports section for a daily listing of local games.

Professional Sports

Leading the list of attractions is the AFC East **Miami Dolphins** football team, which packs 'em in every season at Pro Player Stadium. The Dolphins have played in the Super Bowl five times and in 1972 achieved everlasting glory with the only all-win, no-tie season in NFL history. The season runs from August through December; ticket prices range from $25 to $225 and are available from the stadium box office or Ticketmaster at ☎ 954-523-3309. The stadium is located at 2269 NW 199th Street in North Miami; ☎ 305-620-2578 for more information.

Pro Player Stadium, which hosted its second Super Bowl in 1995, also hosts the annual Blockbuster Bowl college football championship. It's also home to the **Florida Marlins,** 1997 World Series champs. General-admission tickets for Marlins games range from $6 to $175 but average $10–$25. Call the stadium at ☎ 305-626-7400 for home-game dates and additional information on obtaining tickets.

The 20,000-seat American Airlines Arena, located at 601 Biscayne Boulevard, hosts the **Miami Heat,** an NBA team offering fast-paced basketball action. The squad debuted in 1988 and has been to the NBA's Eastern Conference Finals. Ticket prices are $10–$300. Call ☎ 305-577-HEAT for ticket information. The National Hockey League's **Florida Panthers,** who made an incredible run to the Stanley Cup finals in just their third season, play in Sunrise at the Office Depot Arena (2555 SW 137th Way). Ticket prices are $20–$250. For information, ticket prices, and dates for home games, call 954-835-7000.

The **Grand Prix of Miami** is South Florida's premier auto-racing event. Each spring, international drivers compete at speeds of more than 100 mph at Metro-Dade Homestead Motorsports Complex in Homestead. Tickets for three days of racing action range from $105 to $180. For ticket information, call the Homestead-Miami Speedway ticket office at ☎ 305-230-RACE.

To see the best in top-notch international tennis competition, don't miss the **NASDAQ-100 Open,** held for two weeks each March at the International Tennis Center, 7300 Crandon Boulevard, Key Biscayne, in a new, 7,500-seat stadium. The event draws more than

200,000 spectators and is broadcast live each year to more than 30 countries as top players compete for upwards of $4.5 million in prize money. Call ☎ 305-446-2200 or 800-725-5472 for dates and ticket information.

Amateur Sports

Top-flight collegiate sports teams in South Florida include the University of Miami **Hurricanes** football, baseball, and basketball teams. Hurricanes football is played at the famous Orange Bowl from September through November. Sit high up in the stands, and you'll get a great view of Miami while watching the gridiron action. The stadium is located at 1400 NW Fourth Street, west of downtown. For tickets to any Hurricane events ($20–$45), call ☎ 305-284-CANE or 800-GO-CANES; for game information, call ☎ 305-284-CANE.

The Hurricanes baseball team plays about 50 home games a year at Mark Light Stadium on the school's Coral Gables campus. The season lasts from February to May, with both day and evening games on the schedule. Tickets are $6 for adults and $4 for children and seniors. The University of Miami basketball squad plays at the Miami Arena, 701 Arena Boulevard, in downtown Miami. Tickets are $10–$25. For more information on Hurricanes baseball and basketball, call ☎ 305-284-2263.

Florida International University's **Golden Panthers** field a wide range of teams. Basketball is played November through March at Pharmed Arena, on SW Eighth Street and 112th Avenue in Miami. The baseball season runs January through May; home games are played at the University Park Complex, on SW Eighth Street and 112th Avenue. Golden Panthers soccer is played September through November at the University Park Complex. For schedules, call ☎ 305-348-4263.

The Betting Sports: Horse Races, Greyhounds, and Jai Alai

Puppies and ponies and jai alai: South Florida is home to several sports that permit pari-mutuel wagering, the type of gambling in which you bet against other wagerers, not the house. For folks who restrain from betting, the activities can be fun and inexpensive. While no one under age 18 may bet in Florida, children may accompany adults to horse races, greyhound races, and jai alai.

THOROUGHBRED HORSE RACING For more than 50 years Florida has been a center of thoroughbred horse racing. Classy **Hialeah Park,** built in 1925 (2200 East Fourth Avenue, Hialeah; ☎ 305-885-8000) is no longer a venue for racing, but can be visited just to enjoy the gorgeous grounds, a racetrack and coral clubhouse listed on the National Register of Historic Places, and a flock of 400 pink flamingos. Bring binoculars to better see the flamingos on the track's infield. (Nearby, Opa-locka, a planned community that fell on hard times but is experiencing a comeback, is north of Hialeah Park and features some outrageous Moorish-style architecture also worth a peek.)

Gulfstream Park is just over the Broward County line in Hallandale on US 1; ☎ 305-931-RACE.

Calder Race Course's weatherproof track permits racing during the rainy summer; it's located at 21001 NW 27th Avenue, near I-95 and the Dade-Broward border; ☎ 305-625-1311. To see where the ponies are running during your , check the sports section of the *Miami Herald*.

DOG RACING Greyhounds reach speeds of more than 40 miles an hour; you can see the action at two tracks in the Miami area. Like horse racing, the venue rotates throughout the year, so check the *Miami Herald* before heading out. Racing starts around 7:30 p.m.; several days during the week feature matinees starting at 12:30 p.m.

The **Flagler Greyhound Track** is located at 401 NW 38th Court, near Seventh Street and 37th Avenue, southeast of Miami International Airport; ☎ 305-649-3000. In Broward County, the **Hollywood Greyhound Track** is located on US 1 a mile east of I-95, just over the county line in Hallandale; ☎ 954-924-3200.

JAI ALAI Teams compete in the world's fastest sport, a Basque game dating from the 15th century that evokes lacrosse, tennis, and racquetball. The hard ball (called a *pelota*) flung and caught in a long, curved wicker basket (a *cesta*) has been clocked at 180 mph. Teams of two or four compete; the first team to score seven points wins. You can bet on a team to win or on the order in which teams finish.

The **Miami Jai Alai Fronton** is located at 3500 NW 37th Avenue, near Miami International Airport. A *fronton*, by the way, is the 176-foot-long court where jai alai (pronounced "high lie") is played; Miami's, built in 1926, is the oldest in the United States.

The game can be utterly confusing to first-time visitors, yet fascinating to watch even though the atmosphere is redolent with the pungent smell of cigars and beer. Admission is $1; the first game is at 7 p.m. on Wednesday, Friday, and Saturday. Matinees are daily (except Tuesday), noon–5 p.m. Call ☎ 305-633-6400 for more information.

SHOPPING

WHAT WOULD YOU EXPECT IN A CITY RENOWNED for its cosmopolitan mix of cultures and its fashion-magazine photo shoots but an extensive range of stores offering everything from imported hand-rolled cigars to haute couture?

STROLLING AND WINDOW SHOPPING

MIAMI IS A HOTBED OF PEOPLE WATCHING, which goes hand in hand with window shopping. Strolling the city's commercial districts is a great way to get to know Miami—and possibly snag a bargain.

miami shopping

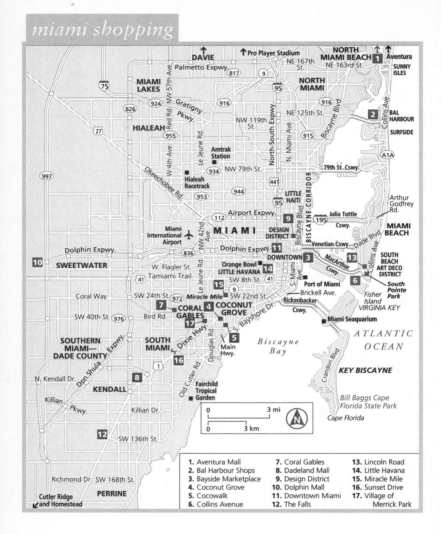

1. Aventura Mall
2. Bal Harbour Shops
3. Bayside Marketplace
4. Coconut Grove
5. Cocowalk
6. Collins Avenue
7. Coral Gables
8. Dadeland Mall
9. Design District
10. Dolphin Mall
11. Downtown Miami
12. The Falls
13. Lincoln Road
14. Little Havana
15. Miracle Mile
16. Sunset Drive
17. Village of Merrick Park

Downtown

Downtown Miami, a curious blend of Art Deco architecture and modern monoliths, contains a wondrous mix of shops, many owned and operated by second- and third-generation Latino families. As with most downtown metropolitan areas, the streets meander, but it's entirely possible to find everything you'll need by staying on the main drag, West Flagler, with a few side-street excursions. Wear sensible shoes, and leave your jewelry in the hotel safe, just to be safe. Finish your downtown shopping before nightfall and you'll be fine.

Jewelry, in fact, is downtown Miami's main lure. For the real thing, visit the venerable **Seybold Building** (37 East Flagler Street; ☎ 305-374-7922), chock-full of jewelers and some wholesalers who sell rough stones and gold and silver by the ounce. Small electronics stores are scattered everywhere, with a deal or two to be found, but when it comes to returning your purchase should you change your mind, you'd be better off at Radio Shack.

South Beach

The current hot spot of South Florida, South Beach is a fine destination for shopping on foot. While the entire district spans a mere 17 blocks, with trendy boutiques and quaint galleries in unlikely places such as hotel lobbies, there are certain streets the *au courant* shopper will not want to miss.

Lincoln Road runs from the ocean to Biscayne Bay, with nine blocks of shopping. In the 1940s, Lincoln Road was a chi-chi strip of elite retail stores including Bonwit Teller, Saks Fifth Avenue, and Lillie Rubin. Today, like everything else on South Beach, it's hip again. With a nod to New York's SoHo, Lincoln Road is a revamped open-air pedestrian mall that is home to artists; boutiques both funky and chic; chain stores such as **Pottery Barn** (1045 Lincoln Road; ☎ 786-276-8889), **BCBG Max Azria** (744 Lincoln Road, Miami Beach; ☎ 888-636-BCBG), **Williams-Sonoma** (1035 Lincoln Road, Miami Beach; ☎ 786-276-9945) and **Anthropologie** (1108 Lincoln Road; ☎ 305-695-0775); and sidewalk cafes. Don't overlook the side streets, which are dotted with worthwhile stores, salons, and cafes one block north and south of Lincoln Road. **Brownes & Co. Apothecary** (841 Lincoln Road; ☎ 305-532-8703) offers a comprehensive selection of toiletries, cosmetics, and grooming aids, from old-fashioned hair pomade to lavender-scented soaps to coconut-flavored lip gloss; its **Some Like It Hot** salon is handy for an impromptu manicure or blow-dry in a spacious setting. Just want a T-shirt to take back home? Stop by **Pink Palm Co.** (737 Lincoln Road; ☎ 305-538-8373) for an unusual greeting card or colorful gift item. For designer clothing, try **En Avance** (734 Lincoln Road; ☎ 305-534-0337), **Chroma** (920 Lincoln Road; ☎ 305-695-8808), and **Base** (939 Lincoln Road; ☎ 305-531 4982). We like **Senzatempo** (1655 Meridian Avenue; ☎ 305-534-5588) for its fascinating selection of vintage watches, furniture, and home accessories. For vintage apparel and accessories, try **Fly Boutique** (650 Lincoln Road; ☎ 305-604-8508) and **Consign of the Times** (1635 Jefferson Avenue; ☎ 305-535-0811), the latter also offering contemporary clothing at bargain prices. Want to rent a video? Go where in-the-know locals and visiting celebs do: **New Concept Video** (1671 Meridian Avenue; ☎ 305-674-1111), where you can find new releases as well as cult classics and a great selection of Euro and domestic magazines and groovy CDs, too. Need a quick bite? Try **David's Café II** (1654 Meridian Avenue, one block north of Lincoln Road; ☎ 305-672-8707) for inexpensive Cuban food and the best *café con leche* in town; **Rosinella** (525 Lincoln Road; ☎ 305-672-8777) for down-home Italian lunches and dinners; and the **Van Dyke Café** (846 Lincoln Road; ☎ 305-534-3600)—Lincoln Road's answer to the renowned News Café—a perennial favorite for casual dining and sidewalk people-watching. Love a good old-fashioned flea market? Many visitors try scheduling their trips around the semi-weekly **Lincoln Road Antiques and Collectibles Market,** held along the intersection of Lincoln Road and Drexel Avenue the second and last Sunday of each month from October to late May. And if Miami's famed weather has wilted your 'do, dash into **Van Michael Miami Salon** (1667 Michigan Avenue; ☎ 305-534-6789) for a blowout or an Aveda humidity-zapping serum.

Española Way intersects Washington Avenue and is situated between 14th and 15th streets. This quaint block of shops includes adorable gift and vintage boutiques, as well as avant-garde art galleries. **South Beach Makeup** (439 Española Way; ☎ 305-538-0805) carries a plethora of makeup as well as the Kiehl's line of products. Check out **Española Way Art Center** (409 Española Way; ☎ 305-672-5305), where the resident artists always have several intriguing projects on display. On Sundays during tourist season, Española Way turns into a street fair–cum–block party, with vendors selling everything from handmade candles to vintage bric-a-brac.

Washington Avenue is South Beach's main commercial artery and is brimming with upscale boutiques, trendy restaurants, and the occasional hardware store. One of the can't-miss stops is **Pop Collectibles** (1151 Washington Avenue; ☎ 305-604-9604) for edgy, provocative tank tops and baby tees, as well as great gag gifts and Florida-themed souvenirs.

Ocean Drive, at once scenic and chaotic, is fine for people watching while sipping overpriced cappuccino, but as far as serious shopping is concerned, you're better off searching out the small boutiques located along its side streets. One exception is **Lilian's Sandals** (800 Ocean Drive; ☎ 305-674-7610), where you'll find the best selection of sequined and colorful flats and platforms for the beach, the pool, or a casual summer night out.

One block west is the **Collins Avenue** fashion district, a three-block stretch (from Sixth to Ninth streets) littered with national boutiques including **Nicole Miller** (656 Collins Avenue; ☎ 305-535-2200), **Banana Republic** (800 Collins Avenue; ☎ 305-674-7079), **Sephora** (721 Collins Avenue, Miami Beach; ☎ 305-532-0904), **Urban Outfitters** (653 Collins Avenue; ☎ 305-535-9726), **Intermix** (634 Collins Avenue; ☎ 305-531-5950), and **Arden B.** (600 Collins Avenue; ☎ 305-534-0317).

Alton Road, South Beach's quietest retail street, is getting increasingly popular as rents in other areas skyrocket. Jewelry buffs will want to check out **MIA Boutique** (1439 Alton Road; ☎ 305-532-6064) for trendy, reasonably priced stone and wood necklaces and gold and sterling silver jewelry. Also on Alton Road, try **Spiaggia** (1624 Alton Road; ☎ 305-538-7949) for an eclectic and ever-changing offering of new and vintage home decor and **Alton Road Nursery** (1239 Alton Road; ☎ 305-532-7939) for a fantastic collection of not only plants but also glorious antiques that the owner accumulates on her travels.

Coral Gables/Miracle Mile

A picturesque business and residential area, Coral Gables contains one of Miami's most historic shopping areas, Miracle Mile. This four-block stretch of outdoor shopping (don't neglect the side streets) contains more than 150 boutiques, with something to satisfy everyone's taste and budget. The area is probably the safest in Miami, as well as the best manicured. Favorite destinations include **Rene Ruiz** (262 Miracle Mile; ☎ 305-445-2352), which sells elegant gowns for *quinceañeras,* cocktail parties, and weddings; **Leather World** (339 Miracle Mile; ☎ 305-446-7888), for every type of small leather good imaginable; **Luminaire** (2331 Ponce de Leon Boulevard, ☎ 305-448-7367), for contemporary furnishings and accessories; and **Books & Books** (265 Aragon Avenue; ☎ 305-442-4408), Miami's favorite independently owned bookstore.

South Miami

About seven minutes south of Coral Gables lies Sunset Drive, a pretty street that's home to some serious shopping. For designer clothing, it doesn't get better than **Steam on Sunset** (5830 Sunset Drive, ☎ 305-669-9991), which carries a well-edited selection of new and established designers. Select shoes to go with your purchase next door at family-owned **Capretto Shoes** (5822 Sunset Drive; ☎ 305-661-7767), in business for two decades. At **Cream** (5820 Sunset Drive, ☎ 305-669-9220), you'll find beauty products to rival those of any major retailer.

Coconut Grove

Miami's hot-spot hippie village of the 1970s, Coconut Grove has retained its antiestablishment charm while continuing to attract young sophisticates. Follow narrow sidewalks down the shady streets and browse the afternoon away. Our favorites include **IOS** (3109 Commodore Plaza; ☎ 305-442-7166), offering sleek hip-chick attire, and **Azul** (3444 Main Highway, Coconut Grove; ☎ 305-443-7268). Need a last-minute manicure, blowout, or makeup application before dinner? Head to **Allure Express Salon** (3405 Main Highway; ☎ 305-461-0020) for exceptional work at reasonable prices.

The **Miami Design District** (just west of Biscayne Boulevard at 40th Street) and Biscayne's Upper East Side are new, less chartered territories for shopping. For fine furniture and home accessories, check out **British Khaki** (180 NE 39th Street, Suite 101; ☎ 305-576-7300) and **Via Solferino** (3930 NE Second Avenue; ☎ 305-572-1182).

MALL SHOPPING

IF IT'S A BIG, GENERIC MALL YOU WANT, Miami's got plenty. **Dadeland** and **Aventura** malls will do just fine, located respectively at 7535 North Kendall Drive (☎ 305-665-6226) and 19501 Biscayne Boulevard, #450, North Miami Beach (☎ 305-935-1110). But it's that Miami flavor you crave, right? Okay, we know just where to send you.

If the thought of a $3,000 knit day dress doesn't send you into convulsions, you'll feel right at home at **Bal Harbour Shops** (9700 Collins Avenue, Bal Harbour; ☎ 305-866-0311). A charming two-floor mall with valet parking (self-parking by the hour is also available), a fleet of security guards, and French cafes serving $35 pasta entrees, Bal Harbour Shops is Miami's toniest mall. Offerings include Chanel, Gucci, Hermès, Neiman Marcus, Prada, Saks Fifth Avenue, Tiffany, Versace, and Yves St. Laurent. For the label conscious, this is paradise found.

Fun for the whole family, the tropical indoor-outdoor **Bayside Marketplace** (401 Biscayne Boulevard [NE Fourth–NE Ninth streets], Miami; ☎ 305-577-3344) is like an international carnival with stores. The lower level is teeming with stalls offering ethnic wares and cute (if largely useless) merchandise such as Flintstones coffee mugs and beach rafts in the image of the Venus de Milo. National chain stores include Brookstone, Gap, The Limited, and Victoria's Secret. Great for gifts is the Disney Store, which stocks everything from Mickey Mouse silk boxer shorts to *101 Dalmatians* charm bracelets. Naturalists will appreciate Art by God, which carries oversized crystals to put on display at home, as well as zebra-skin rugs made from farm-raised herds. Just minutes from downtown Miami, Bayside is easy to find and safe and clean, with plenty of sheltered, if slightly costly, parking.

Resembling a big Mediterranean birthday cake, **CocoWalk** (3015 Grand Avenue, Coconut Grove; ☎ 305-444-0777) is a comprehensive shopping-cum-entertainment complex. Smack in the middle of Coconut Grove, the two-layer mall contains everything the Generation X mall rat craves: music, tapas, loud bands, a multiscreen cinema, and a Gap. Grown-up choices including JW Cooper for Western wear, Victoria's Secret, and a good bookstore.

Probably Miami's most beautiful mall, **The Falls** (US 1 and SW 136th Street, Miami; ☎ 305-255-4570) is tropical and serene, with lots of wood, waterfalls, and leafy foliage. Bloomingdale's is the big draw, but there are also 60 specialty and national boutiques, including Ann Taylor, Banana Republic, Crate and Barrel, and Pottery Barn.

The Village of Merrick Park (358 San Lorenzo Avenue; ☎ 305-529-0200) is Miami's newest addition to the upscale-mall scene. This sprawling open-air Coral Gables mall has all the heavy hitters: Donald J Pliner, Diane von Furstenberg, Etro, Gucci, Hogan, Jimmy Choo, Neiman Marcus, Nordstrom, and Sonia Rykiel, among others.

SPECIALTY SHOPS

ANTIQUES You'll find the greatest concentration of antique stores on NW 27th Street, directly west of South Dixie Highway (an extension of US 1). Whether it's a delicate fauteuil chair or a replacement chandelier crystal you need, chances are you'll find it. **Corinthian Antiques** (2741 SW 27th Avenue; ☎ 305-854-6068), which carries a mix of American, English, and Continental collectibles, is your best bet for shopping the Queen Anne circuit. At **Alhambra Antiques** (2850 Salzedo Street, Coral Gables; ☎ 305-446-1688), you'll find a great selection of reasonably priced French and Italian pieces from the 18th and 19th centuries. For more of the same, plus a beautiful selection of Chinese antiques, visit the sprawling, long-standing **Bonnin Ashley Antiques** (4707 SW 72nd Avenue, Miami; ☎ 305-666-7709). On Miami's Upper East Side, check out **Divine Trash** (7244 Biscayne Boulevard, ☎ 305-751-1973) for secondhand items and art; a rustic collection of colorful South American pottery at South American prices; Haitian and Mexican masks and drawings; vintage clothing; and posters from the 1950s through the 1970s.

ART In addition to Miami's rejuvenated Design District, Coral Gables, South Beach, and Bay Harbor Islands are your key areas for art. On the first Friday of every month, an air-conditioned minibus takes art lovers for a free tour of the Coral Gables galleries. Reservations are not required; just show up in the early evening hours at one of the galleries, such as **Artspace/Virginia Miller Galleries** (169 Madeira Avenue; ☎ 305-444-4493). This area has a fine concentration of American and Latin American paintings.

On the trendy side, Lincoln Road on South Beach is a mini–art row of sorts. Local artists, some of whom attract international recognition, operate studios and galleries alongside well-established Miami art specialists, including **Barbara Gillman** (5582 NE Fourth Court; ☎ 305-759-9155). Artist Romero Britto's gallery, **Britto Central** (818 Lincoln Road; ☎ 305-531-8821), attracts high-profile collectors including Arnold Schwarzenegger and Marisa Tomei. **Lincoln Road's Gallery Walk** is held the second Saturday of the month, 6p.m.–10 p.m.

BARGAINS If labels such as Armani and Moschino entice you, we recommend **Loehmann's Plaza** (2855 NE 187th Street; ☎ 305-932-0520) in North Miami. This location consistently carries the best selection of designer wear at the lowest prices. The tireless bargain-shopper could easily get addicted to Broward County's **Sawgrass Mills** (12801 West Sunrise Boulevard, Sunrise; ☎ 800-356-4557) and **Dolphin Mall**

(NW 12th Street, Miami; ☎ 305-365-7446), located closer to Miami, both megadiscount designer malls.

In the gourmet-food division, one of Miami's secrets is **Alterman's Country Store** (12805 NW LeJeune Road, Opa-locka; ☎ 305-688-3571, x1209), which sells undamaged high-end foodstuffs at a fraction of the retail cost. A friend recently found a five-pound box of Godiva chocolates that retails at approximately $100 for less than half that. Revered goodies like imported cheeses and Maine lobsters turn up now and then. Expect a hit-or-miss inventory.

BOOKSTORES Any bookworm will tell you that everyone's favorite bookstore in Miami is **Books & Books** (three locations: 933 Lincoln Road, South Beach, ☎ 305-532-3222; Bal Harbour Shops, 9700 Collins Avenue, Bal Harbour, ☎ 305-864-4241; and 265 Aragon, Coral Gables, ☎ 305-442-4408). A close second is **Borders Books and Music** (three locations: 9205 South Dixie Highway, Miami, ☎ 305-665-8800; 3390 Mary Street, Coconut Grove, ☎ 305-447-1655; and 19925 Biscayne Boulevard, Aventura, ☎ 305-935-0027), which, like Books & Books, features meet-the-author readings and signings. For out-of-town news periodicals, try **Worldwide News** (1629 NE 163rd Street; ☎ 305-940-4090). **Lambda Passages** (7545 Biscayne Boulevard, Miami; ☎ 305-754-6900), a gay bookstore, has a good selection of biographies, history, and art books. There's sure to be a **Barnes & Noble** near your hotel (152 Miracle Mile, Coral Gables; ☎ 305-446-4152; 18711 Biscayne Boulevard, Aventura; ☎ 305-935-9770; 7710 North Kendall Drive, Miami; ☎ 305-598-7292; 12405 North Kendall Drive, Miami; ☎ 305-598-7727; 5701 Sunset Drive, Suite 196, South Miami; ☎ 305-662-4770).

CIGARS Stogie aficionados will appreciate **Mike's Cigars** (1030 Cane Concourse, Miami Beach; ☎ 305-866-2277), which carries more than 300 brands from all over the globe. Also worthy: the **News Café Store and Restaurant,** on trendy Ocean Drive (800 Ocean Drive; ☎ 305-538-6397), which is 24 hours a day—a real plus for the all-night set.

DESIGNER CLOTHING If you can't find it in Bal Harbour Shops (see "Malls"), chances are it doesn't exist. Do check out, however, the **Versace Jeans Couture Boutique** in South Beach (755 Washington Avenue; ☎ 305-532-5993) for casual wear and home items such as china and lavish $700 silk throw pillows; **En Avance** (734 Lincoln Road, Miami Beach; ☎ 305-534-0337) for some of the hippest labels around, including Miguelina, Juicy Couture, and DSquared; and **Steam on Sunset** (5830 Sunset Drive; ☎ 305-669-9991), where some of Miami's most chic women shop.

ETHNIC GOODS You might as well go to **Bayside Marketplace,** where you can find clothing and items from places as diverse as Jamaica, Africa, and India. The **Caribbean Marketplace** in Miami's Little Haiti district is interesting, but not so safe. **World Resources** (719 Lincoln Road; ☎ 305-535-8987) sells one-of-a-kind items collected from various locales around the world, everything from handwoven tablecloths to crystal earrings and leather knapsacks.

FRESH FISH Seafood makes for Miami's most reliable meals, and the waters around the city teem with more than 60 varieties of commercial fish that you can eventually find parked on a restaurant plate next to a lemon wedge. Some of the most popular saltwater catches are grouper, mahimahi, mullet, pompano, redfish, snapper, and trout.

To buy fresh fish, avoid supermarket seafood counters; most of their goods have been frozen. Instead, opt for fish fresh off the boat at some of the docks around the city. The best time to buy is late afternoon, when all the fishing boats have returned with their day's haul.

On Key Biscayne, the boat docks next to **Sunday's** restaurant are usually lined with fishermen beginning about 3 p.m. The docks are easy to spot on this narrow island. They're on the left at about the midway point.

The stone crab is more than a seafood specialty in Miami; it's an obsession almost. You can share this kingliest of crustaceans with friends back home—for a price. **Joe's Stone Crab Takeaway** will ship iced crabs to the doorstep of your choice by the following morning (☎ 800-780-2722).

FRUIT SHIPPING What's a trip to Florida without a box of rosy oranges and grapefruit to ship back home? **Norman Brothers Produce** (7621 SW 87th Avenue, South Miami; ☎ 305-274-9363) will ship anything you wish from their amazing array of culinary exotica, which includes obscurities such as the dwarfed doughnut apple. Then there's always our favorite standby, **Publix** (numerous locations throughout Miami), which will do the shipping honors for you in season, November through February.

JEWELRY Besides downtown Miami, the **International Jeweler's Exchange** in North Miami (18861 Biscayne Boulevard, behind Loehmann's Plaza; ☎ 305-935-1471) will fill the bill. Fifty stalls are stocked with gold, pearls, and diamonds. Open Monday–Saturday, 10 a.m.–6 p.m., with extended holiday hours.

SWIMWEAR Finding a good swimsuit in Miami should be the least of your worries. **Swim 'n' Sport** (many locations, including The Falls and Bal Harbour Shops) and **Ritchie Swimwear** (160 Eighth Street, Miami Beach; ☎ 305-538-0201) are among the many fine options.

TROPICAL FURNITURE To accommodate and adapt to the humidity and relentless sunshine of Miami, furniture is often made of rattan, wicker, or light woods. In many of the Art Deco hotels on South Beach, 1950s-style furniture, with its whimsy and clean lines, decorates rooms and lobbies. Miami is a furniture-producing Mecca, though the most outstanding and truly local sorts are tropical and vintage furniture. Shipping should present no problem, but be sure to verify with your furniture dealer and remember to insure your purchase. Check out Miami's up-and-coming Design District—located two blocks west of Biscayne Boulevard at 36th Street—for a concentration of unique showrooms.

Rattan Shack (9840 NW 77th Avenue, Hialeah Gardens; ☎ 305-823-9800) is a vast place off the Palmetto Expressway with rattan and wicker furniture for indoors and out. **J&J Rattan** (4652 SW 72nd Avenue, Miami; ☎ 305-666-7503) is another large warehouse that exclusively sells rattan and wicker couches, dining sets, and chairs.

In **Miami's Design District** (west of Biscayne Boulevard at NE 40th Street), you can browse through numerous stores open to both designers and the public.

WINE AND GOURMET FOODS Whether you're browsing for a new imported mustard or in search of the definitive California Cabernet Sauvignon, chances are you'll find it at **Epicure Market** (1656 Alton Road; ☎ 305-672-1861), where the local elite shop for foodstuffs, as well as the freshest of produce, tempting bakery items, and old-fashioned Jewish deli fare.

If you're a hardcore Italian-food-and-wine fan, you'll spend hours at **Laurenzo's,** an Italian-American market and wine emporium (16385 West Dixie Highway, North Miami; ☎ 305-945-6381). The award-winning wine department features vintages from Bordeaux, Burgundy, Spain, California, and Italy, among other regions, as well as more than 40 weekly in-store wine specials. Also noteworthy is **Perricone's Marketplace and Café** (15 SE Tenth Street; ☎ 305-374-9449), where you can also sit down for a meal in the airy dining room.

SIGHTSEEING TIPS *and* TOURS

COLLEGE AND PROFESSIONAL SPORTS, ART SHOWS, street festivals, museums, film festivals, a renowned book fair, a world-class zoo, and fascinating attractions and festivals showcase this subtropical city: Greater Miami is worth exploring, even if it means tearing yourself away from the beach.

SPECIALIZED TOURS

AREA BUS TOURS—ON AIR-CONDITIONED MOTOR coaches with trained tour guides narrating—take visitors to popular tourist areas such as South Beach, Coconut Grove, Brickell Avenue, Coral Gables, Little Havana, and downtown Miami. Many guided tours are all-day or multiday affairs that go to destinations well outside of Miami: the Florida Keys and Key West, the Bahamas, the Everglades, and Walt Disney World.

Here are some tours we recommend. Most require advanced reservations and a deposit; most tour buses can pick you up and drop you off at your Miami or Miami Beach hotel.

Flamingo Tours offers daily narrated bus trips to Key West that pick you up at your Miami Beach hotel at 7 a.m. and bring you back around 11 p.m. The tour includes a breakfast stop at Key Largo, a brief stop at the Seven-Mile Bridge, and an afternoon exploring Key West. Activities include visits to the Hemingway House, Mel Fisher's Treasure Exhibit, and a glass-bottom-boat ride. On the return trip, the bus stops in Islamorada. The price per person is $69; $59 for children ages 3–11.

Other tours offered by Flamingo include one-day daily motor-coach trips to Walt Disney World ($120 for adults and $110 for children ages 3–9). For more information, call Flamingo Tours at ☎ 305-948-3822.

In addition to an all-day bus tour to Key West, **Miami Nice Tours** offers excursions to the Everglades on Tuesday and Saturday, narrated in English and German. The tours stop at the Everglades Alligator Farm near Florida City and include an airboat ride. The bus leaves at 8:30 a.m. and returns at 5 p.m.; the cost is $59 for adults and $49 for children ages 3–9. Call ☎ 305-949-9180 for more information.

Miami Nice also offers daily one-day trips to Walt Disney World and Universal Studios in Orlando. The bus leaves Miami Beach at 6 a.m. and returns around midnight. The motor-coach trip costs $120 for adults and $105 for children ages 3–9; the price includes the entrance fee to one of the parks.

Art Deco Tours offers a wide range of tours, including citywide and shopping tours led by owner Dona Zemo. The most popular is the Art Deco Walking Tour, the official tour of the Miami Beach Chamber of Commerce (MBCC), available Wednesday through Sunday. The cost is $20 per person; the tour lasts two hours, so wear comfortable shoes. Call ☎ 305-531-3484 for more information.

TOURING ON YOUR OWN: OUR FAVORITE ITINERARIES

IF YOU'VE TAKEN A GUIDED TOUR OF THE CITY and you're looking for a less packaged experience, or if you've only limited time to see the sights and still want the full flavor of Miami, here are some suggested itineraries, along with some advice to get you into a South Florida state of mind.

unofficial **TIP**
Rent a convertible (c'mon, this is Miami), set the FM dial to some pulsating Latin rhythms, and crank up the volume. Wear your bathing suit beneath your clothes, and put on some comfortable walking shoes.

For a full one-day dose of Miami-ness, pick and choose from the following:

1. Meander through Coral Gables in the early morning. Stop at the Biltmore Hotel, have a club soda in the courtyard, and peer at the huge, fantastic pool. Drive by the Venetian Pool, carved out of coral rock.

2. Visit Vizcaya Museum and Gardens for another sampling of vintage opulence.

3. On to Coconut Grove for a stroll and some shopping.

4. Check out life on Calle Ocho. Grab a late lunch at a Cuban restaurant: Order *arroz con pollo, café con leche,* and *flan* at La Carreta, Versailles, or Casablanca.

5. Head over to South Beach for a bit of strolling, sunning on the beach, or a visit to the Bass Museum.

6. Head back to the hotel for a shower and a nap—you'll need it.

7. Dine late at an oceanside restaurant on South Beach or in one of the open-air restaurants on Lincoln Road.

8. Dance at one or more of the clubs on South Beach.

If you have just a couple of days, consider this day-two itinerary:

1. Breakfast at an oceanside cafe on South Beach after an early-morning stroll along the beach.

2. Take a walking tour of the Art Deco District, or rent a bike and explore the area. Or check out the Wolfsonian-FIU museum.

3. Head downtown at lunchtime. Take a break from walking on the "People Mover" as it loops around Miami and offers great city views.

4. Eat lunch at one of the many crowded-but-cheap ethnic eateries found throughout downtown or at Bayside.

5. Drive to Key Biscayne for a late afternoon of windsurfing, kayaking, beaching, or tennis.

6. Returning to downtown, board the Heritage of Miami sunset cruise behind Bayside Marketplace to see the city at dusk from a sailboat.

7. Enjoy dinner at one of the many restaurants that dot Coral Gables, Coconut Grove, or Brickell Village.

If your stay in Miami is longer than a couple of days, try to include the following not-to-be-missed attractions on your itinerary: Fairchild Tropical Garden, Parrot Jungle Island, Metrozoo, the Historical Museum of Southern Florida, the Lowe Art Museum, snorkeling at Biscayne National Park or John Pennekamp Coral Reef State Park, a bike ride down Old Cutler Road, and a day trip to the Everglades and/or the Keys.

MIAMI FOR CHILDREN

ALTHOUGH PLACES LIKE SOUTH BEACH ARE definitely adult (some would suggest R-rated) in their appeal and Miami's downtown will appeal chiefly to adults and older children, Miami and its environs offer plenty for youngsters to see and do. Attractions include a world-class zoo, a marine-mammal aquarium, a science museum designed for young folk, and some private "jungles" that will delight the kids.

TEN MIAMI ATTRACTIONS GREAT FOR KIDS

Biscayne National Park

Everglades National Park/Shark Valley Tram Tour

Gold Coast Railroad Museum

Historical Museum of Southern Florida

Metrozoo

Miami Museum of Science/Space Transit Planetarium

Monkey Jungle

Parrot Jungle Island

Seaquarium

Weeks Air Museum

SIGHTSEEING CRUISES

CRUISE BOATS THAT DEPART FROM DOWNTOWN Miami and the marina on Miami Beach give visitors a chance to see the town's most spectacular sights from the water. Most tours are narrated in English and Spanish, and snacks and beverages are sold on board.

From **Bayside Marketplace,** the two-story shopping mall by the water in Bayfront Park in downtown Miami, several large, air-conditioned tour boats whisk visitors on one-and-a-half-hour excursions around placid Biscayne Bay. Tours generally leave every hour, starting at 11 a.m. until about 7 p.m. daily. Tickets cost $16 for adults and $7 for children ages 4–12.

The sights include high-rise buildings downtown and the most conspicuous landmark on the bay: the 65-foot Fender Stratocaster guitar rotating above the Hard Rock Cafe; its reported cost was a cool half-million dollars. Other sights on the cruise include the spiraling metal structure in Bayfront Park that's a monument to the crew of the space shuttle *Challenger,* and tugboats, freighters, and cruise ships tied up at the Port of Miami.

Next, the boats swing by Fisher Island (an exclusive community of high-rise condos that can only be reached by boat or helicopter) and Miami Beach. After you pass under the MacArthur Causeway connecting Miami Beach and the mainland, a number of artificial islands are next, including the aptly named Star Island and Million-aires' Row. Your guide will point out the former homes of Elizabeth Taylor, Don Johnson and Melanie Griffith, Al Capone, and other notables—it seems the elusiveness of fame and the high cost of real estate dictate who stays and who leaves Star Island. The current homes of megastar Gloria Estefan and other celebs are noted.

After passing the Henry Flagler Monument and Palm Island, the tour boats swing back under the Venetian Causeway and complete their circuit of Biscayne Bay.

Sailing aboard a Tall Ship on Biscayne Bay

For the nautically inclined, a sure bet is a two-hour cruise on Biscayne Bay aboard the Heritage of *Miami II,* an 85-foot topsail schooner. Once out on the placid waters of the bay, the engine goes off and wind fills the crimson sails. If the weather cooperates, the skipper might let passengers take the helm for a few minutes while under sail.

unofficial **TIP**
In the winter, sign up for the 4 p.m. sail, which turns into a sunset cruise.

Two-hour sails depart at 1:30 p.m. and 4 p.m.; a one-hour trip leaves at 6:30 p.m. and 8 p.m. All sails depart daily from Bayside Marketplace in downtown Miami. The cost is $15 for adults and $10 for children for the evening trips, and $20 for adults and $15 for children for the afternoon trips. Call ahead for specific schedules, as the *Heritage of Miami II* may be on charter and unavailable for tours; ☎ 305-442-9697.

GREAT VIEWS

CRUISE SHIPS AND HIGH-RISES On weekend nights, drive from Miami Beach to downtown Miami on the MacArthur Causeway, and you'll see a panorama of glittering cruise ships tied up at the Port of Miami and moving out to the Atlantic along Government Cut. The backdrop is the multicolored Miami skyline, which some consider the most spectacular urban cityscape in the United States. Try to spot the CenTrust Building; a circular high-rise designed by I. M. Pei, it changes color on command.

DOWNTOWN FROM A SLIGHTLY DIFFERENT ANGLE Another great view of downtown is available from the Rickenbacker Causeway to Key Biscayne. Park on the left side of the causeway. It's not uncommon to spot a couple stealing kisses here.

ART DECO For an unusual—and spectacular—view of the candy-colored architecture, try this: At sundown, put on a swimsuit, wade out into the surf until you're neck deep . . . and turn around. (Just don't inhale salt water when you gasp at the view.)

THE "PEOPLE MOVER" This fun automated-transportation system scoots people around a 26-block chunk of downtown and provides a spectacular pelican's-eye view of the city, Biscayne Bay, and the Atlantic Ocean. The new Omni Loop provides an excellent view of Government Cut and the Port of Miami. A ride on the People Mover is free.

CRUISE SHIPS AND FREIGHTERS NAVIGATING GOVERNMENT CUT You can see the nautical action from South Pointe Park on the southern tip of Miami Beach. The 38-foot-deep channel means even the largest cruise and container ships can steam in and out of the Port of Miami. Fridays and Sundays are your best bets.

CORAL WAY (SW 24TH STREET) A broad, mainly commercial avenue separated and shaded by giant banyan trees with sprawling roots, Coral Way stretches from the historic 1920s homes of Coral Gables to the luxury high-rises of Brickell Avenue by Biscayne Bay. Start at the Miracle Mile and drive east; on the left, at Douglas Road, is the thoroughly spaced-out-looking Miracle Center, designed by Arquitectonica.

OVERVIEW OF MIAMI Stop by the Greater Miami Convention and Visitors Bureau's main office, at 701 Brickell Avenue, Suite 2700, during regular business hours, pick up a free map, and check out the panoramic views of downtown Miami, the Miami River, Biscayne Bay, the Port of Miami, and the Atlantic Ocean from the office windows. Park free in the basement of the high-rise, and get your parking ticket validated.

SUNRISE Make it a point to get up early one morning to view the pink-and-orange sunrise over the ocean. Better yet, stay up all night dancing at a South Beach club, and greet the rising sun.

SUNSET From Key Biscayne, the Rusty Pelican Restaurant, just over the bridge, has spectacular sunset views of downtown Miami. Also, from Miami Beach, sunsets over Biscayne Bay and the skyline are a treat.

THE EVERGLADES Although it's about an hour's drive west to Everglades National Park on US 41, followed by **a seven-mile tram or bicycle ride,** the Park rewards visitors with one of the best views in South Florida. The view from the top of the 40-foot-plus tower (easily accessible from a ramp) stretches from horizon to horizon across stunning wilderness scenery. Directly below you lies a wide, impressive scene featuring bird life, huge fish, and giant turtles and gators moving through the water.

SCENIC DRIVES

AFTER THE LONG DRIVE OR THE HASSLE PICKING up your rental car, it only makes sense to take advantage of your wheels. Auto tours are great way to see Miami. Just don't leave during rush hour (7–9 a.m. and 3:30–6:30 p.m., weekdays), and be sure to bring a good map.

One of the most memorable sights in Miami is the view of the city from the **MacArthur Causeway**—especially at night, when cruise ships are tied up at the Port of Miami (see above, "Great Views") and the buildings and bridges are edged in colored lights. Farther north on Miami Beach's **Collins Avenue,** starting when intersecting streets number in the 40s, a string of condos and hotels dates from the 1950s. Continue north along **FL A1A** as far as you want; cruising this venerable old highway is a South Florida tradition.

South of downtown, near the Rickenbacker Causeway, Vizcaya, and the Miami Museum of Science, take **Bayshore Drive** for a long, relaxing drive through Coconut Grove, Coral Gables, and points south. As you meander along **Main Highway, Ingraham Highway,** and **Old Cutler Road,** you'll pass some of the most lush tropical scenery in the Miami area, sprawling homes, and glimpses of sparkling Biscayne Bay. The best way to do this drive is to take a map and not worry about getting lost; the area is safe, and you're never too far from a major road.

A perfect destination—and a real treat for outdoors lovers—is Fairchild Tropical Garden; a good turning-back point is **Coral Reef Drive** (SW 152nd Street). That's where the damage from Hurricane Andrew—a noticeable decrease in foliage—starts to appear.

For a look at what all of South Florida used to look like, go west on US 41 toward the Everglades. (In Miami, just west of downtown, **US 41** is Eighth Street, or Calle Ocho, and cuts through the heart of Little Havana.) After you get past Florida's Turnpike, you'll start to see natural flora and an astounding amount of bird life in the canals along the side of the road. Past the Shark Valley entrance to Everglades National Park is Big Cypress National Preserve; the scenery is lush, and you pass several Native American villages on the road.

■¦ ATTRACTIONS

THE FOLLOWING CHART WILL HELP YOU prioritize your touring at a glance. In it you'll find the name, location, and author's rating. Attractions without permanent collections (usually art galleries) are not rated because exhibits change. Each attraction is individually profiled later in this section. Most museum-type attractions offer group rates for ten or more people.

Miami Attractions

NAME	LOCATION	AUTHOR'S RATING
AQUARIUM		
Miami Seaquarium	Miami	★★
GARDENS		
Fairchild Tropical Garden	Miami	★★★★½
Vizcaya Museum and Gardens	Miami	
	mansion	★★★
	gardens	★★★★★

NAME	LOCATION	AUTHOR'S RATING
HOME TOURS		
The Barnacle State Historic Site	**Coconut Grove**	★★½
Deering Estate at Cutler	**South Miami**	
	mansion	★★★
	grounds	★★★★★
Vizcaya Museum and Gardens	**Miami**	
	mansion	★★★
	gardens	★★★★★
MEMORIAL		
Holocaust Memorial of Miami Beach	**Miami Beach**	★★★★
MUSEUMS		
Gold Coast Railroad Museum	**Miami**	★★½
Historical Museum of Southern Florida	**Miami**	★★★★
The Jewish Museum of Florida	**Miami Beach**	★★
Lowe Art Museum	**Coral Gables**	★★★★
Miami Art Museum	**Miami**	n/a
Museum of Contemporary Art	**North Miami**	★★★½
The Wolfsonian-FIU	**Miami Beach**	★★★½
PARKS		
Biscayne National Park	**Between Miami and Homestead**	★★★★
ZOOS/ANIMAL EXHIBITS		
Metrozoo	**Miami**	★★★★★
Monkey Jungle	**Miami**	★★★½
Parrot Jungle Island	**Miami**	★★★★½

ATTRACTION PROFILES

The Barnacle State Historic Site

APPEAL BY AGE	PRESCHOOL	GRADE SCHOOL ★½	TEENS ★½
YOUNG ADULTS ★★		OVER 30 _½	SENIORS ★★½

In Coconut Grove; 3485 Main Highway; ☎ 305-448-9445; www.abfla.com/parks/barnacle/barnacle.html

Type of attraction The oldest home in Dade County on its original site (1891), with a panoramic view of Biscayne Bay and beauty and calm in hectic Coconut

miami area attractions and beaches

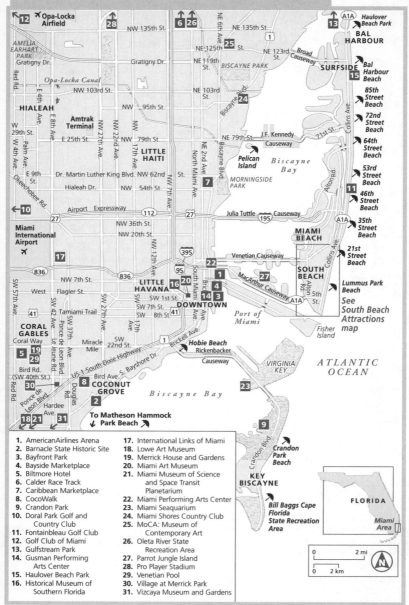

1. AmericanAirlines Arena
2. Barnacle State Historic Site
3. Bayfront Park
4. Bayside Marketplace
5. Biltmore Hotel
6. Calder Race Track
7. Caribbean Marketplace
8. CocoWalk
9. Crandon Park
10. Doral Park Golf and
    Country Club
11. Fontainebleau Golf Club
12. Golf Club of Miami
13. Gulfstream Park
14. Gusman Performing
    Arts Center
15. Haulover Beach Park
16. Historical Museum of
    Southern Florida
17. International Links of Miami
18. Lowe Art Museum
19. Merrick House and Gardens
20. Miami Art Museum
21. Miami Museum of Science
    and Space Transit
    Planetarium
22. Miami Performing Arts Center
23. Miami Seaquarium
24. Miami Shores Country Club
25. MoCA: Museum of
    Contemporary Art
26. Oleta River State
    Recreation Area
27. Parrot Jungle Island
28. Pro Player Stadium
29. Venetian Pool
30. Village at Merrick Park
31. Vizcaya Museum and Gardens

south beach attractions and dining

Attractions
1. Art Deco Welcome Center
2. Collins Park
3. Colony Theater
4. Holocaust Memorial of Miami Beach
5. Jackie Gleason Theater of the Performing Arts
6. Jewish Museum of Florida
7. Lincoln Theater
8. Lummus Park Beach
9. Miami Beach Bicycle Center
10. Miami Beach Post Office
11. Miami Beach Public Courts at Flamingo Park
12. Morris Lapidus Sculptures
13. Wolfsonian-FIU Museum

Restaurants
14. B.E.D.
15. Barton G.
16. Blue Door at the Delano
17. Casa Tua
18. China Grill
19. Icebox Café
20. Jerry's Famous Deli
21. Joe Allen
22. Joe's Stone Crab Restaurant
23. Nemo
24. News Café
25. Nikki Beach Club
26. Pacific Time
27. Pearl
28. Talula
29. Tap Tap
30. Touch
31. Van Dyke Café
32. Vix

south miami-dade county attractions, dining, and nightlife

Attractions ●
1. Coral Castle
2. Deering Estate at Cutler
3. Fairchild Tropical Garden
4. Gold Coast Railroad Museum
5. Metrozoo

6. Miami National Golf Club
7. Monkey Jungle
8. Weeks Air Museum

Restaurants ◆
9. La Pastis
10. Lan Pan-Asian Cafe

11. Red Fish Grill
12. Shorty's
13. Two Chefs

Nightlife ■
14. Gameworks
15. Ozone

Grove. House tours are guided only; tours of the grounds are self guided. **Admission $. Hours** Daily, 9 a.m.–4 p.m.; closed Thanksgiving, Christmas, and New Year's days. **When to go** Anytime **Special comments** Pets on a leash are allowed on the grounds. **Author's rating** A real find for history buffs and folks interested in how the landed gentry lived in South Florida a century ago. It's also a terrific picnic spot with a drop-dead view of Biscayne Bay. ★★½. **How much time to allow** An hour or so for the building tour, or however long it takes to recharge your batteries after a morning of shopping or people watching in the Grove. Allot half an hour to stroll the grounds.

DESCRIPTION AND COMMENTS Ralph Middleton Munroe was a yacht designer and wrecker who earned a living by salvaging ships that ran aground. He first visited South Florida in 1877 and returned in 1886 to purchase 40 acres facing Biscayne Bay. In 1891, he built The Barnacle, a one-story structure raised on wood pilings with a central octagonal room. Today, visitors can tour the unique house, filled with nautical touches, and glimpse an early-Miami way of life. A five-acre tropical-hardwood hammock isolates the grounds from busy Main Highway, giving way to a view that over the years has attracted neighbors such as Sylvester Stallone and Madonna.

TOURING TIPS Guided house tours are free and conducted at 10 a.m., 11:30 a.m., 1 p.m., and 2:30 p.m., Friday–Sunday; meet on the porch of the main house. Tours are limited to the first ten people who show up, so try to arrive a few minutes early. Bring a picnic lunch.

OTHER THINGS TO DO NEARBY The Grove is second only to South Beach for people watching, shopping, and dining. If the Barnacle whetted your appetite for more outdoor enjoyment on the shores of Biscayne Bay, continue south on Main Highway a few miles to Fairchild Tropical Garden.

Biscayne National Park

APPEAL BY AGE	PRESCHOOL ★★	GRADE SCHOOL ★★★	TEENS ★★★½
YOUNG ADULTS ★★★½	OVER 30 ★★★★		SENIORS ★★★★

The Convoy Point Visitor Center, the only part of the park accessible by car, is about 25 miles south of Miami and 6 miles east of US 1 and Homestead; from the Florida Turnpike Extension, take SW 328th Street (North Canal Drive) to the park entrance on the left; ☎ 305-230-7275; to make reservations for snorkel, scuba, and boat trips, call ☎ 305-230-1100; www.nps.gov/bisc

Type of attraction More than 180,000 acres of underwater reefs, islands, and the closest coral-reef snorkeling to Miami; guided and self-guided tours **Admission** Free. A park concession offers three-hour glass-bottom-boat tours of the bay and reef. The cost is $24.50 for adults, $16.50 for children ages 12 and under, and $19.50 for seniors; the trips leave at 10 a.m. daily. Three-hour snorkeling trips to the reef are $30 per person and include all equipment; the boat leaves at 1:30 and 4:30 p.m. daily. Two-tank scuba dives for certified divers are offered at 8:30 a.m. and 1 p.m. on weekends only; the cost is $54. Advance reservations for the boat tour and the snorkel trip are strongly advised; reservations are required for the scuba dives. Canoe rentals are $12 an hour, and kayak rentals are $16 an hour; prices include paddles and life jackets. Rentals are available 9 a.m.–3 p.m. **Hours** Visitor center: daily, 8:30 a.m.–5 p.m. **When to go** Anytime, weather permitting. While mosquitoes and other biting insects are present year-round, their populations are lowest from January to April. Around holiday weekends, call at least three days in advance for a reservation for a boat tour or diving trip. While reservations usually aren't necessary at other times, call ahead to make sure a boat trip isn't canceled due to a chartered event. **Special comments** Because the park is almost completely under water, visitors are at the mercy of the weather; tours and canoe rentals are sometimes canceled in windy conditions. If the air is cold, snorkelers can rent wet suits. Boat schedules change seasonally, so it's always a good idea to call first. **Author's rating** Viewing a coral reef through a face mask or glass-bottom boat sure beats looking at fish through glass in an aquarium. ★★★★. **How much time to allow** Half a day or longer.

DESCRIPTION AND COMMENTS Clear blue water, dark-green foliage, coral reefs, and islands combine to create a subtropical paradise only an hour or so from hectic Miami. Unlike most parks, however, Biscayne is dominated by water—and enjoying it requires renting a canoe or taking a boat excursion.

Parrotfish, finger garlic sponge, goosehead scorpionfish, and peppermint goby populate the shallow-water reefs drenched in sunlight. A reef explorer outfitted in mask, snorkel, flippers, and a life vest can spend hours drifting lazily in the waters above the reefs while watching a procession of astounding marine life.

TOURING TIPS Call at least a day ahead to reserve a boat trip. Exploring the reefs is best on calm, sunny days. Unless you're an experienced snorkeler or diver, go on the group trip, which is run by experts who provide plenty of hand-holding for novices. Canoes are available for rent for exploring the mangrove shoreline along the mainland.

Fishermen can try their luck at saltwater fishing from the jetty; stop at the visitor center for regulations and in Homestead for fishing licenses. The attractive new visitor center has a few small displays on bay ecology, local history, and Hurricane Andrew.

OTHER THINGS TO DO NEARBY Everglades National Park is due west of Homestead. If you haven't had your fill of Florida tourist schlock yet, stop by the Coral Castle, just north of Homestead on US 1. You'll also find a nearly endless selection of fast-food joints along the venerable old highway.

Deering Estate at Cutler

APPEAL BY AGE	PRESCHOOL ★	GRADE SCHOOL ★★★	TEENS ★★
YOUNG ADULTS ★★★★		OVER 30 ★★★★	SENIORS ★★★★

16701 SW 72nd Avenue; South Miami, off Old Cutler Road;
☎ **305-235-1668; www.deeringestate.com**

Type of attraction True Floridiana, with acres of lush foliage, a Florida cracker inn, and an understated mansion; guided and self-guided tours; canoes. **Admission** $7 adults, $5 children ages 14 and under. **Hours** Daily, 10 a.m.–5 p.m.; last admission at 4 p.m. **When to go** Anytime, as both indoor and outdoor pleasures allow for cooling off; moonlit nights are especially delightful respites in summer. **Author's rating** Relatively undiscovered example of true South Florida beauty and history. ★★★★½ **How much time to allow** Minimum of 2 hours; if you partake of outdoor activities, up to half a day.

DESCRIPTION AND COMMENTS   Like Vizcaya, about a 45-minute drive north, this sprawling estate and grounds on Biscayne Bay were created by a wealthy Deering as a winter home. Less well known and more austere than James Deering's Vizcaya, it offers unique Florida charms. James's brother, Charles, bought the property in 1913. A long walk through natural tropical plantings of hardwoods and orchids leads to the smallish coral-rock Mediterranean Revival mansion, completed in 1932. Rooms are sparsely furnished but offer interesting details such as iron gates, copper ceilings, and stone ceilings. Next door, the restored Richmond Cottage displays vintage photos and furnishings. Built in 1900 in true South Florida vernacular, the structure was the first inn to be built between Coconut Grove and Key West.

Much of the property remains natural and unspoiled. Grounds are lush with native vines and trees. Bobcats, foxes, and other critters live on-site, and pelicans and cormorants swoop along the blue bay.

TOURING TIPS   The most special activity is a canoe trip on the bay to nearby Chicken Key (call ahead for details). An environmental center offers programs for adults and children. Guided nature tours explore the property, which is thick with coastal-Florida hardwood hammocks. Scientists have found human remains here from 10,000 years ago, and a fossil pit holds bones of ancient animals, including bison and jaguars.

OTHER THINGS TO DO NEARBY   Fairchild Tropical Garden (see below), Metrozoo, and Matheson Hammock Park are all within 20 minutes away.

Fairchild Tropical Garden

APPEAL BY AGE	PRESCHOOL ★	GRADE SCHOOL ★½	TEENS ★★
YOUNG ADULTS ★★★½	OVER 30 ★★★½		SENIORS ★★★★

10901 Old Cutler Road, Miami; south of Coconut Grove on Old Cutler Road; ☎ **305-667-1651; www.fairchildgarden.org**

Type of attraction 83 lushly landscaped acres containing plants from tropical regions around the world; guided and self-guided tours. **Admission** $15; children under age 12 free; includes a narrated 30-minute open-air tram tour of the garden. **Hours** Park: daily, 9:30 a.m.–4:30 p.m.; closed Christmas Day. Garden Café: daily, 9:30 a.m.–4:30 p.m. **When to go** Anytime, but avoid hot and humid summer afternoons. In the fall, winter, and spring, the late-afternoon sun lights the tropical foliage with a rich glow. The park is seldom crowded, except on weekends. **Author's rating** This manicured garden, filled with lush palms and exotic trees and dotted with man-made lakes, is a knockout. ★★★★½. **How much time to allow** 2 hours minimum; half a day or more for a leisurely exploration.

DESCRIPTION AND COMMENTS Fairchild Tropical Garden is the largest tropical botanical garden in the United States; its mission encompasses education, scientific research, and display. The grounds and plant life are stunning. You don't have to be a certified tree hugger to appreciate the beauty and tranquility found here.

TOURING TIPS The free tram tour leaves on the hour. After taking the tour, go back to areas that interest you. For example, Cycad Circle features the same plants that dinosaurs munched 300 million years ago and an indoor garden houses orchids and other specimens. The 1939 Gate House has been restored and is now a historical museum with permanent exhibits on plant exploration.

The expanded Garden Shop sells tropical gardening books, plants, and unique gifts. Sandwiches, drinks, and snacks are available at the snack bar, where you can eat under a huge sapodilla tree (on weekends only). If you bring your own food, picnic next door at Matheson Hammock Park.

Some evenings, moonlit concerts offer a romantic opportunity to picnic.

OTHER THINGS TO DO NEARBY Coconut Grove is loaded with places to eat, drink, and shop. Matheson Hammock Park features a beach, a marina, and a terrific view of downtown Miami.

Gold Coast Railroad Museum

APPEAL BY AGE	PRESCHOOL ★★★	GRADE SCHOOL ★★★★	TEENS ★★
YOUNG ADULTS ★★½		OVER 30 ★★	SENIORS ★★

South of Miami near the entrance to Metrozoo; take the Florida Turnpike Extension to SW 152nd Street and follow signs to Metrozoo;
☎ **305-253-0063 or 888-608-7246; www.goldcoast-railroad.org**

Type of attraction A museum featuring steam and diesel locomotives, as well as a presidential railroad car; guided and self-guided tours. **Admission** Adults, $5; children under 12, $3. **Hours** Monday–Friday, 10 a.m.–4 p.m.; Saturday and Sunday, 11 a.m.–4 p.m. **When to go** Anytime except hot, humid summer afternoons. **Author's rating** A must-see for railroad buffs and kids. ★★½. **How much time to allow** 1 hour.

DESCRIPTION AND COMMENTS This complex of Navy blimp hangars destroyed in a 1945 hurricane rose again to become a railroad museum—only to be wiped out by Andrew in 1992. The new railroad shed and museum shop are now open again. Visitors can check out an array of historic railroad cars (including one used by former presidents Roosevelt, Truman, Eisenhower, and Reagan) and fascinating memorabilia, and on weekends even go for train rides.

TOURING TIPS The Gold Coast Railroad Museum is a nice diversion before or after visiting Metrozoo, which is right next door. On weekends at 1 p.m. and 3 p.m., rides on the museum's two-foot-gauge railroad are offered; the cost is an additional $2 per person. Rides last 15–20 minutes.

OTHER THINGS TO DO NEARBY Metrozoo, Monkey Jungle, the Weeks Air Museum, and a wide selection of fast-food restaurants are all close by.

Historical Museum of Southern Florida

| APPEAL BY AGE | PRESCHOOL ★★ | GRADE SCHOOL ★★★★ | TEENS ★★★½ |
| YOUNG ADULTS ★★★★ | | OVER 30 ★★★★ | SENIORS ★★★★ |

101 West Flagler Street in downtown Miami, in the Metro-Dade Cultural Center; take the "People Mover" to the Government Center station; ☎ 305-375-1492; www.historical-museum.org

Type of attraction 10,000 years of Florida history on display; a self-guided tour. **Admission** Adults, $5; children ages 6–12, $2; children under age 6, free. **Hours** Monday–Saturday, 10 a.m.–5 p.m.; Thursday, 10 a.m.–9 p.m.; Sunday, noon–5 p.m. **When to go** Anytime. **Author's rating** A spiffy museum that will entertain and educate both kids and adults. ★★★★. **How much time to allow** 1–2 hours.

DESCRIPTION AND COMMENTS Interactive displays feature earphones that let you hear jungle sounds; others are big enough to walk through. Visitors can discover the Florida that existed before tourists—even before people set foot in South Florida. The museum also emphasizes the rich cultural diversity of modern Florida's multiethnic population, ranging from Hispanic to Jewish.

TOURING TIPS Kids will really like the various Colonial-era cannons in the historical exhibits. They'll also like climbing aboard an old 1920s trolley car. The Indies Company, the museum's gift shop, offers a wide range of items that reflect South Florida and the Caribbean, including a large assortment of old poster reproductions.

Discounted parking is available at Cultural Center Parking at 50 NW Second Avenue and at Metro-Dade County Garage at 140 West Flagler Street. Have your parking ticket validated at the admission desk.

OTHER THINGS TO DO NEARBY Couple your visit to the Historical Museum of Southern Florida with a stop at the Miami Art Museum, across the plaza. The Miami Public Library, with an art exhibit on the second floor, is a fine place to relax and read up on Floridiana. If you've never boarded the "People Mover," Miami's automated downtown transportation system, do it now: It's free.

Holocaust Memorial of Miami Beach

| APPEAL BY AGE | PRESCHOOL ★ | GRADE SCHOOL ★★ | TEENS ★★½ |
| YOUNG ADULTS ★★★ | | OVER 30 ★★★★ | SENIORS ★★★★½ |

Dade Boulevard and Meridian Avenue (near the Miami Beach Convention Center) in Miami Beach; ☎ 305-538-1663; www.holocaustmmb.org

Type of attraction A memorial to the 6 million Jews killed in the Holocaust; a self-guided tour. **Admission** Free. **Hours** Daily, 9 a.m.–9 p.m. **When to go** Anytime. **Author's rating** A moving experience. ★★★★ **How much time to allow** 1 hour.

DESCRIPTION AND COMMENTS Miami Beach is home to one of the world's largest populations of Holocaust survivors. Dedicated in 1990 in a ceremony that featured Nobel Prize laureate Elie Wiesel, the Holocaust Memorial utilizes contrasting elements to deliver an emotional punch:

bright Jerusalem stone, somber black granite, the stillness of a reflecting pool, the backdrop of an azure sky, and a stunning 42-foot sculpture of a giant outstretched arm (tattooed with a number from Auschwitz) rising up from the earth. Local architect Kenneth Treister designed it.

For more evidence of Treister's artistry, see Mayfair Shops, a 20-year-old shopping mall in Coconut Grove, and the cavelike, exquisite chapel at Miami's oldest reform synagogue, Temple Israel, on NE 19th Street, off NE Second Avenue.

TOURING TIPS There's more to the memorial than just the dramatic hand that seems to rise from the reflecting pool—but you must get out of your car to experience it. Black granite panels contain a concise history of the Holocaust, plus pictorial representations, text, and maps. After walking through an enclosed space and a narrow passage, the visitor is greeted with a stunning sight: a circular plaza surrounded by shining black granite that mirrors the 42-foot bronze sculpture. Accompanying music seems to reflect the sorrow.

Area parking is scarce (especially if a convention is taking place), but reserved street parking is available on Meridian Avenue for Holocaust Memorial visitors only.

OTHER THINGS TO DO NEARBY The Wolfsonian-FIU, the Bass Museum, and the Jewish Museum of Florida are all nearby in South Beach. And you can always stroll, sit, and sup on Lincoln Road.

The Jewish Museum of Florida

APPEAL BY AGE	PRESCHOOL ★	GRADE SCHOOL ★★	TEENS ★★½
YOUNG ADULTS ★★½		OVER 30 ★★½	SENIORS ★★★

In South Beach; 301 Washington Avenue; ☎ 305-672-5044; www.jewishmuseum.com

Type of attraction More than 200 years of Florida Jewish life on display in a 1936 Art Deco–style building; guided and self-guided tours. **Admission** Adults, $6; seniors and students, $5; $12 for families; free admission on Saturday. **Hours** Tuesday–Sunday, 10 a.m.–5 p.m.; closed Monday, Jewish holidays, and major holidays (except Christmas). **When to go** Anytime.. **Special comments** The neighborhood around this former Orthodox synagogue (which predates the Art Deco District a few blocks north) is rapidly changing as developers move in; enjoy the ambience before high-rise condos take over. **Author's rating** A narrow yet interesting slice of South Florida history; a beautiful interior that's worth a peek. ★★. **How much time to allow** 1 hour.

DESCRIPTION AND COMMENTS This recently restored Art Deco building once served as Miami Beach's first Orthodox synagogue. Today, visitors can enjoy nearly 80 stained-glass windows, a copper dome, the marble *bimah* (Torah reading platform), and many Art Deco features such as chandeliers and sconces. Arranged on the slanted floor (designed so the rabbi could be heard by the congregation) is a collection of temporary exhibits on Jewish life, culture, and history in the Sunshine State.

TOURING TIPS For a more meaningful visit, a docent can enlighten you. Don't miss the 15-minute video that explains the museum's restoration and mission. And look for the window sponsored by notorious gangster Meyer Lansky (it's on the right as you enter the main room), who was a member of the synagogue.

OTHER THINGS TO DO NEARBY Drive south and turn right onto Biscayne Street to reach Joe's Stone Crab, the most famous (and crowded) restaurant in South Florida (open mid-October through mid-May). Watch huge freighters and cruise ships on their way to and from the Port of Miami at South Pointe Park. Explore the Art Deco District, which starts above Fifth Street, two blocks north. Stop at the Wolfsonian-FIU museum, a few blocks north on Washington Avenue.

Lowe Art Museum

APPEAL BY AGE	PRESCHOOL ★	GRADE SCHOOL ★ ★	TEENS ★ ★ ½
YOUNG ADULTS ★ ★ ★		OVER 30 ★ ★ ★ ½	SENIORS ★ ★ ★

Just off US 1 on the Coral Gables campus of the University of Miami; 2 blocks north of the University Metrorail Station; ☎ 305-284-3535; www.miami.edu/lowe

Type of attraction A diverse art collection ranging from antiquities to Renaissance, traditional, contemporary, and non-Western works; a self-guided tour. Admission Adults, $5; seniors and students, $3; children under age 12, free. Slightly higher fees are sometimes charged for special shows. Hours Tuesday, Wednesday, Friday, and Saturday, 10 a.m.–5 p.m.; Thursday, noon–7 p.m.; Sunday, noon–5 p.m.; closed Monday. When to go Anytime. Special comments A 10,000-foot expansion was recently completed. Author's rating A little bit of everything in bite-sized chunks that don't overwhelm; one of the best art museums in the Miami area. ★ ★ ★ ★. How much time to allow At least 1 hour; if the special exhibitions grab you, figure another hour.

DESCRIPTION AND COMMENTS The oldest visual-arts institution in Dade County boasts a collection of 7,000 works of art in its permanent collection, including Baroque art, paintings by Spanish masters such as El Greco, and works by modern artists such as Lichtenstein, Hanson, and Warhol. The Lowe features several special exhibitions each year, further varying the kind of art you'll see on any visit. The museum also emphasizes non-Western art, with exhibits of Southwestern Indian art, Latin American art, Guatemalan textiles, and pre-Columbian objects. For art lovers, the Lowe is a real find.

TOURING TIPS The Lowe Museum of Art is all on one floor, a boon for the elderly and handicapped. The museum store offers unusual gifts, art books, museum publications, and cards. The Lowe Art Festival in January is a popular event where you can gaze and shop for art and artifacts.

OTHER THINGS TO DO NEARBY Coconut Grove is a great place for eating, drinking, shopping, and people watching. The Venetian Pool in Coral Gables is an unusual swimming hole, if you want to cool off in style.

METRO-DADE CULTURAL CENTER

This downtown conglomeration of attractions consists of the Historical Museum of Southern Florida, the Miami Art Museum, and a branch of the Miami-Dade Public Library.

Miami Art Museum (formerly Center for the Fine Arts)
101 West Flagler Street, in the Metro-Dade Cultural Center in downtown Miami; take the "People Mover" to the Government Center station; ☎ 305-375-1700; www.miamiartmuseum.org

Type of attraction An art gallery that features constantly changing exhibitions of a wide range of art from around the world; a self-guided tour. **Admission** Adults, $5; seniors, $2.50; children under 12, free; free on Sunday and the second Saturday of the month. **Hours** Tuesday–Friday, 10 a.m.–5 p.m.; Saturday and Sunday, noon–5 p.m.; Thursday, noon–9 p.m.; closed Monday. **When to go** Anytime **Special comments** Because the museum has no permanent collection and exhibits are constantly changing, it's not possible to rate the gallery by age group. **Author's rating** It's not possible to assign this a reliable rating, but it's a large, comfortable gallery that should be on any art lover's itinerary. The shows are consistently professional and well attended. **How much time to allow** 1–2 hours.

DESCRIPTION AND COMMENTS Visit before or after seeing the Historical Museum of Southern Florida, located across the plaza. The large gallery offers exhibits on two floors. Stop at the admission desk to find out what's on display during your visit, or check Friday's edition of the *Miami Herald.*

TOURING TIPS The Miami Art Museum emphasizes high-quality art and hosts national touring shows. Discounted parking is available at Cultural Center Parking, 50 NW Second Avenue and at Metro-Dade County Garage, 140 West Flagler Street. For free parking, validate your parking ticket at the admission desk.

OTHER THINGS TO DO NEARBY The Miami Art Museum is paired with the Historical Museum of Southern Florida; Metrorail's "People Mover" makes the rest of downtown Miami easy to get to. Gusman Performing Arts Center—an 80-year-old cultural showcase for symphony, dance, and film that is the gem of downtown—is nearby.

Metrozoo

APPEAL BY AGE	PRESCHOOL ★★★★★	GRADE SCHOOL ★★★★★	TEENS ★★★★
YOUNG ADULTS ★★★★	OVER 30 ★★★★		SENIORS ★★★★

South of Miami. Take the Florida Turnpike Extension to the SW 152nd Street exit and follow the signs to the entrance; ☎ 305-251-0400 for a recorded message; ☎ 305-251-0401 for more information; www.miamimetrozoo.com

Type of attraction A "new-style" zoo featuring 800 cageless animals that roam on plots of land surrounded by moats; guided and self-guided tours. **Admission** Adults, $11.50; children ages 3–12, $6.75. **Hours** Daily, 9:30 a.m.–5:30 p.m. **When**

to go Avoid sweltering summer afternoons. "You'll die here midday in July and August," a zoo employee reports. Come before 10 a.m. or after 3:30 p.m. to beat the worst of the heat. Saturday, predictably enough, is the most crowded day, while Sunday morning is usually quiet. Keep in mind, too, that animals are most active early in the morning and late in the day. **Special comments** Southern Florida's semitropical climate makes it possible to build a cageless zoo; it also means that visitors are at the mercy of the weather. Try to plan your day accordingly; Metrozoo doesn't issue rain passes. **Author's rating** This zoo is rated by experts as one of the best in the world, and the absence of cages means that people who normally hate zoos may love this one. ★★★★★. **How much time to allow** 2 hours minimum—although that's enough time to induce heatstroke on a sweltering summer afternoon.

DESCRIPTION AND COMMENTS Wings of Asia is Metrozoo's world-class bird exhibit. The zoo's monorail service makes a complete loop of the park, including a Tiger Temple and the African Plains, and more than 7,000 trees have been planted in the past decade. Other additions include a meerkat exhibit in the children's zoo and an educational court with interactive zoological exhibits.

TOURING TIPS Take the free Zoofari Monorail, which makes a complete loop of Metrozoo. The round-trip takes 20–25 minutes. Then either get off at Station 1 and begin walking toward Station 2, or continue on the train to Station 4 (the last stop) and walk back toward the zoo entrance. Along the way, you'll pass outdoor exhibits featuring gorillas, chimpanzees, elephants, Himalayan black bears, a white Bengal tiger, and other exotic animals. They're all uncaged—and appear content. Some exhibits feature "viewing caves" that let you view animals through plate-glass windows on their side of the moat.

Folks who would like to avoid the stairs or long ramps leading to the monorail stations—or who just don't feel like walking—can take a narrated tram tour ($5). You'll also see some behind-the-scenes areas such as the animal hospital.

At Ecology Theatre in the Children's Zoo, handlers bring out a variety of animals for close-up views. Hedgehogs usually steal the shows, which are free and held at 11 a.m., 1 p.m., and 3 p.m. Kids will love the petting zoo. Chimps and gorillas—the most popular exhibits—are fed at 2 p.m.

OTHER THINGS TO DO NEARBY The Gold Coast Railroad Museum is located outside of the entrance of Metrozoo. Other nearby attractions include the Redland Fruit and Spice Park, Weeks Air Museum, and, closer to Miami, the Fairchild Tropical Garden. (But if you've done justice to Metrozoo, you'll be too tired for more sightseeing.)

Miami Seaquarium

APPEAL BY AGE	PRESCHOOL ★★★★★	GRADE SCHOOL ★★★★★	TEENS ★★★★
YOUNG ADULTS ★★★½		OVER 30 ★★½	SENIORS ★★★

4400 Rickenbacker Causeway (on Virginia Key between Key Biscayne and Miami); ☎ 305-361-5705; www.miamiseaquarium.com

Type of attraction A tropical marine aquarium; a self-guided tour. **Admission** Adults, $25.95 plus tax; children ages 3–9, $20.95 plus tax; children under age 3, free. Parking is $6, and the causeway toll is $1. **Hours** Daily, 9:30 a.m.–6 p.m.; ticket office closes at 4:30 p.m. **When to go** During the high tourist season (Christmas through April), try to arrive at 9:30 a.m. You can catch all of the shows by 1:30 p.m. and miss most of the crowds. Monday is the slowest day. **Special comments** Don't sit too close to the water during the shows, or you'll get soaked by a diving dolphin or killer whale. **Author's rating** Expensive, but a bit worn around the edges—and now you have to pay to park! ★★ **How much time to allow** 4 hours to see all of the shows; 2 hours to see the shows and exhibits that most interest you.

DESCRIPTION AND COMMENTS   The hottest attraction at this South Florida tourist mainstay is Lolita, Seaquarium's killer whale. It's an adrenaline rush you don't want to miss when this 20-foot-long behemoth goes airborne in her smallish tank—and lands with a splash that drenches the first ten rows of spectators. Plan your visit around the Killer Whale Show, usually offered twice daily. Call ahead for the schedule.

Other performances at Seaquarium include the Flipper Show, a reef-aquarium presentation, the Top Deck Dolphin Show, the Golden Dome Sea Lion Show, and a shark presentation. There's also a rain forest, a sea-life touch pool, a wildlife habitat, a crocodile exhibit, and a tropical aquarium to view between shows. You can also take glass-bottom boat tours of Biscayne Bay.

The Seaquarium shows are slick and well orchestrated. But like the disco music played during the performances, this 40-year-old marine-life park struck us as a little worn. And following the dose of consciousness-raising from the *Free Willy* film franchise, a lot of folks may feel a twinge of guilt as they watch these magnificent—but captive—animals.

TOURING TIPS   The food for sale in the aquarium is overpriced, so eat before you come. Don't miss a manatee presentation, usually scheduled twice daily: It may be your only opportunity to see these docile endangered mammals. A staffer talks about the manatees' plight and feeds them. You may also get to see a manatee do its version of a trick—roll over on its back for the trainer. Then go see the Flipper Show for more action. Kids will love the frolicking dolphins.

OTHER THINGS TO DO NEARBY   Key Biscayne has plenty of places to eat and great beaches, too. You can walk right up to where the old Rickenbacker Bridge drawbridge was removed and fish, or just watch the ospreys and pelicans and the sail- and powerboats glide by in the blue. Back on the mainland, Vizcaya, the fabulous estate and gardens, is near the entrance to the Rickenbacker Causeway.

Museum of Contemporary Art (MoCA)

APPEAL BY AGE	PRESCHOOL ★	GRADE SCHOOL ★	TEENS ★★
YOUNG ADULTS ★★★½	OVER 30 ★★★½		SENIORS ★★½

Because the gallery exhibits change regularly, use these ratings as a general guide.

770 NE 125th Street, North Miami; from Miami Beach, take the Broad

Causeway at 96th Street, which becomes NE 125th Street; MoCA is on the left; ☎ 305-893-6211; www.mocanomi.org

Type of attraction The only art museum in Miami solely dedicated to modern art; a self-guided tour. Admission Adults, $5; seniors and students, $3; children under age 12, free. Hours Tuesday–Saturday, 11 a.m.–5 p.m.; Sunday, noon–5 p.m.; closed Monday. When to go Anytime. Special comments All on one level. Author's rating Never a dull moment in Miami's newest museum; a gem. ★★★½. How much time to allow 1 hour.

DESCRIPTION AND COMMENTS MoCA stages large shows of cutting-edge contemporary art. Expect to be stimulated (or, at least, amused) by whatever is on display during your visit. Films, lectures, artists' talks, and excursions are also offered at MoCA.

TOURING TIPS Docent-led tours are available on weekends. The gift shop features handcrafted jewelry and other one-of-a-kind items. You can listen to jazz in the courtyard one Friday night a month; check with the museum.

OTHER THINGS TO DO NEARBY The Museum of Contemporary Art is located in North Miami, infamous for its lack of tourist attractions. The posh shops of Bal Harbour are directly across the Broad Causeway; turn right on NE 123rd Street to get to them. One of Miami's best sushi joints is Tani Guchi's Place, a few miles east in a strip shopping center just west of the Broad Causeway (2224 NE 123rd Street; ☎ 305-892-6744).

Monkey Jungle

APPEAL BY AGE	PRESCHOOL ★★★★★	GRADE SCHOOL ★★★★	TEENS ★★★★
YOUNG ADULTS ★★★	OVER 30 ★★★		SENIORS ★★★

14805 SW 216th Street (Hainlin Mill Drive), about 20 miles south of Miami; take the Florida Turnpike Extension to Exit 11 (SW 216th Street) west and drive 3 miles to the entrance on the right; ☎ 305-235-1611; www.monkeyjungle.com

Type of attraction A primate zoo where visitors walk in screened walkways that pass through large "habitats" (actually, larger cages) that feature 300 monkeys from 25 species roaming free; a self-guided tour. Admission Adults, $19.95; seniors, $16.95; children ages 3–9, $13.95; children ages 2 and under, free. Hours Daily, 9:30 a.m.–5 p.m.; ticket office closes at 4 p.m. When to go Avoid the hottest times of the day by arriving by 10 a.m. or just before 4 p.m. Crowds are lighter during the week than on weekends. Special comments Don't forget mosquito repellent; visitors are outside the entire time. If it rains, pick up a rain pass at the entrance. Author's rating A lot of fun—and it's okay to feed the primates. ★★★½. How much time to allow An hour; 2 hours if you want to catch all the shows.

DESCRIPTION AND COMMENTS A real switch: The monkeys are watching us in cages! Gibbons, spider monkeys, orangutans, a gorilla, chimpanzees, and other primates are close at hand as you walk through screened walkways that wind through a tropical forest. While not all the monkeys roam free— a lot of them reside in large cages located along the walkways—many can be seen when you pass through the larger jungle habitat. Founded in the 1930s, Monkey Jungle is a slice of pre-Disney Florida.

TOURING TIPS Bring quarters; monkey-food dispensers that resemble bubble-gum machines are located along the walkways. Three different shows start at 10 a.m. and run in two intervals featuring swimming monkeys, a gorilla, twin chimpanzees, orangutans, and the Amazon rain forest.

OTHER THINGS TO DO NEARBY Coral Castle, Metrozoo, the Weeks Air Museum, and the Gold Coast Railroad Museum are nearby. For some-thing different—and a little less touristy—stop by the Redland Fruit and Spice Park on SW 248th Street, about five miles away.

Parrot Jungle Island

APPEAL BY AGE	PRESCHOOL ★★★★★	GRADE SCHOOL ★★★★★	TEENS ★★★★½
YOUNG ADULTS ★★★★	OVER 30 ★★★★		SENIORS ★★★★

Watson Island, between Miami and Miami Beach, just east of the MacArthur Causeway; ☎ 305-666-7834; www.parrotjungle.com

Type of attraction A bird sanctuary and botanical gardens that also include trained birds, a flock of pink flamingos, and wildlife shows; a self-guided tour. **Admission** Adults, $24.95; children ages 3–10, $19.95. **Hours** Daily, 10 a.m.–6 p.m. **When to go** Weekends are usually very crowded, so try to arrive before 2 p.m. to beat the worst of the crowds. Monday through Wednesday are the least crowded days. **Special comments** Parrot Jungle moved from South Miami, and reopened on 18.6 acres on the north side of Watson Island (the first island on the way to Miami Beach on the MacArthur Causeway) in 2003. It's a more conve-nient location, with tropical lushness recreated in a new $46 million park. **Author's rating** What a hoot—or, better yet, screech; don't miss it. ★★★★½. **How much time to allow** 2 hours if you want to catch all the shows.

DESCRIPTION AND COMMENTS You'll find a lot more than 2,000 parrots at Par-rot Jungle. Alligators, gibbons, several dozen pink flamingos, tortoises, a children's playground, a petting zoo, and a Miccosukee Indian display are waiting to be discovered in this lush tropical garden. Fortunately, winding paths disperse the crowds. Along the way you'll see more than 1,100 varieties of birds and more than 1,000 types of plants. The two-story aviary, a 17-foot croc, poisonous snakes, and an albino alligator are a few of the special attractions.

TOURING TIPS Don't miss the trained-bird show: Macaws and cockatoos ride bikes, drive trucks, and race chariots. Watch trainers work with young birds in the Baby Bird Training Area, and see nonavian Florida wildlife in the Jungle Theater. In the Bird Posing Area, get your picture taken with a macaw perched on your head; there's no charge.

OTHER THINGS TO DO NEARBY The new Children's Museum is just across the road. Both downtown Miami and South Beach are five minutes away.

Vizcaya Museum and Gardens

APPEAL BY AGE	PRESCHOOL ★	GRADE SCHOOL ★★	TEENS ★★½
YOUNG ADULTS ★★½	OVER 30 ★★★½		SENIORS ★★★★

3251 South Miami Avenue, Miami; near the Rickenbacker Causeway and across from the Miami Museum of Science; ☎ **305-250-9133; www.vizcayamuseum.org**

Type of attraction A magnificent Italian Renaissance–style villa and formal gardens built by the cofounder of International Harvester; guided and self-guided tours. **Admission** Adults, $12; children ages 6–12, $5; children ages 5 and under, free. **Hours** Daily, 9:30 a.m.–4:30 p.m. The gardens close at 5:30 p.m. **When to go** Vizcaya is rarely mobbed. To beat the crowds in the high tourist season (Christmas through April), try to arrive soon after the gates open. **Special comments** Vizcaya is beautifully decorated for the holidays in December. **Author's rating** The mansion displays robber-baron decadence in a stunning setting on Biscayne Bay, but only so-so art and ho-hum guided tours (★★★); the ten acres of formal gardens are fabulous (★★★★★). **How much time to allow** 2 hours.

DESCRIPTION AND COMMENTS Chicago industrialist James Deering built his $20 million winter home on the shores of Biscayne Bay in 1916, an era (not unlike today) when the fabulously rich weren't shy about showing off their wealth. Vizcaya's 34 rooms are loaded with eclectic European period furniture, textiles, sculpture, and paintings from the 15th through the early 19th centuries. The effect is that of a great country estate that's been continuously occupied for 400 years.

Most visitors go on a guided tour of the first floor that lasts 45 minutes. (If no tour guides are available, you're given a guidebook and turned loose.) Highlights of the magnificent rooms include a rug that Christopher Columbus stood on, an ornate telephone booth (check out the early example of a dial telephone), and dramatic carved ceilings and patterned marble floors. The house also has its eccentricities: Mr. Deering didn't like doors slamming from the continuous breeze off the bay, so many were hung at off-angles so they would close slowly. Today, the proliferation of high-rise condos on Biscayne Bay probably blocks much of the wind.

TOURING TIPS Explore the second-floor bedrooms on your own. Then stroll the formal gardens, which feature spectacular views of Biscayne Bay. The Great Stone Barge in front of Vizcaya's East Facade acts as a breakwater and creates a harbor for small boats. And when the Miami moon is full, check out the moonlight garden tours for silvery delight.

OTHER THINGS TO DO NEARBY Seaquarium and Key Biscayne are on the other side of the Rickenbacker Causeway; Coconut Grove—with the Barnacle mansion for a comparison—is the place to go if you're hungry. The Lowe Museum of Art is on the campus of the University of Miami in Coral Gables, just off US 1.

The Wolfsonian-FIU

APPEAL BY AGE	PRESCHOOL —	GRADE SCHOOL ★	TEENS ★½
YOUNG ADULTS ★★½	OVER 30 ★★★½	SENIORS ★★★½

In South Beach; 1001 Washington Avenue; ☎ **305-531-1001; www.wolfsonian.fiu.edu**

Type of attraction A museum of design dedicated to the art, architecture, commercial design, and cultural history of the period 1885–1945; a self-guided tour. **Admission** Adults, $7; seniors, adult students (with ID), and children ages 6–12, $5; free to all on Fridays, after 6 p.m. **Hours** Tuesday, Wednesday, Friday, and Saturday, 11 a.m.–6 p.m.; Thursday, 11 a.m.–9 p.m.; Sunday, noon–5 p.m.; closed Mondays, the Fourth of July, and Thanksgiving, Christmas, and New Year's days. **When to go** Anytime. **Special comments** This place just oozes sophistication. **Author's rating** Design plus art equals Art Deco . . . and who could imagine a more appropriate location for a museum like this than South Beach? ★★★½. **How much time to allow** 1–2 hours.

DESCRIPTION AND COMMENTS   At the Wolfsonian, visitors can delve beneath the surfaces and ponder the meanings that lurk within everyday things such as furniture, household items, model trains, posters, and other objects taken from a collection of more than 70,000 decorative items dating from 1885 to 1945. Major themes in the changing exhibits focus on how design trends function as agents of modernity, how design works as a key element in reform movements, and how design elements are incorporated as vehicles of both advertising and political propaganda. Wear your thinking cap.

Temporary and semipermanent exhibits are housed in this spiffed-up former storage building that has been restored to its original 1920s Mediterranean-style elegance. Most of the building is used for storing the collection; the surprisingly small exhibit spaces are located on the fifth, sixth, and seventh floors. Who collected all this stuff? Mitchell Wolfson Jr., heir to a fortune made in the Florida movie-theater business.

TOURING TIPS   Take the elevator up to the seventh-floor exhibit area and work your way down.

OTHER THINGS TO DO NEARBY   Washington and Collins avenues offer a wide array of shops. Lincoln Road Mall is six blocks north; frenetic Ocean Drive (and the ocean) is two blocks east. Watch out for weaving Rollerbladers, and enjoy the beautiful people and water.

DINING *and* RESTAURANTS

CHOICES, CHOICES

THE MIAMI AREA SUSTAINS A REMARKABLE breadth of restaurants: 6,000 in Miami-Dade County. Given Miami's diverse population— more than 60 percent of its residents are Hispanic, mixed with sizable Asian, Haitian, Indian, and Jamaican communities—it follows that the eateries are as diverse as the population, making for a lively and exciting restaurant scene.

And Miami seems to draw a continuing stream of young chefs— many of them graduates of U.S. culinary schools and top international restaurants.

Local Flavor

Talented chefs are creating a distinct new "Florida" cuisine, sometimes referred to as "Florida-Caribbean," "Floribbean," or "New World" cooking. Pioneers are **Norman Van Aken** of **Norman's; Mark Militello** of **Mark's Las Olas; Allen Susser** of **Chef Allen's; Robbin Haas;** formerly of **Baleen** and now of **Chispa** restaurant in Coral Gables; and **Cindy Hutson** of **Ortanique on the Mile.** The inspired cooking has improved the quality of independent restaurants throughout the area.

Miami restaurants boast a profusion of exotic foods such as plantains, papaya, mangoes, hot chili peppers, malanga, and yuca. Area farmers, along with fishermen, bring their harvests directly to the back doors of Miami's restaurateurs.

Casual Dress

In South Florida, the warm, humid weather inspires flexibility in standards of dress. (Shorts are common at just about any family-friendly or beachside restaurant.) However, this fashion-conscious area takes note of cosmopolitan trends. If you're looking to make a higher-end impression, you either have to dress well or dress up. In this guide, "casual" means a sundress or shorts, jeans, or a skirt, with a decent top; "dressy casual" means a dress, nice pants or skirt, and a decent top; "business casual" means anything you would wear straight from work; and "upscale casual" means an in-style outfit that could be considered casual but is notably trendy and/or expensive. Very few South Florida restaurants require a jacket and tie, and unless you aren't wearing anything else, open-toed shoes won't raise any eyebrows. (In fact, even if you only wore open-toed shoes, you wouldn't be doing anything new: Madonna already pioneered this look on Miami Beach circa 1992.)

Global Tastes

Many Cuban restaurants in Little Havana serve traditional Cuban food, with rice and black beans, plantains, and yuca almost always accompanying the entrees. **Versailles** is a classic favorite. An emerging number of "new Cuban" restaurants offer lighter twists on the traditional, including **Havana Harry's.**

Some of the best ethnic eateries are Italian. Among the best are **Romeo's Cafe, Osteria del Teatro,** and **Casa Tua,** in South Beach and **La Bussola, Cafe Violetto, Randazzo's,** and **Caffe Abbracci** in Coral Gables. **Hosteria Romana** on pretty Española Way is worth a night out. And in North Miami there's **Il Tulipano Centodieci,** arguably the best Italian restaurant in Miami-Dade County.

Among other ethnic groups you'll find the world in this worldly environs. Try **Old Lisbon** for Portuguese; **Tropical Chinese Restaurant** for dim sum; **Matsuri** in West Miami and **Shoji, Bond St. Lounge,** and **Toni's** on the Beach for sushi; and **Bangkok Bangkok** and **Miss Saigon Bistro** in the Gables for Vietnamese.

downtown coral gables, coconut grove, and little havana dining and nightlife

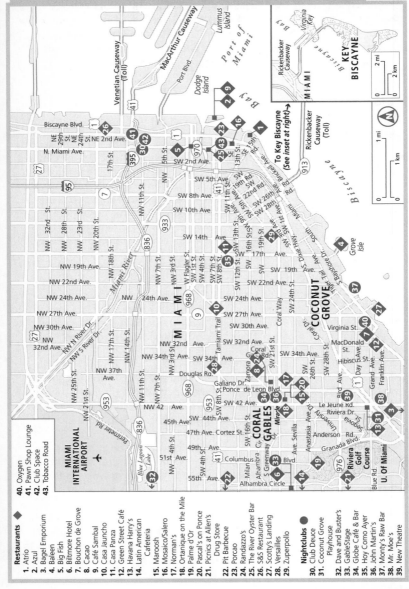

Restaurants ◆
1. Atrio
2. Azul
3. Bagel Emporium
4. Baleen
5. Big Fish
6. Biltmore Hotel
7. Bouchon de Grove
8. Cacao
9. Café Sambal
10. Casa Jauncho
11. Casa Panza
12. Green Street Café
13. Havana Harry's
14. Latin American Cafeteria
15. Maroosh
16. Mosaico/Salero
17. Norman's
18. Ortanique on the Mile
19. Palme d'Or
20. Pascal's on Ponce
21. Picnics at Allen's Drug Store
22. Pit Barbecue
23. Porcao
24. Randazzo's
25. The River Oyster Bar
26. S&S Restaurant
27. Scotty's Landing
28. Versailles
29. Zuperpollo

Nightclubs ●
30. Club Deuce
31. Coconut Grove Playhouse
32. Dave and Buster's
33. GableStage
34. Globe Café & Bar
35. Hoy Como Ayer
36. John Martin's
37. Monty's Raw Bar
38. Mr. Moe's
39. New Theatre
40. Oxygen
41. Pawn Shop Lounge
42. Club Space
43. Tobacco Road

miami beach, north beach, north miami dining and nightlife

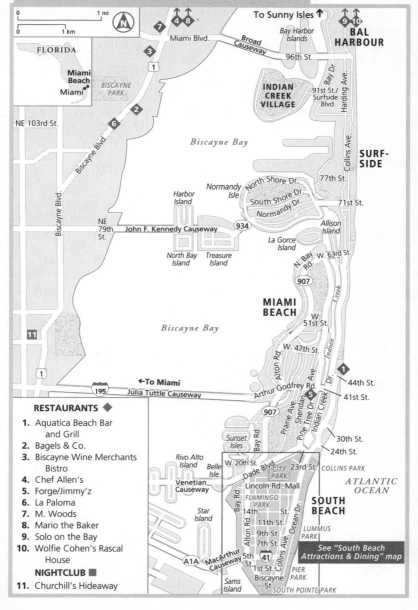

0   1 mi
0   1 km

To Sunny Isles ↑

7 **4** **8**

FLORIDA

Miami
Beach
Miami

BISCAYNE
PARK

3

1

2

NE 103rd St.

6

Biscayne Blvd.

Miami Blvd.

Broad
Causeway

Bay Harbor
Islands

96th St.

9 **10**

**BAL
HARBOUR**

INDIAN
CREEK
VILLAGE

91st St./
Surfside
Blvd.

Bay Dr.

Harding Ave.

Collins Ave.

**SURF-
SIDE**

Biscayne Bay

North Shore Dr.

77th St.

Normandy
Isle

South Shore Dr.

71st St.

Harbor
Island

Normandy Dr.

NE
79th
St.

John F. Kennedy Causeway

934

La Gorce
Island

Allison
Island

North Bay
Island

Treasure
Island

W. 63rd St.

N. Bay
Rd.

907

C. creek

**MIAMI
BEACH**

W.
51st St.

Indian Creek

Biscayne Bay

W. 47th St.

Alton Rd.

Sheridan Ave.

Pine Tree Dr.

Indian Creek Dr.

1

44th St.

11

1

To Miami

195
Julia Tuttle Causeway

Arthur Godfrey Rd.

5

41st St.

907

Prairie Ave.

Sunset
Isles

Bay Rd.

30th St.

24th St.

Rivo Alto
Island

Belle
Isle

W. 20th St.

Dade Blvd.

CITY
PARK

23rd St.

COLLINS PARK

*ATLANTIC
OCEAN*

Venetian
Causeway

Lincoln Rd. Mall

**SOUTH
BEACH**

Star
Island

Bay Rd.

Alton Rd.

FLAMINGO
PARK

14th St.

11th St.

9th St.

7th St.

Ocean Ave.

Collins Ave.

LUMMUS
PARK

A1A

MacArthur
Causeway

5th
St.

1st St.

41

Biscayne
St.

PIER
PARK

See "South Beach
Attractions & Dining" map

Sams
Island

SOUTH POINTE PARK

RESTAURANTS ◆

1. Aquatica Beach Bar
   and Grill
2. Bagels & Co.
3. Biscayne Wine Merchants
   Bistro
4. Chef Allen's
5. Forge/Jimmy'z
6. La Paloma
7. M. Woods
8. Mario the Baker
9. Solo on the Bay
10. Wolfie Cohen's Rascal
    House

NIGHTCLUB ■

11. Churchill's Hideaway

Small Argentinean, Brazilian, Mexican, Nicaraguan, and Peruvian restaurants cluster in Little Havana, the Gables, and along Coral Way. **Porcão** for Brazilian is on Brickell Bay, with a drop-dead view.

Barbecue? **The Pit** and **Shorty's** in Miami and around are longtime favorites. Among the best steak houses are **The Palm, Morton's, Smith & Wollensky, Tuscan Steak,** and **Capital Grille.**

Seafood? Although there are one or two outstanding specialty seafood restaurants, such as **Joe's Stone Crab,** restaurants like **Azul, Nemo, Chef Allen's, Blue Door at Delano, Ortanique on the Mile,** and **1220 at The Tides** usually have their fish delivered to the kitchen door on a daily basis, ensuring impeccable freshness. Funky seafood venues include **Joe's** (not the stone-crab one) and **Garcia's** on the Miami River. **Francesco** in Coral Gables and **Fish Joynt** in Aventura are among the best.

DINING HOT SPOTS

South Beach

Along South Beach, restaurants seem to pop up and disappear faster than tropical showers. A hot new bar or restaurant will draw trendies one month, only to be over the next. Most South Beach restaurants have outdoor terraces or porches, placing tables and chairs on the sidewalk for the overflow; a "see and be seen" scene. On weekends, sightseers can scarcely make their way through the throngs of diners sitting at small tables along Lincoln Road, where the food is mostly mediocre but the festivity is incredible.

Strangely enough, there was little outdoor dining in Miami until the 1980s. Waterfront restaurants offered a porch or terrace, but natives mumbled, "Only tourists would go out in that sun." Many new restaurants throughout Southeastern Florida now offer outdoor dining, and older restaurants are scrambling to do the same.

Unless there is a special event, most restaurants start filling up around 9 p.m.; come when a place opens and you may find yourself alone. You can often get last-minute reservations if you're willing to eat early. (Early-bird in SoBe means seven!)

Parking on South Beach is difficult day and night. Even if you find a space, a valet-parking attendant is apt to inform you that it will cost you $12 or even $18 for the privilege. There may be free parking available if you look hard enough (beware of the parking areas reserved for residents only), but spaces may be several blocks away.

 Most restaurants on Ocean Drive will add a 15%–18% gratuity to your bill. If you are ignorant of this practice and you tip another 15%, don't expect to be informed of your error.

Breakfasts

Though the "most important meal of the day" hardly factors into most tourists' itineraries, a few breakfasts draw both locals and tourists. On South Beach, **News Café, Van Dyke Café,** and **Jerry's Deli** attract more people than there are seating spaces. The **Rascal House,** on North Miami Beach, has been the neighborhood's most steadily popular and busy restaurant through the years. It is a landmark worth visiting if you like deli-style food.

Then, of course, there are the bagel houses, a nod to Miami's Northeast snowbirds. Among the most popular are the **Bagel Emporium** in Coral Gables and **Bagels & Co.** in North Miami on Biscayne Boulevard. Some of the better and more interesting breakfast spots to pop up lately are in renovated hotels such as **Delano, The Tides,** and the **Astor,** all in South Beach.

Cuban coffee and hot, buttered bread (*pan*) are popular all over Little Havana. It's an inexpensive and delicious way to start the morning.

Hotel Dining

In the 1950s and 1960s many hotels downgraded their restaurants. But this downward trend was reversed in the late 1970s and early 1980s, when many hotels hired talented chefs to run their kitchens. Today, hotels house some of the very best restaurants in the area.

The best include the **Blue Door at the Delano; 1220 at The Tides; Azul** at the Mandarin Oriental; **Nobu** and **Ago,** both at the Shore Club; **Bizcaya Grill** at the Ritz-Carlton in Coconut Grove; **Atrio** at the Four Seasons; **Vix** at the Victor on South Beach; and **Palme d' Or** at the Biltmore Hotel.

Business Dining

Coral Gables professionals pour into upscale restaurants. Influenced in part by the Hispanic population, as well as the concentration of businesses in the Gables, lunch is often a leisurely affair, designed for conducting business while enjoying fine food. A similar area for great business lunches is Brickell Avenue and adjacent Brickell Village. **Perricone's, Capital Grille,** and **Morton's** are all favorites there.

If You're Going to the Everglades

Homestead and Florida City in South Dade, near farming communities and a major entrance to the Everglades, offer casual, affordable dining venues. These include **El Toro Taco, White Lion Cafe, Main Street Cafe, Sam's Restaurant,** and **Tiffany's** in Homestead. In Florida City, even closer to the Everglades, you can enjoy good, basic food at **Mutineer Restaurant, Richard Accursio's Capri Restaurant, Farmer's Market Restaurant,** and **Sonny's Real Pit Barbeque.**

A Word About Kids

When it comes to dining and children, keep the following in mind: Clubby South Beach restaurants are not kid friendly, and expensive eateries usually cater to adults. But Asian, Italian, Latin, and other ethnic and bistro-type establishments can be great for families. And most moderately priced restaurants where you can eat outside are not only fine for kids, they're fine for Fido, too. Call ahead if you're not sure—and remember, the earlier you eat dinner, the more kids you'll find.

A Few of Our Favorite Things at Area Restaurants (Not Necessarily the Food)

- Slipping off your shoes and eating in a king-size bed at **B.E.D.** in SoBe (929 Washington Avenue, Miami Beach; ☎ 305-532-9070)
- All that Brazilian-style meat and a water view too at **Porcão** (801 Brickell Bay Drive, Miami; ☎ 305-373-2777)
- Popcorn shrimp served in a popcorn box in the romantic garden at **Barton G.** (1427 West Avenue, Miami; ☎ 305-672-8881)
- Sitting at a terrace table overlooking Ocean Drive at **1220 at the Tides** and nibbling—something—and drinking in the breezy beauty inside and out (The Tides, 1220 Ocean Drive, Miami Beach; ☎ 305-604-5000)
- Floating up to **Big Fish** on the Miami River under the neon-lit highway (55 SW Miami Avenue Road, Miami; ☎ 305-373-1770)
- The bamboo floor and red-velvet cake at **M. Woods** (12953 Biscayne Boulevard, Miami; ☎ 305-895-9962)
- Flamenco nights at **Casa Panza** in Little Havana (1620 SW Eighth Street, Miami; ☎ 305-643-5343)
- Looking into the underwater window to the pool at **Aquatica Beach Bar and Grill** at the Eden Roc Resort (4525 Collins Avenue, Miami Beach; ☎ 305-531-0000)
- All things chocolate (including some main courses) at **Cacao** in the Gables (141 Giralda Avenue, Coral Gables; ☎ 305-445-1001)
- Eating and imbibing among the hundreds of wine bottles at **Biscayne Wine Merchants Bistro** (738 NW 125th Street, North Miami; ☎ 305-899-1997)
- The twinkling city view from the 25th-floor dining room at **Atrio** at the Conrad Miami (1395 Brickell Avenue, Miami; ☎ 305-503-6500)
- Chatting food at communal tables at **Blue Sea** in the Delano Hotel (1685 Collins Avenue, Miami Beach; ☎ 305-672-2000) and **Casa Tua** (1700 James Avenue, Miami Beach; ☎ 305-673-1010)
- Light meals in a lacquered box at **Café Sambal** in the Mandarin Oriental on Brickell Key (500 Brickell Key Drive, Miami; ☎ 305-913-8251)
- The pineapple-infused vodka signature cocktail at **Capital Grille** (444 Brickell Avenue, Miami; ☎ 305-374-4500)
- Mango "bubble tea" at **Lan Pan-Asian Cafe** in South Miami (8332 South Dixie Highway, Miami; ☎ 305-661-8141)

- Brunch outside at the **Green Street Café** in Coconut Grove (3468 Main Highway, Coconut Grove; ☎ 305-444-0244) and (upscale) brunch in the courtyard of the **Biltmore Hotel** in the Gables (1200 Anastasia Avenue, Coral Gables; ☎ 305-445-1926)
- The most romantic, most isolated table for two right by the bay at **Baleen** on Grove Isle (4 Grove Isle Drive, Miami; ☎ 305-860-4386)
- German chocolate cake at **Icebox Café** off Lincoln Road (1657 Michigan Avenue, Miami; ☎ 305-538-8448)
- The early-bird special at **La Paloma** (10999 Biscayne Boulevard, North Miami; ☎ 305-891-0505)
- Mussels and *frites* at an outdoor table at **Bouchon de Grove** (3430 Main Highway, Coconut Grove; ☎ 305-448-6060)
- Bouillabaisse at **La Pastis** in South Miami (7310 SW 57th Avenue, South Miami; ☎ 305-665-3322)
- Garlic rolls and pies at **Mario the Baker** in North Miami (13695 West Dixie Highway, Miami; ☎ 305-891-7641)
- Baba ghanoush and the weekend belly dancers at **Maroosh** in the Gables (223 Valencia Avenue, Coral Gables; ☎ 305-476-9800)
- Rooftop couches and modern Spanish cuisine at **Mosaico/Salero** in Brickell Village (1000 South Miami Avenue, Miami; ☎ 305-371-3473)
- Lit-up teepees and people watching at **Nikki Beach Club** (1 Ocean Drive, Miami Beach; ☎ 305-538-1111)
- Cleavage on the servers and the shag carpet on the chairs at **Pearl** in SoBe (1 Ocean Drive, Miami Beach; ☎ 305-673-1575)
- Breakfasts and banana pudding at **Picnics at Allen's Drug Store** (4000 SW 57th Avenue, Coral Gables; ☎ 305-665-6964)
- Barbecue and biscuits and honey at **Shorty's** (9200 South Dixie Highway, Miami; ☎ 305-670-7732) and **Pit Barbecue** (16400 SW Eighth Street, Miami; ☎ 305-226-2272)
- Seafood salad, meatballs and ricotta, cannoli, and the boxing-champ owner at **Randazzo's** in the Gables (150 Giralda Avenue, Coral Gables; ☎ 305-448-7002)
- Biscayne Bay views at **Red Fish Grill** in Matheson Hammock Park (9610 Old Cutler Road, Coral Gables; ☎ 305-668-8788)
- Cioppino at the **River Oyster Bar** off Brickell (650 South Miami Avenue, Miami; ☎ 305-530-1915)
- Apple pie at the old-fashioned counter at **S&S Restaurant** in downtown Miami (1757 NE Second Avenue, Miami; ☎ 305-373-4291)
- The Haitian art—everywhere from tables to walls to bathrooms—at **Tap Tap** in SoBe (819 Fifth Street, Miami Beach; ☎ 305-672-2898)
- The bay and sailboat views, laid-back atmosphere, and inexpensive fare at **Scotty's Landing** in Coconut Grove (3381 Pan American Drive, Coconut Grove; ☎ 305-854-2626)

- A mojito and the sunset view of the Intracoastal waterway at **Solo on the Bay** on Haulover Beach (10880 Collins Avenue, Miami; ☎ 305-949-3920)

- Live blues till early a.m. and American grub at **Tobacco Road** in Brickell Village (626 South Miami Avenue, Miami; ☎ 305-374-1198)

- Flame-swallowing belly dancers at **Touch** (910 Lincoln Road, Miami Beach; ☎ 305-532-8003)

- The early-bird dinner and imaginative cuisine at **Two Chefs** in South Miami (8287 South Dixie Highway, South Miami; ☎ 305-663-2100)

- Jazz and people watching at **Van Dyke Café** in South Beach (846 Lincoln Road, Miami Beach; ☎ 305-534-3600)

- Accordion music and Uruguayan-style rotisserie chicken at **Zuperpollo** (1247 Coral Way, Coral Gables; ☎ 305-856-9494)

- The Cuban sandwich and mango shake at **Latin American Cafeteria** (2940 Coral Way, Coral Gables; ☎ 305-448-6809)

ABOUT THESE CHOICES

WE HAVE CONFINED OUR LIST TO A SAMPLING of the best, from haute to casual. Few of these restaurants are inexpensive. Check out the list above for a sampling of more casual, less pricey dining. Detailed profiles of each restaurant follow in alphabetical order.

EXPLAINING THE RATINGS

WE HAVE DEVELOPED DETAILED PROFILES for the best restaurants (in our opinion) in town. Each profile features an easily scanned heading that allows you, in just a second, to check out the restaurant's name, cuisine, overall rating, cost category, quality rating, and value rating.

OVERALL RATING The overall rating encompasses the entire dining experience, including style, service, and ambience, in addition to taste, presentation, and food quality. Five stars is the highest rating possible and denotes the best of everything. Four-star restaurants are exceptional, and three-star restaurants are well above average. Two-star restaurants are good. One star is used to denote an average restaurant that demonstrates an unusual capability in some area of specialization—for example, an otherwise-immemorable place that has great barbecued chicken.

COST Our expense description provides a comparative sense of how much a complete meal will cost. A complete meal for our purposes consists of an entree with vegetable or side dish, and choice of soup or salad. Appetizers, desserts, drinks, and tips are excluded.

Inexpensive	$14 or less per person
Moderate	$15–$30 per person
Expensive	$30–$45 per person
Very expensive	$46 or more per person

QUALITY RATING Each heading also includes a quality rating and a value rating. The quality rating is based expressly on the taste, freshness of ingredients, preparation, presentation, and creativity of food served. There is no consideration of price. If you are a person who wants the best food available and cost is not an issue, you need look no further than the quality rating. The quality ratings are defined as:

★★★★★	Exceptional quality
★★★★	Good quality
★★★	Fair quality
★★	Somewhat sub-par quality
★	Sub-par quality

VALUE RATING If, on the other hand, you are looking for both quality and value, then you should check the value rating. The value ratings are a function of the overall rating, the price rating, and the quality rating:

★★★★★	Exceptional value, a real bargain
★★★★	Good value
★★★	Fair value, you get exactly what you pay for
★★	Somewhat overpriced
★	Significantly overpriced

PAYMENT We've listed the type of payment accepted at each restaurant using the following codes:

AE	American Express (Optima)
CB	Carte Blanche
D	Discover
DC	Diners Club
MC	MasterCard
V	Visa

The Best of Miami Area Restaurants

RESTAURANT/TYPE	OVERALL RATING	QUALITY RATING	VALUE RATING	CITY
AMERICAN				
The Forge/Jimmy'z	★★★½	★★★	★★★	Miami Beach
Joe Allen	★★★	★★★	★★★★	Miami Beach
CONTINENTAL/ITALIAN				
Casa Tua	★★★★½	★★★★	★★	Miami Beach
CUBAN				
Versailles	★★★★	★★★	★★★	Miami

The Best of Miami Area Restaurants (continued)

RESTAURANT/TYPE	OVERALL RATING	QUALITY RATING	VALUE RATING	CITY
CUBAN (CONTINUED)				
Havana Harry's	★★★	★★★	★★★	Coral Gables
ECLECTIC				
Vix	★★★★½	★★★★★	★★	Miami Beach
FLORIDA-CARIBBEAN				
Ortanique on the Mile	★★★★	★★★★½	★★★	Coral Gables
FRENCH				
Blue Door at the Delano	★★★★½	★★★★	★★	Miami Beach
Palme D'Or	★★★★½	★★★★½	★★★★	Coral Gables
Pascal's on Ponce	★★★½	★★★★½	★★★	Coral Gables
NEW AMERICAN				
Azul	★★★★★	★★★★★	★★★	Brickell Key
Nemo	★★★★	★★★	★★★	Miami Beach
Talula	★★★★	★★★★	★★★	Miami Beach
NEW FLORIDA				
Chef Allen's	★★★★	★★★★★	★★★	Miami
NEW WORLD				
Norman's	★★★★½	★★★★★	★★★	Coral Gables
PACIFIC RIM				
Pacific Time	★★★★	★★★★½	★★★	Miami Beach
PAN ASIAN				
China Grill	★★★★	★★★★	★★	Miami Beach
SEAFOOD				
Joe's Stone Crab	★★★★★	★★★★½	★★★	Miami Beach
SPANISH				
Casa Juancho	★★★	★★★	★★★	Miami

RESTAURANT PROFILES

Azul ★ ★ ★ ★ ★

NEW AMERICAN   VERY EXPENSIVE   QUALITY ★ ★ ★ ★ ★   VALUE ★ ★ ★

Mandarin Oriental Hotel, 500 Brickell Key Drive, Brickell Key;
☎ **305-913-8288; www.mandarinoriental.com**

Reservations Recommended. **When to go** Anytime. **Entree range** $25–$4. **Payment** AE, DC, MC, V. **Parking** Valet. **Bar** Full service. **Wine selection** Extensive Champagne list; well-selected American and French wines; $7–$15 per glass, $30–$950 by the bottle. **Dress** Casual/business. **Disabled access** Good. **Customers** Young locals, the in crowd, wealthy tourists, celebrities. **Hours** Daily, noon–11 p.m.

MENU RECOMMENDATIONS Sweetbreads and lobster; seared scallops and foie gras; quail cordon bleu; wellington of wild salmon; grilled Kobe beef sirloin; Moroccan lamb; hazelnut-chocolate tart

COMMENTS The setting is the luxurious, minimalist Mandarin Oriental hotel, with floor-to-ceiling windows overlooking the Miami skyline and Biscayne Bay. Expect gracious service and masterful award-winning cuisine, with exceptional wine pairings. Young chef Clay Conley has energized the sumptuous bilevel surroundings of marble open kitchen and rosewood floors with eclectic originality. The tasting menu is the tops, and should you need them, pashminas and reading glasses are yours for the borrowing.

Blue Door at the Delano ★ ★ ★ ★ ½

FRENCH   VERY EXPENSIVE   QUALITY ★ ★ ★ ★   VALUE ★ ★

Delano Hotel, 1685 Collins Avenue, Miami Beach; ☎ **305-674-6400;**
www.delano-hotel.com

Reservations Recommended. **When to go** Anytime. **Entree range** $35–$51. **Payment** AE, DC, MC, V. **Parking** Valet. **Bar** Full service. **Wine selection** Extensive Champagne list; well-selected American and French wines; $7–$15 per glass, $30–$950 by the bottle. **Dress** Casual/business. **Disabled access** Good. **Customers** Young locals, the in crowd, wealthy tourists, celebrities. **Hours** Daily, 7 a.m.–midnight.

MENU RECOMMENDATIONS Thon-Thon (black-and-blue tuna with marinated daikon in lime juice); the foie gras burger; jumbo ravioli filled with taro mousseline and white-truffle oil; *loup cajou* (sea bass in a brown-butter sauce with cashew nuts, garlic, lime, and fresh herbs, served with fresh hearts of palm); osso buco in Thai curry sauce with caramelized bananas and pineapple.

COMMENTS The lobby of the well-hyped Delano takes the visitor past white, gauzy drapery that defines seating alcoves with chinchilla throws, with the terrace, infinity pool, and ocean beyond. The all-white restaurant is a magnet for both celebrities and wannabes. Consulting chef Claude

Troisgros seasonally re-creates the menu, and the fine waitstaff helps make dining here memorable.

Casa Juancho ★ ★ ★

| SPANISH | MODERATE | QUALITY ★ ★ ★ | VALUE ★ ★ ★ |

2436 SW Eighth Street, Miami; ☎ **305-642-2452; www.casajuancho.com**

Reservations Accepted. **When to go** Early. **Entree range** $18–$38. **Payment** AE, DC, MC, V. **Parking** Valet. **Bar** Full service. **Wine selection** Extensive selection of Spanish, South American, and Italian wines; $7–$20 per glass, $19 and up by the bottle. **Dress** Casual/business. **Disabled access** Good. **Customers** Hispanic locals, professionals, internationals. **Hours** Sunday–Thursday, noon–midnight; Friday and Saturday, noon–1 a.m.

MENU RECOMMENDATIONS Spanish roasted peppers stuffed with codfish mousse; baby eels in spicy garlic sauce; garlic soup Castilian-style; chilled whole two-pound Florida lobster with two salsas; grilled snapper fillet over flaming oak logs splashed with fiery garlic and vinegar sauce; rabbit cured in sherry and baked with thyme and creamy brown sauce

COMMENTS A popular Spanish-themed dining spot for active members of the Hispanic community. The mood at night is festive, and the various rooms, decorated with traditional Spanish trappings, are usually crowded. Enjoy tapas, Iberian wines, huge portions of tasty food, and the lively guitar-playing troubadours (who can be a pain and need to be tipped). Spanish is the official language here.

Casa Tua ★ ★ ★ ★ ½

| CONTINENTAL/ITALIAN | VERY EXPENSIVE | QUALITY ★ ★ ★ ★ | VALUE ★ ★ |

1700 James Avenue, Miami Beach; ☎ **305-673-1010;**
www.casatualifestyle.com

Reservations Accepted. **When to go** Early. **Entree range** $9–$46. **Payment** AE, DC, MC, V. **Parking** Valet. **Bar** Full service. **Wine selection** Extensive selection of Spanish, South American, and Italian wines; $6–$7 per glass, $18–$24 by the bottle. **Dress** Casual/ business. **Disabled access** Good. **Customers** Hispanic locals, professionals, internationals. **Hours** Monday–Friday, 11:30 a.m.–11 p.m.

MENU RECOMMENDATIONS Grilled tuna with spring watercress, sugar snaps, orange, fresh tomatoes, and olive sauce; lasagna with lobster and artichokes; grilled lamb chops with sautéed artichokes and smoked eggplant puree; white chocolate and hazelnut mousse.

COMMENTS Superlovely and superexpensive (with lots of supermodels hangin' around), this Mediterranean-style house, built in 1925 on the outskirts of Lincoln Road, is a romantic dining venue. It's hard to choose between the enchanting garden lit with lanterns, the cozy and stylish dining room in the former living area, or the communal table by the open kitchen. Food and service are exceptional—as are sky-high prices.

Chef Allen's ★ ★ ★ ★

| NEW FLORIDA | EXPENSIVE | QUALITY ★ ★ ★ ★ ★ | VALUE ★ ★ ★ |

19088 NE 29th Avenue, Miami; ☎ 305-935-2900; www.chefallen.com

Reservations Accepted. **When to go** Early. **Entree range** $29–$46. **Payment** AE, DC, MC, V. **Parking** Adjoining lot. **Bar** Full service. **Wine selection** Extensive selection of top Americans—a treat of a list: $8–$28 per glass, $27–$1,775 by the bottle. **Dress** Informal, business. **Disabled access** Good. **Customers** Locals, tourists, internationals. **Hours** Sunday–Friday, 6–10:30 p.m.; Saturday, 6–11 p.m.

MENU RECOMMENDATIONS A tasting menu of five courses for $75. Bahamian lobster and crab cakes with tropical-fruit chutney and vanilla beurre blanc; yellowfin tuna tartare with sevruga caviar and a Grey Goose bloody Mary; chai-tea-cured salmon gravlax with cucumber raita; telecherry-pepper-seared French foie gras, crisp pancetta with candied onion, brioche toast, and mango jam; Tribeca veal chop with white beans, wild mushroom ragout, and double-mustard sauce; pistachio-crusted black grouper with a fricassee of rock shrimp, mango, leeks, and coconut rum; crab-crusted mahimahi with spiny lobster risotto, haricots verts, and smoked tomato butter

COMMENTS Operating in a stylish, contemporary art-gallery setting, with a picture window on the kitchen, Susser is one of the most daring and lauded interpreters/innovators of bold New American cuisine, and followers detour to dine here. Service is exemplary, and wines are tops. Order the yummy dessert soufflé early.

China Grill ★ ★ ★ ★

| PAN ASIAN | EXPENSIVE | QUALITY ★ ★ ★ ★ | VALUE ★ ★ |

404 Washington Avenue, Miami Beach; ☎ 305-534-2211; www.chinagrillmanagement.com/chinami

Reservations Necessary. **When to go** Early. **Entree range** $20–$59. **Payment** AE, DC, MC, V. **Parking** Valet. **Bar** Full service. **Wine selection** Fair selection from around the world; $7–$18 per glass, $30–$290 by the bottle. **Dress** Casual to dressy. **Disabled access** Good. **Customers** Locals, professionals, celebrities, tourists. **Hours** Monday–Friday, 11:45 a.m.–midnight; Saturday, 6 p.m.–1 a.m.; Sunday, 6 p.m.–midnight.

MENU RECOMMENDATIONS Broccoli rabe dumplings; crackling calamari salad; Peking duckling salad; sashimi tempura with wasabi-Champagne cream, lobster pancakes; Oriental barbecue salmon; wild-mushroom-profusion pasta with sake-Madeira cream sauce

COMMENTS The Pan-Asian food is as beautiful as the setting. Though prices are high, portions are enormous and are meant to be shared. There's a separate VIP area for celebrities and stars, with gold-threaded draperies, so expect some attitude. The **Dragon,** a private area, serves surprising and creative sushi, such as the Havana Roll with snapper, rum, coconut, and avocado. To end with flair, try the dessert sampler, replete with sparklers.

The Forge/Jimmy'z ★ ★ ★ ★

AMERICAN	EXPENSIVE	QUALITY ★ ★ ★ ½	VALUE ★ ★

432 41st Street, Miami Beach; ☎ 305-534-4536; www.theforge.com

Reservations Accepted. **When to go** Anytime. **Entree range** $20–$90. **Payment** AE, D, MC, V. **Parking** Valet. **Bar** Full service. **Wine selection** The best in Miami; outstanding American and French vintages; $8 and up per glass, $30 and up by the bottle. **Dress** Business, casual-elegant. **Disabled access** Yes. **Customers** Well-heeled locals, tourists. **Hours** Sunday–Thursday, 6–11 p.m.; Friday and Saturday, 6 p.m.–midnight.

MENU RECOMMENDATIONS Chilled jumbo shrimp; shrimp marlin; smoked salmon; yellowfin tuna tartare; chopped salad; the "Super Steak," (voted the number one steak in America by *Wine Spectator* magazine); prime rib; snapper cashew; duck cassis; rack of lamb; chocolate soufflé

COMMENTS The Forge, a lavish, over-the-top dining institution with stained glass, oak paneling, and ornate antiques, offers good food in varied, crowded rooms. With Jimmy'z, an adjacent restaurant and disco, The Forge attracts all night owls. Executive chef Andrew Rothschild has introduced creative dishes to The Forge's classical menu repertoire. More than 300,000 bottles of wine are cellared, and you can sometimes reserve to dine among them.

Havana Harry's ★ ★ ★

CUBAN	INEXPENSIVE/MODERATE	QUALITY ★ ★ ★	VALUE ★ ★ ★

4612 Le Jeune Road, Coral Gables; ☎ 305-661-2622

Reservations Not required. **When to go** Early. **Entree range** $15–$25. **Payment** AE, DC, MC, V. **Parking** Self park in adjacent lot. **Bar** Full service. **Wine selection** Moderate; $6–$8 per glass, $17–$120 by the bottle. **Dress** Casual; a family place. **Disabled access** Good. **Customers** Professionals, locals. **Hours** Monday–Thursday, 11 a.m.–10 p.m.; Friday, 11 a.m.–11 p.m.; Saturday, noon–11 p.m.; Sunday, noon–10:30 p.m.

MENU RECOMMENDATIONS Malanga cream; *tostones rellenos* (green plantains stuffed with beef and seafood); *caldo gallego,* a specialty soup from the Galicia region of northern Spain; Harry's chicken, grilled and topped with avocado sauce, cream, and cheddar cheese, and served with white rice, black beans, and sweet plantains; Caribbean shrimp grilled with mango sauce; salmon with tamarind sauce and sesame seeds, served with mashed potatoes and *mariquitas;* springtime snapper, broiled and covered with crab and avocado sauce

COMMENTS This is an honest family-run operation where everyone shares responsibilities. When you don't feel like going into Calle Ocho, this is a good alternative.

Joe Allen ★ ★ ★

AMERICAN	MODERATE	QUALITY ★ ★ ★	VALUE ★ ★ ★ ★

**1787 Purdy Avenue, Miami Beach; ☎ 305-531-7007;
www.joeallenrestaurant.com**

Reservations Accepted a week in advance. **When to go** Anytime. **Entree range**
$9.50–$28. **Payment** MC, V. **Parking** Ample metered parking. **Bar** Full service.
Wine selection Small but satisfactory; $6–$12 per glass, $20–$45 by the bottle.
Dress Casual. **Disabled access** Good. **Customers** Locals, tourists. **Hours** Daily,
11:30 a.m.–11 p.m.; bar open until 2 a.m. on Friday and Saturday; Sunday brunch,
11:30 a.m.–3:30 p.m.

MENU RECOMMENDATIONS   Gazpacho Andaluzas with spicy croutons; arugula
salad with grilled portobello mushrooms, roasted red peppers, and gorgonzola dressing; great hamburgers with french fries; six varieties of
pizza; grilled New York sirloin with fries; sautéed calf's liver with
mashed potatoes and sautéed spinach; meat loaf with mashed potatoes

COMMENTS   Legendary restaurateur Joe Allen, owner and operator of
namesake establishments in NYC and London, brings his signature style
of informal dining and comfort food to SoBe. The price and value are
great, and the service is as friendly as it gets. On the bayside, in an out-
of-the-way unassuming building, this is a homey alternative when the
nearby Lincoln Road scene seems a bit much.

Joe's Stone Crab Restaurant   ★ ★ ★ ★ ★

SEAFOOD	MODERATE/EXPENSIVE	QUALITY ★ ★ ★ ★ ½	VALUE ★ ★ ★

**11 Washington Avenue, Miami Beach; ☎ 305-673-0365;
www.joesstonecrab.com**

Reservations Not accepted. **When to go** Early. **Entree range** $5–$60. **Payment**
AE, DC, MC, V. **Parking** Valet. **Bar** Full service. **Wine selection** An adequate but
small selection of wines from California and Europe. **Dress** Casual. **Disabled
access** Good **Customers** International tourists, locals. **Hours** Monday, 5–10 p.m.;
Tuesday–Thursday, 11:30 a.m.–2 p.m. and 5–10 p.m.; Friday and Saturday, 11:30
a.m.–2 p.m. and 5–11 p.m.; Sunday, 4–10 p.m.

MENU RECOMMENDATIONS   Though other restaurants serve stone crabs, none
seem to taste quite like Joe's. Nearly essential accompaniments are
hash browns and coleslaw. Also try fried soft-shell crabs; blue-crab
cakes; sautéed fillet of sole; ginger salmon; fried or grilled pompano,
swordfish, or grouper; and New York sirloin or broiled lamb chops for
non-fish eaters.

COMMENTS   South Florida's most popular and famous restaurant is a must
for tourists and a hangout for locals. Waits can be hours (except right at
opening and at lunch time), but it's worth it. Owned and operated by
the original owner's granddaughter, Joan Sawitz Bass, Joe's has a luster

that never diminishes. The no-nonsense servers move quickly through the vast rooms. The sides and both the Key lime and apple pies are worth the trip, even without the main courses. And to avoid the wait, there's always takeout next door, or a tip to the maître d'.

Nemo ★ ★ ★ ★

| NEW AMERICAN | MODERATE/EXPENSIVE | QUALITY ★ ★ ★ | VALUE ★ ★ ★ |

100 Collins Avenue, Miami Beach; ☎ 305-532-4550; www.nemorestaurant.com

Reservations Accepted. **When to go** Early. **Entree range** $11–$39, brunch $29. **Payment** AE, DC, MC, V. **Parking** Valet. **Bar** Full service. **Wine selection** Well-studied and compact selection; excellent for its size; $8–$18 per glass, $22–$450 by the bottle. **Dress** Casual. **Disabled access** Good. **Customers** Young locals, tourists, area professionals. **Hours** Monday–Saturday, noon–3 p.m. and 6:30 p.m.–midnight; Sunday, 11 a.m.–3 p.m. (brunch) and 6 p.m.–midnight.

MENU RECOMMENDATIONS   Polenta fries (a must); garlic- and ginger-cured salmon rolls with tobiko caviar and wasabi mayo; crispy prawns with spicy *salsa cruda* and mesclun greens; sautéed mahimahi with asparagus and orange-basil citronette; spicy pork loin with caramelized onions and papaya relish; grilled swordfish with white beans, tomato, and broccoli rabe; curried lentil stew with sweet caramelized onions and wilted greens.

COMMENTS   Executive chef Mike Sabin creates "South Beach casual." The courtyard under the trees is a great place to watch models and hangers-on stroll by in SoFi, though the interior is charming as well. The raw bar is extolled, as is brunch.

Norman's ★ ★ ★ ★ ½

| NEW WORLD | EXPENSIVE | QUALITY ★ ★ ★ ★ ★ | VALUE ★ ★ ★ |

21 Almeria Avenue, Coral Gables; ☎ 305-446-6767; www.normans.com

Reservations Accepted. **When to go** Early. **Entree range** $30–$40. **Payment** AE, DC, MC, V. **Parking** Valet. **Bar** Full service. **Wine selection** Very good; $8–$40 per glass, $28–$1,500 by the bottle. **Dress** Casual, business. **Disabled access** Good. **Customers** Locals, business leaders, tourists. **Hours** Monday–Thursday, 6–10 p.m.; Friday and Saturday, 6–10:30 p.m.

MENU RECOMMENDATIONS   Foie gras wafers on a Cuban-bread "short stack" with an exotic-fruit caramel; jerk chicken skewer on pigeon-pea salsa; bacalao fritters with ancho–black olive aioli; yuca-stuffed shrimp with sour-orange mojo, greens, and tartar salsa; rum- and pepper-painted grouper on mango-habanero mojo with boniato-plantain mash *en poblano;* palomilla strip steak au poivre with *cabrales crema,* blistered bell peppers, stacked sweet potato torta, and West Indian pumpkin

COMMENTS   Norman Van Aken is the much-awarded forerunner in the development of contemporary Florida cuisine. He sets a stylish, sophis-ticated, and unique tone with both his cuisine and restaurant setting.

Service is polished, even though tables always fill in the airy room, and the open kitchen is a glimpse into a world of culinary mastery.

Ortanique on the Mile ★ ★ ★ ★

FLORIDA-CARIBBEAN	EXPENSIVE	QUALITY ★ ★ ★ ★ ½	VALUE ★ ★ ★

278 Miracle Mile (next to the Actor's Playhouse), Coral Gables;
☎ **305-446-7710**

Reservations Accepted. **When to go** Early. **Entree range** $20–$40. **Payment** AE, MC, V. **Parking** Valet. **Bar** Full service. **Wine selection** Well-selected American, European, and New World wines; unusual finds and values; $11–$16 per glass, $30–$400 by the bottle. **Dress** Casual **Disabled access** Good. **Customers** Young residents, professionals, tourists. **Hours** Monday–Wednesday, 11:30 a.m.–2:30 p.m. and 6–10 p.m.; Thursday and Friday, 11:30 a.m.–2:30 p.m. and 6–11 p.m.; Saturday, 6–11 p.m.; Sunday, 5:30–9:30 p.m.

MENU RECOMMENDATIONS Tropical mango–and–fresh hearts of palm salad; assorted Caribbean ceviches, including Caicos Island conch ceviche, *ceviche del mar,* and button-mushroom ceviche; jerk tuna tataki with mango-papaya relish; roasted-cumin-and-coriander–encrusted mahi-mahi on spicy tomato eggplant; pan-seared Bahamian black grouper marinated in teriyaki with Ortanique orange liqueur–Bacardi Limon sauce; filet mignon au poivre with shiitake mushrooms, port sauce, and the chef's mashed potatoes

COMMENTS Named for a tropical fruit, Ortanique, under the direction of chef Cindy Hutson, has received the highest accolades from food critics and the public. A bit cramped and noisy, with tropical decor and friendly servers, it has tables that spill onto Miracle Mile. Delectable in taste and setting, Ortanique is a South Florida classic, well named.

Pacific Time ★ ★ ★ ★

PACIFIC RIM	MODERATE/EXPENSIVE	QUALITY ★ ★ ★ ★ ½	VALUE ★ ★ ★

915 Lincoln Road, Miami Beach; ☎ **305-534-5979; www.pacifictime.biz**

Reservations Accepted; recommended on weekends. **When to go** Early. **Entree range** $28.50–$38. **Payment** AE, DC, MC, V. **Parking** Adjoining lot. **Bar** Full service. **Wine selection** Outstanding California wines with great by-the-glass options; $8–$13 per glass, $28 and up by the bottle. **Dress** Casual. **Disabled access** Good. **Customers** Locals, tourists, internationals. **Hours** Sunday–Thursday, 6–11 p.m.; Friday and Saturday, 6 p.m.–midnight. Opens seasonally for lunch.

MENU RECOMMENDATIONS Grilled giant squid with locally grown Asian greens and hot-and-sour vinaigrette; pan-seared Hudson Valley foie gras with California port, red, and plum wines; wok-sautéed local yellowfin tuna with roasted sesame rice, avocado, and fresh Malpeque oyster sauce; whole ginger-stuffed Florida yellowtail snapper tempura with steamed ribbon vegetables and sizzling dipping sauce; grilled Angus beef with Indochine spices, shiitake mushrooms, bok choy, sugar snaps, sweet sake, and baked Idaho fingerling potatoes

COMMENTS Owner Jonathan Eismann was originally at Manhattan's China Grill. He fuses Asian skills with the tastes of the Caribbean and offers an outstanding wine list, providing superb results and artistic presentations. Whether inside in the minimalist setting with blue ceiling and open kitchen, or at an outside table watching the passing scene, you'll agree with the reputation: best on Lincoln Road. And check out the pretheater menu for a great deal.

Palme d'Or ★ ★ ★ ★ ½

FRENCH	EXPENSIVE	QUALITY ★ ★ ★ ★ ★	VALUE ★ ★ ★

1200 Anastasia Avenue, Biltmore Hotel, Coral Gables; ☎ **305-913-3201; www.biltmore.com**

Reservations Highly recommended. **When to go** Early. **Entree range** Tasting plates, $39–$70. **Payment** AE, MC, V. **Parking** Valet and street. **Bar** Beer and wine. **Wine selection** Small but carefully selected, with affordable top buys; $8–$15 per glass, $25–$192 by the bottle. **Dress** Casual/dressy. **Disabled access** Yes. **Customers** Locals, tourists. **Hours** Tuesday–Thursday, 6–10:30 p.m.; Friday and Saturday, 6–11 p.m.

MENU RECOMMENDATIONS Morel-mushroom soup with smoked duck breast; lobster–and–crème fraîche cappuccino; veal osso buco with polenta; seared rack of lamb; tomato confit–and–fennel salad with basil-lime sorbet

COMMENTS This elegant restaurant offers a frescoed ceiling, cherry-wood floors, crystal chandeliers, and a view of the huge, legendary Biltmore hotel pool. But the food is even better—three, four, or five plates of the chef's wine-tasting pairings of appetizer-sized French nouvelle cuisine. French chef Philippe Ruiz lets you mix and match tartars, terrines, mollusks, citrus, custards, and chocolate for a total of 28 choices. Original and sublime. A vegetarian menu is also offered.

Pascal's on Ponce ★ ★ ★ ½

FRENCH	MODERATE/EXPENSIVE	QUALITY ★ ★ ★ ★ ½	VALUE ★ ★ ★

2611 Ponce de Leon Boulevard, Coral Gables; ☎ **305-444-2024**

Reservations Highly recommended. **When to go** Early. **Entree range** $10.50–$33.95. **Payment** AE, MC, V. **Parking** Valet and street. **Bar** Beer and wine. **Wine selection** Small but carefully selected, with affordable top buys; $7–$18 per glass, $35–$250 by the bottle. **Dress** Casual/dressy. **Disabled access** Yes. **Customers** Locals, tourists. **Hours** Monday–Thursday, 11:30 a.m.–2:30 p.m. and 6–10:30 p.m.; Friday, 11:30 a.m.–2:30 p.m. and 6–11 p.m.; Saturday, 6–11 p.m.

MENU RECOMMENDATIONS Lobster bisque with quenelles flavored with brandy; pan-seared crab cake with roasted-pepper butter; braised baby artichoke hearts Barigoule; sautéed yellowfin tuna tournedos, pommes puree, and green-peppercorn sauce; tenderloin sautéed with snails, wild mushrooms, and garlic with a bordelaise sauce; mustard-crusted rack of lamb, potato boulangère, and stuffed Mediterranean vegetables; steamed Atlantic salmon, blanquette of shrimp, and scallops with saurelle cream

COMMENTS Pascal Oudin cooks simple, light, and impeccable French cuisine in a small but charming space with a gracious feel. Service is smooth, and the welcome genuine. End your fine meal with *tarte tatin* or a classic cheese course (or both!).

Talula ★ ★ ★ ½

NEW AMERICAN	EXPENSIVE	QUALITY ★ ★ ★ ★ ½	VALUE ★ ★ ★ ★

210 23rd Street, Miami Beach; ☎ 305-672-0778; www.talulaonline.com

Reservations Suggested. **When to go** Early. **Entree range** $20–$35. **Payment** AE, MC, V. **Parking** Valet. **Bar** Full service. **Wine selection** Upscale yet affordable Italians emphasizing Super Tuscans; $9–$15 per glass, $30–$500 by the bottle. **Dress** Casual. **Disabled access** Good. **Customers** Young residents, professionals, tourists. **Hours** Tuesday–Thursday, noon–2:30 p.m. and 6:30–10:30 p.m.; Friday, noon–2:30 p.m. and 6:30–11:30 p.m.; Saturday, 6:30–11:30 p.m.; Sunday, 6–10 p.m.

MENU RECOMMENDATIONS Grilled Sonoma Valley foie gras; fried Chesapeake Bay oysters; grilled shrimp tamale; crispy yellowtail snapper; lavender-crusted venison loin; barbecue-spiced duck breast

COMMENTS Husband-and-wife team Frank and Andrea Curto Randazzo have created one of the area's best restaurants. The garden is charming, and a seat in the dark main room by the kitchen offers a view of a constantly moving kitchen, where great creative American cooking comes forth. The mood is comfortable and cool, and the top reputation is earned.

Versailles ★ ★ ★ ★

CUBAN	EXPENSIVE	QUALITY ★ ★ ★	VALUE ★ ★ ★

3555 SW Eighth Street, Miami; ☎ 305-444-0240

Reservations Accepted. **When to go** Early. **Entree range** $40–$60. **Payment** AE, MC, V. **Parking** Valet. **Bar** Full service. **Wine selection** Upscale yet affordable Italians emphasizing Super Tuscans; $7.50–$12.50 per glass, $30–$500 by the bottle. **Dress** Casual. **Disabled access** Good. **Customers** Young residents, professionals, tourists. **Hours** Sunday–Thursday, 6 p.m.–midnight; Friday and Saturday, 6 p.m.–1 a.m.

MENU RECOMMENDATIONS Fried plantains; *sopa de platanos;* roast pork; *arroz con pollo; ropa vieja; palomilla;* Moors and Christians (black beans, white rice); fried whole fish; *picadillo; tres leches* cake

COMMENTS The mirrors reflect the French palace (kind of), and the chandeliered rooms are vast, but the food and clientele are down-home Cuban all the way. Businesspeople sip Cuban coffee and power-broke during the day, but in the evening local families fill this classic, kitschy Calle Ocho venue. There may be a line, but that's part of the fun, as this is a place to sample a culture as well as a cuisine.

Vix ★ ★ ★ ★ ½

ECLECTIC	EXPENSIVE	QUALITY ★★★★★	VALUE ★★

**1144 Ocean Drive, Miami Beach; ☎ 305-779-8888;
www.hotelvictorsouthbeach.com**

Reservations Accepted. **When to go** Early. **Entree range** $40–$60. **Payment** AE,
MC, V. **Parking** Valet. **Bar** Full service. **Wine selection** Upscale yet affordable Italians
emphasizing Super Tuscans; $7.50–$12.50 per glass, $30–$500 by the bottle. **Dress**
Casual. **Disabled access** Good. **Customers** Young residents, professionals, tourists.
Hours Sunday–Thursday, 6 p.m.–midnight; Friday and Saturday, 6 p.m.–1 a.m.

MENU RECOMMENDATIONS Grilled mojito beef salad; tasting of three ceviches;
baked hot-and-sour rock shrimp; foie gras two ways; pan-roasted Osaka
black cod; seafood hot pot; duck-and-lobster chow mein; selection of
cheeses; passion fruit–mango fritters

COMMENTS Diners will find exquisite seasonal food at this eclectic dining
venue in The Victor, a supertrendy Ocean Drive hotel of the moment.
Dine on the terrace or inside in an updated Art Moderne setting,
maybe at the chef's table facing the kitchen. Chef James Wierzelewski
is inspired by "the sensual world of the legendary spice route." Lots of
spicy bling needed here, but that doesn't faze guests, including Shaq
and P. Diddy (or whatever he's calling himself these days).

ENTERTAINMENT *and*
NIGHTLIFE

MIAMI IS A CITY THAT NEVER SLEEPS, even when the sun comes
up. Whether it's because the residents and visitors of this dynamic
city are easily bored or easily amused is a toss-up. The fact is,
Miami's social side is like a multifaceted theme park, full of wondrous amusements for all ages that bring out the child in everyone.

There are enough worthwhile diversions in Miami to keep people
busy around the clock, which could explain the city's extreme fond-
ness for *colada*, the Cuban espresso coffee so eye-opening it is doled
out in thimble-sized cups. There are parties, then after-parties, and
then after-hour parties, which start at the hour most good suburban-
ites are already in the carpool lane.

There are supper clubs, coffeehouses, dance companies, symphonies, drag shows, discos, strip joints, comedy clubs, concert halls,
jazz venues, pubs, gay clubs, gallery walks, and rock halls to suit
every taste and then some. It's only a matter of finding the time.
Miami nightlife can be divided into three basic categories: theater
and other cultural pursuits; live jazz, Latin, R&B, and rock music;
and the restaurant-cum-disco scene. Noteworthy establishments are
described in the following pages. After that, we provide individual

south beach nightlife

To Central Miami Beach

1. B.E.D.
2. Casa Tua
3. Clevelander Bar
4. Club Madonna
5. Crobar
6. Jackie Gleason Theater of the Performing Arts
7. Jazid
8. Mac's Club Deuce
9. Mango's Tropical Café
10. Metro Kitchen and Bar
11. Miami Beach Cinematheque
12. Mynt Ultra Lounge
13. New World Symphony
14. Nikki Beach Club
15. Nobu Bar
16. Opium Garden
17. Pearl
18. Privé
19. Rok Bar
20. Rumi
21. Score
22. SkyBar at the Shore Club
23. Tantra
24. Touch
25. Twist
26. Van Dyke Café
27. Vix
28. Wolfsonian
29. Yuca

club profiles of the best places Miami has to offer. For those venues with live music, we advise calling ahead for scheduling information and reservations.

Nightly, weekly, and monthly schedules of live music clubs, theatrical productions, and special events are printed in the *Miami Herald* on Friday as well as community newspapers, including *Miami New Times* and the *Miami Sunpost,* and free local hip sheets such as *Wire.* You'll also want to grab a copy of the city's glossy monthly, *Ocean Drive Magazine,* for a rundown on the current hot nightclubs and restaurants, as well as upcoming chic cultural affairs.

THEATER AND OTHER CULTURAL PURSUITS

THE PERFORMING-ARTS WORLD IN MIAMI boasts a broad array of offerings, from legitimate local theater to national touring companies. Tickets tend to be reasonably priced for evenings and events, and the venues run the gamut from offbeat playhouses to grander locales, such as the renovated **Jackie Gleason Theater** (1700 Washington Avenue, Miami Beach; ☎ 305-673-7300; **www.gleasontheater. com**), the site of touring Broadway productions, national ballet companies, and the occasional pop-music concert. Miamians take full advantage of the cultural possibilities, so make every effort to investigate ticket availability early.

Quality theater abounds in Miami. The **Coconut Grove Playhouse** (3500 Main Highway, Coconut Grove; ☎ 305-442-2662; box office ☎ 305-442-4000; **www.cgplayhouse.com**) is a popular venue for national tours. You'll find more-intimate theater in the Playhouse's **Encore Room** (box office ☎ 305-442-4000). For local talent and productions with an edge, **New Theatre** (4120 Laguna Street, Coral Gables; ☎ 305-443-5909; **www.new-theatre.org**) offers first-class production values, with a sense of the avant garde, under the direction of Rafael de Acha. **GableStage** (1200 Anastasia Avenue, Coral Gables; ☎ 305-446-1116; **www.gablestage.org**), located at the historic Biltmore Hotel, is known for classical contemporary productions that both confront today's issues and entertain.

Classical music spills out from a number of renowned concert halls and associations. The highly acclaimed **New World Symphony** (541 Lincoln Road, Miami Beach; ticket office, ☎ 305-673-3330; **www.nws.edu**) is the country's largest training orchestra and offers a wide range of concerts, including a Sunday afternoon series. The **Concert Association of Florida** (CAF offices at 1470 Biscayne Boulevard, Miami Beach; ☎ 877-433-3200 or 305-808-7446; **www.concertfla.org**) has been Miami's foremost presenter of symphonies, ballets, and opera divas for the past 38 years. CAF concerts are held at various venues throughout Miami.

The dance divine can be caught at the **Miami City Ballet** (performances at the Jackie Gleason Theater, 1700 Washington Avenue,

Miami Beach; call ☎ 305-929-7010 for tickets; **www.miamicityballet.org**) under the inspired artistic direction of Edward Villella. For fluid moves, try the **Momentum Dance Company** at different locations in Miami. (☎ 305-858-7002; **www.momentumdance.com**).

For a more modern approach to the performing arts, **Miami Light Project** (at various venues; call ☎ 305-576-4350; **www.miamilightproject.com**) imports the freshest talents in the world of dance, music, and theater.

Once a year, for ten days in February, the Miami Film Society presents the **Miami International Film Festival** (☎ 305-237-FILM; **www.miamifilmfestival.com**). An internationally acclaimed event that showcases brilliant filmmaking from around the world, the festival has featured many avant-garde directors, including new-wave Spanish filmmaker Pedro Almodóvar, who was introduced to American audiences at the festival in 1984 with his film *Dark Habits*. The **Miami Beach Cinematheque** (512 Española Way, Miami Beach; ☎ 305-673-4567; **www.mbcinema.com**), home of the Miami Beach Film Society and headquarters for February's Miami Beach Film Festival, feeds South Beach's hunger for the unusual with special cinema-themed events. The propaganda-arts-themed **Wolfsonian Museum** (1001 Washington Avenue, Miami Beach; ☎ 305-531-1001; **www.wolfsonian.org**) features exhibitions and screenings of movie classics such as Fritz Lang's *Metropolis*.

LIVE ENTERTAINMENT, CAFE CLUBS, AND CONCERT CLUBS

MIAMI OFFERS NOT ONLY UNUSUAL SMALL concert clubs but also cafes-cum-clubs, and these are some of the best nightlife bets in the area. Restaurants that feature live performances of salsa, jazz, and just about everything else run rampant. Impromptu dancing on tabletops is not uncommon. Local, regional, and less mainstream national talent can be found every night all over Dade County. Miami being Miami, the Latin music is unbeatable, and the Latin jazz is among the best in the world. **Yuca** (501 Lincoln Road, Miami Beach; ☎ 305-532-9822), a restaurant whose name is not only a popular root vegetable used in Cuban cuisine but also an acronym for its clientele (Young Urban Cuban Americans), serves up Latin vocalists in its upstairs concert space.

In the cafe-club category, **Monty's Raw Bar** (2550 South Bayshore Drive, Coconut Grove; ☎ 305-856-3992; **www.montysstonecrab.com**) is an oasis of fun with calypso and reggae throughout the week, right on the waterfront. **John Martin's** (253 Miracle Mile, Coral Gables; ☎ 305-445-3777; **www.johnmartins.com**) features fantastic and hard-to-find Irish music on Saturdays and Sundays. The intimate upstairs space at the **Van Dyke Café** (846 Lincoln Road, Miami Beach; ☎ 305-534-3600; **www.thevandyke.com**) offers live jazz nightly in a candlelit setting. **Globe Café & Bar** (377 Alhambra Circle, Coral Gables; ☎ 305-445-3555) features live jazz on Saturday nights and a very popular happy hour on Fridays.

In the heart of South Beach, check out **Mango's Tropical Café** (900 Ocean Drive, Miami Beach; ☎ 305-673-4422; **www.mangostropical-cafe.com**) and the **Clevelander Hotel** (1020 Ocean Drive, Miami Beach; ☎ 305-531-3485; **www.clevelander.com**). At the exotic restaurant-lounge **Tantra** (1445 Pennsylvania Avenue, Miami Beach; ☎ 305-672-4765; **www.tantrarestaurant.com**), diners can have a taste of the fabulous with their meal (the place is swarming with models, trendies, and movie stars on any given night). In a similar vein, **Touch** (910 Lincoln Road, Miami Beach; ☎ 305-532-8003; **www.touch restaurant.com**) serves up glamour and belly dancing with its $34 entrees. At the "it" spot, **Pearl** (at Penrod's Beach Club, 1 Ocean Drive, Miami Beach; ☎ 305-673-1575), the modern orange-and-white interior and round Champagne bar are a suitable backdrop for the restaurant-lounge's fashionable crowd. At the wildly popular **Rumi** (330 Lincoln Road, Miami Beach; ☎ 305-672-4353; **www. rumimiami.com**), trendies dine downstairs in chic Zen surroundings, then sojourn to the upstairs lounge for DJ-enhanced cocktailing. Enjoy a saketini and the spicy shrimp appetizer at **Nobu Bar**—adjacent to Nobu restaurant at the Shore Club Hotel (1901 Collins Avenue, Miami Beach; ☎ 305-695-3232; **www.shoreclub.com**)—where Miami Beach's jet-set scene is at its glamorous best. New Hotel Victor's in-house dining room, **Vix** (1144 Ocean Drive, Miami Beach; ☎ 305-428-1234) is a rich, whimsically designed restaurant with a spicy European-Mediterranean menu. Local nightlife promoter Michael Capponi hosts a popular, highly social dinner party on Thursday nights. Intimate 80-seat **Casa Tua** (1700 James Avenue, Miami Beach; ☎ 305-673-1010; **www.casatualifestyle.com**) restaurant, bar, and lounge serves delicious, delicate Italian fare amid one of the most romantic milieus in town. On weekends, a DJ plays bossa nova and Latin rock in the sometimes lively, sometimes mellow upstairs lounge. Reservations are difficult to land, so have your hotel concierge book it or call far in advance. Chic boutique Hotel Astor has long been a South Beach hot spot for cocktails in the breezy outdoor courtyard or the tiny, sleek lobbyside bar. But take a walk downstairs through its in-house **Metro Kitchen + Bar** (956 Washington Avenue, Miami Beach; ☎ 305-672-7217; **www.metrokitchen bar.com**)—especially after 10 on popular Tuesday or Saturday nights—and you'll get a glimpse of the most glamorously debauched dinner party in town. That is . . . until Wednesday, when **B.E.D.** (929 Washington Avenue, Miami Beach; ☎ 305-532-9070; **www.bedmi-ami.com**)—an acronymn for "beverage, entertainment, dining"—throws its most popular dinner and dancing soiree. There are no chairs, only mattresses, so invite some friends you'd be proud to say you "went to bed with" the next morning. Another popular Wednesday night dinner party takes place at the 35-year-old **Forge** restaurant (432 41st Street, Miami Beach; ☎ 305-538-8533; **www.theforge.com**), replete with tuxedo-clad waiters who theatrically remove the silver cover from their signature 16-ounce Super Steaks. The grand dining room is adorned with museumesque 17th-century artwork and stained glass. After indulging your appetite, hit adjacent club **Jimmy'z,** where you'll party to the hottest Latin and European dance music and satiate the rest of your senses.

Concert clubs in Miami feature an eclectic and diverse lineup. **Tobacco Road** (626 South Miami Avenue, Miami; ☎ 305-374-1198; **www.tobacco-road.com**) is not only undeniably lively, it holds the title of Miami's oldest club. The nightly live music ranges from Latin jazz to rock and R&B. Hardcore rock fans will appreciate **Churchill's Hideaway** (5501 NE Second Avenue, Miami; ☎ 305-757-1807; **www.churchillspub.com**), an English-themed rock 'n' roll pub showcasing local bands and serving traditional pub grub. For jazz and R&B in a dimly lit boîte, check out **Jazid** (1342 Washington Avenue, Miami Beach; ☎ 305-673-9372; **www.jazid.net**), which offers live solo and group performances downstairs and billiards upstairs, seven nights a week. For live Latin music with dancing, **Hoy Como Ayer** (2212 SW Eighth Street, Miami; ☎ 305-541-2631; **www.hoycomoayer.net**), a tiny club in Little Havana, is full of youthful Latinos moving to Afro-Cuban grooves. Come Friday and Saturday nights for the live Latin bands. At **Mr. Moe's** in Coconut Grove (3131 Commodore Plaza, Coconut Grove; ☎ 305-442-1114; **www.mrmoes.com**), in addition to live country music on Wednesdays, you'll find a mechanical bull, karaoke, billiards, 30 television screens, and yummy slow-cooked barbecue all week.

THE NIGHTCLUB CONNECTION

IN MIAMI (AND PARTICULARLY SOUTH BEACH), hot spots change monthly, if not every weekend. As one of the nightclub capitals of the world, celebrities mingle with models and striking socialites dance with boys and girls next door. Besides reading the listings in local magazines and newspapers, ask hotel concierges and maître d's for the lowdown on the latest nightclubs and restaurants: Sometimes it's not only a matter of what's still cool, but what's still *open* since the last time you checked. The scene shifts and regroups constantly. Whenever possible, call ahead for information on theme nights and specials.

Most of the action, of course, is on South Beach. Fortunately, many clubs are concentrated along Washington Avenue, South Beach's main commercial artery. While there are very few clubs per se on famed Ocean Drive or the seven-block shopping-and-dining stretch of Lincoln Road, there are numerous restaurants with sidewalk seating that feature a jazz or blues vocalist. A sprightly walk along the oceanfront strip reading the menus and sidewalk marquees will give you all the info you need. The nightclub circuit is unpredictable at best, with new developers taking over spaces at a moment's notice, so there's a good chance that your favorite dance club last year is now a parking lot, or will be soon.

Since most of the area nightclubs don't get going until at least 11 p.m., an afternoon nap (or, as locals call it, a "disco coma") is advised. Once refreshed, venture out to one of the many options. **Crobar** (1445 Washington Avenue, Miami Beach; ☎ 305-672-8084; **www.crobar. com**) caters to the trendier-than-thou crowd, offering a complexly designed industrial dance club that features myriad bars, VIP rooms, and balcony seating areas that overlook the strobe-lit dance floor. When it's so late you don't think you can stay awake another second, the crowd is just sauntering in at **Club Space** (142 NE 11th Street, Miami; ☎ 305-375-0001; **www.clubspace.com**), downtown Miami's hot after-hours club. Nurse a cocktail under the stars at **SkyBar at Shore Club** (1901 Collins Avenue, Miami Beach; ☎ 786-276-6772; **www.shoreclub.com/skybar**), where the sprawling poolside garden area offers sumptuous white beds for lounging. A block away the party continues into the wee hours at **Mynt** (1921 Collins Avenue, Miami Beach; ☎ 786-276-6132; **www.myntlounge.com**), a modernist lounge where the beautiful, fashionable, and famous congregate. Just around the corner, Mötley Crüe drummer Tommy Lee opened **Rok Bar** (1905 Collins Avenue, Miami Beach; ☎ 305-538-7171; **www. rokbarmiami.com**) as a tiny spot for South Beachers to rock out to their favorite classic and hard rock hits of the 1980s and 1990s. Although it features a punky rock 'n' roll theme, it still attracts an upscale crowd and serves pricey drinks. If you've ever dreamed of dancing on a bar, here's the spot to do it.

On the other end of town—in the southernmost area of Miami Beach known as South Pointe—lies **Nikki Beach Club** (1 Ocean Drive, Miami Beach; 305-538-1111; **www.nikkibeach.com**), a Saint Tropez–inspired outdoor lounge on the sand. You'll drink Champagne while sauntering the sprawling, tiki-torch-laden grounds—especially busy on Sundays at sunset. Across the street, **Privé** (136 Collins Avenue, Miami Beach; ☎ 305-531-5535; **www.theopiumgroup.com** or **www. opiummiami.com**) caters to a late-night VIP crowd of European dance- and hip-hop-loving young models and hipsters: Getting past the velvet ropes is tough, so come early (around 11), go with tuned-in locals, or prepare to wait. Adjacent club **Opium Garden** is larger, open-air, and less A-list (that is, you'll have a better chance of getting inside).

Miami is enjoying a renaissance of its downtown area, with new real estate projects underway and new hot spots such as **Pawn Shop Lounge** (1222 NE Second Avenue, Miami; ☎ 305-373-3511; **www. pawnshoplounge.com**) springing up. This former pawn shop features a spacious dance floor and whimsical interior accents, including a former school bus, an "airport lounge" (featuring real airline seats), and a mobile home. Saturdays attract an upscale local crowd with pop and dance music, while Friday's Revolver party brings in an edgier, younger, alternative crowd.

In Coconut Grove, you'll find **Oxygen** (2911 Grand Avenue, Coconut Grove; ☎ 305-476-0202; **www.oxygenlounge.biz**), booming with top-40 music and a mix of locals, University of Miami students, and visitors. Come for Friday's Latin night, a young locals' scene.

On a less-than-wholesome note, there are the clubs where the charm is measured by how much skin is showing. Most of these clubs are concentrated on Biscayne Boulevard, just north of 163rd Street. **Club Madonna** (1527 Washington Avenue, Miami Beach; ☎ 305-534-2000; **www.clubmadonna.com**), for example, is slick and stocked with lovely ladies, including centerfold celebs.

THE GAY SCENE

MIAMI, ESPECIALLY SOUTH BEACH, HAS BEEN described as a gay Mecca. Its active and involved gay community is evident on many levels. From lawyers to drag divas, the crowds congregate in a variety of bars and clubs. Endless theme offerings at these clubs include men's nights, women's nights, drag shows, strip shows, and many things of which you may never have heard.

South Beach serves as a central spot for much of Miami's gay society. An always-happening spot is **Twist** (1057 Washington Avenue, Miami Beach; ☎ 305-538-9478; **www.twistsobe.com**), whose two floors of bar space make it perfect for late-night gossip and cocktails. **Score** (727 Lincoln Road, Miami Beach; ☎ 305-535-1111; **www.score bar.net**) is much more casual, even featuring cafe tables set up along Lincoln Road, which the club fronts. Several of South Beach's big mainstream clubs also feature gay nights, including Sundays at Crobar. And off the Beach, the action continues at a number of clubs. **Ozone** (6620 SW 57th Avenue, Miami; ☎ 305-667-2888) draws devotees from all over Miami with excellent dance music, nightly specials, and a powerful pace.

FOR THE ENTIRE FAMILY

Dave and Buster's in the Dolphin Mall (11481 NW 12th Street, Miami; ☎ 305-468-1555; **www.daveandbusters.com**) is a family-oriented mega-entertainment complex, with 65,000 square feet of fun, including an American-themed restaurant, virtual-reality game room with bar, billiards room featuring 13 world-class billiard tables, and a 30,000-square-foot entertainment room holding every video game imaginable. Parents can enjoy a beer while racing on motorcycle games as the kids challenge each other on the snowboard machines. **Gameworks** in South Miami (5701 Sunset Drive, Miami;

☎ 305-667-4263; **www.gameworks.com**) offers fun for adults and kiddies alike with 31,000 square feet of entertainment, including a full-service restaurant, high-energy bar scene, and interactive games such as Indy 500, where six players can race head to head.

The Best of Miami-Area Clubs

NAME	COVER	COST	CITY
BARS			
Club Deuce	None	Inexpensive	Miami Beach
DANCE CLUBS			
Crobar	$25–$30	Expensive	Miami Beach
Hoy Como Ayer	$7–$15	Moderate	Miami
Jimmy'z	$15 (none for members)	Expensive	Miami Beach
Mynt Ultra Lounge	$25	Expensive	Miami Beach
Nikki Beach Club	$20; Sat., none	Expensive	Miami Beach
Oxygen	$10–$20	Moderate	Coconut Grove
Pawn Shop Lounge	$10–$20	Expensive	Miami
Privé	$20	Expensive	Miami Beach
Rok Bar	Sometimes $20	Expensive	Miami Beach
GAY CLUBS			
Ozone	None	Moderate	Miami Beach
Score	$5	Moderate	Miami Beach
Twist	None	Moderate	Miami Beach
LIVE MUSIC			
Churchill's Hideaway	$5–$15	Inexpensive	Miami
Clevelander Bar	None	Moderate	Miami Beach
Mr. Moe's	None	Moderate	Coconut Grove
Tobacco Road	$5–$8, weekends only	Inexpensive	Miami
LOUNGES			
Mynt Ultra Lounge	$25	Expensive	Miami Beach

NAME	COVER	COST	CITY
LOUNGES (CONTINUED)			
Opium Garden	$20	Expensive	Miami Beach
SkyBar	None	Expensive	Miami Beach

NIGHTCLUB PROFILES

Clevelander Bar

OCEANFRONT HOTEL BAR, GYM, AND OUTDOOR NIGHTSPOT

Clevelander Hotel, 1020 Ocean Drive, Miami Beach; ☎ 305-531-3485; www.clevelander.com

Cover None. **Minimum** None. **Mixed drinks** $8–$12. **Wine** $5–$8. **Beer** $5–$8. **Food available** Full menu until 3 a.m., from burgers to surf 'n' turf; live lobster tank. **Hours** Daily, 11 a.m.–5 a.m.

WHO GOES THERE Ages 21–45; restless youth, locals, European tourists, Causeway crawlers, bikini babes

WHAT GOES ON A high-energy melting pot of nationalities, with scantily clad babes and bronzed hunks parading around the pool-bar of this popular oceanfront hotel. Live bands nightly and omnipresent DJs keep the rambunctious spirit going. Needless to say, this is prime cruising territory.

COMMENTS Smack on trendy Ocean Drive, this outdoor bar is studded with palm trees and Jetsonian obelisks. Ten TVs inside and out ensure you'll never miss a music video or major sporting event—not that you won't get distracted by the onslaught of physical beauty on display. You'll see all forms of beachwear, from bikinis with sarongs to shorts and sandals to Levi's on a breezy night. This is one place where less is more. Also a good spot to start the night before you hit the clubs. On Wednesdays, Happy Hour goes from 3 to 7 p.m. with half-price drinks and $5 snacks on a happy-hour menu.

Club Deuce

OLDEST, LEAST PRETENTIOUS LOCALS BAR ON SOUTH BEACH

222 14th Street, Miami Beach; ☎ 305-673-9537

Cover None. **Minimum** None. **Mixed drinks** $3–$5. **Wine** $4. **Beer** $2.50–$3.25. **Food available** Mini-pizzas, pickled eggs. **Hours** Daily, 8 a.m.–5 a.m., 365 days a year.

WHO GOES THERE Hip and not-so-hip locals, pool junkies, barflies, tattooed bikers, drag queens, film crews, unfazed normal folk, New Yorkers

WHAT GOES ON Since 1926, the constant stream of nightcrawlers taking their place at the wraparound bar has served as the main attraction. The best training a novice barfly could get.

COMMENTS Wouldn't win any design awards, but then, it's not that kind of place. Assorted neon beer signs dot the walls; a worn pool table sits off to a corner. A decently stocked jukebox and cigarette machine get lots of use. The big-screen TV is the only trace of modernism. Smoky and dim, but not so dark that you can't see the elements around you, which is a good thing. Dress is inexplicably casual, although we once saw a woman wearing a pink-taffeta pea coat. Weekday happy hours offer two-for-one drink specials.

Crobar

TRENDIER-THAN-THOU DANCE CLUB FOR THE *TRÈS CHIC*

1445 Washington Avenue, Miami Beach; ☎ 305-672-8084; www.crobar.com

Cover $25 Thursdays, Sundays, and Mondays; $30 Fridays and Saturdays. **Minimum** None, except at tables, where there is a 2-bottle minimum. **Mixed drinks** $7–$12. **Wine** $7 and up. **Beer** $4 and up. **Food available** None. **Hours** Thursday–Monday, 10 p.m.–5 a.m.

WHO GOES THERE Celebrities, models, locals, and beautiful people with plenty of lunch money

WHAT GOES ON The scene doesn't get much trendier in South Beach, especially on weekends. On Mondays, the locals party Back Door Bamby goes full tilt till the wee hours. The Show, Thursdays at Crobar, is a well-known hip-hop party for those ready to dance the night away. Expect to wait in line, as this branch of the award-winning Chicago club is the perennial favorite of visiting celebrities and local hipsters. Guest DJs from around the country can often be found spinning the latest house music.

COMMENTS Industrial-chic architects have transformed the historic Art Deco Cameo Theater into a complex, voyeuristic space. There is plenty of tucked-away seating within its two levels so that you'll never feel spied upon, plus a large strobe-lit dance floor and requisite VIP room.

Hoy Como Ayer

MIAMI VERSION OF A CUBAN NIGHTCLUB OF YORE

2212 SW Eighth Street, Miami; ☎ 305-541-2631; www.hoycomoayer.net

Cover $7–$15, price depends on artist performing. **Minimum** None. **Mixed drinks** $6–$8. **Wine** $5–$6; bottle service available. **Beer** $4–$5. **Food available** Tapas menu until 2 a.m. **Hours** Thursday–Sunday, 9 p.m.–5 a.m.; call or visit the Web site for events schedule.

WHO GOES THERE Ages 25–45; an international and artistic Latin crowd; sexy gringos with happy feet

WHAT GOES ON Many will reminisce about the heyday of Havana, even those born after the fall of Cuba. In Miami, Café Hoy Como Ayer, the small SW Eighth Street club that translates, appropriately, to "today like yesterday," is located in the trendy-but-still-in-transition neighborhood of Little Havana. People come for comfort, entertainment, or to dance madly to live Afro-Cuban bands that take the stage at 10:30 p.m. on Fridays and Saturdays. If you can't manage to fudge some odd version of salsa or merengue, just wiggle in your seat and smile a lot. Every night, Latin bands play several sets interspersed with a DJ to keep people dancing. Most individuals sit at cocktail tables or crowd around one of the two bars, if they aren't on the dance floor. The newest addition to the club, the bar known as **El Cuarto de Tula,** is a quieter spot for those who want a private area to chat and smoke cigarettes or cigars. At Thursday night's party, known as Fuácata, a DJ mixes Afro-Cuban rhythms with hip-hop, reggae, and other sounds accompanied by an improvising trio of saxophone, trombone, and timbales that packs the house.

COMMENTS All nightclubs once looked like this—tiny tables, dark corners, intimate lighting, and an inviting bar. Cuban songsters from the 1950s, such as Celia Cruz and Cachao, are featured in original campy videos on an overhead screen. Spanish is by far the language of choice among patrons and staff, but feel free to order your drinks in English. There is an extensive list of wines and liquors sold by the bottle at affordable prices. Hoy Como Ayer is a mix of modern and classic cabaret decor with Cuban artwork adorning the walls. Glowing from the club's dark walls are painted takes of La Caridad del Cobre, Cuba's patron saint, depicted in the nude. Dress is casual: Men are not required to wear jackets, and the younger crowd is typically in tight jeans and ensembles where the exposure of skin plays a supporting role.

Jimmy'z

EURO DISCO/TRANCE, DISCO, TOP-40

432 41st Street, Miami Beach; ☎ 305-538-8533; www.theforge.com

Cover $10–$20. **Minimum** Yes. **Mixed drinks** $8–$10. **Wine** $7.50. **Beer** $6. **Food available** Yes. **Hours** Wednesday–Saturday, 10:30 p.m.–5 a.m.

WHO GOES THERE Ages 21–50; a Felliniesque mix of models, Euroboys in crested blazers, celebs, upscale barflies, young women with bionic décolletés, and hip-hop lovers on certain nights

WHAT GOES ON Régine Choukroun, the legendary Queen of the Night, is the impresaria of the club, which caters to the junior jet set. There are theme nights galore, from combos and full Latin bands to whimsical soirees named for exotic destinations the average Joe will never see, but the privileged know firsthand. Wednesday is alarmingly popular, with a loyal contingent for the weekly theme party that has been around for 11 years, as well as spillover from the adjoining luxury restaurant, The Forge.

COMMENTS Sophisticated yet full of character—like Régine herself—Jimmy'z doesn't lack for color. There are red walls, gilt-edged mirrors, a chandelier as large as a Mustang, and a bed done up in rich jewel tones by one of the bars. Concerning attire, the wilder the better for this sexy crowd.

Mynt Ultra Lounge

UPSCALE, EXCLUSIVE SOUTH BEACH LOUNGE THAT GETS MORE RAUCOUS AS THE HOURS TICK BY

1921 Collins Avenue; ☎ 786-276-6132; www.myntlounge.com

Cover $25. **Minimum** 2 bottles for a VIP table on Fridays and Saturdays. **Mixed drinks** $10–$12. **Wine** $8. **Beer** $6. **Food available** None. **Hours** Wednesday–Saturday, 11 p.m.–5 a.m.

WHO GOES THERE Ages 21–50; models, visiting celebrities, hip locals, young women with a penchant for dancing on couches for the amusement of their dates

WHAT GOES ON The Grand Lounge, complete with 40-foot-long bar, is open to all, but the Plexiglas-shrouded Ultra Lounge is reserved for special attendees (read: the famous and connected). DJs spin house and hip-hop grooves so danceable that couch and tabletop gyrations are an inevitable occurrence as the night advances. Even the most beautiful and trendy of mortals may have to suffer temporarily at the hands of the handsome yet attitudinal doormen ("fire marshal's orders" is the running explanation), but celebrities such as Lenny Kravitz, Sean "P. Diddy" Combs, Enrique Iglesias, Martin Lawrence, Justin Timberlake, and Cameron Diaz are able to glide in via the heavily guarded back-door alley entrance.

COMMENTS The later it gets, the harder it is to get in. If you're staying at a hotel with a concierge, by all means have him/her call for you to get you on the guest list (which, by the way, is no guarantee it'll happen). Dress sharp, show up by midnight, and walk up to the doorman with confidence. You'll leave with enough stories to last you a year.

Nikki Beach Club

SOUTH BEACH'S ANSWER TO A ST. TROPEZ–STYLE BEACH CLUB

1 Ocean Drive, Miami Beach; ☎ 305-538-1111; www.nikkibeach.com

Cover $20; no cover on Saturday for the Ibiza Beach Party. **Minimum** On Fridays and Saturdays, a 2-bottle minimum for table service. **Mixed drinks** $9–$13. **Wine** $9 and up; bottle service available. **Beer** $6–$8. **Food available** Fridays 6–9 p.m. there is a clambake, with 2-for-1 drinks and clams; open for lunch daily. **Hours** Thursday–Sunday, 11 p.m.–5 a.m.

WHO GOES THERE Nightlife impresarios, college kids, tourists, beach bums—including island-loving outdoorsy types with glistening bronzed bodies who spend their days bike riding, landscaping, antiquing, and basking in the sun—and South Beach's hot, shaggy, creative types

WHAT GOES ON It's a hammock-, palm-tree-, and tiki-torch-laden party outdoors and on the sand. Sunday is the club's busiest day—come late afternoon and stay until midnight for drinks and dancing to the newest European trance at a scene that feels, smells, and tastes like Saint Tropez. Friday night is Latin Night, when all the music is Latin influenced.

COMMENTS The party can be hot—especially during the summer—so consider booking a dinner reservation at the chic orange-and-white indoor restaurant upstairs, Pearl, as a midevening cooldown.

Opium Garden

EURO-FLAVORED LOUNGE WITH DANCING, DINING, AND (MUCH) POSING

136 Collins Avenue, Miami Beach; ☎ **305-531-5535;**
www.theopiumgroup.com or www.opiummiami.com

Cover $20. **Minimum** On Fridays and Saturdays, a 2-bottle minimum for table service. **Mixed drinks** $10–$12; bottles of liquor, $225–$2,750. **Wine** $9 and up; Champagne, $180–$,5000+; bottle service available. **Beer** $6–$8. **Food available** None. **Hours** Thursday–Sunday, 11 p.m.–5 a.m.

WHO GOES THERE Sprite models with deeply tanned playboys; urban sophisticates from ages 21–40; visiting celebs and rock stars after their Miami concert gigs

WHAT GOES ON Dancing, necking, and often-indiscreet displays of affection—even among the famous—are not an unusual scene at Opium. Champagne consumption is usual among beautiful, attitudinal, and somewhat reckless types who care not what tomorrow brings. The young are gorgeous and know it, so everyone's basically happy, if rather clannish, preferring that you keep to your side of the double banquette, thank you very much. Celebrity sightings include Cindy Crawford with designers Roberto Cavalli and Esteban Cortazar, Jay-Z, Britney Spears, P. Diddy, Daisy Fuentes, Beyoncé Knowles, Anna Kournikova, and Justin Timberlake, to name a few.

COMMENTS As its name implies, the spacious club is addictive, with an infectious energy and cozy VIP table area for those craving some privacy. The catch, though, is that you have to buy a bottle (vodka or Champagne are typical) in order to qualify to sit in one, and it doesn't come cheap—Champagne bottles start at $180, spirits at $225. The lighting is mercifully dim, which, with the rampant hedonism in this crowd, is a very good thing. Wearing Chanel, Gucci, or Prada will cut down the risk of your having to wait in line, an unfortunate (and unfortunately very common) occurrence here. And don't even think of wearing non-designer denim unless you happen to be very good-looking or very famous.

Pawn Shop Lounge

FORMER PAWN SHOP GETS A FRESH MAKEOVER

1222 NE Second Avenue, Miami (downtown Wynwood district); ☎ **305-371-9278; www.thepawnshoplounge.com**

Cover Varies but can run up to $20. **Minimum** On Fridays and Saturdays, a 2-bottle minimum for table service. **Mixed drinks** $9–$13. **Wine** $9 and up; bottle service available. **Beer** $6–$8. **Food available** None. **Hours** Thursday–Saturday, 11 p.m.–5 a.m.

WHO GOES THERE Hot kids with Mohawks, wealthy Latin American business students, artists, models, and fashion-and-entertainment media types galore (read: everyone!)

WHAT GOES ON Thursdays are barbecue and kegs. Friday night's Revolver party attracts a punky young crowd, while Saturday draws a more mature 20- and 30-something group letting their hair down. VIPs congregate in banquettes near the trailer; the "Airline Lounge" is a great spot for a private party.

COMMENTS This former pawn shop is now a hip hangout thanks to accents the owners found on eBay—including a real school bus, trailer, and airline seats—and a great roster of weekly parties. Because the nightclub is located in a burgeoning (i.e., still decrepit) neighborhood in downtown Miami, take a cab, get dropped off, or appoint a designated driver. You don't want to be walking around this part of town after midnight!

Privé

VIP LOUNGE OF THE VAST OPIUM GARDEN COMPLEX

136 Collins Avenue, Miami Beach; ☎ 305-674-8630; www.theopiumgroup.com or www.opiummiami.com

Cover $20. **Minimum** On Fridays and Saturdays, a 2-bottle minimum for table service. **Mixed drinks** $9–$13. **Wine** $9 and up; bottle service available. **Beer** $6–$8. **Food available** None. **Hours** Thursday–Sunday, 11 p.m.–5 a.m.

WHO GOES THERE A consistent weekly slew of the biggest rock stars, socialites, hip-hop moguls, fashion designers, and Latin pop icons

WHAT GOES ON Thursdays bring the Betty Ford party, filled with artists and alternative kids; Fridays are packed with A-list friends and followers of powerhouse promoters: Ingrid Casares reels in the statuesque model boys and sinewy starlets the *New York Post*'s Page Six will be talking about next month; Michael Capponi attracts a loyal clan of local designer-clad A-listers; and Antonio Misuraca lures sexy, cleavage-touting gaggles of eye candy galore.

COMMENTS A slick lounge where intimate alcoves and banquettes surround the dance floor. Under no circumstances pronounce this club as a one-syllable word rhyming with "jive"; its name is French (translates to "private"), and the accent goes atop the "e" for a reason. Outside can get chaotic, so dress your best and come with an equal number of girls and guys (or more girls than guys) for an easier time getting in.

Rok Bar

ROK BAR TAPS INTO OUR INNER ROCK STARS, GIVING US A TINY, COMFORTABLE SPACE TO LET LOOSE

1905 Collins Avenue, Miami Beach; ☎ 305-538-7171; www.rokbarmiami.com

Cover Sometimes $20, sometimes nothing; depends on the night of the week and the promoter. **Minimum** On Fridays and Saturdays, a 1-bottle minimum for table service. **Mixed drinks** $9–$13. **Wine** $9 and up; bottle service available.

Beer $6–$8. Champagne is also available. **Food available** None. **Hours** Tuesday–Saturday, 11 p.m.–5 a.m.

WHO GOES THERE Twiggy 20-something models kissing each other on the dance floor; local entrepreneurs sipping bubbly on the sofa; fun-loving (and good-looking) artists and musicians downing beers at the bar

WHAT GOES ON The kind of jump-up-and-down dancing you'd normally only do at a rock concert; screaming at the top of your lungs to Warrant; and dancing atop the sexy, long bar.

COMMENTS It's a tiny, upscale-yet-punky bar and lounge—awash in florescent pink and black—where you'll hear your favorite heavy metal, hip hop and 1980s rock favorites. Former groupies, prepare yourselves: Club co-owner Tommy Lee (of Mötley Crüe) and friends such as Kid Rock often show up to party or take over the DJ table and spin impromptu sets.

Tobacco Road

NOTED MIAMI INSTITUTION, NEIGHBORHOOD BAR FEATURING LIVE MUSIC; HOME OF AN ANNUAL BLUES FESTIVAL

626 South Miami Avenue, Miami; ☎ 305-374-1198; www.tobacco-road.com

Cover Usually $5–$8, weekends only. **Minimum** None. **Mixed drinks** $3.25–$3.75. **Wine** $3.50. **Beer** $2.50–$3.75. **Food available** Lunch and dinner in the American vein: steaks, burgers, chicken wings, lobster, grilled rack of lamb, ribs, and nachos, plus daily specials. **Hours** Daily, 11:30 a.m.–5 a.m.; kitchen open until 2 a.m., except Sundays kitchen closes at midnight.

WHO GOES THERE Ages 21–45; hepcats, rockers, bikers, modern bohemians

WHAT GOES ON A Miami hot spot since 1912, this New Orleans–type bar is the city's oldest, and holds Miami's first liquor license. Perennially popular with locals, Tobacco Road was among the first to showcase local and national blues acts. The theme nights are among the best: Monday night is a blues jam; Wednesday it's live jazz. Once a year, in October, the bar sponsors Blues Fest, showcasing 20 bands in the rear parking area.

COMMENTS Charmingly quaint, the wooden-frame structure has the feel of a roadhouse. There are two stories, each with a stage; often both are in use simultaneously. Outside, the wooden deck is shaded by a huge oak tree; thatched tiki-style huts and colored patio lights complete the bohemian picture. Rags range from tuxedoes to Harley gear—anything goes. Weekday happy hour is 5–8 p.m. with $1–$2 appetizer plates.

Twist

PARTY PALACE JUST FOR THE BOYS

1057 Washington Avenue, Miami Beach; ☎ 305-538-9478; www.twistsobe.com

Cover None. **Minimum** None. **Mixed drinks** $4 and up. **Wine** $5 and up. **Beer** $4 and up. **Food available** None. **Hours** Daily, 1 p.m.–5 a.m.

WHO GOES THERE Ages 21–45; the young, tan, and built—your basic gay Greek gods

WHAT GOES ON Twist yourself into a quiet corner or contort yourself on the dance floor. Twist offers a number of very different atmospheres to suit your mood. Very popular with locals, this relatively long-standing gay bar-club satisfies a wide variety of tastes. Depending on which of the six bars you select, it can be a place for a romantic drink on a first date or a spot to let loose to throbbing music on the packed dance floor. And, of course, this being Florida, there is an outdoor deck bar that makes you realize Key West is only several hours away. Essentially, all kinds of people go for all kinds of reasons. Wednesdays are female-impersonator night; Thursdays are two-for-one drinks and domestic beers; and Fridays from 6–8 p.m., a complimentary barbecue buffet is served.

COMMENTS Detailed painted murals combine with eclectic decor—but frankly you won't remember much about the decor because it will be packed to the gills. You'll probably have too much fun, too. Nonetheless, don't end your experience at the first-level bars, which is where the chatty locals hang out with flippant (but cute) bartenders and overhead videos. Venture up the staircase, and you can scam drinks, play pool, or dance before heading outside to the terrace. Attire is South Beach casual—jeans, T-shirts (frequently removed), or more exotic apparel announcing availability, such as a scrap of leather.

PART FOUR

THE FLORIDA KEYS

WELCOME *to the* **KEYS**

DUCK, SNIPE, RAMROD, CRAWL, KNIGHT, No-Name, Pigeon, Missouri, Ohio, Greyhound, and Fat Deer. These are only a few of the quirky names given to the mangrove-fringed keys of the curving archipelago south of the Everglades, at the southern tip of the continental United States. Forty-five of these tiny islands are inhabited and 43 bridges span them, bringing you to a blue-sky, blue-water area unlike any other in the world.

The Florida Keys are home to old movies, hard-drinking writers, anglers, ex-hippies, gay folk, and artists in laid-back fishing towns. But mainly, the Keys are a tourist, diving, and sportfishing destination that draws more than a million visitors each year. In the past 25 years, the Keys' sleepy, rum-soaked image was pushed aside by restoration, revitalization, and the good intentions of the tourist industry, and the crowds have followed. Today you'll find both shimmering aqua waters and traffic jams, a constantly complicated compilation of the best and worst of a sought-after region.

THE END OF THE ROAD

THIS IS, AFTER ALL, THE END OF THE ROAD—literally. US 1 stretches for more than 100 miles beyond the tip of mainland Florida, linking this string of islands that form a natural barrier between the Atlantic Ocean and the Gulf of Mexico, and ends up closer to Cuba than to the U.S. mainland.

While PR copy sometimes overstates the romance, intrigue, and hipness of the Keys, remnants of charming shabbiness remain—in Key West anyway. Here you'll find a sense of escape and open-mindedness. While many Keys are increasingly touristy and overdeveloped, most of these tiny islands still afford a comfortable abode for oddballs and dropouts, artists and writers, gay men and lesbians, and anyone else not in lockstep with the conventional American dream.

A GEOGRAPHIC OVERVIEW

PHYSICALLY, THE FLORIDA KEYS ARE A 150-MILE chain of fossilized coral rock. In the 18th and 19th centuries, pirates buried treasure here, fortunes were made scavenging sea wrecks on the reef, and smugglers and slave traders plied the waters, finding cover in the lush dark-hardwood hammocks located on the islands.

A few miles offshore lies the oceanic equivalent of a rain forest: the coral reef. Thousands of sea plants and animals thrive in and around the reef in water anywhere from 10 to 60 feet deep. The cracks and holes in the reef provide protection or homes for all types of marine animals.

The sea life on display is a moving kaleidoscope of colors and shape for divers and snorkelers. The living, slow-growing reef is extremely fragile; visitors must not stand on, sit on, or touch the coral, lest it die (and touching coral almost always results in a painful scratch anyway).

EARLY HISTORY

NOT LONG AFTER CHRISTOPHER COLUMBUS set foot in the New World in 1492, Spanish explorers Ponce de León and Antonio de Herrera were the first Europeans to sight the Florida Keys, on May 15, 1513. Over the next few centuries, pirates were the only Europeans to visit the string of islands.

Key West was not settled until 1822, and development in the rest of the Keys came even later. Early settlers farmed productive groves of Key limes, tamarind, and breadfruit. Years later, pineapple farms flourished in the Lower Keys, and a large processing factory supplied canned pineapple to most of the eastern United States.

The real money, however, was not in agriculture but in salvaging cargo from ships sunk on nearby reefs. As a result of the efforts of the "wreckers," Key West became one the wealthiest U.S. cities in the early first century of the American republic. Later, sponge fishermen developed a thriving market for the high-quality sponges harvested in the waters off Key West. Later still, cigar makers from Cuba built factories in the city.

DECADES OF BOOM AND BUST

HENRY FLAGLER, THE ASSOCIATE OF John D. Rockefeller who opened his railroad along the east coast of Florida at the end of the 19th century, extended his tracks to the Keys in 1905. The Overseas Railroad—also called "Flagler's Folly"—was an incredible engineering feat for its time. The greatest technical achievement was the Seven-Mile Bridge, which links Marathon to the Lower Keys. The railroad reached Key West in 1912, and wealthy visitors took the train to vacation there.

The Depression years were bleak in the Keys, and the city of Key West declared bankruptcy in 1934. More bad luck: While Flagler's bridges took everything Mother Nature threw their way, the Labor Day hurricane of 1935 tore up the railroad; the bridges later were adapted for roadways. In 1938, the Overseas Railroad became the Overseas Highway.

The new road opened up hope for the renewal of tourism, but World War II intervened. During the war, the opening of a submarine base in Key West started an economic revival, boosted by the development of a commercial shrimp industry. President Harry Truman spent time here at his "Little White House." Ernest Hemingway and other notable writers and artists called Key West home—at least some of the year—and enhanced its reputation as a tropical paradise for creative types.

The most recent, tourist-fueled economic upswing began in the early 1980s—and, judging by the size of the crowds on Duval Street, especially when the cruise ships are in, it shows no signs of letting up.

HOW *and* WHEN *to* SEE *the* KEYS

ABOUT 1.5 MILLION PEOPLE VISIT THE KEYS EACH YEAR, basking in the laid-back atmosphere and enjoying the islands' unique location between the Atlantic Ocean and the calmer Gulf of Mexico. The mingling results in a fantastic array of marine life—and world-class sportfishing.

Visitors dive and snorkel in gin-clear waters and view the only coral reef in the continental United States. Others explore the Keys' local birds and fauna. One drawback, however, is the absence of naturally occurring sand, hence few beaches. It takes waves to make sand, and the offshore reef eliminates the surf action. If you focus on swimming and lazing on the beach, you may be disappointed.

DAY-TRIPPING

THE KEYS OFFER A DRAMATIC—AND USUALLY appreciated—contrast to the high-octane pace of hot, hot, hot Miami. The Upper Keys aren't much more than an hour's drive away from the city, so a day trip there is a feasible, if rushed,

unofficial **TIP**
Leave enough time for the long drive—it takes about half a day to get from Miami to Key West. We don't recommend it, but if you only have a day yet insist on visiting Key West, we suggest a bus tour and a commuter flight from Miami. See the section on specialized tours, page 244, for information on commercial tours to Key West.

getaway. The middle and lower Keys are too far for day-tripping and require at least one overnight for a satisfying experience.

WHEN TO VISIT

LOCALS SAY THE BEST MONTHS TO VISIT are September, October, and early spring, when the weather is warm, crowds are down, and lodging is affordable.

The tourist season in the Florida Keys mirrors that of Miami and the rest of South Florida. The winter season begins in mid-November and ends around Easter; during Christmas and Easter hotels, motels, restaurants, and other tourist-dependent facilities jam. In summer months the Keys are a popular destination for South Florida residents seeking relief from heat and humidity; the Keys are typically ten degrees cooler than Miami—and breezier. Floridians crowd US 1 on Friday afternoons and evenings; most of them return on Sunday evening. Try to avoid weekend traffic crushes.

Summer is increasingly popular with foreign visitors, especially those from Asia, Germany, and Latin America; rooms are generally cheaper and Key West is less crowded. Key West is a port of destination on mini-cruises leaving from Miami and Fort Lauderdale, increasing crowds by the literal boatload but fortunately not clogging the highway even more.

While tarpon migrate past the Keys April through June, don't expect to find a last-minute fishing guide just because it's the off season; they're usually booked—unless you get lucky and there's a cancellation.

GATHERING INFORMATION

FOR ADDITIONAL INFORMATION ON KEY WEST and the Florida Keys, call 800-FLA-KEYS, or check the Web at **www.fla-keys.com.** If you're planning on visiting Key West, for example, you can get free guides listing hotels, motels, bed-and-breakfasts, rental properties, and real estate agents.

ARRIVING *and* TRAVELING THROUGH *the* KEYS

BY PLANE

WHILE BOTH KEY WEST (THE END OF THE LOWER KEYS) and Marathon (in the Middle Keys) have small commercial airports, most folks rent a car and drive to their final destination.

If you fly into Miami International Airport, you are west of Miami near FL 836, a major east–west highway that connects with

Florida's Turnpike Homestead Extension. You can literally be in the Upper Keys within an hour after landing at MIA—if you didn't check any baggage and the line at the rental car agency is short. If your final destination is Key West, figure on about a four-hour drive from the airport, or longer if it's a Friday afternoon.

At the rental-car agency, get explicit driving directions. Most people will take LeJeune Road south to FL 836 West. After you get on FL 836, it's about six miles to Florida's Turnpike. Take it south to Homestead, another 12 miles or so.

CONTINUING TO THE KEYS BY CAR

FROM THE END OF FLORIDA'S TURNPIKE AT Florida City, US 1 heads south toward the tip of Florida through stands of tangled mangrove and thick trees; the mile markers count down from 127, just south of Homestead, to 00 in Key West.

Say good-bye to four-lane expressways: US 1 is a mostly two-lane road as it heads over land and water on its way to Key West. Traffic on the narrow road can be a bear, and multihour backups are routine.

After passing Florida City, you can make a more dramatic entrance to the Keys than ho-hum US 1 by hanging a left onto **Card Sound Road** (FL 905A). You'll miss most of the tourist traffic heading south, and the toll bridge over Card Sound offers a great view of undeveloped Key Largo and Florida Bay. Savor the view—farther south on Key Largo, commercialism is rampant.

DRIVING SOUTH TOWARD KEY WEST: THE UPPER KEYS

AFTER MERGING BACK WITH US 1 (now also called the Overseas Highway), continue south on to **Key Largo.** Only a few scenes of the eponymous late-1940s flick starring Bogart, Bacall, and Robinson were actually filmed here. Still, in a case of life imitating art, local flaks changed the name of the town from Rock Harbor to Key Largo to cash in on the publicity.

More-tenuous links with Tinseltown await at the local Holiday Inn, where the original *African Queen*, the small, steam-powered boat used in the film of the same name starring Bogie and Katharine Hepburn, is on display in the hotel's marina (when it's not on promotional tours). Needless to say, that movie wasn't made here—it was filmed in England and Africa.

unofficial **TIP**
When driving to the Keys, try to leave on Friday morning and return on Monday to beat the worst of the weekend traffic.

Welcome Back to Suburbia

From US 1, don't expect to bask in the Keys' legendary ambience. Key Largo is close enough to Homestead and the southern 'burbs of Miami to serve as a bedroom community to the city, and strip malls, restaurants, gas stations, and fast-food joints line the highway. For more-impressive scenery, you've got to get off the island.

Luckily, that's easy to do. **John Pennekamp Coral Reef State Park** (☎ 305-451-6300; **www.pennekamppark.com**), located at Mile Marker 102.5, offers an easy escape for snorkeling, diving, and glass-bottom-boat trips. In addition, a small, sandy beach (a rarity in the Keys) and a visitor center make this unusual park a worthwhile stop. The park is a major draw for the million-plus divers who come to Key Largo each year, making it the "Diving Capital of the U.S." Check out the 4,000-pound underwater bronze statue *Christ of the Deep*. The 510-foot *Spiegel Grove*, a retired Navy vessel, is the largest ship ever intentionally sunk to create a reef. (See page 258 for more information.)

Another snorkeling option is **Jules Undersea Lodge** (Key Largo Undersea Park), an acre-wide enclosed lagoon where snorkelers can swim with more than 100 marine species. Other attractions include an unusual underwater hotel, a working undersea marine-research center, marine-archaeology experiments, and an underwater art studio.

First-time snorkelers get expert supervision, extensive preswim instruction, and time in the placid waters of the inshore lagoon. The park is open daily from 9 a.m. to 3 p.m.; admission is free, and self-guided tours are $15 (which includes use of a mask, snorkel, fins, and life vest). The rate for a family of four is $50. Scuba diving in the lagoon costs $30 for a one-tank dive without equipment and $50 per person with all the required equipment. For directions and more information, call ☎ 305-451-2353 or visit **www.jul.com**.

Tavernier is the next town south on US 1. **Harry Harris Park,** located on the left at Mile Marker 92.5, is a county park offering a sandy beach, a tidal pool, barbecue pits, picnic tables, a playground—and an excuse to pull over and relax.

Past Tavernier is a 20-mile stretch of islands collectively known as Islamorada (pronounced EYE-la-ma-RAHD-a). It means "Purple Isles," probably because of the profuse bougainvillea; it is also known as the "Sportfishing Capital of the World." Indeed, this is big-time deep-sea fishing country, as the many marinas and bait-and-tackle shops along the road attest. As throughout the Keys, the snorkeling and diving at offshore reefs is excellent. Stop in any dive shop along the highway for more details.

Theater of the Sea, a fish-and-sea-mammal emporium at Mile Marker 84.5, is the second-oldest marine park in the world. Sea lions, dolphins, glass-bottom-boat tours, saltwater aquariums, and ongoing shows make this a worthwhile stop, especially for kids. The cost is $23.95 for adults and $15.95 for children ages 3–12. For more information, call ☎ 305-664-2431 or visit **www.theaterofthesea.com**.

Long Key State Recreational Area, at Mile Marker 68.5, offers canoe rentals, camping, and another excuse to get out of the car, smell the salt air, and unwind. Two nature trails on boardwalks offer views of mangrove forests and tropical hammocks. For more information, call ☎ 305-664-4815 or visit **www.floridastateparks.org.**

THE MIDDLE KEYS

SOUTH OF LONG KEY ARE THE MIDDLE KEYS, about halfway to Key West. Here, water views spread out on both sides of the highway, and you get the feeling that you've actually left the North American continent.

The next town is Marathon, the second-largest community in the Keys; it even has an airport. While the waters offshore are a big draw with the fishing and boating crowd, the town itself doesn't exude much personality.

A unique experience—especially for fans of stone crabs—is a crab cruise, provided by **Keys Fisheries,** a commercial-fishing venture on Marathon's bay side. On this half-day adventure, you'll sample what a commercial fisherman goes through in a grueling 12-hour day. But it's not for the squeamish. On the 50-foot commercial fishing boat, you'll trap the crabs into underwater cages, then pry their claws off before returning them to the water, where they regenerate their missing parts. For more information, call ☎ 305-743-4353 or visit **www.keysfisheries.com.**

The big payoff: You can keep up to eight pounds of the claws you catch, over a $70 value—plus the marina's casual dockside restaurant will cook your catch. These special excursion cruises go out in months with "R" (September–April). The cost for up to six people is $450 for three to three and a half hours between 6:30–10 a.m., 10:30 a.m.–2 p.m., and 2:30 p.m.–6 p.m.; reserve ahead and come hungry; ☎ 305-743-4353.

At the **Dolphin Research Center,** a nonprofit educational facility located at Mile Marker 59, you can spend time with researchers and dolphins; one-hour guided walking tours leave five times daily between 9 a.m. and 4 p.m. Tickets are $19.50 for adults, $16.50 for seniors age 55 and older, $13.50 for children ages 4–12; free for children ages 3 and under. No reservations are required; for more information, call ☎ 305-289-1121 or visit **www.dolphins.org.**

The **Museum of Natural History of the Florida Keys** at Mile Marker 50.5 is a small museum offering exhibits on the history, geology, and biology of the Keys; there's also a short nature trail and a children's museum. For more information, call ☎ 305-743-9100 or visit **www.cranepoint.org.**

For a quick dip, **Sombrero Beach,** off the Overseas Highway at Mile Marker 50 on the ocean, offers a small grassy park and picnic tables.

Next is the Seven-Mile Bridge connecting Marathon to the Lower Keys, built in the early 1980s for $45 million. To the right is the original bridge, built by Henry Flagler for his Overseas Railroad in the early years of the 20th century. Now it's a popular fishing and jogging pier, and a refreshing place just to stop, sit, and enjoy the view.

THE LOWER KEYS

THE ISLANDS OF THE LOWER KEYS ARE HEAVILY wooded, primarily residential, and decidedly noncommercial.

Bahia Honda State Recreation Area, located at Mile Marker 37, is one of the loveliest spots in the Keys. Attractions in the 300-acre park include a nationally renowned white-sand beach, nature trails, plentiful bird life, snorkeling, and diving. Key Westers—or Conchs (pronounced "conks," after the shells)—come here for day trips. For more information, call ☎ 305-872-3210.

Big Pine Key is home to canine-sized Key deer, an endangered species under federal protection since 1952; the miniature white-tailed deer are only found on Big Pine Key and 16 surrounding keys.

The **Key Deer National Wildlife Refuge** is the only wildlife refuge in the Keys accessible without a boat ride. Take Key Deer Boulevard to Watson Boulevard to pick up information at the refuge headquarters, open Monday–Friday, 8 a.m.–5 p.m. Your best chances to see the deer are in the early morning, late afternoon, or early evening. For more information, call ☎ 305-872-2239 or visit **www.nationalkeydeer.fws.gov.**

From Big Pine, you can kayak in the protected waters of adjacent Coupon Bight. Mangrove clusters shelter innumerable birds, including cormorants and egrets, and underwater creatures such as nurse sharks and stingrays.

The key is about a half-hour boat ride from **Looe Key National Marine Sanctuary,** a five-square-mile area of submerged reef six miles southwest of Big Pine Key, considered the best reef in the Keys for snorkeling, diving, fishing, and boating. Limpid waters reveal brain coral, tall coral pillars rising toward the surface, and other interesting formations. To visit the reef, make arrangements at any of several area dive shops. For more information, call ☎ 305-292-0311.

KEY WEST

THE END OF THE ROAD, KEY WEST IS DUBBED by some locals the "Conch Republic." As US 1 enters Key West, a sign for the far right lane reads: "Right Lane Go at All Times." Follow these directions, and North Roosevelt Boulevard leads to Duval Street and Old Town Key West, full of bars, restaurants, hotels, bed-and-breakfasts, museums, galleries, blocks of charming old homes, and congested, narrow streets.

If you ignore the sign above and go left as you enter Key West, you'll pass Houseboat Row, the Atlantic Ocean, snazzy resorts, Key West International Airport, Southernmost Point, and then Old Town.

AN ORIENTATION TOUR

PARK AT THE WELCOME CENTER NEAR THE intersection of US 1 and North Roosevelt Boulevard, and sign up for the next Conch Tour

Train: an open-air trolley with narrator—really an open-air bus—
that transports visitors around Key West and gives them an overview
of the town.

Is it corny? You bet. The vehicle's engine is a diesel-powered truck
disguised as a locomotive, and the "train" even has a whistle. But the
90-minute tour is fun and informative.

The rich, complicated history of Key West can be difficult for
first-time visitors to appreciate. A ride on the Conch Tour Train
offers insight into the ups and downs of this town of 30,000—from
the boom years of the wreckers in the early 1800s to the depths of the
Great Depression of the 1930s (the city declared bankruptcy in 1934)
to its attempted secession from the United States in the 1980s. It also
explains Key West's roles in the Civil War and the Cuban missile crisis of 1962, and reveal insights into why people such as John James
Audubon, Ernest Hemingway, Harry Truman, Tennessee Williams,
and Robert Frost sought out the town. The tour will also help you
understand the town's physical layout and preview attractions that
you can go back and visit later on your own.

The annual three-night Ernest Hemingway Look-alike
Contest in late July has hundreds of wannabe "Papas"
walking the Key West streets. Winners are announced at
Sloppy Joe's Bar, where Hemingway imbibed during his decade-long
residence in the 1930s.

The Conch Tour Train leaves every 30 minutes from 9 a.m. to 4:30
p.m. daily. You can board at the Roosevelt Boulevard location or in Old
Town's Mallory Square. Tickets are $20 for adults and $10 for children
ages 4–12. Passengers can get off in Old Town, wander around or get
lunch, and catch the next "train" 30 minutes later. For more information, call ☎ 305-294-5161 or visit **www.conchtourtrain.com**.

Another option for guided tours is the **Old Town Trolleys,** open-air
buses that shuttle visitors on a 90-minute narrated tour of Key West.
The trolleys let passengers disembark at any of 12 marked stops on
the tour route and reboard another trolley later; many hotels are on
the route. The tours depart every 30 minutes from 9 a.m. to 4:30 p.m.
from Mallory Square. The tour is $25 for adults and $12 for children
ages 5–12. For more information, call ☎ 305-296-6688.

An Eclectic Sampling of Key West Events and Whimsy

Late April–early May CONCH REPUBLIC INDEPENDENCE CELEBRATION
Commemorates the founding of the "Conch Republic" on April 23,
1982, when the U.S. Border Patrol erected a roadblock that halted
traffic in and out of the Keys. The residents protested and (light-
heartedly) "seceded from the Union." The secession lasted for one
minute but is celebrated every year.

May 5 ANNUAL CINCO SWIM Celebrate Mexico's independence as
each contestant jumps off the Sunset Pier with a margarita in hand,

then attempt to swim around the pier in the shortest amount of time, spilling the least amount of his or her cocktail.

Early May **ANNUAL KEY WEST SONGWRITER'S FESTIVAL** Showcases Nashville's top talent, performing at the famous Hog's Breath Saloon.

Late May **ANNUAL SCHOONER WHARF MINIMAL REGATTA** Folks build a boat from minimal materials and compete against others in the Key West Bight. The craziest regatta you'll ever see.

Early June **PRIDEFEST** Honors diversity, openness, and freedom in a city that is one of the world's top gay and lesbian vacation destinations.

Mid-June **CUBAN AMERICAN HERITAGE FESTIVAL** This annual event showcases the culture and customs of the Cuban community in Key West.

Late July **HEMINGWAY DAYS FESTIVAL** The legendary Key West resident's work and lifestyle are highlighted, along with a look-alike contest.

Late July–early August **SUMMER FOOD AND WINE FESTIVAL** Experience the best restaurants Key West has to offer, along with some of the finest wines from around the world.

Mid-September **ANNUAL CONCH POKER RUN (AKA BIKER WEEKEND)** Tens of thousands of people see thousands of the best and flashiest in motorcycles and their riders.

Late October **FANTASY FEST, FEATURING ANNUAL LIVING ART AIRBRUSH EXPO** Spotlights the finest airbrush artists from around the country as they create using the human form as a living canvas. Not for the tame of heart!

Mid-November **OFFSHORE SUPER SERIES POWERBOAT RACES AND SUPER BOAT INTERNATIONAL RACES** Some of the fastest and most exciting powerboats race around Key West.

Late November–early December **PIRATES IN PARADISE** Historic Fort Taylor and other venues throughout Key West are transformed into pirates' strongholds with mock sea battles; a thieves' market features arts, crafts, and more.

Late November **ANNUAL SUNSET PIER THANKSGIVING TURKEY SHOOT** Competitors toss frozen turkeys into colorful inner tubes floating in the water.

December 31 **ANNUAL KEY WEST NEW YEAR'S EVE, FEATURING FUNKY NEW YEAR ON THE SUNSET PIER** An outdoor party with live music, food, and cool libations.

Old Town Key West

Compact Old Town, a square mile of restored houses that makes up the heart of Key West, is best viewed on foot or by bicycle. While main avenues are frequently jammed, side streets still offer the peculiar Key West charm of gingerbread Victorian houses, tropical foliage, and funky atmosphere. As the many bike rental shops attest, Key West is bicycle friendly. It's easiest on these side streets to walk or ride a bike.

While there's kitsch on the main drags, residential streets reveal glimpses of the anarchic spirit of its residents—even if it's only the sound of Bob Dylan's "Blonde on Blonde" blasting from a hippie crash pad at nine in the morning. And much of the architecture is vintage, with lots of ornately carved Victorian trim.

Key West's tolerant spirit has fueled its latest economic revival. The large population of gay people in Key West heavily supports restoration efforts, pushing up the price of real estate and giving the town a solid economic boost.

Today's main tourist strip is Duval Street, renovated with well-manicured boutiques, T-shirt shops, bars, T-shirt shops, restaurants, T-shirt shops, galleries, beachwear shops, and other essentials for vacationing tourists. (Did we mention T-shirt shops?) Duval Street serves as an anchor as it cuts a swath across the island from the Gulf of Mexico to the Atlantic Ocean.

Everyone's Doing It

On the Gulf end of Duval Street is Mallory Square, famous for its daily sunset celebration. The "square" is in fact a cramped old concrete wharf that hosts a mini–street festival late each afternoon. During high tourist season, it's shoulder-to-shoulder along the dock with tourists, cruise-ship passengers, and street vendors selling everything from fruit-and-yogurt shakes to Southernmost falafels.

Key West–style free entertainment may include a troupe of trained cats (most impressive), a bowling ball juggler, an escape artist, innumerable Dylan clones strumming guitars, and the "Southernmost Bag Piper" (least impressive). You'll have trouble seeing any of this, though, because of the throngs.

For folks expecting a re-creation of Haight-Ashbury during the mid-1960s, Mallory Square is a letdown: No hippies pass joints to toast the setting sun, and no seafaring bohemians pass around a bottle of rum to mark the end of another day. Our opinion is that this famous "ritual" is touristy and overrated . . . at least when the crowds are overpowering.

On the Atlantic side of Duval Street—actually, a block over on parallel Whitehead Street—is Southernmost Point, another example

unofficial **TIP**
If crowds are not your thing, get up early one morning and check out the Key West sunrise on the east side of the island, over the Atlantic. Just as beautiful as the sunset, and a lot less noisy.

of Key West hype. A huge buoy perched on land and a placard mark the spot. But as any schoolchild will readily point out, the land continues south a few yards to the water's edge—the real southernmost point. Still, you can't deny the draw of this otherwise-undistinguished place: it's usually packed with tourists getting their picture taken in front of the buoy.

Cruise Ships

Speaking of crowds, huge cruise ships dock at the foot of Whitehead Street, near Mallory Square. Not that you'll have any trouble seeing them—the bigger ships tower over the docks and look as if they could accommodate the entire population of Key West. The presence of one or more of the big ships could mean even bigger crowds along Duval and Whitehead streets, so try to tour away from the dock area until the ships leave. Restaurants, however, aren't usually affected, as many of the cruise passengers return to their ships for meals.

Beyond the Hype

Behind the tourist schlock and commercialization, Key West still retains a true and quixotic charm. Our advice: Get off Duval Street, wander the back roads, visit the unique and interesting museums, get a handle on the rich and unusual history and local culture. Art galleries abound with handblown glass, oils, and watercolors. Cottages with carved wooden trim are covered in purple bougainvillea, and the smell of conch chowder wafts from kitchen windows. Bike bells ring down winding alleys. Take it slow and take in the soft, sensory details of this small town at the far southeastern end of the States.

Stop at an outdoor cafe for a two-hour lunch and hang out in bars that don't have T-shirt shops on the premises (which rules out Sloppy Joe's and Jimmy Buffett's Margaritaville). See a play at the **Waterfront Playhouse** (☎ 305-294-5015; **www.waterfrontplayhouse.com**) or **The Red Barn Theatre** (☎ 305-296-9911; **www.theredbarntheatre. com**). Listen to local musicians—who make music in the street, as well as watering holes. Slow the pace, give it a chance, and you'll soon discover Key West's innumerable charms.

AT *the* SEASHORE

THE KEYS ARE, GEOGRAPHICALLY SPEAKING, in a unique position: between the Atlantic Ocean and the Gulf of Mexico. For outdoor enthusiasts, there's world-class snorkeling and scuba diving, deep-sea fishing, sight fishing, and exploring the Dry Tortugas and Fort Jefferson, a 19th-century coastal fortification 70 miles west and only accessible by boat or seaplane. Because they are on the seam of two huge bodies of water, the Keys are washed with tremendous tidal forces twice daily. The result is wonderful feeding and breeding grounds for aquatic wildlife—and tremendously clear water. So while beaches are few and far between, water recreation abounds.

If you want to laze on historic Key West sand, try **Higg's Beach,** near Atlantic Boulevard and Reynolds. Here in 1860, the U.S. Navy rescued 1,432 Africans from three American-owned ships that were illegally transporting slaves to Cuba, 90 miles away. Almost 300 captives died soon after the rescue and are buried in a nearby mass grave.

DIVING AND SNORKELING

NUMEROUS KIOSKS AND DIVE SHOPS IN Key West offer half-day snorkeling and diving trips to the reef. Shop around for the best price and most convenient departure time. If you have your own gear, you can snorkel right from the beach at **Fort Zachary Taylor State Historic Site** (☎ 305-292-6713), located in the Truman Annex at Whitehead and Southard streets in Old Town Key West.

Certified scuba divers, however, can dive anywhere on their own. The Keys offer both beginning and experienced divers plenty of great scenery in protected, relatively shallow waters (60 feet deep and less). At the only living coral barrier reef off continental North America, giant brain coral grows up to six feet high, elkhorn coral six to ten feet high, and mountainous star coral to five feet or more across and up to ten feet high.

Popular dive sites include **John Pennekamp Coral Reef State Park,** in Key Largo, **Looe Key National Marine Sanctuary** (near Big Pine Key in the Lower Keys), and the **Marquesas** (22 miles west of Key West). Snorkeling is an option at these parks as well. For those in need of rental equipment, dive shops are located all along US 1 and throughout Key West.

Seaplanes of Key West offers full- and half-day flights to Fort Jefferson and the Dry Tortugas that include coolers, ice, sodas, and snorkeling gear—all you need to bring are a towel and a camera. The 70-mile flight is 40 minutes each way; the plane flies at low altitude, so passengers can view the clear waters, shipwrecks, and marine life. You spend two and half hours on the island. Four-hour trips leave at 8 a.m. and noon daily; prices are $189 for adults, $139 for children ages 7–12, and $109 for children ages 2–6. Full-day trips are $325 for adults, $245 for children ages 7–12, and $190 for children ages 2–6. For reservations, call ☎ 800-950-2359 or visit **www.seaplanesofkeywest.com.**

Another option for visiting Fort Jefferson and the Dry Tortugas is the **Fort Jefferson Ferry,** which sails out of Lands End Marina (251 Margaret Street in Key West) for full-day excursions. The 100-foot *Yankee Freedom II* boasts a large air-conditioned salon with a chef's galley, a cash bar, a snack bar, a large sundeck, and freshwater showers for swimmers, snorkelers, and divers. The ferry departs daily at 8 a.m. and returns at 5:30 p.m.; it's three hours each way, and visitors can enjoy about four hours on the island (including a complete tour of the fort). The price for the all-day trip is $134 for adults; $124 for seniors age 62 and older, military with ID, and students with ID; and $89 for children ages 4–16; breakfast and lunch included in price. For schedule and booking information, call ☎ 800-634-0939 or 305-294-7009; **www.yankeefreedom.com.**

FISHING

ANGLERS LOOKING FOR REPUTABLE GUIDES AND fishing-boat charters available at Key West marinas can stop by the **Saltwater Angler** at the Hilton Resort and Marina, 243 Front Street, and talk to Captain Jeff Cardenas, who spent ten years guiding flats fishermen in the Keys before opening his custom rod shop. He's an expert on the outdoors around Key West and happy to offer advice. For more information, call ☎ 800-223-1629 or 305-296-0700 or visit **www.saltwaterangler.com.**

You'll also find a discussion on the hows, whys, and wheres of South Florida sportfishing in "Deep-Sea Fishing" in Part One, Planning Your Visit.

BOATING

BILL KEOGH OF **Big Pine Kayak Adventures** in Big Pine Key has guided visitors for 18 years on kayak trips to the Keys' backcountry. No experience is necessary to paddle the calm, shallow waters in stable, easy-to-paddle sea kayaks on tours that emphasize seeing wildlife. You'll view birds, animals, and marine life in the Great White Heron and Key Deer wildlife refuges; snorkeling is another popular option. Trips are $50 per person and last about three hours; tour times vary. A guide, equipment, instruction, and a snack are provided. Big Pine Key is 30 miles from Key West.

Big Pine Kayak Adventures is based at Old Wooden Bridge Fishing Camp adjacent to No-Name Key Bridge. For a sailing ecoadventure, try a trip on a 26-foot catamaran that takes visitors and their kayaks into shallow-water areas; half-day trips cost $300, and full-day outings are $450 (prices are for parties of six or less). For more information or to make a reservation, call ☎ 305-872-7474 or visit **www.keyskayaktours.com.**

The **MV Discovery,** a glass-bottom boat with an underwater viewing room that puts you at eye level with marine life, offers trips at 10:30 a.m., 1:30 p.m., and sunset in the winter, and 11:30 a.m., 2:30 p.m., and sunset in the summer. Tickets for the two-hour trip are $35 for adults and $16 for children (plus tax); kids sail free on the first trip of the day. The ship is located at the Lands End Marina, 251 Margaret Street in Key West. For more information, call ☎ 800-262-0099 or 305-293-0099 or visit **www.discoveryunderseatours.com.**

Sebago Watersports offers catamaran cruises and solo or tandem parasailing. For more information call ☎ 305-292-4768 or 800-507-9955 or visit **www.keywestsebago.com.**

ATTRACTIONS

WHILE MOST VISITORS TO THE FLORIDA KEYS are outdoor enthusiasts who come to enjoy a unique subtropical area between the Gulf and the Atlantic, there's more to do on this string of islands than just fish, dive, snorkel, and boat. Organized by category, the following chart will help you prioritize your touring at a glance. You'll find the name, location, and author's rating. Each attraction is individually profiled in detail later in this section. Most museum-type attractions offer group rates for ten or more people.

Florida Keys Attractions

NAME	LOCATION	AUTHOR'S RATING
AQUARIUM		
Key West Aquarium	Key West	★★½
CEMETERY		
Key West Cemetery	Key West	★★★
FUNHOUSE		
Ripley's Believe It or Not	Key West	★★
HISTORIC SITE/FORT		
Fort Zachary Taylor State Historic Site	Key West	★★★★
HOME AND GARDEN TOURS		
Audubon House and Tropical Gardens	Key West	★★★
Ernest Hemingway Home and Museum	Key West	★★★★
Harry S. Truman Little White House Museum	Key West	★★½
Heritage House Museum and Robert Frost Cottage	Key West	★★★★½
LIGHTHOUSE		
Key West Lighthouse Museum	Key West	★★★★
MUSEUMS		
East Martello Museum	Key West	★★★
Flagler Station Over-Sea Railway	Key West	★★★★

Florida Keys Attractions (continued)

NAME	LOCATION	AUTHOR'S RATING
MUSUEMS (CONTINUED)		
The Key West Museum of Art and History	Key West	★★★½
Key West Shipwreck Historeum	Key West	★★★★
Mel Fisher's Maritime Heritage Society and Museum	Key West	★★½
Museum of Natural History of the Florida Keys	Marathon	★★½
PARKS		
Bahia Honda State Park	Bahia Honda Key	★★★
John Pennekamp Coral Reef State Park	Key Largo	★★★★★
Theater of the Sea	Islamorada	★★★½

ATTRACTION PROFILES

Audubon House and Tropical Gardens

APPEAL BY AGE	PRESCHOOL ★	GRADE SCHOOL ★½	TEENS ★★
YOUNG ADULTS ★★½	OVER 30 ★★★		SENIORS ★★★½

205 Whitehead Street, Key West; ☎ 877-294-2470 or 305-294-2116; www.audubonhouse.com

Type of attraction Restored three-story home dedicated to the famed early 19th-century bird illustrator and lived in by a Key West harbor pilot and wrecker; a self-guided tour. **Admission** Adults, $10; students of any age, $6.50; children ages 6–12, $5; children age 6 and under, free. **Hours** Daily, 9:30 a.m–5 p.m. **When to go** Anytime. **Special comments** You must climb three sets of stairs; the second-floor gallery of Audubon porcelains is air-conditioned **Author's rating** A beautifully restored house and gardens. ★★★. **How much time to allow** 1 hour.

DESCRIPTION AND COMMENTS The house commemorates Audubon's 1832 trip here to draw local birds. The house belonged to Captain George H. Geiger, an early Key West harbor pilot and wrecker who, like many Key West residents, made a fortune salvaging cargo from ships wrecked on the reef. Captain Geiger and his heirs lived in this house for more than 120 years, but in 1958 the deteriorating structure was slated for demolition. Through the efforts of local conservationists, the house was saved and restored, decorated with exquisite period pieces collected in

florida keys attractions and dining

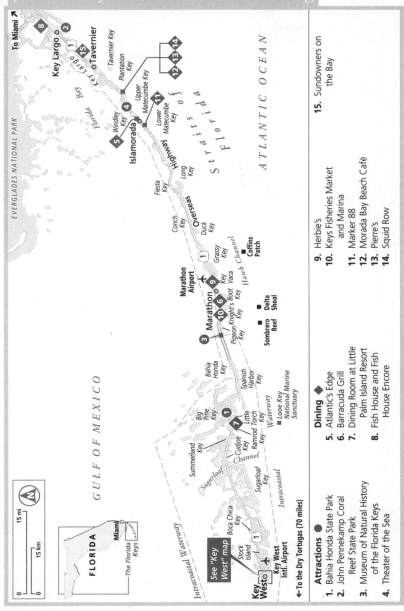

Attractions ●

1. Bahia Honda State Park
2. John Pennekamp Coral Reef State Park
3. Museum of Natural History of the Florida Keys
4. Theater of the Sea

Dining ◆

5. Atlantic's Edge
6. Barracuda Grill
7. Dining Room at Little Palm Island Resort
8. Fish House and Fish House Encore

9. Herbie's
10. Keys Fisheries Market and Marina
11. Marker 88
12. Morada Bay Beach Café
13. Pierre's
14. Squid Row
15. Sundowners on the Bay

Europe, and dedicated as a museum commemorating the Key West visits of painter and ornithologist John James Audubon. The restoration of the house inaugurated a movement that saved many historically significant Key West buildings.

TOURING TIPS   You may find the voices in the audio tour a bit much, but don't miss the children's room on the third floor; two pairs of 19th-century roller skates look like forerunners of the in-line skates popular today. Outside, orchid-filled trees and rare plantings evoke the wealthy, cosmopolitan lifestyle of early Key West residents. Check out the duplex outhouse in the corner of the garden.

OTHER THINGS TO DO NEARBY   The Heritage House Museum, the Harry S. Truman Little White House, the Key West Shipwreck Historeum, and Mel Fisher's Treasure Exhibit are all within a few blocks.

Bahia Honda State Park

APPEAL BY AGE	PRESCHOOL ★★	GRADE SCHOOL ★★★	TEENS ★★★½
YOUNG ADULTS ★★★		OVER 30 ★★★	SENIORS ★★★

US 1 at MM 37.5, Bahia Honda Key; ☎ 305-872-2353; www.bahiahondapark.com

Type of attraction Beach with natural land and water activities and camping. **Admission** $5 per vehicle. **Hours** Daily, 8 a.m.–sunset. **When to go** Anytime. **Author's rating** The best beach in the Keys. ★★★. **How much time to allow** 3–4 hours.

DESCRIPTION AND COMMENTS   Just off the Seven-Mile Bridge, 524 lush acres of dunes, mangroves, hammocks, trails, and sand sprawl on both the Gulf and the ocean. The narrow two-and-a-half-mile natural beach is a rarity in the Keys. Waterside picnicking and grilling, hiking, bird-watching, biking, kayaking, boating and wade-in snorkeling are popular pastimes. There's a concession stand, marina, campgrounds, snack bar, gift shop, and marina.

TOURING TIPS   Guided nature walks are available. If you're coming from/returning to the Miami area, time this stop to break up your drive to or from Key West. Bring your bathing suit and gear. Or you can camp here.

OTHER THINGS TO DO NEARBY   Boat from Bahia Honda concessions to snorkel or dive off Looe Key National Marine Sanctuary, four miles offshore. From the old Bahia Honda railroad bridge, you can fish for tarpon or just enjoy the panoramic view of the Atlantic and Gulf.

East Martello Museum

APPEAL BY AGE	PRESCHOOL ★★★★	GRADE SCHOOL ★★★★	TEENS ★★★½
YOUNG ADULTS ★★★		OVER 30 ★★★	SENIORS ★★★

3501 South Roosevelt Boulevard, Key West, near the airport; ☎ 305-296-3913; www.kwahs.com/martello

Type of attraction A Civil War fort converted to an eclectic museum; a self-guided tour. **Admission** Adults, $6; students, $4; children under age 6, free. **Hours** Daily, 9:30 a.m.–4:30 p.m.; closed Christmas Day. **When to go** Anytime. **Special**

comments The climb up the lookout tower requires negotiating a steep spiral staircase. **Author's rating** A bizarre museum with a little bit of everything. ★★★. **How much time to allow** 1–2 hours.

DESCRIPTION AND COMMENTS It might be easier to catalog what you *won't* find here. The low brick ceilings and arches of this old fort contain a horse-drawn hearse and a wicker casket (circa 1873), ship models, exhibits on Native Americans, Civil War and Spanish American War military artifacts, a hotel safe, a deep-sea diver's air suit and wooden air pump, and a crude raft used by Cubans to escape the Castro regime. Book lovers will enjoy the display of books by Key West authors, including seven Pulitzer Prize winners.

Ankle biters can play in the "junior museum"—a tiny house that adults must stoop to enter—located on the well-manicured grounds. There's also an art museum that features temporary exhibits.

TOURING TIPS On the way up the spiral staircase leading to the lookout tower, with the payoff of a great view, stop at the exhibit of odd and whimsical "junkyard art" by Stanley Papio.

OTHER THINGS TO DO NEARBY In the West Martello tower of the ruined fort, tropical gardens are maintained by the Key West Garden Club. The Atlantic Ocean is directly across Roosevelt Boulevard.

Ernest Hemingway Home and Museum

| APPEAL BY AGE | PRESCHOOL ★ | GRADE SCHOOL ★★ | TEENS ★★½ |
| YOUNG ADULTS ★★★ | OVER 30 ★★★½ | | SENIORS ★★★★ |

907 Whitehead Street, Key West; ☎ 305-294-1136; www.hemingwayhome.com

Type of attraction The stone house and gardens of Nobel Prize–winning author Ernest Hemingway; guided and self-guided tours. **Admission** Adults, $11; children ages 6–12, $6; children ages 5 and under, free. **Hours** Daily, 9 a.m.–5 p.m. **When to go** In the morning during hot weather; the house isn't air-conditioned. **Special comments** Hemingway loved cats, and about 40 of their alleged descendants (some with six or seven toes per foot) lounge around the 1-acre grounds; yet some experts dispute the local legend that says these cats are the descendants of the great writer's pets. Either way, folks not fond of (or allergic to) felines, beware. Visitors must climb two sets of steep stairs on the tour. **Author's rating** An interesting piece of American literary and Key West history. ★★★★. **How much time to allow** 1 hour.

DESCRIPTION AND COMMENTS Ernest Hemingway owned this Spanish Colonial house, built in 1870, from 1931 until his death in 1961. In his study in the loft of his pool house, he wrote some of his most famous novels and short stories, including *A Farewell to Arms,* "The Snows of Kilimanjaro," and *For Whom the Bell Tolls.* The spacious mansion gives visitors a glimpse into genteel life in the 1930s. Much (but not all) of the furniture and the memorabilia on display behind glass cabinets belonged to Hemingway.

TOURING TIPS Don't skip the optional 30-minute guided tour; the tour leaders are witty and literate, and they tell great stories about the writer, whom many critics consider America's greatest writer. Lots of Key West firsts in the house—indoor plumbing, fireplace, and the 65-foot saltwater swimming pool—look for the penny in the cement; part of the cats' water fountain, located between the house and the pool, is a urinal rescued by the writer from Sloppy Joe's Bar.

OTHER THINGS TO DO NEARBY The Key West Lighthouse Museum is across the street.

Flagler Station Over-Sea Railway Historeum

APPEAL BY AGE	PRESCHOOL ★½	GRADE SCHOOL ★★	TEENS ★★
YOUNG ADULTS ★★★½		OVER 30 ★★★★	SENIORS ★★★★

901 Caroline Street, Key West; ☎ 305-295-3562

Type of attraction Concise collection of memorabilia, documents, and video footage and documentaries pertaining to the construction of the over-sea railway. **Admission** Adults, $5; children ages 12 and under, $2.50 **Hours** Daily, 9 a.m.–5 p.m. **When to go** Anytime. **Author's rating** Good films tout an interesting piece of not-so-widely known history; ★★★★. **How much time to allow** 45 minutes.

DESCRIPTION AND COMMENTS This small collection of clothing, contracts, photos, building materials, and other bits of history is accented by three highly enjoyable and informative films about Henry Flagler's drive to build the first railway from Miami to Key West. The first film is 13½ minutes long and runs continuously, with a four-minute interval between screenings. The film, entitled *The Day the Train Arrived,* is about Flagler's personal drive and the actual building of the railway. The second film, *The Seven-Mile Bridge,* lasts 3½ minutes and is a synopsis of bridge and railroad construction—especially as it related to this specific project. The last film, *A Trip down the Florida Keys,* is an 8½-minute narrative of life in the Keys before and after construction of the railway.

TOURING TIPS The Historeum is a pleasant stroll down Caroline Street, just a few blocks from the crowds of Duval Street. As the exhibit is actually outside on the back-porch area of the enclosed, air-conditioned gift shop, it would be wise to head here to wind-down—around 3 p.m. or so.

Two of the three films have limited seating and viewing areas, and since it doesn't matter which order they are viewed, choose based on which screen you can see best.

OTHER THINGS TO DO NEARBY Walk back down to Duval Street, and have a cocktail or window-shop until sunset; then head over to Mallory Square to applaud the sundown.

kids Fort Zachary Taylor State Historic Site

APPEAL BY AGE	PRESCHOOL ★★★★★	GRADE SCHOOL ★★★★★	TEENS ★★★★
YOUNG ADULTS ★★★★		OVER 30 ★★★★	SENIORS ★★★★

Southard Street (in the Truman Annex), Key West; ☎ 305-292-6713; www.forttaylor.org

Type of attraction A partially restored Civil War fort and museum; the best beach in Key West; guided and self-guided tours. **Admission** $5 per carload; $2 for pedestrians and bicyclists. **Hours** Daily, 8 a.m.–sundown. **When to go** Anytime, but it's elbow-to-elbow on the beach on weekends. **Author's rating** A triple hit: a neat fort, interesting history, and a beach you can snorkel from. ★★★★. **How much time to allow** Half a day. Budget 30 minutes to 1 hour to tour the fort, spend the afternoon on the beach, then catch the best view of the sunset in Key West.

DESCRIPTION AND COMMENTS For 150 years, Fort Zachary Taylor defended the harbor of Key West. During the Civil War, it was one of four Union forts in Confederate territory that never fell into Southern hands. As a result, hundreds of cannons trained on the nearby shipping lanes kept ships bottled up in Key West throughout the Civil War. The craftsmanship of the exquisite brickwork throughout the fort would be difficult to duplicate today.

TOURING TIPS Don't miss the free 30-minute guided tour of the fort, offered daily at noon and 2 p.m., which gives visitors a quick education on the evolution of seacoast fortification through the 19th and 20th centuries. You'll also hear some interesting anecdotes from the park ranger who leads the tour. For example: Many ten-inch cannons were so loud that local merchants demanded a 15-minute warning before practice firing so they could rush home and open their windows—the concussion of the big guns could shatter glass.

There's also a fine view of the Gulf of Mexico from the top of the fort. The ocean beach is made of coral and is great for swimming, snorkeling, and sunbathing; the west side of the 87-acre park offers anglers a wide variety of saltwater fish (a Florida fishing license is required). Shaded picnic areas, tables, grills, several outdoor showers, and a bathhouse are available to visitors. On the first weekend in March, you can participate in costumed Civil War Days reenactments.

OTHER THINGS TO DO NEARBY The Harry S. Truman Little White House is on the grounds of the adjacent Truman Annex.

Harry S. Truman Little White House Museum

APPEAL BY AGE	PRESCHOOL ★	GRADE SCHOOL ★½	TEENS ★½
YOUNG ADULTS ★★	OVER 30 ★★★	SENIORS ★★★★★	

111 Front Street (one block up Caroline Street through the presidential gates), Key West; ☎ 305-294-9911; www.trumanlittlewhitehouse.com

Type of attraction The restored vacation home of President Harry Truman; a guided tour. **Admission** Adults, $11; children ages 12 and under, $5. **Hours** Daily, 9 a.m.–5 p.m. Guided tours leave every 15 minutes or so. **When to go** Anytime. **Special comments** Visitors must negotiate a set of steep stairs on the tour. **Author's rating** A nostalgia trip for folks old enough to remember "Give 'Em Hell" Harry. ★★½. **How much time to allow** 1 hour.

DESCRIPTION AND COMMENTS President Harry Truman spent 175 vacation days during his presidency (1945–53) at this house in Key West. Today, the building is completely redone to posh 1949 standards, although most of the furnishings aren't original (one exception is the custom-made mahogany poker table). The guide tells visitors that while Truman disapproved of gambling in the White House, playing poker with "the boys" was a major form of relaxation for the president when he vacationed in Key West.

TOURING TIPS The tour begins with a ten-minute video that evokes the Truman era and primes visitors for the tour. The guides offer interesting tidbits about Truman's personal life when vacationing in Key West. For example, Bess Truman didn't often accompany her husband because she preferred their home in Independence, Missouri. Don't miss the gift shop, which sells aprons inscribed with, you guessed it, "If you can't stand the heat, get out of the kitchen."

OTHER THINGS TO DO NEARBY Mel Fisher's Treasure Museum, the Key West Aquarium, and the Audubon House are all within a comfortable walk.

Heritage House Museum and Robert Frost Cottage

APPEAL BY AGE	PRESCHOOL ★	GRADE SCHOOL ★½	TEENS ★★
YOUNG ADULTS ★★★		OVER 30 ★★★½	SENIORS ★★★★

**410 Caroline Street, Key West; ☎ 305-296-3573;
www.heritagehousemuseum.org**

Type of attraction An 1830s sea captain's home full of literary memorabilia and antique furnishings from the China trade; a guided tour. **Admission** $15. **Hours** Monday–Saturday, 10 a.m.–4 p.m.; guided and self-guided tours; closed Sundays and Christmas Day. **When to go** Anytime **Author's rating** Fascinating stuff— don't miss it. ★★★★½. **How much time to allow** 30 minutes.

DESCRIPTION AND COMMENTS Unlike many old Key West homes open to visitors, this residence never needed restoration; it's exactly as its owner left it after her death in 1972. Former owner Jessie Porter, a granddaughter of one of Key West's founders, hosted celebrities including Gloria Swanson and Tallulah Bankhead and was a friend to famous writers such as Ernest Hemingway, Tennessee Williams, and Robert Frost. In addition to photos of a few of America's great literary stars and some original manuscripts, this old house bursts with priceless artifacts, unique furnishings, musical instruments, exquisite silk kimonos, and other treats. In a backyard cottage, poet Robert Frost spent many winters. While this building is not open to the public, the tour guide plays a tape of Frost reading one of his poems.

TOURING TIPS Look for the marijuana leaves imprinted in the handmade tiles around the fireplace. The freshwater well outside the front door was used by Native Americans as early as the 12th century.

OTHER THINGS TO DO NEARBY The Audubon House, the Harry S. Truman Little White House, and the Key West Shipwreck Historeum are all close.

kids John Pennekamp Coral Reef State Park

APPEAL BY AGE	PRESCHOOL ★★★★	GRADE SCHOOL ★★★★	TEENS ★★★★
YOUNG ADULTS ★★★★★		OVER 30 ★★★★★	SENIORS ★★★★★

**On US 1 at Mile Marker 102.5, Key Largo (about a 90-minute drive south of Miami); ☎ 305-451-1621; reservations 305-451-6300;
www.pennekamppark.com**

Type of attraction A 178-square-mile underwater park featuring snorkeling tours, scuba diving trips, and glass-bottom-boat trips **Admission** The entrance fee to the park is $2.50 per car and driver, $5 for 2 people, and 50 cents per additional person up to 8 people. Snorkeling tours are $28.95 plus tax for adults and $23.95 plus tax for children under age 18. Tours leave at 9 a.m., noon, and 3 p.m. Mask, snorkel, and fins rent for an additional $2 each (you keep the snorkel); ☎ 305-451-6300. 4-hour guided scuba trips are $45 per person and leave at 9:30 a.m. and 1:30 p.m. Rental of 2 air tanks for 2 1-hour dives is $20. Complete rental and instruction are available for scuba diving. 3-day certification courses cost $450; a "resort" course that lets you dive with an instructor or dive master takes a full day and costs $160. For more information, call the dive center at ☎ 305-451-6322. 4-hour sailing and snorkeling trips on a 38-foot catamaran are $33.95 for adults and $28.95 for children under age 18 and leave at 9 a.m. and 1:30 p.m; ☎ 305-451-6322. 2½-hour glass-bottom-boat tours on the *Spirit of Pennekamp* cost $22 plus tax for adults and $15 for children under age 12 and depart at 9:15 a.m., 12:15 p.m., and 3 p.m. From 8 a.m. to 3:45 p.m., you can rent canoes for $12 an hour, sea-kayak singles for $12 an hour, and doubles for $17 an hour. **Hours** Daily, 8 a.m.–sunset **When to go** Anytime to visit the park; on weekends during the winter for diving and snorkeling trips to the reef. Reservations should be made several weeks in advance; call at least a day ahead of time during the week to reserve a spot. **Special comments** All trips are subject to weather conditions and a minimum number of paying customers. Only certified divers can go on the scuba trips; anybody who can swim can go on a snorkeling tour. **Author's rating** Find out why Key Largo is the dive capital of the United States. ★★★★★. **How much time to allow** Half a day or longer.

DESCRIPTION AND COMMENTS   The 78 miles of living coral reef in this park are only a small portion of one of the most beautiful reef systems in the world. We recommend taking the snorkel tour, which focuses on shallow water. After the 30-minute boat ride to the reef, it's over the side for up-close views of aquatic life. The boat crew coaches snorkeling. All snorkelers must wear inflatable life vests, which are provided.

TOURING TIPS   If swimming with the fish and coral don't appeal, take the two-and-a-half-hour glass-bottom-boat tour. Other facilities in the park include hiking trails, a small swimming beach, a bathhouse with freshwater showers, an aquarium, canoe rentals, and a visitor center featuring ecological displays on Keys flora and fauna. The reef is a protected, fragile area, and nothing may be taken from the water.

OTHER THINGS TO DO NEARBY   Theater of the Sea is 18 miles south in Islamorada. Key Largo has plenty of places to eat, sleep, and shop.

kids Key West Aquarium

APPEAL BY AGE	PRESCHOOL ★★★★★	GRADE SCHOOL ★★★★	TEENS ★★★½
YOUNG ADULTS ★★★		OVER 30 ★★½	SENIORS ★★

1 Whitehead Street, Key West; ☎ 305-296-2051;
www.keywestaquarium.com

Type of attraction An old-fashioned aquarium featuring sea life from both the Atlantic and the Gulf of Mexico; guided and self-guided tours. **Admission** Adults,

$10; children ages 4–12, $5; children ages 3 and under, free. Tickets are good for 2 days. **Hours** Daily, 10 a.m.–6 p.m.; guided tours and feedings at 11 a.m., 1 p.m., 3 p.m., and 4:30 p.m. **When to go** Anytime. **Author's rating** Great for the kiddies, but otherwise a bit ho-hum. ★★½. **How much time to allow** 1 hour.

DESCRIPTION AND COMMENTS   This aquarium, built in 1934, is small but comfortable, and will especially please younger children. At the touch tank, kids can handle conch, starfish, and crabs. You'll probably never get closer to a shark unless you hook one.

TOURING TIPS   This is a browsing kind of place with long rows of backlit fish tanks at eye level. The moray eels look especially creepy, and you'll see specimens of smaller sharks such as lemon, blacktip, and bonnethead, which are especially interesting at feeding time, on guided tours. If you're on a short visit to Key West, spend your valuable touring time elsewhere and come back on a later visit.

OTHER THINGS TO DO NEARBY   You're in the heart of downtown Key West: Mel Fisher's Treasure Exhibit, the Audubon House, and Mallory Square are within a few blocks' walk.

Key West Cemetery

APPEAL BY AGE	PRESCHOOL ★	GRADE SCHOOL ★	TEENS ★★
YOUNG ADULTS ★★★	OVER 30 ★★★		SENIORS ★★★

The main gate is at Margaret and Angela streets, Key West;
☎ **305-292-8170**

Type of attraction The final resting place of many prominent—and unusual—Key West residents; guided and self-guided tours. **Admission** Free. **Hours** Daily, 7 a.m.–sunset. **When to go** Anytime, but avoid the middle of the day in hot weather. **Author's rating** A unique piece of Key West history that's managed to avoid the rest of the island's rampant commercialism. ★★★. **How much time to allow** 1 hour, although it could take much of the day to explore the entire 25 acres.

DESCRIPTION AND COMMENTS   A high water table and tough coral rock explain the unusual burial practices in this corner of paradise—everyone here is "buried" above ground in mausoleums. As a result, the cemetery is filled with coffin-shaped tombs, many of them stacked on top of one another like mortuary condominiums. Nevertheless, it's not a ghoulish place. In addition, pets are often entombed next to their owners.

TOURING TIPS   Guided tours depart the main gate Tuesday and Thursday mornings at 9:30 a.m.; the cost is $12 per person.

Seek out the most inspired headstone inscription in the cemetery, that of famous Key West hypochondriac Mrs. B. P. Roberts: "I told you I was sick."

OTHER THINGS TO DO NEARBY   The cemetery is at the edge of Old Town Key West; explore some of the quiet, shaded streets lined with charming houses that range from shacks to Victorian masterpieces. Some are lovingly restored, while others seem as if they haven't been touched since Hemingway lived here. Look in the yards for concrete cisterns, which were once the chief source of fresh water on the island.

Key West Lighthouse Museum

APPEAL BY AGE	PRESCHOOL ★★	GRADE SCHOOL ★★★★	TEENS ★★★★
YOUNG ADULTS ★★★★		OVER 30 ★★★★	SENIORS ★★★

938 Whitehead Street, Key West; ☎ 305-294-0012;
www.kwahs.com/lighthouse

Type of attraction An 1848 lighthouse and a museum that tells the story of light-houses in the Florida Keys; a self-guided tour. **Admission** Adults, $8; children ages 6–12, $4. **Hours** Daily, 9:30 a.m.–4:30 p.m.; closed Christmas Day. **When to go** Anytime. **Special comments** Folks who aren't in shape or don't like heights should skip the climb to the top of the 90-foot lighthouse. **Author's rating** A great view and interesting history. ★★★★. **How much time to allow** 1 hour.

DESCRIPTION AND COMMENTS Next to doing "12-ounce curls" (drinking beer) at Sloppy Joe's, a climb to the lantern at the top of the lighthouse is the most rewarding workout in Key West. The 88 steps to the top of the tower lead to an impressive view of the Atlantic Ocean, the Gulf of Mexico, and cruise ships docked in the harbor. This structure was originally built in 1822 on Whitehead Point but was reconstructed after a hurricane demolished the original building in 1846. Pirates who frequently looted stranded ships were put out of business when this lighthouse shined its beam on the waters.

TOURING TIPS The nearby museum (formerly the Keeper's Quarters when this was an operating lighthouse) is small, dark, cool, and filled with fascinating artifacts from the days when the big light atop the tower guided navigators through the treacherous waters outside Key West.

OTHER THINGS TO DO NEARBY The Hemingway House is directly across White-head Street.

The Key West Museum of Art and History at the Custom House

APPEAL BY AGE	PRESCHOOL ★★★	GRADE SCHOOL ★★★	TEENS ★★★
YOUNG ADULTS ★★★★		OVER 30 ★★★★	SENIORS ★★★

281 Front Street, Key West; ☎ 305-295-6616;
www.kwahs.com/customhouse.htm

Type of attraction A small collection of permanent and traveling works located in the beautifully restored Custom House in the heart of old Key West. **Admission** Adults, $10; seniors 65+ and locals, $8; children ages 7–17, $5; children ages 6 and under, free. **Hours** Daily, 9 a.m.–5 p.m. **When to go** Anytime. **Special comments** Be sure to bring the kids—they'll love Stanley Papio's "junkyard art." **Author's rating** Beautiful architecture housing varied and interesting works. ★★★½ **How much time to allow** 1 hour.

DESCRIPTION AND COMMENTS Key West became the richest city in Florida in the early 1800s, when salvagers could legally claim sunken treasure and bring it through this custom house. The Key West Museum of Art and History here has several permanent exhibits. These include a room dedicated to (and funded by) Wilhelmina Harvey, who calls herself Key West's most famous political celebrity. You can also find the work of Stanley Papio, who sculpts amusing characters from all sorts of scrap metal and junk, and the woodcarvings of local artist Mario Sanchez, who creates intricately carved three-dimensional scenes representing different aspects of life in Key West in a folk art style. Additionally, the permanent collection of art and historical artifacts from Key West encompasses the history and restoration of the Custom House. This includes pieces of the formerly permanent exhibit, the U.S.S. *Maine,* that related to the history of Key West.

TOURING TIPS   As the Custom House is a relatively small arena for art display, look for art in places you wouldn't expect—leading to the third-floor office area, on the walls and floors behind the volunteers' posts, and down the hallway to the restrooms, to name a few.

OTHER THINGS TO DO NEARBY   Include a pass through the Custom House during your Duval Street/Mallory Square sightseeing; it's in the middle of everything and is easier to access on foot than trying to park nearby.

Key West Shipwreck Historeum

APPEAL BY AGE	PRESCHOOL ★½	GRADE SCHOOL ★½	TEENS ★★★
YOUNG ADULTS ★★★★	OVER 30 ★★★★		SENIORS ★★★★

1 Whitehead Street at Mallory Square, Key West; ☎ 305-292-8990; www.shipwreckhistoreum.com

Type of attraction A self-guided tour through a replica of an 1856 Key West wreckers' warehouse, where skits, films, laser technology, and actual artifacts combine to present a picture of 19th-century Key West life and explain how the wrecking profession influenced the island's society. **Admission** Adults, $10; children ages 4–12, $5; children under age 4, free. **Hours** Daily, 9:45 a.m.–4:45 p.m.; shows begin 15 minutes before and after the hour. **When to go** Anytime. **Special comments** The Historeum is not wheelchair accessible. You must descend several stairs to see the movie, and the museum tour involves several flights of stairs. The lookout tower provides an incredible view of the historic district and the barrier reef, but it requires visitors to climb nine flights of stairs. Those afraid of heights might want to skip this part of the attraction. **Author's rating** Talented actors, interesting history, and impressive booty. ★★★★. **How much time to allow** About 45 minutes for the entire tour.

DESCRIPTION AND COMMENTS   Drift back in time as Asa Tift, a famous 19th-century Key West wrecker, greets you as a potential crew member in his warehouse. Listen to the story of how Key West became the richest city in the U.S.A. when the vessel *Isaac Allerton* sank in 1856. A 20-minute video depicts the life of the wreckers and their fight to save lives and precious cargo from ships doomed by the dangerous reefs. Much of the story is told through comments and stories from some of Key West's prominent figures of the time.

TOURING TIPS   The *Isaac Allerton* was the richest shipwreck in our history, caught in an 1856 hurricane, and artifacts from the wreck are prominently featured on this self-guided museum tour—the ship was headed for New

Orleans loaded with expensive and precious items intended to decorate the city's Customs House. Asa Tift (who originally owned the house that Hemingway later lived in) seems busy at work in the room where you begin the museum tour, but he will be happy to stop and answer all your questions. The actor playing Tift will make it worth your time to stop and chat—our guide was loaded with interesting Key West tidbits. Don't forget about Tift's Wrecker's Lookout, which marks the end of the tour. If you're up for the climb, you will be rewarded with a spectacular view.

OTHER THINGS TO DO NEARBY You're in the heart of Mallory Square and only a few blocks' walk from the Aquarium, the Audubon House, and Mel Fisher's Treasure Exhibit.

Lofton B. Sands African-Bahamian Museum

APPEAL BY AGE	PRESCHOOL ★	GRADE SCHOOL ★★	TEENS ★★★
YOUNG ADULTS ★★★		OVER 30 ★★★	SENIORS ★★★

324 Truman Avenue, Key West; ☎ 305-295-7337

Type of attraction Museum highlighting history and contributions of African-Americans to the Keys. **Admission** Call for current prices; donation suggested (usually $5). **Hours** Vary; tours conducted by appointment. **When to go** Anytime. **Author's rating** A source of valuable historic insight. ★★★. **How much time to allow** 1 hour.

DESCRIPTION AND COMMENTS Exhibits in this simple 1928 house at the edge of Bahama Village—once known as Black Town or Africa Town—show nearly 200 years of life in the Keys through the lens of the African American experience, with vintage photos of weddings, funerals, and other social history. Outdoor displays trace local events through the civil rights era, sometimes with craft demonstrations. The inside market carries jewelry and trinkets.

TOURING TIPS Regardless of your ethnicity, this is an informative museum, and a reminder of the long Afro-Caribbean influence in South Florida.

OTHER THINGS TO DO NEARBY Bahama Village is home to many residents who trace their roots to the Bahamas and, ultimately, slavery. (The area is called "Le Africa" on old maps.)

Mel Fisher's Maritime Heritage Society and Museum

APPEAL BY AGE	PRESCHOOL ★★★	GRADE SCHOOL ★★★★	TEENS ★★★★
YOUNG ADULTS ★★★½		OVER 30 ★★★	SENIORS ★★★½

200 Greene Street, Key West; ☎ 305-294-2633 or 800-434-1399; www.melfisher.org/museum

Type of attraction A display of treasure recovered from two Spanish galleons sunk off Key West in a 1622 hurricane; a self-guided tour. **Admission** Adults, $10; children ages 6–12, $5; AAA and AARP discounts available. **Hours** Daily, 9:30 a.m.–5 p.m.; the last video presentation is at 4:30 p.m. **When to go** Anytime. **Author's rating** Impressive booty, a small exhibit, and plenty of self-promotional schlock. ★★½. **How much time to allow** 1 hour.

DESCRIPTION AND COMMENTS Ever dream of finding a treasure trove worth hundreds of millions? Well, Mel Fisher, the best-known salvager in the Keys, did, and he accomplished his goal after many years of searching. Bars of solid silver, a solid-gold dinner plate, doubloons, a cedar chest, and cannons and sailors' artifacts from the 17th century are among the items on display in this small museum. You can even pick up an almost-seven-pound solid gold bar. Exhibits also explain how modern treasure hunters find the ancient wrecks and bring up loot from the bottom of the sea. Yet the relentless self-promotion and commercialism of this private museum—not to mention its small size—are a letdown.

TOURING TIPS *The Margarita,* part of a fleet of ships sunk in a hurricane en route from Havana, Cuba, to Spain in 1622, was discovered in 1980. But it wasn't until 1985, when Mel Fisher located the hull structure and cargo of the fleet's flagship *Nuestra Señora de Atocha* that the bulk of the treasure was found; a dated 20-minute video tells the story.

OTHER THINGS TO DO NEARBY The Key West Aquarium, the Harry S. Truman Little White House, and the Audubon House are all within a few blocks.

kids Museum of Natural History of the Florida Keys

APPEAL BY AGE	PRESCHOOL ★★★★	GRADE SCHOOL ★★★★★	TEENS ★★★
YOUNG ADULTS ★★½		OVER 30 ★★½	SENIORS ★★½

On US 1, at Mile Marker 50.5, in Marathon; ☎ 305-743-9100; www.cranepoint.org

Type of attraction A child-friendly museum emphasizing the natural history and ecology of the Florida Keys; a self-guided tour. **Admission** Adults, $7.50; seniors, $6; students, $4; children ages 6 and under, free. **Hours** Monday–Saturday, 9 a.m.–5 p.m.; Sunday, noon–5 p.m. **When to go** Anytime. **Special comments** Don't forget mosquito repellent before walking the quarter-mile nature trail. **Author's rating** A small museum geared for children, who will love it. ★★½. **How much time to allow** 1–2 hours.

DESCRIPTION AND COMMENTS Exhibits feature ancient Indians, pirates, wreckers, and the railroaders who built the rail line to Key West. Kids will like the re-creation of an underwater cave, as well as the 15,000-gallon salt-water lagoon and tanks featuring spiny lobsters, an iguana, and a parrot. A separate children's museum features touch tanks that let kids handle spiny sea urchins and other creatures, and a corner with books and a chair for reading.

TOURING TIPS The nature trail leads to a rare tropical-palm hammock, home to some uncommon and unusual plants.

OTHER THINGS TO DO NEARBY The Seven-Mile Bridge, an engineering marvel when it was completed in 1910, is a few miles south. Farther south at Mile Marker 37, Bahia Honda State Park offers weary travelers a real sand beach, a nature trail, and a respite from the highway.

kids Ripley's Believe It or Not

| APPEAL BY AGE | PRESCHOOL ★★ | GRADE SCHOOL ★★★★ | TEENS ★★★★ |
| YOUNG ADULTS ★★★ | | OVER 30 ★★ | SENIORS ★½ |

108 Duval Street, Key West; ☎ 305-293-9939; www.ripleyskeywest.com

Type of attraction A carnival funhouse for youngsters and loony adults featuring exhibits from *Ripley's Believe It or Not;* a self-guided tour. **Admission** Adults, $14.95 plus tax; children ages 5–12, $11.95 plus tax; children ages 4 and under, free. **Hours** Daily, 9 a.m.–11 p.m. **When to go** Anytime. **Special comments** A number of exhibits are right out of a roadside carnival, so be ready for unsettling special effects—both optical and physical—such as wobbly decks and lunging "sharks." **Author's rating** Tacky, tasteless, and often hilarious, as well as expensive. ★★. **How much time to allow** 1 hour for adults, 2 for youngsters.

DESCRIPTION AND COMMENTS Is it really Ripley, returned from the dead, who materializes at his desk and invites visitors to explore his museum? Or is it a hologram of an actor who looks vaguely like Christopher Walken wearing a smoking jacket? Who cares?

Join in the fun on an exploration of this ridiculous—and funny—"museum." You'll find oddities of questionable authenticity (like "shrunken" heads), endlessly repeating film clips of human bizarreness (a guy blowing up a balloon through his eye), grainy film clips with corny narration of New Guinea natives chowing down on grubs and a roast crocodile (gross, but not so shocking in light of *Fear Factor*), lots of juvenile sex-teasers (walk by in one direction and you get a glimpse of a naked lady's backside, but walk by in the other direction and she's gone).

TOURING TIPS This is a perfect rainy-day kind of place. You don't have to be a kid, but having one along would certainly increase the fun. And don't ask yourself what any of this has to do with Key West.

OTHER THINGS TO DO NEARBY Duval Street must offer more T-shirts for sale than any other place in the universe. Knock down a you-know-what at Jimmy Buffett's Margaritaville (across the street), or stretch your legs for a stroll to the Southernmost Point; hang a left as you leave Ripley's. Is the sun low in the sky? Then head for Mallory Square and the sunset celebration; it's to the right.

kids Theater of the Sea

| APPEAL BY AGE | PRESCHOOL ★★★ | GRADE SCHOOL ★★★½ | TEENS ★★★ |
| YOUNG ADULTS ★★★ | | OVER 30 ★★★ | SENIORS ★★★½ |

84721 Overseas Highway on US 1 at Mile Marker 84.5, Islamorada; ☎ 305-664-2431; www.theaterofthesea.com

Type of attraction A marine park offering continuous shows featuring sea lions and dolphins, "bottomless" boat rides, snorkeling trips, an aquarium, and opportunities to swim with dolphins. **Admission** Adults, $23.95; children ages 3–12, $15.95; children under age 3, free. Group rates are available Price of admission does not include the dolphin swim, boat rides, or snorkeling trips. **Hours** 9:30 a.m.–4 p.m. **When to go** Anytime. **Special comments** If you're interested in a dip with the dolphins, call ahead for reservations; note that this is your only opportunity to swim at the park. **Author's rating** ★★★½. **How much time to allow** At least 2½ hours, half a day for leisurely exploration.

DESCRIPTION AND COMMENTS Established in 1946, Theater of the Sea is the world's second-oldest marine park. Here you can explore the surroundings of the deep in a natural lagoon setting. Activities such as bottomless-boat rides, aquatic shows, and lagoon tours will entertain guests of all ages as well as educate them about marine life. Other programs offer a chance to swim with rays, dolphins, and sea lions. Children are especially drawn to the touch tank, where they can pet a shark or kiss a sea lion. Also, children of all ages are invited to take part in the shows.

TOURING TIPS To escape the crowds and the heat, the best time to go is early in the morning during the week. Show up at 8:30 a.m. for a four-hour snorkeling trip and 13-mile boat cruise. The boat leaves the dock at 9 a.m. daily; the cost is $65 for adults and $40 for children ages 6–12. Snorkeling equipment can be rented. There is also an afternoon trip; plan to arrive by 1 p.m.

OTHER THINGS TO DO NEARBY The Tiki Bar is right next door. Adults can refresh themselves with a cocktail and a little calypso music, while the kids play in the pool. Float and Jet Ski rentals are also available.

DINING *and* RESTAURANTS

ONCE A CULINARILY CHALLENGED AREA EXCEPT for fish restaurants, the Florida Keys has nurtured an exciting regional cuisine called "Floribbean," which mixes local ingredients with a fusion of Latin American, Asian, and traditional American influences. Seafood still rules, but Keys cuisine has developed beyond conch chowder, stone crabs, and Key lime pie: You'll find dozens of fine ethnic restaurants as well. From shacks with sunset views, killer margaritas, and raw bars (in more ways than one) to elegant Floribbean venues with artful platings and fine wines, eating in the Keys delights the senses and the imagination.

The restaurants listed in this section are among the best, but the average check for dinner in the Keys (with the exception of Little Palm Island and a couple of other high-enders) remains the lowest in South Florida.

A FEW QUIRKY NOTABLES FOR KEYS AMBIENCE

FUNKY ATMOSPHERE ABOUNDS IN INFORMAL eateries in the Keys, especially in Key West. Maybe it's the end-of-the-road environment, but creative juices flow like margaritas. Check out these establishments, for fun if not for food.

key west attractions, dining, and nightlife

↑To Airport

Pearl St.
Angela St.
Newton St.
Petronia St.
Pine St.
Florida St.
Georgia St.
White St.
Virginia St.
Duncan St.
United St.
Tropical Ave.
Palm Ave.
Ashe St.
Varela St.
Seminary St.
South St.
Washington St.
Von Phister St.
Flagler St.
Johnson St.
Casa Marina Ct.
Atlantic Blvd
Frances St.
Watson St.
James St.
Eaton St.
Grinnell St.
1847 CEMETERY
Grinnell St.
Packer St.
Reynolds St.
Margaret St.
Margaret St.
Key West Bight
William St.
Windsor Ln.
William St.
Fleming St.
Elizabeth St.
Alberta St.
KEY WEST MARINE PARK
Front St.
Greene St.
Caroline St.
Simonton St.
Olivia St.
Catherine St.
Louisa St.
Vernon Ave.
ATLANTIC OCEAN
Wall St.
Duval St.
Southard St.
Angela St.
Petronia St.
Truman Ave.
Virginia St.
United St.
Amelia St.
Mallory Square
Whitehead St.
TRUMAN ANNEX
Thomas St.
Terry Ln.
Julia St.
BAHAMA VILLAGE
Howe St.
Emma St.
Fort St.

(i) **Information**

0 .... 1/4 mi
0 .... 1/4 km

FORT ZACHARY TAYLOR STATE PARK

Attractions
1. Audubon House and Tropical Gardens
2. East Martello Museum
3. Ernest Hemingway Home and Museum
4. Flagler Station Over-Sea Railway Historeum
5. Fort Zachary Taylor State Historic Site
6. Harry S. Truman Little White House Museum
7. Heritage House Museum and Robert Frost Cottage
8. Key West Aquarium
9. Key West Cemetery
10. Key West Lighthouse Museum
11. Key West Museum of Art and History at the Custom House
12. Key West Shipwreck Historeum
13. Lofton B. Sands African-Bahamian Museum
14. Mel Fisher's Maritime Heritage Society and Museum
15. Ripley's Believe It or Not

Dining
16. Alice's Key West
17. Antonia's
18. Bagatelle
19. Blue Heaven
20. Café Marquesa
21. Café Sole
22. La Trattoria
23. Louie's Backyard
24. Mangoes
25. Meteor Smokehouse
26. One Duval
27. Seven Fish
28. Shula's on the Beach
29. Square One

Nightlife
30. The Blu Room
31. Captain Tony's Saloon
32. Green Parrot Bar
33. Rick's/Durty Harry's Entertainment Complex
34. Schooner Wharf Bar
35. Sloppy Joe's Bar

- **Bo's Fish Wagon**
  Sandwiches 801 Caroline Street, Key West; ☎ 305-294-9272
  Decor includes lobster traps, fishing nets, a muffler-shop sign, and an old pickup truck.

- **Dennis Pharmacy**
  Luncheonette 1229 Simonton Street, Key West; ☎ 305-294-1577
  To the left, a pharmacy; to the right, a mid-20th-century lunchroom with soda fountain. Said to be the inspiration for Jimmy Buffett's "Cheeseburger in Paradise."

- Harpoon Harry's
  Diner   832 Caroline Street, Key West; ☎ 305-294-8744
  Just about everything (including the kitchen sink), is harpooned to the ceiling, and all around. Mickey Mouse glasses, sleds, roller skates, carousel horses, and so on—employees donated their collectibles—spill out onto the ceiling, walls, and floor.

- Jimmy Buffett's Margaritaville
  Cafe   424-A Fleming Street, Key West; ☎ 305-296-9089;
  www.margaritaville.com
  Props from Buffett tours, including iguanas, his seaplane mock-up, and a huge meat sandwich with all the fixin's create a Buffet paradise. Parrothead music is a given, as are the cheeseburgers.

- Kelly's Caribbean Bar, Grill & Brewery
  Cafe   301 Whitehead Street, Key West; ☎ 305-293-8484;
  www.kellyskeywest.com
  The former Pan Am building, filled with airline memorabilia from the 1920s on. Old airplane seats, airplane-motor ceiling fans—you get it. Owners are actress Kelly McGillis and her husband, Fred Tillman.

- Turtle Kraals Restaurant and Bar
  231 Margaret Street, Key West; ☎ 305-294-2640; www.turtlekraals.com
  A former turtle cannery with an enclosure for injured sea life heals, informs, and amuses. Museum adjacent.

- Iguana Café
  Cafe   425 Greene Street, Key West; ☎ 305-296-6420
  Mr. Iggy, a live iguana, is on hand as CEO and mascot, so iguana is not on the menu. Alligator burgers are.

ABOUT THESE CHOICES

WE HAVE INCLUDED A MIX OF RESTAURANTS here and have tried to provide something for everyone. Some of our choices are low profile, or even low end, but all offer something special. Here in the Keys, the dress code is relaxed, and some of the best food comes out of dives. That's a proud part of the laid-back scene.

For more about South Florida dining and an overview of our restaurant-profile format, including abbreviations and ratings, see page 208 in the Miami-Dade County dining section. Enjoy.

The Best of the Keys Restaurants

RESTAURANT/TYPE	OVERALL RATING	QUALITY RATING	VALUE RATING	CITY
BARBECUE				
Meteor Smokehouse	★★★	★★★★	★★★	Key West

RESTAURANT/TYPE	OVERALL RATING	QUALITY RATING	VALUE RATING	CITY
ECLECTIC				
Pierre's	★★★★★	★★★★½	★★★	Islamorada
Alice's Key West	★★★½	★★★★	★★	Key West
Seven Mile Grill	★★★½	★★★½	★★★	Marathon
Squid Row	★★★	★★★★	★★★	Islamorada
FLORIDA-CARIBBEAN (FLORIBBEAN)				
Morada Bay Beach Café	★★★★	★★★★	★★★	Islamorada
Bagatelle	★★★	★★★	★★★	Key West
Blue Heaven	★★★	★★★★½	★★★	Key West
FRENCH				
Café Sole	★★★★	★★★★★★	★★★	Key West
Mo's	★★	★★★★½	★★★★	Key West
ITALIAN/CONTINENTAL				
Antonia's	★★★★	★★★★★★	★★	Key West
La Trattoria	★★★★	★★★★½	★★★	Key West
Marker 88	★★★★	★★★★	★★★	Islamorada
NEW AMERICAN WITH CARIBBEAN INFLUENCE				
Louie's Backyard	★★★★★	★★★★½	★★★	Key West
Barracuda Grill	★★★★½	★★★	★★★	Marathon
Café Marquesa	★★★★	★★★★½	★★★	Key West
Dining Room at Palm Island Resort	★★★★	★★★★★★	★★★	Little Torch Key
One Duval	★★★★	★★★★	★★	Key West
Square One	★★★★	★★★★	★★★	Key West
Atlantic's Edge	★★★½	★★★★	★★★	Islamorada
Mangoes	★★★½	★★★½	★★★	Key West
SEAFOOD				
Sundowners on the Bay	★★★½	★★★★	★★	Key Largo
Fish House and Fish House Encore	★★★	★★★★	★★★½	Key Largo
Seven Fish	★★★	★★★★½	★★★	Key West
Herbie's	★★	★★★★	★★★★	Marathon
Keys Fisheries	★★	★★★★	★★★★	Marathon
STEAKHOUSE				
Shula's on the Beach	★★★½	★★★★	★★★	Key West

RESTAURANT PROFILES

Alice's Key West ★ ★ ★ ½

ECLECTIC	EXPENSIVE	QUALITY ★★★★	VALUE ★★

1114 Duval Street, Key West; ☎ 305-292-5733; www.aliceskeywest.com

Reservations Accepted. **When to go** Early. **Entree range** $8–$20. **Payment** AE, CB, D, DC, MC, V. **Parking** Street. **Bar** Full service. **Wine selection** Good California selection; $7–$15 by the glass, $20–$45 by the bottle. **Dress** Casual. **Disabled access** Yes. **Customers** Tourists, locals, anglers, celebrities. **Hours** Daily, 8:30 a.m.–11 p.m.

MENU RECOMMENDATIONS Mushroom-and-goat-cheese omelette; Monte Cristo sandwich; macadamia-coconut–crusted shrimp with honey wasabi; marinated ostrich with black beans, corn-avocado salsa, and coconut rice; cappuccino bread pudding

COMMENTS "Fusion Confusion" is the term Alice Weingarten uses for her truly original and eclectic breakfasts, lunches, and dinners, and good food is what makes her a witty star chef here.

Antonia's ★ ★ ★ ★

REGIONAL ITALIAN	EXPENSIVE	QUALITY ★★★★★	VALUE ★★

615 Duval Street, Key West; ☎ 305-294-6565; www.antoniaskeywest.com

Reservations Suggested. **When to go** Early. **Entree range** $15–$32. **Payment** AE, CB, D, DC, MC, V. **Parking** Behind restaurant. **Bar** Full service. **Wine selection** Northern Italian and American. **Dress** Casual. **Disabled access** Yes. **Customers** Tourists, locals, anglers, celebrities. **Hours** Daily, 6–11 p.m.

MENU RECOMMENDATIONS Focaccia; *zuppa di pesce;* rack of lamb in rosemary sauce; veal marsala; shellfish in tomato sauce; filet of beef with mushrooms, brandy, and cream; handmade pastas; *panna cotta;* chocolate fondant; crème brûlée

COMMENTS Watch pasta being created at the marble table in the window. A dress-up kind of place (for the Keys), with a menu that changes daily. Owners Antonia Berto and Phillip Smith travel regularly to Italy to authenticate their selections.

kids Atlantic's Edge ★ ★ ★ ½

NEW AMERICAN	EXPENSIVE	QUALITY ★★★★	VALUE ★★★

Cheeca Lodge, Overseas Highway US 1, Mile Marker 81, Islamorada; ☎ 305-664-4651; www.cheeca.rockresorts.com

Reservations Accepted. **When to go** Anytime. **Entree range** $19–$32. **Payment** AE, DC, MC, V. **Parking** Valet. **Bar** Full service. **Wine selection** Good global selections; $8–$14 per glass, $24–$160 by the bottle. **Dress** Casual. **Disabled access** Good. **Customers** Tourists, locals. **Hours** Daily, 6–10 p.m.

MENU RECOMMENDATIONS Indian River blue-crab cake; Caribbean mojo duck tostones with golden pineapple, Hudson Valley foie gras, and Peruvian lime essence; Key lime–marinated local-seafood ceviche; Wild West rubbed beef tenderloin; onion-crusted yellowtail snapper

COMMENTS Atlantic's Edge is the formal dining room in the best resort in Islamorada, but despite linen tablecloths and crystal goblets, the dress code remains casual. Try for a table outside or by a floor-to-ceiling window overlooking the namesake ocean. And if kids are along (or even if not), check out the Dirt Cup dessert: chocolate pudding and crumbled Oreos, topped by a gummi worm.

Bagatelle ★ ★ ★

FLORIDA-CARIBBEAN   MODERATE/EXPENSIVE   QUALITY ★ ★ ★   VALUE ★ ★ ★

115 Duval Street, Key West; ☎ 305-296-6609;
www.bagatelle-keywest.com

Reservations Accepted. When to go Anytime. Entree range $18–$25. Payment AE, DC, MC, V. Parking Nearby lots. Bar Full service. Wine selection Good. French and American wines; $8–$14 per glass, $20–$180 by the bottle. Dress Casual. Disabled access Adequate. Customers Tourists, locals Hours 11 a.m.–4 p.m. (light menu, 3–4 p.m.) and 5–11 p.m.

MENU RECOMMENDATIONS Conch ceviche marinated with lime juice, cilantro, and Scotch bonnet peppers; escargot Martinique in puff pastry with mushrooms and shallots in brandy crème sauce; grilled jumbo shrimp with garlic-herb butter over pasta; pan-fried snapper; macadamia-crusted fish sautéed with a mango butter sauce

COMMENTS This two-story Classical Revival house in Old Town Key West is a charmer. Dine on one of the wraparound verandas overlooking the noisy Duval scene or indoors among the paintings.

kids Barracuda Grill ★ ★ ★ ★ ½

NEW AMERICAN   MODERATE/EXPENSIVE   QUALITY ★ ★ ★   VALUE ★ ★ ★

US 1, Mile Marker 49.5, Marathon; ☎ 305-743-3314;
www.barracudagrill.com

Reservations Not accepted. When to go Early. Entree range $15–$40. Payment AE, CB, D, DC, MC, V. Parking Alongside building. Bar Full service. Wine selection Mainly from California. Dress Casual. Disabled access Yes. Customers Tourists, locals, anglers, celebrities. Hours Monday–Saturday, 6:25 p.m. until closing (varies).

MENU RECOMMENDATIONS Tipsy olives; calamari; Caicos Gold conch; mangrove snapper and mango salsa; chargrilled veal chop; ribeye steak; rack of lamb with black-raspberry sauce

COMMENTS Jan and Lance Hill have turned a blah-looking place into a winner, with original seafood concoctions, great service, and a family atmosphere. (Kids enjoy funny specialties, including Fish Have Fingers.) No reservations allowed, so it's hard to get into on weekends.

Blue Heaven ★ ★ ★

FLORIBBEAN	MODERATE	QUALITY ★ ★ ★ ★ ½	VALUE ★ ★ ★

729 Thomas Street, Key West; ☎ 305-296-8666

Reservations Accepted for 10 or more. **When to go** Early. **Entree range** Breakfast, $5–$13; lunch, $7–$14; dinner, $10–$36. **Payment** AE, CB, D, DC, MC, V. **Parking** Alongside building. **Bar** Full service. **Wine selection** Large selection of imported and domestic bottles; $8–12 by the glass. **Dress** Casual. **Disabled access** Yes. **Customers** Tourists, locals, anglers, celebrities. **Hours** Monday–Saturday, 8–11:30 a.m., noon–3 p.m., and 6–10:30 p.m.; Sunday, brunch 8 a.m.–2 p.m. and 6–10:30 p.m.

MENU RECOMMENDATIONS Homemade granola; seafood Benedict; tropical-fruit beer-batter pancakes; shrimp and grits; curried soup; Jamaican jerk chicken; pork tenderloin; fresh fish; Caribbean shrimp; vegetable stew; Key lime pie; Banana Heaven

COMMENTS The garden is heavenly indeed—for cats, dogs, chicks, roosters, and lizards, as well as patrons who eat great food at backyard picnic tables amid the animals and dirt floors. Formerly a bordello, boxing ring, pool hall, water tower, ice-cream parlor, and cockfighting venue (Hemingway frequented cockfights), it's now a Keys favorite, especially for breakfast.

Café Marquesa ★ ★ ★ ★

NEW AMERICAN	EXPENSIVE	QUALITY ★ ★ ★ ★ ½	VALUE ★ ★ ★

600 Fleming Street, Key West; ☎ 305-292-1919; www.marquesa.com/cafe

Reservations Recommended. **When to go** Early. **Entree range** $23–$28. **Payment** AE, D, DC, MC, V. **Parking** Small lot or street. **Bar** Full service. **Wine selection** Very good; $8–$13 per glass, $28–$300 by the bottle. **Dress** Casual, business. **Disabled access** Good. **Customers** Tourists, locals, and internationals. **Hours** Daily, 6:30–11 p.m.

MENU RECOMMENDATIONS Feta and pine nut–crusted rack of lamb with rosemary natural demiglace, polenta, and eggplant caponata; seared peppercorn-dusted yellowfin tuna with saffron risotto and mélange of roasted vegetables and spinach pesto; vegetarian delight (Asian vegetables with grilled basil sauce and black Thai rice). Bread and desserts are made on the premises.

COMMENTS Locals splurge here, and the open kitchen is set behind a giant trompe l'oeil wall painting of a kitchen scene. Mahogany-framed mirrors reflect on a small 50-seat dining room, where you can listen to other diners rave about the cuisine.

Café Sole ★ ★ ★ ★

FRENCH	EXPENSIVE	QUALITY ★ ★ ★ ★ ★	VALUE ★ ★ ★

1029 Southard Street, Key West; ☎ 305-294-0230; www.cafesole.com

Reservations Accepted. **When to go** Early. **Entree range** $8–$59. **Payment** AE, CB, D, DC, MC, V. **Parking** Street. **Bar** Full service. **Wine selection** Extensive; $7–12 by the glass, $28–230 by the bottle. **Dress** Casual. **Disabled access** Yes. **Customers** Tourists, locals, anglers, celebrities. **Hours** Daily, 11 a.m.–2:30 p.m. and 5:30–10 p.m.

MENU RECOMMENDATIONS Conch carpaccio; hog snapper; grouper Romanesco; bouillabaisse; rack of lamb; filet mignon Casanova with wild mushrooms and foie gras

COMMENTS In a residential neighborhood but worth finding, this indoor-outdoor charmer combines Provençal touches with a Keys twist. Charming chef John Correa mingles with delighted guests, who extol the fare. Check out the prix fixe menu for special value.

Dining Room at Little Palm Island Resort ★ ★ ★ ★ ★

NEW AMERICAN/CARIBBEAN **VERY EXPENSIVE** **QUALITY ★ ★ ★ ★ ★** **VALUE ★ ★ ★**

28500 Overseas Highway US 1, Mile Marker 28.5, Little Torch Key;
☎ **305-872-2551; www.littlepalmisland.com**

Reservations Required. **When to go** Anytime. **Entree range** $15–$50. **Payment** AE, DC, MC, V. **Parking** At reception area. **Bar** Full service. **Wine selection** Good; $8–$25 per glass, $25–$300 by the bottle. **Dress** Casual. **Disabled access** Adequate. **Customers** Professionals, tourists, celebrities. **Hours** Daily, 8–10 a.m., 11:30 a.m.–2:30 p.m., and 6:30–9:30 p.m.; Sunday brunch.

MENU RECOMMENDATIONS Chili-spiced chilled lobster with cucumber slaw and pineapple jasmine rice; wild mushrooms, duck confit, and foie gras duxelle with ginger scallion crêpes and corn-truffle cream; a caviar selection; pan-seared yellow snapper and red lobster dumplings with watermelon relish and tamarind-pineapple sauce; Adam's crab cakes with asparagus and tomato-truffle salad

COMMENTS Ferrying the 15 minutes from Little Torch Key to the Great House in a coconut grove on exclusive Palm Island has to be one of the world's best restaurant entrances. The private five-acre island is a 30-mile drive from Key West. This Robbin Haas restaurant concept with a menu executed by chef Adam Votaw allows you to dine memorably—under a palm; on the beach, deck, or porch; by torchlight; or even inside. Service is exceptional wherever. Reserve well ahead.

Fish House and Fish House Encore ★ ★ ★

SEAFOOD **INEXPENSIVE/MODERATE** **QUALITY ★ ★ ★ ★** **VALUE ★ ★ ★ ½**

US 1, Mile Marker 102.4, Key Largo; ☎ **305-451-HOOK (Fish House), 305-451-0650 (Encore); www. fishhouse.com**

Reservations Accepted. **When to go** Early. **Entree range** $17–$30. **Payment** AE, CB, D, DC, MC, V. **Parking** Ample. **Bar** Full service. **Wine selection** A wide selection; $5 and up by the glass. **Dress** Casual. **Disabled access** Adequate. **Customers** Tourists, locals, anglers, celebrities. **Hours** Sunday–Thursday, 5–10 p.m.; Friday and Saturday, 5–10:30 p.m.

MENU RECOMMENDATIONS Conch salad; Jamaican jerk; ceviche; smoked fish; shrimp and lobster creole; Fish Matecumbe

COMMENTS Seafood served in this nautical setting of buoys and fishnets is fresh and prepared deliciously. Yes, the atmosphere couldn't be fishier—you may feel like a crammed sardine on weekends, when crowds arrive. You can sit outdoors or go next door to the pricier and less-crowded Encore, with a more formal dining room and a karaoke bar.

Herbie's ★ ★

SEAFOOD	INEXPENSIVE	QUALITY ★ ★ ★ ★	VALUE ★ ★ ★ ★

US 1, Mile Marker 50.5, Marathon; ☎ 305-743-6373

Reservations Accepted. When to go Early. Entree range $2.25–$26. Payment AE, CB, D, DC, MC, V. Parking Lot. Bar Beer and wine only. Wine selection Good. Dress Casual. Disabled access Yes. Customers Tourists, locals, anglers, celebrities. Hours Tuesday–Saturday, 11 a.m.–10 p.m.

MENU RECOMMENDATIONS Conch chowder; fried oysters; fish baskets; burgers

COMMENTS A place named Herbie's just has to offer casual Keys cuisine, and so it does. They will happily cook your catch or serve up fried fish, a burger, or a special dish. You'll find more-creative fare at dinner. Picnic tables, an open porch, and basic decor make this a classic US 1 end-of-the-road roadhouse.

Keys Fisheries Market and Marina ★ ★

SEAFOOD	INEXPENSIVE	QUALITY ★ ★ ★ ★	VALUE ★ ★ ★ ★

3502 Gulfview Drive, Mile Marker 49, Marathon; ☎ 305-743-4353; www.keysfisheries.com

Reservations Accepted. When to go Early. Entree range $9–$23. Payment AE, CB, D, DC, MC, V. Parking Lot. Bar Full service. Wine selection $8–12 by the glass. Dress Casual. Disabled access Yes. Customers Tourists, locals, anglers, celebrities. Hours Daily, 11:30 a.m.–9 p.m.

MENU RECOMMENDATIONS Lobster chowder; local shrimp and fish; golden crab special; stone crabs; lobster Reuben; ice cream

COMMENTS You eat outdoors—with Fido, if you wish, under the plastic canopy. Pick up the superfresh seafood at the market takeout window, park yourself at a picnic table overlooking the harbor fishing boats, and dig in. Tuesday nights are all-you-can-eat fish frys. A real deal, and the real deal.

La Trattoria ★ ★ ★ ★

ITALIAN	MODERATE/EXPENSIVE	QUALITY ★ ★ ★ ★ ½	VALUE ★ ★ ★

524 Duval Street, Key West; ☎ 305-296-1075; www.latrattoria.us

Reservations Accepted. When to go Early. Entree range $10–$37. Payment AE, CB, D, DC, MC, V. Parking Street. Bar Full service. Wine selection $8–$15 by the glass, $23–$94 by the bottle. Dress Casual. Disabled access Yes. Customers Tourists, locals, anglers, celebrities. Hours Daily, 5:30–11 p.m.

MENU RECOMMENDATIONS Antipasti; stuffed mushroom caps; seafood salad; eggplant stuffed with ricotta and roast peppers; lamb with fresh rosemary; cannelloni stuffed with veal and spinach; tiramisu

COMMENTS This southern Italian outpost in the Keys is relaxed, pleasant, and popular. And when you're as stuffed as a ravioli, there's live jazz till the wee hours in their cocktail lounge around the corner.

Louie's Backyard ★ ★ ★ ★ ★

NEW AMERICAN/CARIBBEAN	EXPENSIVE	QUALITY ★★★★½	VALUE ★★★

700 Waddell Avenue, Key West; ☎ 305-294-1061; www.louiesbackyard.com

Reservations Highly recommended. When to go Early. Entree range $18–$50. Payment AE, DC, MC, V. Parking Alongside restaurant. Bar Full service. Wine selection A fair, mostly American selection; $6–$30 per glass, $24–$100 by the bottle. Dress Casual. Disabled access Good. Customers Tourists, locals, internationals. Hours Monday–Saturday, 11:30 a.m.–3 p.m. and 6–10 p.m.; Sunday, (brunch) 11:30 a.m.–3 p.m. and 6–10 p.m.

MENU RECOMMENDATIONS Crisp-fried cracked conch with red-pepper jelly and pickled-ginger slaw; Bahamian conch chowder; pan-seared shrimp and chorizo with whiskey corn cream and corn muffins; pan-cooked Atlantic salmon with sweet soy, wakame salad, shiitake mushrooms, and spinach; grilled tamarind-glazed Key West shrimp, roasted yam barbecue sauce, and cayenne-dusted plantain chips; grilled Black Angus steak with Rioja wine sauce

COMMENTS The backyard is prime Atlantic oceanfront, and the cuisine lives up to the setting. Nestled amid bougainvillea and hibiscus, the Victorian house looks out on a beachfront dining deck where the waves practically lap your toes. This romantic restaurant typifies Key West's dreamiest character. Reserve way ahead.

Mangoes ★ ★ ★ ½

CARIBBEAN	MODERATE/EXPENSIVE	QUALITY ★★★½	VALUE ★★★

700 Duval Street, Key West; ☎ 305-292-4606; www.mangoeskeywest.com

Reservations Accepted. When to go Early. Entree range $10–$27. Payment AE, DC, MC, V. Parking Street. Bar Full service. Wine selection $7–$14 by the glass, $24–80 by the bottle. Dress Casual. Disabled access First floor only. Customers Tourists, locals, anglers, celebrities. Hours Daily, 11 a.m.–1 a.m.

MENU RECOMMENDATIONS Conch chowder; pizza from a wood-fired oven; lobster dumplings with Key lime sauce; grilled shrimp with spicy mango chutney; snapper with passion fruit; Cuban Coffee Pork with vanilla bean–butter sauce and banana-blackcurrant chutney

COMMENTS Known for its creative cuisine (especially Garlic and Lime Pinks—a half pound of local shrimp with a roasted-garlic-and-lime glaze), Mangoes presents seafood in original guises. This corner charmer offers three meals on a brick patio under white umbrellas and banyan trees, or indoor dining with candles and flowers. Either way, this is a relaxing haven off busy Duval Street.

Marker 88 ★ ★ ★ ★

ITALIAN/CONTINENTAL MODERATE/EXPENSIVE QUALITY ★ ★ ★ ★ VALUE ★ ★ ★

Overseas Highway, US 1, Mile Marker 88; Islamorada; ☎ 305-852-9315 or 305-852-5503

Reservations Accepted. **When to go** Early. **Entree range** $24–$35. **Payment** AE, CB, D, DC, MC, V. **Parking** Alongside building. **Bar** Full service. **Wine selection** Well rounded from California and Europe; $8–$15 per glass, $23–$400 by the bottle. **Dress** Casual. **Disabled access** Good. **Customers** Tourists, locals, anglers, celebrities. **Hours** Daily, 11 a.m.–10 p.m.

MENU RECOMMENDATIONS   Conch ceviche with red onions and sweet-and-sour sauce; oysters Moscow topped with caviar and creamy horseradish; Cuban black bean soup; conch steak; yellowtail, snapper, grouper, dolphin, or pompano prepared fried, sautéed meunière, broiled, poached, grilled, Grenoblaise, or blackened; shrimp Milanesa with angel hair pasta; Apalachicola soft-shell crabs fried, sautéed, or served with garlic butter

COMMENTS   This rustic, weathered building overlooking Florida Bay is looking better inside. The mix of dishes, from conch fritters to rack of lamb Provençale, arrives in huge portions, and the water views are superb.

Meteor Smokehouse ★ ★ ★

BARBECUE MODERATE QUALITY ★ ★ ★ ★ VALUE ★ ★ ★

404 Southard Street, Key West; ☎ 305-294-5602; www.meteorsmokehouse.com

Reservations Accepted. **When to go** Early. **Entree range** $8–$23. **Payment** AE, CB, D, DC, MC, V. **Parking** Lot. **Bar** Full service. **Wine selection** $6 and up by the glass. **Dress** Casual. **Disabled access** Yes. **Customers** Tourists, locals, anglers, celebrities. **Hours** Monday–Thursday, 11 a.m.–10 p.m.; Friday and Saturday, 11 a.m.–11 p.m.; and Sunday, noon–11 p.m.; happy hour, daily, 4–7 p.m.

MENU RECOMMENDATIONS   Dry-rubbed hickory-smoked ribs; pulled pork; brisket; spicy beans; cole slaw; cornbread

COMMENTS   Real good pit barbecue here, which you can eat in or carry out, with all the requisite fixin's. And if you get really thirsty, the famed old Green Parrot bar is right next door.

Morada Bay Beach Café ★ ★ ★ ★

FLORIBBEAN MODERATE/EXPENSIVE QUALITY ★ ★ ★ ★ VALUE ★ ★ ★

US 1, Mile Marker 81, Islamorada; ☎ 305-664-0604

Reservations Accepted. **When to go** Early. **Entree range** $22–$40. **Payment** AE, CB, D, DC, MC, V. **Parking** Street. **Bar** Full service. **Wine selection** Extensive imported and domestic selections; $7–12 by the glass, $23 and up by the bottle. **Dress** Casual. **Disabled access** Yes. **Customers** Tourists, locals, anglers, celebrities. **Hours** Sunday–Thursday, 11:30 a.m.–10 p.m.; Friday and Saturday, 11:30 a.m.–11 p.m.

MENU RECOMMENDATIONS Dolphin fingers; chicken with jerk-rum glaze; tuna tartare; Thai ribs; fresh fish

COMMENTS Clyde Butcher black-and-white photos of the Everglades decorate the walls of this popular Conch hangout. The beach on Florida Bay is strewn with Adirondack chairs, and everyone seems in a frolicking mood—especially at the monthly full-moon party, and when there's live music and dancing by the palms and tiki torches. More fun and less haute than sibling Pierre's next door, this is a tapas kind of place.

One Duval ★ ★ ★ ★

NEW AMERICAN/CARIBBEAN	EXPENSIVE	QUALITY ★★★★	VALUE ★★

Pier House Hotel, 1 Duval Street, Key West; ☎ 305-296-4600; www.pierhouse.com

Reservations Suggested for dinner. **When to go** Anytime. **Entree range** $10–$36. **Payment** AE, D, DC, MC, V. **Parking** Adjoining lot. **Bar** Full service. **Wine selection** Well rounded and global; $8–$15 per glass, $24–$300 by the bottle. **Dress** Casual. **Disabled access** Good. **Customers** Tourists, winter residents, celebrities. **Hours** Daily, 7 a.m.–10:30 p.m.

MENU RECOMMENDATIONS Guava shrimp cocktail; coconut grouper; grilled lobster flatbread; achiote chicken; paillard

COMMENTS The inventive cuisine is "New Calypso Harvest" and emphasizes the coastal southeastern United States. Located in Key West's most famous hotel, One Duval features a deck from which you can watch the sun set over the Gulf—much more pleasant than watching from the noisy pier next door. Try for a window seat if you dine inside.

Pierre's ★ ★ ★ ★ ★

ECLECTIC	MODERATE/EXPENSIVE	QUALITY ★★★★½	VALUE ★★★

US 1, Mile Marker 81.6, Islamorada; ☎ 305-664-3225

Reservations Accepted. **When to go** Early. **Entree range** $28–$41. **Payment** AE, CB, D, DC, MC, V. **Parking** Street. **Bar** Full service. **Wine selection** $9–$16 by the glass, $23–$120 by the bottle. **Dress** Casual. **Disabled access** Yes. **Customers** Tourists, locals, anglers, celebrities. **Hours** Tuesday–Sunday, 6–11 p.m.

MENU RECOMMENDATIONS Lotus root–crusted yellowtail; tempura lobster tail
COMMENTS Up sweeping stairs to candlelit tables and a sunset view over the water, you'll have a truly fine dinner in an ultra-romantic setting—either indoors or on the covered porch. Antiques abound, service is refined, and the decor evokes a touch of Britain.

Seven Fish ★ ★ ★

SEAFOOD   MODERATE/EXPENSIVE   QUALITY ★ ★ ★ ★ ½   VALUE ★ ★ ★

632 Olivia Street, Key West; ☎ 305-296-2777; www.7fish.com

Reservations Accepted. **When to go** Early. **Entree range** $15–$28. **Payment** AE, MC, V. **Parking** Free behind restaurant. **Bar** Full service. **Wine selection** Mainly California selections; $5–$8 per glass, $26–$44 per bottle. **Dress** Casual. **Disabled access** Yes. **Customers** Tourists, locals, anglers, celebrities. **Hours** Wednesday–Monday, 6–11 p.m.

MENU RECOMMENDATIONS Shrimp salsa; penne with crawfish and scallops; crab–shiitake mushroom pasta; gnocchi with blue cheese, meat loaf, and mashed potatoes; snapper in Thai curry sauce; Key lime cake

COMMENTS You'll find a wide array of good, homey dishes here, not just namesake fish. Cozy and hard-to-find, this local favorite is often crowded; reserve if possible.

Shula's on the Beach ★ ★ ★ ½

STEAKHOUSE   EXPENSIVE   QUALITY ★ ★ ★ ★   VALUE ★ ★ ★

Reach Resort, 1435 Simonton Street, Key West; ☎ 305-296-6144; www.donshula.com/onthebeach/keywest

Reservations Accepted. **When to go** Anytime. **Entree range** $18–$36. **Payment** AE, DC, MC, V. **Parking** Valet. **Bar** Full service. **Wine selection** Good, mostly American; $8–$15 per glass, $23–$140 by the bottle. **Dress** Casual. **Disabled access** Good. **Customers** Tourists, locals. **Hours** Sunday–Thursday, 6–10:30 p.m.; Friday and Saturday, 6–11 p.m.

MENU RECOMMENDATIONS Oysters Rockefeller; lobster bisque; barbecued shrimp stuffed with fresh basil wrapped in applewood bacon; certified Angus beef selections, including the 16-ounce New York strip, 12-ounce filet mignon, 24-ounce porterhouse, and 22-ounce cowboy steak; gigantic lobsters; and steak Mary Anne—two 5-ounce filet mignons with a creamy peppercorn sauce.

COMMENTS Reach Resort offers a meaty experience. Excellent service and fine china and crystal add elegance, while huge cuts of meat and six-pound lobsters can be savored while watching the Keys' sunset.

Square One ★ ★ ★ ★

NEW AMERICAN/CARIBBEAN   EXPENSIVE   QUALITY ★ ★ ★ ★   VALUE ★ ★ ★

1075 Duval Street at Duval Square, Key West; ☎ 305-296-4300; www.squareonerestaurant.com

Reservations Recommended. **When to go** Anytime. **Entree range** $20–$32. **Payment** AE, MC, V. **Parking** Self parking in the streets. **Bar** Full service. **Wine selection** Down-to-earth wine list; $7–$10 per glass, $23–$250 by the bottle. **Dress** Casual. **Disabled access** Good. **Customers** Tourists, winter residents. **Hours** Tuesday–Sunday, 8:30 a.m.–3 p.m. and 6–10:30 p.m.; Monday, 6–10:30 p.m.

MENU RECOMMENDATIONS Mixed-greens salad with fried Camembert and a sherry-walnut vinaigrette; steak tartare; grilled marinated pork tenderloin with saffron risotto and banana-guava chutney; roast honey-lacquered white duck breast and leg confit with a native-orange–Grand Marnier glaze; sautéed Key West pink shrimp with a roasted-pepper sauce; pecan-crusted snapper served with Cuban bananas and Key lime rum butter; Caribbean paella with baked lobster, shrimp, clams, chicken, and Andouille sausage simmered in Caribbean herbs, yellow rice, and spicy saffron broth

COMMENTS One of the locals' favorite spots for tropical gourmet fare. Owner Michael Stewart created this restaurant with floral murals, polished wood, and green carpet—a casually sophisticated look, enhanced with piano music and solid food.

Squid Row ★ ★ ★

ECLECTIC	MODERATE	QUALITY ★ ★ ★ ★	VALUE ★ ★ ★

US 1, Mile Marker 81.9, Islamorada; ☎ 305-664-9865; www.keysdining.com/squidrow

Reservations Accepted.**When to go** Early.**Entree range** $8–$37.**Payment** AE, CB, D, DC, MC, V.**Parking** Lot.**Bar** Full service.**Wine selection** Domestic and imported; $4–$12 by the glass, $17–$145 by the bottle. **Dress** Casual. **Disabled access** Yes. **Customers** Tourists, locals, anglers, celebrities.**Hours** Daily, 11:30 a.m.–11 p.m.

MENU RECOMMENDATIONS Bahamian Borscht (conch chowder); burgers; fried or grilled seafood; Toll House pie

COMMENTS Bring your own fish and they'll cook it up and serve it with Key lime butter. Or enjoy good, basic Keys food. There's no view from this wood-paneled diner, but friendly service, big portions, fair prices, and no-nonsense quality make up for it. Finish the bouillabaisse and you'll get a free slice of Key lime pie. You have to love a playful place that dishes up desserts called chocolate-covered oysters and caramel-covered squid.

Sundowners on the Bay ★ ★ ★ ½

SEAFOOD	MODERATE	QUALITY ★ ★ ★ ★	VALUE ★ ★

US 1, Mile Marker 104, Key Largo; ☎ 305-451-4502; www.sundownerskeylargo.com

Reservations Accepted.**When to go** Early.**Entree range** $17–$40.**Payment** AE, DC, MC, V.**Parking** Lot. **Bar** Full service. **Wine selection** $6–$10 by the glass, $22–60 by the bottle. **Dress** Casual. **Disabled access** Yes. **Customers** Tourists, locals, anglers, celebrities.**Hours** Daily, 11 a.m.–10 p.m.

MENU RECOMMENDATIONS Fish sandwich with sautéed onions and cheese; blackened tuna Alfredo; Mermaid's Delight with shrimp and scallops; snapper seven ways

COMMENTS You can boat right up to this restaurant on Blackwater Sound. As the name suggests, come when the sun is setting for the best effect, and sit on the patio or deck, enjoying the breezes and good food.

ENTERTAINMENT *and* NIGHTLIFE

IN KEY WEST, WHERE LAID-BACK BARS—many of which feature a combination of reggae and karaoke—rule instead of the flashy disco scene favored in Miami, among the more popular haunts is the open-air **Schooner Wharf Bar** (202 William Street; ☎ 305-292-3302), open daily 8 a.m.–4 a.m. with live music daily. The **Green Parrot Bar** (see profile, page 282) is another good choice for a little piece of Key West, with prime people-watching. The Sunday evening tea dance, from 7 to 11 at the **Atlantic Shores Resort** (510 South Street; ☎ 305-296-2491), features a disco overlooking the pier and a largely gay clientele. Martini bars such as **The Blu Room** (422 Appelrouth Lane; ☎ 305-296-6667) and cocktail lounges such as **Virgilio's** (524 Duval Street; ☎ 305-296-8118) offer an alternative to the traditional Margaritaville scene—yet hold a happy hour 9 p.m.–4 a.m., every night of the week.

The Best of Key West's Nightclubs

NAME	COVER	COST
ADULT ENTERTAINMENT		
Rick's/Durty Harry's Entertainment Complex	None	Moderate
BARS		
Captain Tony's	None	Inexpensive
Green Parrot Bar	None	Inexpensive
Sloppy Joe's Bar	None, except special events	Inexpensive
Schooner Wharf Bar	None	Inexpensive
DANCE CLUBS		
Rick's/Durty Harry's Entertainment Complex	None	Moderate
The Blu Room	None	Moderate
KARAOKE		
Rick's/Durty Harry's Entertainment Complex	None	Moderate
LIVE MUSIC		
Captain Tony's	None	Inexpensive

NAME	COVER	COST
LIVE MUSIC (CONTINUED)		
Rick's/Durty Harry's Entertainment Complex	None	Moderate
LOUNGE		
The Blu Room	None	Moderate

NIGHTCLUB PROFILES

The Blu Room

CITIFIED, CLUBBY LOUNGE O' THE MOMENT

422 Appelrouth Lane, Key West; ☎ 305-296-6667

Cover On weekends and special events. **Minimum** None. **Mixed drinks** $5 and up. **Wine** $5–$6.50. **Beer** $3.50–$5. **Food available** None. **Hours** Wednesday–Sunday, 9 p.m.–4 a.m.

WHO GOES THERE 25–35, hip out-of-towners and locals, both gay and straight, looking for a little urban decorum (or not) in relaxed Key West

WHAT GOES ON Evenings start on a relatively mellow note at this five-year-old establishment, with well-dressed patrons sipping cocktails and oversized martinis. The scene gradually progresses into a frenzied nightclub, with self-liberated souls dancing on banquettes and every other available surface. Local DJs spin house music every night, with national DJs making guest appearances when in the area.

COMMENTS This urban-cocktail-lounge-meets-dance-club is tiny but packs in 250 people on a weekend night. Chinese-red-lacquered walls, booths shaped in a horseshoe, and lit cocktail tables combined with a dance platform give The Blu Room the look of a sleekly modern bordello. In the back, **420 Lounge,** an outside courtyard bar, serves cheap drinks and provides relief for locals needing to escape the chaos and remember they are indeed in tropical Key West while listening to alternative rock. Happy hour runs 3 p.m.–4 a.m. on weekdays and 1 p.m.–4 a.m. on Saturdays and Sundays.

Captain Tony's Saloon

LOCAL WATERING HOLE WITH ECLECTIC LIVE MUSIC

428 Greene Street, Key West; ☎ 305-294-1838; www.capttonyssaloon.com

Cover None. **Minimum** None. **Mixed drinks** $4–$6. **Wine** $4. **Beer** $2.75–$4. **Food available** None. **Hours** Monday–Saturday, 10 a.m.–2 a.m.; Sunday, noon–2 a.m.

WHO GOES THERE Locals and tourists 25–40, spring breakers

WHAT GOES ON This is one of the Keys' legendary bars, owned since 1962 by local character Captain Tony, who is 86, has been married seven times, has 13 children, and has even served as mayor (1988–91). The bar's namesake, who originally came to the Keys as a fisherman in the 1940s, occasionally drops by the bar, amusing patrons with incredible stories, such as how he used to give Jimmy Buffett $10 a day plus all he could drink. In case Captain Tony doesn't show, there are live musical acts daily starting in the afternoons. Music is truly eclectic, ranging from Nirvana to the top-40 hits of the 1950s. In case you experience déjà vu, the bar site is the former location of the original Sloppy Joe's before it moved to Duval Street.

COMMENTS An amusing hodgepodge of bar patrons past have left mementos stuffed everywhere: wall-to-wall business cards, musical instruments, license plates, celebrity bar stools, a plane propeller, and even a bra dangling from the ceiling. You can wear cutoffs and flip-flops, and shoes and shirts are not required at night. Try the house pirate's punch, a gin, rum, and fruit-juice concoction served in a 22-ounce souvenir jug.

Green Parrot Bar

KEY WEST'S OLDEST BAR

601 Whitehead Street, Key West; ☎ 305-294-6133;
www.greenparrot.com

Cover None. **Minimum** None. **Mixed drinks** $3.50–$5. **Wine** $3–$5. **Beer** $2.50–$4.50. **Food available** None. **Hours** Monday–Saturday, 10 a.m.–4 a.m.; Sunday, noon–4 a.m.

WHO GOES THERE Locals, tourists, New Yorkers escaping the rat race

WHAT GOES ON A Key West landmark open since 1890, this popular bar features live entertainment every Friday and Saturday, with reggae, rock, or blues from 10 p.m. to 2 a.m. Several years back, the bar's propensity for attracting the most eligible bachelors in town was noted in *Playboy* magazine.

COMMENTS This is an open-air bar known to display bold (if not quality) art, with the outside walls covered in various eclectic themes (sports, slice-of-life, Jamaica). Two pool tables, a deluxe pinball machine, a dart board, and a variety of arcade games are available. According to the management, "the the best stocked jukebox found in the Keys" adds to the bar's breezy, laid-back charm. Dress in Key West casual for a happy hour: 4–7 p.m., seven days a week, with $3 mixed drinks and $1.50 domestic draft beer.

Rick's/Durty Harry's Entertainment Complex

LONG-RUNNING KEY WEST DANCE/COMEDY/KARAOKE/LIVE MUSIC/ADULT ENTERTAINMENT VENUE

202 Duval Street, Key West; ☎ 305-296-4890; www.rickskeywest.com

Cover None. **Minimum** None. **Mixed drinks** $3.50 and up. **Wine** $3.75–$5.25.

Beer $2.75. **Food available** Peanuts. **Hours** Monday–Saturday, 11 a.m.–4 a.m.; Sunday, noon–4 a.m.

WHO GOES THERE A cross-section of Key West humanity, 21- to whatever-somethings, college-aged karaoke-holics, thirsty tourists

WHAT GOES ON You'll never be bored at this ten-bars-in-one entertainment complex, which features live performers daily 9 p.m.–4 a.m. at Durty Harry's Bar and at Rick's noon–midnight; there's karaoke at Rick's downstairs bar from midnight to closing. Additionally, the complex offers dancing at three bars and an open deck upstairs at Rick's; adult entertainment on two stages, a bar, and a private dance floor at the 21-and-older Red Garter Saloon; and alfresco cocktailing at the Tree Bar, which fronts Duval Street. Local comedian-musician Steven Neil performs Thursday through Sunday evenings. Musical offerings are typically reggae and rock. This entertainment complex combines a rock 'n' roll venue, a comedy parody lounge, and a high-energy dance club.

COMMENTS New-rustic decor here includes dark-wood bars—the one in Rick's is so massive it spans the entire length of the space—and dim lighting, relying on the local color for aesthetics.

Schooner Wharf Bar

A LAST LITTLE PIECE OF OLD KEY WEST THAT JUST KEEPS GETTING BETTER WITH TIME

202 William Street, Key West; ☎ 305-292-3302; www.schoonerwharf.com

Cover None. **Minimum** None. **Mixed drinks** $3.75 and up. **Wine** $4. **Beer** $2.50 and up. **Food available** Full menu of seafood, salads, burgers, etc. **Hours** Monday–Saturday, 8 a.m.–4 a.m.; Sunday, noon–4 a.m.

WHO GOES THERE A favorite of the locals and tourists alike, with a colorful mix of patrons and their pets.

WHAT GOES ON This island institution is located on the site of an old shrimp factory, attracting both tourists and locals with a unique mix of delicious cuisine, live music, and special events. The site of numerous special events throughout the year, including the Lighted Boat Parade (December), the Minimal Regatta (Memorial Day weekend), the Wrecker's Cup Race Series, the Barbecue Cook-off, the Chili Cook-off, and one of the Keys' favorite local events, the Battle of the Bars. Don't miss the Keys' quintessential musical storytellers during the day and nighttime favorites, because you are sure to stumble on live entertainment at all times. And yes . . . dancing is encouraged!

COMMENTS Known for its unique nautical decor and open-air proximity to sweet ocean breezes, this is Key West's best kept secret. The place offers outdoor thatched-umbrella tables, a covered full bar, and indoor games, including billiards and darts. The friendly bar staff are always pleased to serve up specialty drinks such as Schooner Lemonade, Rumrunners, and mango daiquiris; those are the most popular drinks during the bar's three happy hours, which run 8 a.m.–noon, 5–7 p.m., and 2–4 a.m.

Sloppy Joe's Bar

FAMOUS AND INFAMOUS KEY WEST WATERING HOLE THAT PAPA HEMINGWAY USED TO CALL HOME

201 Duval Street, Key West; ☎ 305-294-5717; www.sloppyjoes.com

Cover None, unless it's a special event. **Minimum** None. **Mixed drinks** $6–$7.50. **Wine** $5. **Beer** $3.25–$5.50. **Food available** Light menu including appetizers, salads, and sandwiches. **Hours** Monday–Saturday, 9 a.m.–4 a.m.; Sunday, noon–4 a.m.

WHO GOES THERE A mix of humanity, from local barflies to Midwestern tourists

WHAT GOES ON Famed for being the local watering hole of Ernest Hemingway, this bar has gained a following with both locals and the international tourist crowd. The bar continues to host the outrageous Hemingway Look-alike Contest in mid-July in celebration of the author's birthday; the event brings more than 100 bearded men from all over the world to Key West annually. Entertainment goes on day and night, with a varied selection of country, rock, and blues.

COMMENTS Everything about the bar reads "Sit back, relax, and have fun." There is an enormous amount of memorabilia on Hemingway and George Russell (Hemingway's friend and the bar's former owner). The original long, curving bar, ceiling fans, and jalousie doors open onto busy Duval Street. Note the Depression-era mural of Russell, Hemingway, and "Big" Skinner, who tended bar at Sloppy Joe's for more than two decades. Check out the constant drink specials, including the bar's Pop Double, Hemingway Hammer, and Key Lime shooter (prices start at $6).

PART FIVE

PALM BEACH COUNTY

WELCOME *to* PALM BEACH

TRUMP AND THE BREAKERS, TRUMPETS AT the Philharmonic, and breaking the bank are people and things associated with mostly rarefied, sometimes vilified, but always fascinating Palm Beach.

Palm Beach County is larger than Delaware, but most visitors are aware only of the opulent "Gold Coast," from Palm Beach to Boca Raton. But there are 37 other municipalities and unincorporated areas, and the county includes 47 miles of beaches on the east, and Lake Okeechobee and the Everglades on the west.

Delray Beach, between Boca and Palm Beach, has become a lively, desirable place to play and live. West Palm Beach is becoming a shopping and entertainment destination in itself, far less stuffy than its rich neighbor across Lake Worth. And west of the coast, past the suburban communities, are citrus groves, ranches, and wildlife refuges.

A BRIEF HISTORY

THE COUNTY'S EARLIEST KNOWN RESIDENTS were Native Americans, but the region was claimed for Spain in 1513. The nascent United States purchased the territory of Florida three centuries later. The Seminole Indian tribe's famous resistance to forced relocation prompted three wars. The third, fought between 1835 and 1842, ended Indian control of the area. The county's oldest nonnative settlement, Jupiter, was founded as a wartime fort in 1836. The Jupiter Lighthouse began operating in 1860 and continues to the present.

In the 1890s, visionary Henry Flagler, a founding partner of Standard Oil, built the Florida East Coast Railway system from Jacksonville to Key West to open the state as a winter paradise. He also built two large hotels, the Royal Poinciana and The Breakers, plus his own grand winter home, Whitehall, which is now the Flagler Museum.

The Town of Palm Beach was incorporated in 1911 on a barrier beach. The area grew as a fashionable winter retreat, and workers arrived to supply the needs of wealthy vacationers. A legend tells of the African American workers who lived in shacks on the beach. Developers wanted to use this land but couldn't oust the settlers. Supposedly, they organized a huge party for the workers with food, drink, and entertainment. During the festivities, a "mysterious" fire broke out, burning down the shacks. The workers were moved to new, mainland housing in West Palm Beach.

Today, Palm Beach's Ocean Boulevard is lined with millionaires' estates, home to such gilded families as Vanderbilt, Whitney, and Kennedy. Perhaps the most recognizable is Donald Trump's 118-room mansion, Mar-a-Lago, built for cereal heiress Marjorie Merriweather Post, and now a private club across the road from the ocean.

Walkways have been built beneath the road to link the mansions and the beach. But, because the beaches are public, there's nothing to stop you from accessing Palm Beach Municipal Beach—say, at the foot of Worth Avenue—and strolling along for some mansion-gazing and celeb-watching. Just don't expect public bathrooms.

Many other stops along Flagler's railroad route blossomed as well. For instance, Boca Raton was settled in 1896. It became noteworthy because of the foresight of architect Addison Mizner. His 100-room hotel, The Cloister, built in 1925, is now part of the world-renowned Boca Raton Resort and Club. The lobby retains the grand architectural elements and antiques.

Unfortunately, visitors can't pop into the Boca Raton Resort and Club to glimpse the period opulence unless they're registered guests. However, as a nonguest you may view the amazing lobby and public rooms of The Breakers in Palm Beach, and even dine there (for big bucks, of course).

Buildings built or influenced by Mizner blend Mediterranean, Spanish, and Moorish elements. The buildings are often painted in Boca pink—a calamine-lotion hue.

PALM BEACH TODAY

PALM BEACH COUNTY WRESTLED WITH CLASS and social divisions well into the late 20th century. Schools here weren't integrated until 1971; the Everglades Club was notorious for its policy denying membership to blacks and Jews, who were not welcome even as guests for lunch or dinner. Socialite C. Z. Guest reportedly brought cosmetics queen Estée Lauder to the club for lunch. Even though Lauder denied her Jewishness at the time, Guest's tennis privileges were temporarily revoked as punishment for the infraction. In 1985, the late choreographer Jerome Robbins (who was also Jewish) canceled a scheduled cocktail party honoring the New York City Ballet when he learned of the club's exclusionary policy.

Today, diversity is the rule, but inequalities drawn along the color line linger. The county's Hispanic presence increased following 1992's Hurricane Andrew, which destroyed many homes in Dade County and prompted a northward flow. And Palm Beach's Raymond F. Kravis Center for the Performing Arts honors a philanthropic Jewish family.

A blossoming big-business presence in the county, including offices for IBM in Boca Raton and Motorola in Boynton Beach, prompts young families to relocate to the area. Boca is now home to manicured country clubs, condominiums, and shops and restaurants catering to both full- and part-time residents. Boynton Beach is sprouting homes on every available parcel of land, and Jupiter is the latest area to experience drastic growth. The most recent population figures for Palm Beach County count over a million residents, about 10% of whom are winter-only residents.

GATHERING INFORMATION

FOR GENERAL TOURIST INFORMATION, CONTACT **Palm Beach County Convention and Visitors Bureau** (1555 Palm Beach Lakes Boulevard, Suite 800, West Palm Beach 33401; ☎ 561-233-3000; fax 561-471-3990; **www.palmbeachfl.com**).

Summer offers savings on many fronts. Request the coupon book "$1,000 Worth of the Palm Beaches for Free" to save on many dining, shopping, sightseeing, and sports attractions. Call ☎ 800-554-PALM. Many hotels provide a seventh night free, and restaurants often reduce prices to attract customers when the tourist and snowbird seasons wind down.

ARRIVING

IF YOU ARE ARRIVING IN SOUTH FLORIDA VIA one of the larger airports—in Fort Lauderdale or Miami—check the appropriate section for advice on navigating the airport and getting to your hotel.

BY PLANE

PALM BEACH INTERNATIONAL AIRPORT (PBI), though still relatively small, is a three-level modern facility with all the amenities of other large city airports, and it's serviced by most major airlines. The international status is primarily because of flights to the Bahamas, but a landing-strip expansion and direct-highway connection from

I-95 should lure more international airlines. Southwest Airlines, Jet-Blue, and Delta Express offer service. Rental-car agencies have desks conveniently located in the luggage-retrieval area. For more information, call ☎ 561-471-7400.

BY CAR

MOST DRIVERS ENTER PALM BEACH COUNTY from the north, either via Interstate 95 (with well-marked signage) from the northeast or Florida's Turnpike (with its service plazas) from Orlando. Some visitors drive east from the Gulf Coast via FL 70 and FL 710 (70 becomes 710), skirting north of Lake Okeechobee. But don't expect to see much of the country's second-largest freshwater lake unless you leave the highway. The scenery consists of large sugar plantations with fields of waving sugar cane, and not much else.

BY TRAIN OR BUS

THE AMTRAK STATION IS IN A LOVELY OLD Spanish Renaissance–style building near the Kravis Center and CityPlace at 201 South Tamarind Avenue, West Palm Beach; ☎ 561-832-6169.

Tri-Rail is an underused commuter-train service running among Miami-Dade, Broward, and Palm Beach counties (☎ 800-874-7245), with stops in West Palm Beach, Delray Beach, and Boca Raton. Extra trains are added for major events such as football games.

Greyhound Bus Lines has terminals in West Palm Beach (205 South Tamarind Avenue; ☎ 561-833-8536) and Lake Worth (929 North Dixie Highway; ☎ 561-588-5002).

GETTING AROUND

DRIVING YOUR CAR

SPEED LIMITS VARY THROUGHOUT SOUTH Florida: 30 mph is common in congested areas, around hotels, or in heavily populated neighborhoods; 40 or 45 mph commercial areas; and 65 or 70 mph on highways. Florida's seat-belt law requires everyone to buckle up.

Many South Florida roadways have two names. US 1, for example, is also called Federal Highway. It runs from Maine down to Key West, so when referenced here we mention the nearest municipality.

The main north–south arteries within Palm Beach County are the **Florida Turnpike** and **I-95.** Although the turnpike usually offers a smoother drive, it's several miles west of the county's major destinations. And the toll cost for using the turnpike adds up, especially in the county's northern reaches (it costs $2.20–$3 to drive a car from Boca Raton to Jupiter). I-95 generally has more traffic, particularly trucks.

Although its road network is relatively simple in comparison to southern neighbors Broward and Miami-Dade, construction is endemic to Palm Beach—lanes are regularly added to handle the influx of 1,000 immigrants to Florida per day. When an accident occurs, traffic grinds to a halt—and there's often terrible start-and-stop movement in the opposite direction as myriad rubberneckers brake.

FL A1A, despite the stops and the slow traffic, offers a delightful, leisurely ride along the ocean, providing glimpses here and there of gorgeous beach vistas, lush vegetation, and millionaires' mansions. In some spots it narrows considerably, so you can watch the boat action on the Intracoastal Waterway and the seaside.

Pay Attention

Note the license plates on the cars you pass— New Jersey, Quebec, Ohio, Texas, New York, Indiana, Louisiana, Mississippi. They're all exploring new roads, just as you are. Use your turn signals, stay in the left lane unless you are passing, and avoid a heavy hand on the horn.

Road rage is a fact of life today, and South Florida's tropical climate seems to exacerbate tempers, especially on I-95. We suggest using hand signals that are socially acceptable and avoiding all others. If another driver lets you into a line of traffic, signal your thanks.

Many traffic accidents result from carelessness, using a cell phone while driving, speeding, or running red lights. Be cautious.

BY BUS

Palm Tran (☎ 561-841-4200; **www.pbcgov.com/palmtran**) operates a fleet of buses—each seats 42—throughout the county, with numerous stops. Schedules are available on any bus or at any county library (note that city libraries are not county operated). Fares are $1.25 for adults or 60 ¢ for seniors age 60 and over, students, and disabled citizens (you must show a valid ID to receive an age-based reduced fare); unlimited day passes are $3, or $2 reduced.

OTHER OPTIONS

Palm Beach Water Taxi (98 Lake Drive, Palm Beach Shores; ☎ 561-683-8294 or 800-446-4577) is the latest—and probably most pleasant—way to get around near the Intracoastal Waterway. Choose among guided tours or shuttle service to Clematis Street and waterfront restaurants.

unofficial **TIP**
By all means avoid rush hours and use parallel roads such as **Congress Avenue, Military Trail,** and **Jog Road/Powerline Road** (the last one is inconsistently named in different sections). And if you plan to park on a shopping street or at a public beach, remember to bring heaps of quarters for the meters. Some municipalities along the coast now provide special ticket machines or cards.

unofficial **TIP**
For a water-and-land experience, try the popular **Diva Duck,** an amphibian craft that takes you from the streets of Palm Beach and West Palm to the waters of the Intracoastal. Along the way, you'll enjoy the gawkers from your high perch, make duck noises with your special whistle, and even get an aria or two from the guide.

A free trolley also connects West Palm Beach's City Place and the Clematis Street district.

AT *the* SEASHORE

THE BEACHES

MAJOR HOTELS BOAST OCEANFRONT BEACHES. The Boca Raton Resort and Club offers registered guests the beach at its Boca Beach Club property, but frequent trams and Mizner's Dream, a period boat, bring guests from other buildings. Hotel concierge desks provide the schedule.

Numerous strands dot the ocean side of FL A1A, luring young families and retirees. Remember, always heed warnings of riptides and sea lice. The beaches listed below offer bathrooms and outside showers.

One of the most popular Boca Raton beaches is the small **South Beach Pavilion** at Spanish River Boulevard, with free parking for just 17 cars; there's additional public parking on Palmetto Park Road.

unofficial **TIP**
Limited free parking for Red Reef Park is available on Spanish River Boulevard, on both sides of the Intracoastal Bridge. Paid parking is inside the park; daily rates are $16 weekdays and $18 weekends per car.

North up the road is the larger **Red Reef Park,** featuring picnic tables and barbecue grills; it's accessible from the parking lot on the west side of FL A1A through three underground tunnels ($8 per car weekdays, $10 weekends and holidays). This beach particularly draws the young singles set.

In **Delray Beach,** a long stretch of narrow beach is accessible north and south of Atlantic Avenue. Several eateries and beach-supply shops are located on the west side of FL AIA. Bring lots of quarters for the parking meters.

At Lake Avenue in **Lake Worth,** a large complex provides lovely beaches, a municipal pool, a children's playground, a fishing pier, fast-food restaurants, John G's (which has lines around the block at times—see the restaurant profile), and tourist-oriented shops. Parking here costs 25¢ per 15 minutes, with a maximum of ten hours. Arrive early for the closest parking. The city of Lake Worth runs three trolleys to the pier, leaving every hour on the hour from the City Hall depot at Lake Avenue and H Street. Fares are $1; 50¢ for those under 18 and over 60. Printed schedules are available at City Hall and the Chamber of Commerce, or call ☎ 561-586-1600.

South of Indiantown Road on FL A1A, the huge complex at **Carlin Park** in Jupiter draws many families. Parking is complimentary. The 3,000-foot beach competes with other activities, including a baseball field, tennis courts, a playground, and bocce and volleyball courts. There are picnic tables and grills. The nearby Lazy Loggerhead Cafe (☎ 561-747-1134) is open for most meals daily, has patio and inside seating, and dishes up fast fare alongside more ambitious meals. It was recently named "Best Takeout Dining" by the Palm Beach Post.

For information on additional town beaches within Palm Beach County, call Boca Raton Parks and Recreation at ☎ 561-393-7806; Delray Beach Parks and Recreation Department at ☎ 561-243-7250; Jupiter Parks and Recreation at ☎ 561-746-5134; and Palm Beach Gardens Parks and Recreation at ☎ 561-775-8270.

DIVING

REEF DIVING IS TOPS HERE. THE SAME coral reef that extends along Broward and Miami-Dade counties extends this far north, except it's extremely deep off the Palm Beach coast. And there are artificial reefs made with all manner of sunken items, including (in typical Palm Beach fashion) a Rolls Royce.

Contact the **Scuba Club** (4708 North Flagler Drive, West Palm Beach; ☎ 561-844-2466 or 800-835-2466). Join the two-hour trips aboard a 40-foot boat with equipment available for rent. Trips leave Tuesday–Sunday; times vary. Cost is $28 to $50 per person.

Another option is **Force-E Dive Centers,** family-owned since 1976 and with two locations: 2181 North Federal Highway, Boca Raton, ☎ 561-368-0555; and 155 East Blue Heron Boulevard, West Palm Beach, ☎ 561-845-2333.

Each center uses ten boats and operates daily (except when seas are rough). The most frequently requested trips are two-tank dives, which cost $40–$55. Equipment is sold and rented, and Jacques Cousteau wannabes may take courses at these Professional Association of Diving Instructors (PADI) five-star facilities.

American Dive Center (176-B Glades Road, Boca Raton; ☎ 561-393-0621) is a full-service PADI outfit, providing rentals, reef trips on seven boats, and lessons. Boats go out daily, and trips cost $45–$53; equipment rental is separate.

Snorkeling

Force-E Dive Centers (see above) also offer snorkeling. The average price is $30 for four hours, depending on which boats are used and whether equipment is included or not. American Dive Center (176-B Glades Road, Boca Raton; ☎ 561-393-0621) is another option; they usually offer snorkeling trips on weekends. A four-hour trip costs $45.

FISHING

FLORIDA FISHING LICENSES ARE ALWAYS REQUIRED, whether you drop a line off the nearest bridge or go out on a party boat. Licenses are available at area sporting-goods stores, tackle shops, and K-Marts. A saltwater license is $13.50 a year for Florida residents; it's

292 PART 5 PALM BEACH COUNTY

$6.50 for three days and $16.50 for seven days for nonresidents. A freshwater fishing license is $13.50 a year for Florida residents and $16.50 for seven days for nonresidents.

Drift Boats

The Sir Lawrence, based at the Riviera Beach Marina, makes night drift-fishing trips. Tickets are $50. Reservations are suggested. Call ☎ 561-252-6779. Price includes everything participants need to fish: bait, rods, and a fishing license.

The **B-Love Fleet** (314 East Ocean Avenue, Lantana; ☎ 561-588-7612) offers two boats that take three four-hour trips daily. Prices include a fishing license, bait, and tackle. The cost is $30 for adults and $20 for children age 12 and under. Seniors fish for $25 on day trips Monday–Friday. A six-hour trip costs $40.

The 72-foot-long *Sea Mist* (Ocean Avenue, Boynton Beach; ☎ 561-732-9974) also sails three times a day. Cost is $30 for adults, $20 for children age 12 and under, and $25 for seniors over age 65. Fees include everything you'll need for fishing: rods, reels, bait, tackle, and a fishing license.

BOATING

Sailboating and Sailing Courses

Few sailboat rentals are available in Palm Beach County because the Boca Inlet has become extremely difficult to navigate—and it takes a long time to reach a better inlet. The major hotels still schedule sailing outings because their captains go through the inlet daily.

Fast Break Sailing Charters (400-A North Flagler Drive, West Palm Beach; ☎ 561-659-4472) heads down through the Hillsboro Inlet. Its 41-foot-long classic boat has been in the Palm Beach area for almost 20 years. They schedule only private charters with one to six sailors and won't join passengers from one group with another. A three-and-a-half-hour trip costs $350; a seven-hour trip costs $500 and includes lunch.

Canoeing and Kayaking

A world of wildlife opens when you rent canoes and kayaks, which take you into shallow areas inaccessible to big boats. Check conditions before arriving, however, since droughts force some enterprises to temporarily cease operations.

Loxahatchee Canoe Rentals (10216 Lee Road, Boynton Beach; ☎ 561-733-0192) rents canoes at the Arthur R. Marshall Loxahatchee National Wildlife Refuge. Boaters will see sawgrass, swamp hibiscus, and arrowroot, plus alligators and ibis; if you're lucky, you may spot otters, storks, and white-tailed deer. Cost is $32 per canoe. Each canoe holds three to four people. Call for directions (it's somewhat hard to find). Open on the weekends by reservation only.

Canoes and kayaks are available for rent at the **Jupiter Outdoor Center** on the Intracoastal Waterway (1000 Coastal A1A, Jupiter; ☎ 561-747-9666). Paddlers pass mangroves and may spot birds such as great blue herons and osprey; you might even catch sight of a manatee or resident Smoky the dolphin. Rates for singles run $30 per day. For doubles it's $40 per person, adults and children.

The center also offers 50 guided tours. The most popular is the Saturday night tour, which focuses on stargazing and ends with a campfire (bring your own food and drink). Cost is $37 for adults and $22 for children.

Another guided tour is the four-hour Indian River Lagoon Kayak Adventure, which goes to the Nature Conservancy at Blowing Rock, where participants may see sea turtles and manatees. Admission is included in the price of $37 for adults and $30 for children.

Jonathan Dickinson State Park (US 1, Jupiter; ☎ 772-546-2771) also rents canoes and kayaks. Rowers paddle up the northwest fork of the Loxahatchee River. You may see little blue herons, greenback herons, osprey, and manatees (which are usually more plentiful in winter)—and maybe even an alligator. *Loxahatchee* means "river of turtles," and you're very likely to see some of the local variety, peninsular cooters. Canoes, which usually hold two adults and one small child, cost $10 for the first two hours and $4 each additional hour. Single kayaks rent for $15 for the first two hours and $6 each additional hour. Double kayaks go for $20 for the first two hours and $6 each additional hour.

SPORTS *and* RECREATION

FITNESS CENTERS AND AEROBICS

THOUGH YOU MAY CHOOSE TO PUMP UP in the hotel's fitness center, that's not always an option. Or, you might enjoy mixing with locals who are similarly fitness-focused.

One of the most popular spots is **Ultima Fitness** (downtown at 400 Clematis Street, West Palm Beach; ☎ 561-659-1724). It boasts 20,000 square feet with 40 varieties of cardiovascular equipment (Life Fitness cross-trainers, treadmills, recumbent and upright bikes, and Tetrix StairMasters), Cybex machines, Hammer Strength and Strive machines, and free weights. There are 45 aerobics classes weekly, including kickboxing, plus yoga classes. Other attractions include dry saunas, on-site nursery care with a minimal charge ($5 per child up to two hours), and a health-food restaurant. Cost is $15 per day for members and guests.

A hit with young, local professionals (because it's located near large business complexes) is the **Athletic Club Boca Raton** (1499 Yamato Road, Boca Raton; ☎ 561-241-5088). This whopping facility—

78,000 square feet—offers cardiovascular equipment; indoor and outdoor pools; racquetball, handball, basketball, and squash courts; an indoor track; aerobics, spinning, and yoga classes; a sauna, steam room, and whirlpool; and a restaurant. Nonmembers may purchase a one-day pass for $23.50, five-day for $100, and ten-day for $185.

Gold's Gym and Aerobic Center, started in 1965 in California, has several branches in Palm Beach County. The Palm Beach Gardens facility (9910 Highway A1A; ☎ 561-694-6727) boasts more than 50 pieces of cardio equipment, including treadmills, bikes, and Stairmasters. Open 24 hours, Gold's offers free day care for little ones, a sauna, adults' and kids' karate, a juice bar, and personal trainers. Guests may receive complimentary fat-composition evaluations. Other locations include: 2101 Palm Beach Lakes Boulevard, West Palm Beach, ☎ 561-471-8880; 11427 West Palmetto Park Road, Boca Raton, ☎ 561-470-9494; and 499 NE Spanish River Boulevard, Boca Raton, ☎ 561-362-6001. Daily rates are $10; weekly rates $35.

World Gym Fitness Center (6832 Forest Hill Boulevard, West Palm Beach; ☎ 561-966-4653) offers Bodymaster, Hammer Strength, Nautilus, Hoist, Star Trek, Life Cycle, and Life Step equipment. Rates for visitors are $10 daily, $32 weekly. Other branches with similar prices are at 4762 Congress Avenue, Boynton Beach, ☎ 561-964-6676; 14550 South Military Trail, Delray Beach, ☎ 561-638-9980; and 4430 North Lake Boulevard, Palm Beach Gardens, ☎ 561-630-3933.

The **YMCA** (6631 Palmetto Circle South, Boca Raton; ☎ 561-395-9622) offers reciprocal, complimentary use to members of other Ys; nonmembers may buy temporary memberships for $10 per day or $30 per week. The YMCA has Stairmasters, treadmills, cross trainers, saunas, free weights and machines, a pool, and day care ($3 per day). There is another facility at 9600 South Military Trail, Boynton Beach. There, members of other Ys may use the facilities free for two weeks. Nonmembers may buy short-term memberships for $15 a day or $30 a week; there are also children's and family rates. For more information, call ☎ 561-738-9622.

The **Jewish Community Center** (9801 Donna Klein Boulevard, Boca Raton; ☎ 561-852-3200) offers six free visits to members of other JCCs. Daily guest passes cost $35 for up to five days or $10 for just one day. Equipment in the 80,000-square-foot athletic facility includes Precor EFX elliptical cross trainers, bikes, Stairmasters, Cybex machines, and a full free-weight facility; racquetball and basketball courts, aerobics classes, sauna and steam baths, and two pools are also available.

Other JCC locations are 8500 Jog Road, Boynton Beach, ☎ 561-740-9000 and 3151 North Military Trail, West Palm Beach, ☎ 561-689-7700; both offer five free visits for members of other JCCs and $10 per day access for nonmembers.

TENNIS

SOUTH FLORIDA'S WEATHER ALLOWS FOR YEAR-ROUND tennis, which is why so many former and aspirant champions relocate here. Palm Beach County in particular offers world-class tennis facilities and lessons. In Boca Raton, world-famous champion Chris Evert runs the **Evert Tennis Academy** at 10334 Diego Drive South; ☎ 561-488-2001 or 800-417-3783. The complex boasts 9 hard courts, 12 clay courts, and 2 red-clay courts. A day's lesson, held 9–11:30 a.m., costs $80; three days of lessons run $225; 5 days, $350. If you're looking for a special gift for a tennis buff, consider a fantasy clinic with Chris. Note: Adult clinics are suspended during the summer from mid-June to the first week of August.

Also in Boca, **Patch Reef Park** (NW 51st Street; ☎ 561-997-0881) has 17 lighted hard courts and is open 7:30 a.m.–10 p.m., but closes Sunday at 5 p.m. Non–Palm Beach County residents pay $6 per person for one and a half hours of play. Lessons are available.

The **City of Boca Raton Memorial Park** (271 NW Second Avenue; ☎ 561-393-7978) is open 7:30 a.m.–10 p.m. The four hard courts and six clay courts are lighted. Nonresident adults pay $6.50 to play the clay courts for one hour before 2:30 p.m. or one and a half hours after 2:30 p.m.; hard courts run $6 for one hour. Juniors pay $5 for clay, $4 for hard courts, with the same time restrictions. Lessons are available.

The **Boca Del Mar Tennis and Golf Club** (6200 Boca Del Mar Drive; ☎ 561-392-8118) holds junior clinics Monday, Wednesday, and Friday, 4:30–6:30 p.m. Nonmember rates for one day per week (4 classes) are $85; two days per week (8 classes) run $170; three a days week (12 classes) are $255. Family discounts are also available.

Northward up the coast, the area's top tennis center is the **Delray Beach Tennis Center** (201 West Atlantic Avenue, Delray Beach; ☎ 561-243-7360). Besides watching exciting professional matches, normal players may also call "game, set, and match" on 7 hard courts and 14 clay courts. Nonresidents pay $10–$13 for one and a half hours; children pay $6.75–$9.25. There are adult and children's clinics and classes as well.

In Boynton, the **Boynton Beach Tennis Center** (3111 South Congress Avenue; ☎ 561-742-6575) has 4 hard courts and 17 Har-Tru courts. Open to the public Monday–Friday, 8 a.m.–9 p.m.; Saturday and Sunday, 8 a.m.–dusk. Fees for one-and-a-half hours are $7 on clay courts and $3 on hard courts. Juniors under 18 pay $2 for one and a half hours on any court. There's a $4 light fee per court at night.

The city of West Palm Beach has five courts open to the public daily 8 a.m.–8 p.m. at no charge. At the **South Olive Park Tennis Learning Center** (345 Summa Street; ☎ 561-540-8831), Michael Baldwin runs a program of tennis lessons for peewees through teens, adults, and seniors. Lessons are given mornings, afternoons, and evenings. This facility has four all-weather lighted courts.

Also operated by the city with no pay-for-play fees: **Gaines Park Tennis Court** (1501 Australian Avenue; ☎ 561-659-0735) has six all-weather lighted courts; **Howard Park Tennis Club** (901 Lake Avenue; ☎ 561-833-7100) offers five clay courts and two all-weather lighted courts; **Phipps Park** (4301 Dixie Highway; ☎ 561-835-7025) has four all-weather lighted courts; and **Vedado Park** (3710 Paseo Andalusia; ☎ 561-835-7035) has one unlighted all-weather court.

Farther north in Jupiter, the **Jupiter Bay Tennis Club** (353 South US 1; ☎ 561-744-9424) offers seven clay courts, three of them lighted; rates are $16 per person, $12 each with a friend for nonmembers; $10 with a member for one and a half hours. Clinics are conducted for juniors and adults.

North Palm Beach Tennis Club (951 US 1, North Palm Beach; ☎ 561-626-6515) offers ten lighted clay courts; it's open 7 a.m.–9 p.m. The daily guest fee for nonresidents is $10 per adult, $3 for juniors. An adult clinic is available.

GOLF

PALM BEACH IS ONE OF THE GREAT GOLF DESTINATIONS in the world, luring duffers with more facilities per capita than just about any place except Scotland. Visitors probably won't find themselves teeing off alongside the rich and infamous—private courses flourish here—but everyone from beginners to club champions will find a course to meet their needs.

Atlantis Country Club

ESTABLISHED: 1972   STATUS: RESORT/SEMIPRIVATE COURSE

190 Atlantis Boulevard, Atlantis 33462; ☎ 561-965-7700; www.atlantiscountryclub.com

Tees
- **Gold: 6,610 yards, par 72, USGA 72.2, slope 137**
- **Blue: 6,060 yards, par 72, USGA 69.3, slope 130**
- **Red: 5,242 yards, par 72, USGA 67.6, slope 122**
- **White: 5,701 yards, par 72, USGA 67.6, slope 122**

Fees $45–$85 per person

Facilities Dining room, driving range, snack bar, locker rooms, 24-room inn

Comments Soft spikes only. Although there's a misconception that Atlantis has only a private course, this one has been open to the public 25 years.

Belle Glade Golf Course

ESTABLISHED: 1989   STATUS: PUBLIC COURSE

FL 7, Belle Glade 33430; ☎ 561-996-6605

Tees

- **Blue: 6,558 yards, par 72, USGA 70.0, slope 116.**
- **White: 6,044 yards, par 72, USGA 70.0, slope 112.**
- **Red: 5,182 yards, par 72, USGA 69.8, slope 112.**

Fees $36 for 18 holes. Greens fees are $25 off-season.

Facilities Although it's a pretty bare-bones operation, Belle Glade does offer a driving range, practice tee, pro shop, and restaurant.

Comments A popular course with locals

Boca Dunes Golf and Country Club

ESTABLISHED: 1977   STATUS: SEMIPRIVATE COURSE

1400 Country Club Drive, Boca Raton 33428; ☎ 561-451-1600; www.bocadunes.com

Tees

- **Gold: 7,093 yards, par 72, USGA 73.1, slope 134**
- **Blue: 6,803 yards, par 72, USGA 72.2, slope 126**
- **Red: 5,743 yards, par 72, USGA 71.1, slope 121**
- **White: 6,422 yards, par 72, USGA 71.5, slope 123**

Fees $33 with cart for 18 holes

Facilities Clubhouse, driving range, lockers, bar, grill

Comments Soft spikes only

Boca Raton Municipal Golf Course

ESTABLISHED: 1982   STATUS: PUBLIC COURSE

8111 Golf Course Road, Boca Raton 33434; ☎ 561-483-6100 (automated tee times); www.ci.boca-raton.fl.us/parks/golf/brmgc.html

Tees

- **Blue: 6,514 yards, par 72, USGA 70.5, slope 126.**
- **White: 6,115 yards, par 72, USGA 68.5, slope 119.**
- **Red: 5,306 yards, par 72, USGA 69.8, slope 114.**
- **Gold: 5,575 yards, par 72, USGA 69.5, slope 123.**

Fees Greens fees: 9 holes, $16.75; 18 holes, $25.25. With cart: 9 holes, $20.50–$25; 18 holes, $29–$35.50

Facilities Practice range, lockers, snack bar

Comments Soft spikes only

Boca Raton Resort and Club (Resort Course)

ESTABLISHED: 1997   STATUS: RESORT COURSE

501 East Camino Real, Boca Raton 33432; ☎ 561-447-3000 or 888-491-BOCA; www.bocaresort.com

Tees

- **Gold: 6,253 yards, par 71, USGA 69.3, slope 128**
- **Blue: 5,902 yards, par 71, USGA 67.6, slope 124**

- Green: 5,142 yards, par 71, usga 64.3, slope 107
- White: 5,588 yards, par 71, usga 66.4, slope 119
- Red: 4,503 yards, par 71, usga 65.5, slope 112

Fees $100–$155 per person

Facilities Driving range, clubhouse, locker rooms, and restaurant completed in 200.

Comments Soft spikes only. Available only to registered guests and club members

Boca Raton Resort and Club (Country Club Course)

ESTABLISHED: 1985   STATUS: RESORT/PRIVATE COURSE

17751 Boca Club Boulevard, Boca Raton 33487; ☎ 561-447-3600 or 888-491-boca; www.bocaresort.com

Tees

- Gold: 6,585 yards, par 72, usga 72.6, slope 130
- Blue: 6,564 yards, par 72, usga 71.0, slope 121
- White: 5,608 yards, par 72, usga 67.9, slope 131
- Red: 5,449 yards, par 72, usga 72.1, slope 127

Fees $100–$155 per person

Facilities New clubhouse with pro shop, locker rooms, fitness center, restaurant, bar

Comments Soft spikes only. Available only to registered guests and club members

The Breakers Ocean Course

ESTABLISHED: 1897   STATUS: PRIVATE COURSE

1 South County Road, Palm Beach 33480; ☎ 561-659-8407; www.thebreakers.com/golf

Tees

- Championship: 6,167 yards, par 72, usga 68.1, slope 127
- Ladies': 5,254 yards, par 72, usga 69.0, slope 123

Fees $50 for 18 holes, $35 for 9 holes; slight reduction in summer

Facilities New clubhouse, pro shop, small fitness center, restaurant, bar, putting green, driving range, golf academy

Comments Soft spikes only. Only hotel guests and members may play.

The Club at Winston Trails

ESTABLISHED: 1993   STATUS: SEMIPRIVATE COURSE

6101 Winston Trails Boulevard, Lake Worth 33463; ☎ 561-439-3700

Tees

- Championship: 6,838 yards, par 72, usga 73.0, slope 130.
- Men's: 6,443 yards, par 72, usga 71.1, slope 128.
- Ladies': 5,309 yards, par 72, usga 70.0, slope 119.

Fees Monday–Friday, $27–$30; weekends, $29–$35; all fees include cart.
Facilities Clubhouse, fitness center, restaurant, bar, snack bar
Comments A concessionaire drives around selling drinks. Soft spikes only

Delray Beach Golf Club

ESTABLISHED: 1923   STATUS: PUBLIC COURSE

2200 Highland Avenue, Delray Beach 33445; ☎ 561-243-7380;
www.jcdsportsgroup.com/delray_beach_golf_club/index.html

Tees

- **Gold: 6,907 yards, par 72, USGA 73.0, slope 126.**
- **Blue: 6,360 yards, par 72, USGA 70.2 slope 119.**
- **White: 5,189 yards, par 72, USGA 69.8, slope 117.**

Fees $16.90–$25.35, nonresidents; $16.90–$22.54, Delray Beach residents
Facilities Clubhouse, restaurant, bar, lockers, driving range, pro shop
Comments Soft spikes only

Golf Club of Jupiter

ESTABLISHED: 1980   STATUS: SEMIPRIVATE COURSE

1800 Central Boulevard, Jupiter 33458; ☎ 561-747-6262

Tees

- **Blue: 6,235 yards, par 70, USGA 69.9, slope 117**
- **White: 5,649 yards, par 71, USGA 67.4, slope 114**
- **Red: 5,150 yards, par 71, USGA 69.5, slope 118**

Fees $29, 7 a.m.–noon; $25, noon–3 p.m.; $20, after 3 p.m.
Facilities Luncheonette, bar, lockers, putting green, club storage
Comments Course driving range has a pond.

Lacuna Golf Club

ESTABLISHED: 1985   STATUS: SEMIPRIVATE COURSE

6400 Grand Lacuna Boulevard, Lake Worth 33460; ☎ 561-433-3006

Tees

CHEAP

- **Blue: 6,813 yards, par 71, USGA 71.9, slope 128**
- **White: 6,428 yards, par 71, USGA 70.4, slope 121**
- **Red: 5,527 yards, par 71, USGA 69.7, slope 118**

Fees $15–$20 during the week; $20-25 on weekends
Facilities Restaurant, pro shop, putting green
Comments Course is popular with locals year-round and with seasonal
tourists in winter.

Lake Worth Municipal Golf Course

ESTABLISHED: 1980   STATUS: PUBLIC COURSE

1 Seventh Avenue North, Lake Worth 33460; ☎ 561-582-9713;
www.lakeworth.org

Tees

- **Blue: 6,120 yards, par 70, USGA 68.9, slope 119**
- **White: 5,654 yards, par 70, USGA 67.3, slope 115**
- **Red: 5,100 yards, par 70, USGA 69.5, slope 114**

Fees In season: $40 per person with cart until noon, $32 without; $35 with cart after noon, $28 without; $28 with cart after 2:30 p.m., $23 without. In summer: $22–$25 until 3 p.m., $17 after 3 p.m.

Facilities Clubhouse, restaurant, lockers, pro shop, chipping area

Comments Yet another popular course with locals year-round and tourists in season

The Links at Boynton Beach

ESTABLISHED: 1984   STATUS: PUBLIC COURSE

8020 Jog Road, Boynton Beach 33437; ☎ 561-742-6507; www.boynton-beach.org

Tees

- **Professional: 6,231 yards, par 71, USGA 70.4, slope 132.**
- **Back: 5,831 yards, par 71, USGA 68.3, slope 124.**
- **Middle: 5,040 yards, par 65, USGA 64.9, slope 108.**
- **Forward: 4,763 yards, par 72, USGA 68.9, slope 113.**

Fees $26 for 18 holes, including cart

Facilities Clubhouse, restaurant, driving range, practice green, putting and chipping greens, lockers

Comments Soft spikes only

Mizner Trail Golf Club

ESTABLISHED: 1972   STATUS: SEMIPRIVATE COURSE

22689 Camino Del Mar, Boca Raton 33433; ☎ 561-392-7992; www.miznertrailgolfclub.com

Tees

- **Championship: 6,842 yards, par 72, USGA 73.3, slope 135.**
- **Other: 6,202 yards, par 72, USGA 70.1, slope 128.**
- **Middle: 6,528 yards, par 72, USGA 71.70, slope 131.**
- **Forward: 5,174 yards, par 72, USGA 69.70, slope 121.**

Fees Weekdays: before 1 p.m., $33; after 1 p.m., $29. Weekends: before 11 a.m., $35; after 11 a.m., $21; after 1 p.m., $29

Facilities Clubhouse, restaurant, bar, pro shop, putting green, driving range, chipping green

Comments Soft spikes only

North Palm Beach Country Club

ESTABLISHED: 1956   STATUS: SEMIPUBLIC—A MUNICIPAL COURSE FOR MEMBERS AND NONMEMBERS

**951 US 1, North Palm Beach 33408; ☎ 561-691-3433;
www.village-npb.org/cclub.htm**

Tees

- **Blue: 5,781 yards, par 72, USGA 63.3, slope 113**
- **Ladies': 5,033 yards, par 72, USGA 68.9, slope 114**

Fees $30 for 18 holes with cart before 3 p.m.; $19 for 18 holes with cart after 3 p.m.

Facilities Clubhouse, restaurant, bar, lockers, putting green, driving range

Comments Soft spikes only. For an additional charge, golfers may use the Olympic-size pool and lighted tennis courts.

Palm Beach Gardens Golf Club

ESTABLISHED: 1991 STATUS: PUBLIC COURSE

**11401 Northlake Boulevard, Palm Beach Gardens 33418;
☎ 561-626-7888; www.pbgfl.com/resident/golf/golf.asp**

Tees

- **Gold: 6,454 yards, par 72, USGA 71.2, slope 131**
- **Blue: 6,013 yards, par 72, USGA 69.1, slope 122**
- **White: 5,400 yards, par 72, USGA 66.5, slope 111**
- **Red: 4,690 yards, par 71, USGA 70.6, slope 122**

Fees $27 weekday and $31 weekends; rates slightly lower after noon

Facilities Clubhouse, restaurant, bar, driving range

Comments Always busy—one of the region's most popular courses.

PGA National Members Club

ESTABLISHED: 1980 STATUS: PRIVATE

**1000 Avenue of the Champions, Palm Beach Gardens 33418;
☎ 561-627-1800 or 561-627-1614; www.pgamembersclub.com**

Tees

CHAMPIONSHIP COURSE

- **Black: 7,048 yards, par 72, USGA 75.3, slope 147**
- **Gold: 6,721 yards, par 72, USGA 73.3, slope 144**
- **Blue: 6,379 yards, par 72, USGA 71.6, slope 137**
- **White: 5,984 yards, par 72, USGA 69.9 slope 129**
- **Red: 5,145 yards, par 72, USGA 72.3, slope 136**

ESTATE COURSE

- **Blue: 6,694 yards, par 72, USGA 71.8, slope 137**
- **White: 6,122 yards, par 72, USGA 69.1, slope 125**
- **Red: 4,943 yards, par 72, USGA 68.9, slope 123**

GENERAL COURSE

- **Blue: 6,768 yards, par 72, USGA 73.1, slope 134**
- **White: 6,219 yards, par 72, USGA 70.4, slope 128**
- **Red: 5,327 yards, par 72, USGA 71.3, slope 123**

HAIG COURSE

- **Blue: 6,806 yards, par 72, USGA 73.5, slope 139**
- **White: 6,335 yards, par 72, USGA 71.3, slope 134**
- **Red: 5,645 yards, par 72, USGA 73.1, slope 129**

THE SQUIRE

- **Blue: 6,465 yards, par 72, USGA 71.8, slope 139**
- **White: 6,000 yards, par 72, USGA 69.1, slope 131**
- **Red: 4,875 yards, par 72, USGA 70.2, slope 131**

Fees Champion, Haig, General, and Squire Courses, $105–$225; Estate Course, $105–$130; slight fee reduction in summer

Facilities Clubhouse, pro shop, lockers, restaurant, bar, 9 putting greens, 2 driving ranges

Comments You must be a guest of the resort to play.

Polo Trace Golf Club

ESTABLISHED: 1989   STATUS: SEMIPRIVATE COURSE

13397 Hagen Ranch Road, Delray Beach 33446; ☎ 561-495-5300 or 866-465-3765 (tee-time service); www.polotracegolf.com

Tees

- **Championship: 7,182 yards, par 72, USGA 74.8, slope 139.**
- **Back: 6,725 yards, par 72, USGA 72.6, slope 133.**
- **Forward: 5,445 yards, par 72, USGA 71.6, slope 125.**
- **Members: 6,331 yards, par 72, USGA 70.3, slope 129.**

Fees $49 Sunday–Thursday, $59 Friday and Saturday

Facilities Pro shop, locker rooms, restaurant, bar and lounge, driving range open to players that day only

Comments Soft spikes only

Villa Delray Golf Club

ESTABLISHED: 1972   STATUS: SEMIPRIVATE COURSE

6200 Via Delray, Delray Beach 33484; ☎ 561-498-1444

Tees

- **Blue: 6,151 yards, par 71, USGA 71.0, slope 128**
- **White: 5,843 yards, par 71, USGA 68.8, slope 126**
- **Red: 5,442 yards, par 71, USGA 67.0, slope 119**

Fees In season: $48 with cart

Facilities Driving range, restaurant, pro shop, lockers, putting green, bag storage

Comments A full-service club catering to seniors.

The Village Golf Club

ESTABLISHED: 1980   STATUS: SEMIPRIVATE   COURSE

**122 Country Club Drive, Royal Palm Beach 33411; ☎ 561-793-1400;
www.thevillagegolfclub.com**

Tees

- **Championship: 6,900 yards, par 72, USGA 73.3, slope 134**
- **Men's: 6,582 yards, par 72, USGA 70.7, slope 128**
- **Ladies': 5,455 yards, par 72, USGA 71.7, slope 12.**

Fees   Greens fees run $16–$39.

Facilities   Clubhouse, restaurant, bar, lockers, putting green, driving range, pro shop. Swimming pool and tennis are available.

Comments   Soft spikes only

Westchester Golf and Country Club

ESTABLISHED: 1988   STATUS: SEMIPRIVATE COURSE

12250 Westchester Club Drive, Boynton Beach 33437; ☎ 561-734-6300

Tees

GOLD COURSE

- **Gold: 6,657 yards, par 72, USGA 72.3, slope 134**
- **Blue: 6,166 yards, par 72, USGA 69.9, slope 129**
- **White: 5,736 yards, par 72, USGA 67.9, slope 122**
- **Silver: 5,119 yards, par 72, USGA 65.1, slope 106**
- **Red: 4,808 yards, par 72, USGA 70.0, slope 120**

RED COURSE

- **Gold: 6,772 yards, par 72, USGA 72.9, slope 134**
- **Blue: 6,281 yards, par 72, USGA 70.4, slope 129**
- **White: 5,876 yards, par 72, USGA 68.5, slope 122**
- **Silver: 5,219 yards, par 72, USGA 65.6, slope 106**
- **Red: 4,750 yards, par 72, USGA 70.3, slope 120**

BLUE COURSE

- **Gold: 6,735 yards, par 72, USGA 72.8, slope 137**
- **Blue: 6,223 yards, par 72, USGA 70.3, slope 133**
- **White: 5,768 yards, par 72, USGA 68.4, slope 123**
- **Silver: 5,100 yards, par 72, USGA 65.1, slope 108**
- **Red: 4,728 yards, par 72, USGA 69.7, slope 121**

Fees $38–$55; after noon, $31

Facilities   Restaurant, driving range, locker room, 18-hole par 3

Comments   Soft spikes only; three championship 9-hole courses

WALKING, RUNNING, AND HIKING

PALM BEACH COUNTY'S MAJOR PARKS offer trails for walking and running. An outstanding choice is the **Lake Trail** on Palm Beach. Most area communities lack sidewalks; however; walking or jogging alongside FL AIA (from Deerfield to Delray Beaches) is feasible if you don't mind the traffic.

Many walkers trek in air-conditioned shopping malls, which open earlier than the stores. Most major strolling takes place in Boca Raton's Mizner Park and West Palm Beach's CityPlace. And, of course, window shopping along Palm Beach's Worth Avenue is mandatory. The Athletic Club Boca Raton boasts an indoor track (see Fitness Centers and Aerobics). Those who run outside usually choose early morning or late afternoon; midday gets too hot.

South Florida has no hills to hike, but several trails provide access to nature's unique wonders. One especially fine way to experience the Everglades is to hike any of the five trails at **Arthur R. Marshall Loxahatchee National Wildlife Refuge** (10216 Lee Road, Boynton Beach; ☎ 561-732-3684).

BICYCLING

FLAT FLORIDA IS IDEAL FOR BIKERS, ESPECIALLY in the mornings and late afternoons. For unique bicycling, visit the **Palm Beach Bicycle Trail Shop** (223 Sunrise Avenue, in the Palm Beach Hotel; ☎ 561-659-4583). Rental rates are $10 per hour, $25 for 4 hours, $30 per day, $45 for 2 days, $55 for 3 days, and $70 per week. The shop is open Monday–Saturday, 9 a.m.–5:30 p.m.; and Sunday, 10 a.m.– 5 p.m. The business started here 28 years ago.

Bikers cycle along the paved Lake Trail between millionaires' homes and the Intracoastal Waterway, spotting boats and dog walkers along the way. At its southern end, the trail starts at the Flagler Museum and continues for about one mile. Then, near the rental shop, it continues northward from Sunrise Avenue for another nine miles to Palm Beach Inlet. The shop also rents helmets and children's bikes. Guided tours, which point out famous residents' homes, are available by reservation only.

An extremely popular trail parallels FL A1A (Ocean Boulevard) in Boca Raton and Highland Beach; bikers sometimes glimpse the ocean or Intracoastal. **Richwagen's Delray Beach Bicycles** (217 East Atlantic Avenue, Delray Beach; ☎ 561-243-2453) rents a variety of bikes, from single speeds and hybrids to tandem bikes and children's bikes. One of the most popular is the seven-speed cruiser, costing $10 per hour, $25 per day, or $45 per week. Open Monday–Friday, 10 a.m.–6 p.m., and Saturday, 10 a.m.–5 p.m.

Most large parks boast bicycle trails and bicycle racks, along with other athletic facilities and picnic areas. There are bicycle paths at **Carlin Park** in Jupiter (south of Indiantown Road on FL A1A; ☎ 561-746-5134); **John Prince Park** (2700 Sixth Avenue South, Lake Worth; ☎ 561-966-6600), which also offers a 1.2-mile fitness trail; and **Okeeheelee Park** (7715 Forest Hill Boulevard, West Palm Beach; ☎ 561-966-6600), which also has a lighted water-ski course. There are also bicycle trails at **Jonathan Dickinson State Park** (16450 SE Federal Highway, Hobe Sound; ☎ 772-546-2771) (see Attractions, page 322).

SPECTATOR SPORTS

TENNIS At the **Delray Beach Tennis Center** (201 West Atlantic Avenue, Delray Beach; ☎ 561-243-7360) you can watch such exciting matches as the Citrix Tennis Championships and the Chris Evert Pro-Celebrity in the top-notch facilities at the center stadium court.

The **Boca Raton Resort and Club** (☎ 561-395-3000) hosts the EMC2 Skills Challenge in alternate years; past participants included Jack Nicklaus and Arnold Palmer.

SHOPPING

AMONG THE NUMEROUS OPPORTUNITIES IN shop-till-you-drop Palm Beach County, you will find the latest styles from Paris and Milan, as well as more-reasonable duds for the masses. You may even find a bargain castoff—maybe last season's style—from a socialite's closet in one of several "thrift" shops.

STROLLING AND WINDOW SHOPPING

Worth Avenue on the island of Palm Beach is one of the country's most glamorous and unique shopping streets; even natives of Beverly Hills say it's more beautiful than Rodeo Drive. Most buildings are only one or two stories high, and the architecture is Mizner-style Mediterranean, with hidden lanes, arcades, tiled stairways, public art, and blooming bougainvillea all about. Don't miss the famous doggie watering trough outside **Phillips Galleries** at 318 Worth Avenue. Streetside meters and valet parking are available at the Apollo parking lot just north of Worth Avenue, off Hibiscus Avenue, as well as at the Esplanade's parking garage, at the southeast end of the Avenue, near **Saks Fifth Avenue** (172 Worth Avenue, Palm Beach; ☎ 561-833-2551).

Worth Avenue, befitting its name, offers such worthy shops as **Armani, Brooks Brothers, Cartier, Chanel, Gucci, Hermès,** and **Ungaro.** Along with antique and other collectibles shops are some long-standing icons, such as **Trillion** (315 Worth Avenue; ☎ 561-832-3525), which has featured a splayed rainbow display of men's sweaters for nearly 20 years; the individual garments are changed frequently to showcase different colors.

unofficial **TIP**
Worth Avenue businesses often host unadvertised after-season sales—discreetly noted by tiny, tasteful signs in the window. These sales start in April.

Don't miss the opportunity to stroll down the "vias," small but charming alleyways with specialty boutiques and outdoor cafes. Here, for instance, is **Morgan Terry Hats** (313-A Worth Avenue, Palm Beach; ☎ 561-659-0771), a spot to find the perfect Palm Beach straw hat. The whimsical chapeaux range from about $130 to $200.

Mizner Park (430 Plaza Real, Boca Raton; ☎ 561-362-0606) is an upscale outdoor shopping area anchored by **Jacobson's** and filled with fashionable boutiques, galleries, and restaurants. The charming and immaculate Mediterranean-style village also houses offices and residences.

In West Palm Beach, the city that developed to provide service for Palm Beach residents, **CityPlace** (Okeechobee Boulevard; ☎ 561-366-1000) is a multiuse complex with shops, restaurants, bars, and homes. Some standout shops: **Banana Republic** (700 South Rosemary Avenue, West Palm Beach; ☎ 561-833-9841) and **Gianna Christine Salon, Spa, and Wellness** (700 South Rosemary Avenue, West Palm Beach; ☎ 561-742-8858).

Preserved in the 1926 Spanish Colonial Revival church is the **Harriet Himmel Gilman Theatre,** which features original details such as cypress doors and beams and is used for cultural events. Outside, the church bell announces choreographed water displays at the Palladium Plaza fountains. Free outdoor concerts are held Friday and Saturday nights, which often prompt spontaneous dancing. There's no additional number for "The Harriet" (as it's now dubbed); for information, contact the CityPlace Information Line at ☎ 561-366-1000.

The CityPlace complex incorporates several of the previous streets and includes sherbet-colored townhouses and apartments—embellished with wrought-iron railings and barrel-tiled roofs—reminiscent of a Riviera city. The complimentary trolley service connecting CityPlace with Clematis Street transports 40,000 people a month. Clematis itself, a low-rise street similar to Las Olas in Fort Lauderdale, has become a great place to stroll: an early-Florida treasure of shops, galleries, and restaurants.

MALL SHOPPING

LOCAL MALLS KEEP GETTING MORE ELABORATE, and they're especially crowded when the weather is rainy or cloudy. **Boynton Beach Mall** (801 North Congress Avenue, Boynton Beach; ☎ 561-736-7900) appeals to both retirees and the younger set, offering 135-plus stores. It's looking perkier since the Simon Property Management Group took over, and it's anchored by Macy's, Gap, Sears, Dillard's, and JCPenney.

Palm Beach Mall (1801 Palm Beach Lakes Boulevard, West Palm Beach; ☎ 561-683-9186) draws a lot of locals with its 125 specialty shops. Anchors are Burdines, Dillard's, JCPenney, Borders Books, and Sears.

The Gardens of the Palm Beaches (3101 PGA Boulevard, Palm Beach Gardens; ☎ 561-775-7750) is a lovely two-story mall with an open, sunny, gardenlike atmosphere. Among its 150-plus stores are anchors Macy's, Nordstrom, Sears, Bloomingdale's, and Saks Fifth Avenue.

Town Center at Boca Raton (6000 Glades Road, Boca Raton; ☎ 561-368-6000) is an upscale enclosed center with shops totaling 220. Anchors include Bloomingdale's, Saks Fifth Avenue, Brookstone, Sears, Neiman Marcus, and Nordstrom. Valet parking is available.

SPECIALTY SHOPS

ANTIQUES Think South Florida residents decorate their homes in modern pastels? Think again. You'll find a gaggle of antiques stores (about 45) located on **Antique Row,** on South Dixie Highway (two blocks north of Southern Boulevard) in West Palm Beach. Pop into any of the stores on the six-block stretch for a printed map showing locations and types of merchandise.

Wardall Antiques (3709 South Dixie Highway; ☎ 561-832-0428) offers an eclectic mix of American and European antiques. **Pierre Anthony** (3300 South Dixie Highway; ☎ 561-650-1344) specializes in period antiques from the 17th, 18th, and 19th centuries. **Cassidy's Antiques** (3621 South Dixie Highway; ☎ 561-832-8017) offers museum-quality 17th- and 18th-century Spanish and Italian pieces.

Art, Architecture, and Antiques in West Palm and Lake Worth

The **Clematis Street Historic District** is crammed with fabulous buildings. The 500 block of Clematis is a real gem; you'll see Art Deco and Venetian, Greek, and Mediterranean Revival buildings from the 1920s and 1930s recycled into galleries, restaurants, and boutiques. On Saturdays, from 7 a.m. to 1 p.m., you can enjoy the nearby **West Palm Beach Green Market** (Second and Narcissus Streets between Oliver and Flagler; ☎ 561-644-7292).

Ragtops Motorcars (2119 South Dixie Highway; ☎ 561-655-2836) has three buildings—and outside space—devoted to classic cars, including 75-year-old LaSalles. If you couldn't care less, you'll still enjoy Bumpers Diner on-site—even though it doesn't serve any food.

In nearby Lake Worth, the **Palm Beach Institute of Contemporary Art** (601 Lake Avenue; ☎ 561-582-0006; **www.palmbeachica.org**) has excellent visiting exhibitions. The **Lake Worth Historical Museum,** in the Old City Hall, built in 1929, has seven rooms of memorabilia—a delightful, giant community attic (414 Lake Avenue; ☎ 561-586-1700).

Antiquing is fun on **South Dixie Highway,** especially south of Monroe Drive, in shops where ritzy Palm Beach residents tend to leave their prized possessions. You'll find outrageous things at sometimes reasonable prices.

Art, Architecture, and Antiques in West Palm and Lake Worth *(continued)*

Check out the **El Cid Historic District** in West Palm Beach. Barcelona, Belmont, and Grenada roads here are filled with Mediterranean-style homes built in the 1920s. The **Ann Norton Sculpture Gardens** (25 Barcelona Road, ☎ 561-832-5328) show off over 300 species of palms, and the artist's work fills her house and studio. North on Olive Avenue is **Mango Promenade,** a tiny historic district with charming bungalows in a variety of styles. Makes for a great walk.

Longtime names around tony **Worth Avenue** include **Christian Du Pont Antiques** (353 Peruvian Avenue, Palm Beach; ☎ 561-655-7794), specializing in intricate 17th- through 19th-century French marquetry and sparkling crystal chandeliers.

ART **Wally Findlay Galleries** (165 Worth Avenue, Palm Beach; ☎ 561-655-2090) has long been a bastion of fine art on Palm Beach. **Wentworth Galleries** has two locations representing international contemporary painters and sculptors: **Town Center Mall** (Boca Raton; ☎ 561-368-6000) and The Gardens mall (Palm Beach Gardens; ☎ 561-775-7750). At **Art & Frame Co.** (51 Glades Road, Boca Raton; ☎ 561-750-1554), you'll find vintage posters from the 19th and 20th centuries, primarily French and Italian, plus Art Deco and Art Nouveau originals. If you can't pay big bucks for originals, contemporary copies are also for sale.

BAIT Overpasses along the Intracoastal Waterway host a constant stream of anglers. Fishing is such a popular pastime in these parts that most bait and tackle shops have been on board for decades.

Boynton Fisherman Supply (618 North Federal Highway, Boynton Beach; ☎ 561-736-0568), a family-owned business for 18 years, carries fresh and saltwater bait and fishing tackle—lures, hooks, rods, and reels.

Perk's Bait and Tackle (307 North Fourth Street, Lantana; ☎ 561-582-3133) appeals to many who fish at the Boynton Beach Inlet. Family-owned for 55 years, it boasts everything for offshore fishing. They even sell custom-made rods. Most of their customers are locals who fish year-round, but they'll tell you the best fishing is March–November. Remember to pick up your fishing license when you stop by.

BARGAINS Long familiar to savvy New York bargain hunters, **Loehmann's** has two locations (8903 Glades Road, Boca Raton, ☎ 561-852-7111, and 4100 PGA Boulevard, Palm Beach Gardens,

☎ 561-627-5575). Don't forget to pop into The Back Room for special-occasion glam. Sales on swimwear and shoes begin in May, after the tourist season.

Near Palm Beach's Worth Avenue is a high-class consignment shop, **Déjà Vu** (219 Royal Poinciana Way, Palm Beach; ☎ 561-833-6624), where shopaholics might find a cast-off glitzy gown formerly owned by a local celeb or society type. Maxie Barley and her co-owner and sister, Marilyn Lanham, recycle duds from socialites who dare not wear the same outfit twice. The most popular items requested are Chanel designs; the shop sells $500–$1,000 bouclé suits that were originally $3,000. Spend the money you save on a lavish dinner befitting your new outfit.

BOOKSTORES Barnes & Noble Booksellers (1400 Glades Road, Boca Raton, ☎ 561-750-2134; 333 North Congress Avenue, Boynton Beach, ☎ 561-374-5570; and 700 Rosemary Avenue, West Palm Beach, ☎ 561-514-0811) offers books, a vast selection of magazines and out-of-town newspapers, and CDs, DVDs, and videos. They also host book clubs and have a cheerful section for youngsters (where they hold a preschool story time). There's a cafe for that caffeine jolt, and best-sellers are usually offered at a 40% discount.

Books-A-Million (1630 South Federal Highway, Delray Beach, ☎ 561-243-3395; and 6370 West Indiantown Road, Jupiter, ☎ 561-743-8094) is a chain that sells books, newspapers, and magazines; each shop also features a cafe.

Borders Books, Music and Cafe stores (9887 Glades Road, Boca Raton, ☎ 561-833-5854; 525 North Congress Avenue, Boynton Beach, ☎ 561-734-2021; and 1801 Palm Beach Lakes Boulevard, West Palm Beach, ☎ 561-689-4112) are massive, offering books, newspapers, magazines, CDs, DVDs, videos, and, of course, coffee. They discount their own list of best-sellers (not the *New York Times* list).

The Bookworm (4111 Lake Worth Road, Lake Worth; ☎ 561-965-1900) has been here since 1966. Room after room opens up to reveal about 200,000 books—almost entirely used—and thousands of used magazines. (Owner Judith DeWitt says 99% of the books are used, but they must carry some new tomes for insurance purposes.)

Rand McNally Map and Travel Store (The Gardens mall; ☎ 561-775-7602) not only has tons of travel books but also everything travelers could wish for, be they backpackers or armchair travelers: games (to keep the kids occupied on those endless car rides), maps, travel kits, luggage, electrical adapters, and mini-pillboxes.

ETHNIC GOODS You'll want to *mange* at **Doris Italian Market and Bakery** (9101 Lakeridge Boulevard, Boca Raton; ☎ 561-482-0770) when you see and smell the savory Italian groceries, cheeses, top-grade olive oils, pastas, and sauces. The butcher carries high-grade Italian meats and fresh-frozen homemade dinners. At the bakery, you'll find popular

Italian pastries, including baba au rhum, cannoli, and tiramisu, all fresh-baked on the premises.

At **King's Italian Market** (1900 North Military Trail, Boca Raton; ☎ 561-368-2600), foodies find more than just Italian angel hair. Choose from top-quality exotic produce, goodies from the in-house bakery, the finest prime meats and name-brand deli items, dozens of varieties of cheese, and 50 gourmet prepared salads.

Flakowitz Bake Shop (8202 Glades Road, Boca Raton; ☎ 561-488-0900), serves traditional Jewish breads like eggy braided challah and dense pumpernickel rye, as well as pastries like apple strudel.

Wolfie Cohen's Rascal House (2006 Executive Center Drive, Boca Raton; ☎ 561-982-8899)—besides being a sit-down restaurant—maintains a reputation as the area's top Jewish deli, with lox, corned beef, and deli fare. Their chopped liver ain't chopped liver, either.

Tulipan Bakery (704 Belvedere Road, West Palm Beach; ☎ 561-832-6107) dispenses Hispanic baked goods—you'll shout *"¡Olé!"* for the guava pastries. They also offer prepared meat-filled pastries and classic Cuban sandwiches (filled with pork, ham, cheese, and pickles).

FLEA MARKETS The **Delray Swap Shop and Flea Market** (2001 North Federal Highway, Delray Beach; ☎ 561-276-4012) is a bargain lover's paradise, with 124 merchants indoors and 76 outdoors. Open Thursday–Monday, 9 a.m.–4 p.m. Closed on Monday in summer.

At the **Uptown Downtown Flea Market and Outlet Mall** (5700 Okeechobee Boulevard, West Palm Beach; ☎ 561-684-5700), approximately 200 merchants vie for sales in an enclosed mall. The outlet is open Monday–Thursday, 10 a.m.–6 p.m.; Friday and Saturday, 10 a.m.–8 p.m.; and Sunday, noon–6 p.m. The flea market is open Tuesday–Friday, 10 a.m.–5 p.m.; Saturday, 10 a.m.–6 p.m.; and Sunday, noon–6 p.m. Hours are reduced in the summer.

FRESH FISH Many area fish and seafood markets closed their doors in response to dwindling supplies and rising prices. **Captain Frank's** (435 Boynton Beach Boulevard, Boynton Beach; ☎ 561-732-3663) still offers fresh fish and shellfish bought directly from fishing-boat anglers or flown in fresh (except king crab legs, which are frozen). They also offer a fisherman's catch of homemade goodies: crab cakes from Maryland blue crabs, lake cakes (the lobster meat shipped in fresh from Maine), and fish chowders. Most of Captain Frank's customers are locals, which says lots about the store's power to please.

Delray Seafoods (120 SE Fourth Avenue, Delray Beach; ☎ 561-278-3439) offers locally caught fresh fish such as dolphinfish (aka mahimahi—not Flipper's relatives), grouper, and tuna, as well as fresh flown-in varieties like salmon and Chilean sea bass. Shellfish include local blue crabs. The firm, located here since 1960, purchases directly from local fishing boats.

FRESH PRODUCE AND FRUIT SHIPPING The Blood family at **Blood's Hammock Groves** (4600 Linton Boulevard, Delray Beach; ☎ 561-498-3400 or 800-255-5188) has 50 years' experience in the Florida citrus business. Customers can view the fruit processing from an observation deck. Fresh-picked oranges, grapefruits, and pomelos (which resemble giant lemons) are sold, along with company-made marmalades and fruit baskets. The bakery offers scones and breads. They ship fruit and gourmet baskets.

At **Knollwood Groves** (8053 Lawrence Road, Boynton Beach; ☎ 561-734-4800 or 800-222-9696), the original trees were planted in 1930 by comedians Charles Correll and Freeman Gosden, stars of the long-running radio show *Amos 'n' Andy*. Oranges and grapefruits are sold, plus other fresh produce, juice, and fruit pies made on-site. A tram ride takes visitors to see the groves and packing house and to watch an alligator show. Oranges and grapefruits are shipped according to which is in season. Closed Sundays in summer.

The **West Palm Beach Green Market** (Narcissus Avenue and Second Street, West Palm Beach; ☎ 561-659-8003) is open Saturdays from late October to late April and offers free parking. The 60-plus vendors sell only Palm Beach County–grown fruits, vegetables, and plants (from palm trees to orchids), along with honey, cakes, and pastries made by five local bakeries.

JEWELRY Big spenders might head toward Palm Beach's elegant Worth Avenue for some jaw-dropping baubles at **Cartier** (214 Worth Avenue, Palm Beach; ☎ 561-655-5913), **Tiffany & Co.** (259 Worth Avenue, Palm Beach; ☎ 561-659-6090), or **Van Cleef and Arpels** (249 Worth Avenue, Palm Beach; ☎ 561-655-6767).

Those in search of value more than name head for **International Jewelers Exchange** (8221 Glades Road, Boca Raton; ☎ 561-488-0648), which claims to be Florida's largest and oldest jewelry exchange. The complex houses 60 vendors displaying a glittering array of gold, gemstones, and pearls—just like New York's 47th Street. And all below retail. Open Tuesday–Saturday, 10 a.m.–5 p.m.; open daily from Thanksgiving to Christmas.

unofficial **TIP**
Our favorite vendor at the International Jewelers Exchange is **ABS Gems,** where a registered gemologist knows the ropes.

SPAS Need to relax and beautify? Masseuses are just waiting to get their hands on you. The **PGA National Resort and Spa** (400 Avenue of the Champions, Palm Beach Gardens; ☎ 561-627-2000) offers spa day programs to the public, as well as packages for registered guests. Costs for men's and women's half-day packages run $275–$285; full-day packages are $350–$470. With certain spa packages, daily guests may have access to the fitness facility as well. The **Ritz-Carlton Palm Beach** (100 South Ocean Boulevard, Palm Beach; ☎ 561-533-6000) permits nonregistered guests to enjoy massage treatments for no charge beyond the massage itself. Additionally, half-day packages run $180–$220 and full-day packages $310–$360. And during summer only, spa guests may use the pool or beach.

The Breakers Hotel (1 South County Road, Palm Beach; ☎ 561-655-6611) offers nonregistered guests the opportunity to book a treatment in the spa (such as a facial or massage), which then includes access to the fitness center, four pools, and the beach. Prices vary depending on the treatment.

SWIMWEAR Swimland (Royal Palm Plaza, known locally as the Pink Plaza, 200 SE First Avenue, Boca Raton; ☎ 561-395-4415) has racks and racks of teeny-weeny bikinis and stunning Gottex outfits for ladies. Most women are sure to find something in their size. The shop features major brands such as Jantzen, Serena, and Gideon Oberson. An annual sale begins before Memorial Day and ends shortly before Thanksgiving.

The high-action crowd heads to surfboard central at **Nomad Surf Shop** (4655 North Ocean Boulevard, Boynton Beach; ☎ 561-272-2882). This surfers' heaven, which opened in 1968, features room after room of beachwear for men and women from such makers as Nomad, Volcom, and Quicksilver. And, of course, they sell surfboards—even custom-made jobs. There's a sale the weekend before Memorial Day and a half-price sale the second week of October.

TOYS Kids ages 3–103 will flip over the **Build-A-Bear Workshop** (The Gardens mall; ☎ 561-630-7734). In this interactive store, customers start at the Dress Me station and choose which outfits they want their teddy bear to wear—perhaps a basketball outfit or a bridal ensemble; next they add accessories such as shoes, hats, and so on. Patrons then give their bears an "air bath" and go home with self-styled teddies.

USED YACHTS AND BOATS Rybovich is an internationally known name in custom boats. Visitors are welcome at the newly renovated, enlarged **Rybovich Spencer** (4200 North Flagler Drive, West Palm Beach; ☎ 561-844-1800) and may join a free one-hour tour. Tours are held Thursdays at 4 p.m. (except during summer); guests must make reservations 24 hours ahead. You'll see the full-service marina and new sportfishing boat under construction; two boats are under construction at all times. They're all custom-made, each taking 18–24 months to complete. The yard also brokers used boats and offers full-service marina facilities.

unofficial **TIP**
If you're serious about getting a boat, pick up a copy of *Boat Trader*, a weekly black-and-white magazine that lists hundreds of photos and pertinent information, or *Yacht Trader*, its sister publication; both are available at most convenience stores for $2.50.

Steer to **HMY Yacht Sales** (2401 PGA Boulevard, Palm Beach Gardens; ☎ 561-775-6000) for used yachts. It's currently berthing vessels from 31 to 105 feet. For something smaller, make your way to **Inflatable Experts** (155 East Blue Heron Boulevard, West Palm Beach; ☎ 561-848-5588), which handles new inflatables such as Zodiacs and accepts used inflatables on trade-ins.

WINE AND GOURMET FOODS At **Chocolates by Mr. Roberts** (505 NE 20th Street, Boca Raton; ☎ 561-392-3007), Heinz Robert Gold-schneider is called "Mr. Roberts" because Henry Fonda—who played that character—adored his handmade chocolates when his acting work took him to New York. Goldschneider, a septuagenarian gentleman who learned his techniques in Switzerland before immigrating to the United States, continues to turn out some two dozen varieties of handmade truffles—plus dipped chocolates and nuts—daily.

Crown Wine and Spirits has five branches (22191 Powerline Road, Boca Raton, ☎ 561-391-6009; 3500 North Federal Highway, Boca Raton, ☎ 561-392-6366; 737 South Federal Highway, Boca Raton, ☎ 561-394-3828; 911 SE Sixth Avenue, Delray Beach, ☎ 561-278-2100; and 564 SE Woolbright Road, Boynton Beach, ☎ 561-734-9463). They offer an array of liquors, chilled wines, and imported beer, plus gourmet cheeses and chocolates.

Another option is **Good Life Wine, Spirits and Gourmet** (1536-B South Federal Highway, Delray Beach; ☎ 561-276-3838). At **Hampton Liquors** (257 Royal Poinciana Way, Palm Beach; ☎ 561-832-8368), you might spot a bronzed and beautiful Palm Beach celebrity.

And **ABC Fine Wine and Spirits** (1531 Boynton Beach Boulevard, Boynton Beach; ☎ 561-732-0794) has a large range of alcohol, both wine and liquor. It boasts a wine cellar (actually a glassed-in area that's temperature and humidity controlled) and a wine vault, where customers may store their wines. It also offers imported cheeses and caviar and other gourmet goodies.

ATTRACTIONS

BECAUSE OF THE WIDE RANGE OF PALM BEACH County attractions, we've provided the following chart to help you prioritize your touring at a glance. Organized by category, in it you'll find the name, location, and author's rating (from one star to five stars). Some attractions, usually art galleries without permanent collections, weren't rated because exhibits change. Each attraction is individually profiled later in this section. Most museum-type attractions offer group rates for ten or more people.

SOME OF OUR PALM BEACH COUNTY FAVORITES

- Walking in Boca Raton's **Mizner Park,** because there are so many outdoor activities in this city block—among them an open-air cinema, an amphitheater with top concerts, and free music by the fountain. Speaking of Addison Mizner, some of his greatest Mediterranean architecture from the 1920s is in Palm Beach. Don't miss **Casa de Leoni** (450 Worth Avenue) and **Via Mizner** (337–339 Worth Avenue).

- The **Jupiter Inlet Lighthouse,** for the best view in Palm Beach County
- **Clematis by Night,** a Thursday-night West Palm Beach concert series by the fountain, including an international bazaar
- After sunset, from May till August, watch sea turtles crawl onto moonlit beaches above the high-tide line, dig holes with their flippers, and bury up to 120 eggs. At **John D. MacArthur Beach State Park,** rangers escort sea turtles on evening walks on the beach.
- The award-winning **South Florida Fair,** the county's largest and oldest outdoor event, in late January
- Delray Beach's **Atlantic Avenue,** a magnet for strollers who enjoy the Old Florida architecture, shops, galleries, and restaurants.
- The **Lake Trail,** a ten-mile stretch along Palm Beach dedicated to bicyclists, Rollerbladers, joggers, and walkers. It begins at the Society of Four Arts Museum on Royal Palm Way.

Palm Beach County Attractions

NAME	LOCATION	AUTHOR'S RATING
AMUSEMENT/WATER PARKS		
Boomers	Boca Raton	★★★
Rapids Water Park	West Palm Beach	★★
AQUARIUMS/NATURE EXHIBITS		
Gumbo Limbo Environmental Complex	Boca Raton	★★½
Lion Country Safari	Loxahatchee	★★★★½
Red Reef Park	Boca Raton	★★½
CHOCOLATE FACTORY		
Hoffman's Chocolate Shoppe and Gardens	Lake Worth	★★
CITRUS GROVES		
Blood's Hammock Groves	Delray Beach	★★½
Knollwood Groves	Boynton Beach	★★
Palm Beach Groves	Boynton Beach	★★½
COAST GUARD STATION TOUR		
Peanut Island Tour	Phil Foster State Park	★★★

NAME	LOCATION	AUTHOR'S RATING
CULTURAL CENTER		
Old School Square Cultural Arts Center	**Delray Beach**	★★½
GARDENS		
Mounts Botanical Garden	**West Palm Beach**	★★★
Pan's Garden	**Palm Beach**	★★★
GLIDER RIDE		
Barry Aviation Florida	**West Palm Beach**	★
INDUSTRIAL TOUR		
Florida Crystal Sugar and Rice Tours	**Boca Raton**	★★★
LIGHTHOUSE		
Jupiter Inlet Lighthouse	**Jupiter**	★★★
MUSEUMS		
Boca Raton Museum of Art	**Boca Raton**	★★
The Flagler Museum	**Palm Beach**	★★★
Morikami Museum and Japanese Gardens	**Delray Beach**	★★★★
Norton Museum of Art	**West Palm Beach**	★★★
South Florida Science Museum	**West Palm Beach**	★★★
PARKS AND REFUGES		
Arthur R. Marshall Loxahatchee National Wildlife Refuge	**Boynton Beach**	★★★
John D. MacArthur Beach State Park	**North Palm Beach**	★★★
Jonathan Dickinson State Park	**Jupiter**	★★★
Loxahatchee Everglades Tours	**Boca Raton**	★★★★
SPORTS VENUES		
Palm Beach Kennel Club	**West Palm Beach**	★★★
Palm Beach Polo	**Wellington**	★★★
Roger Dean Stadium	**Jupiter**	★★★
ZOO		
Palm Beach Zoo at Dreher Park	**West Palm Beach**	★★★

palm beach and west palm beach attractions

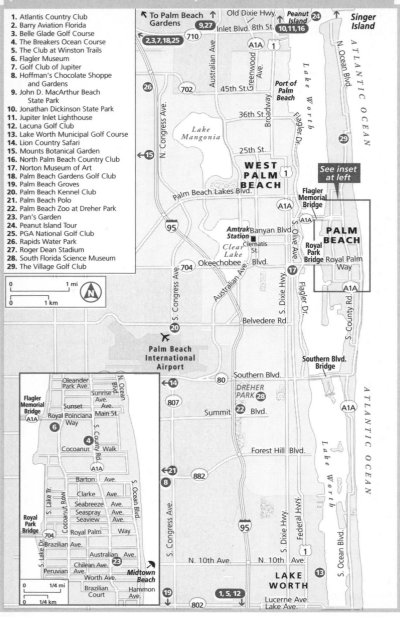

1. Atlantis Country Club
2. Barry Aviation Florida
3. Belle Glade Golf Course
4. The Breakers Ocean Course
5. The Club at Winston Trails
6. Flagler Museum
7. Golf Club of Jupiter
8. Hoffman's Chocolate Shoppe
   and Gardens
9. John D. MacArthur Beach
   State Park
10. Jonathan Dickinson State Park
11. Jupiter Inlet Lighthouse
12. Lacuna Golf Club
13. Lake Worth Municipal Golf Course
14. Lion Country Safari
15. Mounts Botanical Garden
16. North Palm Beach Country Club
17. Norton Museum of Art
18. Palm Beach Gardens Golf Club
19. Palm Beach Groves
20. Palm Beach Kennel Club
21. Palm Beach Polo
22. Palm Beach Zoo at Dreher Park
23. Pan's Garden
24. Peanut Island Tour
25. PGA National Golf Club
26. Rapids Water Park
27. Roger Dean Stadium
28. South Florida Science Museum
29. The Village Golf Club

boca raton and delray beach attractions

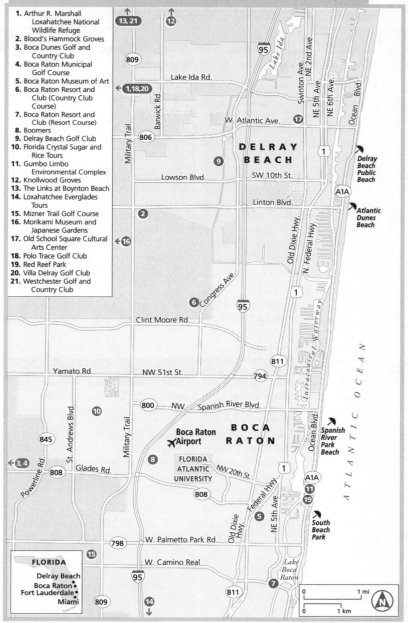

1. Arthur R. Marshall Loxahatchee National Wildlife Refuge
2. Blood's Hammock Groves
3. Boca Dunes Golf and Country Club
4. Boca Raton Municipal Golf Course
5. Boca Raton Museum of Art
6. Boca Raton Resort and Club (Country Club Course)
7. Boca Raton Resort and Club (Resort Course)
8. Boomers
9. Delray Beach Golf Club
10. Florida Crystal Sugar and Rice Tours
11. Gumbo Limbo Environmental Complex
12. Knollwood Groves
13. The Links at Boynton Beach
14. Loxahatchee Everglades Tours
15. Mizner Trail Golf Course
16. Morikami Museum and Japanese Gardens
17. Old School Square Cultural Arts Center
18. Polo Trace Golf Club
19. Red Reef Park
20. Villa Delray Golf Club
21. Westchester Golf and Country Club

ATTRACTION PROFILES

Arthur R. Marshall Loxahatchee National Wildlife Refuge

APPEAL BY AGE	PRESCHOOL ★	GRADE SCHOOL ★★★	TEENS ★★★
YOUNG ADULTS ★★★	OVER 30 ★★★		SENIORS ★★★★

10119 Lee Road, Boynton Beach 33437; ☎ **561-734-8303;**
loxahatchee.fws.gov

Type of attraction Everglades walking tours. **Admission** $5 per vehicle, $1 per pedestrian. **Hours** Refuge: daily, 6 a.m.–7 p.m.; Visitors Center: weekdays, 9 a.m.–4 p.m.; Saturday and Sunday, 9 a.m.–4:30 p.m.; closed Monday and Tuesday, May–October. **When to go** Anytime. **Author's rating** ★★★. **How much time to allow** 2–4 hours.

DESCRIPTION AND COMMENTS The park includes 221 square miles of wetlands and fits most visitors' concept of a real swamp. This is one of three water-retention areas outside the Everglades, designed to prevent flooding. Fascinating options include climbing a 20-foot observation tower, canoeing along an overgrown trail, fishing for bass or panfish, and walking the boardwalk or four other trails through the cypress marsh. You'll spot live alligators, cypress knees, and abundant bird life.

TOURING TIPS Summer is hot, and there's not as much to see; stick to the other seasons.

OTHER THINGS TO DO NEARBY A short drive to the Morikami Museum immerses visitors in a different culture entirely.

Barry Aviation Florida

APPEAL BY AGE	PRESCHOOL —	GRADE SCHOOL ★	TEENS ★★★
YOUNG ADULTS ★★★	OVER 30 ★★★		SENIORS ★★★★

11600 Aviation Boulevard, West Palm Beach 33412; ☎ **561-624-3000;**
www.barryaviation.com

Type of attraction Glider rides. **Admission** $75 for 20-minute flight; $160 for 40 minutes; $199 for 1 hour. **Hours** Wednesday–Sunday, 9 a.m.–4 p.m. **When to go** On clear days, when you can see the beach. Weekends are most crowded; weekdays permit more flexibility. **Special comments** Passengers must be age 10 or older, 14 to solo. Repeat customers include some over age 70. **Author's rating** ★. **How much time to allow** 1–2 hours.

DESCRIPTION AND COMMENTS Want to feel like a bird? Flights leave from North County General Aviation Airport and sometimes extend to the beach.

TOURING TIPS Appointments are necessary.

OTHER THINGS TO DO NEARBY Not a lot, since it's way out west toward the Everglades, but it's about a 15-minute drive to The Gardens mall.

Blood's Hammock Groves

APPEAL BY AGE	PRESCHOOL ★★	GRADE SCHOOL ★★★	TEENS ★★
YOUNG ADULTS ★★		OVER 30 ★★½	SENIORS ★★½

4600 Linton Boulevard, Delray Beach 33445; ☎ **561-498-3400;**
www.bloodsgroves.com

Type of attraction Citrus groves. **Admission** Free. **Hours** 8:30 a.m.–5 p.m. daily; closed end of June–November 1. **When to go** Anytime. **Author's rating** ★★½. **How much time to allow** 1 hour maximum.

DESCRIPTION AND COMMENTS Watch as citrus fruit is cleaned and prepared for shipping at this 50-year-old family-owned outfit. Sample and purchase fresh fruits and juices.

TOURING TIPS Surprisingly interesting if you've never seen a citrus plant. You'll never drink a glass of OJ in quite the same way.

OTHER THINGS TO DO NEARBY Morikami Museum

Boca Raton Museum of Art

APPEAL BY AGE	PRESCHOOL ★	GRADE SCHOOL ★★	TEENS ★★
YOUNG ADULTS ★★★		OVER 30 ★★	SENIORS ★★★

501 Plaza Real, Mizner Park, Boca Raton 33432; ☎ **561-392-2500;**
www.bocamuseum.org

Type of attraction Art museum. **Admission** Adults, $8; seniors, $6; students, $4; children under age 12, free (prices increase for special exhibits). **Hours** Tuesday, Thursday, and Friday, 10 a.m.–5 p.m.; Wednesday and Saturday, 10 a.m.–9 p.m.; Sunday, noon–5 p.m. **When to go** Anytime. **Author's rating** ★★. **How much time to allow** 1–1½ hours.

DESCRIPTION AND COMMENTS The museum, in a striking building at Mizner Park, showcases items representing well-known artists such as Degas, Klee, Modigliani, Matisse, and Picasso, plus other 19th- and 20th-century modern masters. Traveling exhibits included a 100-piece Picasso show, aboriginal art from Australia's Western Desert, and a juried Florida-artists show. On the second floor, a permanent collection includes pre-Columbian and African works. Children will enjoy the interactive gallery.

TOURING TIPS The museum stages cultural events, such as music by the Boca Pops (a local orchestra) or a jazz quartet in the sculpture garden one Sunday each month.

OTHER THINGS TO DO NEARBY Window shopping at Mizner Park

Boomers

APPEAL BY AGE	PRESCHOOL ★★★	GRADE SCHOOL ★★★★	TEENS ★★★½
YOUNG ADULTS ★★		OVER 30 ★★	SENIORS ★★

3100 Airport Road, Boca Raton 33431; ☎ **561-347-1888;**
www.boomersparks.com/parks/bocaraton

Type of attraction Amusement park. **Admission** $10 on Tuesday and Thursday; all other days, pay as you go. **Hours** Daily, noon–10 p.m.; summer hours, 10 a.m.–midnight; Sunday, 10 a.m.–10 p.m. **When to go** Anytime. **Author's rating** ★★★. **How much time to allow** 2–4 hours.

DESCRIPTION AND COMMENTS This fun park provides hours of activities for families and area grandparents entertaining visiting grandchildren. Activities include bumper boats, a race track, and two 18-hole miniature golf courses.

TOURING TIPS Adults accompanying children must pay admission. Check out "Ten-buck Tuesdays."

OTHER THINGS TO DO NEARBY Muvico Theater

The Flagler Museum

APPEAL BY AGE	PRESCHOOL ★	GRADE SCHOOL ★★	TEENS ★★
YOUNG ADULTS ★★★	OVER 30 ★★★		SENIORS ★★★½

1 Whitehall Way, Palm Beach 33480; ☎ **561-655-2833; www.flagler.org**

Type of attraction Millionaire's winter mansion with priceless furnishings and collections. **Admission** Adults, $10; children ages 6–12, $3; children under age 6, free. **Hours** Tuesday–Saturday, 10 a.m.–5 p.m.; Sunday, noon–5 p.m. **When to go** Anytime. **Author's rating** ★★★. **How much time to allow** 1–2 hours.

DESCRIPTION AND COMMENTS Here's a peek at how the wealthiest Palm Beachite once wintered. Henry Morrison Flagler, a founding partner with John D. Rockefeller of Standard Oil, built several of Florida's earliest grand hotels (including the Palm Beach Inn, later known as The Breakers). His Florida East Coast Railway opened the state for development as far as Key West. Flagler built this extraordinary 55-room mansion, Whitehall, in 1902—in the Beaux Arts style—as a wedding gift for his third wife. The *New York Herald* then called it "grander and more magnificent than any other private dwelling in the world."

The building opened as the Whitehall Hotel in 1925; it was reopened as a museum in 1960. Air-conditioning now prevents further deterioration of woodwork and furnishings from humidity. Most visitors take the 45-minute guided tour, which reveals the country's largest Gilded Age marble room, silk-covered walls, period furnishings, a 1,200-pipe organ, Baccarat crystal chandeliers, and frescoed ceilings. Photographs and mementos, opulent architecture, and art objects add up to a meaningful South Florida experience.

TOURING TIPS Indulge in the elegant Gilded Age Tea held noon–3 p.m., when finger sandwiches (such as watercress and goat cheese) and pastries (including scones) are served on silver platters—within sight of the Intracoastal Waterway. Cost is $10 per person. Visitors may also step inside Flagler's private 1886 railcar, in which he traveled to Key West.

OTHER THINGS TO DO NEARBY Norton Museum of Art, Kravis Center, and Worth Avenue

Florida Crystal Sugar and Rice Tours

APPEAL BY AGE	PRESCHOOL ★	GRADE SCHOOL ★★★	TEENS ★★★
YOUNG ADULTS ★★½		OVER 30 ★★½	SENIORS ★★★

NW 24th Way, Boca Raton 33431; ☎ 954-971-5657

Type of attraction Industrial tours. **Admission** Adults, $17; children ages 7–18, $14; children under age 7 not permitted. **Hours** Call to schedule. **When to go** Tours are given four times a week in season, twice a week in summer. **Author's rating** ★★½. **How much time to allow** 2 hours.

DESCRIPTION AND COMMENTS Sugar cane has been an important Florida crop for centuries, and this one-hour tour of the Sem-chi rice mill and packaging plant and half-hour tour of the Okeelanta sugar-packaging plant give you a real understanding of the process. Visitors learn how sugar cane is pressed and the juice evaporated to make organic sugar; rice is grown here as a rotation crop and milled on-premises.

TOURING TIPS Open for tours since 1996, the El Joy Tours firm specializes in group tours but accepts individuals.

OTHER THINGS TO DO NEARBY Lion Country Safari

Gumbo Limbo Environmental Complex

APPEAL BY AGE	PRESCHOOL ★	GRADE SCHOOL ★★	TEENS ★★
YOUNG ADULTS ★★		OVER 30 ★★½	SENIORS ★★½

1801 North Ocean Boulevard, Boca Raton 33432; ☎ 561-338-1473; www.gumbolimbo.org

Type of attraction Saltwater aquariums and nature exhibits. **Admission** Free. **Hours** Monday–Saturday, 9 a.m.–4 p.m.; Sunday, noon–4 p.m. **When to go** Anytime. **Author's rating** ★★½. **How much time to allow** 1–2 hours.

DESCRIPTION AND COMMENTS Four indoor saltwater tanks hold turtles, sharks, stingrays, and more. Some displays feature baby sea turtles. There are also two outdoor boardwalk trails and a 50-foot tower to observe the watery scene.

TOURING TIPS Make reservations to join an organized turtle watch or walk. From May until August, female sea turtles lay and bury their eggs. The mother turtle returns to the ocean, leaving the hatchlings to fend for themselves. About two months later, the baby turtles hatch, dig their way out of the nest, and begin their journey to the ocean.

OTHER THINGS TO DO NEARBY Spend time at the beach.

kids Hoffman's Chocolate Shoppe and Gardens

APPEAL BY AGE	PRESCHOOL ★★	GRADE SCHOOL ★★★	TEENS ★★
YOUNG ADULTS ★★		OVER 30 ★★	SENIORS ★★★

5190 Lake Worth Road, Lake Worth 33463; ☎ 561-967-2213 and 888-281-8800; www.hoffmans.com

Type of attraction Chocolate factory and gift shop. **Admission** Free. **Hours** Weekdays, 9 a.m.–4:30 p.m. **When to go** Busiest times are around Christmas and Easter, so avoid them if you don't want to compete with lots of onlookers. **Author's rating** ★★. **How much time to allow** 1–2 hours.

DESCRIPTION AND COMMENTS Visitors watch through a window as chocolate goodies are made by hand. At Christmastime, a large outdoor display of lights, trains, and other exhibits excites little ones. The retail store offers outstanding chocolates and gift baskets.

TOURING TIPS Don't come into this establishment if you're on a diet!

OTHER THINGS TO DO NEARBY Enjoy your chocolate!

 John D. MacArthur Beach State Park

APPEAL BY AGE	PRESCHOOL ★★	GRADE SCHOOL ★★★★	TEENS ★★★
YOUNG ADULTS ★★★★		OVER 30 ★★★	SENIORS ★★★

10900 FL 703 (A1A), North Palm Beach 33408; ☎ 561-624-6950; www.macarthurbeach.org

Type of attraction Natural-habitat park and beach. **Admission** $4 per vehicle with up to 8 passengers; additional passengers $1 each; admission includes guided tours; visitors may come and go during the same day. **Hours** 8 a.m.–sundown daily. **When to go** When it's cooler, fewer bugs hang around. **Author's rating** ★★★. **How much time to allow** Half day to all day.

DESCRIPTION AND COMMENTS The park covers 225 acres of uplands and 535 acres under water, including marine hammocks and mangroves. Boardwalks allow exploration of almost two miles of subtropical coastal habitat. The park also offers good access to the beach. Picnic tables and grills are available. Three types of turtles nest here in June and July.

TOURING TIPS Visitors may use their own canoes (no motorboats). They may also bring snorkeling equipment for observing the reef; dive flags are available for rental. Kayaks and bicycles may be rented. Volunteer-led walks along Lake Worth take place weekdays at 10 a.m. and some weekends at 10 a.m. and 1 p.m.; call for a schedule. A nature center provides further information.

OTHER THINGS TO DO NEARBY Sightseeing boat rides at Phil Foster State Park

Jonathan Dickinson State Park

APPEAL BY AGE	PRESCHOOL ★★	GRADE SCHOOL ★★	TEENS ★★
YOUNG ADULTS ★★★		OVER 30 ★★★	SENIORS ★★★

US 1, Jupiter 33455; ☎ 561-546-2771 (phone is extremely busy in season); for river-tour and cabin-rental information, call ☎ 561-746-1466; www.floridastateparks.org/jonathandickinson

Type of attraction Marine and mangrove habitat and campgrounds. **Admission** $4 per car (maximum 8 people), $1 per person on bicycle, bus, or foot. River tour fare (☎ 561-746-1466), adults, $12; children ages 6–12, $7; children under age

6, free. Canoe rentals: $10 for 2 hours; $4 each additional hour. **Hours** Park open daily 8 a.m.–dusk. River tours depart daily at 9 a.m., 11 a.m., 1 p.m., and 3 p.m. Canoe rentals available 9 a.m.–3:30 p.m. Trapper Nelson's Interpretive Site closed Monday and Tuesday. **When to go** Anytime. **Special comments** Call ahead, because sometimes the tidal river is too shallow for transport boats to reach the station. Campgrounds are booked up to 11 months in advance. **Author's rating** ★★½. **How much time to allow** 2 hours—all day.

DESCRIPTION AND COMMENTS The park covers 12,000 acres, including the Loxahatchee River. Bald eagles, scrub jays, and sandhill cranes are among the birds thriving amid the park's native plant life, including red mangroves, sabal palms, and gumbo limbo trees. Several walking trails include 18 miles of the Florida Trail.

Guided tours depart to Trapper Nelson's station, started in 1936 on the Loxahatchee River, accessible only by 40-passenger pontoon boat (no reservations taken). Nelson made scads of money trapping beavers and other animals and bought land encompassing the park's present territory with more than $1 million remaining to leave to his heirs. Visitors may join a ranger-led tour and walk through the log- and tin-roofed original buildings.

TOURING TIPS You can roam on your own or take ranger-led trips. During rainy periods, the three types of mosquitoes here can make visitors' lives miserable, especially at sunrise and sunset and in shady areas like hammocks. Though they're not as bad as in the Everglades, come prepared with insect repellent.

OTHER THINGS TO DO NEARBY Jupiter Inlet Lighthouse and the beach

Jupiter Inlet Lighthouse

APPEAL BY AGE	PRESCHOOL ★	GRADE SCHOOL ★★	TEENS ★★
YOUNG ADULTS ★★	OVER 30 ★★★		SENIORS ★★★

805 North US 1, Jupiter 33477; ☎ 561-747-8380; www.lrhs.org

Type of attraction Lighthouse-museum. **Admission** $6 per person; children under age 6, free **Hours** Sunday–Wednesday, 10 a.m.–4 p.m.; closed Thursday and Friday. Lighthouse tours are conducted every 20 minutes. **When to go** Weekdays host a lot of school classes and camp groups, so families and seniors are better off going on weekends. **Author's rating** ★★½. **How much time to allow** 1–2 hours.

DESCRIPTION AND COMMENTS Visit this museum in the Oil House, the county's oldest standing structure (completed in 1860), to view artifacts such as musket balls and old photos of ships and lighthouse keepers. For excellent views, you can also climb inside the restored 105-foot-tall red-brick lighthouse, built by Civil War general George Meade.

TOURING TIPS To ascend the lighthouse, visitors must be at least four feet tall and in good health; they must also wear closed-back shoes.

OTHER THINGS TO DO NEARBY Jonathan Dickinson State Park

Lion Country Safari

| APPEAL BY AGE | PRESCHOOL ★★½ | GRADE SCHOOL ★★★★ | TEENS ★★½ |
| YOUNG ADULTS ★★ | | OVER 30 ★★ | SENIORS ★★½ |

2003 Lion Country Safari Road, Loxahatchee 33470 (18 miles west of I-95 on Southern Boulevard); ☎ 561-793-1084; www.lioncountrysafari.com

Type of attraction Drive-through African "safari." **Admission** Ages 10 and up, $19.95; children ages 3–9, $15.95; seniors 65 or older, $17.95; children under age 2, free. **Hours** Daily, 9:30 a.m.–5:30 p.m.; last car admitted at 4:30 p.m. **When to go** Anytime except following lunch (when the animals have just been fed; often they're napping or lethargic). **Special comments** No pets or convertibles allowed; guests may rent appropriate vehicles if theirs don't qualify. **Author's rating ★★. How much time to allow** 1 hour for drive-through safari only, but many families stay 3 hours.

DESCRIPTION AND COMMENTS More than 1,300 animals—including chimpanzees and zebras—roam this cageless 500-acre drive-through zoo. It has wowed guests since 1967. Kids of all ages are thrilled as hippopotamuses walk past their car, or a group of elephants surround a baby for protection when a feeding truck arrives. Kiddie rides, paddleboats, a stroller-accessible walk-through section for smaller animals, and miniature golf add further appeal; there's even a real, live elephant ride.

Guests remain in their cars and slowly drive through seven habitats—such as Serengeti Plain and Lake Nakuru—of elephants, lions, ostriches, and other major animals.

TOURING TIPS Both a restaurant and picnic areas provide for lunches.

OTHER THINGS TO DO NEARBY Florida Crystal Sugar and Rice Tours

Loxahatchee Everglades Tours

| APPEAL BY AGE | PRESCHOOL ★ | GRADE SCHOOL ★★½ | TEENS ★★★ |
| YOUNG ADULTS ★★★ | | OVER 30 ★★★★ | SENIORS ★★★★½ |

15490 Loxahatchee Road, Boca Raton 33076; ☎ 561-482-8026 and 800-683-5873; www.evergladesairboattours.com

Type of attraction Airboat rides in the Everglades. **Admission** Adults, $30; children ages 6–12, $15; children ages 5 and under, free. **Hours** Daily, 9:30 a.m.–4 p.m.; first tour begins at 10 a.m.; closed Thanksgiving, Christmas, and New Year's Day. **When to go** Anytime. **Author's rating ★★★★. How much time to allow** 1 hour; tour is 6–8 miles long.

DESCRIPTION AND COMMENTS The Everglades is a unique attraction worldwide, but it's not choreographed by Disney, so viewings can't be guaranteed. Participants may see alligators swimming, nests of alligator babies, American bald eagles, and unusual tropical birds. They'll also learn about sawgrass, pickerel weed, and marsh flowers.

TOURING TIPS Those with hearing problems and very young children might find the engine noise overpowering, even though participants are given earplugs.

OTHER THINGS TO DO NEARBY The Coconut Cove Water Park with fun for all ages is located within South County Regional Park (11200 Park Access Road, Boca Raton; ☎ 561-274-1140). It's three and a half miles west of the Florida Turnpike's Glades Road exit.

Morikami Museum and Japanese Gardens

APPEAL BY AGE	PRESCHOOL ★	GRADE SCHOOL ★★★	TEENS ★★
YOUNG ADULTS ★★½	OVER 30 ★★★★		SENIORS ★★★★

4000 Morikami Park Road, Delray Beach (off Jog Road south of Linton Boulevard) 33446; ☎ 561-495-0233; www.morikami.org

Type of attraction Japanese culture and history, particularly as related to Palm Beach County. Admission Adults, $9; seniors over age 65, $8; children ages 6–18 and college students, $6; children under age 6, free. Hours Tuesday–Sunday, 10 a.m.–5 p.m. When to go Anytime, for serene places to ponder life. Author's rating ★★★★. How much time to allow 2–4 hours.

DESCRIPTION AND COMMENTS This 200-acre park, honoring an early Japanese settlement of farmers here, lures visitors with six stunning and tranquil gardens nearly a mile in length. There are nature trails, ponds, waterfalls, and a bonsai garden. The two museum buildings feature changing and permanent exhibitions, a 225-seat theater, a library, Japanese tea ceremonies, and a cafe.

TOURING TIPS Special events are scheduled, such as the annual Hatsume Fair in February celebrating spring with bonsai exhibits, drum performances, and flower arranging; the Bon Festival in August honors ancestors. The Children's Day Celebration (*Kodomo no hi*) in April provides fun for youngsters within a Japanese cultural context, including sessions in making origami and opportunities to participate onstage in Japanese folk stories.

OTHER THINGS TO DO NEARBY Check out the oranges and grapefruit at Blood's Hammock Groves or opt for additional natural flora and fauna at Arthur R. Marshall Loxahatchee National Wildlife Refuge. Also near Morikami is the American Orchid Society.

Mounts Botanical Garden

APPEAL BY AGE	PRESCHOOL ★	GRADE SCHOOL ★★★	TEENS ★★
YOUNG ADULTS ★★	OVER 30 ★★★		SENIORS ★★★★

531 North Military Trail, West Palm Beach 33415; ☎ 561-233-1749; www.mounts.org

Type of attraction Gardens for learning and relaxation. Admission Free (except during special events). Hours Monday–Saturday, 8:30 a.m.–4:30 p.m.; Sunday and holidays, 1–5 p.m. When to go Anytime, but tours are conducted Saturday at 11 a.m. and Sunday at 2:30 p.m. Author's rating ★★½. How much time to allow 1–3 hours.

DESCRIPTION AND COMMENTS Begun as part of the Palm Beach County Cooperative Extension Service in 1954, plantings in these 14 acres have been continuously enhanced. Some exotic plants and trees are huge, such as the kapok and rainbow eucalyptus.

Several gardens, such as the aromatic herb garden and citrus area, teach visitors about different types of plants (unfortunately, many of the identification signs are broken or missing).

TOURING TIPS Picnic tables and lakeside contemplation spots are available. The rain forest and butterfly gardens are special.

OTHER THINGS TO DO NEARBY If you're up for seeing animals after the flowers, stop at the Palm Beach Zoo at Dreher Park. The South Florida Science Museum is another option.

Norton Museum of Art

APPEAL BY AGE	PRESCHOOL ★	GRADE SCHOOL ★★	TEENS ★★
YOUNG ADULTS ★★★	OVER 30 ★★★		SENIORS ★★★½

1451 South Olive Avenue, West Palm Beach 33401; ☎ 561-832-5196; www.norton.org

Type of attraction Art museum. **Admission** Adults, $8; children ages 13–21, $3; children under age 12, free. Traveling exhibits may raise the ante considerably. **Hours** Tuesday–Saturday, 10 a.m.–5 p.m.; Sunday, 1 p.m–5 p.m. **When to go** Anytime. **Author's rating** ★★★. **How much time to allow** 2–4 hours.

DESCRIPTION AND COMMENTS This ever-expanding art museum boasts a permanent but small collection of gems, including works by Monet, Gauguin, Picasso, Cézanne, Bellows, O'Keeffe (whose sister lived in Palm Beach), Hopper, Shahn, and Pollock. Chinese, pre-Columbian, and Southwest sections add additional interest. A children's learning center helps develop budding talent. National traveling exhibitions, like "The Triumph of French Painting," expand the permanent collections. The outdoor covered loggia and library are fine for contemplation, but the most beautiful building element is the intricate colored-glass ceiling by famed artist Dale Chihuly.

TOURING TIPS Rent an audiotape for professional explanations of the artwork. Free guided tours are given daily at 2 p.m. The museum store offers great gift items, including many geared to kids; free children's programs (with paid general admission) lure families on Sunday and sometimes other days.

OTHER THINGS TO DO NEARBY Flagler Museum

Old School Square Cultural Arts Center

APPEAL BY AGE	PRESCHOOL ★	GRADE SCHOOL ★★	TEENS ★★
YOUNG ADULTS ★★	OVER 30 ★★★		SENIORS ★★★

51 North Swinton Avenue, Delray Beach 33444; ☎ 561-243-7922; www.oldschool.org

Type of attraction Cultural center. **Admission** Adults, $3; children ages 6–14, $2; seniors, $4; children under age 6, free. **Hours** Cornell Museum: Tuesday–Saturday, 11 a.m.–4 p.m.; Sunday, 1–4 p.m. **When to go** Anytime. **Author's rating** ★★½. **How much time to allow** 1–3 hours

DESCRIPTION AND COMMENTS The Cornell Museum offers exhibits in all media, such as paintings, sculpture, and photography. Traveling theatrical groups perform in the Crest Theatre.

TOURING TIPS Keep youngsters occupied by enrolling them in some of the courses; interactive programs appeal to little ones, while Saturday art classes are conducted for teens.

OTHER THINGS TO DO NEARBY Stroll along Delray's Atlantic Avenue, popping into art galleries or enjoying a cool drink at an outdoor cafe. Check out the lobby of the Colony Hotel, built in 1926. Delray has become hot, hot, hot!

Palm Beach Groves

| APPEAL BY AGE | PRESCHOOL ★★½ | GRADE SCHOOL ★★½ | TEENS ★★ |
| YOUNG ADULTS ★★ | OVER 30 ★★★ | | SENIORS ★★★ |

7149 Lawrence Road, Boynton Beach 33436; ☎ 561-965-6699; www.pbgroves.com

Type of attraction Citrus groves. Admission Free. Hours Daily, 8:30 a.m.–5:30 p.m.; closed Christmas and Thanksgiving. When to go Anytime. Author's rating ★★½. How much time to allow 1–1.5 hours.

DESCRIPTION AND COMMENTS Take the free 20-minute tram ride through the citrus groves November–April, then watch the fruits being processed. There's also a 5–10-minute walk on a nature trail.

TOURING TIPS Check out the 50-year-old sausage tree and the strolling peacocks. Bring a picnic lunch to enjoy the grounds.

OTHER THINGS TO DO NEARBY Take a break to cool off at Boynton Beach Mall.

Palm Beach Kennel Club

| APPEAL BY AGE | PRESCHOOL ★★ | GRADE SCHOOL ★★ | TEENS ★★ |
| YOUNG ADULTS ★★★ | OVER 30 ★★★ | | SENIORS ★★★½ |

1111 North Congress Avenue, West Palm Beach 33409; ☎ 561-683-2222; www.pbkennelclub.com

Type of attraction Greyhound racing Admission 50 ¢ for first-floor general admission; $1 for second-floor general admission; kids free with adults. Hours Monday, Wednesday, Friday, and Saturday, post times are 12:40 p.m. and 7:30 p.m.; Sunday, 1 p.m. When to go Anytime. Author's rating ★★★. How much time to allow 3–4 hours.

DESCRIPTION AND COMMENTS This kennel is expressly for greyhound racing, and the dogs' needs are attended to by veterinarians. Guests may dine in the second-floor Paddock Restaurant while watching races or choose a more casual meal on the Terrace. A poker room and simulcast wagering also draw gamers.

TOURING TIPS Dining in the Paddock Room requires reservations; no shorts or jeans are permitted, and men must wear collared shirts.

OTHER THINGS TO DO NEARBY It's about a 20-minute drive to the Palm Beach Zoo at Dreher Park and the South Florida Science Museum.

kids Palm Beach Zoo at Dreher Park

APPEAL BY AGE	PRESCHOOL ★★★	GRADE SCHOOL ★★★½	TEENS ★★½
YOUNG ADULTS ★★½		OVER 30 ★★½	SENIORS ★★★

1301 Summit Boulevard, West Palm Beach 33405; ☎ 561-547-WILD or 561-533-0887; www.palmbeachzoo.org

Type of attraction Zoo. **Admission** Adults, $10.95; seniors, $7.95; children ages 3–12, $6.95; children under age 3, free. **Hours** Daily, 9 a.m.–5 p.m.; closed Thanksgiving and Christmas. **When to go** Anytime. **Author's rating** ★★★. **How much time to allow** 2–4 hours.

DESCRIPTION AND COMMENTS Although it's small by zoo standards—23 acres—the park keeps youngsters amused and learning for hours. More than 400 animals of 125 species live here, including locals such as the Florida panther. The petting zoo, otter exhibit, rain forest with Mayan ruins, aviary, and reptile exhibit are big hits. Tropical birds, kangaroos, and tigers have their audiences, but all kids love the prairie dogs.

TOURING TIPS Despite the lush plantings, it can get steamy; plan to bring or buy lots of liquids. Wheelchairs and strollers have easy access on the paved walks; strollers may also be rented.

OTHER THINGS TO DO NEARBY Visit the South Florida Science Museum.

Pan's Garden

APPEAL BY AGE	PRESCHOOL ★	GRADE SCHOOL ★★	TEENS ★
YOUNG ADULTS ★★		OVER 30 ★★	SENIORS ★★

386 Hibiscus Avenue, Palm Beach; ☎ 561-832-0731

Type of attraction Vest-pocket garden off busy Worth Avenue. **Admission** Free. **Hours** Daily, 9 a.m.–5 p.m.; May 15–November 15, open Monday–Friday, 10 a.m.–2 p.m. **When to go** Anytime. **Author's rating** ★★½. **How much time to allow** 15 minutes–1 hour.

DESCRIPTION AND COMMENTS This serene, lush garden and pond offer benches for resting weary feet and studying the flowers and birds. Note the whimsical sculptures.

TOURING TIPS Photography is allowed.

OTHER THINGS TO DO NEARBY Shop or window shop on Worth Avenue.

Peanut Island Tour

APPEAL BY AGE	PRESCHOOL ★★	GRADE SCHOOL ★★	TEENS ★★
YOUNG ADULTS ★★★		OVER 30 ★★★½	SENIORS ★★★

55 Blue Heron Boulevard at Phil Foster State Park for water taxi to island; ☎ 561-845-4445; for water taxi, 561-683-TAXI; www.pbmm.org

Type of attraction 45-minute tour of former Coast Guard station and site of bomb shelter during President Kennedy's term. **Admission** Water-taxi sightseeing ride and tour of island: adults, $17; seniors over age 60, $14; children ages 5–17, $13.

Island tour only (many reach the island via private boats): adults, $7; seniors, $6; students age 5–17, $5; children under age 5, free. **Hours** Water taxis leave the park every hour on the hour for the 15-minute ride and leave Peanut Island every hour on the half hour. However, if enough passengers gather, they make extra runs. **When to go** Mornings are cooler on the island, although there's often a breeze. **Author's rating** ★★★. **How much time to allow** 2 hours–all day.

DESCRIPTION AND COMMENTS The most fascinating part of a visit here is the bomb shelter, built in 1961 for President John F. Kennedy's safety in case of enemy attack. The man-made island was named for the 1917 peanut-oil storage facility here, but hurricanes and the 1929 stock market crash destroyed that.

TOURING TIPS Families often come to spend the day, but nostalgia seekers and history buffs come just for the sights. For disabled visitors, call ahead and transportation will be provided on the ferry boat rather than by water taxi.

OTHER THINGS TO DO NEARBY Many people picnic and spend time at the island's beach. Wooden walks and restrooms are available.

kids Rapids Water Park

APPEAL BY AGE	PRESCHOOL ★★	GRADE SCHOOL ★★★	TEENS ★★★
YOUNG ADULTS ★★		OVER 30 ★★	SENIORS ★★

6566 North Military Trail, West Palm Beach 33407; ☎ 561-842-8756; www.rapidswaterpark.com

Type of attraction Water theme park. **Admission** $28; children under age 2, free. **Hours** Park opens at 10 a.m. and closes at sunset, which varies from 5–8 p.m. Open daily March 17–April 22 and May 19–Labor Day; weekends only April 23–May 18. Parking is $5. **When to go** Weekdays are least crowded. **Author's rating** ★★. **How much time to allow** 4–5 hours.

DESCRIPTION AND COMMENTS All sorts of water-related amusements on 22 acres, including water slides, a wave pool, and rubber-tube flumes.

TOURING TIPS Participants must wear bathing suits—cutoff jeans not permitted—but cannot wear water shoes on the rides (must go barefoot).

OTHER THINGS TO DO NEARBY It's a ten-minute drive from Palm Beach Gardens Mall or CityPlace.

Red Reef Park

APPEAL BY AGE	PRESCHOOL ★★	GRADE SCHOOL ★★★	TEENS ★★
YOUNG ADULTS ★★		OVER 30 ★★	SENIORS ★★★

1400 Ocean Boulevard, Boca Raton 33432; ☎ 561-393-7974; www.ci.boca-raton.fl.us/parks/redreef.cfm

Type of attraction Marine-life park **Admission** Weekdays, $16 per vehicle; weekends and holidays, $18 per vehicle. **Hours** Daily, 8 a.m.–10 p.m. **When to go** The nature center is open Monday–Saturday, 9 a.m.–4 p.m.; and Sunday, noon–4 p.m. **Author's rating** ★★½. **How much time to allow** 2 hours–all day.

DESCRIPTION AND COMMENTS At this 39.7-acre City of Boca Raton park, visitors may look for sea turtles, ospreys, pelicans, and manatees in their natural habitat or snorkel around the rocks. The park extends from the Intracoastal Waterway to the Atlantic Ocean.

TOURING TIPS Besides school groups, many European tourists come here—but American travelers don't seem to know about it. Picnic area available. Lifeguards on duty.

OTHER THINGS TO DO NEARBY Stop at the free 15-acre Gumbo Limbo Nature Center across the street (☎ 561-338-1473) to see live snakes, fish, and turtles; there's a beehive with live bees behind glass. If you just want to relax, bring a picnic lunch or play at the beach.

Roger Dean Stadium

APPEAL BY AGE	PRESCHOOL ★	GRADE SCHOOL ★★	TEENS ★★★
YOUNG ADULTS ★★★	OVER 30 ★★★		SENIORS ★★★½

4751 Main Street, Jupiter 33458; ☎ 561-775-1818; www.rogerdeanstadium.com

Type of attraction Baseball spring-training stadium. Admission $7–$20 a ticket; call Ticketmaster at ☎ 561-966-3309 or visit **www.ticketmaster.com.** Hours Monday–Friday, 8:30 a.m.–6 p.m. When to go March for spring training, April–September for Jupiter Hammerheads games. Author's rating ★★★. How much time to allow 5–6 hours.

DESCRIPTION AND COMMENTS This stadium is spring-training home of the Montreal Expos, St. Louis Cardinals, and Florida State League Jupiter Hammerheads (AA team of the Montreal Expos). There are plans to inaugurate baseball fantasy camps in the future. The Tommy Hutton Baseball Academy started in June 2001.

TOURING TIPS The area is experiencing tremendous growth; a large shopping mall provides further entertainment.

OTHER THINGS TO DO NEARBY Plan to spend a few hours at Jonathan Dickinson State Park.

South Florida Science Museum

APPEAL BY AGE	PRESCHOOL ★★	GRADE SCHOOL ★★★	TEENS ★★★
YOUNG ADULTS ★★	OVER 30 ★★		SENIORS ★★

4801 Dreher Trail North, West Palm Beach 33405; ☎ 561-832-1988; www.sfsm.org

Type of attraction Hands-on science museum. Admission Adults, $7; children, $5. Daily planetarium shows (1 p.m. and 2 p.m.) cost $2 additional; daily laser shows (3 p.m. and 4 p.m.) cost $4 additional. Hours Monday–Friday, 10 a.m.–5 p.m.; in June, July, and August, Monday–Saturday, 10 a.m.–9 p.m.; Sunday, noon–6 p.m. When to go Anytime Author's rating ★★½. How much time to allow 1–4 hours.

DESCRIPTION AND COMMENTS Although it's a small museum, imaginative exhibits on light, energy, the environment, and the space program keep youngsters occupied for hours. A planetarium, aquarium, and laser shows with music by Led Zeppelin and Pink Floyd turn kids on. Hands-on experiences include brain teasers and a live frog exhibit; there's also an outdoor science trail. You'll find family-oriented activities for all ages.

TOURING TIPS Call for directions; it's hard to find the entrance otherwise.

OTHER THINGS TO DO NEARBY Palm Beach Zoo at Dreher Park

DINING *and* RESTAURANTS

EVER SINCE HARRY FLAGLER FIRST LAID TRACKS in Palm Beach County, well-off snowbirds, tristate transplants, internationals, and retirees have demanded of South Florida the good taste to which they have grown accustomed. Increasingly, more local chefs are graduates of culinary schools, including Johnson & Wales University in North Miami and the Florida Culinary Institute in West Palm Beach.

The best ingredients, preparations, and service are obviously labor intensive and therefore costly to produce. The result is that Boca Raton and Palm Beach have the highest concentrations of high-quality dining and decor: marble bathrooms, designer light fixtures, and fusion menus have become de rigueur in these areas; it's harder to find a truly bad dining experience than it is to find a fairly good one. Bad service or the rudeness of competitive fellow diners, not bad food, are more often than not the cause of any dining woes—especially during "the season" (November to March). Whenever possible, make reservations, and be advised that many busy South Florida restaurants won't seat you until your entire party is present. Also, give yourself extra time to find a parking space or bring cash for the valet (almost all highly trafficked restaurants have them). Be aware that smoking was recently banned for all Florida restaurants.

ABOUT THESE CHOICES

ALTHOUGH PALM BEACH IS A BASTION OF fine dining, our selections reflect the full range of dining options open to vacationers, including low-profile local haunts and family-friendly establishments. We have chosen restaurants that, while we can't guarantee their staying power, have proven to operate successfully for some time and have a following among local professionals, residents, and tourists.

Detailed profiles of each restaurant follow in alphabetical order. For more about South Florida dining and an overview of our restaurant-profile format, including abbreviations and ratings, see page 208 in the Miami-Dade County dining section. *Bon appétit!*

palm beach and west palm beach dining and nightlife

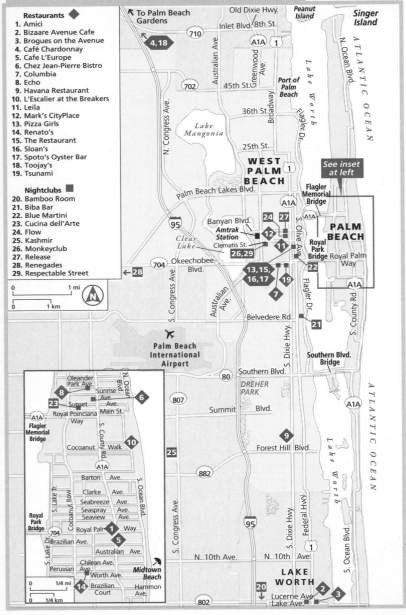

Restaurants ◆
1. Amici
2. Bizaare Avenue Cafe
3. Brogues on the Avenue
4. Café Chardonnay
5. Cafe L'Europe
6. Chez Jean-Pierre Bistro
7. Columbia
8. Echo
9. Havana Restaurant
10. L'Escalier at the Breakers
11. Leila
12. Mark's CityPlace
13. Pizza Girls
14. Renato's
15. The Restaurant
16. Sloan's
17. Spoto's Oyster Bar
18. Toojay's
19. Tsunami

Nightclubs ■
20. Bamboo Room
21. Biba Bar
22. Blue Martini
23. Cucina dell'Arte
24. Flow
25. Kashmir
26. Monkeyclub
27. Release
28. Renegades
29. Respectable Street

boca raton and delray beach dining and nightlife

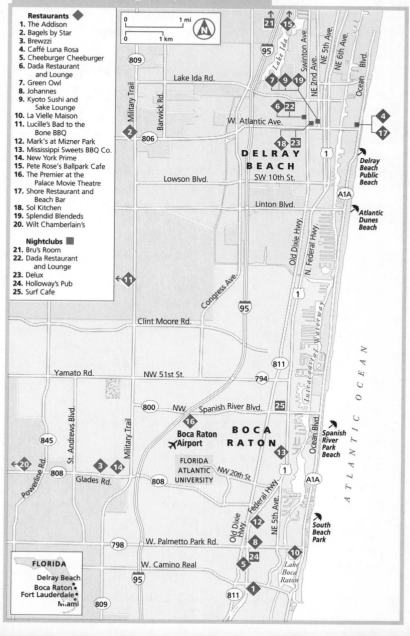

Restaurants
1. The Addison
2. Bagels by Star
3. Brewzzi
4. Caffé Luna Rosa
5. Cheeburger Cheeburger
6. Dada Restaurant
   and Lounge
7. Green Owl
8. Johannes
9. Kyoto Sushi and
   Sake Lounge
10. La Vieille Maison
11. Lucille's Bad to the
    Bone BBQ
12. Mark's at Mizner Park
13. Mississippi Sweets BBQ Co.
14. New York Prime
15. Pete Rose's Ballpark Cafe
16. The Premier at the
    Palace Movie Theatre
17. Shore Restaurant and
    Beach Bar
18. Sol Kitchen
19. Splendid Blendeds
20. Wilt Chamberlain's

Nightclubs
21. Bru's Room
22. Dada Restaurant
    and Lounge
23. Delux
24. Holloway's Pub
25. Surf Cafe

The Best of Palm Beach County Restaurants

RESTAURANT/TYPE	STAR RATING	QUALITY RATING	VALUE RATING	CITY
AMERICAN/CONTEMPORARY				
The Restaurant	★★★★★	★★★★★	★★★★★	Palm Beach
The Addison	★★★★	★★★★	★★★★	Boca Raton
Cafe Chardonay	★★★½	★★★★½	★★★★	Palm Beach Gardens
Shore Restaurant and Beach Bar	★★★½	★★★★	★★★	Delray Beach
The Premier at the Palace Movie Theatre	★★★½	★★★½	★★★★★	Boca Raton
Bizarre Avenue Café	★★★	★★★★	★★★★	Lake Worth
Brewzzi	★★★	★★★★	★★	Boca Raton, West Palm
Dada Restaurant and Lounge	★★★	★★★½	★★★★	Delray Beach
Wilt Chamberlain's	★★★	★★★	★★★	Boca Raton
Cheeburger Cheeburger	★★½	★★★	★★★★	Boca Raton, West Palm, Delray Beach
Pete Rose's Ballpark Café	★★	★★★	★★★	Boynton Beach
CONTINENTAL				
Johannes	★★★★★	★★★★★	★★★★½	Boca Raton
Cafe L'Europe	★★★★½	★★★★½	★★★★	Palm Beach
Mark's CityPlace	★★★★	★★★★½	★★★★	West Palm
CUBAN/LATIN				
Columbia	★★★½	★★★★	★★★	West Palm
Havana Restaurant	★★★	★★½	★★★	Lake Worth
DELI/CAFÉ/DINER				
Bagels by Star	★★★★	★★★★★	★★★★	Delray Beach

RESTAURANT/TYPE	STAR RATING	QUALITY RATING	VALUE RATING	CITY
DELI/CAFÉ/DINER (CONTINUED)				
Green Owl	★★★½	★★★	★★★★	Delray Beach
Toojay's	★★★	★★★	★★★	Jupiter, Palm Beach Palm Beach, Lake Worth, Boca Raton
DESSERTS				
Sloan's	★★★	★★½	★★★	West Palm, Boca Raton
FLORIBBEAN				
Splendid Blendeds	★★★½	★★★★	★★★½	Delray Beach
FRENCH				
La Vielle Maison	★★★★★	★★★★★	★★★★★	Boca Raton
L'Escalier	★★★★★	★★★★★	★★★★½	Palm Beach
Chef Jean-Pierre Bistro	★★★★	★★★★	★★★★	Palm Beach
IRISH				
Brogues on the Avenue	★★★	★★★★	★★★	Lake Worth
ITALIAN				
Renato's	★★★★½	★★★★	★★★½	Palm Beach
Caffé Luna Rosa	★★★★	★★★★½	★★★★	Delray Beach
Amici	★★★	★★★★	★★	Palm Beach
Pizza Girls	★★½	★★	★★★★★	West Palm
MIDDLE EASTERN				
Leila	★★★★	★★★	★★★★	West Palm
MEDITERRANEAN				
Mark's at Mizner Park	★★★★	★★★★½	★★★★	Boca Raton

The Best of Palm Beach County Restaurants (continued)

RESTAURANT/TYPE	STAR RATING	QUALITY RATING	VALUE RATING	CITY
PAN-ASIAN				
Echo	★★★★½	★★★★½	★★★★	Palm Beach
Tsunami	★★★½	★★★★	★★★	West Palm
Kyoto Sushi and Sake Lounge	★★★½	★★★	★★★	Delray Beach
SOUTHERN				
Mississippi Sweets BBQ Co.	★★½	★★★	★★★★	Boca Raton, Lake Worth
Lucille's Bad to the Bone BBQ	★★½	★★★	★★★	Boca Raton, Delray Beach, Boynton Beach
STEAK AND SEAFOOD				
New York Prime	★★★★	★★★★★	★★★★	Boca Raton
Spoto's Oyster Bar	★★★½	★★★★	★★★	West Palm
TEX-MEX/FLORIBBEAN				
Sol Kitchen	★★★½	★★★½	★★★½	Delray Beach

RESTAURANT PROFILES

The Addison ★★★★

CONTEMPORARY AMERICAN   EXPENSIVE   QUALITY ★★★★   VALUE ★★★★

**2 East Camino Real, Boca Raton; ☎ 561-395-9335;
www.theaddison.com**

Reservations Suggested. **When to go** Sunday, Monday, or Tuesday. **Entree range** $22–$36. **Payment** AE, D, DC, MC, V **Parking** Free lot, valet. **Bar** Full service. **Wine selection** Excellent. **Dress** Upscale. **Disabled access** Yes. **Customers** Adult diners, couples. **Hours** Daily, 6–10 p.m. (bar opens at 5 p.m. daily and closes an hour later than restaurant).

MENU RECOMMENDATIONS Corn-crusted soft-shell crab with garlic mash, fennel salad, and citrus butter; sesame-seared yellowfin tuna with sticky rice and ponzu-and-daikon-sprout salad

COMMENTS Located in a converted home that used to house the maintenance workers who would work at the Boca Hotel and Resort, The Addison is a Boca fine-dining stalwart with a quaint courtyard and beautiful Mediterranean architecture.

Amici ★ ★ ★

ITALIAN	EXPENSIVE	QUALITY ★ ★ ★ ★	VALUE ★ ★

288 South County Road, Palm Beach; ☎ 561-832-0201; www.amicipalmbeach.com

Reservations Suggested, especially on weekends. **When to go** When you're yearning for fancy Italian in West Palm. **Entree range** $9–$28. **Payment** AE, DC, MC, V. **Parking** Valet (complimentary with dinner). **Bar** Full service. **Wine selection** Good. **Dress** Upscale, dressy and business casual. **Disabled access** Yes. **Customers** Adult diners, couples. **Hours** Monday–Thursday, 11:30 a.m.–3 p.m. and 5:30–10:30 p.m.; Friday and Saturday, 11:30 a.m.–3 p.m. and 5:30–11p.m.; Sunday, 5:30–10:30 p.m.

MENU RECOMMENDATIONS Tagliatelle and Maine lobster with wild mushrooms and tarragon-and-brandy sauce; roasted Long Island duck with sweet potatoes, peas, dried apricot, and *vin santo* glaze

COMMENTS A favorite of locals, this restaurant is a little past its prime but still popular for consistent, predictable upscale Italian cuisine.

Bagels by Star ★ ★ ★ ★

DELI	INEXPENSIVE	QUALITY ★ ★ ★ ★ ★	VALUE ★ ★ ★ ★

5195-D West Atlantic Avenue, Delray Beach; ☎ 561-495-0530

Reservations Not accepted. **When to go** Weekends are always busy, so stop in during the week or order takeout to avoid the crowd. **Entree range** $2–$9. **Payment** Cash only. **Parking** Lot. **Bar** None. **Dress** Casual. **Disabled access** People with walking aids and large medical equipment might have a hard time maneuvering through the tightly packed-in tables. **Customers** Adult diners, couples, families. **Hours** Monday–Saturday, 8 a.m.–4 p.m.; Sunday, 8 a.m.–3 p.m.

MENU RECOMMENDATIONS Nova Platter with a bagel or the Matzoh Brie

COMMENTS Great New York–style bagels and other baked goods made right on the premises. They really pack 'em in here for brunch on the weekends. Small tables, lots of people, and a lot of food for a remarkably low price, though they will charge you $2 to share.

 Bizaare Avenue Café ★ ★ ★

CONTEMPORARY AMERICAN	INEXP/MODERATE	QUALITY ★ ★ ★ ★	VALUE ★ ★ ★ ★

921 Lake Avenue, Lake Worth; ☎ 561-588-4488; www.bizaareavecafe.com

Reservations Not necessary. **When to go** Anytime; a great stop if you're visiting the nearby Palm Beach Institute of Contemporary Art. **Entree range** $10–$17 **Payment** AE, MC, V. **Parking** Street and lot (park in the city hall lot on weekends or after work hours). **Bar** Beer and wine. **Wine selection** Excellent; $3–$18. **Dress** Casual to business casual. **Disabled access** The couches in the front room might cause a tight squeeze. **Customers** Professionals and ladies who lunch, local artsy kids, the occasional celebrity. **Hours** Monday–Thursday, 11:30 a.m.–2:30 p.m. and 5:30 p.m-11 p.m.; Friday and Saturday, 11:30 a.m.–2:30 p.m. and 5:30 p.m.–midnight.

MENU RECOMMENDATIONS Chicken–artichoke heart crêpes; baked Brie; cranberry chicken-salad sandwich; Thai duck salad

COMMENTS With a new brick facade on the south side of Lake Worth's City Hall just up the street from the Palm Beach Institute of Contemporary Art, the cafe has gone from being a small, eclectic neighborhood secret for area hipsters to a place where wealthy older women come for a fun lunch. A recent renovation has made the dining room roomier. The decor is "shabby chic" bohemian–thrift store appliqué. Walls are lined with local artwork. Every knickknack you see is on sale and price-tagged. Little ones will love the robust selection of pizzas and pastas, and the décor keeps young eyes preoccupied. A play box with figurines, markers, and little toys is available upon request. The food is still imaginative and fresh. Take your meal or drink to enjoy on couches with coffee tables in the front room, or eat at a standard four-legged table in the back. Live entertainment after 6 p.m. nightly upstairs.

Brewzzi ★ ★ ★

CONTEMPORARY AMERICAN	MODERATE/EXP	QUALITY ★ ★ ★ ★	VALUE ★ ★

2222 Glades Road, Glades Plaza, Boca Raton; ☎ 561-392-2739
700 South Rosemary Avenue, West Palm Beach; ☎ 561-366-9753;
www.brewzzi.com

Reservations No, but you can call ahead for parties of 4 or fewer. **When to go** 8–9:30 p.m.; both locations are busiest on Friday and Saturday. **Entree range** $9–$35. **Payment** AE, DC, M, V. **Parking** Lot, valet, street. **Bar** Full service, with own beer-brewing facilities on premises. **Wine selection** Good. **Dress** Upscale casual. **Disabled access** Yes. **Customers** Adult diners, couples, families. **Hours** Sunday–Thursday, 11:30 a.m.–10:30 p.m.; Friday and Saturday, 11:30 a.m.–11:30 p.m.; outdoor bar at West Palm Beach location open daily, 11:30 a.m.–2 a.m.

MENU RECOMMENDATIONS Start with the gorgonzola chips and a glass of Boca Blonde, then bite into a Chili Brew Burger, sausage-and-pepper sandwich, farfalle alla vodka, or Pizza Florentina.

COMMENTS A madly popular Italian-American local restaurant whose fans ignore the relatively high prices. Entrees on menu include recommendations for beers from Brewzzi's own microbrewery. The covered outdoor bar between Brewzzi and City Cellar in West Palm's CityPlace is never without a customer and is especially busy on Friday and Saturday nights, when it offers a perfect spot to people-watch at the busy locale, with other bars, clubs, and a movie theater nearby. It's also a lively family restaurant—not a quiet place—which makes it popular with parents and kids, especially on Sunday afternoon in the Boca location. They offer a kids' menu and crayons. Beers are good; the food is decent. Mostly, you're paying for popularity.

Brogues on the Avenue ★ ★ ★

IRISH	INEXPENSIVE/MODERATE	QUALITY ★ ★ ★ ★	VALUE ★ ★ ★

621 Lake Avenue, Lake Worth; ☎ 561-585-1855

Reservations Not accepted. **When to go** Whenever; weekends are busy. **Entree range** $7–$17. **Payment** AE, MC, V. **Parking** Street or municipal lots around downtown Lake Worth. **Bar** Full service, with special attention paid to the whiskey and scotch. **Wine selection** Good. **Dress** Casual. **Disabled access** Yes. **Customers** Adult diners, couples **Hours** Monday–Saturday, 11 a.m.–2 a.m.; Sunday, noon–2 a.m.

MENU RECOMMENDATIONS Chicken curry; Irish breakfast; Brogues burger

COMMENTS A fun Irish pub in the heart of South Florida. The entire interior of the bar was imported from Ireland. They offer live music six nights a week and soccer televised regularly. Check out the beautiful island bar. A great place to stop for a drink on the way back from the beach or to hang out on a Friday night.

Café Chardonnay ★ ★ ★ ½

CONTEMPORARY AMERICAN	EXPENSIVE	QUALITY ★ ★ ★ ★	VALUE ★ ★ ★ ★

4533 PGA Boulevard, Palm Beach Gardens; ☎ 561-627-2662; www.cafechardonnay.com

Reservations Required in season. **When to go** Anytime. **Entree range** $10–$38. **Payment** AE, D, MC, V. **Parking** Lot. **Bar** Wine and beer. **Wine selection** Excellent, $6–$35 a glass. **Dress** Upscale casual. **Disabled access** First floor only. **Customers** Young professionals, tourists. **Hours** Monday–Friday, 11:30 a.m.–2:30 p.m. and 5:30–10 p.m.; Saturday and Sunday, 5:30–10 p.m.

MENU RECOMMENDATIONS Start with a pesto-crusted goat cheese tart with grilled eggplant, roasted portobello mushrooms, and marinated pepper, and follow that with a rack of roasted Australian lamb enhanced by a rosemary-scented port reduction and accompanied by herbed mashed potatoes. For dessert try the warm deep-dish apple pie on a bed of caramel sauce.

COMMENTS At this bilevel restaurant, where modern paintings provide a sophisticated background, wine lovers often sit at the wine bar, choosing from 500 selections.

Cafe L'Europe ★ ★ ★ ★ ½

CONTINENTAL	EXPENSIVE	QUALITY ★ ★ ★ ★ ½	VALUE ★ ★ ★ ★

331 South County Road, Palm Beach; ☎ 561-655-4020; www.cafeleurope.com

Reservations Required. **When to go** Anytime. **Entree range** $14–$40. **Payment** AE, DC, MC, V. **Parking** Valet. **Bar** Full service. **Wine selection** Outstanding (1,225 choices), $7.75–$20.50 by the glass. **Dress** Jackets in dining room; casual in bistro (menu same). **Disabled access** Good. **Customers** Internationals, celebrities, winter residents. **Hours** Tuesday–Saturday, noon–2:30 p.m. and 5:30–10 p.m.; Sunday, 5:30–10 p.m. (closed Saturday in summer).

MENU RECOMMENDATIONS A caviar bar appeals to old-time Palm Beachers. Start with fried sweetbreads and poached pear, followed by a grilled veal chop in a tarragon reduction served with potato-scallion cake or risotto with porcini mushrooms, then for dessert a flourless chocolate cake swathed with praline and served with butter-pecan ice cream.

COMMENTS The elegant dining room has swagged drapes and divine accoutrements. A pianist provides soft background music, and dancers enjoy a jazz quartet on Friday and Saturday nights.

Caffé Luna Rosa ★ ★ ★ ★

ITALIAN	MODERATE/EXPENSIVE	QUALITY ★ ★ ★ ★ ½	VALUE ★ ★ ★ ★

34 South Ocean Boulevard, Delray Beach; ☎ 561-274-9404; www.caffelunarosa.com

Reservations Not accepted. **When to go** Anytime, busiest on nights and weekends. **Entree range** $15–$30. **Payment** AE, MC, V. **Parking** Street, valet around the corner (11 a.m.–11 p.m.). **Bar** Full service. **Wine selection** Award-winning cellar of Italian and fine wines, $6.50–$12. **Dress** Casual. **Disabled access** Good. **Customers** Beachgoers, locals, tourists. **Hours** Daily, 7 a.m.–11 p.m.; brunch Saturday and Sunday, 7 a.m.–3:30 p.m.

MENU RECOMMENDATIONS The house specialty is a best-seller: *costolette di vitello alla Valpolicella*—a 14-ounce milk-fed veal chop topped with fresh basil and imported buffalo mozzarella. The restaurant makes all its pastas fresh in-house.

COMMENTS A favorite with locals and snowbirds alike, Luna Rosa offers good service and gastronomically smart Italian. It's also located right on the ocean. Barring inclement weather, the windows are open, so you always have an unobstructed view. Alfresco seating is offered. Between the traffic both in and out of the restaurant, Luna Rosa gets busy. So if you want a quieter meal, come early on weekends or during the week. Live entertainment Monday–Friday, 7–11 p.m.

Cheeburger Cheeburger ★ ★ ½

AMERICAN	INEXPENSIVE	QUALITY ★ ★ ★	VALUE ★ ★ ★ ★

200 South Federal Highway, Boca Raton; ☎ 561-392-1969
5030 Champion Boulevard, Polo Shoppes, Boca Raton; ☎ 561-241-4472
450 East Atlantic Avenue, Delray; ☎ 561-265-1959
760 South Rosemary Avenue in CityPlace, West Palm Beach;
   ☎ 561-833-1997; www.cheeburger.com

Reservations Not accepted. **When to go** Anytime. **Entree range** Burgers, $5.25–$11.25. **Payment** MC, V. **Parking** Street, lot. **Bar** None. **Wine selection** None. **Dress** Casual. **Disabled access** Yes. **Customers** Shoppers, tourists, beachgoers, families. **Hours** Monday–Thursday, 8 a.m.–10 p.m., Friday–Sunday, 8 a.m.–11 p.m. (Beach Place hours).

MENU RECOMMENDATIONS Milkshakes, fries, onion rings, burgers, pacemaker

COMMENTS Popular with tourists and locals alike, Cheeburger is a great, quick family restaurant located conveniently all throughout Broward County. The menu features milkshakes you need to eat with a spoon and burgers you could nap on—big, juicy, delicious.

Chez Jean-Pierre Bistro ★ ★ ★ ★

FRENCH	EXPENSIVE	QUALITY ★ ★ ★ ★	VALUE ★ ★ ★ ★

132 North County Road, Palm Beach; ☎ 561-833-1171

Reservations Required. **When to go** Dinner, whenever you can get a reservation; try calling a week in advance. **Entree range** $20–$60. **Payment** AE, MC, V. **Parking** Lot, valet. **Bar** Full service. **Wine selection** Excellent. **Dress** Upscale, business, dressy casual. **Disabled access** Yes. **Customers** Adult diners, couples. **Hours** Monday–Saturday, 5:30–10:30 p.m; closed July–August.

MENU RECOMMENDATIONS Osso buco; short ribs; Dover sole, crème brûlée

COMMENTS Family owned, this French restaurant is always heralded as one of the best in the area. The menu doesn't change much, but then, why fix what isn't broken?

Columbia ★ ★ ★ ½

CUBAN-HISPANIC	EXPENSIVE	QUALITY ★ ★ ★ ★	VALUE ★ ★ ★

651 Okeechobee Boulevard, CityPlace, West Palm Beach;
☎ 561-820-9373; www.columbiarestaurant.com

Reservations Suggested for dinner. **When to go** Anytime. **Entree range** $17–25. **Payment** AE, D, DC, MC, V. **Parking** Lot, valet, and garage. **Bar** Full service. **Wine selection** Excellent. **Dress** Dressy, business, and upscale casual. **Disabled access** Yes. **Customers** Well-heeled Hispanic South Floridians, shoppers at CityPlace. **Hours** Daily, 11 a.m.–11 p.m.

MENU RECOMMENDATIONS Deviled-crab croquettes, *croquetas de pollo,* red snapper Alicante, filet mignon Chacho, chocolate Brazo Gitano sponge cake soaked in a syrup with sherry and rolled with a chocolate mousse

COMMENTS This family-owned franchise out of Tampa has been serving elegant Latin cuisine for the last century. The owners went to Spain to hand-select tiles for the interior of this, their newest location. Serves the most elegant Cuban sandwich in Palm Beach County.

Dada Restaurant and Lounge ★ ★ ★

AMERICAN/CONTINENTAL   MOD/EXPENSIVE   QUALITY ★★★½   VALUE ★★★★

52 North Swinton Avenue, Delray Beach; ☎ 561-330-3232; www.closermagazine.com/dada.htm

Reservations Not necessary. **When to go** Bar gets busy around 11 p.m. **Entree range** $8–$24. **Payment** AE, D, MC, V. **Parking** Street, lot—either park along Atlantic Avenue near Swinton, in the lot adjacent to the old schoolhouse, or after hours, in the office lots nearby. **Bar** Full service. **Wine selection** Fair, $6.50–$12. **Dress** Casual or upscale casual. **Disabled access** Yes. **Customers** Pretty much anyone shows up for dinner; the late-night set consists mostly of college kids, young professionals, and local musicians and artists. **Hours** Daily, 6 p.m.–1:30 a.m.

MENU RECOMMENDATIONS Habanero-maple–glazed salmon; lentil soup

COMMENTS Dada is happy to be called a dining alternative. Just north of the beaten path that is Delray's Atlantic Avenue, you'll find this bohemian Bahamian-style house with tiki torches out front. It's a restaurant, lounge, and performance space with a creative decor (visit both bathrooms, if you can). Open mics, poetry slams, local bands, and DJs entertain on alternating nights.

Echo ★ ★ ★ ★ ½

PAN-ASIAN   MODERATE/EXPENSIVE   QUALITY ★★★★½   VALUE ★★★★

230A Sunrise Avenue, Palm Beach; ☎ 561-802-4222; www.echopalmbeach.com

Reservations Suggested. **When to go** Anytime. **Entree range** $9–$36. **Payment** AE, D, DC, MC, V. **Parking** Valet and street. **Bar** Full service. **Wine selection** Very good; $8–$21 a glass. **Dress** Upscale casual; shorts permitted at porch tables. **Disabled access** Good. **Customers** Young locals, professionals, tourists, internationals. **Hours** Sunday, Wednesday, Thursday, 5:30–9:30 p.m.; Friday and Saturday, 5:30–10 p.m.

MENU RECOMMENDATIONS Exquisitely fresh sushi and sashimi are available by the piece. Outstanding interpretations include steamed sea bass with a soy-and-ginger glaze, pad Thai with chicken and shrimp, Peking duck for two, and Vietnamese roasted chicken with lemon grass–chili sauce. A "Sharing Menu" for a table of four at $60 per person provides an exotic Asian trip.

COMMENTS Stunning contemporary design imparts Oriental flavor. The menu, which features Chinese, Japanese, Thai, and Vietnamese, is divided into five elements: wind, fire, water, earth, and flavor.

 Green Owl ★ ★ ★ ½

DELI	INEXPENSIVE	QUALITY ★★★	VALUE ★★★★

330 East Atlantic Avenue, Delray Beach; ☎ 561-272-7766

Reservations Not accepted. **When to go** A weekend brunch hot spot; go early to beat the rush. **Entree range** $3–$10. **Payment** Cash only. **Parking** Street or municipal lots behind Atlantic storefronts. **Bar** None. **Dress** Casual. **Disabled access** Yes, but it's tight. **Customers** Adult diners, couples, families, beachgoers. **Hours** Monday–Friday, 7 a.m.–3 p.m.; Saturday, 7 a.m.–2 p.m.; Sunday, 8 a.m.–midnight.

MENU RECOMMENDATIONS Don't miss the cakes.

COMMENTS For the scruffy, just-rolled-out-of-bed breakfast, brunch, and lunch on weekends. The only breakfast place along Atlantic Avenue, Green Owl has been a family favorite for decades—inexpensive and easy diner food with a come-as-you-are dress code; they offer crayons and coloring things. Good portions. Inexpensive but lots of people. Strollers and walkers alike could have a difficult time maneuvering through the restaurant.

Havana Restaurant ★ ★ ★

CUBAN	INEXPENSIVE/MODERATE	QUALITY ★★½	VALUE ★★★

6801 South Dixie Highway, Lake Worth; ☎ 561-547-9799;
www.havanacubanfood.com

Reservations Not required but suggested. **When to go** Anytime. **Entree range** $10–$17. **Payment** AE, D, DC, MC, V. **Parking** Lot. **Bar** Beer, wine, sangria. **Wine selection** $3. **Dress** Casual. **Disabled access** Yes. **Customers** Hispanic families, bikers, professionals, late-night bar hoppers from Lake Avenue. **Hours** Walk-up window with full menu is open 24 hours—call in advance for pickup.

MENU RECOMMENDATIONS *Maduros* (sweet plantains); *yuca frita; tamal cubano; paella de mariscos.* For a liquid culture fix, take advantage of the juices (orange, guava, mango, papaya, passion fruit) and sodas (Malta, Materva, Jupina, Ironbeer).

COMMENTS Cuban and Hispanic fare served in a clean, casual setting. If you're a little hung over somewhere in central Palm Beach County, we suggest the piping-hot Cuban coffee and a warm Cuban sandwich to cure what ails you. The portions are generous, but be forewarned that the restaurant is stingy with its soda—only one free refill. There's also a coupon on the Havana Web site.

Johannes ★ ★ ★ ★ ★

CONTINENTAL	VERY EXPENSIVE	QUALITY ★★★★★	VALUE ★★★★½

47 East Palmetto Park Road, Boca Raton; ☎ 561-394-0007

Reservations Accepted. **When to go** When you can get in. **Entree range** Prix fixe, $58 or $79. **Payment** AE, MC, V. **Parking** Valet and street. **Bar** Wine only. **Wine selection** Very good, $7.50–$21. **Dress** Elegant. **Disabled access** Good. **Customers** Discriminating diners. **Hours** Tuesday–Sunday, 6–10 p.m.

MENU RECOMMENDATIONS Lobster ravioli in tandoori sauce with red tobiko caviar; the foie gras and venison are always served to perfection.

COMMENTS Possibly one of the most opulent, expensive, hush-hush restaurants in Palm Beach County—and yet it has a lot of flair for a restaurant that's such a secret. Why broadcast the name of your restaurant on a sign when you can be more subtle? A single "J" on the door handle is the only sign on this restaurant, which seats about 30. The restaurant closes for several weeks each summer, usually opening again in October; call in advance.

Kyoto Sushi and Sake Lounge ★ ★ ★ ½

PAN-ASIAN/SUSHI	MODERATE	QUALITY ★ ★ ★	VALUE ★ ★ ★

25 NE Second Avenue; Suite 208, Delray Beach;
☎ **561-330-2275; www.kyotosushisake.com**

Reservations Recommended for parties of 6 or more. **When to go** Anytime. **Entree range** $10–$30. **Payment** AE, D, DC, MC, V (no checks). **Parking** Street, lot, valet. **Bar** Full service. **Wine selection** Very good; $7–$10. **Dress** Casual. **Disabled access** Good. **Customers** Young professionals. **Hours** Monday–Thursday, 11:30 a.m.–late; Saturday, 5 p.m.–late; Sunday, 5–10:30 p.m.

MENU RECOMMENDATIONS For local flavors, try the Mexican roll (with tempura shrimp and spicy mayonnaise) and the salmon–cream cheese roll. The Asian-fusion entrees include nonseafood and vegetarian options.

COMMENTS Everything you would expect from a sushi bar

La Vieille Maison ★ ★ ★ ★ ★

FRENCH	VERY EXPENSIVE	QUALITY ★ ★ ★ ★ ★	VALUE ★ ★ ★ ★ ★

770 East Palmetto Park Road, Boca Raton; ☎ **561-391-6701**

Reservations Recommended. **When to go** For important dates, business or personal. **Entree range** $24–$42. **Payment** AE, D, DC, MC, V. **Parking** Valet. **Bar** Full service. **Wine selection** Excellent, $6.50–$12.75 a glass. **Dress** Dressy casual; jackets in season. **Disabled access** Good. **Customers** Discriminating diners, internationals, well-heeled tourists, celebrators. **Hours** Daily, 6–10 p.m.

MENU RECOMMENDATIONS Sevruga caviar accompanied by blini; wild-mushroom ravioli in lemon grass–scented cream sauce punctuated with tiny clams; a trio of medallions (rosemary-scented lamb, beef teamed with béarnaise sauce, and veal with morel sauce); cornmeal-crusted mahimahi with a Provençal zucchini cake; lemon crêpe soufflé accented with raspberry sauce (although many repeat diners prefer the chocolate "bag")

COMMENTS If you want to know what life was like for the wealthy winter residents of yesteryear, dine at this romantic 1920s mansion. The 25-

year-old restaurant is awash with Mediterranean influences such as Provençal furnishings and lush gardens with gurgling fountains. Loyal servers are knowledgeable without being haughty. Private rooms are available. Summer sees reduced prices.

L'Escalier ★ ★ ★ ★ ★

FRENCH	VERY EXPENSIVE	QUALITY ★ ★ ★ ★ ★	VALUE ★ ★ ★ ★ ½

The Breakers, 1 South County Road, Palm Beach; ☎ 561-659-8480; www.thebreakers.com

Reservations Recommended. **When to go** When celebrating a special occasion or impressing an important client. **Entree range** $32–$40. **Payment** AE, D, DC, MC, V. **Parking** Valet. **Bar** Full service. **Wine selection** Exceptional (6,500 selections, up to an $1,800 bottle), $8–$24 by the glass. **Dress** Dressy. **Disabled access** Good. **Customers** The rich and famous, special-event celebrators. **Hours** Daily, 6–10 p.m.

MENU RECOMMENDATIONS Near-perfect dishes start with a complimentary opener, possibly cranberry beignets with a duck and port sauce, and include grilled beef tournedos and foie gras served with a black truffle–and–wild mushroom reduction and the Floribbean (Floridian-Caribbean) pan-roasted Maine lobster morsels in curried coconut sauce with caramelized banana slices. End your meal with a vanilla crème brûlée.

COMMENTS This regally appointed dining room under a 24-foot-high hand-stenciled ceiling serves arguably the county's best-prepared and most elegantly served meals. Diners know they're in for something special when the bread server presents a basket of four whole loaves (perhaps French, sourdough, multigrain, and cherry-chocolate), then slices the diner's choices. At the meal's finale, the cheese presentation of 18 varieties appears on a cart; the server then describes each, peppering the history with humorous anecdotes. Sunday brunch recalls the Waldorf-Astoria.

Leila ★ ★ ★ ★

MIDDLE EASTERN	MODERATE/EXPENSIVE	QUALITY ★ ★ ★ ★	VALUE ★ ★ ★ ★

120 South Dixie Highway, #101, West Palm Beach; ☎ 561-659-7373; www.leilawpb.com

Reservations Suggested. **When to go** Anytime. **Entree range** $17–$42. **Payment** AE, D, DC, MC, V. **Parking** Lot behind restaurant, free validated parking. **Bar** Full service. **Wine selection** Good. **Dress** Upscale, business, dressy casual. **Disabled access** Yes. **Customers** Adult diners, couples. **Hours** Monday–Wednesday, 11:30 a.m.–10 p.m.; Thursday and Friday, 11:30 a.m.–10:30 p.m.; Saturday, 11:30 a.m.–11 p.m.

MENU RECOMMENDATIONS Feta puffs, simbusik, kibbeh, baba ghanoush
COMMENTS Sleek decor and modern Mediterranean menu with belly dancing and hookah service. Look for "101" on the door, not "120."

Lucille's Bad to the Bone BBQ ★ ★ ½

| SOUTHERN | INEXPENSIVE | QUALITY ★ ★ ★ | VALUE ★ ★ ★ |

3011 Yamato Road, Boca Raton; ☎ **561-997-9557**
710 Linton Boulevard, Delray Beach; ☎ **561-330-6705**
6691 West Boynton Beach Boulevard, Boynton Beach; ☎ **561-742-7499;**
www.badtothebonebbq.com

Reservations Not accepted. **When to go** Before 6 p.m. or after 7:45 p.m. **Entree range** $6–$18. **Payment** AE, MC, V. **Parking** Lot. **Bar** Wine and beer. **Wine selection** Fair. **Dress** Casual. **Disabled access** Good. **Customers** Young families, seniors, experts on Southern-roadhouse eats. **Hours** Boca Raton and Boynton Beach: Daily, 11 a.m.–10 p.m.; Delray Beach: Sunday–Thursday, 11 a.m.–10 p.m.; Friday and Saturday, 11 a.m.–11 p.m.

MENU RECOMMENDATIONS Rotisserie-roasted chicken and St. Louis ribs are major choices, served with zippy barbecue sauce, a baked sweet potato, and pecan pie. Down-homers can order catfish, while finicky kids can always choose hamburgers. Platters include several side dishes. Don't forget to order the Black Bow Root Beer Float.

COMMENTS Decor in this fun spot is funky Dixie roadhouse, where farm implements such as watering troughs and washboards provide local color. The name recalls B. B. King's guitar, Lucille. All-you-can-eat bad-to-the-bone ribs draw bushels of regulars on Tuesday, but locals bring the youngsters on Wednesdays, when kids under 12 eat free; a clown keeps them busy by painting faces and making balloon animals. On Thursdays there is all-you-can-eat catfish.

Mark's at Mizner Park ★ ★ ★ ★

| MEDITERRANEAN/FUSION | VERY EXPENSIVE | QUALITY ★ ★ ★ ★ ½ | VALUE ★ ★ ★ ★ |

344 Plaza Real, Boca Raton; ☎ **561-395-0770; www.chefmark.com**

Reservations Accepted. **When to go** Anytime. **Entree range** $10–$38. **Payment** AE, D, DC, V. **Parking** Valet and street. **Bar** Full service. **Wine selection** Very good, $8–$14 a glass. **Dress** Smart casual. **Disabled access** Good. **Customers** Young locals, professionals, winter residents, tourists. **Hours** Daily, 11:30 a.m.–3:30 p.m. and 5–11 p.m.; Sunday brunch, 11:30 a.m.–2:30 p.m.

MENU RECOMMENDATIONS Dishes that seem commonplace are taken to new heights with the Mark Militello touch: lobster-and-asparagus pizza; grilled-chicken Caesar salad with roasted garlic; pan-roasted duck breast with sun-dried cranberry couscous, asparagus, and Meyer lemon duck jus; seared "rare" yellowfin tuna with udon pad Thai, long beans, and organic soy.

COMMENTS Militello, who started out with restaurateur Dennis Max and branched off with his own highly successful hot spots, created this popular eatery next to Max's Grille in Mizner Park. The interior is dramatically contemporary, featuring ultra-high-back booths, but many choose to sit and sup at outdoor tables. Locals often sit at the seven-seat chef's table to watch the culinary whizzes in action; an appreciation for the intense labor behind a meal's perfect touches makes the high price tag easier to swallow. The noise level is high, in keeping with the boundless excitement.

Mark's CityPlace ★ ★ ★ ★

CONTINENTAL/CONTEMPORARY EXPENSIVE QUALITY ★ ★ ★ ★ ½ VALUE ★ ★ ★ ★

700 South Rosemary Avenue, West Palm Beach; ☎ 561-514-0770; www.chefmark.com

Reservations Necessary for dinner and for parties of 5 or more. **When to go** Anytime. **Entree range** $23–$48. **Payment** AE, DC, MC, V. **Parking** Valet and garage. **Bar** Full service. **Wine selection** Very good, $7.25–$14 a glass. **Dress** Dressy casual. **Disabled access** Very good. **Customers** Professionals, upscale locals, internationals. **Hours** Monday–Thursday, 6–11 p.m.; Friday and Saturday, 6 p.m.–midnight; Sunday, 6–10:30 p.m.

MENU RECOMMENDATIONS Grilled-chicken pizza; black-peppercorn–crusted seared yellowfin tuna. The fresh-made sorbets are heavenly.

COMMENTS A star in much-awarded Mark Militello's galaxy of cutting-edge fusion foods, this is a stunning theater of cuisine. Located on the second floor, it offers outdoor tables and indoor seating beneath dramatic custom-made lighting fixtures and a ceiling that looks like copper-toned crumpled paper—it actually notches down the noise level. A sushi bar features smart-looking glazed pottery serving pieces.

Mississippi Sweets BBQ Co. ★ ★ ½

SOUTHERN INEXPENSIVE QUALITY ★ ★ ★ VALUE ★ ★ ★ ★

2399 North Federal Highway, Boca Raton; ☎ 561-394-6779
6604 Hypoluxo Road, Lake Worth; ☎ 561-432-8555

Reservations Not accepted. **When to go** Before 5:30 p.m. or after 8 p.m. **Entree range** $6–$17. **Payment** MC, V. **Parking** Lot. **Bar** Wine and beer. **Wine selection** House wines only, $3–$5 a glass. **Dress** Casual. **Disabled access** Fair. **Customers** Young locals, seniors, winter residents. **Hours** Monday–Thursday, 11:30 a.m.–9:30 p.m.; Friday and Saturday, 11:30 a.m.–10 p.m.; Sunday, noon–10 p.m.

MENU RECOMMENDATIONS Pulled pork and barbecued chicken are featured, but most folks come for the baby back ribs served with a sweet-tangy barbecue sauce. The best "side road" is the Mississippi Sweets—sweet potatoes sliced paper thin and deep-fried.

COMMENTS This tiny eatery usually has lines waiting outside. The decor recalls life in Mississippi, through pictures of fishing boats and the *Delta Queen* steamboat. Food arrives in baskets and is set on vinyl tablecloths.

New York Prime ★★★★

STEAK AND SEAFOOD   VERY EXPENSIVE   QUALITY ★★★★★   VALUE ★★★★

2350 NW Executive Center Drive, Boca Raton; ☎ **561-998-3881;**
www.newyorkprime.com

Reservations Suggested. **When to go** 8 p.m. **Entree range** $20–$37. **Payment** AE,
DC, MC, V. **Parking** Lot, valet. **Bar** Full service. **Wine selection** Excellent, $8 and up.
Dress Dressy casual or jacket and tie. **Disabled access** Good. **Customers** Discrimi-
nating diners, successful professionals, tourists, snowbirds. **Hours** Daily, 5–11 p.m.

MENU RECOMMENDATIONS Oysters Rockefeller; baked shrimp; lobster cocktail
   rémoulade; center-cut filet; live lobster; creamed spinach
COMMENTS A simple, elegant chop house offering what is possibly the best
   steak in Palm Beach County. Your blood gets bluer as you walk through
   the door. An enormous lobster is wheeled through the dining room on
   its own little red wagon, surrounded by palm trees, slowly waving paddle fans, white-linen tablecloths, and white-jacketed servers.

 Pete Rose's Ballpark Cafe ★★

AMERICAN/CONTINENTAL INEXPENSIVE/MODERATE QUALITY ★★★ VALUE ★★★

1601 North Congress Avenue, Boynton Beach; 561-364-**PETE;**
www.peteroseballparkcafe.com

Reservations Not accepted. **When to go** Anytime. **Entree range** $7–$18. **Payment**
AE, DC, D, MC, V. **Parking** Lot. **Bar** Full service. **Wine selection** $4 and up. **Dress**
Casual. **Disabled access** Good. **Customers** Families, professionals, sports fans.
Hours Sunday–Thursday, 7 a.m.–11 p.m.; Friday and Saturday, 7 a.m.–midnight.

MENU RECOMMENDATIONS Dugout spinach-and-artichoke dip; McGwire's
   grouper sandwich; double-decker brownie
COMMENTS Young kids love the game room; big kids love the pool tables.
   When the arcade gets busy, it looks like a half-pint version of the NYSE
   trading floor. The kids aren't just playing games; they're investing in a potential prize. The money you shell out for games makes this restaurant a
   good candidate for the moderate/expensive list. On Mondays from 6 to
   8 p.m., kids eat free. Every Tuesday night from 6 to 8 p.m., the restaurant
   offers two-for-one tokens night. Also on Tuesday, kids can bring their report cards for free tokens. Check the Web site for updated specials.

 Pizza Girls ★★ ½

ITALIAN   INEXPENSIVE   QUALITY ★★   VALUE ★★★★★

114 Clematis Street, West Palm Beach; ☎ **561-833-4004;**
www.pizzagirls.com

Reservations Not accepted. **When to go** Anytime. **Entree range** $5–$17. **Payment** AMEX, D, DC, MC, V. **Parking** Street. **Bar** Beer by the bottle, $3–$3.55.

Wine selection House wine by the split, $4. **Dress** Casual. **Disabled access** Good. **Customers** Tourists, families, young singles, students. **Hours** Sunday, noon–9 p.m.; Monday–Wednesday, 11 a.m.–10 p.m.; Thursday–Saturday, 11 a.m.–11 p.m.

MENU RECOMMENDATIONS Pies are named after New York landmarks and neighborhoods. Try the Times Square: eggplant Parmesan with tomato slices. Also served are heroes, calzones, pasta, and salads.

COMMENTS Located just near the fountains at the end of Clematis, Pizza Girls is like any New York pizza joint: Order by the pie or by the slice at the counter, then use 90,000 paper napkins to keep your fingers clean after each delicious bite. Also, right next door is Sloan's Ice Cream parlor (see below). Check the Web site for coupons and specials.

The Premier at the Palace Movie Theatre ★ ★ ★ ½

| AMERICAN/CONTINENTAL | MODERATE | QUALITY ★ ★ ★ ½ | VALUE ★ ★ ★ ★ ★ |

3200 Airport Road, Boca Raton; ☎ 561-395-9009; www.muvico.com/main/thepremier.htm

Reservations For premiers, yes; general admission, no. **When to go** Weekends. **Entree range** $14–$32. **Payment** AE, DC, MC, V. **Parking** Street. **Bar** Full service. **Wine selection** Good, $6–$11 a glass. **Dress** Business. **Disabled access** Good. **Customers** Over 21 only. **Hours** Sunday–Thursday, 11 a.m-11 p.m.; Friday and Saturday, 11 a.m.–midnight.

MENU RECOMMENDATIONS Lobster roll; baked crab dip; grouper sandwich

COMMENTS The novelty and convenience of this restaurant make it worth a visit. Eat, then take no more than 30 paces across the marble floor to the theater, where you can digest in plush comfort. You can order sushi and splits of Champagne at the Premier's concession stand or have food delivered by a waiter to your seats.

Renato's ★ ★ ★ ★ ½

| ITALIAN | EXPENSIVE | QUALITY ★ ★ ★ ★ | VALUE ★ ★ ★ ½ |

87 Via Mizner, Palm Beach; ☎ 561-655-9752; www.renatospalmbeach.com

Reservations Suggested. **When to go** Anytime. **Entree range** $14-42. **Payment** AE, D, DC, MC, V. **Parking** Valet for dinner. **Bar** Full service. **Wine selection** Excellent, $9–$17. **Dress** Any. **Disabled access** Good. **Customers** Professionals and professional Palm Beachers. **Hours** Monday–Saturday, 11:30 a.m.–3 p.m. and 6:30–10:30 p.m.

MENU RECOMMENDATIONS Sesame-crusted ahi tuna seared rare, soy-ginger sauce, macadamia-crusted sea bass fillet finished with soy–temple orange glaze, roast rack of lamb with candied-garlic sauce

COMMENTS Professional service, elegant decor, and outside seating draw a well-heeled and business clientele.

The Restaurant ★★★★★

NEW WORLD/CONTEMPORARY   EXPENSIVE   QUALITY ★★★★★   VALUE ★★★★★

**Four Seasons Resort, 2800 South Ocean Boulevard, Palm Beach;
☎ 561-533-3750; www.fourseasons.com/palmbeach/vacations/
dining_78.html**

Reservations Required. **When to go** When in an elegant mood. **Entree range** $30–$45. **Payment** AE, D, DC, MC, V. **Parking** Valet only. **Bar** Full service. **Wine selection** Exceptional (300 labels, up to a $2,700 bottle), $9–$20 by the glass. **Dress** Jackets required. **Disabled access** Good. **Customers** Winter residents, celebrities, young locals celebrating special events. **Hours** Tuesday–Sunday, 6–10 p.m.; closed Mondays and Tuesdays, April 1–December 31.

MENU RECOMMENDATIONS Spice-crusted yellowfin tuna, caramelized daikon, pickled beet–and–Scotch bonnet sugarcane syrup; pecan-crusted double-cut lamb chop; petite lamb shank, crispy corn grits, stewed oven-dried tomatoes, fennel, and a roasted-poblano–Merlot reduction; and the signature dessert, molten chocolate lava cake complemented by Jack Daniel's ice cream. A daily vegetarian option also is available.

COMMENTS This gorgeous, lavish restaurant, overlooking the ocean through floor-to-ceiling windows, has lots more than travertine and stunning fresh-flower arrangements. For ten years, its cuisine has been created by executive chef Hubert Des Marais, a graduate of the Culinary Institute of America who started here when it was the Ocean Grand Hotel. Chef Des Marais insists on the highest-quality ingredients, and he even grows most of the herbs himself. Southern U.S. and Caribbean flavors appear in new incarnations, lovingly presented and garnished.

Shore Restaurant and Beach Bar ★★★½

SEAFOOD-AMERICAN   MODERATE   QUALITY ★★★★   VALUE ★★★

**6 South Ocean Boulevard, Delray Beach; ☎ 561-278-7878;
www.shorerestaurant.com**

Reservations Not accepted. **When to go** When the weather is nice, so you can sit at one of the outdoor tables and people-watch. **Entree range** $13–$26. **Payment** AE, D, MC, V. **Parking** Street, valet, or lot. **Bar** Full. **Wine selection** Good. **Dress** Casual, business casual, dressy casual. **Disabled access** Yes. **Customers** Adult diners, couples. **Hours** Daily, 11:30 a.m.–midnight.

MENU RECOMMENDATIONS Maine lobster roll, truffle-Parmesan fresh-cut fries, pan-roasted and crab-crusted grouper

COMMENTS One of the hippest upscale restaurants in Palm Beach County. Located right on the ocean and serving breakfast, lunch, and dinner, the Shore's preparation and presentation are unique, but the food is still moderately priced. At night, the Shore is more of an adult scene, but during the day, parents and kids on the beach trudge back through the hot sand and plop down at one of the Shore's outdoor tables as if it were an oasis with a wait staff. They offer a kids' menu and "wikki sticks," bendable toys that kids can play with at the table.

Sloan's ★ ★ ★

DESSERTS	INEXPENSIVE/MODERATE	QUALITY ★ ★ ½	VALUE ★ ★ ★

112 Clematis Street, West Palm Beach; ☎ 561-833-3335
329 Plaza Real, Mizner Park, Boca Raton; ☎ 561-338-9887

Reservations Not accepted. **When to go** Sunny afternoons. **Parking** Street, parking garage. **Bar** None. **Dress** Any. **Disabled access** Good—it's a small space, so navigating with Seeing Eye dogs or wheelchairs may be difficult if it's crowded. **Customers** Anyone. **Hours** Sunday–Wednesday, noon–11 p.m.; Thursday–Saturday, noon–midnight.

MENU RECOMMENDATIONS Try Mom's Apple Pie ice cream, cotton candy ice cream, or a hot brownie sundae.

COMMENTS This ice-cream parlor looks like a set from *Willy Wonka and the Chocolate Factory,* and the whimsical interior placates even the crankiest kids. The ice cream is homemade and delicious (though not cheap). If you're on the eastern end of Clematis, it's worth the visit just to see Sloan's bathrooms—see-through glass walls and doors that go magically opaque when you lock the bathroom door.

Sol Kitchen ★ ★ ★ ½

TEX-MEX/FLORIBBEAN	MODERATE	QUALITY ★ ★ ★ ½	VALUE ★ ★ ★ ½

4 East Atlantic Avenue, Delray Beach; ☎ 561-921-0201;
www.solkitchenrestaurant.com

Reservations Accepted. **When to go** To avoid the wait for dinner, go between 5:30–6:30 p.m. **Entree range** $8–$20. **Payment** AE, D, MC, V. **Parking** Valet, street. **Bar** Full service. **Wine selection** Good. **Dress** Dressy casual. **Disabled access** Yes. **Customers** Adult diners, couples. **Hours** Monday–Thursday, 11:30 a.m.–10:30 p.m.; Friday, 11:30 a.m.–11:30 p.m.; Saturday, 5–11:30 p.m.; Sunday, 5:30–10:30 p.m.; closed Mondays in summer.

MENU RECOMMENDATIONS Lunch: Havana press sandwich with mango mustard, pickled serranos, and crispy yuca; dinner: mojo skirt steak with onions and a side of Manny's rice and beans

COMMENTS A colorful, lively little Tex-Mex restaurant across from the old converted school house—the food is as creative and modern as the interior.

Splendid Blendeds ★ ★ ★ ½

FLORIBBEAN	MODERATE	QUALITY ★ ★ ★ ★	VALUE ★ ★ ★ ½

432 East Atlantic Avenue, Delray Beach; ☎ 561-265-1035

Reservations Accepted. **When to go** Anytime. **Entree range** $10–$30. **Payment** AE, DC, MC, V. **Parking** Street. **Bar** Wine and beer. **Wine selection** Good. **Dress**

Casual, dressy casual. **Disabled access** Yes. **Customers** Adult diners, couples. **Hours** Monday–Friday, 11:30 a.m.–10 p.m.; Saturday, 5:30–10 p.m.

MENU RECOMMENDATIONS Yellowtail snapper Française; lobster Française; duck breast; stuffed filet mignon

COMMENTS Don't be confused by the name—Splendid Blendeds is not a beachside smoothie cafe but a small, eclectic eatery on Delray's busy Atlantic Avenue.

Spoto's Oyster Bar ★ ★ ★ ½

AMERICAN/SEAFOOD   MODERATE   QUALITY ★★★★   VALUE ★★★

125 Datura Street, West Palm Beach; ☎ 561-835-1828; www.spotosoysterbar.com

Reservations Not accepted. **When to go** Anytime. **Entree range** $20–$30. **Payment** AE, D, DC, MC, V. **Parking** Lot and street. **Bar** Full; 9 beers on tap. **Wine selection** Good; $6–$14. **Dress** Casual. **Disabled access** Fair. **Customers** Young locals, tourists, winter residents. **Hours** Sunday–Wednesday, 11:30 a.m.–midnight.; Thursday–Saturday, 11:30 a.m.–1 a.m.

MENU RECOMMENDATIONS Oyster varieties on the half shell; New England clam chowder; sesame tuna; chocolate silk pie

COMMENTS Around the corner from Clematis Street, near the Intracoastal Waterway, the wood-paneled, brick-floored Spoto's has a lively bar and tables inside and out, as well as an extremely gracious staff.

Toojay's ★ ★ ★

DELI   INEXPENSIVE   QUALITY ★★★   VALUE ★★★

4050 US 1 South, Jupiter; ☎ 561-627-5555
4084 PGA Boulevard, Palm Beach Gardens; ☎ 561-622-8131
313 Royal Poinciana Way, Palm Beach; ☎ 561-659-7232
419 Lake Avenue, Lake Worth; ☎ 561-582-8684
5030 Champion Boulevard, Boca Raton; ☎ 561-241-5903; www.toojays.com

Reservations Not accepted. **When to go** To avoid lines, come before 11 a.m. for lunch and before 6 p.m. for dinner. **Entree range** $5–$13. **Payment** AE, D, DC, MC, V. **Parking** Lot. **Bar** Beer and wine. **Wine selection** Fair, $4–$6. **Dress** Casual. **Disabled access** Good. **Customers** Locals, tourists, winter residents, kosher eaters. **Hours** Daily, 8 a.m.–9 p.m.

MENU RECOMMENDATIONS Matzo-ball soup; corned-beef sandwich; "killer cake"; rye bread, pitas, and wraps

COMMENTS Where Bubby and Pop-Pop go to nosh, Toojay's has authentic New York Jewish-deli flavor. Although the portions of French fries are sometimes skimpy, the sandwiches are enormous, the corned beef juicy, the bread fresh, and the black-and-white cookies delish.

Tsunami ★ ★ ★ ½

PAN-ASIAN	MODERATE	QUALITY ★ ★ ★ ★	VALUE ★ ★ ★

651 Okeechobee Boulevard, West Palm Beach; ☎ 561-835-9696; www.tsunamirestaurant.com

Reservations Required on weekends; strongly suggested otherwise. **When to go** Dinner, for a drink after a show at the neighboring Kravis Center, or for happy hour on Thursdays, 5:30–7:30 p.m. **Entree range** $9–$40. **Payment** AE, D, DC, MC, V. **Parking** Valet, lot, street. **Bar** Full service. **Wine selection** Good. **Dress** Upscale casual. **Disabled access** Yes. **Customers** Adult diners, couples, families (children's menu). **Hours** Sunday–Thursday, 5–11 p.m.; Friday and Saturday, 5 p.m.–midnight.

MENU RECOMMENDATIONS   If you're ordering sushi, try the spicy sesame tuna roll; beginners: crispy Peking duck wontons with green papaya slaw and a Madras curry reduction; entree: smoked tangerine chicken with a vegetable stir-fry, toasted almonds, and a tangerine-honey reduction, or the chargrilled pesto-rubbed salmon spiral with Chinese long beans, rice noodles, and a spicy citrus-Chile-miso emulsion.

COMMENTS   A megascene restaurant with three-story windows, a six-foot gold-leaf Buddha, and a lit central staircase leading up to the popular mezzanine bar, which offers a sweeping view of the theatrically designed interior

Wilt Chamberlain's ★ ★ ★

AMERICAN/CONTINENTAL	INEXPENSIVE/MODERATE	QUALITY ★ ★ ★	VALUE ★ ★ ★

Somerset Shops, 8903 West Glades Road, Boca Raton; ☎ 561-488-8881; www.wiltsrestaurant.com

Reservations Suggested during season. **When to go** Anytime. **Entree range** $7–$19. **Payment** AE, D, MC, V. **Parking** Lot. **Bar** Full service. **Wine selection** Less than stellar; $4–$8. **Dress** Casual. **Disabled access** Good. **Customers** Families, professionals, sports fans. **Hours** Monday–Thursday, 11:30 a.m.–11:30 p.m.; Friday, 11:30 a.m.–12:30 a.m.; Saturday, 11 a.m.–12.30 a.m.; Sunday, 11 a.m.–11:30 p.m.

MENU RECOMMENDATIONS   Ribs, roasted chicken, pizza
COMMENTS   Extremely family-friendly, Wilt Chamberlain's has a game room adjoining the dining area with more than 40 arcade games as well as a small basketball court and a prize counter where tickets won at games can be redeemed for gifts. The American/international menu keeps adults pretty happy, too. The restaurant features three large-screen TVs plus 30 smaller screens. The bar is a popular happy-hour spot.

ENTERTAINMENT *and* NIGHTLIFE

FINDING THE GOOD TIMES

BECAUSE SOUTH FLORIDA SPRAWLS, TOURISTS are sometimes overwhelmed, frustrated, or just cynical when trying to find a good time off the beach and the beaten path. If this has been, is, or could be you, pay attention to the next few paragraphs, a crash course on finding good times in Palm Beach County.

For the most part, Palm Beach County (and most of South Florida) is an alternating pattern of suburbs, strip malls, office buildings, and movie theaters. But you can generally find clusters of clubs, restaurants, and bars in two zones: downtowns and mixed-use developments.

Downtowns

In southeast florida, a city's "downtown" is normally a lively street (or two) east of I-95 that dead-ends at the ocean. In Palm Beach County, these downtown streets are Atlantic Avenue (Delray Beach, south county), Lake Avenue and Lucerne Avenue (Lake Worth, mid-county), and Clematis Street (West Palm Beach, north county). Park your car along these streets or in one of the adjacent lots, and everything is magically within walking distance, which means you can make a night of it without spinning your wheels—an especially useful thing if you're drinking.

Free festivals and concerts are often held here as well. The largest of these festivals, **Clematis by Night,** is celebrated every Thursday night on Clematis. The street is closed to traffic; there are free concerts (5:30 p.m.–9 p.m.), street performers, and arts and crafts for sale, as well as the already present cornucopia of restaurants, cafes, and bars (**www.clematisbynight.net**).

CityPlace and Mizner Park

In the last decade, private developers in West Palm Beach and Boca Raton have fabricated their own mini "downtowns" east of I-95—high-rise apartment complexes that frame cobblestone streets lined with stores, restaurants, and bars as well as theaters, fountains, and parking garages. (The technical term is "mixed-use" facility.) Boca Raton has **Mizner Park** (**www.miznerpark.org**) and West Palm Beach has **CityPlace** (**www.cityplace.com**). These developments are mellower than the actual city downtowns, making them a favorite stop for professionals, older couples, families, and tourists who are seeking an environment that's more controlled (and less edgy) than in the downtowns. The whole setup is extremely family friendly—both CityPlace and Mizner Park have first-run multiplex movie theaters. Street performers pepper these places on weekends, to make even a relaxed evening just a bit spicier.

CityPlace and Mizner Park also host well-known musical acts. At the north end of Mizner Park, the de Hoernle Amphitheatre housed concerts by Tori Amos, Norah Jones, Lionel Richie, and The Strokes in its first year. The centerpiece of CityPlace is the Harriet Himmel Gillman Theater, which stages adult-contemporary music concerts (think Bruce Hornsby) as well as fine-arts performances. Also, within walking distance of CityPlace is the Raymond F. Kravis Center for the Performing Arts—Palm Beach's preeminent performing arts center (see below).

CINEMA, THEATER, AND OTHER CULTURAL PURSUITS

MOVIEGOING IS A HUGE INDUSTRY IN SOUTH FLORIDA. So much so that you have to plan on a parking-lot holding pattern and lines at the box office if you attend a screening on Friday or Saturday night—which is why many bigger theaters now offer valet services and self-serve ticket machines.

> *unofficial* **TIP**
> If you're headed to a theater on the weekend, it's a good idea to purchase your tickets in advance over the phone or buy them on the Internet.

When **Muvico's Palace 20** (3200 Airport Road, Boca Raton; ☎ 561-395-4695) opened in Boca Raton, it brought cinema viewing to new heights. There's a standard 20-screen movie house with stadium seating, but what really sets the bar is The Premier. While candy may be dandy for suspending your cinematic disbelief, liquor is certainly quicker. The Premier offers its patrons (21 and over) access to a private second floor, which houses a bistro and bar nestled between gourmet snack bars (sushi and Champagne are available alongside candy and the like). People who purchase movie tickets through The Premier have reserved access to plush, balcony-level loveseats as well as free valet parking and complimentary popcorn and soda. There are also tables alongside each loveseat for plates of food and drinks (alcoholic or not), which can be ordered from servers during the movie. Cost is $18 per person after 4 p.m., $14 per person before 4 p.m. Parents or grandparents may use The Premier while leaving children in a supervised fanciful playroom at $9 per child (ages 3–10). There is a $5 charge for each additional child.

At CityPlace, you can catch a flick at the 20-screen Muvico Parisian, fashioned somewhat after the Paris Opera House. This branch also offers a Premier bar and a playroom, but there's no restaurant. This is now the site of the annual **Palm Beach County International Film Festival,** held each April (**www.pbifilmfest.org**). The festival has included guest appearances by Sir Anthony Hopkins, Samuel Jackson, Tommy Lee Jones, Adrian Brody, Selma Hayek, and

Edward Norton. Awards are presented at the Kravis Center. Or catch well-known, national comedy acts at the **West Palm Beach Improv** comedy club and dinner theater (CityPlace, 550 South Rosemary Avenue, Suite 250, West Palm Beach; ☎ 561-833-1812; **www.palm beachimprov.com**).

The state-of-the-art **Raymond F. Kravis Center for the Performing Arts** (701 Okeechobee Boulevard, West Palm Beach; ☎ 561-833-8300 or 800-KRAVIS-1) is the major venue for touring Broadway shows. It's also home to the acclaimed **Ballet Florida**—Palm Beach's resident dance company for 20 years (☎ 561-659-2000 or 800-540-0172; **www.balletflorida.com**), and the respected **Palm Beach Opera** (☎ 561-833-7888; **www.pbopera.org**). The playhouse hosts touring performances by the Miami City Ballet, as well as plays, concerts, and stand-up comedy performances. There are three performance venues: the 2,200-seat Dreyfoos Hall, the intimate, 300-seat Rinker Playhouse, and the Gosman Amphitheatre, an outdoor theater that holds 1,400 people. Call Ticketmaster at ☎ 561-966-3309, or go to **www. ticketmaster.com** for more info on shows at the Sound Advice Amphitheatre as well as other major venues in the county.

The **Royal Poinciana Playhouse** (70 Royal Poinciana Plaza, Palm Beach; ☎ 561-833-0705) is a jewel box of a theater, formerly Palm Beach's only stage for major productions. Limited by size and technical possibilities, it now showcases dramatic performances and one-man shows. The small **Carefree Theatre** (2000 South Dixie Highway, West Palm Beach; ☎ 561-833-7305) hosts artsy films, concerts, and comedians. **Boynton Beach's Club Ovation** is also a good place to catch live rock acts (3637 South Federal Highway, Boynton Beach; ☎ 561-740-7076). The **Caldwell Theatre** (7873 North Federal Highway, Boca Raton; ☎ 561-241-7432 or 800-930-6400) is a small playhouse spotlighting drama, comedy, play readings, and musical nostalgia programs. **Florida Atlantic University's** huge auditorium (777 Glades Road, Boca Raton; ☎ 561-297-3737) seats 2,500.

The *Palm Beach Princess* (One East 11th Street, Riviera Beach; ☎ 561-845-7447; **www.pbcasino.com**), a 421-foot-long cruise ship, leaves the Port of Palm Beach twice daily for five- to six-hour cruises to nowhere. Prices vary but include all food and live entertainment. Gambling costs, of course, are at your own expense. Free bus pickups add to the cruises' popularity.

While you're in town, you can stop at almost any roadside newsstand to pick up a copy of *New Times Broward–Palm Beach* or *City Link* for the weekly goings on. Every Friday, the *Sun-Sentinel* also publishes an arts and entertainment guide for the coming week.

The Best of Palm Beach County Clubs

NAME	COVER	COST	CITY
BARS			
Biba Bar	None	Mod	West Palm Beach
Bru's Room	None	Inexp	Delray Beach Boynton Beach
Cucina Dell'Arte	None	Exp	Palm Beach
Flow	Varies	Mod	West Palm Beach
Holloway's Pub	None	Mod	Boca Raton
Surf Café	Varies	Inexp	Boca Raton
DANCE			
Delux	Varies	Mod/Exp	Delray Beach
Monkeyclub	Varies	Mod	West Palm Beach
Renegades	Varies	Inexp	West Palm Beach
Release	Varies	Mod	West Palm Beach
GAY CLUB			
Kashmir	Varies	Mod	West Palm Beach
LIVE MUSIC			
Bamboo Room	Varies	Mod/Exp	Lake Worth
Dada Restaurant and Lounge	None	Mod	Delray Beach
SINGLES BARS			
Blue Martini	None	Exp	West Palm Beach
Pete's	None	Mod	Boca Raton

NIGHTCLUB PROFILES

Bamboo Room

GET YOUR BLUES ON

25 South J Street, Lake Worth; ☎ 561-585-BLUE;
www.bambooroomblues.com

Cover Free on weekdays, varies according to artist on weekends ($10 and up).
Minimum None. **Mixed drinks** $6.50 and up; $5 cocktail specials. **Wine** $6.50 and
up. **Beer** $4.50–$6 and up; 6 beers on tap; 15 domestic, 24 imported bottles and
9 specialty imports. **Food available** "Booze and blues only" (but there are salty
snacks); smoking is permitted. **Hours** Tuesday–Saturday, 7 p.m.–2 a.m.

WHO GOES THERE People who like blues with their beers

WHAT GOES ON Live music five nights weekly, encompassing Texas blues,
contemporary jazz, and classic R&B; Bo Diddley has stopped by.

COMMENTS Bamboo lines the walls, and the S-shaped bar is topped with
a collection of copper shakers. This is George Thorogood's kind of bar,
with a "trademark acoustic blues act" that's worth the trademark. Un-
pretentious music and drinks in a cool, intimate atmosphere.

Biba Bar

ÜBER-COOL LOUNGE

Hotel Biba, 320 Belvedere Road, West Palm Beach; ☎ 561-832-0094;
www.hotelbiba.com

Cover None. **Minimum** None. **Mixed drinks** $7–$19, $65–$325 bottle service.
Wine $7–$10. **Beer** $7–$10. **Food available** None. **Hours** Opens daily at 6 p.m.
Closes Wednesday, Friday, and Saturday at 2 a.m.; Tuesday and Thursday at mid-
night; and Sunday and Monday at 11 p.m.

WHO GOES THERE People who speak three languages and own sneakers
more complicated than your DVD player—that is, young internationals
and locals hoping to see and be seen

WHAT GOES ON Hipsters chill and chitchat while the music plays.

COMMENTS Located in the swanky Hotel Biba, Biba Bar is on the high end of
cool but too small to be a ridiculous scene. The decor is lovely—a minimalist, midcentury-modern decorating scheme that is novel for the way
it belies the hotel's island-colonial exterior. Even Floridians feel as if
they're on vacation when they walk in.

Blue Martini

CIVILIZED DRINKING FOR CIVILIZED PEOPLE

550 South Rosemary Avenue, CityPlace, West Palm Beach;
☎ 561-835-8601; www.bluemartinilounge.com

Cover None. **Minimum** None. **Mixed drinks** $6.75 and up; martinis $12–$15. **Wine**
$6.75 and up. **Beer** $5 and up. **Food available** Tapas-menu favorites include a beef

tenderloin sandwich, spinach dip, and sushi. **Hours** Sunday–Thursday, 4 p.m.–3 a.m.; Friday and Saturday, 1 p.m.–4 a.m.

WHO GOES THERE Professionals ages 25–50

WHAT GOES ON Mingling professionals sip, munch, and wiggle a bit to live music (nightly 8:30–11:30 p.m.) that runs the gamut: top-40 tunes, jazz, R&B, and electronica.

COMMENTS The bar is made from milky onyx that is lit from beneath—no self-respecting martini would be caught dead in any different lighting. Modern paintings dot the walls, and live trees provide greenery. The standard attire is semidressy; jackets are not required.

Bru's Room

BEER, FOOD, SPORTS, GAMES

35 NE Second Avenue, Delray Beach; ☎ 561-276-3663
1333 North Congress Avenue, Boynton Beach; ☎ 561-739-9332;
www.brusroom.com

Cover None. **Minimum** None. **Mixed drinks** $3–$7. **Wine** $4.50–$8. **Beer** $2.75–$5. **Food available** Standard sports-bar fare, $5–$12. **Hours** Daily, 11 a.m.–2 a.m.

WHO GOES THERE Working stiffs looking to loosen up, sports fans

WHAT GOES ON Games on TV, bar trivia, darts, game-day specials on food and drinks

COMMENTS A favorite with men and women who roll up the sleeves of their business shirts to improve their dart toss. Named after owner and former Miami Dolphin Bob Brudinski. Happy hour is Monday–Friday, 4–7 p.m.; Sunday–Thursday, 11 p.m. to close: margaritas, $3; domestic longnecks, $2; drafts, $1.75; well drinks, $2; house wine, $3.

Cucina dell'Arte

MORE KHAKI THAN A SAFARI

257 Royal Poinciana Way, Palm Beach; ☎ 561-655-0770;
www.cucinadellarte.com

Cover None. **Minimum** None. **Mixed drinks** $8–$12. **Wine** $8–$11. **Beer** $5–$7. **Food available** Lunch menu available 10:30 a.m.–2 a.m. **Hours** Daily, 7 a.m.–3 a.m.—"open 365, with or without power."

WHO GOES THERE Young Palm Beachers, artists, eccentrics, and good-time Joes ages 18–80

WHAT GOES ON In the later hours, this cute little cafe becomes a standby bar for the kids on the island. A certain amount of pedigree is evident; a degree of silliness is encouraged.

COMMENTS An open-minded, eccentric clientele and staff encourage people to "leave their prejudices at the door." The owners are involved in Palm Beach island life, and the bar is justly esteemed, but Cucina mixes people from all over the area.

Dada Restaurant and Lounge

CASUAL BOHEMIAN

52 North Swinton Avenue, Delray Beach; ☎ 561-330-3232

Cover None. **Minimum** None. **Mixed drinks** $8 and up. **Wine** $7–$15. **Beer** $4–$8. **Food available** Yes; $5–$25. **Hours** Daily, 6 p.m.–1:30 a.m.

WHO GOES THERE College kids, young professionals, local musicians and artists, tourists

WHAT GOES ON Music, open mics, drinking, eating, and cruising for hip young things and artistic types

COMMENTS This popular eatery doubles as a nightlife hot spot. For details, see the restaurant profile on page 342.

Delux

ATTITUDE PLUS

16 East Atlantic Avenue, Delray Beach; ☎ 561-279-4792

Cover $5 weekends. **Minimum** None. **Mixed drinks** $7 and up. **Wine** $4 and up. **Beer** $5 and up. **Food available** Lots of restaurants nearby. **Hours** Wednesday–Sunday, 10 p.m.–2 a.m.

WHO GOES THERE Area see-and-be-seensters dance to high-energy electronica and hip-hop.

WHAT GOES ON If you're in southern Palm Beach County, you look good, and you want to show yourself off without driving to Miami or Lauderdale, this SoBe wannabe is your place. The music is generally pretty good—high-beats-per-minute electronica. But if you're sensitive to blasé rudeness from your fellow (albeit good-looking) patrons, stop at one of the other bars in Delray.

COMMENTS Really the only place to dance inDelray, and one of the younger crowds in town. It's an easy stop right after dinner if you're eating on Atlantic Avenue.

Flow

YOUNG PEOPLE WHO NEED PEOPLE—LOTS OF THEM

308 Clematis Street, West Palm Beach; ☎ 561-833-9555

Cover No cover before midnight on weekends; otherwise, it varies by the night. **Minimum** None. **Mixed drinks** $5 and up. **Wine** $3 and up. **Beer** $3 and up. **Food available** None. **Hours** Daily, 10 p.m.–4 a.m.

WHO GOES THERE Lots of 20-somethings who don't mind being crammed like sardines into a tin can

WHAT GOES ON Solid DJs, fine drinks, attractive young people all make for a mob scene of a hot spot. Claustrophobics, this isn't your joint.

COMMENTS Definitely a college scene. Grown-ups, stay away.

Holloway's Pub

ERIN GO DRINK

77 Royal Palm Plaza, Boca Raton; ☎ 561-361-8445

Cover None. **Minimum** None. **Mixed drinks** None. **Wine** $5 and up. **Beer** $3 and up. **Food available** Irish pub food such as shepherd's pie; salmon patties with mustard-dill sauce. **Hours** Monday–Friday, 4 p.m.–2 a.m.; Saturday, noon–2 a.m.; closed Sundays "unless there's an NFL game."

WHO GOES THERE Anybody who is just anybody

WHAT GOES ON A casual, comfy bar where you can relax and have a drink—very simple. Live music on Friday and Saturday. Tuesday is karaoke night.

COMMENTS A good bar for nice people—a bastion of level-headed living in a city of enormous disposable income.

Kashmir

GENDER BENDER, AN "ALTERNATIVE-LIFESTYLE DANCE COMPLEX"

1651 South Congress Avenue, West Palm Beach; ☎ 561-649-5557

Cover Varies with the night. **Minimum** None. **Mixed drinks** $3 and up. **Wine** $4 and up. **Beer** $4 and up. **Food available** None. **Hours** Monday–Sunday, 10 p.m.–5 a.m.

WHO GOES THERE Girls who like girls, boys who like boys, boys who like boys who look like girls, people who like to dance

WHAT GOES ON Palm Beach County's gay and gay friendly drink, mingle, and dance. Kashmir hosts drag and strip shows in addition to DJs.

COMMENTS One of the oldest gay bars in the area

Monkeyclub

DANCE MUSIC FOR THE MASSES

219 Clematis Street, West Palm Beach; ☎ 561-833-6500

Cover Varies. **Minimum** None. **Mixed drinks** $4 and up. **Wine** $5 and up. **Beer** $4 and up. **Food available** None. **Hours** Thursday–Saturday, 9 p.m.–4 a.m.

WHO GOES THERE 20-something singles who like to shake their tail feathers

WHAT GOES ON Rump shaking, glass draining

COMMENTS The jungle-themed Monkeyclub is a very basic dancing-and-drinking club. Ladies' night on Fridays, with free drinks from 9–11 p.m. The dress code prohibits hats and headgear, bold logos, baggy pants, and beach attire; all guests must be 21 or older.

Release

UNDO THE WEEK AND LET IT ALL HANG OUT

311 Clematis Street, West Palm Beach; ☎ 561-366-9100; www.releasenightclub.com

Cover Varies with night. **Minimum** None. **Mixed drinks** $4 and up. **Wine** $3 and up. **Beer** $3 and up. **Food available** None. **Hours** Thursday, 10 p.m.–3 a.m.; Friday and Saturday, 10 p.m.–4 a.m.

WHO GOES THERE Pretty people from Martin and Palm Beach counties and their hangers-on.

WHAT GOES ON Located on downtown hot spot Clematis Street, Release is the latest big dance club in Palm Beach County, where loyalty to dance clubs is fickle. Release is divided into sections: a red room that plays house and trance and a blue room that pumps the hip-hop.

COMMENTS A large-crowd pleaser—not the most upscale club, but it gets the job done if you want to dance.

Renegades

TWO-STEP TONIGHT

4833 Okeechobee Boulevard, West Palm Beach; ☎ 561-683-9555

Cover Varies. **Minimum** None. **Mixed drinks** $3 and up. **Wine** $2 and up. **Beer** $2 and up. **Food available** None. **Hours** Tuesday–Saturday, 7 p.m.–close.

WHO GOES THERE Country-music fans in Palm Beach County

WHAT GOES ON Line dancing to all walks of music, but mostly country. Plus, there's a mechanical bull.

COMMENTS This place has become a hot spot as of late. Come early for a parking space, and wear your friendly clothes, because you'll be mingling with lots of people, from the parking lot to the lines in the bathrooms.

Respectable Street

COOL FOR LOCALS, COOL FOR YOU

518 Clematis Street, West Palm Beach; ☎ 561-832-9999;
www.respectablestreet.com

Cover Varies with performances; none or $5 (under 21) when no show is scheduled. **Minimum** None. **Mixed drinks** $4 and up. **Wine** $3–$6. **Beer** $2 and up. **Food available** None. **Hours** Wednesday and Thursday 9 p.m.–3 a.m.; Friday and Saturday, 9 p.m.–4 a.m.

WHO GOES THERE Musical melting pot—goth kids, punks, fashionistas, you name it

WHAT GOES ON The longest-running alternative dance club in the Southeast and one of the best venues in Palm Beach County for hearing live alternative music

COMMENTS Built in a renovated Salvation Army in 1987, Respectables, as it's known, made a name for itself by hosting the Red Hot Chili Peppers on the eve of their fame (a hole the Peppers' drummer put in the wall remains to this day). If you can recognize and identify at least one good industrial or electroclash band, or if you own any Joy Division albums, you'll know the secret handshake at the door.

Surf Café

SURF AND BOTTOMS ARE BOTH UP

395 NE Spanish River Boulevard, Boca Raton; ☎ 561-392-1965

Cover Varies. **Minimum** None. **Mixed drinks** $4 and up. **Wine** $3 and up. **Beer** $2 and up. **Food available** Typical bar grub. **Hours** Monday–Saturday, 11:30 a.m.–2 a.m.; Sunday, 3 p.m.–2 a.m.

WHO GOES THERE Florida Atlantic University students and local beachgoing regulars

WHAT GOES ON A small bar with a love for local bands and a surf theme, this is a casual hangout for the college crowd.

COMMENTS In the ten years this bar has been around, it has amassed a pretty regular happy-hour crowd of professionals. Wednesday night is reggae night—always popular. Friday and Saturday nights, local bands play—and the clientele varies according to the style of the bands performing.

PART SIX

BROWARD COUNTY

WELCOME *to* BROWARD COUNTY

BROWARD MAY NOT HAVE THE SEXY AURA of its neighbor Miami-Dade, but it flaunts its glorious award-winning coastline like a feathery boa. No longer the "in" place for Spring Break, it's now a paradoxical combo for tourists—sophisticated and sensible, upscale and affordable, laidback and dynamic. There's a mix of opportunities for nature-lovers, art lovers, families, and just about anyone who appreciates the water.

A combination of cities, suburbs, and natural areas, Broward County—now often called "Greater Fort Lauderdale"—stretches 23 miles along the Atlantic Ocean between Palm Beach County on the north and Miami-Dade County on the south. Broward's western boundary is 505,600 acres of Everglades (occupying about two-thirds of the county). In all, the county encompasses 1,197 square miles.

Thirty municipalities with more than 1.5 million people make up Greater Fort Lauderdale/Broward. They include Hallandale, Hollywood, Dania Beach, Fort Lauderdale, Lauderdale-by-the-Sea, Lighthouse Point, Pompano Beach, Hillsboro Beach, Sea Ranch Lakes, and Deerfield Beach. Most are quiet, mainly residential communities by the water. Farther west, new suburban communities continue to edge toward the Everglades.

Fort Lauderdale, a fast-growing city of 150,000, is the county's largest municipality and the seat of government, with an ever-soaring skyline of offices and luxury condos. But natural assets are not forgotten in the midst of today's building boom. The waterways and beaches, museums and art center, and Las Olas Boulevard and River-walk by the New River offer exceptional tourism opportunities.

Dania Beach was once the country's tomato capital. Located just south of Fort Lauderdale/Hollywood International Airport, Dania Beach is now famous for its Antiques Row (along US 1) with a wide collection of antique jewelry, furniture, and housewares, as well as its unspoiled, dune-fringed shore.

Hollywood, seven miles south of Fort Lauderdale, projects both past and present in a comfy, livable mix. The Broadwalk by the ocean and the downtown Circle are popular places to stroll, and the mix of old and new shops and cafes provides for pleasant hours of browsing and people watching.

A BRIEF HISTORY

BROWARD COUNTY WAS, FOR MANY YEARS, a bedroom community for Miami workers. The area began to attract migrants from the Northeast and Midwest and former members of the military who had trained in the area during World War II. Many Georgians and Alabamians also settled in the region. While originally Broward was—like Miami Beach to the south—a community of retirees, current statistics indicate the average age of residents is now under 40.

The traditional pattern of migration to Florida's southeastern coast included a core group of people from the Northeast, particularly from urban centers: Boston, New York, New Jersey, Philadelphia, Baltimore, and Washington, D.C. Although most Midwesterners opted for (and still choose) Florida's southwestern coast over the southeastern coast, some chose the small-town feel of Broward County.

Many migrants were Jews who sought a better life and the promise of a fine climate and sunshine year-round. Signs here once said "no dogs or Jews allowed," but today a hundred varieties of bagels are available at dozens of local bakeries and delis. A rich Jewish cultural life supports some three dozen synagogues, as well as Hebrew day schools and social-service agencies throughout Broward County.

After Hurricane Andrew struck southern Dade County in 1992, another wave of residents came to Broward looking to begin anew. Today the area is also home to many Caribbean-basin and Hispanic immigrants who have settled in Fort Lauderdale's western suburbs, coming from island nations to seek that same "better life."

Tourism too has come in waves. Fort Lauderdale was a spring-break destination for years, a place where young people partied around the clock and tourism honchos and hoteliers developed heartburn after wet T-shirt contests found their way to national television. At its heyday in 1985, the area attracted 350,000 college revelers—a "Maalox moment" for locals. Today, tourists from Canada, Europe, and South America enjoy sun and fun, and Northerners and gay and lesbian travelers have also found the Fort Lauderdale area a welcoming destination.

BROWARD COUNTY TODAY

MORE THAN SEVEN MILLION TOURISTS ENJOY Broward's average year-round temperature of 77° Fahrenheit. And in recent years, Fort Lauderdale has emerged as a growing business center. Downtown Fort Lauderdale has become a center of fine-dining opportunities and home to the Broward Center for the Performing Arts and outstanding museums. And landscaped, architecturally retro Las Olas Boulevard offers boutiques, galleries, and restaurants—and a charming stroll.

Broward County's artificial-reef program is augmenting the underwater ecosystem and renewing both fish and coral life. Angel fish, sergeant majors, sea turtles, octopus, butterflyfish, and barracudas abound—even large fish such as grouper. The reef is a 20-minute boat trip from the beaches, and air service is frequent and economical.

Back on land, trendy hotels and multimillion-dollar mansions along the waterways earn the city its nickname: the "Venice of America." Greater Fort Lauderdale is also called the "Yachting Capital of the World."

And redevelopment and renewal projects—Broward's answer to the popularity of South Beach—have revitalized downtown Hollywood with galleries and restaurants. Realtors have rediscovered the popularity of these older communities with the addition of new amenities that attract younger buyers. And property values are somewhat lower in Broward than in Miami-Dade or Palm Beach.

Greater Fort Lauderdale boasts the second-highest hotel occupancy in the state (Orlando and the mighty mouse, Disney World, rank number one). In recent years, there's been a boom in tourism, population, housing, job growth, and commercial real-estate development.

How do all these new residents and tourists occupy their time? Shopping and dining fill the gaps between sporting and cultural events, with year-round offerings now the norm. The state-of-the-art Office Depot Center in Sunrise is home to the Florida Panthers hockey team. The Fusion major-league soccer team plays at Lockhart Stadium, while Fort Lauderdale Stadium hosts the Baltimore Orioles for spring training. And just over the line in Miami-Dade is Dolphins pro football and Florida Marlins pro baseball.

Once the whole county seemed to close up in the summer, but today venues such as Sunrise Musical Theater, Parker Playhouse, and Broward Center for the Perfoming Arts host some of the world's best entertainers in every season. Shopaholics have their pick of Bloomingdale's, Saks, or Nordstrom, as well as Sawgrass Mills, one of the country's largest outlet malls.

Be prepared to drive to all the shops and venues, however. While Broward's growth spurt has touched each of the county's eclectic neighborhoods, infrastructure (parks, schools, and especially public transportation) struggles to keep pace.

GATHERING INFORMATION

FOR TOURIST INFORMATION ON BROWARD COUNTY, contact the **Greater Fort Lauderdale Convention & Visitors Bureau,** 19850 Eller Drive, Suite 303, Fort Lauderdale 33316; ☎ 800-22-SUNNY ext. 711 (in the United States and Canada); **www.sunny.org.** Available information includes a free CD-ROM about local dive sites. Numerous GFLCVB branch offices are found throughout the United States and elsewhere:

Washington, D.C.
1800 Diagonal Road, Suite 130
Alexandria, VA 22314
☎ 703-684-0456
fax 703-684-6848

Chicago
225 West Scott Street, 2E
Chicago, IL 60610
☎ 312-932-9668
fax 312-932-0221

United Kingdom
Contact Travel Marketing Ltd.
21 Broadway
Maidenhead, Berks SL6 1NJ
☎ 011-44-1628 778863
fax 011-44-1628 676798

ARRIVING

WHILE MANY TRAVELERS STILL CHOOSE TO DRIVE to Florida, or take Amtrak's Auto Train, most people fly into Broward County, to the Fort Lauderdale/Hollywood International Airport. In fact, many visitors going to Florida's Southwest Coast or Miami opt to fly into Fort Lauderdale/Hollywood because it's more user-friendly, and airfares are often cheaper, particularly in comparison to the Fort Myers area.

Some visitors arrive on cruise ships and spend a few days in the region. Port Everglades is just minutes away from the airport and is the second-largest cruise port in the world, serving more five-star cruise ships than any other port in the country.

Among the lines serving Port Everglades are Celebrity, Costa, Crystal, Cunard, Discovery, Holland America, Princess, Radisson Seven Seas, Royal Caribbean, Royal Olympic, Seabourn, Sea-Escape, and Silversea.

Taxi service is available both at the airport and the cruise port.

BY PLANE

IN THE MIDST OF SECURITY CONCERNS AND hassles, the Fort Lauderdale/Hollywood International Airport was one of the few in the country that actually increased flights during the early part of the decade. Located between Interstate 95 on the east and US 1 on the west, and between Griffin Road on the south and FL 84 on the north, the airport is served by most major airlines, including the following carriers: Air Canada, AirTran, America West, American, American Trans Air, Continental, Delta, Delta Express, JetBlue, MetroJet, Midway, Midwest Express, Northwest, Southwest, Spirit, TWA, United, USAirways, and USAirways Express.

It is undergoing an expansion project that is estimated to cost about $1 billion by the year 2012, more than doubling the airport's passenger capacity from 11 million in 1996 to 25 million by 2015. It is a comfortable, easy-to-use airport, well marked and well lit.

After leaving the airport, tourists work their way east to the Atlantic Ocean, west to the suburbs, north to Palm Beach, or south to Miami-Dade. While many local Fort Lauderdale-area hotels offer shuttle service from the airport (telephones are available on the airport's lower level across from the baggage carousels), taxi service and rental cars are also available at the airport (rental-car lots are nearby but off the airport grounds). Rental-car agencies serving the airport and cruise port are Alamo, Avis, Budget, Dollar, Enterprise, Hertz, National, Snappy, Thompson, Thrifty, and Value.

BY CAR

THE MOST DIRECT ROUTE TO FORT LAUDERDALE Beach from the airport is by US 1 North (also called Federal Highway). Take US 1 to the 17th Street Causeway and turn right. This is one of the major beach-access roads, and traffic is always heavy. You will pass over a bridge (which spans the Intracoastal Waterway). The road turns north at FL A1A.

If your destination is, for example, Hollywood Beach, Aventura, or North Miami Beach, take US 1 South. To reach Hollywood Beach, turn left onto Dania Beach Boulevard, passing Dania Jai Alai, and winding up on FL A1A. If you continue south on US 1 (be forewarned: you'll meet with heavy traffic), you will pass the Aventura/Turnberry complex—and the Aventura mega–shopping mall with Bloomingdale's, Macy's, Sears, and JC Penney among its many stores.

When you reach the Lehman Causeway (named for a former well-known and respected state legislator), turn left, heading east toward

unofficial **TIP**
Because the traffic on US 1 can be stop and go, we offer an alternative to getting to Aventura or North Miami. Head south on US 1, turn left at Dania Beach Boulevard, and continue south on FL A1A. To return inland to Aventura, stay in the right-hand lane at Lehman Causeway (aka 192nd Street) to get back to US 1 (Federal Highway).

the ocean. The view is spectacular, and traffic flows well most of the day. Don't let the fact that the highway is called 188th Street in Aventura throw you.

If you're headed to the western area, follow the signs to I-595 and cut through Broward County to Cooper City, Sunrise, Plantation, or half a dozen other western suburbs. I-595 ultimately leads to I-75 and Florida's Gulf Coast. You will pass townhomes, apartments, and country-club communities as well as an eclectic mix of strip malls.

An alternative to I-595 is to take an east–west road such as Griffin or Stirling Street west to Pine Island and then head north to Sunrise, Plantation, and so on.

If, like many travelers, you use Fort Lauderdale as a gateway to Miami, follow the signs to I-595, then onto I-95 south to downtown, Coral Gables, Coconut Grove, and so on.

BY BUS AND TRAIN

GREYHOUND BUS LINES AND TRIRAIL SERVICE Fort Lauderdale and Hollywood. Greyhound provides intercity bus service. The main station is located at 515 NE Third Street, Fort Lauderdale; ☎ 954-763-6551. More than 15 buses a day travel between Fort Lauderdale and Miami-Dade (many stopping in Hollywood). Service starts at 7:50 a.m., and the last bus runs at 11:30 p.m.

TriRail offers train service from Palm Beach County through Broward County and into Miami-Dade to Miami International Airport. Its main station is located at 205 South Andrews Avenue, Fort Lauderdale; ☎ 954-357-8400 or 800-TRI-RAIL. Train service runs frequently throughout the day but less often on weekends. Both the Greyhound and TriRail stations are in marginal areas of town but are patrolled regularly. Be careful and avoid traveling alone at night.

GETTING AROUND

DRIVING YOUR CAR

BEFORE GETTING BEHIND THE WHEEL, REQUEST instructions from your hotel, motel, or host. Let them know where you will be picking up a car (Fort Lauderdale/Hollywood International Airport, Port Everglades, etc.) and get complete directions to the property.

Some cities, Fort Lauderdale, Dania Beach, Hallandale Beach, Pembroke Pines, for example, use a Northwest, Northeast, Southwest, Southeast pattern of street numbers from a core point in the city. Consider Fort Lauderdale: The intersection of Broward Boulevard and Andrews Avenue is effectively ground zero. North of Broward, addresses include "N" followed by an "E" or "W" denoting the direction east or west of Andrews. Streets, terraces, and courts generally run east–west. Avenues run north–south. Some streets run on an angle, however, starting out east and west then turning north or south. We suggest a good map, or better yet a GPS system, as a traveling companion.

Broward County's major north-south arteries are: **A1A,** also called **Ocean Drive** because it runs along the Atlantic Ocean, except for a short run in Fort Lauderdale and Dania Beach where John U. Lloyd Beach State Recreation Area runs inland from the beach); **US 1; I-95,** a classic interstate with on–off ramps and the requisite fast-food outlets, gas stations, and strip malls; **US 441 (FL 7),** a slow-going road lined with auto showrooms, garages, chain restaurants, and seemingly perpetual construction; the Florida Turnpike, also called the **Ronald Reagan Expressway;** and **University Drive,** the major roadway toward suburbs and towns west of Fort Lauderdale and Hollywood. Major north–south arteries in western Broward include **Pine Island Road, Nob Hill Road, Hiatus Road,** and **Flamingo Road.**

East–west traffic is heaviest on **I-595,** a relatively new interstate connecting the airport (and seaport) to the western suburbs. East–west streets that many tourists travel include: **Hallandale Beach Boulevard (FL 858)** from the Atlantic Ocean to University Drive through Hallandale, Hollywood, and Miramar (where it becomes **Miramar Parkway**); **Hollywood Boulevard (FL 820)** through Hollywood and Pembroke Pines (it becomes **Pines Boulevard** at **University Drive**); **Sheridan Street** in Dania Beach, Hollywood, Cooper City, and Pembroke Pines; **Stirling Road (FL 848)** from US 1 through Dania Beach, Hollywood, Pembroke Lakes, Cooper City, and Davie; **Griffin Road (FL 818)** from US 1 through Dania Beach, Fort Lauderdale, Hollywood, Cooper City, and Davie on to Weston; **FL 84** from Fort Lauderdale to I-595 and on to Port Everglades; **Broward Boulevard (FL 842)** from US 1 to Pine Island Drive; **Sunrise Boulevard (FL 838)** between the Atlantic Ocean and Sawgrass Mills Mall; **Oakland Park Boulevard (FL 816)** from the ocean west through Fort Lauderdale and Sunrise; and **Commercial Boulevard (FL 870)** from the Atlantic to Sunrise.

PUBLIC TRANSPORTATION

THOUGH A MAJORITY OF RESIDENTS RELY on automobiles, Broward County Mass Transit runs more than 230 buses, and services the entire county (☎ 954-357-8400). TriRail also provides regularly scheduled train service between Palm Beach, Broward, and Miami-Dade Counties with stops throughout Broward (☎ 800-874-7245).

Fort Lauderdale's popular water taxis crisscross the Intracoastal Waterway and the city's canals (☎ 954-728-8417). These mini-cruises are a great way to get from one point to another amid Fort Lauderdale's primo real estate.

AT *the* SEASHORE

THE BEACHES

WASHINGTON-BASED CLEAN BEACHES COUNCIL, the first environmental beach-certification board in the United States, named five Greater Fort Lauderdale shorelines as Blue Wave Beaches. Hollywood, Dania, Fort Lauderdale, Pompano, and Deerfield beaches are the state's only beaches to meet the standards for safety, cleanliness, and accessibility. All beaches receiving the award have Blue Wave flags, public-information kiosks, and beach-entrance boundary markers. Greater Fort Lauderdale is also frequently named as one of the top diving destinations in the country.

Hollywood Beach is popular because of its Broadwalk, running parallel to the ocean and lined with dozens of little restaurants, many geared to the French Canadian tourists who winter in the area. It's a good family beach with many lifeguard stations. The action generally spreads north and south from the Johnson Street Parking Garage or north from Hollywood's North Beach Park at Sheridan Street. Or for a relaxed setting, check out tiny Charnow Park, with picnic tables, a Vita course, and a playground. About seven blocks south of Las Olas, **Fort Lauderdale Beach** is long and crowded, with a sidewalk promenade that runs alongside it. This popular beach is also a family favorite with plenty of lifeguard stations. Across the road are dozens of watering holes, popular after hours, where you can watch the waves. The area at the foot of Sunrise and FL A1A is nothing but sun, sand, and water, and if you don't need the picnic area or a playground, you'll love it.

Deerfield Beach is much less crowded, but restaurants and cafes aren't as plentiful as along Hollywood or Fort Lauderdale beaches. Deerfield is a trade-off, but great for those who like a less-hectic atmosphere.

Wherever you have beaches you have parking problems. Weekends are especially crowded, so we suggest you arrive early to secure metered parking or opt for pay parking lots/garages. Don't park illegally on the street (it could be a very costly day at the beach). If your hotel is on the ocean, walking is a sensible option.

*un*official **TIP**
Safety should take priority on any water-sports outing, and we heartily recommend three things: don't fool around in the water if you can't swim, take basic lessons, and never mix liquor with water sports.

Beach Activities

Water-skiing, windsurfing, and parasailing classes are available at the more crowded beaches, as are sailboard and Jet-Ski rentals.

SCUBA DIVING

WHEN THE *MERCEDES*, A 197-FOOT GERMAN freighter, was tossed upon a Palm Beach pool terrace in 1985, it was big news and a nuisance to Palm Beach residents.

Today, it resides in 97 feet of water just a mile from Fort Lauderdale Beach, a new habitat for myriad coral and other marine life. Legend tells that it is home to a barracuda so accustomed to divers, it can be hand-fed—if you dare. On clear days, the *Mercedes* can be seen from the dive boat on the surface.

This new artificial reef has helped position Greater Fort Lauderdale as one of the best wreck-diving destinations in the United States and the Caribbean. Coral growth begins right away on sunken ships, and fish soon come to feed. Other nearby wrecks include the *Atria,* a 240-foot freighter lying in 112 feet of water, and the *Marriot,* a DC-4 airplane 71 feet under.

Area divers have their pick of more than 80 different sites, from artificial reefs and the 23-mile-long, 2-mile-wide Fort Lauderdale Reef, which marks the northern end of the ancient living-coral formation that runs from Palm Beach south past the Florida Keys.

For general information on diving certification, see Part One, pages 27–28. In Broward County, contact **Brownie's Third Lung** (1530 Cordova Road, Fort Lauderdale; ☎ 954-524-2112). Brownie's offers rental, air fills, and lessons. Fees are $50 for a four-hour, two-tank dive from a boat. Similar prices prevail at **Scuba Network** (199 North Federal Highway, Deerfield Beach; ☎ 954-422-9982) and at South Florida Diving **"Aquanaut"** (101 North Riverside Drive, Pompano Beach; ☎ 954-783-2299).

BROWARD-AREA REEFS AND DEPTHS	
Suzannes Ledges	13–16 feet
Twin Ledges	30–45 feet
Copenhagen Wreck	15–30 feet
Tenneco Platforms	105–190 feet
Curry Reef	70–75 feet
Osborne Reef	60–75 feet
Dania EroJacks Reef	10–20 feet
Fishamerica	110–115 feet

FISHING

DRIFT FISHING IS POPULAR WITH FAMILIES. Usually boats go out for four hours at a time—in early morning, at noon, and occasionally at night. For a set fee, your hooks are baited, your fish cleaned, and all the gear you need (poles, reels, tackle, and bait) is supplied. Some people call drift boats "party boats," but most of the 30 or 40 people who have paid to head out to sea are there to catch fish.

Operators include **Helen S. Drift Fishing** (101 North Riverside Drive, #107, Pompano Beach; ☎ 954-941-3209); **Sea Legs III** (5400

North Ocean Drive, Hollywood; ☎ 954-923-2109); and **Flamingo Fishing** (801 Seabreeze Boulevard, in Bahia Mar Marina; ☎ 954-462-9194). Rates average about $25 for adults and $16 for children.

Chartering a boat is a more costly option, but one readily available at area marinas such as Bahia Mar in Fort Lauderdale or Harbour Town in Dania Beach. Charters go further out to sea than drift boats and cater to anglers who want to fish all day.

BOATING

ABOUT 40,000 BOATS ARE REGISTERED IN Fort Lauderdale—more per capita than almost anywhere else. Most, but not all, frequent saltwater.

Glass-bottom boat cruises (**A Admiral's Cruise Line,** 801 Seabreeze Boulevard, Bahia Mar; ☎ 954-522-2220) and sailboat rentals (**Palm Breeze Charter,** Hillsboro Boulevard and the Intracoastal; 561-368-3566) allow you to enjoy the ocean without getting sand in your shorts. Canoeing is offered at **Hugh Taylor Birch State Park** (3109 East Sunrise Boulevard, Fort Lauderdale; ☎ 954-564-4521) and **Tree Tops Park** (3900 SW 100th Avenue, Davie; ☎ 954-370-3750). Both canoeing and kayaking are available at **West Lake Park/Anne Kolb Nature Center** (751 Sheridan Street, Hollywood; ☎ 954-926-2410).

SPORTS *and* RECREATION

FITNESS CENTERS AND AEROBICS

MANY BROWARD COUNTY HOTELS OFFER state-of-the-art fitness centers and/or aerobics classes, eliminating the challenge of working out in the heat. Independent gym chains also have facilities that similarly allow you to feel the burn without burning up.

If you can't work out in your hotel, here are some local options. **Gold's Gym Fitness and Aerobic Center** (1427 East Commercial Boulevard, Fort Lauderdale; ☎ 954-491-8314) is a full-service gym. Daily fees are $15. **Bally Total Fitness, Courtrooms** (750 West Sunrise Boulevard, downtown Fort Lauderdale; ☎ 954-764-8666) is another full-service health club. Daily rates vary. Membership at other chain locations is honored here.

TENNIS

IF YOUR HOTEL DOESN'T HAVE TENNIS COURTS, don't worry, there are more than 550 public and private courts throughout Broward County. Consider where tennis champ Chris Evert learned her swing, her father's **James Evert Tennis Center** (701 NE 12th Avenue, Fort Lauderdale; ☎ 954-828-5378), with 18 clay courts and 3 hard courts. Hours are Monday–Friday, 7:45 a.m.–9 p.m.; Saturday and Sunday, 7:45 a.m.–6 p.m. Fees are $5–$6 for doubles and $6–$7 for singles.

Free public courts in Fort Lauderdale are located at **Bay View Park** (4400 Bay View Drive, between Oakland Park Boulevard and Sunrise Boulevard); **Hardy Park** (Andrews Avenue and SW Seventh Street); and **Riverside Park** (500 SW 11th Avenue). All are open from 8 a.m. to dusk and operate on a first-come, first-served basis. For more information, call the Fort Lauderdale Parks and Recreation Department at ☎ 954-828-5346.

Hollywood's **David Park Tennis Center** (510 North 33rd Court, Hollywood; ☎ 954-967-4237) has nine clay and three hard courts. Fees are $6–$7 per person all day; light fees are $1 for every 15 minutes of night play. Hours are Monday–Thursday, 7:30 a.m.–9 p.m.; Friday, 7:30 a.m.–8 p.m.; Saturday and Sunday, 7:30 a.m.–5 p.m. Lessons are available.

Free courts are available 8 a.m.–8 p.m. at Hollywood's **Jefferson Park** (Jefferson Street between 15th and 16th Avenues; ☎ 954-921-3404). Visitors can enjoy free play daily, 8 a.m.–9 p.m., at Hallandale's **Peter Bluesten Park** (501 SE First Avenue, Hallandale; ☎ 954-457-1457) and **Oreste Blake Johnson Park** (745 NW Ninth Street, Hallandale; ☎ 954-457-1453).

GOLF

ALTHOUGH THE "TOURIST" SEASON STARTS somewhere after Thanksgiving and runs through Easter, golf courses are always busy. During the week, it's possible to get in on a game with no-shows. Weekends—when local residents hit the links—are busy year-round, and securing a morning reservation is difficult. Greens fees are reduced at many courses during the off-season. Book in advance through your hotel. Plan on teeing off before 1 p.m., so you're not racing the sun. Sunset occurs around 5 p.m. in the middle of winter, closer to 8:30 p.m. in the summer. Reserve an early-morning or late-afternoon tee time and avoid the links between 11 a.m. and 2 p.m.

Courses throughout South Florida have been designed by some of the game's greatest players and best-known course designers, including Arnold Palmer, Pete Dye, and George and Tom Fazio. South Florida golf courses meet varying skill levels.

Some of the best courses in Broward are profiled below.

Bonaventure Country Club

ESTABLISHED: 1969   STATUS: SEMIPRIVATE/RESORT COURSE, OPEN TO THE PUBLIC

200 Bonaventure Boulevard, Weston 33326; ☎ 954-389-2100; www.golfbonaventure.com

Tees

WEST COURSE

- **Blue: 6,128 yards, par 70, USGA 71, slope 118**
- **White: 5,736 yards, par 70, USGA 70, slope 116**

- **Red: 5,014 yards, par 70, USGA 69.0, slope 114**
  EAST COURSE (INCLUDES SENIORS' TEES)
- **Blue: 7,011 yards, par 72, USGA 74.2, slope 132**
- **White: 6,519 yards, par 72, USGA 72.5, slope 127**
- **Red: 5,207 yards, par 72, USGA, 71.6, slope 122**
- **Gold: 5,742 years, par 72, USGA 68.3, slope 117**

Fees Monday–Thursday, $40–$60 for West, $50–$70 for East. Weekend rates are $20 higher, cart included.

Facilities Pro shop, restaurant and lounge, banquet facilities for 150, lessons, equipment rental

Comments These two popular 18-hole courses are in good shape and used year-round by locals and guests at the nearby Wyndham Resort and Spa.

The Club at Emerald Hills

ESTABLISHED: 1968   STATUS: SEMIPRIVATE COURSE

4100 North Hills Drive, Hollywood 33021; ☎ 954-961-4000; www.theclubatemeraldhills.com

Tees

- **Black: 7,280 yards, par 72, USGA 76.1, slope 146**
- **Blue: 6,683 yards, par 72, USGA 73.4, slope 136**
- **White: 6,249 yards, par 72, USGA 71.2, slope 130**

Fees Weekdays, $45–$140; weekends, $55–$165
Facilities Catering services, restaurant, pro shop.
Comments A qualifying course for Honda and Doral tournaments, this course was completely redone in 2000 and is considered top-quality.

Colony West Country Club

ESTABLISHED: 1970   STATUS: PUBLIC COURSE

6800 NW 88th Avenue (Pine Island Avenue), Tamarac 33321; ☎ 954-726-8430; www.colonywestcc.com

Tees

CHAMPIONSHIP COURSE—MEN'S
- **Gold: 7,312 yards, par 71, USGA 75.5, slope 146**
- **Green: 6,875 yards, par 71, USGA 73.7, slope 142**
- **Blue: 6,420 yards, par 71, USGA 71.7, slope 135**
- **White: 5,462 yards, par 71, USGA 68.2, slope 127**
CHAMPIONSHIP COURSE—LADIES
- **Blue: 6,420 yards, par 71, USGA 77.7, slope 139**
- **White: 5,462 yards, par 71, USGA 73.4, slope 137**
GLADES COURSE—MEN'S
- **Blue: 4,207 yards, par 65, USGA 59.3, slope 89**
- **White: 3,855, par 65, USGA 58.2, slope 84**
GLADES COURSE—LADIES
- **White: 3,855 yards, par 65, USGA 61.0, slope 94**

- **Red: 3,331, par 65, USGA 57.7, slope 88**

Fees Championship course, $28–$55; Glade course, $15.21–$21

Facilities Pro shop, restaurant, snack bar, banquet capacity for 250, outdoor area for parties

Comments Cart required on Championship course, golfers can walk Glades course

Diplomat Country Club and Spa

ESTABLISHED: 2000   STATUS: RESORT COURSE

501 Diplomat Parkway, Hallandale 33009; ☎ 954-883-4444; www.diplomatcountryclub.com

Tees

- **Blue: 6,728 yards, par 72, USGA 71.9, slope 136**
- **Gold: 6,393 yards, par 72, USGA 71.3, slope 129**
- **Red: 5,354 yards, par 72, USGA 71.4, slope 119**
- **White: 6,107 yards, par 72, USGA 69.8, slope 127**

Fees $200 per day, includes cart

Facilities Country club complex, two restaurants, 60 guest rooms, meeting space, yacht slips, pro shop, and two air-conditioned convenience stations

Comments This beautiful course, redesigned by golf architect Joe Lee, is state-of-the-art.

Hollywood Beach Golf and Country Club

ESTABLISHED: 1923   STATUS: PUBLIC

1600 Johnson Street, Hollywood 33020; ☎ 954-927-1751; www.hollywoodbeachgolf.com

Tees

- **Middle: 6,336 yards, par 70, USGA 70, slope 114**
- **Back: 6,024 yards, par 70, USGA 70, slope 117**
- **Forward: 5,484 yards, par 70, USGA 70, slope 112**

Fees $20–$30, reduced after 11 a.m. and 3 p.m.

Facilities Pro shop, clubhouse restaurant, 31-room full-service hotel, locker rooms, pool

Comments Designed by Donald Ross in 1925 and completely renovated in 1995, this course is a golfing tradition, all the more valued because little golf existed in Hollywood prior to the 1920s.

Orangebrook Country Club

ESTABLISHED: EARLY 1950S   STATUS: PUBLIC

400 Entrada Drive, Hollywood 33021; ☎ 954-967-4653; www.orangebrook.com

Tees

WEST COURSE

- **Gold: 6,626 yards, par 71, USGA 70.7, slope 121**

- Blue: 6,208 yards, par 71, USGA 70.7, slope 121
- White: 5,712 yards, par 71, USGA 68.7, slope 134
- Green: 4,680 yards, par 71, USGA 71.3, slope 123
  EAST COURSE
- Blue: 6,574 yards, par 72, USGA 70.6, slope 117
- White: 6,108 yards, par 72, USGA 68.5, slope 115
- Green: 5,509 yards, par 72, USGA 71.6, slope 117

Fees $15–$26; includes cart

Facilities Pro shop, restaurant, lessons available

Comments One of Hollywood's oldest, most popular courses, Orange-brook is just a half mile west of I-95.

Pompano Beach Municipal Golf Course

ESTABLISHED: 1967   STATUS: PUBLIC

1101 North Federal Highway, Pompano Beach 33062; ☎ 954-786-4142; www.mypompanobeach.org/parks/rec/golf/

Tees
  PINES
- Gold: 6,995 yards, par 72, USGA 72.7, slope 120
- Blue: 6,598 yards, par 72, USGA 70.6, slope 116
- White: 6,209 yards, par 72, USGA 69.1, slope 113
- Red: 5,530 yards, par 72, USGA 69.1, slope 109
  PALMS
- Gold: 6,345 yards, par 71/72, USGA 72.7, slope 120
- Blue: 6,035, par 71/72, USGA 70.6, slope 116
- White: 5,787 yards, par 71/72, USGA 69.1, slope 113
- Red: 5,133 yards, par 71/72, USGA 67.8, slope 109

Fees $18 for 18 holes, $14 for 9 holes; $16.50 to walk after 4 p.m.

Facilities Driving range, practice greens, restaurant and bar, locker rooms and showers, pro shop and instruction

Comments A $2 million renovation improved this municipal course. The Pines course is long, while the Palms course, with more doglegs, requires "position golf."

Tournament Players Club at Heron Bay

ESTABLISHED: 1996   STATUS: PUBLIC

11801 Heron Bay, Coral Springs 33076; ☎ 954-796-2000; www.tpc.com/daily/heron_bay

Tees
- Gold: 7,268 yards, par 72, USGA 74.9, slope 133
- Blue: 6,781 yards, par 72, USGA 72.7, slope 128
- White: 6,123 yards, par 72, USGA 69.7, slope 122

- Green: 5,580 yards, par 72, USGA 67.0, slope 114
- Red: 4,961 yards, par 72, USGA 68.7, slope 113

Fees $50–$85, includes cart; $27–$45 after 2 p.m.

Facilities Golf shop, full-service restaurant and lounge, locker rooms, club and shoe rentals

Comments This world-class course is the permanent home of the Honda Classic.

WALKING, RUNNING, AND HIKING

FORT LAUDERDALE IS MORE A WATER CITY than a walking city. You won't see many people walking to pick up a loaf of bread or their dry cleaning. This is a strip-mall environment, with mall after mall and parking lot after parking lot just waiting for South Floridians to perform their errands. However, those who want to walk or jog for exercise will find a variety of venues. One of the prettiest is along the ocean on Hollywood Beach.

The **Hollywood Broadwalk** runs north–south from Sheridan Street to Washington Street, a distance of about four miles, with water on each side for much of the way. Many walkers opt to stroll through air-conditioned malls, and **Broward Mall** at University Drive and Broward Boulevard is popular. Many of the parks and attractions mentioned elsewhere also have nature trails.

Jogging tracks are available at **McTyre Park** (3501 SW 56th Avenue, Pembroke Park; ☎ 954-964-0283); **North Broward Park** (4400 NE 18th Avenue, Pompano Beach; ☎ 954-796-2195); **Brian Piccolo Park** (9501 Sheridan Street, Cooper City; ☎ 954-437-2600); **Plantation Heritage Park** (1100 South Fig Tree Lane, Plantation; ☎ 954-791-1025); and **Tradewinds Park** (3600 West Sample Road, Coconut Creek; ☎ 954-968-3880). Area high schools also allow walkers and runners to use their tracks when school is out.

Nature Trails at **West Lake Park/Anne Kolb Nature Center** (751 Sheridan Street, Hollywood; ☎ 954-926-2410) are mapped out for hikers. Canoe rentals are also available, and don't miss the narrated boat tour through mangrove swamps.

Hiking paths are available at other Broward County parks, including **Brian Piccolo Park** (address above); **Plantation Heritage Park** (address above); **Quiet Waters Park** (401 South Powerline Road, Pompano Beach; ☎ 954-360-1315); and **T. Y. Park** (3300 North Park Road, Hollywood; ☎ 954-985-1980).

Broward County parks offer other activities ranging from horseshoes (**Easterlin Park,** 100 NW 36th Street, Oakland Park; ☎ 954-938-0610) to a target range and pro shop (**Markham Park and Range,** 16001 West FL 84, Sunrise; ☎ 954-389-2000).

For complete Broward County Parks and Recreation Division activities, call ☎ 954-357-8100 or 954-587-2844 (TTY).

BICYCLING

BROWARD COUNTY, LIKE MOST OF FLORIDA, is flat as a lousy cook's soufflé, so it's easy to cover lots of ground on two wheels. Helmets are compulsory.

Bicycling is best done along the ocean or on park bike paths, however, as heavy South Florida traffic doesn't lend itself to road biking. Between the Intracoastal waterway to the west and the ocean to the east is the Broadwalk in Hollywood, where **Bike Shack** (101 North Ocean Drive/FL A1A, Hollywood; ☎ 954-925-2453) rents equipment starting at $5, and bikers must be 18 with a valid driver's license.

Other bicycling options are the Fort Lauderdale Beach, where in-line skaters also do their thing, and through a variety of parks in Broward County. Mountain bikers might want to check out **Quiet Waters Park** in Pompano Beach for a moderate-to-challenging 5.5-mile loop. For more details, contact Quiet Waters Park (401 South Powerline Road; ☎ 954-360-1315). For other nearby off-road options, see *Mountain Bike! Florida* by Steve Jones (Menasha Ridge Press; distributed by Globe Pequot Press; ☎ 800-243-0495).

SPECTATOR SPORTS

YOU COULD HAPPILY VACATION IN FLORIDA and never see the beach. One popular choice is watching major-league sports teams in action. And in the cases of the Florida Panthers and Miami Heat, both teams play in new, state-of-the-art arenas.

The **Miami Dolphins,** the local AFC East football team, play home games just over the county line in Miami-Dade at Pro Player Stadium (2269 NW Dan Marino Boulevard, North Miami; ☎ 888-346-7849). The stadium used to be named for Joe Robbie, and locals still call it that—he was the founder of the Dolphins and the owner when the team had its perfect season in 1972.

Individual tickets range in price from $45 to $70, and they can be purchased at the stadium box office, online at **www.pro-player-stadium.com,** and via Ticketmaster (☎ 954-523-3309). Preseason games start in August. Check the *Miami Herald* or *Sun-Sentinel* for preseason training, which is sometimes open to the public.

The National League **Florida Marlins,** who won the 1997 World Series, also play at Pro Player Stadium. General admission tickets are $6–$85 per seat. Call the stadium (☎ 305-620-2578) or Ticketmaster (☎ 954-523-3309), or check the paper for game dates and information on special promotions.

The **Florida Panthers,** a National Hockey League team, made it to the Stanley Cup finals in their third season. They play in Sunrise at the Office Depot Arena (2555 SW 137th Way, Sunrise). Individual tickets are available only through Ticketmaster (☎ 954-835-8326). Ticket prices range from $20 to $250.

The **Miami Heat,** the local NBA team, play at American Airlines Arena (601 Biscayne Boulevard, Miami). Ticket prices range from $15 to $200, available from Ticketmaster (☎ 954-835-8326).

The **Miami Fusion** (Lockhart Stadium, 2200 West Commercial Boulevard, Fort Lauderdale; ☎ 954-717-2200) plays pro soccer, the rough-and-tumble game picking up steam throughout the United States.

The **Baltimore Orioles** do their spring training at Fort Lauderdale Stadium (5301 NW 12th Avenue, Fort Lauderdale; ☎ 954-776-1921). Tickets are $9–$55.

The Betting Sports: Horse Races, Greyhounds, Harness Racing, and Jai Alai

Pari-mutuel wagering, which enables winners to divide a pot after taking off a fee for management expenses, is a big-bucks business in Florida. Pari-mutuel betting is available at Gulfstream Park Race Track, Hollywood Dog Track, Pompano Park Harness Racing, and Dania Jai Alai. Both newspapers, the *Miami Herald* and *Sun-Sentinel*, print the entrants each day. For further gambling, there's a state lottery, and an armada of gambling boats ply the Gulf Stream and host roulette, poker, blackjack, and craps.

Winter racing is on tap at **Gulfstream Park** (at US 1 and Hallandale Beach Boulevard, Hallandale; ☎ 954-454-7000).

For dog racing try **Hollywood Greyhound Track** (it's actually at 831 North Federal Highway in Hallandale; ☎ 954-924-3200). Greyhounds are sleek animals that reach speeds of more than 40 miles an hour. The season runs through the end of May.

Pompano Park Harness Racing (1800 Race Trace Road, Pompano Beach; ☎ 954-972-2000) offers races November through mid-April on Monday, Wednesday, Friday, and Saturday evenings.

Jai alai is a speed game combining elements of lacrosse, tennis, and racquetball, played with a hard ball called a pelota, and a cesta, a long, curved wicker basket. The *Guinness Book of World Records* says no ball travels faster than the pelota, which reaches speeds over 180 miles per hour. The local venue is **Dania Jai Alai** (301 East Dania Beach Boulevard; ☎ 954-920-1511). Admission is $1.50 (includes parking). for simulcast games and horse races as well as poker; the box office is open Wednesday–Friday, 4–10 p.m.; Saturday, 11 a.m.–4 p.m.; and Tuesday, 11 a.m.–1 p.m.

unofficial **TIP**
Want to take home a unique, unforgettable, and free souvenir? Why not adopt a greyhound? These sleek, intelligent, affectionate dogs are out of luck when the mechanical rabbit stops and their careers end. And in fact, many never get to race at all. Call the tracks to inquire about their greyhound-adoption programs.

SHOPPING

STROLLING AND WINDOW SHOPPING

FORT LAUDERDALE'S **Las Olas Boulevard** is Florida's smart and sassy answer to Rodeo Drive in Beverly Hills, Boulevard Saint-Germain in Paris, and Michigan Avenue in Chicago. Aptly named Las Olas (meaning "the waves" in Spanish) makes waves with savvy shoppers thanks to cutting-edge fashion boutiques, art galleries, charming restaurants, sidewalk cafes, and jazz houses.

Zola Keller (818 East Las Olas Boulevard; ☎ 954-462-3222) has clothed the area's best-dressed women for years with garments from around the globe. Across the street, **Call of Africa's Native Vision Galleries** (807 East Las Olas Boulevard; ☎ 954-767-8737) offers rare and exotic African art, and **Maus & Hoffman's** (800 East Las Olas Boulevard; ☎ 954-463-1472) men's clothing appeals to shoppers from all over the world. At **Genesis Fine Art** (803 East Las Olas Boulevard; ☎ 954-467-6066) paintings are the main attraction. Landscapes and representational work are popular; you'll see watercolors, acrylics, and oils from modern and postmodern schools, but few abstract works.

A variety of gift shops and galleries—some funky, some fabulous—make Las Olas a great day's activity. Diverse eateries range from moderately priced to expensive.

The **Shops & Restaurants of Downtown Hollywood** (Hollywood Boulevard and Harrison Street; ☎ 954-921-3016) is another popular downtown redevelopment; old movie theaters reappeared as restaurants and banks as shopping arcades. Hollywood hosts a collection of clothing boutiques, art galleries and studios, and intimate cafes, with a growing array of nighttime live entertainment.

MALL SHOPPING

Sawgrass Mills

We strongly recommend a visit to **Sawgrass Mills** (12801 West Sunrise Boulevard, Sunrise; ☎ 954-846-2300) just to ooh and aah at its size. Consider **JC Penney** and **Gap Kids** outlets, add **Ann Taylor** and **Carter's** children's wear, **Luggage Express, Samsonite, Chico's,** and **Nine West,** and you've got a trunkful of bargains. The values are there—it just takes some looking. Sawgrass is not for hit-and-run shoppers.

Opened in 1992, Sawgrass is considered a major tourist attraction, with appeal beyond the outlets alone. The Oasis is a 300,000-square-foot entertainment area with more than 30 stores and restaurants. Surfers and surfer wannabes love the clothes and equipment, including surfboards, skateboards, and swimwear at **Ron Jon Surf Shop** (☎ 954-846-1880), a branch of the world's largest chain of surf shops—founded 64 years ago and respected by surfers from all over the world. Valet parking is available.

kids **Wannado City,** a 140,000-square-foot indoor role-playing theme park in the Sawgrass mall, is a major delight for older children. It allows them to act out more than 250 occupations, from surgeon to reporter to police officer to pizza baker, in realistic venues with adult mentors and other kids. (Parents are tolerated on the sidelines, but this is a kid-centric destination, with its own kid money and kid-viewpoint.) Highly popular and truly original, you can contact **www.wannadocity.com** for info and reservations. Kids could happily spend a full day here and may want to return for more right away.

More Malls

Mall-walking is a 21st-century phenomenon especially appropriate in South Florida's tropical climate. Put on your walking shoes, head to the nearest mall, and stroll in air-conditioned comfort. Broward has almost as great a variety of malls as walkers.

Galleria Mall (2414 East Sunrise Boulevard, Fort Lauderdale; ☎ 954-564-1015) is one of those high-end malls with glitzy stores (**Saks Fifth Avenue** and **Neiman Marcus**), designer boutiques, and a huge parking garage—valet service is available.

Also nearby, visit **Harmony Isle Gallery** (902 NE 19th Avenue, Fort Lauderdale; ☎ 954-527-2880) and view work by local artists as well as national presentations, handmade jewelry, and other gift items and souvenirs.

Broward Mall in Plantation (Broward Boulevard and University Drive; ☎ 954-473-8100) is home to **Sears, Dillard's, JC Penney,** and 120 smaller stores, plus a food court. This is classic suburban mall circa 1985, with every chain you can think of. Best thing about it? Four major department stores and plenty of parking.

Nearby is the **Fashion Mall at Plantation** (321 North University Drive; ☎ 954-370-1884) anchored by **Macy's** and **Lord & Taylor.** There's a Sheraton Hotel and a restaurant in the complex, but the mall itself is unremarkable.

The upscale suburb of Coral Springs has its own mall, **Coral Square Mall** (Atlantic Boulevard and University Drive; ☎ 954-755-5550), with major department stores, boutiques, and chains, and one of the best candy stores around, in **Palm Beach Confections** (☎ 954-753-1888).

Many of the shops that once graced the old Hollywood Mall (opened in the early 1960s, closed some 20 years later, and located about ten miles east of the current hot spot) moved to the **Pembroke Lakes Mall** (11401 Pines Boulevard; ☎ 954-436-3520), which offers department stores, boutiques, chains, a food court, and a huge parking lot.

While You're in the Area

In nearby Sunrise, traveling families can check out the baby stuff and children's wear at **Baby Love** (8100 West Oakland Park Boulevard,

Sunrise; ☎ 954-741-2227). This warehouse-like store is paradise for expectant parents, new parents, and grandparents. Grown-ups may prefer **Up, Up & Away** (829 North Nob Hill, Plantation; ☎ 954-475-2002), with lots of artsy gift items, souvenirs, mementos, and charming ceramics. The Plantation/Sunrise area seems be made of strip malls. There's a heavy concentration of children's clothing and toy stores, furniture and decorating shops, and chain after chain after chain.

SPECIALTY SHOPS

ANTIQUES   Dania Beach is known for blocks of antique shops. Kitsch abounds, but so does antique glassware, furniture, jewelry, and more. Like Las Olas, this is a stroll-and-window-shop area, so take the time to explore some of the 250 shops.

Visit the **Antique Center Mall** of Dania (3 North Federal Highway, Dania Beach; ☎ 954-922-5467), with a selection including Paula Schimmel's antique and period jewelry, **Dick's Toys, E & F Antiques and Collectibles,** and **Madeleine France's 19th and 20th Century Past and Pleasure** perfume bottles, furniture, housewares, and gold.

For antique art, try **Kodner Gallery** (45 South Federal Highway, Dania Beach; ☎ 954-925-2550); **Athena Gallery,** which buys antiques and estates (19 South Federal Highway, Dania Beach; ☎ 954-921-7697).

BOAT GEAR   Whether you own a dinghy or a yacht, try **Boat Owners Warehouse.** They carry more than 16,000 items, with locations at 311 SW 24th Street (FL 84), Fort Lauderdale, ☎ 954-522-7998; 750 East Sample Road, Pompano Beach, ☎ 954-946-6930; and 1720 East Hallandale Beach Boulevard, Hallandale, ☎ 954-457-5081.

BOOKSTORES   The **Barnes & Noble** chain operates several free-standing mega-stores in Broward, complete with comfy chairs, couches, and coffee shops. The stores are a great place to go on a rainy day or a free afternoon, and sometimes children's story hours are scheduled to entertain the youngsters. Locations are at 4170 Oakwood Boulevard, Hollywood, ☎ 954-923-1738; 11820 Pines Boulevard, Pembroke Pines, ☎ 954-441-0444; and 2790 University Drive, Coral Springs, ☎ 954-344-6291.

FISHING GEAR   **Outdoor World Bass Pro Shops** (200 Gulf Stream Way, Dania Beach; ☎ 954-929-7710) has an indoor archery range, gun range, restaurant, and all things fishy. Also on site is the **Fishing Hall of Fame & Museum,** and a fresh-fish market, plus a four-story waterfall, aquarium, and trout pool.

FLEA MARKETS   Festival Flea Market (2900 West Sample Road, Pompano Beach; ☎ 954-979-4555) and **Swap Shop of Fort Lauderdale** (3291 West Sunrise Boulevard, Fort Lauderdale; ☎ 954-791-7927) are popular. Festival Flea Market features upscale bargains, a food court, and a full-service beauty salon. The Swap Shop features a circus, food court, and carnival-like ambience, with more than 2,000 vendors—and they offer shuttle-bus service from hotels and downtown locations.

FRUIT SHIPPING   Mack's Groves (locations at 4405 North Ocean Drive, Lauderdale-by-the-Sea, ☎ 954-776-0910; and 1180 North Federal Highway, Pompano Beach, ☎ 954-941-4528 or 800-327-3525) offers fresh citrus from South Florida's best groves. Fruit-basket gift items can be shipped while you enjoy the sunshine. **Publix** supermarkets (found throughout the state) also offer fresh-fruit shipping.

JEWELRY   Across from the Galleria, **Daoud's Fine Jewelry** (2525 East Sunrise Boulevard, Fort Lauderdale; ☎ 954-565-2734) sells unique pieces, estate jewelry, and pre-owned Rolex watches.

Morningstar's (2000 Hollywood Boulevard, Hollywood; ☎ 954-923-2372) sells new and pre-owned jewelry. **Levinson Jewelers** (8139 West Broward Boulevard, Plantation; ☎ 954-473-9700) is considered tops for fine jewelry.

SHOES   Birkenstock Footprints (3526 North Powerline Road, Pompano Beach; ☎ 954-943-3041) has more than 400 colors and styles for adults and kids.

SWIMWEAR   The latest (and briefest) swimwear on Fort Lauderdale or any beach is at **Swimland** (2571 East Sunrise Boulevard, Fort Lauderdale; ☎ 954-561-2824), from Gottex, Anne Klein, Nautica, and all major names.

TWO (OF MANY) FESTIVALS

The **Winterfest Boat Parade** displays hundreds of yachts and mansions along Fort Lauderdale's Intracoastal waterway ablaze in lights. Check out this beloved and balmy December tradition; when most of the country is hoping for snow, "White Christmas" here means lights sparkling on the water (☎ 954-767-0686; **www.winterfestparade.com**).

Beethoven-by-the-Beach is a Greater Fort Lauderdale summer festival highlighting great music under the breezy palms (☎ 954-561-2997).

ATTRACTIONS

A PERFECT DAY

LOUNGING ON THE BEACH WITH A GOOD supply of sunscreen, a cooler of cold drinks, and a novel may be enough for you. Others may want to hit the links and play 18 holes before lunch. Some inveterate shoppers can't buy enough, charging through South Florida's malls, shopping centers, flea markets, and antique shops.

A perfect day might begin with a sunrise walk along the four-mile Broadwalk on Hollywood Beach. Watch the sun come up over the ever-changing Atlantic Ocean and stop for breakfast at one of a dozen or so beachfront restaurants, where the view is incredible and prices are low.

Then head over to the Diplomat Country Club and Spa and reward yourself for that morning walk. The club's full-service, 30,000-square-foot spa offers massage, shiatsu, reflexology, mud and seaweed wraps, hydrotherapies, body scrubs, facials, and a variety of other services. Showers and a sauna help refresh and restore.

Then head west to Sawgrass Mills Mall and enjoy lunch at Wolfgang Puck's. Afterward, stroll through the hundreds of stores for that ideal gift.

Plan on dinner at Giorgio's Mediterranean Restaurant (ask for a table on the deck with the posh boats tied at your feet). Save time to catch a movie at the nearby Regal Oakwood Cinemas.

Or perhaps head up to Butterfly World (in Tradewinds Park off Sample Road) to see the largest live butterfly exhibit in the world. Wander through the three-acre rain forest.

In the late morning, turn back south to Hillsboro Boulevard and the Intracoastal Waterway for a Palm Breeze sail on a 55-foot catamaran, scheduled daily at 12:45 p.m. (and booked in advance).

That's a lot of sun for one day, so grab a late lunch, take a nap, then enjoy a gala dinner at the romantic, luxurious Burt and Jack's, where you can watch the moon shimmer on the water.

A final alternative might include a morning on the beach, followed by lunch at the Islamorada Fish Company in Dania Beach. Walk through the Bass Outdoor store, located in the same building, then head next door to the Fishing Hall of Fame & Museum, where virtual reality allows you to catch a marlin without getting wet.

Make it a museum kind of day with an afternoon visit to the Museum of Discovery and Science and dinner at one of the restaurants at nearby Las Olas River Front in Fort Lauderdale's Historic District.

Because of the wide range of Broward County attractions, we've provided the following chart to help you prioritize your touring at a glance. Organized by category, the chart provides the name, location, and author's rating of each attraction. However, some attractions, usually art galleries without permanent collections, weren't rated because exhibits change. Each attraction is individually profiled in detail following the chart. Most museum-type attractions offer group rates for ten or more people.

Broward County Attractions

NAME	LOCATION	AUTHOR'S RATING
AMUSEMENT PARK		
Boomers/Dania Beach Hurricane	Dania Beach	★★
BOAT RIDE		
Jungle Queen Riverboat	Fort Lauderdale	★★★★
HOME TOUR		
Bonnet House	Fort Lauderdale	★★★★
MUSEUMS		
Ah-Tah-Thi-Ki Museum	Seminole Big Cypress Reservation	★★★
Fort Lauderdale Historical Museum	Fort Lauderdale	★★
Fishing Hall of Fame & Museum	Dania Beach	★★★
International Swimming Hall of Fame	Fort Lauderdale	★★
Museum of Discovery and Science–Blockbuster IMAX Theater	Fort Lauderdale	★★★★
Young at Art	Davie	★★
NATURE CENTERS/EXHIBITS		
Anne Kolb Nature Center	Hollywood	★★★
Butterfly World	Coconut Creek	★★★
PARKS AND REFUGES		
Flamingo Gardens	Fort Lauderdale	★★★
Sawgrass Recreation Park	None	★★

SURPRISING AND FUN THINGS TO DO IN BROWARD COUNTY

- **Five Star Rodeo:** The wild west in southeastern Florida. Yes, on the fourth weekend of every month, you can enjoy a rodeo. Who needs Texas? 4271 Davie Road; ☎ 954-680-3555; **www.fivestarrodeo.com.**

broward county attractions and nightlife

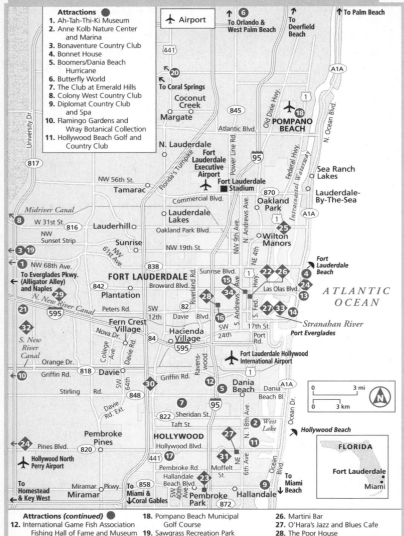

Attractions ●
1. Ah-Tah-Thi-Ki Museum
2. Anne Kolb Nature Center and Marina
3. Bonaventure Country Club
4. Bonnet House
5. Boomers/Dania Beach Hurricane
6. Butterfly World
7. The Club at Emerald Hills
8. Colony West Country Club
9. Diplomat Country Club and Spa
10. Flamingo Gardens and Wray Botanical Collection
11. Hollywood Beach Golf and Country Club

Attractions (continued) ●
12. International Game Fish Association Fishing Hall of Fame and Museum
13. International Swimming Hall of Fame Museum and Aquatic Complex
14. Jungle Queen Riverboat
15. Museum of Discovery and Science–Blockbuster IMAX Theater
16. Old Fort Lauderdale Village & Museum
17. Orangebrook Golf Club

18. Pompano Beach Municipal Golf Course
19. Sawgrass Recreation Park
20. Tournament Players Club at Heron Bay
21. Young at Art Children's Museum

Nightclubs ◆
22. Automatic Slim's
23. Billabong Pub
24. Cafe Iguana
25. Christopher's

26. Martini Bar
27. O'Hara's Jazz and Blues Cafe
28. The Poor House
29. Round Up Country and Western Restaurant and Nightclub
30. Seminole Paradise Hard Rock Hotel and Casino
    Spice Resto-Lounge
31. Swig Bartini
32. Tarpon Bend
33. Voodoo Lounge
34. Voodoo Lounge

SURPRISING AND FUN THINGS TO DO IN BROWARD COUNTY (CONTINUED)

- **Fort Lauderdale Museum of Art:** A permanent collection of artworks from Copenhagen, Brussels, Amsterdam, and Cuba, and a new wing housing the world's largest collection of works by American Impressionist William Glackens is just the start. Watch for exciting visiting exhibits in this downtown Fort Lauderdale museum, near Riverwalk; ☎ 954-525-5500; **www.moafl.org.**

- **Royal Horse Drawn Carriages:** Central Park has nothing on Fort Lauderdale's Las Olas. You can ride in style Wednesday–Sunday nights, starting at 7 p.m., from carriage stands at SE Eighth Avenue and Las Olas Boulevard; ☎ 954-971-9820; **www.royalcarriagesfl.com.**

- **Goodyear Blimp Base:** Get up close to that huge bag of wind, the Stars and Stripes Blimp, at 1500 NE Fifth Avenue (at Copans Road), Pompano Beach.

- **Pompano Park Racing:** Trotters and pacers thunder down the stretch of Florida's only nighttime horse track, which offers simulcast thoroughbred and harness racing as well as jai alai; fine dining and light fare; and free admission and parking. One block south of Atlantic Boulevard, on Powerline Road, Pompano Beach; ☎ 954-972-2000; **www.pompanopark.com.**

- **Stranahan House:** Broward's oldest building is beautifully restored and furnished in period antiques. Built in 1901 for Fort Lauderdale's founder, it's one of several turn-of-the-last-century pioneer buildings by the river; 335 SE Sixth Avenue; ☎ 954-524-4736; **www.stranahan house.com.** Others along SW Second Avenue include the **King Cromartie House** (1907) and **New River Inn** (1905).

  Strolling by these dwellings—ancient by Florida standards—is a good way to enjoy the early-morning balmy breezes and get some exercise. Nearby is the Third Avenue Arts District; ☎ 954-763-8982. And if you enjoy breakfast out, stop by another classic, the **Riverside Hotel,** Broward's oldest, at 620 East Las Olas Boulevard; ☎ 954-467-0671; **www.riversidehotel.com.**

- **Billie Swamp Safari:** A real Everglades experience and a great way to learn about the land, history, and culture of the Seminole Indians on Big Cypress Seminole Reservation; ☎ 800-949-6101; **www.seminole tribe.com/safari.** Swamp buggy ecotours, airboat rides, and snake and gator educational shows operate daily. You can even spend a night in a real Seminole thatch hut.

- **A One-Day Cruise to the Bahamas:** Discovery Cruise Lines lets you experience cruising, gambling, and award-winning cuisine, daily, between Port Everglades and Grand Bahama Island; ☎ 888-213-8253; **www.discoverycruise.com.**

ATTRACTION PROFILES

Ah-Tah-Thi-Ki Museum

APPEAL BY AGE	PRESCHOOL ★★★	GRADE SCHOOL ★★★	TEENS ★★★
YOUNG ADULTS ★★★		OVER 30 ★★★★	SENIORS ★★★★

17 miles north of Alligator Alley (I-75), Exit 49 on the Seminole Big Cypress Reservation; ☎ 863-902-1113; www.seminoletribe.com/museum

Type of attraction A unique perspective on the Seminole Indian Nation. **Admission** Adults, $6; seniors and students, $4; children under age 6, free. **Hours** Tuesday–Sunday, 9 a.m.–5 p.m. **When to go** Mornings are the least busy. **Author's rating** ★★★. **How much time to allow** 2 hours.

DESCRIPTION AND COMMENTS The name means "a place to learn, a place to remember," and here is a great way to learn about native Floridians and their many contributions to the region. Exhibits, artifacts, films, nature trails, and a "living" village entertain and enlighten, but no traditional alligator wrestling (which some people associate with Seminoles) takes place—and that's the whole point of this museum. A 17-minute orientation film and gallery, plus a mile-and-a-half walk through a Seminole village, impart knowledge graciously and thoroughly. Don't miss the opportunity to watch Native American arts and crafts being produced.

The Seminoles continue to maintain a vibrant presence throughout the area (including a Hard Rock Cafe Resort and Casino and two Indian gaming halls in the county that offer bingo and video poker 24 hours a day).

TOURING TIPS Bring your own snacks and drinks. While food and drinks are not allowed in the museum, picnic tables are provided outside.

OTHER THINGS TO DO NEARBY Complete your indigenous experience with a visit to Billie Swamp Safari and Big Cypress Campground; ☎ 800-949-6101 or **www.seminoletribe.com/safari.** These attractions lie in the middle of the Everglades, so come prepared.

Anne Kolb Nature Center and Marina

APPEAL BY AGE	PRESCHOOL ★★	GRADE SCHOOL ★★★	TEENS ★★★★
YOUNG ADULTS ★★★★		OVER 30 ★★★	SENIORS ★★★

751 Sheridan Street, Hollywood 33020; ☎ 954-926-2410

Type of attraction Nature center with canoe and kayak rentals. **Admission** Adults, $1; children under age 6, free. **Hours** Daily, 9 a.m.–5 p.m. **When to go** Mornings or after 3 p.m. **Author's rating** ★★★. **How much time to allow** 2 hours.

DESCRIPTION AND COMMENTS Anne Kolb was a local environmental activist. The Nature Center and Marina named after her encompasses more than 1,500 acres of mangrove wetlands and forest habitat, all minutes from the beach. More than a million dollars has gone into the 27 interactive exhibits, three-level aquarium, and ecology room. You can take narrated boat tours, climb a five-story observation tower for a spectacular view of southern Broward County, view wildlife, or bike, hike, or canoe through the wild. There's also a fishing pier nearby.

TOURING TIPS Drink plenty of water, and wear a hat.

OTHER THINGS TO DO NEARBY Visit Hollywood North Beach Park with its full facilities, or head a few miles south to the refurbished Downtown Hollywood Historic Area, with its galleries, boutiques, and sidewalk cafes.

Bonnet House

| APPEAL BY AGE | PRESCHOOL ★ | GRADE SCHOOL ★★ | TEENS ★★ |
| YOUNG ADULTS ★★★ | OVER 30 ★★★★ | | SENIORS ★★★★ |

900 North Birch Road, Fort Lauderdale 33301 (Sunrise Boulevard and FL A1A); ☎ 954-563-5393; www.bonnethouse.org

Type of attraction Whimsical old Florida home on unspoiled oceanfront grounds. **Admission** Adults, $12; seniors, $11; students ages 6–18, $10; children under age 6, free. **Hours** December 1–April 30: Tuesday–Friday, 10 a.m.–4 p.m.; Saturday, noon–4 p.m.; May 1–November 30: Wednesday–Friday, 10 a.m.–3 p.m.; Saturday, 10 a.m.–4 p.m.; Sunday, noon–4 p.m. **When to go** When it opens or for the last tour, Wednesday–Friday, 1:30 p.m. and Saturday and Sunday, 2:30 p.m. **Author's rating** ★★★★. **How much time to allow** 2 hours including 75-minute guided tour.

DESCRIPTION AND COMMENTS Great for history buffs who enjoy Old Florida, this is a quintessential lush attraction and a not-to-be-missed Florida estate. Watch for the monkeys swinging through the banyan trees, and the black swans in the pool. The house exemplifies a wealthy Florida lifestyle from the early 20th century. Built by painter Frederick Clay Bartlett, the 35-acre beachfront home is a turn-of-the-19th-century beauty; it's Bartlett's personal adaptation of a southern plantation. The art is excellent, the grounds are gorgeous, and the mansion is typically Floridian.

TOURING TIPS More interesting to adults than kids, but young 'uns like the menagerie.

OTHER THINGS TO DO NEARBY A day at the beach is convenient—you're at the edge of the Atlantic. Or wander through nearby Beach Place, an eclectic strip mall/entertainment complex with eateries, boutiques, and clubs.

Boomers/Dania Beach Hurricane

| APPEAL BY AGE | PRESCHOOL ★ | GRADE SCHOOL ★★ | TEENS ★★★ |
| YOUNG ADULTS ★★★★ | OVER 30 ★★★★ | | SENIORS ★★ |

1700 NW First Street, Dania Beach 33304 (just east of I-95 between Griffin and Stirling Roads); ☎ 954-921-1411; www.boomersparks.com

Type of attraction Amusement park. **Admission** Single attractions, $1–$16; value paks, $32–$42. **Hours** Sunday–Thursday, 10 a.m.–midnight; Friday and Saturday, 10 a.m.–2 a.m. **When to go** Anytime. **Author's rating** ★★. **How much time to allow** 2–3 hours minimum.

DESCRIPTION AND COMMENTS The Hurricane, the largest wooden roller coaster in the state, is visible from I-95. Popular with coaster aficionados, the Hurricane reaches speeds up to 60 miles per hour. Otherwise, this is a standard amusement park with midway rides and arcade games. Go-cart racing, minigolf, batting cages, bumper cars, and a bungee-like Sky Coaster ride are popular attractions.

TOURING TIPS Go midweek rather than on the weekend, and stick to morning or late afternoon. The early afternoon is hot, hot, hot.

OTHER THINGS TO DO NEARBY Oakwood Plaza—only minutes away—offers a variety of stores and a multiscreen theater.

Butterfly World

APPEAL BY AGE	PRESCHOOL ★★	GRADE SCHOOL ★★★	TEENS ★★★
YOUNG ADULTS ★★	OVER 30 ★★★		SENIORS ★★★★

3600 West Sample Road, Coconut Creek 33319 (in Trade Winds Park, just west of Florida's Turnpike); ☎ 954-977-4400; www.butterflyworld.com

Type of attraction Butterfly exhibit and aviary. **Admission** Adults, $17.95; children ages 4–12, $12.95; children under age 4, free. **Hours** Monday–Saturday, 9 a.m.–5 p.m.; Sunday, 1–5 p.m. **When to go** Early in the day when it's cooler. **Author's rating** ★★★. **How much time to allow** 2 hours.

DESCRIPTION AND COMMENTS On three acres within Trade Winds Park of gardens and waterfalls, thousands of multihued and iridescent butterflies flutter by. There are also fish, birds, and a 30-foot insectarium with observation decks. This is a tour for the whole family—colorful, beautiful, tropical, and interesting. Little ones love the color, and everyone enjoys the lush foliage, ponds, and tunnels.

TOURING TIPS Wear a hat and drink water. Never underestimate the Florida sun. And be patient; sometimes butterflies hide and rest, and then, surprisingly, flutter by the hundreds.

OTHER THINGS TO DO NEARBY Trade Winds Park is a pretty (and safe) area to visit before heading back to the hotel.

kids Flamingo Gardens and Wray Botanical Collection

APPEAL BY AGE	PRESCHOOL ★★	GRADE SCHOOL ★★★	TEENS ★★★
YOUNG ADULTS ★★★	OVER 30 ★★★★		SENIORS ★★★★

3750 Flamingo Road, Davie–Fort Lauderdale 33330; ☎ 954-473-2955; www.flamingogardens.org

Type of attraction Botanical gardens and wildlife sanctuary. **Admission** Adults, $15; children ages 4–11, $8; discounts for seniors and AAA members. **Hours** Daily, 9:30 a.m.–5:30 p.m.; closed Monday in summer. **When to go** Wildlife encounters at 12:30 p.m., 1:30 p.m., and 2:30 p.m. daily. **Author's rating** ★★★. **How much time to allow** 2–3 hours.

DESCRIPTION AND COMMENTS One of the prettiest sites in Broward. A subtropical rain forest, a free-flight, 25-thousand-foot walk-through aviary, nature trails, and wild animals (including gators, crocs, and otters) coexist on 60 acres of botanical gardens. Rare, exotic plants abound. The half-hour tram tour through citrus groves and wetlands is a comfortable way to see everything, and kids love it. The gardens are outstanding, offering a profusion of tropical flora, and the pioneer Wray home includes an Everglades museum.

TOURING TIPS Take your time. Go early and explore the grounds. Check out the 200-year-old oak hammock.

OTHER THINGS TO DO NEARBY You're close to Nova Southeastern University campus and the Sawgrass Mills Mall—all 270 stores, restaurants, movie theaters, and for kids, Wannado City.

International Game Fish Association Fishing Hall of Fame & Museum

APPEAL BY AGE	PRESCHOOL ★★	GRADE SCHOOL ★★	TEENS ★★
YOUNG ADULTS ★★★	OVER 30 ★★★		SENIORS ★★★

300 Gulf Stream Way, Dania Beach 33004; ☎ 954-922-4212; www.igfa.org

Type of attraction Museum focused on all phases of fishing. Admission Adults, $6; children ages 3–16, $5; seniors, $5. Hours Daily, 10 a.m.–6 p.m.; closed Thanksgiving and Christmas. When to go Anytime. Author's rating ★★★. How much time to allow 2 hours.

DESCRIPTION AND COMMENTS The Tackle Gallery is interesting, and the collection of boats includes a 1933 "Wheeler," sister ship to Ernest Hemingway's *Pilar*. It's pretty much everything you ever wanted to know about fishing—and well done. The museum teaches respect for sea life and the importance of conserving and protecting our valuable natural aquatic resources.

TOURING TIPS See the movie first, which is an excellent orientation for the museum.

OTHER THINGS TO DO NEARBY Shop at Bass Pro Shops Outdoor World, or take a TriRail train ride from the station nearby. Dania antique shops and flea markets are tempting, and Oakwood Plaza is only five minutes away, but the Bass complex (and Islamorada Fish Factory restaurant) can keep you busy most of the day.

International Swimming Hall of Fame Museum and Aquatic Complex

APPEAL BY AGE	PRESCHOOL ★	GRADE SCHOOL ★★	TEENS ★★
YOUNG ADULTS ★★★	OVER 30 ★★★		SENIORS ★★★

1 Hall of Fame Drive, Fort Lauderdale 33316; ☎ 954-462-6536; www.ishof.org

Type of attraction Swimming memorabilia museum. Admission Family, $5; adults, $3; seniors, students, and military, $1. Hours Monday–Friday, 9 a.m.–7 p.m.; Saturday and Sunday, 9 a.m.–5 p.m. When to go Anytime. Author's rating ★★. How much time to allow Minimum 1 hour.

DESCRIPTION AND COMMENTS Look for lots of waterlogged memorabilia featuring U.S. swimmers from Johnny Weissmuller (a film Tarzan of the 1930s and 1940s), Mark Spitz (who won fame at the Munich Olympics), and Olympic gold-medalist diver Greg Louganis.

TOURING TIPS Take it slow—there's lots to see. Look for the display on swimming diva Esther Williams, and go "virtual fishing." The two 10-lane, 50-meter pools can be used when not hosting competitions.

OTHER THINGS TO DO NEARBY Swim at the pool, shop at the retail store, or, inspired by the museum, head for the beach.

Jungle Queen Riverboat

APPEAL BY AGE	PRESCHOOL ★	GRADE SCHOOL ★★	TEENS ★★★
YOUNG ADULTS ★★★	OVER 30 ★★★★		SENIORS ★★★★

801 Seabreeze Boulevard, Fort Lauderdale 33316; ☎ 954-462-5596; www.junglequeen.com

Type of attraction Boat ride. **Admission** Adults, $14; children ages 10 and under, $10. 3-hour sightseeing cruises daily at 10 a.m. and 2 p.m., and a cruise down to Miami's Bayside Marketplace leaves at 9:15 a.m. **When to go** Anytime. **Author's rating** ★★★★. **How much time to allow** 3 hours for the sightseeing cruise.

DESCRIPTION AND COMMENTS This boat ride has been a Fort Lauderdale tradition for more than six decades. A "must-do" for first-timers; even the locals take the tour. The daytime sightseeing cruise is the best choice, and the accompanying live commentary is excellent.

TOURING TIPS Sunscreen and a hat are essential, and don't forget a camera—you'll be passing some of the prettiest real estate in South Florida.

OTHER THINGS TO DO NEARBY Catch a few more rays on the postcard-picture beach. Or take a public water taxi for a less expensive, even more complete circuit of the Fort Lauderdale intracoastal waterways that wend through the city.

Museum of Discovery and Science– Blockbuster IMAX Theater

APPEAL BY AGE	PRESCHOOL ★★★	GRADE SCHOOL ★★★	TEENS ★★★
YOUNG ADULTS ★★★★	OVER 30 ★★★		SENIORS ★★★★

401 SW Second Street, Fort Lauderdale 33312; ☎ 954-467-6637; www.mods.org

Type of attraction Interactive museum and IMAX theater. **Admission** Adults, $14; seniors and students, $13; children, $12; all prices include one IMAX feature. **Hours** Monday–Saturday, 10 a.m.–5 p.m.; Sunday, noon–6 p.m.; closed Thanksgiving and Christmas. **When to go** Anytime. **Author's rating** ★★★★. **How much time to allow** At least 3 hours—more if you see the film.

DESCRIPTION AND COMMENTS The 52-foot Great Gravity Clock, Gizmo City, and Florida Ecoscapes, with a living coral reef, are among the attractions. A well-designed, hands-on, interactive facility with a five-story 3-D IMAX theater, this outstanding museum is sure to be enjoyed by all ages.

TOURING TIPS Take the little ones to the area designed for them first, then see the film before touring the rest of the museum.

OTHER THINGS TO DO NEARBY Visit Las Olas River Riverwalk, or stop in at the beautiful Museum of Art, host to many major international exhibits. The permanent collection features paintings by William Glackens and 20th-century European and American pieces.

Old Fort Lauderdale Village & Museum

APPEAL BY AGE	PRESCHOOL ★	GRADE SCHOOL ★★	TEENS ★★
YOUNG ADULTS ★★	OVER 30 ★★★		SENIORS ★★★

219 SW Second Avenue, Fort Lauderdale 33301 (in the Arts and Science District); ☎ 954-463-4431; www.oldfortlauderdale.org

Type of attraction History museum. Admission Adults, $8; seniors and children, $5; children under age 6, free. Hours Tuesday–Sunday, noon–5 p.m. When to go Anytime. Author's rating ★★. How much time to allow 2 hours.

DESCRIPTION AND COMMENTS You'll gain insight into the lives of early settlers from the Seminoles who chose to make their home near the end of the Florida peninsula and built a thriving civic center on former swampland. Life was often perilous, and a history lesson helps tourists appreciate the area's comfortable hotels and beaches. Includes the King-Cromartie House, the Historical Society's Hoch Heritage Center archives building, and the New River Inn.

TOURING TIPS Avoid school holidays.

OTHER THINGS TO DO NEARBY Visit Las Olas Riverwalk, or consider the Discovery Center.

Sawgrass Recreation Park

APPEAL BY AGE	PRESCHOOL ★	GRADE SCHOOL ★	TEENS ★★
YOUNG ADULTS ★★	OVER 30 ★★		SENIORS ★★★

Turnpike or I-95 to I-595 west to I-75, north to US 27, then north 2 miles; ☎ 888-424-7262; www.evergladestours.com

Type of attraction National wilderness. Admission Adults, $19.50; children, $10; ages 4 and under, free. Hours Daily, 9 a.m.–5 p.m. When to go Anytime. Author's rating ★★. How much time to allow 2 hours for all tours.

DESCRIPTION AND COMMENTS The long trek out here is worth it for a close look at the Everglades and extensive information on Seminole culture. Don't miss the village and the alligator and reptile show. Sawgrass is an amazing example of nature at its most wild, just a few miles from urban South Florida.

TOURING TIPS The airboat tour is exciting, viewing gators, birds, turtles, snakes, and Everglades flora and fauna.

OTHER THINGS TO DO NEARBY You might want to opt for the indoors after all that nature, so take I-595 to 136th Avenue (or Flamingo Road) and Sawgrass Mills, with its game centers, restaurants, and shops.

A Few of Our Favorite Broward Things

- Reaching zero-gravity weightlessness at ZERO-G Experience, based at Fort Lauderdale/Hollywood International Airport. Precision parabolic patterns are like a roller coaster.

- Stolling around Sailboat Bend and Tarpon River, two historic, tree-lined neighborhoods near Las Olas and by the New River, with the charm of Miami's Coconut Grove

- Arriving via water taxi at the Las Olas Riverwalk on a balmy winter night for dinner and a performance at the Broward Center for the Performing Arts

- Hunting for treasures at the Farmer's Market and the Swap Shop, the South's largest flea market

- Taking the glass elevator to the top of the Hyatt Regency Pier 66 to enjoy a view of the waterways, skyline, and Atlantic

- Looking for manatees at Port Everglades from November to April, and experiencing turtle walks on the beach from May to August

- Visiting the Elbo Room on FL A1A and Las Olas, the site of the 1960s movie, *Where the Boys Are*

- Rollerblading on the Fort Lauderdale beachfront Promenade

- Poking into the little Stranahan House museum near Las Olas, Fort Lauderdale's oldest building, built by Frank Stranahan in 1901

- Checking out the Hillsboro Light in Lighthouse Point, the brightest lighthouse in the Southeast. Then driving a couple of miles north along "The Hillboro Mile," a stretch of mansions and tropical foliage between the Intracoastal and the Atlantic

- Shuttling by boat to Deerfield Island Park, an Urban Wilderness Area on hammock islands in the intracoastal near Deerfield Beach.

- Canoeing in West Lake Park in Hollywood

- Watching the cruise ships enter Port Everglades from a kayak at John U. Lloyd Beach State Recreation area in Dania

kids Young at Art Children's Museum

APPEAL BY AGE	PRESCHOOL ★★	GRADE SCHOOL ★★★	TEENS ★
YOUNG ADULTS ★		OVER 30 ★	SENIORS ★★

11584 FL 84, Davie 33325; ☎ 954-424-0085;
www.youngatartmuseum.org

Type of attraction Children's museum and art center. **Admission** Adults and children, $5; seniors, $4.50; children under age 2, free. **Hours** Monday–Saturday,

10 a.m–5 p.m.; Sunday, noon–5 p.m. **When to go** Anytime. **Author's rating** ★★.
How much time to allow 1–2 hours.

DESCRIPTION AND COMMENTS This museum is especially great for children
who have shown interest in any kind of art. Kids can learn computer art,
build sculptures, attend art classes, and explore their imagination and
creativity through many hands-on activities. Themes change three
times a year.

TOURING TIPS Take kids when they are most active—after a nap is ideal. Since
they can bring work home, carry totes or bags.

OTHER THINGS TO DO NEARBY A variety of malls are nearby, as is the campus
of Nova Southeastern University. Or drive through the town of Davie,
a small western-influenced community with horse ranches and an
annual rodeo.

DINING *and* RESTAURANTS

AS WE'VE SAID, BROWARD COUNTY IS THE home of beautiful Fort
Lauderdale, yachting capital of the world. Accordingly, its restaurants
have set their tablecloths like sails to catch tastes blown in from all over
the world. Your mouth can taste the farthest reaches of the globe in one
Broward strip mall. (Fort Lauderdale's Gateway shopping center on
East Sunrise Boulevard and Federal Highway is a good example.)

Broward shares much of its talent and clientele with Palm Beach
County. Frequently, restaurateurs who do well in Broward will open an-
other location in Palm Beach, or vice versa. From November to
March—"the season"—Broward sees its largest influx of visitors.
Whenever possible during these months, make reservations. Leave
yourself extra time to find a parking space, or bring cash for the valet.

ABOUT THESE CHOICES

WE HAVE CHOSEN RESTAURANTS THAT, WHILE we can't guarantee
their staying power, have proven to operate successfully for some time.
We've also selected restaurants with a following among local professionals, residents, and tourists whose travel plans include a trip, for example, to Blue Moon Fish Co. for a romantic, waterfront dinner for
two; to Cheeburger Cheeburger for an overstuffed burger after shopping; to Eduardo de San Angel for their famous crispy duck; to Canyon
Southwest for their notorious Prickly Pear Margarita; and to Le Tub
for real Florida cracker–style seafood. We have included a mix of
restaurants that are well known and some that are low-profile, and in
the process we have tried to provide something for everyone.

Detailed profiles of each restaurant follow in alphabetical order. For
more about South Florida dining and an overview of our restaurant-
profile format, including abbreviations and ratings, see page 208 in the
Miami-Dade County dining section.

The Best of Broward County Restaurants

RESTAURANT/TYPE	STAR RATING	QUALITY RATING	VALUE RATING	CITY
AMERICAN				
Dave and Buster's	★★★	★★★½	★★★★	Hollywood
Dan Marino's Town Tavern	★★★	★★★½	★★	Fort Lauderdale, Coral Springs
The Floridian	★★★	★★★	★★★★	Fort Lauderdale
Georgie's Alibi	★★★	★★★	★★★★	Wilton Manors
Toojay's	★★★	★★★	★★★	Coral Springs, Plantation
84 Diner	★★½	★★★	★★★★★	Davie
Cheeburger Cheeburger	★★½	★★★	★★★★	Fort Lauderdale, Davie, Weston, Pembroke Pines, Lauderhill
ASIAN				
Hong Kong City BBQ	★★★★½	★★★★	★★★★★	Tamarac
Christina Wan's	★★★★	★★★	★★★★★	Hollywood, Fort Lauderdale
BARBECUE				
Tom Jenkins Bar-B-Q	★★★★	★★★★	★★★½	Fort Lauderdale
BRAZILIAN				
Chima Brazilian Steakhouse Fort Lauderdale		★★★★	★★★★	★★★★½
CONTINENTAL				
The River House	★★★★	★★★★½	★★★	Fort Lauderdale
Lester's Diner	★★½	★★★	★★½	Fort Lauderdale
CUBAN				
Little Havana II	★★★★	★★★½	★★★★	Deerfield
DESSERTS				
Kilwin's	★★★★	★★★½	★★★★★	Coral Springs, Fort Lauderdale, Weston

RESTAURANT/TYPE	STAR RATING	QUALITY RATING	VALUE RATING	CITY
FLORIBBEAN				
Johnny V	★★★★★	★★★★★	★★★★	Fort Lauderdale
Rainforest Café	★★★	★★★	★★★	Sunrise
FLORIDIAN				
Café Maxx	★★★★★	★★★★½	★★★	Pompano Beach
ITALIAN				
Casa D'Angelo	★★★★½	★★★★★	★★★★	Fort Lauderdale
Café Martorano	★★★★½	★★★★★	★★★★★	Fort Lauderdale
Il Mulino	★★★★	★★★★	★★★★	Fort Lauderdale
MEDITERRANEAN				
Trina	★★★★	★★★★	★★★★	Fort Lauderdale
Casablanca Café	★★★	★★★★	★★★	Fort Lauderdale
MEXICAN/SOUTHWESTERN				
Eduardo de San Angel	★★★★½	★★★★	★★★	Fort Lauderdale
Canyon Southwest	★★★★	★★★★	★★★★	Fort Lauderdale
Zona Fresca	★★★	★★★	★★★	Fort Lauderdale
POLYNESIAN				
Mai Kai	★★★	★★★★	★★	Fort Lauderdale
SEAFOOD				
Le Tub	★★★★½	★★★★	★★★★★	Hollywood
Blue Moon Fish Co.	★★★★	★★★★	★★★★	Fort Lauderdale
SUSHI/PAN-ASIAN				
Sushi Blues Café and Blue Monk Lounge	★★★★	★★★★½	★★★★	Hollywood
THAI				
Try My Thai	★★★	★★★★	★★★	Hollywood, Fort Lauderdale

broward county dining

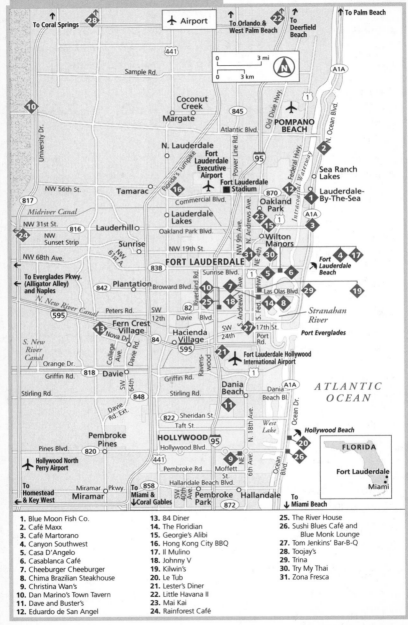

1. Blue Moon Fish Co.
2. Café Maxx
3. Café Martorano
4. Canyon Southwest
5. Casa D'Angelo
6. Casablanca Café
7. Cheeburger Cheeburger
8. Chima Brazilian Steakhouse
9. Christina Wan's
10. Dan Marino's Town Tavern
11. Dave and Buster's
12. Eduardo de San Angel

13. 84 Diner
14. The Floridian
15. Georgie's Alibi
16. Hong Kong City BBQ
17. Il Mulino
18. Johnny V
19. Kilwin's
20. Le Tub
21. Lester's Diner
22. Little Havana II
23. Mai Kai
24. Rainforest Café

25. The River House
26. Sushi Blues Café and
    Blue Monk Lounge
27. Tom Jenkins' Bar-B-Q
28. Toojay's
29. Trina
30. Try My Thai
31. Zona Fresca

RESTAURANT PROFILES

Blue Moon Fish Co. ★★★★

| SEAFOOD | EXPENSIVE | QUALITY ★★★★ | VALUE ★★★★ |

4405 West Tradewinds Avenue, Fort Lauderdale; ☎ 954-267-9888; www.bluemoonfishco.com

Reservations Recommended. **When to go** Lunch, dinner, Sunday brunch. **Entree range** $27–$36. **Payment** AE, D, DC, MC, V. **Parking** Valet. **Bar** Full service. **Wine selection** Excellent. **Dress** Dressy casual. **Disabled access** Yes. **Customers** Adult diners, couples, families. **Hours** Sunday–Thursday, 11:30 a.m.–10p.m.; Friday and Saturday, 11:30 a.m.–11 p.m.

MENU RECOMMENDATIONS Any seafood. It's all good.

COMMENTS The best waterfront dining in Broward County. The intracoastal waterway backdrop is obviously romantic. If you're boating, you can dock out back and head in for lunch or dinner.

Café Maxx ★★★★★

| FLORIDIAN | VERY EXPENSIVE | QUALITY ★★★★½ | VALUE ★★★ |

2601 East Atlantic Boulevard, Pompano Beach; ☎ 954-782-0606; www.cafemaxx.com

Reservations Recommended. **When to go** Weeknights are much less crowded but always busy. **Entree range** $19–$40. **Payment** AE, D, DC, MC, V. **Parking** Valet. **Bar** Beer and wine. **Wine selection** Large; $7–$13 per glass, $25–$800 by the bottle. **Dress** Dressy casual. **Disabled access** Yes. **Customers** Upscale crowd of all ages. **Hours** Monday–Thursday, 5:30–10:30 p.m.; Friday and Saturday, 5:30–11 p.m.; Sunday, 5:30–10 p.m.

MENU RECOMMENDATIONS Filet mignon, shrimp dishes, and grilled salmon are popular and beautifully presented, and the crème brûlée is as good as any in France.

COMMENTS A few years ago this restaurant won many gourmet awards; some critics think it's now living off reputation and is overpriced. But the food isn't bad these days; it's just more commercial. And it's still popular with locals. Ask for a table away from the cramped doorway/hostess station.

Café Martorano ★★★★½

| ITALIAN | EXPENSIVE | QUALITY ★★★★★ | VALUE ★★★★★ |

3343 East Oakland Park Boulevard, Fort Lauderdale; ☎ 954-561-2554; www.cafemartorano.com

Reservations Not accepted; entire party must be present to be seated. **When to go** Superbusy during the season; arrive early. **Entree range** $12–$40. **Payment** AE, MC, V. **Parking** Street. **Bar** Beer and wine. **Wine selection** Good. **Dress** Casual, dressy casual. **Disabled access** Yes. **Customers** Anyone, a few celebrities included. **Hours** Monday–Saturday, 5 p.m.–midnight.

MENU RECOMMENDATIONS No menu. You eat what Martorano tells you to eat, capiche?

COMMENTS Known as the place the Sopranos would eat, if they were in town (the cast actually did eat here during a press junket), pics of Sinatra and other Italian Americans line the walls of Café Martorano. The kitchen is clean; the food is delicious and simple. There is no set menu; Martorano prepares what comes in freshest each day.

Canyon Southwest ★ ★ ★ ★

SOUTHWESTERN/NEW AMERICAN FUSION	MODERATE/EXPENSIVE
QUALITY ★ ★ ★ ★	VALUE ★ ★ ★ ★

1818 East Sunrise Boulevard, Fort Lauderdale; ☎ 954-765-1950; www.canyonfl.com

Reservations Not accepted. **When to go** Dinner (before 8 p.m. to avoid a wait). **Entree range** $21–$32. **Payment** AE, MC, V. **Parking** Lot. **Bar** Full service. **Wine selection** Good. **Dress** Dressy casual (don't wear shorts). **Disabled access** Yes. **Customers** Adult diners, couples. **Hours** Sunday–Thursday, 5:30–10 p.m.; Friday and Saturday, 5:30–11 p.m.; happy hour, Monday–Friday, 5:30–7 p.m.

MENU RECOMMENDATIONS To start, order one of their famous prickly pear margaritas then try the Indonesian spiced ostrich skewers with sweet corn and scotch bonnet blueberry cream. Entrée: ancho chili–crusted tuna with crispy pancetta and white bean ragout, poached garlic vine ripe tomato salsa, and garden basil oil.

COMMENTS This decade-old Fort Lauderdale staple is a favorite for its extensive margarita menu and its proximity to a small movie theater, right next door, that is popular for screening independent and smaller films. A great dinner-and-a-movie date spot.

Casa D'Angelo ★ ★ ★ ★ ½

ITALIAN MODERATE/EXPENSIVE	QUALITY ★ ★ ★ ★ ★	VALUE ★ ★ ★ ★

1201 North Federal Highway, Fort Lauderdale; ☎ 954-564-1234; www.casa-d-angelo.com

Reservations Suggested. **When to go** Anytime, weekdays are generally less busy than weekends. **Entree range** $12–$30. **Payment** AE, D, DC, MC, V. **Parking** Lot. **Bar** Beer and wine. **Wine selection** Good; $7–$12 per glass, $20–$400 by the bottle. **Dress** Casual, dressy casual. **Disabled access** Yes. **Customers** Anyone. **Hours** Daily, 5:30–11 p.m.

MENU RECOMMENDATIONS Tiger prawns, gnocchi, Costoletta di Vitello Alla Milanese—breaded veal on the bone topped with tomato, arugula, endive, and radicchio.

COMMENTS A family feel and great service characterize this establishment. If you're comparing it to Café Martorano, keep in mind that D'Angelo has a permanent menu and accepts reservations.

Casablanca Café ★★★

MEDITERRANEAN	MODERATE	QUALITY ★★★★	VALUE ★★★

3049 Alhambra Street, Fort Lauderdale; ☎ 954-764-3500

Reservations Not accepted. **When to go** If you are looking for a quiet dinner, go during the week; weekends see live music, a livelier crowd, and a wait. **Entree range** $15–$30. **Payment** AE, D, DC, MC, V. **Parking** Street, valet is better. **Bar** Full service. **Wine selection** $5–$7. **Dress** Casual, dressy casual. **Disabled access** Yes. **Customers** Couples, professionals. **Hours** Food service: daily, 11:30 a.m.–11 p.m.; live music and bar: Thursday–Saturday, 9 p.m.–1 a.m.

MENU RECOMMENDATIONS Calimari fritti, Brazilian stew, Vesuvio osso buco.
COMMENTS Located in a freestanding historic house (designed by Frances Abreu), away from the bustle of Las Olas and Beach Place, Casablanca couples decent Mediterranean food with candlelight and a gorgeous oceanside view. It's a great place for a romantic, relaxed dinner.

 Cheeburger Cheeburger ★★½

AMERICAN	INEXPENSIVE	QUALITY ★★★	VALUE ★★★★

Beach Place, 17 South Fort Lauderdale Beach Boulevard, Fort Lauderdale; ☎ 954-769-9953
Fort Lauderdale International Airport Southwest Terminal #1
900 South Federal Highway, Fort Lauderdale; ☎ 954-462-7255
5409 North University Drive, Lauderhill; ☎ 954-749-466
Trafalgar Square, 1853 University Drive, Coral Springs; ☎ 954-346-6666
2010 North Flamingo Road, Pembroke Pines; ☎ 954-441-9799
Sawgrass Mills, 2602 Sawgrass Mills Circle, Davie; ☎ 954-838-7555
1793 Bell Tower Lane, Weston; ☎ 954-659-1115

Reservations Not accepted. **When to go** Anytime. **Entree range** Burgers, $5.25–$11.25. **Payment** MC, V. **Parking** Street, lot. **Bar** None. **Wine selection** None. **Dress** Casual. **Disabled access** Yes. **Customers** Shoppers, tourists, beach-goers, families. **Hours** Monday–Thursday, 8 a.m.–10 p.m.; Friday–Sunday, 8 a.m.–11 p.m. (Beach Place hours).

MENU RECOMMENDATIONS Milkshakes, fries, onion rings, burgers, pacemaker.
COMMENTS Popular with tourists and locals alike, Cheeburger is a great, quick family restaurant located conveniently all throughout Broward County. The menu features milkshakes you need to eat with a spoon and burgers you could nap on—big, juicy, delicious.

Chima Brazilian Steakhouse ★★★★

BRAZILIAN	EXPENSIVE	QUALITY ★★★★	VALUE ★★★★½

2400 East Las Olas Boulevard, Fort Lauderdale; ☎ 954-712-0580; www.chima.cc

Reservations Required. **When to go** Anytime. **Entree range** $40. **Payment** AE, D, DC, MC, V. **Parking** Complimentary valet. **Bar** Full service. **Wine selection**

Good. **Dress** Upscale casual. **Disabled access** Yes. **Customers** Adult diners, couples. **Hours** Monday–Friday, noon–2 p.m. and 5:30–10:30 p.m.

MENU RECOMMENDATIONS The flank steak and Brazilian pork sausages are what this restaurant lives for.

COMMENTS A popular new addition to Las Olas eating, this restaurant is an all-you-can-eat grill fest featuring a bottomless gourmet salad bar and Brazilian gauchos who bring the meat around on skewers. The $40 buffet price offers a lot of food in a high-end setting.

Christina Wan's ★ ★ ★ ★

ASIAN	MODERATE TO EXPENSIVE	QUALITY ★ ★ ★	VALUE ★ ★ ★ ★ ★

2031 Hollywood Boulevard, Hollywood; ☎ 954-923-1688
664 North Federal Highway, Fort Lauderdale; ☎ 954-527-0228
www.christinawans.com

Reservations Recommended on weekends. **Entree range** $13–$20. **Payment** D, DC, MC, V. **Parking** Street and nearby municipal lots. **Bar** Beer and wine. **Wine selection** Limited; $3.50–$6 per glass; $12–$30 by the bottle. **Dress** Casual. **Disabled access** Yes. **Customers** Many have been dining at Wan family restaurants for years; downtown workers and suburban couples and families who like good Chinese food. **Hours** Fort Lauderdale: Monday–Thursday, 11:30 a.m.–10 p.m.; Friday and Saturday, 11:30 a.m.–10:30 p.m.; Sunday, 1–10 p.m.; Hollywood: Tuesday–Thursday, 11:30 a.m.–10 p.m.; Friday and Saturday, 11:30 a.m.–10:30 p.m.; Sunday, 4–10 p.m.; Monday, closed.

MENU RECOMMENDATIONS Mandarin, Szechuan, and Cantonese menus, including chicken and cashews as spicy as you want and garlic eggplant you won't soon forget. There are good vegetarian options.

COMMENTS Some have complained about the food being overpriced, but most don't seem to mind—the portion sizes are generous, and few Asian restaurants have both the comfort and flair this one does.

Dan Marino's Town Tavern ★ ★ ★

AMERICAN	MODERATE	QUALITY ★ ★ ★ ½	VALUE ★ ★

Las Olas Riverfront 300 SW First Avenue, Fort Lauderdale;
☎ 954-522-1313
901 University Drive, Coral Springs; ☎ 954-341-4658
www.danmarinosrestaurant.com

Reservations Recommended. **When to go** Whenever; game days are busy. **Entree range** $8–$16. **Payment** AE, MC, V. **Parking** Valet, lot, street (difficult). **Bar** Full service. **Wine selection** Fair. **Dress** Casual. **Disabled access** Yes. **Customers** Sports fans, professionals, families. **Hours** Sunday–Thursday, 11 a.m.–midnight; Friday and Saturday, 11 a.m.–2 a.m.

MENU RECOMMENDATIONS Dan Marino's sesame seared tuna with ginger soy vinaigrette or the Chicken Daniel. For dessert, you can't go wrong with the almond basket or the Key lime pie.

COMMENTS South Florida will always have a special place in its heart for Dan Marino, so this place is something of a cultural relic: a clean, upscale sports bar with a competent, predictable menu and a counter where you can buy Dolphins memorabilia.

kids Dave and Buster's ★ ★ ★

AMERICAN	MODERATE	QUALITY ★★★½	VALUE ★★★★

3000 Oakwood Boulevard, Hollywood; ☎ 954-923-5505; www.daveandbusters.com

Reservations Special events only. When to go Weekend nights are busiest; go before 8 p.m. Entree range $12–$18. Payment AE, D, DC, MC, V. Parking Lot. Bar Full service. Wine selection Very good, $4.25–$7. Dress Casual. Disabled access Yes. Customers Families, tourists. Hours Sunday–Tuesday, 11:30 a.m.–midnight; Wednesday and Thursday, 11:30 a.m.–1 a.m.; Friday and Saturday, 11:30 a.m.–2 a.m.

MENU RECOMMENDATIONS Jack Daniels rib-eye, honey-glazed mahi mahi, chicken pasta.

COMMENTS A popular national chain, this restaurant has flexible hours and games for the kids, and it's located in a busy shopping center visible from I-95 (at Stirling Road). It's a very easy place to take the family. The game area features exclusive games like Coca Cola Racing Family Cyclone. Note that kids no longer have to leave at 10 p.m., but for every four kids under the age of 21, the restaurant requires at least one adult over the age of 25, during all hours of operation.

Eduardo de San Angel ★ ★ ★ ★ ½

MEXICAN	MODERATE	QUALITY ★★★★	VALUE ★★★

2822 East Commercial Boulevard, Fort Lauderdale; ☎ 954-772-4731; www.eduardodesanangel.com

Reservations Recommended for weekends. When to go Weeknights. Entree range $12–$15. Payment AE, DC, MC, V. Parking Shopping center plaza. Bar Beer and wine. Wine selection Large; $7–$13 per glass, $25–$80 by the bottle. Dress Casual. Disabled access Yes. Customers Upscale. Hours Monday–Saturday, 5:30–10 p.m.

MENU RECOMMENDATIONS Gourmet Mexican menu includes crisply roasted duck with a sauce made with pumpkin seeds and green chiles (the recipe is more than 200 years old). The garlic shrimp are also spectacular.

COMMENTS This romantic restaurant has been designed to look like a small hacienda. Excellent, romantic spot for a dinner for two.

84 Diner ★ ★ ½

AMERICAN DINER	INEXPENSIVE/MODERATE	QUALITY ★★★	VALUE ★★★★★

11432 West FL 84, Davie; ☎ 954-370-8217; www.84diner.com

Reservations Accepted for 8 or more. When to go Anytime; avoid weekend mornings if you don't want a crowd. Entree range $7.25–$26.95. Payment Cash only, but there's an ATM near the register. **Parking** Lot. **Bar** Beer, wine, and select mixed drinks. **Wine selection** House wines only, $3.25 per glass. **Dress** Casual. **Disabled access** Good. **Customers** All of humanity. **Hours** Daily, 6 a.m.–1 a.m.; breakfast served all day.

MENU RECOMMENDATIONS   Omelets, rolled pancakes, traditional Wiener Schnitzel, strawberry cheesecake.

COMMENTS   A real diner's diner. A sign at the counter boasts "Largest diner in South Florida"—the place takes up several storefronts, which means you will almost never have a hard time getting seated in a booth. The servers and staff—hurried, friendly, quick-witted—make the place.

The Floridian ★ ★ ★

AMERICAN DINER	MODERATE	QUALITY ★ ★ ★	VALUE ★ ★ ★ ★

1410 East Las Olas Boulevard, Fort Lauderdale; ☎ 954-463-4041

Reservations Not accepted. **When to go** Anytime, but weekend brunches are busy. **Entree range** $9–$28. **Payment** Cash only. **Parking** Street (along Las Olas), lot, or behind the restaurant. **Bar** Beer and wine. **Wine selection** Fair. **Dress** Beach casual. **Disabled access** No. **Customers** All walks of life—straight and gay, male and female, young and old. **Hours** Daily, 24 hours; breakfast served all day.

MENU RECOMMENDATIONS   One of the few places in South Florida where you can order a juicy turkey burger. The American comfort food—meatloaf, mashed potatoes, chicken—brings grown men to the table like little boys.

COMMENTS   A true Fort Lauderdale tradition, the interior is thrown together—a hodgepodge of pictures hiding the wood-paneled walls, neon lights, mounted televisions broadcasting shows you can't hear with no captions, hanging plants—but the Floridian just makes you happy to be alive and hungry. Note: Those with allergies and asthma may find the air quality a bit dank at times.

Georgie's Alibi ★ ★ ★

AMERICAN	MODERATE/EXPENSIVE	QUALITY ★ ★ ★	VALUE ★ ★ ★ ★

2266 Wilton Drive, Wilton Manors; ☎ 954-565-2526;
www.georgiesalibi.com

Reservations Required. **When to go** Anytime for a drink and a sandwich. **Entree range** $5.25–$7. **Payment** D, DC, MC, V. **Parking** Lot. **Bar** Full service. **Wine selection** House, $4. **Dress** Casual. **Disabled access** Yes. **Customers** Mostly a gay male crowd; the straight and adventurous show up for the drag dinner. **Hours** Sunday–Friday, 11 a.m.–2 a.m.; Saturday, 11 a.m.–3 a.m.

MENU RECOMMENDATIONS   Black Russian sandwich, Philly cheesesteak, awesome burgers.

COMMENTS   This video, cafe, and sports bar is a neighborhood favorite with the local thriving gay community. Georgie's Alibi is a wirelss hot spot with weekly euchre tournaments. Also home to "Lipservice"—a monthly dinner and show served up by saucy drag queens, à la Lucky Cheng's in New York City.

Hong Kong City BBQ ★ ★ ★ ★ ½

ASIAN BBQ	MODERATE	QUALITY ★★★★	VALUE ★★★★★

5301 North FL 7 (441), Tamarac; ☎ 954-777-3832

Reservations Accepted. **When to go** Anytime. **Entree range** $10–$21. **Payment** AE, MC, V. **Parking** Lot. **Bar** None. **Wine selection** None. **Dress** Casual. **Disabled access** Yes. **Customers** Adult diners, couples. **Hours** Monday–Saturday, 11 a.m.–11 p.m.

MENU RECOMMENDATIONS Everyone loves the dim sum.

COMMENTS Locals frequent this no-frills suburban eatery for its consistently yummy take on Chinese cuisine, complete with some surprises, like jellyfish and duck's feet.

Il Mulino ★ ★ ★ ★

ITALIAN	INEXPENSIVE/MODERATE	QUALITY ★★★★	VALUE ★★★★

1800 East Sunrise Boulevard, Fort Lauderdale; ☎ 954-524-1800; www.ilmulinofl.com

Reservations Not accepted. **When to go** Anytime. **Entree range** $9–$20; pizza $8–$10. **Payment** AE, D, DC, MC, V. **Parking** Lot. **Bar** Full service. **Wine selection** Good. **Dress** Dressy casual (don't wear shorts). **Disabled access** Yes. **Customers** Adult diners, couples. **Hours** Sunday–Thursday, 11:30 a.m.–11 p.m.; Friday and Saturday, 11:30 a.m.–midnight.

MENU RECOMMENDATIONS Any of the pizzas will hit the spot, as will the filetto anelli and the zuppa di pesce.

COMMENTS Some think it has the best gourmet-style pizza in the area. Plus, its location near a small movie theater makes it a great time-saver on date night. Free corkage is also available.

Johnny V ★ ★ ★ ★ ★

FLORIBBEAN	EXPENSIVE	QUALITY ★★★★★	VALUE ★★★★

625 East Las Olas Boulevard, Fort Lauderdale; ☎ 954-761-7920; www.johnnyvlasolas.com

Reservations Recommended. **When to go** Anytime; weekdays are less busy for dinner. **Entree range** $15–$40. **Payment** AE, D, DC, MC, V. **Parking** Lot, street, or valet. **Bar** Full service. **Wine selection** Excellent. **Dress** Dressy casual. **Disabled access** Yes. **Customers** Adult diners, couples. **Hours** Monday–Thursday and Sunday, 11:30 a.m.–11 p.m.; Friday and Saturday, 11:30 a.m.–midnight.

MENU RECOMMENDATIONS Make sure to begin with the cheese course. The wild mushroom short stack is wildly fun and delicious, and the yellowtail is a crowd pleaser.

COMMENTS You might want to leave the kids with a babysitter to enjoy a long night of many delicious courses. The service is sometimes inconsistent, but the food is worth the trip.

Kilwin's ★ ★ ★ ★

| DESSERTS | INEXPENSIVE | QUALITY ★ ★ ★ ½ | VALUE ★ ★ ★ ★ ★ |

2758 North University Drive, Coral Springs; ☎ 954-227-5599
809 East Las Olas Boulevard, Fort Lauderdale; ☎ 954-523-8338
Bay 7 Weston Town Centre, Weston; ☎ 954-385-9033;
www.kilwins.com

Reservations Not necessary. **When to go** Anytime. **Dessert range** Prices vary between chains and are subject to change; a single scoop of ice cream starts at about $3. **Payment** AE, MC, V. **Parking** Street, lot behind store. **Dress** Any. **Disabled access** Good, but it's a small store, so navigating with Seeing Eye dogs or wheelchairs may be difficult if it's crowded. **Customers** Anyone. **Hours** Vary according to location; generally Sunday–Thursday, 11 a.m.–10 p.m.; Friday and Saturday, 11 a.m.–11:30 p.m.; may stay open later during the season.

MENU RECOMMENDATIONS Clusters, barks, brittles, fudges, nuts, taffies, turtles, and truffles.

COMMENTS Almost all their chocolates are made fresh on the premises—in the window. If you're on a diet, circumnavigate this dandy storefront by at least 20 feet, because the warm scent of baked goods carries. There are a few outdoor tables—patrons normally grab something to take home or to nibble while they stroll. Kilwin's also serves ice cream and smoothies. It's a great after-dinner spot for dates and families.

Le Tub ★ ★ ★ ★ ½

| SEAFOOD | INEXPENSIVE/MODERATE | QUALITY ★ ★ ★ ★ | VALUE ★ ★ ★ ★ ★ |

1100 North Ocean Drive, Hollywood; ☎ 954-921-9425

Reservations Not accepted. **When to go** On a clear day to enjoy the view. **Entree range** $6–$20. **Payment** Cash only. **Parking** Lot. **Bar** Full service. **Wine selection** Good. **Dress** Casual. **Disabled access** Yes. **Customers** Adult diners, couples. **Hours** Daily, 11 a.m.–4 a.m.

MENU RECOMMENDATIONS Go for a burger or the seafood gumbo and then finish it off with Key lime pie for dessert.

COMMENTS The decor is fun and casually fabulous—a converted gas station, with bathtubs and toilet bowls as planters. If you have time, wait for a seat on the deck. Excellent waterfront view, boat accessible with billiards and a jukebox. The seafood-dominant menu is not very vegetarian friendly.

Lester's Diner ★ ★ ½

| AMERICAN | INEXPENSIVE | QUALITY ★ ★ ★ | VALUE ★ ★ ½ |

250 FL 84, Fort Lauderdale; ☎ 954-525-5641

Reservations Not accepted. **When to go** Anytime. **Entree range** $5–$12. **Payment** AE, D, DC, MC, V. **Parking** Lot; plenty. **Bar** None. **Wine selection** None.

Dress Casual. **Disabled access** Yes. **Customers** Truckers, tourists on their way to the nearby airport, families, workers on their lunch breaks. **Hours** Daily, 24 hours.

MENU RECOMMENDATIONS Diner-style omelets, burgers, and sandwiches.

COMMENTS A Fort Lauderdale tradition, Lester's is a cavernous 1950s-style diner with food to match. What it lacks in atmosphere, it makes up for in comfort food and fast service. Soups are filling and taste like home-made, sandwiches are large enough for two, and desserts are big enough for three or four to share. Daily specials are a great value.

 Little Havana II ★ ★ ★ ★

| CUBAN | INEXPENSIVE/MODERATE | QUALITY ★ ★ ★ ½ | VALUE ★ ★ ★ ★ |

800 South Federal Highway, Deerfield; ☎ 954-427-6000; www.littlehavanarestaurant.com

Reservations Accepted. **When to go** Anytime. **Entree range** $6–$23. **Payment** AE, MC, V. **Parking** Lot. **Bar** Full service. **Wine selection** Good. **Dress** Casual to dressy casual. **Disabled access** Yes. **Customers** Adult diners, couples, families. **Hours** Monday–Thursday and Sunday, 11:30 a.m.–10 p.m.; Friday and Saturday, 11:30 a.m.–11 p.m.

MENU RECOMMENDATIONS "Taste of Havana" appetizer platter; *ropa vieja,* shredded beef in a light tomato sauce. Children's menu available.

COMMENTS They offer live entertainment Tuesday–Sunday, 6 p.m. until closing. It's small, modest, clean, and child and vegetarian friendly.

 Mai Kai ★ ★ ★

| POLYNESIAN | MODERATE | QUALITY ★ ★ ★ ★ | VALUE ★ ★ |

3599 North Federal Highway (NE 31st Street), Fort Lauderdale; ☎ 954-563-3272; www.maikai.com

Reservations Required. **When to go** Dinner. **Entree range** $15–$60. **Payment** AE, D, DC, MC, V. **Parking** Pay lot, valet. **Bar** Full service. **Wine selection** Good. **Dress** Dressy Casual. **Disabled access** Yes. **Customers** Adult diners, couples, families. **Hours** Daily, 5–11:30 p.m.; last seating is at 9 p.m.; happy hour: daily, 5–7 p.m.; Poly-nesian reviews: Sunday–Thursday, 7 and 9:30 p.m.; Friday and Saturday, 7 and 10 p.m.

MENU RECOMMENDATIONS Peking duck, Thai chicken and shrimp with pineap-ple, Szechuan Surf & Turf.

COMMENTS Campy and touristy but still fun, especially for groups. If you want to immerse yourself in a beach mindset while in South Florida, this is a good place to stop—even if it is Polynesian. Children ages 12 and under don't have to pay to see the show (adult charge is $10). The restaurant offers a special kids menu, plus children get tropical fruit punch, a coloring book, and a lei. The Sunday 7 p.m. show is unofficially dedicated to kids; performers bring children onstage to dance.

Rainforest Café ★ ★ ★

FLORIBBEAN   MODERATE   QUALITY ★ ★ ★   VALUE ★ ★ ★

Sawgrass Mills, 12801 West Sunrise Boulevard, Sunrise/Fort Lauderdale;
☎ **954-851-1015; www.rainforestcafe.com**

Reservations Not necessary. **When to go** Anytime. **Entree range** $8–$18. **Payment** AE, D, DC, MC, V. **Parking** Lot (white seahorse at Sawgrass Mills). **Bar** Full service. **Wine selection** Good. **Dress** Casual. **Disabled access** Good. **Customers** Families, tourists, shoppers. **Hours** Daily, 11 a.m.–10 p.m.

MENU RECOMMENDATIONS China Island chicken salad, Cyclone crab-cake sandwich.

COMMENTS This restaurant chain was created with your children in mind. Located at the "white seahorse" entrance of Sawgrass Mills, there's a huge jungle gym outside the restaurant to keep your kids occupied until your "safari guide" leads you through a synthetic, misting rainforest, complete with moving animatronic creatures and periodic thunderstorms. Also, the restaurant donates a portion of its profit to rain-forest conservation.

The River House ★ ★ ★ ★

AMERICAN CONTINENTAL   MODERATE/EXPENSIVE   QUALITY ★ ★ ★ ★ ½ VALUE ★ ★ ★

301 SW Third Avenue, Fort Lauderdale; ☎ **954-525-7661;**
www.ftlauderdaleriverhouse.com

Reservations Accepted. **When to go** Saturday evenings for a quieter dinner; Sunday for brunch. **Entree range** $30–$35. **Payment** AE, D, MC, V. **Parking** Valet. **Bar** Full service. **Wine selection** Good; $12 samplers feature different tastes and styles. **Dress** Professional casual; jackets not required. **Disabled access** Yes. **Customers** Families and professionals. **Hours** Sunday–Thursday, 5:30–10:30 p.m.; Friday and Saturday, 5:30–11 p.m.; Sunday brunch, 11 a.m.–2:30 p.m.

MENU RECOMMENDATIONS Menu changes daily, featuring fresh cuts of beef and fish. Past favorites include chili-rubbed grilled rib-eye steak; bouillabaisse-style Alaskan halibut, rosemary-marinated pork loin, and pan-roasted yellowtail snapper with hot-and-sour mango sauce.

COMMENTS Located along Fort Lauderdale's New River, this historic home (owned by the Bryan family, responsible for bringing the railroad to Fort Lauderdale) is a quaint place for a calm, romantic dinner. The view is really quite lovely. A great spot for a weekend brunch.

Sushi Blues Café and Blue Monk Lounge ★ ★ ★ ★

SUSHI/PAN-ASIAN   MODERATE/EXPENSIVE   QUALITY ★ ★ ★ ★ ½   VALUE ★ ★ ★ ★

2009 Harrison Street, Hollywood; ☎ **954-929-9560;**
www.sushiblues.com

Reservations Recommended. **When to go** Anytime; 8 p.m. or earlier if you don't want a crowd. **Entree range** $8–$30. **Payment** AE, MC, V. **Parking** Lot. **Bar** Full service. **Wine selection** Good. **Dress** Dressy casual. **Disabled access** Yes. **Customers** Adult diners, couples. **Hours** Monday–Thursday, 11:30 a.m.–1:30 a.m.; Friday, 11 a.m.–1:30 a.m.; Saturday, 5:30–1:30 a.m.; Sunday, 5:30–11:30 p.m.

MENU RECOMMENDATIONS Start with the ginger-carrot soup. If you want a traditional entrée, try the garlic-and-ginger-studded tuna steak with smashed honey-ginger sweet potatoes—yum. If you're ordering off the sushi menu, don't miss the "new world sashimi"—paper-thin snapper with fresh ginger and leeks seasoned with a hot olive oil and sesame oil vinaigrette.

COMMENTS This is a well-known jazz and blues hot spot, so don't go on the weekend if you're looking for a quiet dinner. A big menu will please even non-sushi eaters. Overall, this place exudes a fun vibe.

Tom Jenkins' Bar-B-Q ★ ★ ★ ★

BARBECUE	INEXPENSIVE	QUALITY ★ ★ ★ ★	VALUE ★ ★ ★ ½

1236 South Federal Highway, Fort Lauderdale; ☎ 954-522-5046; www.tomjenkinsbbq.com

Reservations Not accepted. **When to go** Anytime. **Entree range** $5–$18. **Payment** Cash only. **Parking** Lot (a bit of a pain). **Bar** None. **Wine selection** None. **Dress** Casual. **Disabled access** Yes, but people with wheelchairs and other equipment may have a hard time navigating the room. **Customers** Adult diners, couples, families. **Hours** Tuesday–Thursday, 11 a.m.–8:30 p.m.; Friday and Saturday, 11 a.m.–10 p.m.

MENU RECOMMENDATIONS Anything with sauce on it.

COMMENTS It's picnic-table sit-down style, which means sometimes sitting next to strangers. Also, you may have to wait in line. The service is known to be standoffish and overworked. People come back to this place because the food is good. Get the best of both worlds and order takeout.

Toojay's ★ ★ ★

DELI	INEXPENSIVE	QUALITY ★ ★ ★	VALUE ★ ★ ★

The Walk at University, 2880 North University Drive, Coral Springs; ☎ 954-346-0006
801 South University Drive, Plantation; ☎ 954-423-1993; www.toojays.com

Reservations Not accepted. **When to go** To avoid lines, come before 11 a.m. for lunch and before 6 p.m. for dinner. **Entree range** $7–$15. **Payment** AE, D, DC, MC, V. **Parking** Lot. **Bar** Beer and wine. **Wine selection** Fair, $3.50–$5.50. **Dress** Casual. **Disabled access** Good. **Customers** Locals, tourists, winter residents, kosher eaters. **Hours** Daily, 8 a.m.–9 p.m.

MENU RECOMMENDATIONS Matzo-ball soup, corned-beef sandwich, "killer cake", rye bread, pitas and wraps.

COMMENTS Where Bubby and Pop-Pop go to nosh, Toojay's has authentic New York–Jewish deli flavor and a lot of elderly and family diners. Although the portions of french fries are sometimes skimpy, the sandwiches are enormous, the corned beef juicy, the bread fresh, and the black-and-white cookies delish.

Trina ★★★★

MEDITERRANEAN	EXPENSIVE	QUALITY ★★★★	VALUE ★★★★

The Atlantic Hotel, 601 North Fort Lauderdale Beach Boulevard, Fort Lauderdale; ☎ 954-567-8070; www.theatlantichotelfortlauderdale.com/trina

Reservations Recommended; call 48 hours in advance. When to go Anytime, but weekends are busy. Entree range $23–$36. Payment AE, D, DC, MC, V. Parking Valet (get your ticket validated and pay $5 instead of $10). Bar Full service. Wine selection Excellent. Dress Dressy casual. Disabled access Yes. Customers Adult diners, couples. Hours Sunday–Thursday, 6:30 a.m.–10 p.m.; Friday and Saturday, 6:30 a.m.–11 p.m.

MENU RECOMMENDATIONS You must order from the flatbread menu—enough for a meal alone. Then, try the pan-roasted diver scallops and sweetbreads with smoked bacon and a black truffle and sherry vinegar sauce. All desserts are good. For breakfast or brunch, dig into the lemon buttermilk pancakes topped with mascarpone, toasted almonds, and blueberry compote or the breakfast panini, with scrambled eggs, pancetta, fontina, and home fries.

COMMENTS A combination of sleek decor, a gastronomically informed and delicious Mediterranean menu, and a pretty beachfront view makes this a very popular spot with the local foodies.

Try My Thai ★★★

THAI	MODERATE	QUALITY ★★★★	VALUE ★★

**2003 Harrison Street, Hollywood; ☎ 954-926-5585
1507 North Federal Highway, Fort Lauderdale; ☎ 954-630-0030**

Reservations Suggested for larger parties. When to go Weeknights, early dinners. Entree range $9–$16. Payment AE, D, DC, MC, V. Parking Public lots, street. Bar Beer and wine. Wine selection Small list; $16–$26 bottle, $5.50–$6.50 per glass. Dress Casual. Disabled access Yes. Customers Businesspeople at lunch; locals and tourists for dinner. Hours Monday–Friday, 11 a.m.–2:30 p.m. and 5–10:30 p.m.; Saturday and Sunday, 5–10:30 p.m. (Fort Lauderdale location closed Monday.)

MENU RECOMMENDATIONS Holy Cow, a spicy mix of Thai basil, chili, and beef; Forever Shrimp, with shrimp, ginger, and vegetables; Thai donuts; Banana Surprise—slices of banana fried crisp and sprinkled with honey and sesame seeds; alligator.

COMMENTS Decorated with ties—yes, neckties—in a variety of colors, fabrics, and styles. Your meal comes with a complimentary appetizer, too.

Zona Fresca ★ ★ ★

MEXICAN	INEXPENSIVE	QUALITY ★ ★ ★	VALUE ★ ★ ★

1635 North Federal Highway, Fort Lauderdale; ☎ 954-566-1777; www.zonafresca.com

Reservations Not accepted. **When to go** Anytime. **Entree range** $3–$7. **Payment** AE, D, DC, MC, V. **Parking** Lot. **Bar** Beer only. **Wine selection** None. **Dress** Casual. **Disabled access** Yes. **Customers** Adult diners, couples. **Hours** Sunday–Thursday, 11 a.m.–9 p.m.; Friday and Saturday, 11 a.m.–10 p.m.

MENU RECOMMENDATIONS Baja "Ranchero," taco "sabroso," taquitos, and chili rellenos.

COMMENTS Fresh, fast Mexican food—all natural, no preservatives, no MSG. Look for the big yellow neon letters when you're trying to find it.

ENTERTAINMENT *and* NIGHTLIFE

FINDING THE GOOD TIMES

SANDWICHED BETWEEN MIAMI-DADE AND Palm Beach counties, Broward is known by proponents as less pretentious than Palm Beach County and more "just be" than "SoBe." Many residents and in-the-know vacationers, particularly those who tire of jet-setters racing to plant their flags in the sands of South Beach, find Fort Lauderdale to be more accessible, slightly less expensive, and just as much fun.

Generally, Broward's layout is similar to Palm Beach County's in the sense that most of the action happens in clusters east of I-95. For the most part, these clusters offer the same things—bars, shops, restaurants, and clubs—but they do have discriminating features:

*un*official **TIP**
Beach Place gouges you with the parking fee at its garage, since it's the only convenient place to park. The lot also closes at 2 a.m. If you plan to stay later, park in one of the street lots around Beach Place or in the city lot at the corner of Las Olas and FL A1A (a rather long walk from Beach Place).

- Second Street is close to the Broward Center for the Performing Arts and the Science Museum. Of all three locales, it's probably the least touristy.
- Las Olas Riverfront (**www.riverfrontfl.com**) is an outdoor mall that has a 15-screen movie theater and Riverfront cruises, as well as a charter service that tours the city's intracoastal waterway.
- Las Olas Boulevard (**www.lasolasboulevard.com**) offers art galleries, antique shops, and salons. It's the most gentrified commercial area of Fort Lauderdale. It's also the city's location of choice for street festivals.

- Beach Place (**www.gobeachplace.com**) is an outdoor mall right across the street from the ocean. With a welcome center on the ground level, it anticipates tourists.

Certainly, there are great clubs and restaurants outside these areas, and we include some of them here. But if you're looking to get the most done with the least amount of driving, you can pick one of these spots and stick with it.

CONCERTS, THEATER, AND OTHER CULTURAL PURSUITS

BROWARD COUNTY IS COMMITTED TO LIVE music. The most notable new live music venue in the area is **Revolution**—a well-renovated old nightclub that has gone through many incarnations at its location (200 West Broward Boulevard; ☎ 954-727-0950) and now draws big-name Clear Channel acts like Snoop Dogg, as well as smaller independent acts like Kings of Leon or The Roots. You can also catch national rock acts almost every night of the week at **The Culture Room** (3045 North Federal Highway, Fort Lauderdale; ☎ 954-564-1074) and **The Factory** (both in Fort Lauderdale). **Center Court** at Beach Place is a little nest for local musicians of all genres—from rock to jazz to flamenco.

After Fort Lauderdale, Hollywood Beach is the city that offers the most to do in Broward County. Hollywood's **Young Circle** resembles a small town's Main Street, with restaurants, coffee shops, bars, and the like. The city of Hollywood also goes out of its way to provide live music for its residents. Almost every night of the week, there are live musicians at the **Hollywood Beach Theater** (Johnson Street and Broadwalk, Hollywood; ☎ 954-921-3404).

unofficial **TIP**
Your best bet for tracking the dates and times of the concerts at sea, as well as any other concert in the area, is to look up "Fort Lauderdale, FL" on **www.pollstar.com**.

Music-themed cruises also sail regularly out of Fort Lauderdale—like the annual weeklong Jam Cruise through the Caribbean, which has featured acts like Bela Fleck and the Flecktones, or the Rhythm and Blues Cruise, which has showcased acts like Taj Mahal and Tab Benoit.

There's an endless market for cultural events catering to Broward's retirees from northern cities, young professionals and families, and tourists. Whether you prefer Bob Fosse or Ellen DeGeneres, Eminem or Andrea Bocelli, your options in Broward are numerous.

Call the Broward Ticketmaster line at ☎ 954-523-3309 or visit **www.ticketmaster.com** to see who's performing in the greater Fort Lauderdale area; the company sells tickets for the **Broward Center of the Performing Arts** (home to shows by major artists catering to more mature crowds), **Office Depot Center** (likely spot for big, national concert tours), **Sunrise Musical Theater, Parker Playhouse,** and other venues. While you're in town, stop at almost any newsstand to pick up a copy of *New Times Broward/Palm Beach* or *City Link* for the weekly goings-on.

FUN AND GAMES

IF YOU'RE LOOKING FOR A HIGH-STAKES KIND of nightlife, you're going to love the new **Seminole Hard Rock Casino** (441 between Sterling and Griffin; ☎ 954-288-8691), an 86-acre resort that boasts a 130,000-square-foot casino. Of course, there's always the less showy **Seminole Casino** (4150 North FL 7, Hollywood; ☎ 866-222-7466 or 866-2-CASINO), which stays open 24 hours. Opened in 1979, Seminole was the first high-stakes gaming facility of its kind in the country. Veteran slot-pullers and fun-seeking first-timers can try their luck at high-stakes bingo, lightning bingo, poker (48 tables), and slots. If all that fails to get your blood racing, Seminole Casino hosts live boxing matches (**www.warriorsboxing.com**).

For a family-friendly spin on gaming, try **Gameworks** (Sawgrass Mills, in the Oasis, 2608 Sawgrass Mills Circle, Sunrise; ☎ 954-845-8740), a state-of-the-art game room, full-service restaurant, and bar created by film honcho Steven Spielberg. It appeals equally to families, young couples, and singles. **Dave and Buster's** (3000 Oakwood Boulevard, Hollywood; ☎ 954-923-5505) is a restaurant-cum-video game mecca attracting kids of all ages. **Boomers Dania Beach** (1801 NW First Street, Dania Beach; ☎ 954-921-1411) offers go-kart racing, mini-golf, and video games.

NIGHTCLUBS

IN THE LAST COUPLE OF YEARS, BROWARD COUNTY has really stepped up its nightclub inventory, which wasn't bad in the first place. There are more than a few places where you can go low key to grab a beer, like the unadorned **Poor House** (110 SW Third Avenue, downtown Fort Lauderdale; ☎ 954-522-5145), or clubs where the crowd needs to dress to be let in, like the **Voodoo Lounge** (111 SW Second Avenue (Moffat Street), downtown Fort Lauderdale; ☎ 954-522-0733; **www.voodooloungeflorida.com**).

But the biggest news in Broward nightlife is the recent addition of the **Seminole Hard Rock Casino,** which has ten beautifully decorated on-site bars, clubs, and lounges, including the gorgeous Pangaea lounge and the high-energy, multilevel Passion, which draws decent guest DJs when residents DJ George Acosta and Erik Velez aren't spinning. In addition to having the Seminole Hard Rock, the city of Hollywood also enjoys a busy downtown. The joint is jumpin' at **Sushi Blues** (1836 South Young Circle, Hollywood; ☎ 954-929-9560), with dinner at 6 p.m. and live jazz Thursday–Saturday.

THE GAY SCENE

GAY-FRIENDLY GREATER FORT LAUDERDALE HAS more than 100 gay-owned establishments, including hotels, bars, clubs, and restaurants, plus the second-largest **Metropolitan Community Church** congregation in the country (Sunshine Cathedral; ☎ 954-462-2004), a **Gay and Lesbian Community Center** (1717 North Andrews Avenue; ☎ 954-463-9005; **www.glccsf.org**), and several gay and lesbian publications, including *HotSpots!*, *TWN*, *411*, *The Independent*, and *The Express*. Gay clubs and bars are more numerous than usual lately. The boys who want to dance can choose between the daddy of Broward dance clubs, **The Copa** (2800 South Federal Highway, Fort Lauderdale; ☎ 954-463-1507; **www.copaboy.com**), and the young upstart, **Coliseum** (2520 South Miami Road, Fort Lauderdale; ☎ 954-832-0100; **www.coliseumnightclub.com**). Women who like women also have plenty of options (mostly low-key bars), like the Latin-infused **Elements** (3073 NE Sixth Avenue, Wilton Manors; ☎ 954-567-2432), **Cloud 9** (7126 Stirling Road, Davie; ☎ 954-499-3525; **www.thecloud9online.com**), and **J's** (2780 West Davie Boulevard, Fort Lauderdale; ☎ 954-581-8400).

There are about a dozen other gay and lesbian clubs in the area, including video bars **Chase Video Lounge** (2736 North Federal Highway, Fort Lauderdale; ☎ 954-763-8219) and the always popular **Cathode Ray** (1307 East Las Olas Boulevard, Fort Lauderdale; ☎ 954-462-0291; **www.cathoderayusa.com**), as well as leather bars like **Ramrod** (1408 NE Fourth Avenue, Fort Lauderdale; ☎ 954-763-8219).

Wilton Manors, a city located just outside Fort Lauderdale, has a large concentration of gay residents and two of the most popular gay bars in the area: **Georgie's Alibi** for him (2266 Wilton Drive, Wilton Manors; ☎ 954-565-2526) and **New Moon Bar** for her (2440 Wilton Drive, Wilton Manors; ☎ 954-563-7660).

The Best of Broward County Clubs

Name	Cover	Cost	City
BARS			
Automatic Slim's	None	Inexp	Fort Lauderdale
Billabong Pub	Varies	Inexp	Hallandale
Martini Bar	None	Mod	Fort Lauderdale
Swig Bartini	None	Mod/Exp	Weston
COUNTRY AND WESTERN			
Round Up Country and Western Restaurant and Nightclub	$5–$10	Mod	Davie

Name	Cover	Cost	City
DANCE CLUBS			
Cafe Iguana	Varies	Inexp	Fort Lauderdale, Hollywood
Spice Resto-Lounge	None	Inexp	Hollywood
Voodoo Lounge	Varies	Mod	Fort Lauderdale
EIGHT-NIGHTCLUBS-IN-ONE			
Seminole Paradise Hard Rock Hotel and Casino	Varies	Mod	Hollywood
JAZZ AND BLUES			
O'Hara's Jazz and Blues Cafe	None	Mod	Fort Lauderdale, Hollywood
The Poor House	None	Inexp	Fort Lauderdale
SINGLES			
Christopher's	Varies	Exp	Fort Lauderdale
Tarpon Bend	None	Mod	Fort Lauderdale

NIGHTCLUB PROFILES

Automatic Slim's

INDIE HIPSTERS, YOUR SHIP HAS COME IN

**15 West Las Olas Boulevard, Las Olas Riverfront, Fort Lauderdale;
☎ 954-522-8585; www.automatic-slims.com**

Cover None. **Minimum** None. **Mixed drinks** $5 and up. **Wine** $3 and up. **Beer** $3 and up. **Food available** None. **Hours** Monday–Saturday, 9 p.m.–4 a.m.

WHO GOES THERE Spillovers from the rest of the Riverfront, billiard lovers, and young professionals looking to cruise.

WHAT GOES ON This Coyote Ugly–esque bar (yes, the female employees are attractive and dance on things) is modeled after a Nevada desert park—complete with airstream-trailer DJ booth and wayward neon drive-in sign; its motto is "where beautiful people come to get ugly." The pool tables are a favorite, and the music is mostly dance-driven—hip-hop, electronica, rock, and pop. Sometimes the doormen have something to prove, so if you don't, you might want to find a less scene-y bar. On Wednesdays, the club sets up a half-pipe outside for area skaters who've signed their waivers.

COMMENTS At best, a great mix of alt-sportspeople, good, loud music, and cheap beer for an indie crowd. At worst, an "it spot" infiltrated by scene-going oglers who don't embody the bar's laid back sensibility.

Billabong Pub

WHERE BEER LOVERS GO TO DRINK BEER

3000 Country Club Lane, Hallandale (west of the train tracks near Mattress Giant); ☎ 954-985-1050; www.billabongpub.com

Cover Saturday nights there's live music and a cover of $4–$5. Minimum None. Mixed drinks $5 and up. Wine $3.50–$4.50. Beer The best beer selection in South Florida—drafts, $4; bottles, $3–$12—with hard-to-find labels like Chimay and LaTrappe. Food available Greasy American grub like sandwiches and fries. Hours Monday–Friday, 11:30 a.m.–1 a.m.; Saturday, 11:30 a.m.–2 a.m.; Sunday, 4 p.m.–midnight.

WHO GOES THERE College kids, local hipsters, old-time bar stoolies.

WHAT GOES ON This family-owned and -operated pub welcomes customers of all ages. Happy hour runs 5–7 p.m. on weekdays. During NFL season, the pub opens at 12:30 p.m. for football fans.

COMMENTS One of the bars with renewable street cred, year after year, due mostly to its commitment to live, local rock musicians and good beer. Not at all a pretty people scene.

Cafe Iguana

DISCO DE LA MER

17th Street/Fort Lauderdale Beach Boulevard, Beach Place, Fort Lauderdale; ☎ 954-763-7222.
8358 Pines Boulevard, Hollywood; ☎ 954-433-8787; www.cafeiguanapines.com

Cover Varies according to specials and events, generally $5 after 10 p.m. Minimum None. Mixed drinks $3 and up. Wine $4 and up. Beer $2 and up. Food available None. Hours Daily, noon–4 a.m.

WHO GOES THERE Tourists, locals looking for popular dance music; Spring Breakers.

WHAT GOES ON Latin house and rap rule the sound system for young singles on the prowl.

COMMENTS The Beach Place location overlooks the Atlantic Ocean. Iguana is a favorite with tourists. It's like a little bit of Cancun in South Florida. Parking can be difficult, and during the winter crowds are pretty thick at Beach Place. Park at the (expensive) garage on the third floor, but be careful—this place is open later than the garage, which closes at 2 a.m. Dress code enforced, kids. "Dress to impress."

Christopher's

NOT A CLUB FOR COLLEGE KIDS

2587 East Oakland Park Boulevard, Fort Lauderdale; ☎ 954-561-2136; www.christophersnightclub.com

Cover Generally none (though there is a charge for special events like Hot Latin Sunday). **Minimum** None. **Mixed drinks** $3–$8; $80–$1,000 bottle service. **Wine** $5–$9. **Beer** $4–$6. **Food available** Full American-Continental menu. **Hours** Sunday–Thursday, 8 p.m.–2 a.m.; Friday and Saturday, 8 p.m.–3 a.m.

WHO GOES THERE Singles ages 25–55—mostly a mature, upscale, professional crowd.

WHAT GOES ON Singles swinging Tom Jones style.

COMMENTS Dancing, eating, drinking. This is possibly the oldest, most reliable over-30 singles scene in South Florida. Ladies must be 23 and over, guys 25.

Martini Bar

GOOD TASTE AND GOOD MARTINIS

300 SW First Street, Las Olas Riverfront (second floor);
☎ **954-764-4345; www.martinibarfla.com**

Cover None. **Minimum** None. **Hours** Wednesday, Thursday, and Saturday 8 p.m.–4 a.m.; Friday, 5 p.m.–4 a.m.

WHO GOES THERE Adults who don't like to push and shove at a club.

WHAT GOES ON Live music and a late-night menu accommodate an over-30 singles crowd getting cozy.

COMMENTS A great late-night spot for mature professionals.

O'Hara's Jazz and Blues Cafe

THE JOINT IS ALWAYS JUMPIN', BUT THE ATTITUDE ISN'T

722 East Las Olas Boulevard, Fort Lauderdale; ☎ **954-524-1764**
1903 Hollywood Boulevard, Hollywood; ☎ **954-925-2555;**
www.oharasjazzcafe.com

Cover None. **Minimum** None. **Mixed drinks** $5 and up. **Wine** $6.50–$8. **Beer** $4.50–$6. **Food available** Yes. **Hours** Sunday, noon–2 a.m.; Monday–Thursday, 11:30 a.m.–2 a.m.; Friday and Saturday, 11:30 a.m.–3 a.m.

WHO GOES THERE An over-30 crowd and jazz fans of all ages (over 18).

WHAT GOES ON Live music is the main draw at this laid-back, friendly Broward County mainstay. An older crowd comes to drink and, mostly, to enjoy the sound. Don't go if you're looking for a bar that let's you talk while musicians play. Live R&B, funk, classic rock, blues, and jazz every night. Food is served Sunday through Thursday, 6 p.m. to midnight and Friday and Saturday, 5 p.m.–2 a.m. You can smoke there, too.

COMMENTS An old faithful for jazz fans in the area; one of the most stalwart live music venues in Broward County. If you don't like what you're hearing at either location, both are located within proximity to other bars.

The Poor House

NOT A POOR HOUSE, IT'S A POOR HOME

110 SW Third Avenue, downtown Fort Lauderdale;
☎ **954-522-5145**

Cover None. **Minimum** None. **Mixed drinks** $3 and up. **Wine** $3 and up. **Beer** Microbrews $2 and up. **Food available** None. **Hours** 8 p.m.–2 a.m.

WHO GOES THERE Laid-back types who like music and don't brawl when they drink.

WHAT GOES ON Live rock and blues every night; chitchat on the outdoor patio.

COMMENTS A comfortable, no-frills place for live music and drinking. Park on the street or use the valet on 2nd and 2nd in front of Tarpon Bend. Leave the pretension at home—this is not a club for pretty boys and divas.

Round Up Country and Western Restaurant and Nightclub

GOOD OLE BOYS' AND GIRLS' CLUB

9020 West FL 84, Davie; ☎ 954-423-1990; www.roundupcountry.com

Cover $5, Thursday $10. **Minimum** None. **Mixed drinks** $4 and up. **Wine** $5 and up. **Beer** $3.50 and up. **Food available** American menu. **Hours** Wednesday–Sunday, 6 p.m.–4 a.m.

WHO GOES THERE Country music fans of all colors and creeds.

WHAT GOES ON Heralded as the best country bar in all of South Florida, the Round Up offers live acts, line dancing (with lessons on Thursday and Saturday), beers, Stetsons and a menu with a lot of fried foods. Simple.

Seminole Paradise Hard Rock Hotel and Casino

MORE NIGHTLIFE THAN YOU CAN LIVE IN ONE NIGHT

1 Seminole Way, Hollywood; ☎ 866-502-PLAY; www.seminolehardrockhollywood.com

Cover Varies. **Minimum** Varies. **Mixed drinks** $4 and up. **Wine** $4 and up. **Beer** $4 and up. **Food available** Yes, at various restaurants throughout the hotel and casino; check the Web site for more details. **Hours** Sunday–Thursday, 11 a.m.–2 a.m.; Friday and Saturday, 11 a.m.–3 a.m.

WHO GOES THERE Hotel guests and see-and-be-scenesters from all over Broward and Palm Beach counties.

WHAT GOES ON Everything you need to have a full night is at this brand new and very popular mega-facility, where the masses lined up outside the nightclub doors can get restless. Sometimes it's a tense scene. But the décor is unbeatable, the drinks are creative, and the music is good and loud. "Dress to impress" for all the nightclubs. If you're wearing sneakers and a baseball hat, you won't get in anywhere except the Irish pub and the pool hall.

COMMENTS **88s Dueling Piano Bar** (☎ 954-584-8868; **www.88sduelingpianos.com**) features piano pranksters who take requests and spoof well-known songs. **Pangaea and Gryphon** (☎ 954-581-5454; **www.pangaea-lounge.com**) is an African-inspired modern lounge with an adjoining high-energy dance club. If you're looking to relax and be entertained, try **The Improv Comedy Club** (☎ 954-981-5653; **www.improvftl.com**), which features regional and local comedians. At **Jazziz Live** (☎ 954-583-8335; **www.jazzizbistro.com**) patrons can enjoy live jazz and blues. For a more casual spot, check out **Knight Time Billiards** (☎ 954-587-6155; **www.knighttimebilliards.com**), the Hard Rock's pool hall du jour. **Murphy's Law Irish Pub** (☎ 954-791-4782; **www.themurphyslaw.com**) has brews and brogues on tap. **Passion** (☎ 954-321-3443; **www.passionnightclub.com**) is a multilevel facility with theme nights and a theater (requiring additional admission) housing an all-male stripper review. And last but not least, **Spirits,** modeled after the A-list Miami dance meccas, is the newest addition to the Hard Rock and provides a little bit of South Beach in a more accessible form.

Spice Resto-Lounge

MUSICA, MUSICA! BAILA, BAILA!

1934 Hollywood Boulevard, Hollywood; ☎ 954-923-3888

Cover None. **Minimum** None. **Mixed drinks** $4 and up. **Wine** $3 and up. **Beer** $3 and up. **Food available** Yes. **Hours** Daily, 4 p.m.–4 a.m.

WHO GOES THERE People whose grandmother from Cuba taught them how to Salsa, and the people who just like the mojitos.

WHAT GOES ON A restaurant with a twist, Spice Resto-Lounge offers live Latin music every night and the occasional dance performance. Diners normally clear the check then head for the dance floor.

COMMENTS A must for people looking to experience the Latin-American flavor of South Florida, especially on Friday and Saturday nights.

Swig Bartini

MARTINIS, MUSIC, MUNCHING, MINGLING

1744 Main Street, Weston; ☎ 954-349-2102; www.swigbartini.com

Cover None. **Minimum** None. **Mixed drinks** $5 and up; martinis $8 and up. **Wine** $5 and up. **Beer** $5 and up. **Food available** Eclectic menu with pizzas, pastas, appetizers; the kitchen stops serving at 1:30 a.m. on weekends. **Hours** Daily, 3 p.m.–3 a.m.

WHO GOES THERE Mature, chic west-Broward professionals.

WHAT GOES ON A civilized sip-and-be-seen spot with live music.

COMMENTS This is one of the best bets for mature professionals in far West Broward.

Tarpon Bend

LAND-LOCKED FISHING-THEMED BAR

200 SW Second Street, Fort Lauderdale; ☎ 954-523-3233; www.tarponbend.com

Cover None. **Minimum** None. **Mixed drinks** $5 and up. **Wine** $6 and up. **Beer** $2.50 and up. **Food available** Sandwiches, seafood, some steaks and chicken offerings. **Hours** Sunday and Tuesday, 11 a.m.–midnight; Monday and Thursday, 11 a.m.–2 a.m.; Wednesday, 11 a.m.–1 a.m.; Friday and Saturday, 11 a.m.–3 a.m.; happy hour every night features 2-for-1 mixed drinks.

WHO GOES THERE Lauderdale's young professionals and singles.

WHAT GOES ON Nouveau yuppies getting their drink on and trying to snag a catch.

COMMENTS A good all-in-one spot for night crawling: food, drinks, acoustic music, and people who need people. Parking is difficult on this corner—give yourself time to find a space or use the valet on 2nd and 2nd in front of the club.

Voodoo Lounge

PUTS THE "TRANCE" INTO MAKING AN ENTRANCE

111 SW Second Avenue (Moffat Street), downtown Fort Lauderdale; ☎ 954-522-0733; www.voodooloungeflorida.com

Cover Varies; generally none before midnight, then $5 for women and $10 for men. **Minimum** None. **Mixed drinks** $4–$7, $140–$1,000 bottle service. **Wine** $4. **Beer** $5–$6. **Food available** None. **Hours** Wednesday and Friday–Sunday, 10 p.m.–4 a.m.

WHO GOES THERE The kind of people you see in music videos—attractive and well-dressed (or half-dressed) club kids ages 20–40.

WHAT GOES ON DJs, hip-hop, house, electronica, and the occasional 1980s night. On Ladies' Night (Wednesday), women get in free and can consume well and domestic drinks for free midnight to 4 a.m. and on Fridays, 10 p.m. to midnight.

COMMENTS A local favorite and one of Fort Lauderdale's "velvet rope" clubs.

PART SEVEN

SOUTHWEST FLORIDA

WELCOME *to* SOUTHWEST FLORIDA

SOUTHWEST FLORIDA IS AN ALLURING, LAID-BACK travel alternative to those well-known tourist destinations east of the Everglades. Less developed than the Atlantic Coast, Southwest Florida offers tranquility rather than glitz, with great resorts and unspoiled wilderness areas, charming towns, and a relaxing atmosphere.

This superb vacation destination on the Gulf of Mexico, known best for Fort Myers and Naples, is growing rapidly as the world discovers its natural charms and unspoiled beaches. Peak season is January through April, when reservations are essential.

Ecotourism

To appreciate the region's burgeoning ecotourism industry, just consider a few outstanding examples of Southwest Florida's unspoiled wetlands:

- J. N. "Ding" Darling National Wildlife Refuge, Sanibel Island
- Sanibel-Captiva Nature Conservation Foundation
- Calusa Nature Center and Planetarium, Fort Myers
- Lovers Key State Park, Black Island (just south of Fort Myers Beach)
- Matanzas Pass Wilderness Preserve, Estero Island
- Mound Key, accessible only by boat from Estero Island
- Babcock Wilderness Adventures, North Fort Myers
- Corkscrew Swamp Sanctuary, Bonita Springs
- Everglades National Park and Big Cypress National Preserve, home of the National Audubon Society (a short day-trip from anywhere in the region)

A BRIEF HISTORY

FORT MYERS, LOCATED ON THE WONDERFULLY named Caloosahatchee River, has a history connected strongly to Native Americans, Spanish colonials, and Cubans who fished the rich waters of the Gulf of Mexico (which leads into the Caloosahatchee). One such fisherman, Manuel Gonzalez, sailed from Spain for Cuba looking for fishing grounds. He missed the island nation and settled in the Fort Myers area, later moving on to Key West. Southwest Florida's ties to Cuba are deep. For example, the boundaries of area reservations were deliberately set inland during the Indian Wars to prevent Native Americans from fishing and trading with Cubans, who sold them arms.

In the 1830s, the area was home to little more than alligators, a few bears, and Cubans who fished off the barrier islands. Then in 1841, the U.S. military built a fort near the mouth of the Caloosahatchee to supply another fort that had been hit badly by a hurricane. Eventually the new fort was named for Lt. Col. Abraham Charles Myers, an Army quartermaster.

Cattle were sold and shipped to Cuba from Lee County from 1868 to 1878; Fort Myers was the last leg on the journey on land. Herds were driven to Punta Rassa, the shipping center. Jacob Summerlin, "King of the Cowmen," built a causeway connecting the mainland to the island of Punta Rassa in 1868, but when the Cuban rebellion against Spain ceased, the price of cattle dropped.

The town of Fort Myers grew nevertheless, and in the latter part of the 19th century, shipped 20 boxcars of fruit a day during the picking season. The historic freeze that struck Florida in 1894 prompted outsiders to discover citrus from the Caloosahatchee region. Prices soared to as much as $200 for the fruit of one tree, and Fort Myers gained a nationwide reputation as a citrus-farming center.

One early tourist was inventor Thomas Edison, who came to Fort Myers on doctor's orders after a rainy and cold spell in Saint Augustine sent him scurrying for sunshine and warmth during the winter of 1884–85. He spent 46 winters in Lee County, enjoying the mild climate and encouraging friends such as Henry Ford and Harvey Firestone to come visit.

During World War II there were more military personnel than residents in the Fort Myers area. And many of those servicemen and -women chose to settle here.

SOUTHWEST FLORIDA TODAY

Lee Island Coast

Nicknamed the "City of Palms" and "Florida's Tropical Island Getaway," Fort Myers is one of the state's prime growth areas, with a population of about half a million. It welcomes close to 2 million tourists annually, and growth continues as new hotels, shopping centers, and condominium complexes seem to pop up overnight.

The area has long appealed to retirees from the Midwest. Today, visitors come from all over the world to enjoy this beautiful South Florida "frontier."

The Lee Island Coast (**www.leeislandcoast.com**) is an area of unspoiled communities and nature preserves between Naples and Sarasota. It includes such popular tourist destinations as Boca Grande on Gasparilla Island, Bonita Springs and Beaches, Cabbage Key, Cape Coral, Captiva Island, Cayo Costa State Park, Fort Myers, Fort Myers Beach on Estero Island, Lehigh Acres, North Captiva Island, North Fort Myers, Pine Island, Sanibel Island, and Useppa Island—a total of 652,000 acres with 590 miles of shoreline, 50 miles of beaches, and more than 100 barrier and coastal islands in the Gulf of Mexico.

The islands of the Lee Coast are even more laid-back than the mainland, and a couple of them are uninhabited. A visit by boat conjures the beauty, serenity, and charm of a deserted tropical island.

Sanibel and Captiva

Local history goes back to the Calusa tribe, who fished these barrier islands, but today Sanibel is especially known for world-class shelling, with some 200 varieties constantly deposited on the beaches. The shell-hunting posture is known as the "Sanibel Stoop," and truly dedicated shellers even don head-mounted flashlights in order to be the first on the beach after especially high or low tides.

Legend says that Sanibel was originally named Santa Isabella by Ponce de León, after Spain's Queen Isabella. Even more fanciful is a tale claiming that the name *Captiva* comes from the kidnapped women kept by the notorious pirate José Gaspar. What is known for sure is that farmers settled these lush, isolated islands of palms and pines at the end of the 19th century, growing Key limes and coconuts, and the only way to get to them was by boat. Today you can still arrive that way, but a three-mile-long causeway connects to the mainland and nearby Fort Myers, bringing residents and tourists, and the required trappings.

Both Sanibel and Captiva still offer wooded, unspoiled settings much appreciated by nature lovers. The late Anne Morrow Lindbergh wrote her best-selling memoir *A Gift from the Sea* on Captiva. The beauty remains.

Fort Myers Beach, on Estero Island, lures families with its recreational activities, gently sloping shoreline, and powdered-sugar sand. The quiet southern end consists mostly of cottages, condos, and small motels, but the north end, which locals call Times Square, invites a more raucous crowd for a moderately priced sun-and-fun scene.

During winter months, the commercial-fishing area of Matanzas Pass is home port for a large shrimping and fishing fleet. Protected Estero Bay, an aquatic preserve, separates the island from the mainland.

Lesser-known North Captiva and Cayo Costa State Park offer lush, often-deserted coastlines and great shelling. Some shell seekers opt for guided excursions to these islands because competition is much less fierce than on Captiva or Sanibel.

Useppa Island consists of high-end homes but also offers a historical museum. Cabbage Key is a laid-back destination: 100 acres of seclusion where celebs from Ernest Hemingway to Walter Cronkite to Julia Roberts to Jimmy Buffett have chilled out. In 1938, mystery writer Mary Roberts Rinehart helped her son build a home here that has since become a landmark six-room inn. The bar in the library–turned–dining room is papered in thousands of autographed dollar bills worth about $30,000 today. Rumor has it that the custom began when a thirsty fisherman left his bill taped to the wall, ensuring a cold drink the next time he stopped by. Today, most visitors leave a green calling card.

Naples and Marco Island

Refined and relaxed Naples (**www.naples-florida.com**), minutes south of Fort Myers in Collier County, appeals to tourists and residents who look for fine dining; cultural events; a carefree, well-groomed atmosphere; and posh shopping opportunities. Eleven miles of beach and nature preserves line the Gulf of Mexico. Two local beaches—Clam Pass and Delnor-Wiggins—have been included in the Top 20 National Beaches Survey compiled by Dr. Stephen Leatherman, a professor at Miami's Florida International University. Naples is also known as the "Golf Capital of America," and these appealing elements help make the county one of the fastest growing in the country, especially for retirees.

More than 50 fine golf courses, as well as ecotourism, fishing, nature preserves, and parks, draw Naples visitors into the Florida sun; a steadily growing arts scene balances out the natural delights. Those seeking a faster pace, a younger crowd, and a more exciting atmosphere may find Florida's southeastern coast a better fit, but low-key pleasures keep Naples special and charming despite the threats of growing traffic jams and increasing crowds.

Naples has been around awhile. Beginning in 1887, Naples was surveyed and plotted, and lots were sold, mainly to midwesterners. Debt brought further development to a halt until Memphis-born millionaire Barron Gift Collier dipped into his fortune to introduce paved roads, electricity, and other conveniences in the 1920s. A pier and hotel were among the first attractions of the district known today as Olde Naples, and beachfront mansions were built along what became known as Millionaires' Row. This historic area retains its charms in a city that now sprawls north and east with high-rise condos and real estate developments.

Collier County was incorporated in 1923. Five years later, Collier completed the Tamiami Trail (connecting Miami-Dade County with the state's west coast), increasing the potential of the agricultural and tourist industries.

Development took off after World War II and steadily grew. Vanderbilt Beach, north of Olde Naples, a popular resort community nestled between preserves, is typical of the steady growth here in the late 20th century. Major hotels, such as the Ritz-Carlton in Naples, came into the region in the 1980s, as the area once again turned upscale.

Marco Island (**www.marco-island-florida.com**), with its crescent-shaped beach, is the largest of Florida's Ten Thousand Islands, sometimes described as the Western Gateway to the Florida Everglades. Another golfer's delight, Marco has also established a reputation as an angler's paradise, especially for tarpon and backwater fishing. Shells blanket nearby uninhabited barrier islands. And the Cushing archeological site has yielded 3,000-year-old artifacts.

But because development really began in the 1960s, charm and history aren't the selling points here. The end-of-the road atmosphere and quiet lifestyle are what draw people, along with the Gulf sunsets and accessible Everglades wildlife. If you don't boat or fish and you enjoy a livelier nightlife than staring at the stars, consider staying elsewhere.

GATHERING INFORMATION

GENERAL FLORIDA INFORMATION IS AVAILABLE from a variety of sources: Call ☎ 888-7FLA-USA or visit **www.visitflorida.com,** or write the Visit Florida Headquarters, P.O. Box 1100, Tallahassee, FL 32302-1100. Vacation guides are available for domestic and international visitors, including versions in German, French, and Spanish.

Southwest Florida Information Sources

Greater Naples/Marco Island/Everglades
Convention and Visitors Bureau
3050 North Horseshoe Drive, Suite 218
Naples, FL 34104
☎ 800-688-3600
www.paradisecoast.com

Lee County Alliance of the Arts
10091 McGregor Boulevard
Fort Myers, FL 33919
☎ 239-939-2787
www.artinlee.org

Lee County Visitor and Convention Bureau
2180 West First Street, Suite 100
Fort Myers, FL 33901
☎ 800-237-6444 or 239-338-3500
www.leeislandcoast.com

Marco Island Chamber of Commerce
1102 North Collier Boulevard
Marco Island, FL 34145
☎ 239-394-7549
www.marcoislandchamber.org

Southwest Florida Hispanic Chamber of Commerce
3343 Palm Beach Boulevard
Fort Myers, FL 33916
☎ 239-334-3190
www.swflhispanicchamber.org

ARRIVING

BY CAR

FROM PALM BEACH YOU CAN TAKE THE FLORIDA TURNPIKE (also known as the Ronald Reagan Expressway) south to US 595 (aka "Alligator Alley"), or the Sawgrass Expressway to Interstate 75 North, then straight into Fort Myers. I-75 South from the Tampa Bay area is also a major roadway into the Fort Myers area. This latter route is the road most often taken from the Midwest, a primary source of area tourism. Miami's Tamiami Trail (US 41) leads into Fort Myers and Naples. Alligator Alley and US 41 east of Naples are the key east–west highways.

unofficial **TIP**
This is a long, flat state, and driving can be tedious, so many vacationers tie in a trip to South Florida or the Southwest Coast with visits to more-northern parts of the state. If you plan to break up your trip by visiting other areas, leave plenty of time. Driving distances are far, and attractions are many. Avoid overcrowding your itinerary; it's better to explore the state regionally.

BY PLANE

THE AREA'S MAJOR AIRPORT, SOUTHWEST FLORIDA International Airport, is approximately one mile east of I-75 Exit 131. A new Midfield Terminal Complex has 30 gates operational, with potential for 65 more. Based at Southwest Florida are Air Canada, AirTran Airways, American Airlines/American Eagle, American Trans Air, Cape Air, Condor German Airlines, Continental Airlines/Continental Express, Delta Air Lines/Delta Connection, Frontier Airlines, Independence Air, JetBlue, LTU International Airways, Midwest Airlines, Northwest Airlines/KLM, Song, Spirit Airlines, Sun Country Airlines, United Airlines, US Airways, and

SAMPLE DISTANCES AND DRIVE TIMES TO NAPLES	
Daytona Beach	243 miles (five-hour drive)
Jacksonville	348 miles (six-hour dive)
Miami	110 miles (two-hour drive)
Orlando	189 miles (four-hour drive)
Tampa	134 miles (three-hour drive)

USA 3000 Airlines. To reach Marco Island, Everglades, or Naples from the airport requires a brief drive south on I-75.

Visitor Services Centers are located near the baggage-claim areas to help travelers with questions regarding attractions, accommodations, beaches, and parks. German is spoken at the center in the LTU International Airways terminal. For more information, call ☎ 239-768-1000 or visit **www.flylcpa.com.**

Naples Municipal Airport offers commuter and direct flights, private charters, and regularly scheduled flights to the Florida Keys, Key West, and Miami. For more information, call ☎ 239-643-0733 or visit **www.flynaples.com.** Marco Island Executive Airport offers commuter and charter flights to and from nearby international airports. For more information, call ☎ 239-394-3355.

Taxi and limousine services are available at the airports. Taxi fares to area beach resorts are about $40 from Southwest Florida International Airport and about $20 from Naples Municipal Airport. Fares from Miami International Airport run to $150. Reservations are not required for taxis and limos. Travelers simply make arrangements upon arrival at the ground-transportation booth, located in the median between the airport terminal and the parking lot.

Rental-car companies operating at the airports include Alamo, Avis, Budget, Dollar, Enterprise, Hertz, National, Ro-Lin, and Thrifty.

GETTING AROUND

TRAFFIC

THOUGH NOT AS CONGESTED AS THE LARGER CITIES to the east, Southwest Florida still offers travelers the opportunity to get lost. To avoid that, obtain a detailed map and get driving instructions from your hotel, motel, or host; let them know where you will be picking up a car, and get complete directions to the property.

Speed limits vary throughout South Florida: 30 mph is common in congested areas, around hotels, and in heavily populated neighborhoods; 40 or 45 mph in other areas; and 65 or 70 mph on the Turnpike and on I-75. Florida has a seat belt law requiring everyone to buckle up, and state law requires that children under age 8 be in booster seats as well.

MAJOR ROADWAYS

US 41 (THE TAMIAMI TRAIL) RUNS EAST–WEST from Miami and is a two-lane road through much of the route. While this highway is picturesque, with canals filled with birds and gators behind protected shoulders, it takes at least three hours to get from Miami to Naples on the Tamiami. This infamous road may be more daunting to drive than other major routes: Keep your headlights on at all times and stay alert, be aware that cell phones may not work well, and know that you may be refueling at a Miccosukee reservation.

At Naples, US 41 runs north and south between here and Fort Myers. This route is very slow going and heavily traveled, and for many years was the only highway connecting South Florida's east and west coasts. What's more, construction along US 41 is constant. Although **I-75,** which also runs north–south from Naples, was built to handle the overflow and speed traffic through Collier and Lee counties, it doesn't do the job. Rush hours can find both major roadways clogged.

Fort Myers and Surrounding Areas

US 41 and I-75 carry the bulk of the north–south traffic in the area (they also lead northwest to the Tampa Bay area). A series of one-way streets in downtown Fort Myers tends to confuse visitors, but signage is clear if you pay attention.

The Caloosahatchee and Edison bridges span the Caloosahatchee River, and **FL 8,** also called Palm Beach Road, parallels the curve of the bay. FL 80 accesses I-75 at Exit 141.

The major routes to Fort Myers Beach and Sanibel and Captiva islands are across **McGregor Boulevard** or **Summerlin Road.** Both roads lead to the Summerlin Bridge. You can also take **San Carlos** and **Estero boulevards** to Fort Myers Beach; Estero Boulevard, also called FL 865, also leads to Bonita Beach.

Naples and Marco Island

Three exits from I-75 reach Naples: Exit 101 is **Golden Gate,** a main Naples exit; Exit 107, **Pine Ridge Road,** leads directly to US 41; and Exit 111, **Immokalee Road,** leads to North Naples to the west and the National Audubon Society's famed Corkscrew Swamp Sanctuary to the east. Corkscrew is 18 miles northeast of Naples. To get to Marco Island, take Exit 101 (Golden Gate) off I-75, and head south on Collier Boulevard for 20 miles.

The Naples–Marco Island area is smaller than Fort Myers, and a turn to the west takes you to the beaches as well as hotels, restaurants, and local attractions. Naples's **Third Street South** is a remnant of the town's old central commercial district. Third Street is at the western edge of **Fifth Avenue South,** Naples' main street. It is the heart of Olde Naples, and local legend has it that Charles and Anne Morrow Lindbergh often landed their plane on a strip at the corner of Fifth Avenue and Third Street to have Sunday lunch at the Naples Hotel. Today, Third Street South is listed on the National Register of Historic Places and is home to more than 100 shops, galleries, outdoor cafes, and restaurants.

Marco Island is a serene outpost on the Gulf of Mexico where you can get around by bicycle or trolley. You can get there via **FL 951** (Isle of Capri Road). Day cruises leave from Marco Island to Key West (Key West Express, 951 Bald Eagle Drive, Marco Island; ☎ 239-394-9700; **www.keywestshuttle.com**).

These counties and municipalities are well aware they are tourist destinations, and every road is clearly marked with signs.

ALTERNATIVE TRANSPORTATION

IF YOU DON'T WANT THE HASSLE OF TRAFFIC JAMS and scarce parking, consider other means of getting around the area.

Bike rentals are available all across the islands; customers are provided with detailed maps and highlighted waypoints. We suggest **Bike Route** (2330 Palm Ridge Road, Sanibel Island; ☎ 239-472-1955; **www.bikeroute.com**); **Billy's Rentals** (1470 Periwinkle Way, Sanibel Island; ☎ 239-472-5248; **www.billysrentals.com**); **Finnimore's Cycle Shop** (2353 Periwinkle Way, Sanibel Island; ☎ 239-472-5577; **www.finnimores.com**); and **Trikes & Bikes Professional Shop** (3451–53 Fowler Street, Fort Myers; ☎ 239-936-1851).

Trolley tours are also popular and provide guides with knowledge of the region. **Adventures in Paradise** (1159 Causeway Road, Sanibel; ☎ 239-472-8443; **www.adventureinparadise.com**) offers a historic nature tour of Sanibel Island that departs at 10 a.m.; the cost is $20 for adults, $15 for children; ages 3 and under are free. Kayak nature tours are also offered.

LeeTran (see "Public Transportation," below) buses and trolleys offer transportation to Bonita Beach Park on Little Hickory Island, leaving from the Kmart store at Bonita Beach Road and US 41 in Bonita Springs. Cost is 25¢; **www.rideleetran.com.**

Captiva offers cruises to Cabbage Key and Useppa Islands, as well as shelling cruises and a late-afternoon cruise to view dolphins and wildlife. For more information, contact **Captiva Cruises** (11401 Andy Rosse Lane, Captiva Island; ☎ 239-472-5300) or **Captiva Kayak and Wildside Adventures** (11401 Andy Rosse Lane, Captiva Island; ☎ 239-395-2925).

PUBLIC TRANSPORTATION

LEETRAN'S LOCAL BUS SERVICE RUNS Monday to Saturday from 5 a.m. to 9:45 p.m.; limited service to the beach is available Sundays from 6 a.m. to 9:20 p.m. LeeTran also offers airport service hourly 6 a.m.–9:20 p.m. to a transfer point at Daniels Parkway and US 41, with connections to other routes. Fare is $1 for adults, 50¢ for seniors and disabled citizens, and free for children under 42 inches tall. For more information on LeeTran, call ☎ 239-275-8726 or check the Web at **www.rideleetran.com.**

LEETRAN TICKET OUTLETS

LeeTran Administration Building: 10715 East Airport Road

Lee County Administration Office: Monroe and Second Streets

Edison Community College: Student Services Building

Cape Coral City Hall: Country Club at Nicholas

Cape Coral McCrory's: Leonard at Cape Coral Parkway

AT *the* SEASHORE

THE BEACHES

SOUTHWEST FLORIDA IS WELL KNOWN FOR ECOTOURISM opportunities, myriad golf and tennis venues, and, especially, outstanding sugar-sand beaches along the turquoise Gulf of Mexico. Below we list some of the most outstanding beaches in the region.

Fort Myers Area

Lakes Regional Park (7330 Gladiolus Drive, Fort Myers; ☎ 239-432-2000) consists of 279 acres of Florida foliage and summertime fresh-water swimming. Other water sports and picnic tables are also available. Expect a $3-per-person fee to ride the miniature train. Parking is 75 ¢ per hour, $3 maximum per day.

Lovers Key State Park (8700 Estero Boulevard, Fort Myers; ☎ 239-463-4588; **www.floridastateparks.org/loverskey**), between Fort Myers Beach and Bonita Beach, is the state's newest park, with 2.5 miles of white-sand beaches, shelling, swimming, bridge-top and back-bay fishing, bird-watching, and more. The entry fee is $3 per person in a car, two to eight people in one vehicle costs $5, and walk-ins and bicyclists are charged $1 per person.

Bonita Beach Park in Bonita Springs is a full-service beach with plenty of parking. Alternatively, you can park at the Big K at Bonita Beach Road and US 41 in Bonita Springs and take the bus or trolley for 25 ¢.

Seventeen-acre **Bowditch Point Regional Park,** on Estero Island, is designed to provide a total day at the beach. Free parking is available at Main Street, and a trolley will deliver you to the beach for small change; handicapped parking is available inside the park.

Cayo Costa State Park, between North Captiva and Boca Grande, is a secluded island accessible only by boat, with unique plantings that are purportedly the same as they were 500 years ago. (That's not documented, but this is an uninhabited park and a little-known hideaway.) Tent camping and cabins are available, and there is a $1 admission fee per person. (Call ☎ 941-964-0375 or visit **www.florida stateparks.org/cayocosta/default.cfm** for more information.)

Sanibel and Captiva

Bowman's Beach, on Sanibel Island, is a city-operated beach with picnic areas, showers, and parking. Nearby, **Gulfside City Park** offers swimming, picnicking, showers, and restrooms. The beach at 100-year-old **Sanibel Lighthouse** has picnic facilities and pier fishing.

Big-time shelling awaits between Sanibel and Captiva islands on **Turner Beach.** Foot showers, handicapped parking, and restrooms are available. This is one of the most popular beaches, and parking is limited: Come early or after high tide for the best choices, and bring a bag. (Harvesting shells with live animals within is illegal.)

Naples and Marco Island

Delnor-Wiggins Pass State Park, just north of Naples, is an unspoiled beach where the sand has a unique white color and contains whole seashells. Sea oats, sea grapes, and cabbage palms dot the sand dunes. The entry fee is $3 per person in a car, two to eight people in one vehicle cost $5, and walk-ins and bicyclists are charged $1 per person. Visit **www.floridastateparks.org/delnor-wiggins** for more information.

Another outstanding natural beach at the south end of Naples is **Clam Pass.** Gentle waves and a shallow, sandy bottom make it a good place to take children. Kids hunting for seashells could find the alphabet cone, apple murex, Atlantic giant cockle, Florida fighting conch, horse conch, lettered olive, lightning whelk, pear whelk, sand dollar, sunray Venus, thorny sea star, and more.

The white-sand crescent beaches of **Marco Island** teem with excellent seashell varieties—some 400 in all. Shellers say the choices are great and include cockles, fighting conchs, and lion's paws.

SCUBA DIVING AND SNORKELING

THE GULF OF MEXICO ALONG THE SOUTHWEST Florida coast offers dive sites with visibility approaching 50 feet. Artificial reefs are plentiful and include old culverts, the old Edison Reef, and a ship called the *Pegasus.* The **Caloosa Dive Club** (**www.diveclub.org**) has been exploring underwater sites for three decades. For more information, contact **Scuba Quest** (11705 Cleveland Avenue, Fort Myers;

☎ 239-936-7106; **www.scubaquestusa.com**) or **Seahorse Scuba** (15630 McGregor Boulevard, Suite 104, Fort Myers; ☎ 239-454-3111; **www.seahorsescubaftmyers.com**).

FISHING

ANGLERS ON THE GULF COAST HAVE THEIR choice of casting from a boat, shore, or swamp, and the area is known for world-class tarpon fishing; even Teddy Roosevelt came here. Crevalle, jack, mangrove snapper, redfish, sheepshead, snook, spotted sea trout, and other varieties of fish can be caught in mangrove shorelines; over the open flats; and around bridges, piers, and docks. Barracuda, blackfin tuna, bonito, cobia, grouper, permit, shark, and Spanish and king mackerel can be caught over natural or artificial reefs offshore.

Anyone can fish from beaches, piers, bridges, or docks. A saltwater license is required for nonresidents over the age of 16 and can be obtained from the **Lee County Tax Collector** (☎ 239-339-6000; **www.leetc.com**) or through **Florida Marine Patrol** (☎ 239-332-6966). The Marine Patrol also provides information on fishing regulations and closed seasons for specific types of fish.

During April, May, and June, tarpon migrate by the thousands from Boca Grande Pass to the reefs off Sanibel Island and Fort Myers Beach. They can be fished many ways. In Boca Grande Pass, known as the world capital of tarpon fishing, anglers in 20- or 30-foot boats employ a controlled drift-fishing technique with heavy tackle using live bait. Along the beaches of Boca Grande, Cayo Costa, North Captiva, and Sanibel and Captiva islands, as well as the backcountry, anglers pursue tarpon in smaller boats and flat skiffs, using light tackle with live crabs or 11- to 15-weight fly rods with various flies. On the reefs in water 20 feet deep or more, anglers use live bait and heavy tackle.

Freshwater fishing targets bass, bluegill, catfish, crappie, oscars, and shell crackers, using poles, plug-casting outfits, spinning reels, or fly rods. Bait includes plastic worms, wild shiners, artificial lures, crickets in the spring season, and fly-fishing flies.

FISHING GUIDE REFERRAL SERVICES

Boca Grande Fishing Guides Association: ☎ 941-964-1711; www.bocagrandefishing.com

Pro Guides Co-op of Southwest Florida: www.guidescoop.com

Drift Boats

No fishing license is required on drift, or party, boats, and fishers of any age can go out. Tackle is supplied, and boats are usually 60–100 feet with a restroom and a small galley. The average cost for a half day is $25 per person ($40 for a full day).

Charter Boats

No fishing license is required, and anglers can charter a captain and boat for a half day or full day. Tackle is supplied; costs range from $150 for a half day to $400 for a full day.

More than 50 marinas are available on the Lee Island Coast alone. Here's a sampling of those offering bait, charters, fishing equipment, and customized trips.

Southwest Florida Marinas

MARINA	LOCATION	INFORMATION
SANIBEL AND CAPTIVA ISLANDS		
Santiva Saltwater Fishing Team	Tween Waters Marina	☎ 239-472-1779; www.tween-waters.com
Castaways Marina	6460 Sanibel-Captiva Road	☎ 239-472-1112; www.castawayssanibel.com
Sanibel Marina	634 North Yachtsman Drive	☎ 239-472-2723; www.sanibelmarina.com
South Seas Resort	Yacht Harbour	☎ 239-472-5111; www.south-seas-resort.com
Tarpon Bay Recreation	900 Tarpon Bay Road	☎ 239-472-8900
FORT MYERS BEACH (ESTERO ISLAND)		
Fish Tale Marina	7225 Estero Boulevard	☎ 239-463-3600; www.fishtalemarinagroup.cc
Island Lady Deep Sea Fishing	702 Fisherman's Wharf	☎ 239-482-2005
Moss Marine	450 Harbor Court	☎ 239-463-6137
FORT MYERS		
Adventures in Paradise	14341 Port Comfort Road	☎ 239-472-8443; www.adventuresinparadiseinc.com
Mullock Creek Marina	18501 Mullock Creek Lane	☎ 239-267-3717
CAPE CORAL		
Cape Coral Yacht Basin	5819 Driftwood Parkway	☎ 239-574-0809

Southwest Florida Marinas *(continued)*

MARINA	LOCATION	INFORMATION
BONITA SPRINGS AND BEACHES		
Bonita Bay Marina	27598 SE Marina Point Drive	☎ 239-495-322; www.bonitabay.com
Captain Ron LePree	9971 Puopolo Lane	☎ 239-498-9992; www.backcountryfishing.com
NORTH FORT MYERS		
Captain Van Hubbard, Let's Go Fishin' Inc.	P.O. Box 146	☎ 941-697-6944; www.captvan.com

BOATING

Sailboating and Sailing Courses

Sailing on the Gulf of Mexico is exhilarating, and thousands of sailors have learned their skills at the **Offshore Sailing School** (16731 McGregor Boulevard, Fort Myers; ☎ 239-454-1700; **www.offshoresailing.com**), founded 26 years ago by Olympic and America's Cup winner Steve Colgate. Offshore teaches at **South Seas Resort** on Captiva Island (☎ 239-454-1700) and **Hawk's Cay** in the Florida Keys, as well as at other locations throughout the Caribbean and United States.

Other sailboat renters and schools include **Captiva Kayak Company and Wildside Adventures** (11401 Andy Rosse Lane, Captiva Island; ☎ 239-395-2925; **www.captivakayaks.com**) and **Florida Sailing and Cruising School** (3444 Marinatown Lane, Northwest #19, North Fort Myers; ☎ 239-656-1339; **www.flsailandcruiseschool.com**).

Canoeing and Kayaking

Sanibel and Captiva islands have found their way onto *Paddler* magazine's list of the ten best kayaking destinations in the nation. The area's temperate climate is great for year-round kayaking, and its easy access and close proximity to other areas are ideal for paddlers.

For more information, contact the following: **Captiva Kayak Company and Wildside Adventures** (11401 Andy Rosse Lane, Captiva Island; ☎ 239-395-2925; **www.captivakayaks.com**); **Estero River Outfitters** (20991 South Tamiami Trail, Estero; ☎ 239-992-4050); **Gulf Coast Kayak** (The Olde Fish House Marina, 4530 Pine Island Road, Matlacha; ☎ 239-283-1125; **www.gulfcoastkayak.com**); **Tropic Star of Pine Island** (13921 Waterfront Drive, Pineland; ☎ 239-283-0015); or **Conservancy Nature Centers of Southwest Florida** (1450 Merrihue Drive, Naples; ☎ 239-262-0304; **www.conservancy.org**).

SPORTS *and* RECREATION

SOUTHWEST FLORIDA IS RENOWNED FOR ITS golf courses. On the Lee Island Coast alone, a golfer can play 18 holes a day, seven days a week, and not play the same hole twice for nearly two months.

Tennis, fishing, swimming, and water sports also abound throughout the area. Picnic grounds and bike trails, nature walks, and birding areas help complete this outdoor haven.

FITNESS CENTERS

MOST OF TODAY'S NEW HOTELS HAVE fitness centers on-site. You may find only two or three treadmills and a cycling machine, or you may find state-of-the-art cardiovascular equipment geared to keeping you buff. Plus, many hotels do not charge for the use of their fitness equipment.

If your hotel doesn't offer a fitness program, however, you have several options for day-use fitness facilities, each with a selection of aerobic and weight-training equipment: **NCH Wellness Center South** (300 Goodlette Road, Naples; ☎ 239-436-6770) costs $10 a day; **YMCA of Collier County** (5450 YMCA Road, Naples; ☎ 239-597-3148) costs $15 a day; **Fitness on the Move** (13010 Metro Parkway, Fort Myers; ☎ 239-561-1177) costs $10 a day; and **Asylum Fitness Club** (13211 McGregor Boulevard, Fort Myers; ☎ 239-437-3488) costs $12 a day.

TENNIS

SOUTHWEST FLORIDA IS A PARADISE FOR THOSE who routinely shovel snow, bundle up children, and fight the freezing elements to the north. And although golf might seem most popular, tennis nevertheless offers a faster game along the Gulf Coast.

Sanibel Harbour Resort and Spa provides a 5,550-seat stadium court with eight lighted clay courts. Tennis greats like Andre Agassi, Jimmy Connors, John McEnroe, and Pete Sampras have all played here. Agassi says, "It's the prettiest place I've played in United States. Playing may be a bit hot, but . . . when you're done, you can go swimming in the pool or at the beach. It's ideal."

Sundial Beach and Tennis Resort and **Sanibel Harbour Resort and Spa,** on Sanibel Island, offer outstanding beachfront tennis facilities, both clay and hard lighted courts. **South Seas Resort and Yacht Harbour** has 21 courts (7 lighted) and has been honored by trade magazines for outstanding facilities.

Marco Island is another tennis haven. The **Racquet Club of Marco Island** (1275 San Marco Road; ☎ 239-394-5454) and the **Hilton, Marriott, and Radisson Hotels** all have tennis facilities available for tourists and locals.

Local public courts in Fort Myers include **Alva Community Center** (21471 North River Road, Alva; ☎ 239-728-2882), **Bay Oaks Recreation**

Center (2731 Oak Street, Fort Myers Beach; ☎ 239-765-4222), **Boca Grande Community Center** (131 West First Street, Boca Grande; ☎ 941-964-2564), **Hancock Park** (1526 Oak Drive, Fort Myers; ☎ 239-656-7748), **Judd Park** (1297 Driftwood Drive, North Fort Myers; ☎ 239-656-5138), **Olga Community Center and Park** (2325 South Olga Drive, Fort Myers; ☎ 239-694-0355), and **Waterway Estates Park** (5820 Poetry Lane, North Fort Myers; ☎ 239-656-5138).

GOLF

IN THE FORT MYERS–NAPLES REGION, GOLF COURSES number around 125; the area is believed to have more golf holes per capita than anyplace else in the world. In less than ten years, 47 courses have opened in Lee (Fort Myers) and Collier (Naples) counties, offering something for every skill level—from less difficult executive courses to championship courses. And while rates are higher (and courses busier) during the peak-season months of January through April, off-season golfing allows you to play entire courses in half the time for less. In high season, try to play at odd times of the day: late afternoon (which is ideal in summer) or early morning.

unofficial **TIP**
If your trip is during the spring or autumn shoulder seasons, call ahead to find out which courses will be offering their summer rates. Those on tight budgets can play 18 holes at a low-season fee in the morning, then catch another 18 for the afternoon fee at a course still charging high-season rates.

Courses include the 6,400-yard, par-72 Eastwood course, which has been ranked among the top 50 public courses in the nation by golf publications for many years. Other municipal courses on the Lee Island Coast include the 6,100-yard, par-71 Fort Myers Country Club, a course about 90 years old, and designed for walkers; and the 6,623-yard, par-72 Coral Oaks Course in Cape Coral. Many courses in the area are practically on the shores of the Gulf of Mexico and provide some of the most scenic rounds in the country.

Naples itself has about 50 golf courses and has been called the "Golf Capital of the World," while Marco Island is another popular area for the sport.

Alden Pines Country Club

ESTABLISHED: 1980 STATUS: PUBLIC COURSE

14261 Clubhouse Drive, Bokeelia 33922; ☎ 239-283-2179

Tees

- **Championship: 5,600 yards, par 71,** usga 65.4, slope 136
- **Men's: 5,130 yards, par 71,** usga 65.2, slope 116
- **Ladies': 4,500 yards, par 71,** usga 64.4, slope 116

Fees Weekdays $15, weekends $17

Facilities Snack bar, bar, club rental, GPS system on each cart

Comments This gorgeous course has paved cart paths, although alligators and wildlife share the fairways. The greens, nurtured by brackish water, are plush.

Bay Beach Golf Club

ESTABLISHED: 1975   STATUS: PUBLIC COURSE

4200 Bay Beach Lane, Fort Myers Beach 33905; ☎ 239-463-2064; www.baybeachgolfclub.com

Tees

- **Men's: 3,091 yards, par 61, USGA 57.4, slope 99**
- **Ladies': 2,632 yards, par 61, USGA 48, slope 99**

Fees Vary by season; run about $23 for 18 holes with cart

Facilities Snack bar

Comments On lovely and serene Estero Island, Bay Beach is one of the area's oldest courses, set in a charming beach community.

Beachview Golf and Tennis Club

ESTABLISHED: 1974   STATUS: PUBLIC COURSE

1100 Par View Drive, Sanibel 33957; ☎ 239-472-2626; www.beachviewgolfclub.com

Tees

- **Championship: 6,320 yards, par 71, USGA 70.8, slope 127**
- **Men's: 5,838 yards, par 71, USGA 67.8, slope 118**
- **Ladies': 4,937 yards, par 71, USGA 67.6, slope 114**

Fees Vary by season and time of day: early morning, $46, afternoon, $36. All prices include cart.

Facilities Pro shop, restaurant, lockers

Comments One block from the Gulf of Mexico, the course is dotted with little ponds and lakes and provides one of the most natural golf settings in the region.

Burnt Store Marina and Country Club

ESTABLISHED: 1982   STATUS: SEMIPRIVATE COURSE; 27-HOLE COURSE (PELICAN AND HERON COURSES AVERAGED BELOW)

5000 Burnt Store Road, Punta Gorda 33955; ☎ 941-637-1577

Tees

- **Championship: 3,918 yards, par 60, USGA 60.5, slope 104**
- **Men's: 3,542 yards, par 60, USGA 60.0, slope 105**
- **Ladies': 3,118 yards, par 60, USGA 60.9, slope 107**

Fees $30, including cart; $20 after 2 p.m.

Facilities Driving range, snack bar (beer and wine only), rental clubs

Comments This course is located right on Charlotte Harbor in a gated community of homes and condos.

Country Creek Country Club

ESTABLISHED: 1989 STATUS: SEMIPRIVATE COURSE

21131 Country Creek Drive, Estero 33928; ☎ 239-947-3840

Tees

- **Championship: 3,871 yards, par 61, USGA 60.3, slope 102**
- **Men's: 3,462 yards, par 61, USGA 58.3, slope 97**
- **Ladies': 2,531 yards, par 61, USGA 55.3, slope 86**

Fees High season, $40; low season, $20 before 11 a.m. and $15 after 11 a.m. Prices include cart.

Facilities Pro shop (lessons available), lockers, restaurant

Comments Designed by Gordon Lewis, this young-executive course is set in a golf community.

Dunes Golf and Tennis Club

ESTABLISHED: 1973 STATUS: SEMIPRIVATE COURSE

949 Sandcastle Road, Sanibel 33957; ☎ 239-472-3355 (clubhouse),
☎ 239-472-2535 (golf pro shop); www.dunesgolfsanibel.com

Tees

- **Championship: 5,600 yards, par 70, USGA 68, slope 124**
- **Men's: 5,249 yards, par 70, USGA 66.5, slope 111**
- **Ladies': 4,002 yards, par 70, USGA 64.5, slope 111**

Fees High season, $125; low season, $60. Prices include cart.

Facilities No lockers, large pro shop (lessons available)

Comments Two minutes from the beach, this course is set on 140 acres with wildlife; alligators, bald eagles, and other local species are always evident. The popular course features 70 acres of water.

Eastwood Golf Course

ESTABLISHED: 1977 STATUS: PUBLIC COURSE

4600 Bruce Herd Lane, Fort Myers 33905; ☎ 239-275-4848;
www.cityftmyers.com/attractions/golf/eastwood.aspx

Tees

- **Championship: 6,772 yards, par 72, USGA 73.3, slope 130**
- **Men's: 6,234 yards, par 72, USGA 70.7, slope 125**
- **Ladies': 5,116 yards, par 72, USGA 68.4, slope 116**

Fees $27 before 1 p.m.; $23 after 2 p.m.; $17.50 after 5 p.m. Prices include cart.

Facilities Snack bar, driving range

Comments At this very popular course, designed by Devlin Von Haage, more than 75,000 rounds of golf are played annually.

El Rio Golf Club

ESTABLISHED: 1970S   STATUS: PUBLIC COURSE; SIX EXECUTIVE PAR-4 COURSES—
THREE ON THE FRONT, THREE ON THE BACK

1801 Skyline Drive, North Fort Myers 33903; ☎ 239-995-2204

Tees

- **Men's: 3,219 yards, par 70, USGA 60.7, slope 90**
- **Ladies': 3,021 yards, par 70, USGA 55.3, slope 81**

Fees $15 with cart; $14 without cart

Facilities Clubhouse, snack bar, rentals

Comments An old favorite, this executive course is one of the area's most popular.

Sabal Springs Golf and Racquet Club Ltd.

ESTABLISHED: 1989   STATUS: SEMIPRIVATE COURSE; AN EXECUTIVE COURSE WITH
TWO NINE-HOLE COURSES AND LIMITED PAR 4S

3251 Sabal Springs Boulevard, North Fort Myers 33917; ☎ 239-731-0101

Tees

- **Men's: 3,279 yards, par 60, USGA 58.9, slope 95**
- **Ladies': 2,196 yards, par 60, USGA 53.0, slope 83**

Fees $15.90 with cart

Facilities Snack bar, club rental

Comments The course was designed by Gordon Lewis and is located five miles north of the Caloosahatchee Bridge.

Tiburón Golf Club

ESTABLISHED: 1998   STATUS: SEMIPRIVATE COURSE

2620 Tiburón Drive, Naples 34109; ☎ 239-594-2040;
www.ritzcarlton.com/resorts/naples_golf_resort/golf

Tees

- **Championship: 7,288 yards, par 72, USGA 74.7, slope 137**
- **Men's: 7,005 yards, par 72, USGA 74.2, slope 147**
- **Ladies': 5,140 yards, par 72, USGA 70.6, slope 124**

Fees $225 for morning tee times during high season; $85 during low season (May 14–September). Prices include cart.

Facilities Putting green, chipping green, golf academy, restaurants, bar, locker rooms

Comments The club was designed by Greg "The Shark" Norman; *tiburón* means "shark" in Spanish.

WALKING AND HIKING

SEVERAL PARK AND WILDLIFE PRESERVES offer boardwalks and walking/hiking trails. See the Attractions section of this chapter for profiles on **Corkscrew Swamp Sanctuary, J. N. "Ding" Darling National Wildlife Refuge, Lakes Regional Park,** and others. Also notable for walking, hiking, or running are **Mackle Park** (1361 Andalusia Terrace, Marco Island; ☎ 239-642-0575) and **Conservancy Nature Centers of Southwest Florida** (1450 Merrihue Drive, Naples; ☎ 239-262-0304; **www.conservancy.org**).

And the miles of white-sand beaches offer beautiful walks. In Naples, for example, the most popular walking area is directly on the beach, but there's also a popular four-and-a-half-mile walk along the North Loop of Gulfshore Road from Admiral Ty Point to Seagate Drive.

BICYCLING

SANIBEL ISLAND IS LINED WITH BIKE ROUTES, and several roads (Summerlin is one) in Fort Myers and others in Naples and Marco Island are designated bike paths. Before you rent a bike, request a map of the bike trails.

Watch the traffic and enjoy some of the outstanding cycling routes in the region. Bike-rental shops include **Bike Route** (locations at 2330 Palm Ridge Road, Sanibel, ☎ 239-472-1955; and at 14530 South US 41, Fort Myers, ☎ 239-481-3376), **Finnimore's Cycle Shop** (2353 Periwinkle Way, Sanibel; ☎ 239-472-5577), and **Trikes & Bikes Professional Shop** (3451–53 Fowler Street, Fort Myers; ☎ 239-936-1851). **Colliers Seminole State Park** (20200 East Tamiami Trail, Naples; ☎ 239-394-3397) offers additional biking opportunities.

BIRD-WATCHING

BIRDERS ENJOY MARCO ISLAND'S SMALLER, uninhabited sister islands, which are home to a wide range of rare and endangered wading birds. Adjacent **Everglades National Park,** one of the nation's largest wildlife sanctuaries, is home to more than 200 species of birds: egrets, herons, ibis, osprey, and the American bald eagle. Cape Coral has the state's largest number of burrowing owls—estimated at about 10,000 pairs. They grow to about 9 inches and have a wingspan of more than 20 inches.

Some birders claim 300 species live on this coast. We think **J. N. "Ding" Darling National Wildlife Refuge** on Sanibel Island affords some of the best birding in the state (if not the country), but the Everglades and other nature parks all over the area are rife with birders.

SPECTATOR SPORTS

Baseball

Southwest Florida has been a baseball hotbed for more than 100 years, and "batter up" is a cry heard year-round. The area hosts 2 of the 20 major-league teams in the Florida Grapefruit League, a Winter Baseball League team, and a Florida State League team.

The first baseball team in Lee County was organized in January 1896, playing its first game the following July 4. Baseball continued as a major player in the region, and in 1925 the Philadelphia Athletics became the first major-league club to train in Fort Myers. Cornelius McGillicuddy, better known as Connie Mack, was the team manager (his grandson, Connie Mack III, is a former U.S. senator from Lee County). From 1939 to 1940, the Cleveland Indians made Fort Myers their spring training headquarters. And in 1955, the Pittsburgh Pirates came to town.

Terry Park comprises three lit baseball fields—but don't expect playground equipment or picnic facilities. This is, however, the headquarters for **Lee County Parks and Recreation** (3410 Palm Beach Boulevard, Fort Myers; ☎ 239-461-7400; **www.leeparks.org**). Terry Park does have quite a history, including its role as the site of the annual Lee County Fair for some 50 years. It was also home to the Kansas City Royals' spring training from 1968 to 1988.

The **Lee County Sports Complex** in South Fort Myers (which includes the William H. Hammond Stadium) is spring-training headquarters for the **Minnesota Twins** and the summer home to the minor-league **Fort Myers Miracle.** The 7,500-seat stadium opened in 1991 and boasts four regulation major-league practice fields, two half fields, four softball practice fields, ten indoor batting cages (four in the main stadium), and 30 practice pitching areas with mounds. The handicapped-accessible stadium is located at 14100 Six Mile Cypress and Daniels Parkway, Fort Myers; ☎ 239-768-4270 or 239-768-4210.

The Minnesota Twins are the fifth team in more than 65 years to train in Lee County; call ☎ 239-768-4270 for tickets. The Class-A Fort Myers Miracle are affiliated with the Twins. Actor Bill Murray and songwriter Jimmy Buffett are part-owners of the Miracle and have been known to attend games; call ☎ 239-768-4210 for tickets.

The **City of Palms Park** (2201 Edison Avenue, Fort Myers; ☎ 239-334-4700) in downtown Fort Myers is the spring training home of the **Boston Red Sox.** The ten-year-old, 7,000-seat stadium resembles Chicago's Wrigley Field and Boston's Fenway Park.

Hockey

In 1998, hockey came to Southwest Florida when the **Florida Everblades** made their permanent home at Germain Arena. The Everblades belong to the East Coast Hockey League and compete with 26 other franchises in the eastern half of the country. The Germain Arena is located at 11000 Everblades Parkway, Estero; ☎ 239-948-7825.

▌ SHOPPING

STROLLING AND WINDOW SHOPPING

IN FORT MYERS, **Edison Mall** (4125 Cleveland Avenue; ☎ 239-939-5464) is the largest shopping center in the region, with Macy's, Dillard's, and the usual mall standards. **Tanger Sanibel Factory Outlet Stores** (20350 Summerlin Road, just before the Sanibel Causeway; ☎ 239-454-1974 or 888-471-3939) offers 55 shops. The upscale Mediterranean-style **Bell Tower Shops** (corner of US 41 and Daniels Parkway; ☎ 239-489-1221), which houses Saks Fifth Avenue, dozens of other name retailers, and a variety of restaurants, recently underwent a multimillion-dollar renovation.

Miromar Outlets (10801 Corkscrew Road, Estero; ☎ 239-948-3766) hosts Bose, Calvin Klein, Coach, Ellen Tracy, and Nike outlets; and the **Promenade at Bonita Bay** (4200 Gulf Shore Boulevard North, Naples; ☎ 239-261-6100) is a not-to-be-missed rainy-day destination.

On Marco Island, expect to find numerous resort boutiques and bathing suit shops, as well as stores for sandals, sunglasses, and sunscreen, such as **The Beach House** (1300 Third Street South; ☎ 239-261-1366).

In Naples, the area's preeminent shopping city, **Third Street South** and **Fifth Avenue South** are both glamorous streets for strolling, window shopping, buying the perfect gift, or relaxing in a cafe. Shoppers love these thoroughfares—the Southwest Coast's closest equivalent to Palm Beach's Worth Avenue—with their colorful array of shops, galleries, boutiques, and restaurants. Most clothing stores feature a collection of pricey leisure and golf wear (often in bright Florida Deco hues).

Other popular stores in the region offer golf gear for men and women and fishing clothes and accoutrements, and there are galleries galore. Many stores are branches of outfitters from Martha's Vineyard, Nantucket, Palm Beach, and other resort centers. Shops generally close between 5 p.m. and 6 p.m., but some are open until 9 p.m. on Thursday, Friday, and Saturday. Some stores are open on Sundays during high season; others stay closed on Sundays year-round. Call ahead to check if you're doubtful about a store's hours.

Fifth Avenue South is home to **Back of the Bay** (555 Fifth Avenue South; ☎ 239-263-4233), which specializes in one-of-a-kind women's sweaters and outerwear, plus hand-painted apparel, shoes, and jewelry. **GH Collections** (727 Fifth Avenue South; ☎ 239-649-4356) features men's and women's clothing and original artwork by Guy Harvey, a famous marine-wildlife artist.

Other Fifth Avenue South shops include **Giggle Moon** (720 Fifth Avenue South, Suite 105; ☎ 239-643-3833), a children's boutique featuring local and European designs. For shells and a coral gallery (we're talking high quality), try **The Blue Mussel** (478 Fifth Avenue South; ☎ 239-262-4814).

Dennison-Moran Gallery (696 Fifth Avenue South; ☎ 239-263-0590) and **Gallery on Fifth** (680 Fifth Avenue, South, ☎ 239-430-9200) are but two of the many fine art galleries on the street. Both stock contemporary pieces.

Tin City in Naples (1200 Fifth Avenue South at East Goodlette Road; ☎ 239-262-4200) is a collection of 40 waterfront restaurants and shops. Of course, there are the ubiquitous T-shirt shops, souvenirs, jewelry, and tourist-tempting stuff, but the beachside setting makes this a pleasant place to pass the time.

Other shopping opportunities include **Coastland Center** (1900 Tamiami Trail North, Naples; ☎ 239-262-7100), built in a Key West style; **Third Street South,** with a group of stores now on the National Register of Historic Places; and **Waterside Shops at Pelican Bay** (5415 Tamiami Trail North, Suite 320, Naples; ☎ 239-598-1605), an expanded upscale mall, anchored by Saks Fifth Avenue and Jacobson's department stores (other tony tenants include Burberry, Gucci, Hermès, and Tiffany & Co.). **Prime Outlets** (6060 Collier Boulevard, Suite 121, Naples; ☎ 239-775-8083) has more than 40 stores, including **Coach** (☎ 239-732-5009), **Harry & David** (☎ 239-417-5530), **Mikasa** (☎ 239-793-7171), and **Jones New York** (☎ 239-774-5113).

SPECIALTY SHOPS

ANTIQUES World Antiques (1111 Fifth Avenue South, Naples; 239-263-0609) features global antique furniture and decorative arts for serious collectors and gift buyers alike.

BOOKS Barnes & Noble (13751 South Tamiami Trail, Fort Myers; ☎ 239-437-0654) has more than 100,000 book titles and CDs. **MacIntosh Books and Paper** (2365 Periwinkle Way, Sanibel Island; ☎ 239-472-1447), the **Book Trader** (170 Tenth Street North, Naples; ☎ 239-262-7562), and **The Wise Old Owl** (826 Neapolitan Way, Naples; ☎ 239-263-3249) are other good options.

CIGARS Timmy Tobacco (852 Fifth Avenue, South, Naples; ☎ 239-403-3550) has the oldest walk-in cigar humidor in the area.

FLEA MARKETS Visit **Fleamasters Flea Market** (FL 82, one-and-one-quarter mile west of I-75 at Exit 138, Fort Myers; ☎ 239-334-7001) for kitschy Florida souvenirs, T-shirts (tacky and trendy alike), produce, and craft items.

FRUIT Sun Harvest Citrus (14810 Metro Parkway, Fort Myers; ☎ 239-768-2686 or 800-743-1480) sells gift packs and fresh Florida fruits and food for shipping to the folks back home.

SHELLS In an area known for its shelling, what could be a better souvenir than a seashell? **The Shell Factory** (2787 North Tamiami Trail, North Fort Myers; ☎ 239-995-2141) has been one of the region's most famous shopping experiences for more than five decades. The megastore claims to have the world's largest collection of rare shells, sponges, and fossils from the Seven Seas.

Sprawling across more than 65,000 square feet, The Shell Factory has shell jewelry (ranging from costume to fine) and shell magnets, T-shirts, night-lights, chimes, mobiles, keychains, towels, and candles. It's not as pretty as Sanibel Island, but the shells are easier to find!

SHOES Visit **Ellie's Pricey Shoes** (16520 South Tamiami Trail, at Island Park Plaza, Fort Myers, ☎ 239-432-2384) for discounted big-name shoes. **Naples on the Run** (2128 Ninth Street North, Naples; ☎ 239-434-9786) has a good selection of running shoes, and **Pratt's Shoe Salon of Naples** (1183 Third Street South, Naples; ☎ 239-261-7127) has a wide assortment of dressy and casual shoes.

SWIMWEAR Swim World (13300-53 South Cleveland Avenue, Fort Myers; ☎ 239-481-3350) offers a variety of swimwear in the latest styles, fabrics, and colors.

ATTRACTIONS

ON FLORIDA'S SOUTHWEST COAST, A PERFECT DAY might include golf on one of more than 100 golf courses or sea fishing for tarpon. (The sport of tarpon fishing actually originated in Southwest Florida's Pine Island Sound in the late 1880s, and in Boca Grande Pass, the opening between Cayo Costa and Gasparilla islands. This area is considered the "tarpon fishing capital of the world.") Other ideal days could be spent luxuriating at a posh spa, browsing galleries and shopping till you drop, or just enjoying the sun and sea with a cool drink at your elbow on any of the calm beaches along the Gulf of Mexico.

Unlike other parts of the Sunshine State, where "nature" is relegated to landscaping at high-end hotels or restaurants, nature lovers in the Fort Myers–Naples area can explore numerous facilities where wildlife and the environment take center stage. Local parks include more than 1 million acres of nature sanctuaries—most with paths or boardwalks—which permit visitors to see unspoiled wetlands and experience the beauty of the state in pristine condition.

Destinations and outfitters include Babcock Wilderness Adventures, Big Cypress National Preserve, Calusa Nature Center, Carl E. Johnson Park at Lovers Key, Corkscrew Swamp Sanctuary, Everglades National Park, Gulf Coast Kayak, J. N. "Ding" Darling National Wildlife Refuge, Matanzas Pass Wilderness Preserve, Ostego Bay Foundation, and the Sanibel-Captiva Nature Conservation Foundation. For most parks, a flat fee is charged for parking or entry for a car full of people. Some request donations from visitors.

Sure, there are malls, movie theaters, restaurants, museums, historic sites, and dozens of shopping centers (described previously), but nature is big business in this part of Florida—even outside the protected lands. Other spots to visit include **Sun Harvest Citrus** (14810 Metro Parkway; ☎ 239-768-2686), a huge fruit-packing house that allows a look at Florida's citrus industry, and **Mound Key** (just east of Lovers Key, Fort Myers Beach; ☎ 239-992-0311), one of more than 100 islands dotting the Lee Coast. The Calusa tribe, who lived here from about AD 100–AD 1750, probably built the island from shells more than 1,000 years ago. You can visit by boat; amateur and professional archaeologists research on the site.

As most of the attractions are nature oriented and many are outdoors, you should wear sunscreen, hats, comfortable shoes, and carry plenty of water.

---

kids **A FEW OTHER FAVORITE SOUTHWEST FLORIDA WATER-RELATED SURPRISES (ESPECIALLY FOR FAMILIES!)**

- The **Dolphin Watch and Wildlife Adventure Cruise, offered by Captiva Cruises,** is a delightful and informative 90-minute narrated tour by boat. You'll see pods of dolphins, flocks of birds, and an occasional manatee: wonderful, natural family fun (☎ 239-472-5300; **www.captivacruises.com**).

- Weekdays at 11 a.m., the public is invited to **C.R.O.W.** (Clinic for Rehabilitation of Wildlife). The hospital and ten-acre sanctuary on Sanibel are dedicated to helping and releasing native and migratory creatures (☎ 239-472-3644; **www.crowclinic.org**).

- The **Ostego Bay Marine Center,** on Fort Myers Beach's Fisherman's Wharf, highlights touch tanks, aquariums, and unusual marine exhibits. It's great for young kids (☎ 239-765-8101).

- **Four Mile Cove Ecological Preserve** in Cape Coral is a 365-acre saltwater preserve on the Caloosahatchee River. There are scenic canoe trails, wooded paths, and lots of marine wildlife (☎ 239-574-7395).

We've tried to prioritize your touring at a glance. You'll find the type of attraction and location, plus the author's rating of each profiled attraction in the chart below and further details in the profiles that follow. Most museum-type attractions offer group rates for ten or more people.

southwest florida attractions

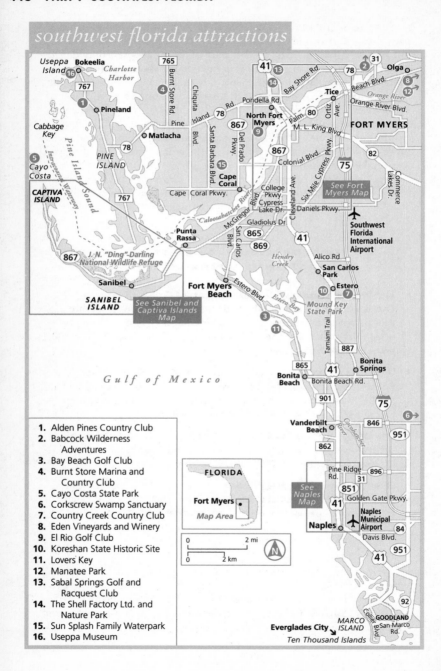

1. Alden Pines Country Club
2. Babcock Wilderness Adventures
3. Bay Beach Golf Club
4. Burnt Store Marina and Country Club
5. Cayo Costa State Park
6. Corkscrew Swamp Sanctuary
7. Country Creek Country Club
8. Eden Vineyards and Winery
9. El Rio Golf Club
10. Koreshan State Historic Site
11. Lovers Key
12. Manatee Park
13. Sabal Springs Golf and Racquest Club
14. The Shell Factory Ltd. and Nature Park
15. Sun Splash Family Waterpark
16. Useppa Museum

FLORIDA

Fort Myers

Map Area

0   2 mi

0   2 km

fort myers attractions, dining, and nightlife

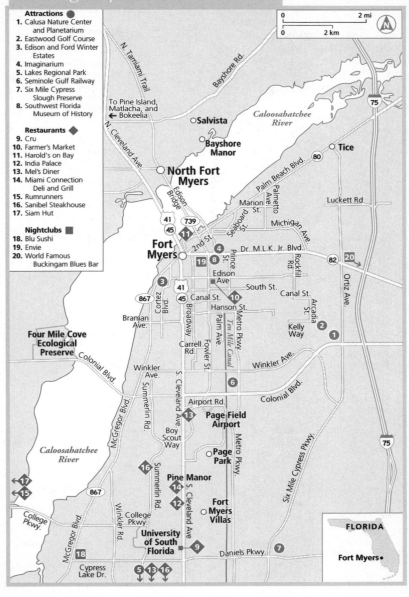

Attractions ●
1. Calusa Nature Center and Planetarium
2. Eastwood Golf Course
3. Edison and Ford Winter Estates
4. Imaginarium
5. Lakes Regional Park
6. Seminole Gulf Railway
7. Six Mile Cypress Slough Preserve
8. Southwest Florida Museum of History

Restaurants ◆
9. Cru
10. Farmer's Market
11. Harold's on Bay
12. India Palace
13. Mel's Diner
14. Miami Connection Deli and Grill
15. Rumrunners
16. Sanibel Steakhouse
17. Siam Hut

Nightclubs ■
18. Blu Sushi
19. Envie
20. World Famous Buckingam Blues Bar

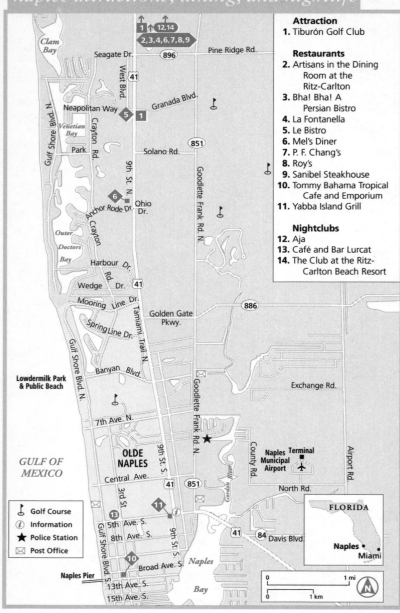

naples attractions, dining, and nightlife

Attraction
1. Tiburón Golf Club

Restaurants
2. Artisans in the Dining Room at the Ritz-Carlton
3. Bha! Bha! A Persian Bistro
4. La Fontanella
5. Le Bistro
6. Mel's Diner
7. P. F. Chang's
8. Roy's
9. Sanibel Steakhouse
10. Tommy Bahama Tropical Cafe and Emporium
11. Yabba Island Grill

Nightclubs
12. Aja
13. Café and Bar Lurcat
14. The Club at the Ritz-Carlton Beach Resort

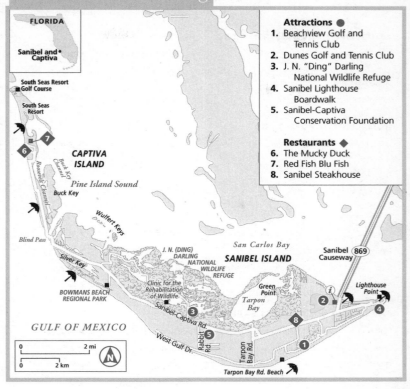

sanibel and captiva attractions and dining

FLORIDA

Sanibel and Captiva

South Seas Resort Golf Course

South Seas Resort

CAPTIVA ISLAND

Buck Key Channel

Roosevelt Channel

Pine Island Sound

Buck Key

Wulfert Keys

Blind Pass

Silver Key

BOWMANS BEACH REGIONAL PARK

GULF OF MEXICO

J. N. (DING) DARLING NATIONAL WILDLIFE REFUGE

Clinic for the Rehabilitation of Wildlife

Sanibel-Captiva Rd

West Gulf Dr.

Rabbit Rd.

Tarpon Bay Rd.

San Carlos Bay

SANIBEL ISLAND

Sanibel Causeway

869

Green Point

Tarpon Bay

Lighthouse Point

0   2 mi
0   2 km

N

Tarpon Bay Rd. Beach

Attractions ●
1. Beachview Golf and Tennis Club
2. Dunes Golf and Tennis Club
3. J. N. "Ding" Darling National Wildlife Refuge
4. Sanibel Lighthouse Boardwalk
5. Sanibel-Captiva Conservation Foundation

Restaurants ◆
6. The Mucky Duck
7. Red Fish Blu Fish
8. Sanibel Steakhouse

Southwest Florida Attractions

NAME	LOCATION	AUTHOR'S RATING
AMUSEMENT PARK/PETTING ZOO		
The Shell Factory	Fort Myers	★★
AQUARIUM		
Imaginarium	Fort Myers	★★
HOME AND GARDEN TOUR		
Edison and Ford Winter Estates	Fort Myers	★★★
LIGHTHOUSE		
Sanibel Lighthouse Boardwalk	Sanibel Island	★★
MUSEUMS		
Calusa Nature Center and Planetarium	Fort Myers	★★
Imaginarium	Fort Myers	★★
Southwest Florida Museum of History	Fort Myers	★★★
Useppa Museum	Useppa Island	★★
PARKS AND WILDERNESS EXPERIENCES		
Babcock Wilderness Adventures	Punta Gorda	★★★½
Cayo Costa State Park	Cayo Costa Island	★★
Corkscrew Swamp Sanctuary	Naples	★★
J. N. "Ding" Darling National Wildlife Refuge	Sanibel Island	★★
Koreshan State Historic Site	Estero	★★
Lakes Regional Park	Fort Myers	★★
Lovers Key State Park	Fort Myers Beach	★★
Manatee Park	Fort Myers	★★
Six Mile Cypress Slough Preserve	Fort Myers	★
PLANETARIUM		
Calusa Nature Center and Planetarium	Fort Myers	★★
TRAIN EXCURSION		
Seminole Gulf Railway	Fort Myers	★

NAME	LOCATION	AUTHOR'S RATING
VINEYARD AND WINERY		
Eden Vineyards and Winery	**Alva**	★
WATER PARK		
Sun Splash Family Waterpark	**Cape Coral**	★★

ATTRACTION PROFILES

Babcock Wilderness Adventures

APPEAL BY AGE	PRESCHOOL ★★	GRADE SCHOOL ★★★★	TEENS ★★★
YOUNG ADULTS ★★★	OVER 30 ★★★		SENIORS ★★★

**8000 FL 31, Punta Gorda 33982; ☎ 800-500-5583;
www.babcockwilderness.com**

Type of attraction Wildlife, woods, and waters of Telegraph Cypress Swamp. **Admission** Adults, $17.95; seniors, $14.95; children ages 3–12, $10.95. **Hours** November–May, daily, 9 a.m.–3 p.m.; June–October, mornings only—call for times. **When to go** Early morning or late afternoon **Special comments** The Crescent B Ranch has won an Environmental Stewardship Award due to its dedication to working in harmony with nature. **Author's rating ★★★½. How much time to allow** Minimum of 3 hours.

DESCRIPTION AND COMMENTS One of the best of the nature trips in the region, with a museum, snack bar, and 90-minute swamp-buggy tour. The tour provides glimpses of panthers, bison, alligators, exotic birds, and boar, and an amazing overview of the exciting wilderness that has belonged to the same family since 1914 and is the largest cattle ranch east of the Mississippi.

TOURING TIPS Bring water and pick up snacks at the snack bar. Be sure to make reservations. Note: The swamp-buggy tour may be rough on those with bad backs.

OTHER THINGS TO DO NEARBY Head back west over the bridge and spend the rest of the day at The Shell Factory—a 20-minute ride from Babcock—or stop by Manatee Park.

Calusa Nature Center and Planetarium

APPEAL BY AGE	PRESCHOOL ★	GRADE SCHOOL ★★	TEENS ★★★
YOUNG ADULTS ★★★	OVER 30 ★★★		SENIORS ★★★

**3450 Ortiz Avenue, Fort Myers 33905; ☎ 239-275-3435;
www.calusanature.com**

Type of attraction Natural history concentrating on the background of the Calusa Indians and their place in the history of the Southwest Coast. **Admission** Adults, $8; children ages 3–12, $5 **Hours** Monday–Saturday, 9 a.m–5 p.m.; Sunday, 11 a.m.–5 p.m. **When to go** Anytime. **Special comments** Handicapped accessible. **Author's rating** ★★. **How much time to allow** 2 hours.

DESCRIPTION AND COMMENTS A great display of Southwest Florida's history, including information on the Calusa Indians, who inhabited the area from AD 800 to AD 1700.

TOURING TIPS If you have little ones, take the stroller onto the mile-long boardwalk. There's a laser show offered on the first Friday of the month. Call for times.

OTHER THINGS TO DO NEARBY Hit the Edison Mall for air-conditioned comfort and shopping.

Cayo Costa State Park

APPEAL BY AGE	PRESCHOOL ★★	GRADE SCHOOL ★★	TEENS ★★
YOUNG ADULTS ★★★	OVER 30 ★★★		SENIORS ★★★

Cayo Costa Island between North Captiva and Boca Grande in the Gulf of Mexico; accessible only by boat; ☎ 239-964-0375; www.floridastateparks.org/cayocosta/default.cfm

Type of attraction State park. **Admission** Parking is $1 per person an hour, maximum of $3. **Hours** Daily, 8 a.m.–sunset. **When to go** Anytime. **Author's rating** ★★. **How much time to allow** At least 2–4 hours.

DESCRIPTION AND COMMENTS Lying in a transitional area between the temperate southeastern coastal plain and subtropical South Florida, Cayo Costa is one of the largest uninhabited barrier islands in the state. If you love the outdoors, natural beauty, pine flats, oak-palm hammocks, and grassy areas, and you enjoy swimming, fishing, hiking, and camping, this one's for you.

TOURING TIPS Take the ferry from Pine Island (☎ 239-283-0015). The island has restrooms, cold showers, and drinking water. Bring everything else with you, including snacks, hats, and sunscreen.

OTHER THINGS TO DO NEARBY Nothing much—this is a true tropical island, so don't expect a Burger King around the corner or a supermarket on the next block. It makes a nice day's outing.

Corkscrew Swamp Sanctuary

APPEAL BY AGE	PRESCHOOL ★	GRADE SCHOOL ★★	TEENS ★★
YOUNG ADULTS ★★★	OVER 30 ★★★		SENIORS ★★★

375 Sanctuary Road West (Exit 111 of I-75), Naples 34120; ☎ 239-348-9151; corkscrew.audubon.org

Type of attraction Natural forest. **Admission** Adults, $10; college students, $6; National Audubon Society members, $5; children ages 6–18 years, $4; children under age 6, free. **Hours** April–September, Daily, 7 a.m.–7:30 p.m.; October–April, Daily, 7 a.m.–5:30 p.m. **When to go** Anytime; early in the day or late in the afternoon to avoid sun exposure out on the boardwalk. **Author's rating ★★. How much time to allow** 2–3 hours.

DESCRIPTION AND COMMENTS 180 degrees from the hectic sun and fun of Florida's beaches, this watershed is owned and operated by the National Audubon Society. It features wading and migratory birds and other wildlife on a two-mile trail though the largest virgin bald-cypress forest in the country. The birds are magnificent, but younger children might get bored, so bring binoculars for spottings. The boardwalk through the pinelands, hammock, and cypress ponds offers some spectacular natural sites.

TOURING TIPS Go early. Our usual precaution: It gets hot quickly, so don't forget to bring water, a hat, and your camera.

OTHER THINGS TO DO NEARBY Head for an outing in Bonita Springs or Naples after your tour of Corkscrew. It might be a good time to head to the beach and veg out. After the passive joys of hanging out with the herons, go to Clam Pass Beach and enjoy the sun, sand, and shelling.

J. N. "Ding" Darling National Wildlife Refuge

APPEAL BY AGE	PRESCHOOL ★★	GRADE SCHOOL ★★	TEENS ★★★
YOUNG ADULTS ★★★	OVER 30 ★★★★		SENIORS ★★★★

1 Wildlife Drive, Sanibel Island 33957; ☎ 239-472-1100; www.fws.gov/dingdarling

Type of attraction Wildlife preserve. **Admission** Cars, $5; walkers or bikers, $1; visitor center is free. **Hours** Saturday–Thursday, 7:30 a.m.–sunset; closed Friday. Education Center, January–April 9 a.m.–5 p.m. and May–December 9 a.m.–4 p.m. **When to go** Anytime, but the best times for viewing wildlife are early morning, late afternoon, and at low tide. **Author's rating ★★ How much time to allow** 2 hours.

DESCRIPTION AND COMMENTS Named after an early conservationist (who also happened to be a newspaper cartoonist), this 6,000-acre wildlife refuge occupies more than half of Sanibel, on the northeast side of the island. "Ding" Darling was chief of the U.S. Biological Survey—the forerunner of the U.S. Fish and Wildlife Service—and saw the need to protect natural habitats.

TOURING TIPS Check out the visitor center for tide listings and other info. The five-mile drive is best done slowly to enjoy the surroundings and wildlife. You'll see alligators, roseate spoonbills, snow egrets, great blue herons, and more. And you don't see no-see-ums, so bring insect repellent.

OTHER THINGS TO DO NEARBY Shelling—again! This is Sanibel, you know. Pick and choose from one of the widest varieties of shells in the country.

Eden Vineyards and Winery

APPEAL BY AGE	PRESCHOOL ★★	GRADE SCHOOL ★★	TEENS ★★
YOUNG ADULTS ★★	OVER 30 ★★★		SENIORS ★★★

19709 Little Lane (Exit 141 off I-75), Alva 33920; ☎ 239-728-9463; www.edenwinery.com

Type of attraction Vineyard and winery. **Admission** Adults, $3 **Hours** Daily, 11 a.m.–4 p.m., last tasting at 3:30 p.m. **When to go** Anytime. **Special comments** Adults only, of course. And it helps if you enjoy wine. **Author's rating** ★ **How much time to allow** 1 hour.

DESCRIPTION AND COMMENTS Set on 20 acres, this vineyard has been operated by the Kiser family for more than 25 years and is the country's southernmost winery. Take an informal tour and sample the six wines produced here. While Southwest Florida isn't known for vineyards, the wine is pretty good. One, made from tropical star fruit, has been called Florida's alternative to California blush. If you've never been to a winery and want a change of pace, this is ideal.

TOURING TIPS Eden Vineyards wines make nice gifts. Groups of 12 or more must be arranged by prior appointment.

OTHER THINGS TO DO NEARBY Visit Manatee Park to watch the endangered West Indian manatee—the elephant of the sea—in its natural environment.

Edison and Ford Winter Estates

APPEAL BY AGE	PRESCHOOL ★	GRADE SCHOOL ★★	TEENS ★★★
YOUNG ADULTS ★★★★	OVER 30 ★★★★		SENIORS ★★★★

2350 McGregor Boulevard, Fort Myers 33901; ☎ 239-334-3614; www.edison-ford-estate.com

Type of attraction Old homes of a tycoon and an inventor, plus the laboratory and gardens. **Admission** Adults, $16; children ages 6–12, $8.50; children under age 6, free. Last tour is at 4 p.m. **Hours** Monday–Saturday, 9 a.m.–5:30 p.m.; Sunday, noon–5:30 p.m. **When to go** Anytime. **Author's rating** ★★★ **How much time to allow** 2 hours or more.

DESCRIPTION AND COMMENTS In 1884 Thomas Alva Edison, whom we thank for inventing the lightbulb, phonograph, and dozens of other things electrical, decided to make his winter home in Fort Myers. The home he called Seminole Lodge was built in 1886 and donated to the city of Fort Myers in 1947 by his second wife and widow, Mina Miller Edison. See not only his home, laboratory, experimental gardens, and museum but also rare antique cars and some 200 Edison phonographs among the memorabilia. Edison convinced his buddy Henry Ford to visit Fort Myers, and the auto magnate also became a winter resident. Mangoes, the bungalow-style house that Ford and his wife, Clara, built next door in 1916, is furnished as it was in the 1920s. A gate between the two properties is called Friendship Gate.

TOURING TIPS Take a guided tour so you don't miss anything. Costumed actors portray the wealthy snowbirds and friends. Check out the gigantic banyan tree out front near the entry. A gift from Harvey S. Firestone (the tire mogul), the tree was planted in 1925 when it was only four feet tall. It's now more than 400 feet around.

OTHER THINGS TO DO NEARBY The Southwest Florida Museum of History will put things in perspective—not all settlers lived so well. You can also ride on the river in the *Reliance,* a replica of Edison's electric boat.

Imaginarium

APPEAL BY AGE   PRESCHOOL ★★   GRADE SCHOOL ★★★   TEENS ★★
YOUNG ADULTS ★★★   OVER 30 ★★   SENIORS ★★★★

2000 Cranford Avenue, Fort Myers (4 miles west of I-75, Exit 138 in downtown Fort Myers) 33916; ☎ 239-337-3332; www.cityftmyers.com/attractions/imaginarium.aspx

Type of attraction Hands-on museum and aquarium. **Admission** Adults, $7; students and seniors, $6; children under age 13, $4; children under age 3, free. **Hours** Monday–Saturday, 10 a.m–5 p.m.; Sunday, noon–5 p.m. **When to go** Anytime. **Author's rating** ★★. **How much time to allow** 2 hours.

DESCRIPTION AND COMMENTS Good for all ages, but kids will especially enjoy this interactive learning center geared to exploring the principles of science. At this former city water plant, see a giant Pipe-O-Saurus at the wetland area entry, stand in a Florida thunderstorm without getting wet, and surf the Internet or broadcast the weather from a TV center.

TOURING TIPS Take your time. This can be fun for the whole family.

OTHER THINGS TO DO NEARBY Visit the Southwest Florida Museum of History.

Koreshan State Historic Site

APPEAL BY AGE   PRESCHOOL ★   GRADE SCHOOL ★★   TEENS ★★★
YOUNG ADULTS ★★★   OVER 30 ★★★   SENIORS ★★★

South US 41, Estero 33928; ☎ 239-992-0311; www.floridastateparks.org/koreshan/default.cfm

Type of attraction State park. **Admission** $4 per vehicle, up to 8 people; $3 for single-occupancy car. **Hours** Daily, 8 a.m.–sunset. **When to go** Anytime. **Author's rating** ★★. **How much time to allow** 2 hours minimum.

DESCRIPTION AND COMMENTS These 300 acres on the narrow Estero River once hosted the quirky Koreshan Unity Movement. This religious sect was headed by Dr. Cyrus Teed, a Union Army Medical Corps veteran inspired by a vision, or "divine illumination," which prompted him to change his name to Koresh (Hebrew for "Cyrus") in 1894 and move his followers to Southwest Florida. He thought he'd create a city of 10 million people, but the settlement drew only 250 residents. Thirteen of the original 60 buildings are left, including Teed's home. A one-of-a-kind globe illustrates the Koreshan belief that man resides on the inside surface of the earth, gazing at the solar system within. A state park offers nature trails, boat ramp, canoeing, fresh- and saltwater fishing, and camping.

TOURING TIPS Wear comfortable shoes, a hat, and sunscreen, especially if you picnic on the wooded grounds.

OTHER THINGS TO DO NEARBY Canoe along safe, marked river trails to Mound Key. You are 15 miles south of Fort Myers, right on the Tamiami Trail, which offers a smorgasbord of restaurants, shops, movie theaters, and more, all within minutes of Koreshan.

Lakes Regional Park

APPEAL BY AGE	PRESCHOOL ★	GRADE SCHOOL ★★	TEENS ★★
YOUNG ADULTS ★★★	OVER 30 ★★★		SENIORS ★★★

7330 Gladiolus Drive, Fort Myers 33908; ☎ 239-432-2000

Type of attraction Park. **Admission** Parking is 75 ¢ an hour or $3 for all-day parking; admission is free. **Hours** Daily, 8 a.m.–sunset; closed Christmas Day. **When to go** Anytime. **Special comments** Includes a Fragrance Garden for the sight-impaired. **Author's rating** ★★. **How much time to allow** 3 hours.

DESCRIPTION AND COMMENTS Diversions include swimming, nature trails, bike and boat rentals, and picnic areas with barbecue grills and showers. Check out the Fragrance Garden, created especially for persons with visual impairments—names of herbs are printed in braille and include chamomile, basil, sage, and rosemary.

TOURING TIPS The park is a dream family destination. We recommend it as a multigenerational chance to enhance the senses and enjoy nature in a lovely setting.

OTHER THINGS TO DO NEARBY Anything on US 41; you're just a half mile away. Wander through any of the dozen strip-mall shopping centers. Kids will love the Ted E. Bear Shoppe, and a variety of golf and tennis shops will appeal to sports enthusiasts.

Lovers Key State Park

APPEAL BY AGE	PRESCHOOL ★★	GRADE SCHOOL ★★	TEENS ★★
YOUNG ADULTS ★★★	OVER 30 ★★★		SENIORS ★★★

8700 Estero Boulevard, Fort Myers Beach 33931; ☎ 239-463-4588; www.floridastateparks.org/loverskey/default.cfm

Type of attraction State park. **Admission** 1 person, $3; 2–8 people in vehicle, $5; walk-ins and bicyclists, $1 per person. **Hours** Daily, 8 a.m.–sunset. **When to go** Anytime. **Author's rating** ★★. **How much time to allow** All day if possible.

DESCRIPTION AND COMMENTS This romantically named park with 2.5 miles of white-sand beaches offers excursions to view endangered West Indian manatees and bottlenose dolphins. Loggerhead sea turtles nest along the beach from May to October, when 300-pound mama turtles come ashore nightly to dig their nests above the high-tide line along the beach. Sixty days later, the babies break out of their ping-pong-ball–sized eggs. A lights-out policy is in effect during nesting and hatching periods on Fort Myers Beach and year-round on Sanibel. Fishing, bird-watching, and various boat rides are also on tap on Lover's Key.

TOURING TIPS Don't forget the sunscreen, hat, and comfortable shoes. Canoe and kayak excursions are a fun way to see wildlife up close.

OTHER THINGS TO DO NEARBY Visit another beach, or stop off at one of the shopping centers dotting the Tamiami Trail.

Manatee Park

APPEAL BY AGE	PRESCHOOL ★★	GRADE SCHOOL ★★		TEENS ★★★
YOUNG ADULTS ★★★	OVER 30 ★★★		SENIORS ★★★	

**10901 FL 80, Fort Myers 33905; ☎ 239-694-3537;
www.captiva.com/stateparks/manatee.htm**

Type of attraction Marine park. **Admission** Parking is 75 ¢ per hour; $3 maximum per day. **Hours** April–September, daily, 8 a.m.–8 p.m.; October–March, 8 a.m.–5 p.m. **When to go** Anytime; in winter to see manatees, though daily climate and weather conditions determine whether they will be resting or feeding on the river. **Author's rating** ★★. **How much time to allow** 2 hours.

DESCRIPTION AND COMMENTS See the endangered West Indian manatee in its natural habitat from three observation decks during the winter months. Year-round facilities include picnic areas, fishing, and canoeing. The park's restored native plant habitats and butterfly gardens are lovely.

TOURING TIPS Bring a picnic basket and enjoy. Dress for the outdoors—comfy shoes are a must.

OTHER THINGS TO DO NEARBY Eden Vineyards and Babcock Wilderness Adventures are two good possibilities.

Sanibel Lighthouse Boardwalk

APPEAL BY AGE	PRESCHOOL ★	GRADE SCHOOL ★★		TEENS ★★
YOUNG ADULTS ★★★	OVER 30 ★★★		SENIORS ★★★	

East tip of Sanibel Island, at Periwinkle Way, 33957; ☎ 239-472-6477

Type of attraction Lighthouse. **Admission** Parking is $2 an hour. **Hours** Daily, 8 a.m.–sunset. **When to go** Anytime. **Author's rating** ★★. **How much time to allow** 1 hour.

DESCRIPTION AND COMMENTS This 94-foot tower, probably one of the most photographed spots on this scenic island, has been a landmark in San Carlos Bay since 1884. Lightkeepers used to live in the cottage at its base, but the lighthouse is now automatic.

TOURING TIPS The boardwalk is 400 feet long and wheelchair accessible. You can't enter the lighthouse, but bring your camera to take photos of the exterior and grounds. Park in the fishing pier lot.

OTHER THINGS TO DO NEARBY Shelling on any of the nearby beaches.

Seminole Gulf Railway

APPEAL BY AGE	PRESCHOOL ★	GRADE SCHOOL ★		TEENS ★★
YOUNG ADULTS ★★★	OVER 30 ★★★		SENIORS ★★★	

Metro Mall Station, at Colonial Boulevard and Metro Parkway, Fort Myers 33919; ☎ 239-275-8487 or 800-736-4853; www.semgulf.com

Type of attraction Train excursions. **Admission** Varies. **Hours** In summer, the train operates Wednesday–Sunday, but call for locations and exact departure times. Visit the Web site above for more information. **When to go** Check schedules. **Author's rating** ★. **How much time to allow** Varies, depending on whether you take the dinner tour, murder-mystery tour, or train ride; evening tours are 3½ hours long.

DESCRIPTION AND COMMENTS   A unique take on the area's history while riding in a 1930s–1950s vintage railroad car that originally ran between Fort Myers and Naples. Today it chugs south to Bonita Springs and north across the river. The dinner tour offers a five-course meal with wine and other beverages. The daytime tour provides narration and a snack bar.

TOURING TIPS   Take the evening trip if you like eating in the dining car and feeling you're a character in an Agatha Christie mystery.

OTHER THINGS TO DO NEARBY   Spend the day outdoors or at the beach before you take the dinner train. The train leaves around 6:30 p.m., so you can still see the passing scenery.

The Shell Factory and Nature Park

APPEAL BY AGE	PRESCHOOL ★★	GRADE SCHOOL ★★		TEENS ★★★
YOUNG ADULTS ★★★	OVER 30 ★★★			SENIORS ★★★

2787 North Tamiami Trail, Fort Myers 33903; ☎ 239-995-2141; www.shellfactory.com

Type of attraction Amusement park, petting zoo, and shops. **Admission** Museum: free; Nature Park: adults, $6; seniors ages 55 and older, $5; Children ages 4–12, $4; children under age 4, free. **Hours** Museum: Monday–Saturday, 10 a.m.–9 p.m.; Sunday, 10 a.m.–8 p.m. Nature Park: Monday–Friday, 11 a.m.–6 p.m.; Saturday and Sunday, 10 a.m.–6 p.m. **When to go** Anytime. **Special comments** A little bit of this, a little bit of that, and hundreds of thousands of shells of every size, shape, and description. **Author's rating** ★★. **How much time to allow** 1–2 hours.

DESCRIPTION AND COMMENTS   A railroad museum, a video arcade, bumper and paddleboats, a gallery of African art, two restaurants, and a petting zoo are part of this eclectic experience. The Shell Factory is a little tacky, but it's worth wandering through the enormous main building and outbuildings. Never before has such a big area been dedicated to seashells, corals, and sponges. (Except, of course, for the glorious natural beaches outside.)

TOURING TIPS   Because Southwest Florida is best known for its shelling, this property pays homage to the shell—and shell novelties, many of them under $10. Buy your shell souvenirs here—the choices are many, from lamps to earrings. Skip the video, games but enjoy the bumper boats and petting zoo.

OTHER THINGS TO DO NEARBY   This might be the day to head out to Babcock Wilderness Adventures and commune with nature (including a swamp-buggy ride with a trained naturalist discussing the bison, deer, and alligators you'll see throughout Telegraph Cypress Swamp) before shell shopping.

Six Mile Cypress Slough Preserve

APPEAL BY AGE	PRESCHOOL ★	GRADE SCHOOL ★★	TEENS ★
YOUNG ADULTS ★★	OVER 30 ★★		SENIORS ★★

7751 Penzance Crossing (off Six Mile Cypress Parkway), Fort Myers 33912;
☎ **239-432-2004; www.captiva.com/stateparks/sixmilecypress.htm**

Type of attraction Nature park. **Admission** Parking is 75 ¢ an hour, $3 maximum. **Hours** Times vary by season, call first; open in summer 8 a.m.–8 p.m., with guided tours at 9 a.m. on Wednesdays. **When to go** Anytime. **Author's rating** ★. **How much time to allow** 1–2 hours.

DESCRIPTION AND COMMENTS Watch for turtles, alligators, river otters, white-tailed deer, and blue herons, among other wildlife. In the flora department, you can see five distinct plant communities, including the cypress swamp. This wetland ecosystem with a 1.2-mile-long boardwalk offers self-guided and free guided walks year-round.

TOURING TIPS Take a camera.

OTHER THINGS TO DO NEARBY For even more nature action, check out Calusa Nature Center and Planetarium.

Southwest Florida Museum of History

APPEAL BY AGE	PRESCHOOL ★★	GRADE SCHOOL ★★★	TEENS ★★★
YOUNG ADULTS ★★★	OVER 30 ★★★		SENIORS ★★★

2300 Peck Street, Fort Myers 33901; ☎ **239-332-5955;**
www.cityftmyers.com/attractions/historical.aspx

Type of attraction Local-history museum. **Admission** Adults, $9.50; seniors, $8.50; children, $4. **Hours** Tuesday–Saturday, 9 a.m.–4 p.m. **When to go** Anytime. **Author's rating** ★★★. **How much time to allow** 2–3 hours.

DESCRIPTION AND COMMENTS This eclectic museum of Floridiana is housed in an old Mediterranean-style Atlantic Coast Line railroad station built in 1923 (next door there's Esperanza, the longest private Pullman rail car). The museum offers a comprehensive record of the region's history: a Calusa settlement, Spanish conquistadors, military outposts, agricultural beginnings, cattle drives and cowboys (who were the first "Florida crackers," so nicknamed for cracking their whips), an increased military presence—and remnants of a plane—from World War II (servicemen outnumbered civilians), and a growth boom these last 50 years. A collection of carnival and Depression glass is one of the first gifts to the museum.

TOURING TIPS Go on a guided tour and take your time. It's worth it.

OTHER THINGS TO DO NEARBY Spend the rest of the day touring the Edison and Ford Winter Estates and see how the famed millionaire inventors lived.

Sun Splash Family Waterpark

APPEAL BY AGE	PRESCHOOL ★	GRADE SCHOOL ★★	TEENS ★★★
YOUNG ADULTS ★★★	OVER 30 ★★		SENIORS ★★

400 Santa Barbara Boulevard, Cape Coral; ☎ 239-574-0557; www.sunsplashwaterpark.com

Type of attraction Water theme park. **Admission** Adults and children 48" and taller, $11.95; smaller children, $9.95; seniors ages 55 or older, $5.95; children ages 2 and under, $2.95. Parking is $1. **Hours** 11 a.m.–5 p.m., March–September; open weekends at beginning and end of season and daily during summer. **When to go** Early in the day. **Author's rating** ★★. **How much time to allow** 2–3 hours.

DESCRIPTION AND COMMENTS Zoom Flume, Cape Fear (a popular tube slide), and the new Electric Slide are the main attractions here, but don't overlook the inner-tube river and children's play area. Outside food and beverages are not allowed in the water park proper; however, you can eat and drink all you want at the picnic area outside the gates. U.S. Coast Guard life jackets are the only ones approved for use in the park (a limited supply is available at the park).

TOURING TIPS Pack a lunch, enjoy it at the outside picnic area, then attack the slides.

OTHER THINGS TO DO NEARBY You won't need more.

Useppa Museum

APPEAL BY AGE	PRESCHOOL ★	GRADE SCHOOL ★★	TEENS ★★
YOUNG ADULTS ★★	OVER 30 ★★★		SENIORS ★★★

Useppa Island; P.O. Box 640, Bokeelia 33922; ☎ 239-283-9600

Type of attraction Historical museum. **Admission** $5. **Hours** Daily, 12:15–2 p.m. **When to go** Anytime. **Special comments** The island is accessible only by boat. **Author's rating** ★★. **How much time to allow** 1 hour.

DESCRIPTION AND COMMENTS Learn about the Calusa natives and see 4,000-year-old artifacts. A 30-minute audio tour is available, and don't miss a forensic restoration of Useppa Man, taken from a skeleton found during an archaeological dig in 1989.

TOURING TIPS Tie in a Captiva Island visit.

OTHER THINGS TO DO NEARBY Head back to Captiva, which will seem exciting after visiting quiet Useppa.

▮ DINING *and* RESTAURANTS

KNOWN PRIMARILY AS A LAID-BACK SUN-AND-SURF destination, Southwest Florida has burgeoning restaurant scene with many of the usual suspects, as well as a multitude of gastronomic surprises. With a year-round population of more than 500,000 as well as nearly 4 million visitors a year, the area hosts ever more major chain eateries, along with scores of smaller establishments. Visitors will find many old reliables—Applebee's, Bennigan's, Perkins, Steak & Shake, TGIFriday's, and Tony Roma's—providing familiar menus particularly helpful to families with finicky eaters. But don't limit yourself to these standbys: Southwest Florida offers much more.

The area's culinary stature rose several points in 1999, when Roy Yamaguchi, the celebrated Hawaiian chef, opened his first restaurant east of the Mississippi in Bonita Springs, a small city between Fort Myers and Naples. Known for innovative style that fuses Californian, Hawaiian, and Pacific Rim ingredients, **Roy's** has become one of the region's most popular dinner destinations.

For lovers of Italian food, there are dozens of restaurants from which to choose. Options range from the big boys, such as **Carrabba's** and **Buca di Beppo,** to mom-and-pop affairs that seem to have been lifted whole from New York or Chicago and set down in the subtropics. In virtually all of them, expect large portions and relatively modest prices. Almost as plentiful are steak houses such as **Outback** and **Lone Star,** along with several upscale versions, including **Don Shula's** and **Fleming's** in Naples, and accomplished local concerns with multiple locations, such as **Sanibel Steakhouse** in Bonita Springs, Fort Myers, Naples, and Sanibel. Many ethnic cuisines are well represented, with Chinese, Japanese, and Mexican most prevalent.

EATING LIKE A NATIVE

DINERS LOOKING FOR LOCAL FLAVOR SHOULD SEEK out a restaurant specializing in fresh seafood or Floribbean fare (a blend of Florida and Caribbean flavors) and menu items that incorporate local ingredients. Florida seafood includes grouper, a lean, firm fish frequently served in sandwiches as well as grilled, fried, or blackened; Florida lobster tails, which are not as rich than their New England counterparts and are actually large crawfish tails; and the much-heralded stone-crab claws, which are taken from crabs without killing them, allowing the crustaceans to regenerate their limbs. The claws, in season from mid-October through mid-May, can be eaten hot or cold and are served much the same way as lobster: partially cracked, with a shell cracker, cocktail fork, lemon, and drawn butter. Don't be alarmed at the sight of dolphinfish on the menu—this is not the mammal, but the fish species better known as mahimahi. Most good seafood houses also serve fresh shrimp (Gulf pink is considered the premium variety), tuna, yellowfin, salmon, snapper, and swordfish. Depending on how busy they are, some restaurants will cook a customer's fresh catch. Call first to make sure.

It takes some searching, but there are a few restaurants that serve another local species, found in abundance both in the wild and at commercial farms: Florida gator. While it has a well-earned reputation for toughness, gator tail can be a tasty alternative protein when prepared by an expert. It's often served fried, although it appears in chowders as well.

Not surprisingly, many people want to dine where there's a water view. There are quite a few restaurants located on such high-rent real estate. Many, however, seem to believe that by offering a great view, customers will fail to notice that the food is below average while the prices are not.

For a glimpse of the inspiration behind Jimmy Buffett's hit "Cheeseburger in Paradise," hop a water taxi for a trip to Cabbage Key, a small barrier island off the coast accessible only by boat. The walls of the island's only dining establishment, generally known as the Cabbage Key restaurant, are lined with thousands of signed dollar bills left by past patrons. The somewhat pricey lunch menu features shrimp and (you guessed it) cheeseburgers.

CHOOSING A TIME AND PLACE

AS IS THE CASE AT STORES AND ON STREETS and beaches, the area's restaurants are more crowded from Christmas to Easter, when winter residents and sun-seeking vacationers flock to the area. During the winter tourist season, it's wise to make a reservation if the restaurant accepts them. Otherwise, expect to wait. A growing number of establishments now offer call-ahead seating. Phone before heading out. They will put you on the list and let you know roughly when to arrive.

Given its reputation as a prime beach-resort area, Southwest Florida embraces the casual lifestyle. As a result, even most of the nicest establishments have few regulations regarding dress beyond requiring shoes and shirts. Only a few suggest that gentlemen wear jackets.

That doesn't mean there's no place to go for a special occasion. The Ritz-Carlton in Naples has three acclaimed restaurants known for superior food, service, and atmosphere. **Artisans in the Dining Room,** where jackets are recommended, has been a repeat winner of both Mobil's Four-Star and AAA's Five Diamond awards. **The Grill Room** next door has won widespread praise as well, and **Lemonia,** the tony Tuscan-style restaurant at the Ritz-Carlton Golf Resort, also in Naples, has earned high marks, too. Other special-event-worthy choices are **Cru** in South Fort Myers, and **Roy's** in Bonita Springs.

At the other end of the scale are lots of little eateries serving on-the-run food—such as pizza and hot dogs—for those who don't want to waste a second of precious beach time indoors.

ABOUT THESE CHOICES

WE HAVE CHOSEN RESTAURANTS THAT, WHILE we can't guarantee their staying power, have proved to operate successfully for some time. We've also selected restaurants with a following among local professionals, residents, and tourists to make for a mix of well-known and low-profile choices. In the process, we have tried to provide something for everyone.

Detailed profiles of each restaurant follow in alphabetical order. For more about South Florida dining and an overview of our restaurant-profile format, including abbreviations and ratings, see page 208 in the Miami-Dade County dining section.

The Best of Southwest Florida Restaurants

RESTAURANT/TYPE	OVERALL RATING	QUALITY RATING	VALUE RATING	CITY
AMERICAN				
Mel's Diner	★★★½	★★★★	★★★★★	Fort Myers, South Fort Myers, Bonita Springs, Naples
BRITISH-STYLE PUB				
The Mucky Duck	★★★½	★★★★	★★★★	Captiva Island
CARIBBEAN				
Tommy Bahama's Tropical Cafe & Emporium	★★★★	★★★★½	★★★★	Naples
CHINESE				
P. F. Chang's	★★★★½	★★★★½	★★★★	Naples
EURO-ASIAN				
Roy's	★★★★½	★★★★★	★★★	Bonita Springs
EUROPEAN				
Artisans in the Dining Room	★★★★★	★★★★★	★★★★	Naples
FRENCH				
Le Bistro	★★★★½	★★★★★	★★★★	Naples
INDIAN				
India Palace	★★★★	★★★★	★★★★	Fort Myers

The Best of Southwest Florida Restaurants *(continued)*

RESTAURANT/TYPE	OVERALL RATING	QUALITY RATING	VALUE RATING	CITY
INTERNATIONAL				
Cru	★★★★½	★★★★½	★★★★	Fort Myers
ITALIAN				
La Fontanella	★★★★	★★★★½	★★★★	Bonita Springs
KOSHER-STYLE DELI				
Miami Connection Deli & Grill	★★★½	★★★½	★★★½	Fort Myers
MIDDLE EASTERN				
Bha! Bha! A Persian Bistro	★★★★	★★★★½	★★★	Naples
NEW AMERICAN				
Red Fish Blu Fish	★★★★½	★★★★½	★★★½	Captiva
Harold's on Bay	★★★★	★★★★½	★★★	Fort Myers
Rumrunners at Cape Harbour	★★★★	★★★★	★★★	Cape Coral
SOUTHERN				
Farmer's Market	★★★★	★★★★½	★★★★★	Fort Myers
STEAK HOUSE				
Sanibel Steakhouse	★★★★	★★★★½	★★	Sanibel Island, Fort Myers, Naples, Bonita Springs
THAI				
Siam Hut	★★★★	★★★★½	★★★★	Cape Coral
TROPICAL				
Yabba Island Grill	★★★★	★★★★½	★★★	Naples

❚ RESTAURANT PROFILES

Artisans in the Dining Room at the Ritz-Carlton ★ ★ ★ ★ ★

FRENCH/MEDITERRANEAN   EXPENSIVE   QUALITY ★ ★ ★ ★ ★   VALUE ★ ★ ★ ★

280 Vanderbilt Beach Road, Naples; ☎ 239-598-3300; www.ritzcarlton.com/resorts/naples/dining

Reservations Required. **When to go** Dinner or Sunday jazz brunch. **Entree range** 3 courses, $68; 4 courses, $75; 5 courses, $80; 8-course blind tasting menu, $85–$130. **Payment** AE, D, MC, V. **Parking** Free lot with valet-only parking. **Bar** Full service. **Wine selection** Encyclopedic—the list comes with a table of contents; $12–$29 per glass, $30–$10,500 by the bottle. **Dress** Very dressy. **Disabled access** Good. **Customers** Hotel guests, knowledgeable and well-heeled locals, celebrants. **Hours** Tuesday–Saturday, 6–10 p.m.; Sunday brunch, 10:30 a.m.–2:30 p.m.

MENU RECOMMENDATIONS Selections change frequently to take advantage of seasonal ingredients. Highlights from the past include salad of Maine lobster warmed in beurre blanc; seared halibut wrapped in squash blossom; roasted turbot with chanterelle mushrooms, salsify, and vanilla-Sauternes sauce; Kobe beef ribeye, and chocolate soufflé.

COMMENTS This is the ultimate in service and gracious ambience, both of which measure up to the inventive menu. For a special occasion, it's hard to top. The Sunday brunch is elegant, complete with a jazz trio. Expect expert pampering at this consistent Mobil Four-Star and AAA Five Diamond restaurant. Jackets are recommended for men.

Bha! Bha! A Persian Bistro ★ ★ ★ ★

MIDDLE EASTERN   MODERATE   QUALITY ★ ★ ★ ★ ½   VALUE ★ ★ ★

Pavilion Shopping Center, 847 Vanderbilt Beach Road, Naples; ☎ 239-594-5557

Reservations Recommended. **When to go** Lunch or dinner. **Entree range** $17–$25. **Payment** AE, MC, V. **Parking** Free lot. **Bar** Beer and wine. **Wine selection** Not large but nicely varied; $6–$8 per glass, $24–$100 by the bottle. **Dress** Stylishly casual. **Disabled access** Wheelchair accessible. **Customers** The culinarily adventurous and gourmets in the know. **Hours** Monday–Friday, 11:30 a.m.–3 p.m. and 5–10 p.m.; Saturday, 11:30 a.m.–2:30 p.m. and 5–10 p.m.; Sunday, 11:30 a.m.–2:30 p.m. and 5–9 p.m.

MENU RECOMMENDATIONS Roasted butternut squash soup; duck in pomegranate-and-walnut sauce; charbroiled lamb drizzled with homemade yogurt; swordfish kebab with couscous, squash jewel cakes, and hibiscus-lemon sorbet

COMMENTS Except during the busiest winter months, expect entertainment by a belly dancer on Thursdays and a fortune-teller on Fridays. The menu includes some Middle Eastern classics as well as innovations by chef-owner Michael Mir, who prepared a Persian New Year's dinner at the prestigious James Beard House in New York City in the spring of 2003. The decor reflects the diversity of the menu. Servers are usually well informed and helpful.

Cru ★ ★ ★ ★ ½

| INTERNATIONAL | EXPENSIVE | QUALITY ★ ★ ★ ★ ½ | VALUE ★ ★ ★ ★ |

Bell Tower Shops, 13499 South US 41, Fort Myers; ☎ 239-466-3663

Reservations Recommended. **When to go** Anytime. **Entree range** $14–$38. **Payment** AE, D, MC, V. **Parking** Free lot. **Bar** Full service. **Wine selection** More than 80 wide-ranging choices; $7–$21 by the glass, $26–$250 by the bottle. **Dress** Stylishly casual. **Disabled access** Good. **Customers** Discerning diners and oenophiles, well-heeled professionals, and well-known singles. **Hours** Sunday and Monday, 5–9 p.m.; Tuesday–Thursday, 5–10 p.m.; Friday and Saturday, 5–11 p.m.

MENU RECOMMENDATIONS Selections change with the seasons but always include a variety of wild game and organic vegetables. Past highlights have included spicy crab rolls; heirloom-tomato salad with Grana shavings and basil vinaigrette; grilled chilled beef and ostrich hand rolls; New Zealand elk chop; grilled Panokette Farms free-range ostrich; baked escargot; paella; and raspberry–and–goat cheese pie.

COMMENTS From the moment this South Beach–style restaurant and bar opened in the spring of 2004, it has been the place to see and be seen dining and drinking. Its motto is "Lush wines and pure foods," and it delivers on both, along with top-flight service. With a dining room awash in vibrant red walls adorned with bold Cuban paintings, the energy is high, and the volume is, too. Frequent wine dinners showcase the talents of its chefs as well as visiting chefs and accomplished vintners.

Farmer's Market ★ ★ ★ ★

| SOUTHERN | INEXPENSIVE | QUALITY ★ ★ ★ ★ ½ | VALUE ★ ★ ★ ★ ★ |

2736 Edison Avenue, Fort Myers; ☎ 239-334-1687

Reservations Not accepted. **When to go** Anytime. **Entree range** $6–$12. **Payment** Cash only. **Parking** Free parking lot. **Bar** None. **Wine selection** None. **Dress** Casual to Sunday best. **Disabled access** Good. **Customers** Florida natives, Sunday after-church crowd, professionals, construction workers. **Hours** Monday–Saturday, 6 a.m.–8 p.m.; Sunday, 6 a.m.–7 p.m.

MENU RECOMMENDATIONS Southern fried chicken; meat loaf; barbecued ribs; chicken and dumplings; corn muffins; collard greens; black-eyed peas; mashed potatoes with gravy; coconut cream pie

COMMENTS Southern hospitality reigns at this Fort Myers institution, where heaping helpings of classic down-home fare are complemented by a cheery and clean dining room that's usually full. Don't be discouraged;

turnover is fairly rapid. Arrive hungry. Large entrees come with three vegetables plus corn muffins and rolls.

Harold's on Bay ★ ★ ★ ★

NEW AMERICAN	EXPENSIVE	QUALITY ★ ★ ★ ★ ½	VALUE ★ ★ ★

2224 Bay Street, Fort Myers; ☎ 239-226-1686

Reservations Recommended. **When to go** Lunch or dinner. **Entree range** $23–$34. **Payment** AE, D, MC, V. **Parking** Free street parking. **Bar** Full service. **Wine selection** Well-chosen assortment with broad range; $6–$10 per glass, $30–$120 per bottle. **Dress** Business casual. **Disabled access** Good. **Customers** The downtown crowd, well-heeled locals. **Hours** Monday, 6–10 p.m.; Tuesday–Thursday, 11:30 a.m.–10 p.m.; Friday, 11:30 a.m.–11 p.m.; Saturday, 6–11 p.m.

MENU RECOMMENDATIONS Sweet potato–bourbon bisque; crab-and-banana spring roll; warm seafood salpicon; sautéed yellowtail over lobster succotash; grilled Colorado lamb chops; house-made Chardonnay-caramel ice cream

COMMENTS Diners can choose from among a selection of small plates as well as standard-sized entrees. The dining room is intimate and stylish, and customers frequently start or end the evening with a stop at either the jazz-and-blues-themed Brick Bar on the third floor or a sunset cocktail at the Sky Bar, which offers a prime view of the nearby Caloosahatchee River and sunset.

India Palace ★ ★ ★ ★

INDIAN	MODERATE	QUALITY ★ ★ ★ ★	VALUE ★ ★ ★ ★

Avenue Shops, 11605 Cleveland Avenue, Fort Myers; ☎ 239-939-2323

Reservations Yes. **When to go** Anytime. **Entree range** $10–$18. **Payment** AE, D, MC, V. **Parking** Free lot. **Bar** Full service. **Wine selection** Mostly Californian; $4–$5 per glass, $14–$50 by the bottle. **Dress** Casual. **Disabled access** Wheelchair accessible. **Customers** Indian expatriates, professionals, young and old. **Hours** Monday–Saturday, 11:30 a.m.–2:30 p.m. and 5–10 p.m.; Sunday, 5–10 p.m.

MENU RECOMMENDATIONS *Dal* (lentil soup); chicken or vegetable curry; eggplant *bartha; naan* (bread); tandoori dinner for one

COMMENTS The restaurant sits back quite a way from the highway, so look for the new sign for Avenue Shops. With numerous meatless dishes, it's a prime pick for vegetarians, and the prices make it a popular choice with budget-minded college students. Take care when ordering dishes hot: Even the mild dishes have a distinct bite. Service can be a bit slow on busy weekends, but customers are never rushed out of their tables.

La Fontanella ★ ★ ★ ★

ITALIAN AND SEAFOOD	MODERATE	QUALITY ★ ★ ★ ★ ½	VALUE ★ ★ ★ ★

Shoppes at Pelican Landing, 24600 Tamiami Trail, #204, Bonita Springs; ☎ 239-498-6808; www.lafontanellarestaurant.com

Reservations Recommended. **When to go** Dinner. **Entree range** $15–$24. **Payment** AE, D, MC, V. **Parking** Free lot. **Bar** Beer and wine. **Wine selection** Wide ranging, with emphasis on Italian vintages; $8–$15 per glass, $22–$250 by the bottle. **Dress** Stylish casual. **Disabled access** Good. **Customers** Romantic couples, discerning gourmets. **Hours** Daily, 5–10 p.m.

MENU RECOMMENDATIONS Wild-mushroom soup; charcoal-grilled calamari served over arugula; sauteed chicken breasts with porcini mushrooms; pan-sautéed salmon with shiitake mushrooms

COMMENTS Do not be put off by the restaurant's location in the midst of a busy shopping center. Inside it's miles from suburbia, with a gracious waitstaff, an inspired kitchen, and a romantic dining room with a rich earth-tone decor and soft, subdued lighting. Both the wine list and the menu are extensive for a restaurant of this size; both also include familiar items and some surprises. The chef has a predilection for wild mushrooms and works them into a number of dishes. This is a good choice for a tasteful adults-only night out.

Le Bistro ★ ★ ★ ★ ½

COUNTRY FRENCH	EXPENSIVE	QUALITY ★ ★ ★ ★ ★	VALUE ★ ★ ★ ★

842 Neapolitan Way, Naples; ☎ 239-434-7061

Reservations Strongly recommended. **When to go** Dinner before curtain at the nearby Philharmonic Center for the Arts. **Entree range** $20.50–$34.50. **Payment** AE, D, MC, V. **Parking** Free lot. **Bar** Beer and wine. **Wine selection** Substantial list of primarily French and Californian labels; $7–$10 by the glass, $26–$225 bottle. **Dress** Stylishly casual. **Disabled access** Wheelchair accessible. **Customers** Theater crowd, Francophiles. **Hours** Monday–Saturday, 5:30 p.m.–last seating 8:30 p.m.

MENU RECOMMENDATIONS Lobster bisque; mussels with cream sauce; bouillabaisse Marseillaise; roasted duck à l'orange; grilled swordfish; crème caramel; poached pear with vanilla ice cream and cinnamon sauce

COMMENTS Le Bistro is worth finding in a busy shopping center. Cool Mexican-tile floors, crisp white-linen tablecloths, and a bubbling fountain soothe the soul while classic French food nourishes the body. Service is friendly and efficient without being chummy. Make reservations, as the dining room is small and the clientele large.

Mel's Diner ★ ★ ★ ½

AMERICAN	INEXPENSIVE	QUALITY ★ ★ ★ ★	VALUE ★ ★ ★ ★ ★

4820 South Cleveland Avenue (US 41), Fort Myers; ☎ 239-275-7850
19050 Tamiami Trail (US 41), South Fort Myers; ☎ 239-985-2220
28601 Trails Edge Boulevard, Bonita Springs; ☎ 239-949-3080
3650 Tamiami Trail (US 41), Naples; ☎ 239-643-9898
www.melsdiner.com

Reservations Not accepted. **When to go** Anytime. **Entree range** $4–$13. **Payment** MC, V. **Parking** Free lot. **Bar** Beer and wine. **Wine selection** Minimal; $4

per glass. **Dress** Casual. **Disabled access** Good. **Customers** Retirees, families, diner devotees. **Hours** Daily, 6:30 a.m.–9 p.m.

MENU RECOMMENDATIONS Homemade chicken-noodle soup; Greek salad; roasted-chicken sandwich with mashed potatoes and gravy; burgers; onion rings; mile-high banana pie; chocolate bread pudding

COMMENTS All locations but the Fort Myers branch are new, cheery Art Deco buildings with the classic silver diner exterior. Inside, the 1950s reign, with pictures of period celebrities everywhere. Service is folksy and efficient. Portions are generous.

Miami Connection Deli & Grill ★ ★ ★ ½

KOSHER-STYLE DELI	MODERATE	QUALITY ★ ★ ★ ½	VALUE ★ ★ ★ ½

11506 Cleveland Avenue, Fort Myers; ☎ 239-936-3811

Reservations Not accepted. **When to go** Breakfast or lunch. **Entree range** $5–$14. **Payment** AE, D, MC, V. **Parking** Free lot. **Bar** None. **Wine selection** None. **Dress** Casual. **Disabled access** Wheelchair accessible. **Customers** Transplanted northeasterners, families, professionals, blue-collar workers. **Hours** Monday–Friday, 6 a.m.–3 p.m. and Saturday and Sunday, 7 a.m.–2 p.m.

MENU RECOMMENDATIONS Piled-high pastrami or corned beef on rye bread; potato knishes; rugalach (small pastries with cinnamon and nuts) or halvah (sesame-seed-paste–based candy)

COMMENTS A long-time favorite with locals who crave a two-fisted sandwich, this deli is almost always busy. Hurricane Charley tore the roof off in 2004, but a complete makeover transformed the plain-Jane deli into a real looker with expanded seating.

The Mucky Duck ★ ★ ★ ½

BRITISH-STYLE PUB	MODERATE	QUALITY ★ ★ ★ ★	VALUE ★ ★ ★ ★

11546 Andy Rosse Lane, Captiva Island; ☎ 239-472-3434;
www.muckyduck.com

Reservations Not accepted. **When to go** For sunset dinner. **Entree range** $17–$33. **Payment** AE, D, MC, V. **Parking** Free lot. **Bar** Beer and wine. **Wine selection** Primarily domestic, $13 by the glass; $3–$8 per glass, $15–$120 by the bottle. **Dress** Casual. **Disabled access** Wheelchair accessible. **Customers** Tourists, island residents. **Hours** Monday–Saturday, 11:30 a.m.–3 p.m. and 5 p.m.–9:30 p.m.

MENU RECOMMENDATIONS Barbecued shrimp with bacon; duck fingers; grouper Café de Paris; roast duckling à l'orange

COMMENTS There's almost always a lively crowd—with charismatic owner Victor Mayeron often leading the pack—at this popular waterfront pub. Because of its prime sunset view, seats are hardest to get just before dusk. Within, it's filled with wood and British memorabilia. Outdoors, tables overlook the beach and the Gulf of Mexico. This is a good choice for families who don't want to worry about how much noise the kids will make. The volume's generally high enough that it won't matter. To get a seat during the winter season, plan to get there early and sit outside on the beach or picnic benches. Once the restaurant opens, beverages and appetizers can be ordered at the bar and carried outdoors.

P. F. Chang's   ★ ★ ★ ★ ½

CHINESE	MODERATE	QUALITY ★ ★ ★ ★ ½	VALUE ★ ★ ★ ★

10840 Tamiami Trail North (US 41), Naples; ☎ 239-596-2174; www.pfchangs.com

Reservations Accepted. **When to go** Anytime. **Entree range** $10–$18. **Payment** AE, D, MC, V. **Parking** Free lot. **Bar** Full service. **Wine selection** 50 options arranged from sweetest to least sweet and all available by the glass or the bottle; $6–$15 by the glass, $24–$60 by the bottle. **Dress** Business casual. **Disabled access** Good. **Customers** Young and old, locals and those passing through. **Hours** Sunday–Thursday, 11 a.m.–11 p.m.; Friday and Saturday, 11 a.m.–midnight.

MENU RECOMMENDATIONS Shanghai street dumplings; peanut chicken salad; coconut-curry vegetables; Cantonese roasted duck; kung pao scallops; oolong marinated sea bass; orange-peel beef; the Great Wall of Chocolate

COMMENTS There are lots of Chinese restaurants around, but no one does it better, or with more style, than Chang's. Portions are generous, ingredients are fresh, service is attentive, and the dining room is downright chic.

Red Fish Blu Fish   ★ ★ ★ ★ ½

NEW AMERICAN	EXPENSIVE	QUALITY ★ ★ ★ ★ ½	VALUE ★ ★ ★ ½

14970 Captiva Drive, Captiva; ☎ 239-472-1956

Reservations Recommended for dinner and Sunday brunch. **Entree range** $8–$12 (all menu items are small plates). **Payment** AE, MC, V. **Parking** Free lot. **Bar** Beer and wine. **Wine selection** Exceptional, with many rare boutique selections; $7–$9 by the glass, $15–$600 by the bottle. **Dress** Casual. **Disabled access** Fair. **Customers** Island residents, savvy tourists, and wine lovers. **Hours** Tuesday–Sunday, 11 a.m.–3 p.m.; Tuesday–Saturday, 6–9:30 p.m.

MENU RECOMMENDATIONS Hamachi carpaccio with yuzu vinaigrette; chicken breast and crispy dumpling with truffle sauce; snapper with sage butter and green-olive sauce; loin of lamb with celeriac puree and lemon-ginger sauce

COMMENTS "See Art. Eat Art. Be Art" is the theme of this island newcomer that rose out of the ruins of Hurricane Charley. Storm debris was fashioned into dining room art. The ambience is fanciful, but the food—served in tapas-sized portions—is serious, with fresh ingredients expertly prepared and artfully presented. Wine lovers will thrill at the breadth of this little restaurant's sophisticated wine offerings.

Roy's   ★ ★ ★ ★ ½

EURO-ASIAN	EXPENSIVE	QUALITY ★ ★ ★ ★ ★	VALUE ★ ★ ★

The Promenade at Bonita Bay; 26831 South Bay Drive, Bonita Springs; ☎ 239-498-7697; www.roysrestaurant.com

Reservations Recommended well in advance. When to go Dinner. Entree range $5–$28. Payment AE, D, MC, V. Parking Free lot. Bar Full service. Wine selection Extensive, including some specially bottled for Roy's; $7–$22 per glass, $20–$280 by the bottle. Dress Casual chic. Disabled access Good. Customers Trendsetters, organized sorts who make reservations well in advance. Hours Sunday–Thursday, 5:30–9 p.m.; Friday and Saturday, 5:30–9:30 p.m.

MENU RECOMMENDATIONS Crispy coconut tiger-shrimp sticks with spicy pineapple-chili sauce; teriyaki short-rib pizza; blackened rare ahi tuna; chocolate soufflé for dessert

COMMENTS The large dining room tends to be noisy when full, which is most of the time. The 160-seat restaurant has an artfully designed dining room with big multilayered ceilings, recessed lighting, and a tantalizing view of the kitchen. A good-sized bar up front provides a strategic spot for people watching..

Rumrunners at Cape Harbour ★ ★ ★

NEW AMERICAN	MODERATE	QUALITY ★ ★ ★ ★	VALUE ★ ★ ★

5848 Cape Harbour Drive, Cape Coral; ☎ 239-542-0200; www.capeharbourmarina.com/restaurant.htm

Reservations Recommended. When to go Anytime. Entree range $11–$27. Payment AE, D, MC, V. Parking Free lot. Bar Full service. Wine selection Not huge, but well chosen; $5–$9 by the glass, $18–$210 by the bottle. Dress Casual chic. Disabled access Good. Customers Locals, boaters, devotees of alfresco dining. Hours Daily, 11:30 a.m.–9 p.m.

MENU RECOMMENDATIONS Steamed fresh mussels Provençal; Ralph's killer shrimp; Todd's meat loaf; crispy Thai chicken; Caribbean bronzed salmon; seafood potpie

COMMENTS The chef and other principal players have long set the trend in restaurants from Fort Myers to Naples and have put Cape Coral on the fine-dining map. Dine inside or out—there are separate outdoor areas for smokers and nonsmokers. Boaters can tie up at the restaurant's dock. Service can be spotty, but the food is consistently good.

Sanibel Steakhouse ★ ★ ★

STEAK HOUSE	EXPENSIVE	QUALITY ★ ★ ★ ★ ½	VALUE ★ ★

1473 Periwinkle Way, Sanibel Island; ☎ 239-472-5700
13401 Summerlin Road, Fort Myers; ☎ 239-437-8325;
www.sanibelsteakhouseftmyers.com
24041 North Tamiami Trail, Bonita Springs; ☎ 239-390-0400
8990 Fontana Del Sol Way, Naples; ☎ 239-597-7832

Reservations Strongly Recommended. When to go Dinner. Entree range $20–$55. Payment AE, D, DC, MC, V. Parking Free lot. Bar Full service. Wine selection Wide range of wines, including Champagne; $5.75–$12.95 per glass, $22–$495 by the bottle. Dress Stylishly casual to dressy. Disabled access Good. Customers Theatergoers, tourists, beef devotees. Hours Daily, 5–10 p.m.

MENU RECOMMENDATIONS Jumbo lump-crab cakes; tuna sashimi; surf and turf; filet mignon; Kobe beef; crab-stuffed Gulf grouper

COMMENTS All locations emphasize good service and aged beef. Since the opening of the Naples branch in early 2003, the menu has been expanded (except at the Sanibel branch) to include Kobe beef and exotic game such as kangaroo and elk. As is the case at many steak houses, everything on the menu is à la carte. Raised panels, muted colors, and subtle lighting create a clubby feel. The Fort Myers branch is convenient to the Barbara. B. Mann Performing Arts Hall.

Siam Hut ★ ★ ★ ★

| THAI | MODERATE | QUALITY ★ ★ ★ ★ ½ | VALUE ★ ★ ★ ★ |

4521 Del Prado Boulevard, Cape Coral; ☎ 239-945-4247

Reservations Recommended on weekends. **When to go** Lunch or dinner. **Entree range** $9–$18. **Payment** MC, V. **Parking** Free lot. **Bar** Beer and wine. **Wine selection** Limited to sake, house wine, and plum wine; $4–$5 per glass, $13–$16 by the carafe. **Dress** Casual. **Disabled access** Wheelchair accessible. **Customers** Multi-ethnic melting pot. **Hours** Monday–Friday, 11:30 a.m.–3 p.m. and 5–10 p.m.; Saturday, 5–10 p.m.

MENU RECOMMENDATIONS *Tom kha gai* (a fragrant coconut-milk soup); Siam rolls (spring rolls); pad thai; Panang curry; green beans in hot-and-spicy chili paste with chicken or tofu

COMMENTS A nondescript storefront belies the well-appointed dining room within that includes two tables at which customers sit (for a 20% surcharge) on the floor with their legs resting in a recessed space below the table. The management is careful to prepare dishes as mild or spicy as desired. Children will feel as welcome as their parents here, with lots of finger foods and familiar offerings such as fried rice and wonton soup. The management has even been known to pick up fussing infants and whisk them off to the kitchen, where they are doted upon while Mom and Dad enjoy dinner.

South Beach Grille ★ ★ ★ ½

| NEW AMERICAN | EXPENSIVE | QUALITY ★ ★ ★ ½ | VALUE ★ ★ ★ |

Santini Marina Plaza, 7205 Estero Boulevard, Fort Myers Beach; ☎ 239-463-7770

Reservations Recommended. **When to go** Any evening. **Entree range** $17–$40. **Payment** AE, MC, V. **Parking** Free lot. **Bar** Full service. **Wine selection** Interesting and evolving; $6.25–$7.95 by the glass, $30–$160 by the bottle. **Dress** Stylishly casual. **Disabled access** Good. **Customers** Beach residents, visitors, the young and the restless. **Hours** Daily, 4 :30–10 p.m.

MENU RECOMMENDATIONS Panko-crusted fried oysters; coconut fried shrimp; snapper with mango and papaya beurre blanc; prime rib; white chocolate–Key lime–raspberry cheesecake

COMMENTS Fort Myers Beach has never been known for chic dining—until now. The dining room is a sherbet-hued delight reminiscent of the trendy Miami Beach neighborhood for which it's named. The atmosphere is lively, so those envisioning an intimate dinner might want to look elsewhere. Early birds can experience the grille for less from 4:30 p.m. to 6 p.m., when entrees are $15–$17.

Tommy Bahama's Tropical Cafe & Emporium ★ ★ ★ ★

CARIBBEAN	MODERATE	QUALITY ★ ★ ★ ½	VALUE ★ ★ ★ ★

1220 Third Street South, Naples; ☎ 239-643-7920; www.tommybahama.com

Reservations Limited, subject to weather conditions. When to go On a sunny day or starry night. Entree range $17–$27. Payment AE, MC, V. Parking Street. Bar Full service. Wine selection Concise, with low- to moderately priced labels, $14 by the glass; $4.25–$6.75 per glass, $18–$65 by the bottle. Dress Casual. Disabled access Wheelchair accessible. Customers Everyone. Hours Daily, 11 a.m.–11 p.m.

MENU RECOMMENDATIONS Cooper Island crab bisque; Fandango Mango chicken salad; St. Bart's BLT; Tommy's Tahitian tacos (wonton shells stuffed with grilled mahimahi, black rice, and mango salsa); piña colada cake; Tommy's original bread pudding

COMMENTS With most of its seating along the broad expanse of sidewalk, this restaurant affords a great view, as well as a chance to savor the great outdoors provided the weather is good. When it isn't, tables can be hard to come by. Despite the island theme, the decor is understated and tasteful. Check out the adjoining his-and-hers boutiques featuring the Tommy Bahama clothing line.

Yabba Island Grill ★ ★ ★ ★

TROPICAL	MODERATE	QUALITY ★ ★ ★ ½	VALUE ★ ★ ★

711 Fifth Avenue South, Naples; ☎ 239-262-5787; www.yabbaislandgrill.com

Reservations Yes. When to go Dinner. Entree range $17.95–$26.95. Payment AE, MC, V. Parking Street. Bar Full service, including 50 types of rum. Wine selection Upwards of 120 choices, 26 by the glass; $5.25–$13 per glass, $22–$150 by the bottle. Dress Stylishly casual. Disabled access Good. Customers Social butterflies, searching singles, people watchers. Hours Sunday–Thursday, 5–10 p.m.; Friday and Saturday, 5–11 p.m.

MENU RECOMMENDATIONS Tuna Negril appetizer; Jamaican classic jerk chicken; seared mahi, lobster, and mussels; sweet-chili–glazed and wasabi-pea–crusted Chilean sea bass; grilled New York strip; Key lime cheesecake

COMMENTS Eat indoors or out at this trendy, high-volume restaurant in Old Naples. Inside, the dining room sports a tin ceiling and walls awash in vivid azure and lime. Service can suffer during peak times, such as weekend nights. This isn't the place for an intimate dinner for two, but it fills the bill for a lively night out and is next door to the Sugden Theatre.

ENTERTAINMENT *and* NIGHTLIFE

THE PARTY-ALL-NIGHT SCENE MAY FLOURISH on Miami Beach, but in Southwest Florida, after-dark activities are considerably more staid and limited. In most cases, the people you'll find out on the Gulf beaches in the wee hours are volunteer members of the sea turtle patrol, keeping a protective eye out for egg-laying turtles that come ashore, along with their tiny hatchlings that must swim out to sea on summer nights.

On Sanibel and Captiva islands, in fact, where there aren't any traffic signals, streetlights, or neon signs, nightlife generally consists of going out for dinner after watching the sunset. But for those who simply must find a place to drink, dance, and/or carouse, the larger hotels have clubs that stay open later than most island establishments.

THE CLUB SCENE . . . WHAT THERE IS OF IT

BY LAW, BARS MUST CLOSE BY 2 A.M., AND most shut down before then. While there are a great many scattered along US 41, clusters of clubs can be found in historic Old Naples; in downtown Fort Myers; and along Estero Boulevard, the main drag through Fort Myers Beach (which is at its wildest during March, when chilled northern college students head south for spring break). In any of these places, it's possible to park and travel by foot from club to club. Beware of driving while intoxicated, however: The police know where the clubs are, too, and are vigilant about enforcing the 0.08 blood-alcohol limit.

The Naples club scene tends toward a slightly older demographic: 30- and 40-something professionals, energetic retirees, and patrons of the arts. By night, inhabitants of downtown Fort Myers can range from the youthful pierced-and-tattooed set to tourists who took a wrong turn to the beach. On Fort Myers Beach, the heart of the action is Times Square, where singles in their late teens and early 20s mingle while looking for a match.

THEATER AND OTHER CULTURAL PURSUITS

SOUTHWEST FLORIDA OFFERS AN INCREASED awareness of the fine arts with new venues and opportunities. In February 1992, the Lee County Alliance of the Arts opened the 12,100-square-foot, $1 million **William R. Frizzell Cultural Center.** The Center consists of an exhibition gallery, the 200-seat Claiborne and Ned Foulds Theatre, an outdoor amphitheater, and the Gladys G. Land School of Arts. Many festivals take place on the grounds. Theatre Conspiracy, a community-theater troupe that specializes in original and offbeat productions, is based inside the Frizzell.

The **Philharmonic Center for the Arts** in Naples (5833 Pelican Bay Boulevard; ☎ 239-597-1900 or 800-597-1900) and the **Barbara B. Mann Performing Arts Hall** in Fort Myers (8099 College Park Way; ☎ 239-481-4849) provide forums for national touring companies of big stage productions such as *Les Misérables, Phantom of the Opera,* and *Miss Saigon.* Well-known comedians, musicians, and dance troupes perform there, too.

There are more than a dozen theater companies between Naples and Fort Myers, including professional and amateur groups. The primary theater season is November through April, and several groups produce summer shows. The **Broadway Palm Dinner Theatre** in Fort Myers (1380 Colonial Boulevard; ☎ 239-278-4422) and the **Naples Dinner Theatre** (1025 Piper Boulevard; ☎ 239-514-7827) operate year-round, serving up buffets and plays, most often musicals. **Florida Repertory Theatre** (2267 First Street; ☎ 239-332-4488), based in Fort Myers' historic downtown Arcade Theatre, is an equity company that produces Broadway shows. Most first-run movies debut locally in a timely fashion, but foreign and art films are in short supply.

Money to Burn?

Gamblers should hit the **Naples–Fort Myers Greyhound Track** in Bonita Springs (10601 Bonita Beach Road; ☎ 239-992-2411); the **Big "M" Casino** (end of Third Street, Fort Myers Beach; ☎ 239-765-7529), a boat that spends a few hours in international waters; and the **Seminole Indian Casino** (506 South First Street, Immokalee; ☎ 239-658-1313 or 800-218-0007), a bare-bones casino near Naples that's one of the few places open all night.

The Best of Southwest Florida Clubs

NAME	COVER	COST	CITY
BARS			
Blu Sushi	None	Moderate	Fort Myers
Café and Bar Lurcat	None	Expensive	Naples
Envie	$0–$5	Moderate	Fort Myers
DANCE CLUB			
Aja	$5–$10	Moderate	Bonita Springs

The Best of Southwest Florida Clubs *(continued)*

NAME	COVER	COST	CITY
LIVE MUSIC			
Chillers at the New Snug Harbor	None	Moderate	Fort Myers Beach
World Famous Buckingham Blues Bar	None	Inexpensive	Fort Myers
LOUNGE			
The Club at the Ritz-Carlton	None	Expensive	Naples

NIGHTCLUB PROFILES

Aja

NIGHTCLUB FOR SOPHISTICATES

The Promenade at Bonita Bay, 26821 South Bay Drive, Bonita Springs; ☎ 239-948-1186

Cover $5–$10. **Minimum** None. **Mixed drinks** $4–$8. **Wine** $5–$10. **Beer** $3–$5. **Food available** None. **Hours** Tuesday–Saturday, 6 p.m.–2 a.m., Sunday, 8 p.m.–2 a.m.

WHO GOES THERE   The 35-to-55 crowd from opening until 10 p.m.; then 20-somethings take over.

WHAT GOES ON   There's no dance floor, so partiers groove to the beat wherever they can find space.

COMMENTS   Aja is a favorite among professionals and other more-mature types until about 10 p.m., when the 20-somethings crank up the volume and pace with hip Miami DJs playing a mix of Euro, progressive, and tribal dance tunes. Even the computerized lights dance to the music. For a special night on the town for you and 30 friends, book the VIP room, which has its own bar, server, and sound system. Mature patrons get their own night out on Tuesdays, when the Singles Club of Bonita shows up for dancing to an oldies beat.

Blu Sushi

HIP NIGHTSPOT FOR MARTINI AND SUSHI LOVERS

13451 McGregor Boulevard, Fort Myers; ☎ 239-489-1500
1170 Third Street South, Naples; ☎ 239-403-9901
www.blusushi.com

Cover None. **Minimum** None. **Mixed drinks** $8–$10. **Wine** $6–$16 per glass (43 varieties available), $32–$1,375 by the bottle. **Beer** $6–$8. **Food available** All manner of sushi and sashimi, salads, and a limited number of cooked dishes. **Hours** Monday–Thursday, 11:30 a.m.–2 p.m. and 5–10 p.m.; Friday, 11:30 a.m.–2 p.m. and 5–11 p.m.; Saturday, 5–11 p.m.; the bar stays open later.

WHO GOES THERE Young singles, older singles, families, raw-fish devotees

WHAT GOES ON A whole lot of drinking, flirting, and sushi consumption at little tables, the sushi bar, and all around the place, including the patio out front.

COMMENTS Blu Sushi looks like a little club that wandered away from Miami's artsy South Beach district. Energetic young servers do a good job of keeping the fish and beverages flowing. Although the name touts the sushi, the full bar is well stocked with inventive martinis (including the red, white, and blue Blu Liberty), eight types of sake, and 18 primarily California wines available by the glass or bottle.

Café and Bar Lurcat

OH-SO-CHIC NIGHTSPOT WITH A PRONOUNCED SOUTH BEACH FEEL

494 Fifth Avenue South, Naples; ☎ 239-213-3357; www.cafelurcat.com

Cover None. **Minimum** None. **Mixed drinks** $6.50–$10. **Wine** $6–$30 by the glass; $18–$300 by the bottle. **Beer** $3.50–$5. **Food available** A variety of small plates. **Hours** Daily, 5 p.m.–1 a.m.

WHO GOES THERE Trendy night owls seeking the hottest downtown hangout

WHAT GOES ON The beautiful people—locals and out-of-towners alike—are irresistibly drawn to the bar's urban chic ambience, with its well-upholstered couches and chairs and green-glass–topped bar where you'll find potent mojitos (white rum, mint, simple syrup, and a splash of club soda), 330-plus wines by the glass, and an intriguing tapas menu that includes mini-burgers and cinnamon doughnuts. The crowd gets younger as the night grows older.

COMMENTS This is a prime pick for those who like to dress smartly for a night on the town. The tony upstairs restaurant offers a larger food and wine menu, but the lively downstairs bar allows for better people watching along Fifth Avenue, the city's most social stomping ground. Musical selections feature chill tunes and trip-hop.

Chillers at the New Snug Harbor Restaurant

LIVELY BAR WITH INDOOR-OUTDOOR ACCESS AND A PRIME VIEW OF THE WATER

1131 First Street, Fort Myers Beach; ☎ 239-463-8077; www.snugharborrestaurant.com/chillers

Cover None. **Minimum** None. **Mixed drinks** $5–$10. **Wine** $6–$12. **Beer** $4–$6. **Food available** Pizzas and bar fare. **Hours** Daily, 11:30 a.m.–until (closing varies).

WHO GOES THERE Beach dwellers, tourists, and a growing number of mainlanders

WHAT GOES ON Drinks and music flow freely at the new digs of this longtime beach establishment. There's dancing, mingling, and plenty of room outdoors to take in the sunset and stars over the tranquil bay.

COMMENTS Options abound at this striking new venue, with seating (and access to the bar) inside and out. The second-story location makes for great stargazing. The music's a mixed bag, ranging from rock to blues to steel drums.

The Club at the Ritz-Carlton Beach Resort

SOPHISTICATES SEEKING SAME FOR DANCING, ROMANCING

280 Vanderbilt Beach Road, Naples; ☎ 239-598-3300; www.ritzcarlton.com/resorts/naples

Cover None. **Minimum** None. **Mixed drinks** $7–$12. **Wine** $8–$19. **Beer** $5.50. **Food available** None. **Hours** Sunday–Thursday 8:30 p.m.–12:30 a.m., Friday and Saturday, 8:30 p.m.–1:30 a.m.

WHO GOES THERE Well-heeled travelers, conventioneers, people watchers

WHAT GOES ON Mature singles check one another out, business deals get sealed, locals work hard at seeing and being seen, and special occasions are celebrated.

COMMENTS This is not the place to slouch in to after a day on the beach— business casual is the minimum, but dressier attire is just fine. The music matches the fine service and subdued lighting. Tables are set far enough apart to allow easy access to the dance floor when the mood strikes. Given that it's located inside the marble- and chandelier-bedecked resort, servers are well versed at making customers feel pampered.

Envie

CHIC DOWNTOWN NIGHTSPOT

2213 Main Street, Fort Myers; ☎ 239-337-0909

Cover $5 when there is one. **Minimum** None. **Mixed drinks** $6.50–$9.50. **Wine** $6–$8 by the glass, $28–$185 by the bottle. **Beer** $3.50–$4.50. **Food available** Tapas menu. **Hours** Wednesday–Friday, 5 p.m.–2 a.m.; Saturday, 8 p.m.–2 a.m.

WHO GOES THERE Trendy professionals

WHAT GOES ON Dancing, drinking, and socializing in an oh-so-cosmopolitan setting to a chill-out soundtrack emanating from a $30,000 sound system. The roomy lounge downstairs is outfitted with a dark-wood bar, tables, and leather-upholstered seats. Upstairs there's another bar, more overstuffed furniture, and a bed from which partiers get a great view of the whole place.

COMMENTS Each table has a built-in ice bucket, so it's possible to buy bottles of liquor and mixers and mix your own as you go. Leave the T-shirts, shorts, and hats behind when planning an Envie-ous evening.

World Famous Buckingham Blues Bar

THE REGION'S PREEMINENT SPOT TO HEAR LIVE BLUES

5641 Buckingham Road, east of Fort Myers; ☎ **239-693-7111;**
www.buckinghambar.com

Cover None. **Minimum** None. **Wine coolers** $3–$5. **Beer** $1.50–$2. **Food available** None. **Hours** Monday–Thursday, 10 a.m.–2 a.m.; Friday and Saturday, 7 a.m.–2 a.m.

WHO GOES THERE Bikers, professionals, neighborhood residents, and blues lovers from all over

WHAT GOES ON Live blues, Live blues jams, darts and pool tournaments, monthly outdoor concerts

COMMENTS "Gritty" might best describe the ambience of this out-of-the-way establishment that draws blues lovers from throughout the region. The draws are the live blues (Fridays and Saturdays), live blues jams in which anyone can play (Wednesdays), and various tournaments.

PART EIGHT

THE EVERGLADES

WELCOME *to the* RIVER *of* GRASS

EVERGLADES NATIONAL PARK, SOUTH FLORIDA'S vast, watery, magnificent backyard, touches both coasts down to the Keys and embraces a complex of other national and state preserves and parks. No visit to South Florida is complete without a visit to this natural treasure.

Whether you spend days or hours for your visit, including all or some parts of the complex, the Glades is easily accessible to any visitor. From Palm Beach County or Broward County, you are nearest the north entrance at Shark Valley; from Miami or the Keys, the Royal Palm Visitor Center; on the west coast, Everglades City.

Only a few minutes from the Everglades entrances, Homestead and Florida City to the east, and Marco Island and Everglades City to the west, provide varied chain hotels, motels, inns, RV parks, and other lodging options.

Within the park, lodging is limited. About 50 campsites are scattered throughout, some deep in the park, where you can really feel the solitude. The only motel within the park is the Flamingo Lodge, described later.

The Tamiami Trail (US 41) starts in Coral Gables and goes west through the Everglades and Big Cypress National Preserve. To the west of the park, the highway wends to Fakahatchee Strand Preserve State Park and Collier-Seminole State Park. You can easily drive the entire route

unofficial **TIP**
We don't recommend visiting the Everglades April through October, when mosquitoes are biting. Also, in winter you'll see more wildlife; it's the dry season, and a vast array of animals—especially alligators and birds—congregate and sun themselves. But even in winter, be sure to apply insect repellent on an Everglades visit.

everglades

29 Ochopee
Everglades City — 41 *Tamiami* — Monroe Station
Gulf Coast Visitor Center
Big Cypress National Preserve Visitor Center

Tiger Key
Picnic Key
TEN THOUSAND ISLANDS
Chokoloskee — Sunday Bay Chickee

BIG CYPRESS NATIONAL PRESERVE
94

Lopez River
Rabbit Key
Sweetwater Bay Chickee

The Watson Place
Pavilion Key
Darwins Place
Mormon Key
New Turkey Key & Turkey Key
Plate Creek Bay Chickee — Lostmans Five Bay

Willy Willy

EVERGLADES

South Lostmans
Rogers River Bay Chickee
Highland Beach
Wilderness Waterway
Camp Lonesome

Harney River Chickee
Canepatch

Graveyard Creek
Shark River Chickee
Watson River Chickee — North River Chickee
Roberts River Chickee

Gulf of Mexico

Oyster Bay Chickee
Joe River Chickee
Wilderness Waterway
Lane Bay Chickee

CAPE SABLE
South Joe River Chickee

Mrazek Pond
Middle Cape
Eco Pond
East Cape — Clubhouse Beach — Flamingo
Flamingo Visitor Center

FLORIDA
Map Area Miami

0   10 mi
0   10 km
N

⬚ Campground

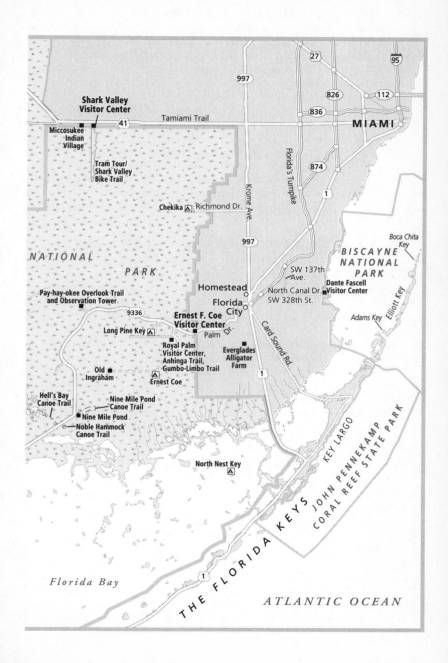

Shark Valley
Visitor Center

Miccosukee
Indian
Village

Tamiami Trail

41

27

997

826

112

836

MIAMI

Tram Tour/
Shark Valley
Bike Trail

Chekika Richmond Dr.

Krome Ave.

Florida's Turnpike

874

1

997

NATIONAL

PARK

BISCAYNE
NATIONAL
PARK

Boca Chita
Key

SW 137th
Ave.

Dante Fascell
Visitor Center

Elliott Key

Pay-hay-okee Overlook Trail
and Observation Tower

Homestead

North Canal Dr.
SW 328th St.

9336

Florida
City

Adams Key

Ernest F. Coe
Visitor Center

Long Pine Key

Palm Dr.

Royal Palm
Visitor Center,
Anhinga Trail,
Gumbo-Limbo Trail

Everglades
Alligator
Farm

Card Sound Rd.

1

Old
Ingraham

Ernest Coe

Hell's Bay
Canoe Trail

Nine Mile Pond
Canoe Trail

Nine Mile Pond

Noble Hammock
Canoe Trail

KEY LARGO

JOHN PENNEKAMP
CORAL REEF STATE PARK

North Nest Key

THE FLORIDA KEYS

1

Florida Bay

ATLANTIC OCEAN

1

through the parks in a day, with numerous stops and a possible stay-over at either the east or west end.

A couple of hours' drive along the Tamiami Trail between the coasts offers a glimpse of seemingly endless sawgrass, interspersed with hammocks of mahogany and cypress. Gators and osprey may be sunning themselves on the protected shoulders, and eagles may circle overhead in a big sky.

But even the apparently empty spaces teem with life and activity. The Everglades is a complex result of climate, topography, and vegetation, and to really find out what's so unique, you've got to get out of your car. We recommend that you dedicate at least a day to hike or bike the trails, go on a walk in the muck (also known as a "slough slog"), or canoe the waters, maybe to a backcountry campsite. If you stay overnight you can watch the sun set impossibly low, tingeing the grassy waters pink, and arise to hear the birds greet the morning and fly in flocks above the water.

ON THE EDGE: NEARBY PARKS AND PRESERVES

FOR THE ULTIMATE SOUTH FLORIDA NATURE experience, you can include visits to other nearby wildlife areas. Just to the north of the Everglades, **Big Cypress National Preserve** was established by Congress in 1974 for preservation and recreation. Here you can hunt within marsh, prairie, and forested swamp; drive or tram through; or visit an Indian enclave.

Biscayne National Park, just to the southeast of the Everglades, was designated a national park in 1980. Mostly underwater, it is the nation's largest marine park and provides coastland, islands, and coral reefs in Biscayne Bay and the Atlantic for an exceptional snorkeling experience.

Ten Thousand Islands, an undervisited fishing paradise known especially for tarpon, includes Marco Island (which is the largest of the islands) and is just to the west of the Everglades.

ABOUT THE EVERGLADES: IT'S NOT A SWAMP

THE SPANIARDS CALLED IT EL LAGUNO DE Espiritu Sanctu—the Lake of the Holy Spirit. But the Everglades is really a slow-moving river.

In this mysterious expanse of hammocks and mangroves, big-city noise is replaced by the cries of herons, the splash of leaping fish, and the wind rippling through sawgrass. Manatees, bobtail deer, otters, and rare Florida panthers all reside here in a world of silvery water and varied shades of green.

Everglades National Park, established in 1947 as a protected wet-lands, encompasses a major chunk of South Florida: at 2,100 square miles, it is the second largest national park (after Yellowstone) in the lower 48 states. However, the 1.5 million acres of Everglades

National Park, originating south of Lake Okeechobee and ending in Florida Bay, lie within an ecosystem seven times that size.

This 50-mile-wide river is only knee-deep and moves so slowly that a drop of water may take eight months to travel from its northern to southern ends. Within this huge expanse of water, sawgrass, clumps of trees called hammocks, and pockets of tropical jungle thrive.

This unparalleled wildlife sanctuary contains an astounding variety of mammals, reptiles, birds, and fish, including roseate spoonbills, egrets, wood storks, osprey, and both alligators and crocodiles—the only place in the world where both species reside.

For eons, the overflow of Lake Okeechobee to the north has moved south slowly over this land nearly as flat as a pool table, into Florida Bay, nourishing millions of acres of sawgrass as the water ebbs and flows.

A THREATENED WILDERNESS

THIS SEEMINGLY PLACID AREA WAS EASY TO ignore by locals, and was disparaged by most visitors as a mosquito-filled swamp until about 50 years ago. Today it is designated a World Heritage Site, an International Biosphere Preserve, and a Wetland of International Importance.

In her best-selling 1947 book *The Everglades: River of Grass,* Florida environmentalist Marjory Stoneman Douglas popularized the notion of the Everglades as a river. Douglas, who died in 1998 at the age of 108, continued to write and speak out about preserving this unique ecosystem until the end of her life. She did so because the Everglades is in serious danger of destruction.

The Everglades used to encompass everything south of Lake Okeechobee, but encroaching civilization has pushed its perimeter back so that today it's only a fraction of its former size. Only the one-seventh of what's left is federally protected as Everglades National Park.

Initiatives to save this unique ecosystem include $200 million in funds provided by Congress in 1996 and a $7.8 billion, 30-year restoration plan approved by Congress in 2000.

But true restoration, experts say, is a long-term goal and will be extremely expensive. The *Miami Herald* routinely prints news articles on the raging controversies surrounding efforts to protect the remaining—and seriously threatened—portions of this unique environment.

WHERE *to* GO

FROM THE NORTHEAST: SHARK VALLEY

FROM FLORIDA'S EAST COAST, THE CLOSEST entrance to Everglades National Park is Shark Valley, on US 41 (the Tamiami Trail) about 35 miles west of downtown Miami. To avoid a seemingly endless procession of traffic lights on SW Eighth Street (US 41 in the city), take FL 836 (the Dolphin Expressway) west to the Florida Turnpike, and go south one exit to US 41 West.

Admission to the park is $10 per car and is good for a week at this and other park entrances. For more information, call Everglades National Park at ☎ 305-242-7700.

Take the Tram

If a day trip to Shark Valley is your only visit to the Everglades, our advice is to take the two-hour motorized-tram tour that leaves from the Shark Valley parking lot on the hour from 9 a.m. to 4 p.m. daily in the winter and at 9:30 a.m., 11 a.m., 1 p.m., and 3 p.m. daily in the summer. The cost is $13.25 for adults, $12.25 for seniors, and $8 for children under age 12. Try to arrive early; the parking lot is small, and this is a popular visitor destination. Reservations are recommended for tram tours; call ☎ 305-221-8455.

You will be taking the loop which cuts through Big Cypress National Preserve. Soon after the open-air tram leaves the visitor center, you'll discover what all the excitement is about as you view flocks of birds resting in trees and fluttering away as a group, alligators resting beside the narrow road, and a surreal, endless landscape of open sky and shallow, vegetated water. Well-informed and enthusiastic guides do a good job of explaining the unique topography and pointing out the unusual fauna. The tram stops often to let visitors view and photograph wildlife and terrain.

The tram follows the 15-mile paved loop road. At the halfway point, visitors disembark at an observation tower for one of the best views in South Florida: a 360-degree, 18-mile panorama of the Everglades. Restrooms, vending machines, and water fountains are available at the 20-minute stop.

Rental Bikes and Binoculars

When visiting Shark Valley, consider renting a bicycle at the visitor center. Biking along a trail through the Glades is one of the most memorable rides you can take. Single-speed bikes rent for $5.75 an hour between 8:30 a.m. and 3 p.m.; bikes must be returned by 4 p.m. And don't forget to bring binoculars, or rent a pair at the visitor center.

Airboats

Another highlight of a Shark Valley excursion: taking an airboat ride. While the motorized contraptions are illegal inside the national park, small airboat operations found all along US 41 offer visitors 30-minute rides into the Glades. Airboats are so incredibly loud that customers are given wads of cotton to stuff in their ears—you need them. Very small children may be frightened by the noise. The price for an hour-long ride ranges from $17 to $33 per person. Some environmentalists criticize the boats for their noise and size, but a ride is fun.

Most drivers make a stop at a hammock (a small, wooded island) that features a re-creation of an Indian village. Your driver will often try to locate some alligators, maybe tossing marshmallows or pieces of bread into the water to attract the critters. Not the most natural experience. If you seek a more placid water ride, try canoes, available at some park campsites and visitor centers.

An Indian Village

The Miccosukee Indians are descendants of Seminole Indians who retreated into the Everglades to escape forced resettlement during the 19th century. They hunted and fished the Everglades by canoe and lived on hammocks in open-sided *chickees*—thatched-roof huts built from cypress. They also learned how to handle alligators.

At the **Miccosukee Indian Village,** on US 41 a mile or so west of the Shark Valley entrance to the park, alligators are the stars of the show—and if you're day-tripping, this is your chance to see an alligator do more than snooze in the sun. Alligator-wrestling exhibitions are offered at 11 a.m., 12:30 p.m., 1:30 p.m., 3 p.m., and 4:40 p.m.; admission to the attraction is $10 for adults, $9 for seniors, and $5 for children ages 4–12. Airboat rides are $10 per person. The hours are 9 a.m.–5 p.m. daily. For more information, call ☎ 305-480-1924.

In addition to watching a Miccosukee Indian put a live gator to sleep (by rubbing its undersides), you'll get a peek at indigenous culture and life on a tour of the village (a small collection of open-air chickees and alligator pens) and at a small museum. Lots of crafts and souvenirs are also offered for sale.

At the **Ah-Tah-Thi-Ki Museum,** which has been constructed near historical ceremonial grounds, you can learn about the culture and heritage of the unconquered Seminole Tribe of Florida. The museum features a five-screen film about the history of the Seminoles, rare artifacts from the Smithsonian National Museum of the American Indian, displays featuring life in the Everglades in the 1800s, a 1.5-mile nature boardwalk, and a living village with Seminole Tribal members at work. Admission: $6 adults and $4 students and seniors, call ☎ 863-902-1113.

At **Billie Swamp Safari,** the ecoheritage wildlife park of the Florida Everglades, you can glide through a cypress dome on an airboat or take a swamp-buggy ecotour out into the land where the Seminole lived. Visit a reconstructed authentic Seminole camp; or learn about the history of the Seminoles, medicine plants, flora and fauna, and the native and exotic wildlife that roams the area. You can even spend the night in an authentic thatched-roof chickee. Activities range from $3 to $27; call ☎ 800-949-6101.

FROM THE SOUTH: THE ROYAL PALM VISITOR CENTER

AN EXCELLENT ARRIVAL OPTION FOR BOTH DAY-TRIPPERS and folks who want to spend a few days in the natural Everglades is south of Miami near Homestead and Florida City at the Royal Palm Visitor Center, located at the park's main entrance; call ☎ 305-242-7770. To get there, take FL 9336 from US 1 at Homestead for ten miles to the gate; admission is $10 per car and is good for a week.

The visitor center features interactive displays, a small theater, and an enclosed walkway to a "borrow"—a water-filled pit created by coral excavation. Visitors can pick up free brochures, view educational displays, obtain information on boat tours and canoe rentals, and get maps to the many trails that intersect with the 38-mile main road to Flamingo.

unofficial **TIP**
No matter the length of your stay, to best enjoy the subtle beauty here, you've got to relax. Get away from your car, and walk one of the trails or rent a canoe.

While Flamingo is a stretch for day-trippers, the village there is the park's largest visitor complex, featuring a motel, a restaurant, a small grocery store, campgrounds, boat tours, a marina, and another visitor center.

Easy Walks

The two-lane road also serves as the jumping-off point for short walking explorations into the Everglades.

unofficial **TIP**
This southeastern end of the park is the better destination for folks who prefer walking and exploring on their own over the guided tram tour offered at Shark Valley, to the north.

A well-planned day here will quickly reveal a fascinating overview of the Everglades. The nearby Anhinga Trail is a half-mile boardwalk that takes visitors through areas teeming with wildlife and shows off the subtle beauty of the region. The adjacent one-third-mile asphalt-covered Gumbo Limbo Trail takes visitors through a dense jungle unique to South Florida.

Other special stops along the road to Flamingo include the Pa-hay-okee Overlook; Mahogany Hammock, home to the largest stand of mahogany trees in the United States; and ponds offering views of bird life that may be unequaled anywhere else in the world. All the trails are on boardwalks, so there's no need to worry about wet feet.

Flamingo

The end of the road is the village of Flamingo, which offers boat rides on Florida Bay, canoe rentals, birding cruises, backcountry boat excursions, a restaurant, a marina, and the only overnight sleeping facilities in the park (outside of primitive camping). If you've got the time and interest, it's a great place for an extended visit. Note that services are limited in Flamingo during the summer.

Overnight visitors should plan to take a sunset cruise on the *Bald*

Eagle, a large pontoon boat that cruises Florida Bay for 90 minutes several times a day. Huge flocks of birds fly across the water, through the light of the setting sun, to roost on uninhabited keys. The views of the bay, dense mangrove forests, and shoreline are spectacular.

The sightseeing tour of the bay costs $20 for adults and $10 for children ages 6–12. Other means of exploring the Flamingo area include canoe rentals ($25–$35 for a half-day and $35–$45 for a full day) and bicycle rentals ($8 for a half day and $14 all day).

Rates at the Flamingo Lodge Marina and Outpost Resort's comfortable (but not fancy) motel range from $100 to $135. Fully equipped cottages and houseboats are also available for rent. Call the lodge at ☎ 239-695-3101 for more information and at ☎ 800-600-3813 to make reservations, or visit the Web site at **www.flamingolodge.com.**

An Alligator Farm

Outside the park entrance, near Florida City, the **Everglades Alligator Farm** is another small, private attraction worth stopping by. Among the creatures residing in this minizoo are more than 2,500 alligators (most of them little guys in "grow out" pens), a collection of snakes and crocodiles (including an eight-and-a-half-foot-long speckled caiman), two mountain lions, two lynxes, and a black bear. The farm is located on SW 192nd Avenue; follow the signs out of Florida City.

The two main attractions are a 20-minute alligator show (a handler "wrestles" a gator and answers questions from visitors) and the only airboat rides on this end of the Everglades (no airboats are allowed inside the national park). Alligator feedings, alligator shows, and snake shows alternate on the hour. Don't plan to stick around for all three shows, though—this attraction is too small to invest that much time.

The park is open 9 a.m.–6 p.m. daily; admission is $17 for adults, $10 for children ages 4–11, and free for children ages 4 and under, which includes a 30-minute airboat ride. Skip the ride and admission is $11.50 for adults and $6.50 for kids. For more information, call the gator farm at ☎ 800-644-9711 or 305-247-2628.

FROM THE WEST: EVERGLADES CITY

THIS OUTPOST TOWN JUST OFF THE TAMIAMI TRAIL on the Gulf Coast, just above the western edge of Everglades National Park, was once the seat of Collier County—a good place to start an Everglades adventure from the west. Known as the "Stone Crab Capital of the World," it has several processing facilities.

Here you'll find the park's Gulf Coast Visitor Center, with narrated boat rides into the water and mangrove islands of the park. An observation tower rises 400 steps from a boardwalk, offering a 360-degree panorama of the surrounding bay.

The weathered **Museum of the Everglades** is just off the circle in the center of town, near US 41 and FL 29. It presents the story of 2,000 years of human habitation with Indian artifacts, period photographs, and palm-thatched chickee huts. Education programs, lectures, and events are presented throughout the year. Opened in 1998, the museum is in the Old Laundry, which dates to when the Tamiami Trail's construction began in 1927. Built by Barron Gift Collier as part of his planned community, the laundry served the people of the new city of Everglades.

The museum is open Tuesday–Saturday, 10 a.m.–4 p.m., and is located at 105 West Broadway. Call ☎ 239-695-0008 for more information. There is no admission fee; a $4 donation is requested.

Within Everglades City (or nearby) are Native American reservations; the world's smallest post office, in Ochopee; famed Everglades photographer Clyde Butcher's Big Cypress Gallery; and airboat rides, swamp-buggy tours, canoe and kayak adventures, alligator farms, and great backcountry fishing.

Ten Thousand Islands

Everglades City is also a great starting point for visiting one of the 10,000 islands (give or take a thousand or so) that hug the tip of Florida, from the Gulf of Mexico to Florida Bay. Backcountry fishing here reels in pompano, redfish, snook, tarpon, and trout, and includes flats fishing and deep-sea charters in the Gulf of Mexico. The shallow waters and miles of trails through mangrove islands require local knowledge to navigate. Local guides are recommended.

You can take an airplane ride from a landing strip here for an overview of the unspoiled wetlands of rugged, isolated keys and mangrove isles.

Chokoloskee Island has been called one of Florida's last frontiers. About 2,000 years ago, the earliest inhabitants began altering the landscape with mounds of oyster shells and canals. Native Americans expanded the mounds, fished, hunted, and farmed the rich soil. Moving south from conflict in North Florida and Georgia, the Seminole Indians were the last native peoples to make the Everglades their home.

Near the end of the 19th century, plume, hide, and fur hunters arrived, quickly followed by families who combined seasonal hunting, fishing, and farming. The settlement brought a need for goods and mail, and in 1906 the **Smallwood Store** trading post served remote Chokoloskee Island, buying hides, furs, and farm produce and providing goods.

Ted Smallwood's store was placed on the National Register of Historic Places in 1974, and remained open and active until 1982. When the doors were shut, 90 percent of the original goods remained. Smallwood's granddaughter has reopened the store as a museum—a time capsule of Florida pioneer history (360 Mamie Street, Chokoloskee Island; ☎ 239-695-2989). The hide room has been turned into exhibit space, telling the history of the pioneers of Southwest Florida. Open daily. Admission: $2.50; over age 55, $2; under age 12, free.

ACCOMMODATIONS INDEX

DINING AND RESTAURANTS INDEX

Note: Page numbers in **bold face** indicate a restaurant profile.

SUBJECT INDEX